HEGEL'S

PHENOMENOLOGY OF SPIRIT

PHENOMENOLOGY
OF SPIRIT

BY

G. W. F. HEGEL

Georg ilhelm riedrich

━━━

Translated by A. V. Miller
with Analysis of the Text
and Foreword by
J. N. Findlay, F.B.A., F.A.A.A.S.

CLARENDON PRESS · OXFORD
1977

Oxford University Press, Walton Street, Oxford OX2 6DP

OXFORD LONDON GLASGOW NEW YORK
TORONTO MELBOURNE WELLINGTON CAPE TOWN
IBADAN NAIROBI DAR ES SALAAM LUSAKA ADDIS ABABA
KUALA LUMPUR SINGAPORE JAKARTA HONG KONG TOKYO
DELHI BOMBAY CALCUTTA MADRAS KARACHI

© *Oxford University Press 1977*

This translation of Hegel's *Phänomenologie des Geistes* has been made from the fifth edition, edited by J. Hoffmeister, Philosophische Bibliothek Band 114 © Felix Meiner Verlag, Hamburg, 1952

British Library Cataloguing in Publication Data
Hegel, Georg Wilhelm Friedrich
   Phenomenology of spirit.
   Index.
   ISBN 0-19-824530-0
   1. Title 2. Miller, Arnold Vincent 3. Findlay,
John Niemeyer
   110   B2928.E/
   Metaphysics

*B
2928
.E5
M54*

*Printed in Great Britain
by Butler & Tanner Ltd
Frome and London*

FOREWORD

THE *Phenomenology of Spirit*, first published in 1807, is a work
seen by Hegel as a necessary forepiece to his philosophical system (as later set forth in the *Encyclopaedia of the Philosophical
Sciences in Outline* of 1817, 1827, and 1830), but it is meant to
be a forepiece that can be dropped and discarded once the
student, through deep immersion in its contents, has advanced
through confusions and misunderstanding to the properly
philosophical point of view. Its task is to run through, in a scientifically purged order, the stages in the mind's necessary progress from immediate sense-consciousness to the position of a
scientific philosophy, showing thereby that this position is the
only one that the mind can take, when it comes to the end of
the intellectual and spiritual adventures described in the book.
But this sort of history, he tells us in *Encyclopaedia* §25, necessarily
had to drag in, more or less out of place and inadequately
characterized, much that would afterwards be adequately set
forth in the system, and it also had to bring in many motivating
connections of which the adventuring mind was unaware,
which explained why it passed from one phase of experience
or action to another, and yet could not be set forth in the full
manner which alone would render them intelligible.

Hegel also, in preparing for republication of the work before
his death in 1831, wrote a note which throws great light on
his ultimate conception of it. It was, he writes, a peculiar earlier
work (*eigentümliche frühere Arbeit*) which ought not to be revised,
since it related to the time at which it was written, a time
at which an abstract Absolute dominated philosophy. (See the
final paragraph of the first section of Hoffmeister's Appendix
Zur Feststellung des Textes in the 1952 edition.) This note indicates that, while Hegel undoubtedly thought that the sequence
of thought-phases described in the *Phenomenology*—phases experienced by humanity in the past and recapitulated by Hegel
in his own thought-adventures up to and including his own advance to the position of Science in about 1805—was a necessary

sequence, he still did not think it the only possible necessary sequence or pathway to Science, and certainly not the pathway to Science that would be taken by men in the future, or that might have been taken in other cultural and historical settings. For Hegel makes plain by his practice, as well as in some of his utterances, that he does not confuse the necessary with the unique, that he does not identify a necessary sequence of phases with the *only* possible sequence that can be taken. Hegel was obviously familiar with the branching variety of alternative proofs, all involving strictly necessary steps, that are possible in mathematics, and it is plain that he did not think that a similar branching of proofs was impossible in his dialectical reasoning. Dialectic is, in fact, a richer and more supple form of thought-advance than mathematical inference, for while the latter proceeds on lines of strict identity, educing only what is explicit or almost explicit in some thought-position's content, dialectic always makes higher-order comments upon its various thought-positions, stating relations that carry us far beyond their obvious content. What is obvious, for example, in Being is not its identity with Nothing, and what is obvious in Sense-certainty is not its total lack of determinateness. If mathematical identities can thus follow different routes to the same or to different goals, dialectical commentaries can even more obviously do the same, and Hegel in his varying treatment of the same material in the two Logics and in the *Phenomenology* shows plain recognition of this fact. A necessary connection, whether mathematical or dialectical, is not psychologically compulsive: it represents a track that the mind may or may not take, or that it may or may not prefer to other tracks, on its journey to a given conclusion. There is no reason then to think that Hegel thought that the path traced in the *Phenomenology*, though consisting throughout of necessary steps, was the only path that the conscious spirit could have taken in rising from sensuous immediacy to absolute knowledge. It was the path that *had* been taken by the World Spirit in past history, and that had been rehearsed in the consciousness of Hegel, in whom the notion of Science first became actual. But this involved no pronouncement as to what pathway to Science would be taken by men in the future, nor as to what pathway would have been taken in other thinkable world-situations. For Hegel admits an element of the sheerly contingent, and therefore also of the sheerly possible, in nature and history.

The sequence of phases to be studied in the *Phenomenology* therefore involves a fine blend of the contingently historical and the logically necessary. Its successive phases bring out what is logically implicit in its earlier phases, in the Hegelian sense of representing throughout an insightful, higher-order comment on previous contents, but they also only bring out a series of implications actually embodied in past history and in Hegel's own thought-history. Hegel, we know, did not desire to step out of his own time and his own thought-situation: the philosopher, as he was later to say on page 35 of the Preface to the *Philosophy of Right*, is necessarily a son of his own time, and his philosophy is that time comprehended in thought. To seek to transcend one's time is only, he says, to venture into the 'soft element' of fancy and opinion. The pathway to Science taken in the future may therefore differ profoundly from the one studied in the *Phenomenology*: it may involve many abbreviations and alternative routings. It is not, however, profitable to consider such for us empty possibilities. The path to be considered is the one actually taken in the past and terminating in the present. It is, however, for all that, a path involving necessary implications and developments which will be preserved in all paths taken in the future and in the terminus to which these lead. For, on Hegel's view, all dialectical thought-paths lead to the Absolute Idea and to the knowledge of it which is itself.

It is necessary, in considering the *Phenomenology*, as in considering all Hegel's other writings, to stress this initial point that, though Hegel may mention much that is contingent and historical, and may refuse to break wholly loose from this, his concern is always with the *Begriffe* or universal notional shapes that are evinced in fact and history, and with the ways in which *these* align themselves and lead on to one another, and can in fact ultimately be regarded as distinguishable facets of a single all-inclusive universal or concept. (See, for example, *Phenomenology*, §§6, 12 (pp. 12, 16)[1]; *Encyclopaedia* §§163–4.) For Hegel

---

[1] Page references to Hegel's *Phenomenology of Spirit* given within parentheses in the Foreword are to the German edition edited by J. Hoffmeister (F. Meiner, Hamburg, 1952). The paragraph numbers are those used in A. V. Miller's translation published in this volume.

the universal is no strengthless, arbitrary distillation of the common features of what is individual and empirical; it is rather what must be conceived as realizing itself in what is individual and empirical, and as responsible both for the being and intelligibility of the latter. But what is thus universal will not necessarily align together what are contiguous in space and history, and hence in the *Phenomenology* the conceptual treatment can jump wildly from one factual, empirical scene to the other, from, for example, the scientific universals behind phenomena to the fellow minds which discover them in phenomena, from the antique Stoics and Sceptics, who entrenched themselves in cogitative abstraction from contingent content, to the medieval devotees who located their explanatory abstractions beyond all such content, from the compassion which enables the man of conscience to forgive the sin-soiled man of action to the religious spirit which can see the divine in all men, and so on.

It is also necessary to stress here that the dialectical development which Hegel sees as connecting his phenomenological phases is a logical growth of notions out of notions, given to *us* who consider the cultural past of humanity as resumed in ourselves, but not given as a logical growth to those who, including ourselves, went through the actual cases of such notions, and not even exactly following the order of the corresponding particularizations. The mind of humanity in the past did not, for example, see the necessary logical step from the kingdom of laws behind nature to the kingdom of subjects who consider nature, nor did they in fact historically pass from the one to the other. It is we, the phenomenological students of the shapes of Spirit, who see the logical connections between them, and therefore also for phenomenological purposes the order in which they must be arranged. It is important, therefore, that from the very beginning we frame viable conceptions of the logical 'movements' our notional shapes of Spirit must undergo, movements of which temporal sequences are often only inadequately and misplaced reflections. (See, for example, *Phenomenology*, §801) (p. 558); *Encyclopaedia* §258.) Subjectively, of course, as we have said, all these movements involve a species of reflection, a retreat to the vantage-point of a higher-order and, as we might now say, metalogical examination, and the consequent bringing into view of what can be truly predicated of a thought-phase, though not necessarily what is 'meant' or intended in its explicit content. But objectively what are thus brought into view are *other* thought-phases, thought-phases which in a very wide sense negate it or go beyond it, and which involve relations as various to the thought-phase in question as being its necessary correlate or complement or opposite, or as being what is true of it though not at all part of its content and perhaps contradicting the latter, or as being a more explicit and perfect form of what some phase obscurely prefigures, or as being some inclusive whole or unity of which the phase in question can only be an excerpt. The logical 'movement' which the *Phenomenology*, like the rest of the system, exhibits, is throughout the logic of the 'side' or 'aspect' or 'moment', of that which, while it can be legitimately distinguished in some unity, and must in fact be so distinguished, nevertheless represents something basically incapable of self-sufficiency and independence, properties which can only be attributed to the whole into which sides, aspects, or moments enter, and a reference to which is accordingly 'built into' each such side. On Hegel's basic assumptions negation, in a wide sense that covers difference, opposition, and reflection or relation, is essential to conception and being: we can conceive nothing and have nothing if we attempt to dispense with it. But negation in this wide sense always operates within a unity, which is not as such divisible into self-sufficient elements, but is totally present in each and all of its aspects, and we conceive nothing and have nothing if we attempt to dispense with this unity. This unity in a sense negates the former or primary negation: it changes what in a sense *tried* to be an independent element into a mere aspect or moment. This second sort of negation is not, however, comparable with the first: it involves a reversal of direction, which does not, however, annul the primary direction that it reverses. The distinctions are still there, but only as 'moments' and no longer as independent elements.

It is, further, in retrospect, the unity which reverses the first negation which also made that first negation possible. It is because a unity indivisibly underlies distinct sides, that each such side can acquire a certain relative self-sufficiency and independence, can after a fashion assert itself in opposition to the whole. But it is this unity also which forces the mind (and also

the thing) onward from one of its one-sided aspects to another
aspect necessary to its completion, and which ultimately builds
all sides into a single integrated or reasonable totality. From
the point of view of the phenomenological student, we have here
a dialectical process or sequence. This is always initiated by
the Understanding, that seemingly marvellous faculty (see
Phenomenology §32, (pp. 29–30)) that is able, as it were, to segre-
gate aspects in an indivisible whole, and to endow the non-independent with a certain quasi-independence. This segregation
is carried on by a dialectical phase in which other aspects then
either negate, oppose, supplement, or are put into necessary
relation with the first segregated aspect, which then loses itself
with the other aspects in a many-sided but truly indivisible
whole. From the point of view of the notional phases here concerned, they grow out of and into one another, not in the derived temporal sense in which the parts of an organism grow
out of one another, but rather in the primary sense in which,
for example, the whole series of numbers grows out of certain
basic arithmetical principles. The notional integration thus indicated ends, according to Hegel, in Absolute Knowledge or
the Absolute Idea, the test of whose absoluteness consists simply
in the fact that nothing further remains to be taken care of.
Even the contingencies and loosenesses of connection that
obtain in the world are such as the sort of system we are con-
structing does and must involve. That Hegel *does* achieve this
final integration is, of course, what many would dispute.

There is, however, yet another sense in which the *Phenomenology* is concerned only with notions or concepts, i.e. with the
universal shapes of Spirit, and only indirectly with the individual instances of such shapes. This depends on Hegel's view
that conscious Spirit or subjectivity is itself exhaustively analys-
able in terms of the three conceptual moments of universality,
specificity, and singularity, and that it represents, in fact,
merely an extreme form of these three notional functions, a
severance or an alienation of them from one another which is,
of course, inseparable from their fruitful and necessary coming-
together. For Hegel does not believe in the subject as being some
detached, substantival entity standing in varying relations to
other substantival entities which are its objects. The subject is,
as said in the *Encyclopaedia*, the active or self-active universal,

the universal in a peculiar form in which it distinguishes itself
from what is specific and individual, from what is perhaps given
sensibly, and yet goes forth from itself and interprets and con-
trols what thus confronts it objectively. In so doing, moreover,
it makes its objects its own, and is thereby enabled to return
to self and to achieve consciousness of self. (See *Phenomenology*
§18 (p. 20), also *Encyclopaedia* §§20–3.) The thinking Ego is,
further, in another place (*Phenomenology* §235 (pp. 178–9))
closely connected and in fact identified, much as by Kant in
the Transcendental Deduction, with the category or categories
used in the synthetic constitution of objects by the understanding, and, at the end of the *Phenomenology*, the conceptualization
of all objects, and their subjection to universals, is not seen as
different from the imposition on them of the *form of self* (*Phenomenology* §803 (p. 560)). The subject or Ego is thus for Hegel
not what we ordinarily understand by a personal thinker, but
the logical function of universality in a peculiar sort of
detachment from its species and instances. The mind for Hegel,
as for Aristotle, is thus the place of forms, a bustling Agora
where such forms are involved in endless transactions and con-
versations, and though it is by the intermediation of such forms
that there is a reaching-out to their individual instances, they
none the less enjoy a relative independence there, a detachment
in the thought-ether, that they never enjoy elsewhere. Universals, of course, on Hegel's view, enjoy a sunken, implicit existence *in* natural objects (see *Encyclopaedia* §24), and they also
enjoy some sort of being *beneath* the surface of natural objects,
as the essences or forces which explain them (*Phenomenology* §152
(p. 117)). They are also, in the Logic, given as having a status
as 'pure essentialities' or as 'notional shadows' without sensuous
concretion, in some sense prior to the existence of nature and
finite spirit. But however much universals, and that Universal
of all Universals, the Idea, may exist apart from subjects, in
any ordinary sense of the latter, the fact remains that they
achieve their full development and truth in the self-consciousness of Spirit, in which all universal patterns of logical and
natural being are reactivated and resumed.

The life then of conscious Spirit, whether in the *Phenomenology
of Spirit* or the later *Philosophy of Spirit*, is arguably only a series
of phases in which one or other of the moments of the Notion

is detached, as subjective, from the rest, which are thereby
extruded into objectivity, and which are then again reintegrated with the moments remaining in the subject, again
extruded and again reintegrated in an endlessly developing
rhythm. Those who know Hegel well, and are aware of the profound connections of the *Phenomenology* with the later system
(which is in fact all there in the Jena writings), will know how
mistaken are all those who think of the *Phenomenology* as merely
a contribution to existential phenomenology, to which the later
system is largely irrelevant. From first to last Hegel conceived
everything in terms of the self-active *Begriff* and *Idee*, and his
thought is as remote from the personally concerned thought of
the existentialists as from that of the grandiose suprapersonal
Ego of Fichte. These types of thought can, of course, be found
encapsulated in Hegel if one likes to look for them, since he
includes what he transcends and even includes what he will
transcend once his epigoni have formulated it. (Compare, for
example, his dialectical anticipations of Mill's views on induc-
tion and of the logical atomism of Wittgenstein and Russell.)
But what Hegel brings in as a phrase in an ongoing dialectic
is not, of course, his last word on a subject.

One more word before we begin our introductory survey of
the actual content of the *Phenomenology*. Since the *Phenomenology*
studies a particular path from immediate sense-experience to
all-grasping *Wissenschaft* which is also the path distilled in
Hegel's experience from the previous experiences of the World
Spirit, there will be much in that path that would be illuminated by knowledge of the personal history of Hegel: we ought
to know why he was impressed by certain notional entailments
and affinities and not by others. In part we do have considerable
light on this topic. We understand, for example, how the love
between him and his sister Christina caused him to stress the
role of sisters in ethical life, we understand his interest in the
Antigone from his schoolboy studies at Stuttgart, and we understand his interest in the French Enlightenment and Revolution
from the provincial position of continental Germany: both historical phases counted for much less in Britain. There are also
difficult allusions in his treatment of the Unhappy Consciousness which Rosenkranz convincingly illuminated. But there
remains much in the *Phenomenology* which is enigmatic, and one

cannot always see why the route to Absolute Knowledge should
wind through just these peculiar thickets. Hegel was in fact a
writer of literary genius, and one swayed in his choice of words
by a burgeoning unconscious. Once he departed from the dis-
piriting atmosphere of Berne and Frankfurt, and ceased writing
such relatively dull, much over-studied writing as he produced
there, an afflatus seized him in the Jena lecture-rooms, an
afflatus perhaps unique in philosophical history, which affected
not only his ideas but his style, and which makes one at times
only sure that he is saying something immeasurably profound
and important, but not exactly what it is. (I am in this position,
despite help, regarding the two intelligible worlds in the section
on Force and Understanding.) To comment on Hegel fully
would therefore require the same sort of psychological and
metapsychological treatment that has long been practised on
an essentially rapt man like Shakespeare or on such a Gallic
genius as Rimbaud or Mallarmé. Despite the sensitive work of
Jean Hyppolite, we are far from having anything like a really
full commentary on the *Phenomenology*. The general remarks
that I shall now make will therefore yield only a very inadequate prefatory illumination.

We shall begin our treatment of the *Phenomenology* with the
Introduction, ignoring the beautiful and famous Preface, which
was in fact only added when the book was complete, and which
was meant to introduce not only the *Phenomenology*, but the
whole system. The point of the Introduction is simply to give
a preliminary conception, justified only when the work would
be complete, as to *how* a study of the shapes of mind leading
one on from immediate experience to what claimed to be scientific knowledge could succeed in dissipating doubt as to the real
possibility of the whole venture. Might not the finally corrected
shape which emerged from such a process be as remote from
things 'as they in themselves are' as the first, uncorrected, immediate shape? And how could the projected work abolish
Kant's view that an examination of human knowledge only
shows, not that such knowledge can really reach some standpoint where 'the Absolute' or 'the Thing in Itself' will be accessible
to it, but that this is for ever and in itself impossible, that there
are and must be aspects of things that we can indeed conceive
negatively, or perhaps have beliefs about, but of which we can

never have knowledge? Hegel's criticism of this critical view
of knowledge is simply that it is self-refuting, that it pronounces,
even if negatively, on the relation of conscious appearances to
absolute reality, while claiming that the latter must for ever
transcend knowledge. To this self-refuting view Hegel opposes
the view that the distinction between what things in themselves
are, and what things only are for consciousness or knowledge,
must itself be a distinction drawn within consciousness, that the
former can be only the corrected view of an object, while the
latter is merely a view formerly entertained but now abandoned
as incorrect. The progress of knowledge will then consist in the
constant demotion of what appeared to be the absolute truth
about the object to what now appears to be only the way that
the object appeared to consciousness, a new appearance of absolute truth taking the former's place.

Hegel, however, assumes that this progress *must* have a final
term, a state where knowledge need no longer transcend or correct itself, where it will discover itself in its object and its object
in itself, where concept will correspond to object and object to
consciousness (see §80 (p. 69)). Such a conception might seem
to go too far, for surely an endless inadequacy of knowledge to its
object would not destroy all meaning and validity in such knowledge, nor would this vanish were there to be aspects of things of
which, as Kant held, we could only frame negative, regulative
conceptions, but of which we could never have definite knowledge? Hegel will, however, marvellously *include* in his final notion
of the final state of knowledge the notion of an endless progress
that can have no final term. For he conceives that, precisely
in seeing the object as an endless problem, we forthwith see it
as not being a problem at all. For what the object in itself is,
is simply to be the other, the stimulant of knowledge and practice, which in being for ever capable of being remoulded and
reinterpreted, is also everlastingly pinned down and found out
being just what it is. The implication of all this is that the teleological view of objectivity as being intrinsically destined to be
interpreted and controlled by consciousness will prove, on a sufficiently deep examination, to be so wholly appeasing and
satisfying that no shadow of the hidden or inexplicable will
remain to haunt us. We shall then be in a fit state to investigate
the essentialities of being as set forth in the Logic, and the sub-

sequent self-externalization of these essentialities in the philosophies of Nature and Spirit. Whether this Hegelian view of the role of the object as a mere inspirer of spiritual effort is valid may of course be questioned: there would certainly seem to be obscurities, inconsequences, and dysteleologies in our world which demoralize, rather than stimulate, spiritual effort. We shall not, however, consider these contemporary depressants, which Hegel, as a German Romantic, could not have envisaged.

The Introduction in its final paragraphs (§§86–9 (pp. 71–5)) makes the further important point that the lessons that consciousness learns in its continued experience of objects are not *for it* a continuous course of lessons: it conceives that it is constantly passing to some new and unrelated object, when it is really only seeing its previous object in some novel, critical light. It is not, for example, aware, as previously said, that the consciousness of an order of mutually conscious persons is what was implicit in the awareness of laws, forces, and other essentialities behind the phenomena of nature: it is *we*, the phenomenological students, who see the deep notional continuity in what is for it a kaleidoscope of objects. It is important, in what follows, that we should always distinguish between the actual transitions occurring in conscious experience and the *logical* transitions that the phenomenologist elicits from these latter.

In Section A on Consciousness Hegel explores three relations of conscious subjectivity to its object: the *Sense-certainty* which merely confronts an object in what seems to be its rich individuality without making anything definite of it, the Perception where it begins to distinguish properties or qualities in the immediately given, but is unable to integrate them in the unity of the perceived thing, and finally the Understanding, where the natures of things are seen as fixed patterns of mutual interference and interaction behind their manifest, phenomenal surface. Sense-certainty is dialectically flawed by its claim to qualitative richness and individual immediacy, since it is impossible to pin down the qualities which are thus felt to be rich and various or the individuality which is thus felt to be wholly unique. For in the flux of experience one quality is constantly yielding place to another, and it is impossible to seize what is individual by pointing gestures or by demonstrative words such

as 'This', 'Here', 'Now', 'I', etc., which are all irremediably
general in meaning. Perception, likewise, is dialectically flawed
by its incapacity to integrate the separate characters it picks out
with the unified individuality of the object to which it seeks
to attribute them. Both lead on to Understanding, where the
universal in terms of which immediacies are to be understood
is both a complex pattern unifying a number of discriminable
characters and also involves the distinction of the manifest and
the dispositional, the latter being part and parcel of such
notions as permanent nature, specific essence, force, and law.
But the realm of the essential and dispositional is dialectically
flawed by its inability to explain the comprehensive dovetailing
of essential natures, forces, and laws into one another, so as to
form only one system of interacting essentialities. It is by recognizing something akin to the explanatory unity imparted by
conscious mind to all that it considers, that this dialectical flaw
is removed, and that the consciousness of objects is replaced
by self-consciousness or by a consciousness *of* consciousness. It
is important to realize that the sensing, perceiving, understanding, and self-conscious mind does not perceive the logical connections which lead from each of these stages to the next. It
is *we*, the phenomenologists, who perceive them. To consciousness itself there is simply a blurred, sensuous confrontation with
unseizable, qualified particulars, which becomes clarified into
a perception of things which in some manner mysteriously unite
different aspects or characters, and which then becomes
organized in the sense of a number of regularly recurrent
'natures' making dynamic impacts upon us and upon one
another. From this the glance simply switches to the rational
creatures around oneself, who are all interpreting the same
objects, without identifying their interpretative acts with the
interpretations embedded in things. It is the watching phenomenologist who discerns all these transitions, and who above
all performs the difficult, non-formal transition from 'Things
are interacting in a manner X' to '*We all* are understanding
things as interacting in a manner X'.

From Consciousness, A, we have therefore jumped to B, Self-
consciousness, where our object is now a conscious Ego, an actively functioning, categorically synthetic universal, looking
about for fully specified and individualized contents to interpret

intellectually and to master practically (§177 (p. 140)). Practical
desire which transforms the object is at this stage more important than intellectual interpretation.) But the active universality of the subject Ego is at first unwilling to see in the
active Universality of the object Ego a just reflection of itself.
It at first tries to demote the object Ego to one that will indeed
recognize *it* as subject Ego, but whom *it* in its turn will *not* fully
recognize as an active subject (§185 (p. 143)). This demotion
of object Egos by subject Egos then inevitably leads to what
Hegel calls a Life-and-death struggle: each subject wishes to
be the sole centre of active universality and to risk all in asserting his claims. Such a policy, however, threatens to deprive
each subject of the recognition he demands, and hence the
struggle develops into one for a sovereign position among actively universal subjects, all others being wholly subordinated
to this one (Lord and Bondsman). But this one-sided aspiration
is also self-frustrating, since the recognition one receives from
a pale reflex of oneself can be no true recognition, and will in
fact impoverish the receiver, whereas the recognition the serf
accords to his lord, and the work he does for him, will raise
him to a far higher consciousness of active universality than the
lord can ever enjoy. Obviously the flawed, imperfect universality where *every* subject desires sovereignty only for *himself*
(the second occurrence of the variable not being independently
quantified) necessarily corrects itself in the unflawed universality where *every* subject recognizes and promotes active
universality in *every* subject, where all men equally recognize
and co-operate with one another.

This stage must, however, at first be present as an inner ideal
to which the particularity of interpersonal existence will not
as yet conform: the world is not as yet so arranged that all can
be servants and thus also lords to one another. The self-active
universal therefore withdraws *stoically* into the emptily abstract
fortress of reason and virtue, or, recognizing this emptiness, into
a similar impractically *sceptical* fortress which commits itself to
nothing whatever, whether theoretical or practical. Finally we
have an extreme, pathological form of spiritual withdrawal in
which consciousness, unable to disengage itself from irrational
particularity, simply identifies itself with the latter, and is then
led to extrude the rational universality which is its true self into

a mystical, unattainable Beyond. Consciousness in this last
pathology makes itself the universal serf, while the lord in his
perfection becomes no one and dwells nowhere. Such a strained
separation of moments that necessarily belong together cannot
but break down. Consciousness must pass from a wallowing self-
abasing mysticism to a *reasonable* frame of mind. It must see the
world, in all its natural and social arrangements, as something
to be known, enjoyed, and improved by all, since it embodies
the same universality that is active in each subject. Here again
we must stress that the logical sequence of phases from the Life-
and-death-struggle to Reason is not a logical sequence for those
who live through it. They pass from Hobbesian egoism to various forms of abstract intersubjectivity, then to a despair which
locates all shared universality infinitely above and beyond
themselves, and then on to a confidence born from the sheer
absurdity of such despair, all without seeing the secret logical
links which link one such attitude to another.

   The next section of the *Phenomenology* (§§231–437), devoted
to various forms of *Vernunft* or Reasonableness, gets off, after
a short discussion of the Hegelian meaning of 'idealism' (§§231–
40 (pp. 175–82))—as a philosophy which discovers the same
universality in the world as in subjective thought—to a consideration of various forms of scientific empiricism and experi-
mentation. (This is not the same as the projections of the Understanding studied in §§132–65 (pp. 102–29), since the scientific
understanding is now conscious and confident, even if
obscurely, of its own methodological procedures.) We start with
the observational study of nature, in which the universal in the
mind divines its own presence in the world, and is guided by
an 'instinct of reason' to see what that presence may in detail
involve. Hegel goes into a long discussion of various forms of
observational description and classification, and the passage
from these to the formulation of laws which involve unmanifest
and dispositional factors. The discovery of such laws is wholly
successful in the inorganic realm, but can only be partially successful in the organic realm, where all laws are laws of tendency,
and involve contingencies introduced by that 'universal individual', the Earth, as well as all the systematic indefinitenesses
of teleology. The observational urge therefore directs itself inward to the true home of self-determining universality, and in-

vestigates, first the principles of a logic conceived in purely psy-
chologistic terms, and then the wider psychologism which deals
in contingent mental traits and faculties. This treatment of
conscious inwardness as if it had the contingency and the
singularity of external, natural being, leads, however, inevitably to attempts to physicalize consciousness, to identify it with
a thing, or a set of things, that we find out there in the natural
world. Had Hegel lived in the present age we should now have
had a long treatment of the behaviourisms of Watson and Tol-
man and Skinner: as it is, we are treated to a repulsively long
discussion of the crude physiognomic speculations of Lavater
and the phrenological fantasies of Gall. All that is important
in Hegel's long attempt to make dialectical sense of these primitive exercises is the final outcome: that if self-consciousness can
be reduced to something like a bone or a bone-structure, then
a bone or a bone-structure must be credited with all the in-
tentional negativity, and the negation of this negativity, involved in self-consciousness. The manœuvres of reductionism
are accordingly vain: if mind can be modelled by matter, matter must be possessed of every intricate modality of mind. Nothing has been achieved by the 'reduction', and, since the phenomena of self-consciousness are richer and more intrinsically intelligible than the limited repertoire that we ordinarily ascribe
to matter, it is matter rather than mind that is thereby reduced.
This conclusion is what Bertrand Russell would call 'malicious'.
Hegel, however, is not ashamed of the vengeful ingratitude of
consciousness and spirit: it overreaches its pitiable 'other', and
reduces it to itself.

Hegel now characteristically moves from a reasonableness
concerned to *discover* itself in objects to a reasonableness concerned to *impose* itself on objects through overt action. After a
few initial moves (§§347–58 (pp. 254–61)), which anticipate
what will really only emerge at the stage of the Spiritual, Hegel
begins by discussing the hedonistic approach to the world, the
reasonableness which makes everything in the world, including
the body and soul of another person, minister to one's own satisfaction. This attitude breaks down in a manner analogous to
the seeming fulness of sense-certainty: it condemns the hedonist
to an endless, hollow search for new pleasures, which never provide a lasting content for self-consciousness. The hedonistic life

therefore dissolves into the romantic life of the heart, the life
which espouses grand projects, which in their extravagance
measure up to the sweeping universality of self-consciousness,
but which inevitably clash with the equally grand life-projects
of others. The game of the heart then yields place to the greater
game of virtue, of the keeping of oneself pure in quixotic scruple
and total indifference to 'the way of the world'. This game,
however, also interferes with the parallel quixotism of others,
and with the sensible non-quixotism of the ordered social world,
which is more truly universal than the cult of personal virtue.
The dialectic then swings over from arbitrary subjectivity to
the arbitrary objectivity of *Sachlichkeit*. A man identifies himself
with a *Sache*, a thing or a task, which is his own, and which
he pursues without regard to external success or approval.
Everyone else is similarly supposed to be devoting himself to
his own *Sache*. Such disinterested fulfilment of tasks rests, however, on self-deception. Its disinterestedness is always held up
for the admiration of others, and is really a form of personal
exhibitionism. When this is exposed, disinterestedness shifts to
a moralistic form, setting up absolute prescriptions of various
simple sorts (Tell the truth, Help others, etc.). These can, however, never achieve the complete exceptionlessness to which
they aspire. Reasonableness then finally assumes the Kantian
form of identifying the universal with the formally universaliz-
able or self-consistent. This, Hegel shows, is as vacuous as the
universalism of the Stoics or Sceptics, since any way of life can
be rendered formally self-consistent. We therefore move to a
universalism which is *substantial* as well as subjective, the universalism of the ethical life of an actual community, whose laws
and customs clothe the bare bones of ethical prescriptions with
living flesh, and make the universalizing life genuinely possible.
We pass from the merely Reasonable (*Vernunft*) to the higher
stage of the Spiritual (*Geist*).

Hegel finds the exemplary material for his first, rudimentary
form of spirituality in the ethical world of Greek tragedy, with
which he had come into vivid contact in his Gymnasium studies
at Stuttgart. Rudimentary spiritual life is not the life of an undivided community with which the individual subject identifies himself whole-heartedly: it is essentially bifocal,
and centres as much in the family, with its unwritten prescrip-

tions dimly backed by dead ancestors, as in the overt power
of the State, with its openly proclaimed, 'daylight' laws. The
law of the family is a divine law, a law stemming from the
underworld of the unconscious, and interpreted by the intuitive
females in the family: the state law is on the contrary human,
and is proclaimed and enforced by mature males. Hegel makes
plain that these two laws must at times clash—the theme of
the *Antigone* and other tragedies: in the case of such clashes,
the individual incurs guilt whatever he may do. Obviously
Hegel has here seized on a very profound source of disunity
in ethical spiritual life: the clash between a self-transcendence
which is deep, but also tinged with contingent immediacy, and
a self-transcendence which can be extended indefinitely,
but in that very extensibility necessarily lacks depth.
The truly moral life to which we must advance will be as deep
in its care for individual problems and circumstances as
it is wide in its concern for anyone and everyone. For the time
being, however, the rent life of the primitive ethical community must yield place to a spiritual life where all intimacy is
dissolved.

Hegel here chooses for his illustration the atomistic life of Imperial Rome (§§477–83 (pp. 342–6)), where every man counts
as no more than a property-owner and the state laws merely
concern the ownership and transmission of property. Such an
atomistic community, to which all individual needs and characters are indifferent, necessarily culminates in a more or less arbitrarily selected Imperator or World-master, whose relation to
the community is external, and quite void of anything like
family depth and warmth. The removal of intimacy, of warmth
or soul, from the mutual recognition of the community's
members, must, however, necessarily give rise to a sense of distance, of estrangement or alienation from the community. The
latter may represent the individual's true self, but he cannot
find himself in it. If Hegel has chosen Imperial Rome as his
first example of such alienation, he now leaps to seventeenth-
and eighteenth-century continental Europe, with its dazzling
French centre, for one of his most fascinating and brilliant
phenomenological studies. The jump here taken shows how
little the *Phenomenology* is an eidetic reconstitution of history,
and how much it is concerned with spiritual stances that are

very widely scattered, for example in Hellenistic Greece, India in the time of Buddha, contemporary America, etc.

In the immense central section of Spirit (§§488–595 (pp. 347–422)) in which Hegel discusses alienated spirituality, there are two central focuses: the focus of Enlightenment (*Aufklärung*), representing the abstract communal life of a mutual recognition and shared use of facilities which never becomes intimate, and the focus of Faith or Belief (*Glaube*), which in a dim and confused way strives to overcome the abstraction which leads to alienation, and to return to the intimate concreteness of tribal and family life. It seems clear that in this section Hegel is really characterizing the spiritual life of Germany, that eternal servitor among nations, condemned to admire and imitate the brilliant, brittle universalism of French life and culture, while always hankering after the integrity and concreteness of a simpler, sturdier, more peasant-like vision, the vision which expressed itself, for example, in the Rhineland masters or in countless religious sculptors and wood-carvers. The German eighteenth century was one of the high-points of such alienation: if it was the age when Voltaire and Maupertuis plumed themselves at Frederick's court, it was also the age of the pietists, so strong an influence in the early life of Kant and Hegel, the simple, good people who scorned all but the precepts and transforming example of the 'Holy One of the Gospels'. The simple man of virtue and good sense, whom Hegel depicts as struck dumb by the ruthless wit of the French salons (§§523–4 (pp. 373–4)), is arguably the eternal German visitor, struggling to unify the cultivated negations of a disintegrating society, which he admires but only half understands, with the simple standards and principles that the 'folks at home' still rely on and live by.

The spirituality of the Enlightenment is first sketched in a section entitled Enlightenment and its Realm of Actuality (§§488–526 (pp. 350–76)). This spirituality is characterized as being essentially one of Culture (*Bildung*), by which nothing immediate or natural is reckoned as of importance. Its universality is that of the open variable: one must always be ready to progress further, to develop talents and possibilities, to replace one's initial constants with others. This open variability reveals itself, on the one hand, in the infinitely ramifying structure of the state bureaucracy, culminating in the Monarch, and, on the other hand, in the endless open variability of economic life, in which enterprises always expand or decline, fortunes go up and down, and extreme wealth always goes flanked by abject penury. This spirituality is also always one of divided values: residues of feudal loyalty still attach to the bureaucracy and the monarch, while new values, whether favourable or unfavourable, circulate about money-making and money-changers. In the inner life of those who live in this alienated regime the divided values appear in two new forms: in sophisticated, Voltairian 'insight' on the one hand, and in the deliberate unsophistication of pious belief (*Glaube*) on the other. These are discussed through §§527–81 (pp. 376–411), and Hegel is mainly concerned to stress that the whole fight between these seemingly irreconcilable opponents is really a sham fight, since the generalized insights of Voltairianism mean nothing without their concrete implementation in such lives as those of good, God-fearing people, just as the 'simple' faith of the latter is really, in its indifference to anything merely outward or literal, as full of critical negativity as the enlightenment of Voltaire. The Voltairian thinks religious piety is intent on icons or wafers, or historical events which never happened, whereas religious piety is as critical of vain observances or of external signs as the Voltairian, and believes only in religious events that can be re-enacted in the believer's heart. And, if the Voltairian regards the God of pious worship as a mere projection of its thought, the pietist agrees with him in worshipping a God felt not to be alien to his own spirituality, but as being the universality of which he represents only the contraction (§549 (pp. 390–1)). The various abstractions posited by the enlightened, whether going by the names of 'matter' or 'the supreme being', are likewise mere projections of the enlightened person's thought, only more empty and the same in their total emptiness.

The alienated spirituality of the Enlightenment is not, however, able to achieve a true synthesis of abstractly universalistic insight and pious unsophistication: its most positive achievement in this direction is the thin notion of *Nützlichkeit*, Utility (§579 (pp. 410–11)). Everything in the world has then its sole justification in its usefulness towards human ends, which, like anything merely concrete, generate an endless series of performances and arrangements, each exciting purely for the sake of something else. But the two abstractions of individual subjectivity on the one hand, with its intimately felt demands, and the indifferent, external, bureaucratic-economic machine on the other, have necessarily to come together, and this is at first brought about in an abstraction which liquidates both, much as emptily restless Becoming in the Logic is the joint outcome of emptily abstract Being and emptily abstract Nothingness. The pure self-assertion of the individual person, the element always passed over by the whole alienated society, storms the Bastille and creates a society which will reflect and express his absolute self alone. It does not, however, take Hegel long to exhibit the purely destructive and ultimately self-destructive profile of this spiritual stance (§§528–95). Spiritual sansculottism can have no programme but the downing and doing-away of everything and everyone: it can generate no principle of self-differentiation, it can throw up no genuine or permanent leadership. It is a government by junta, by cabal and intrigue, and can achieve only the universal suppression and liquidation of individuality. It would have been interesting if, instead of this dialectical criticism of the relatively innocuous and transient synthesis of Liberty, Equality, and Fraternity, dismembered almost as soon as formed, we had had Hegel's criticisms of the far more adhesive pitch-like abstractions of the *Communist Manifesto*, in which the feet of humanity would seem as if for ever entangled.

The third of Hegel's studies of Spirituality is entitled Spirit Sure of Itself or Morality (§§596–671 (pp. 424–72)). Here we have a study of dutiful subjectivity, by which Hegel understands neither the personal cult of Virtue, a superseded form of egoistic Reasonableness, nor the blind obedience to the daylight or underground laws of the substantial ethical community, but rather a set of practically oriented attitudes representing the individual's own deep reflection on conduct, balanced by a deep respect for the parallel reflections of others. The moral view of the world sees the fulfilment of duty not only as the whole task of man, but also as the whole purpose of nature, and also of a continuation of life and consciousness beyond the limits of our present state. Such a view requires supplementation by theological postulates: we must posit a God who will guarantee the indefinite survival that will make endless moral

progress possible, and who will also complete the moral good
of virtue with the natural good of happiness. Such a view is
at once involved in peculiar contradictions, and in the bad faith
and hypocrisy (*Verstellung*) used to cover up such contradictions. It must alternate like Sisyphus between seeming on the
point of pushing the stone of its sensuousness on to the high
plateau of perfect virtue, and then realizing that this would destroy, rather than perfect, virtue, and so sinking back once
more to the bottom of the hill. (See, for example, §623 (p. 439).)
These self-contradictory postulations, and these hypocritical
self-deceptions, are then all cured in the spiritual stance of pure
Conscientiousness, where the subject makes his goal the simple
doing of his duty *as he sees it*, without worrying about its relations
to the natural or supernatural order, or without raising the unreal issue of what he should do once he has achieved perfection.
Conscientiousness so defined has its standard of certainty in
itself: it is undisturbed by the conflict of prima facie duties, since
it is the sole arbiter as to which must override which (§635 (p.
447)). It is also undisturbed by the conflict between different
men's consciences, since it is not part of the idea of conscience
that it should pronounce identically to different men. The cult
of conscience is a religion, a religion at once lonely, yet at a
higher level communal. My conscience in its absolute majesty
legislates *for me* and for me alone, but its legislation *for me* is
recognized as valid by all conscientious persons, and so in a
sense becomes a law for all (§§655–6 (pp. 460–2)).

Hegel's analysis is here very profound, and wholly true to
what we actually think and say. It is superior to analyses which
argue that where consciences differ, one or other must be mistaken, failing to see that they thereby remove the one solvent
virtue of conscientiousness, that it can decide issues which are
in the abstract undecidable. This solvent virtue of conscientiousness is, however, open to other difficulties: though inerrant in
what it proclaims, it can at times be thought to be enunciating
duties when it is not really pronouncing clearly on anything,
or when its presumed voice is really that of some external authority, or of some private interest, or some intellectual confusion.
And, while the communion of conscientious persons must
always respect my conscience, they may at times doubt whether
some pronouncement really springs from my conscience,

whether it is not the expression of some hypocritical personal interest (§661 (pp. 464–5)). Faced with this new fear of self-deceit, conscience readily takes refuge in a passive concern with 'problems': it prefers to wring its hands in beautiful impotence, rather than do something that *may* be wrong, and so violate the law of conscience (§658 (p. 462)). This impotent beauty of soul then confronts the other species of conscientiousness, which has dared to make difficult decisions, and perhaps goes on to condemn it, thereby, however, implicitly condemning itself. For the refusal to take a decision is itself a decision, even if of higher order. The confrontation may, however, lead on to a higher spiritual reconciliation, that of mutual understanding and forgiveness among men, who have nevertheless decided differently. At this stage, Hegel tells us, morality becomes religious: we experience a spirit at once present in, yet transcending, the difference of conscientious agents, and which is rightly thought of as suprapersonal and divine (§671 (pp. 471–2)). If the quarrel of consciences really ended, there would be no place for God: God exists and is active because He lives beyond any form of reasoned consensus.

Hegel's phenomenology of Religion (§§672–787 (pp. 473–520)) runs through all the forms in which men have conceived, and must necessarily conceive, a spirituality which transcends their own, and which as much lies behind nature as behind the personal and social life of men. He writes beautifully of the Iranian religion of Light, of the Indian pantheisms which place the malign and sinister alongside the beautiful and good, of the Egyptian religion of the Understanding, with its passion for geometrical forms and for enigmatic sculptural combinations of human rationality with animality. From all these we pass on to the 'Art-Religion' of Greece, which, if tinged, in Hegel's account, with eighteenth-century German sensibility and romanticism, is still described with aptness and beauty. The sculptured god represents to Hegel a fine fusion of rational self-consciousness with sensuous externality, and the same applies to the hymn and the rite, to the athlete with his glorious, public body, and to the semi-religious performances of tragedy and comedy. All forms of religion, which unite the self-consciously human with what transcends it, must, however, suffer decay and attrition in a period when man becomes alienated from his deeper self, a period such as that of Rome under the Caesars, or again of Europe in the eighteenth century, and so on. It was at such a point in time that Christianity, the absolute and revealed religion, first made its appearance, a religious stance in which human spirituality strives upwards towards and becomes one with a spirituality which transcends the human, while the latter likewise is seen as coming down into and trans-figuring human spirituality. If this spiritual identification of two natures was conceived of as first occurring in the historic person of Jesus, it was also thought of as being capable of being shared by a whole society of believers, to whom the Divine Spirit at work in Jesus could be further communicated. Such a union of the individual and the specific with the transcen-dently universal is of course for Hegel the sense and 'truth' of everything. It is not necessary nor pertinent for us here to enter into a long assessment of Hegel's merits or demerits as a Christian theologian. Plainly he saw as merely pictorial much that orthodox Christians would see as essential to their faith. But his philosophical reconstitution of Christianity strays no further from his original than, for example, the Aristotelian–neo-Platonic reconstitution of Aquinas: in some respects it keeps closer to it. For the Christianity of Germany, as witnessed by countless, infinitely affecting altar-pieces, has always been one that could best distil beauty from agony, and which could see what was most divine in the lifting of the ordinary griefs, frustrations, and pathetic needs of men into a region that trans-cends the human. The Christian God is essentially redemptive, and Hegel's philosophy is essentially a philosophy of redemp-tion, of a self-alienation that returns to self in victory. If Hegel was nothing better, he was at least a great Christian theologian.

The phenomenological drama now draws to its close. Con-sciousness has confronted the world through the senses, de-scribed it perceptually, and construed it quasi-scientifically. It has learnt, after some initial distortions, to put itself on a level with others, and has proceeded with their aid to classify and explain the phenomena of nature and mind. It has also tried to contribute distinctively to interpersonal life by various per-sonal programmes of a hedonistic, sentimental, improving, absorbedly practical, and analytically ethical sort. It has become aware of the community of conscious persons as united, and also dirempted, by the close bonds of common ancestry and family love, and also more loosely but widely held together by governmental and economic ties. It has experienced the tensions of social positions where men are subjected to external legal and economic pressures, where their need for a more profound communion has to be displaced to the higher plane of faith. It has worked through the various stages and syndromes of a conscientiousness that has learnt to cut Gordian knots in its practical decisions and to respect others whose decisions have cut these differently. It has risen to a religion for which the active universality, the Spirit which informs the teleology of nature and history, is also felt and pictured as a principle which achieves self-consciousness in a paradigmatic man, and, through the Spirit there present, in all men. What will now be achieved is *das absolute Wissen*, the perfect knowledge only consummated in philosophy, and here spoken of with a brevity and a modesty which accords with Hegel's simple sense of its all-importance. For absolute knowledge is simply the realization that all forms of objectivity are identical with those essential to the thinking subject, so that in construing the world conceptually it is seeing everything in the form of self, the self being simply the ever-active principle of conceptual universality, of categorial synthesis. In its conceptual grasp of objects it necessarily grasps what it itself is, and in grasping itself it necessarily grasps every phase of objectivity. These are the claims obscurely stated in Kant's transcendental deduction, but there given a one-sidedly subjective slant which is here for ever done away with. (See §§798–800 (pp. 556–7).)

Prior to this final conceptual grasp there has been a long process in time during which the extruded concept, the self alienated from self, has been steadily enriched in its determinations until, when the process was completed, the extruded concept simply came into coincidence with the self which studies it, and Time, in which the process was completing itself, was abolished, made wholly irrelevant (§801 (pp. 557–8)). The beginnings of absolute knowledge occurred at a point in time when the religious view of the Middle Ages yielded to the first stirring of modern post-Renaissance thought, when Descartes made his celebrated connection of thinking with being. It continued through Spinoza's attribution of thought and extension

to a single substance, and through Leibniz's further diremption
of this substance into countless points of individual spirituality.
Then followed the Enlightenment with its stress on utility—
the unmentioned empiricists are not here seen as helping on
'conceptual grasp'—and this in its turn gave rise to the Kantian
subordination of all practical ends to the demands of the
rational will—the transcendental deduction here also goes unmentioned—and this to the philosophy of Fichte, where the
pure self necessarily opposes itself to, yet also identifies itself
with, the flux of time, and is further opposed to the frozen differentiation of space. From this the thought of Schelling developed, where substantial being and subjective thought were
alike thrown back into the abyss of the Absolute, and neither
enjoyed an unquestioned priority. Out of all these thought-
stances the final form of conceptual grasp emerged, where the
self or subject saw itself as itself the Absolute, externalizing itself
in substantial, objective nature, yet conscious of itself in this
very act of self-externalization, and of itself, in fact, as simply
being its own act of self-identification in and through such externalization. (The packed thought of §§803–4 (pp. 560–1) defies
reproduction in terms other than its own, and one is quite un-
sure that one has got the full gist of it.) At this stage of grasp
the whole distinction between objective truth and subjective
certitude vanishes: the Notion or Concept unites both aspects
in itself. We are therefore in a position to develop the scientific
system which has been our goal from the first, where notions
develop purely out of notions in virtue of their own inner
oppositions and mediations. Obviously what Hegel is here an-
ticipating (§805 (p. 562)) is the Logic or Metaphysics which
is the first part of his system. He tells us that this system must
then go on to exhibit the self-externalization of his purely logical
categories in the sensuous shows of nature and in the contingencies which fill space and time (§§806–7 (p. 563)), and that
it must then study itself returning to itself out of nature's externality, a return which will restate the content of the phenomenology in the form of a real history of spirit, i.e. in the Philosophy of Spirit which will form the third part of the system (§808
(pp. 563–4)). What has further happened at this point is that
the phenomenological 'We' that has been examining and ordering the shapes of consciousness has itself become one of their

number, has revealed itself as being the final shape of consciousness. As such it now appropriates and remembers the whole content of the development that it has been studying, and can go on to study alignments of shapes which are as much shapes of being as of its own conscious certitude.

We might at this point go on to analyse the superb *Vorrede* or Preface, which Hegel wrote early in 1807 as an Introduction, not only to the *Phenomenology*, but to the whole system. We shall, however, abstain from doing this, and shall leave the reader with a task which he should be able to perform with pleasure, provided he reads the rest of the book before the Preface. What we have said in this Foreword is only meant to be a sketch, a preliminary help, and the same applies to the analyses that have been added to the translated paragraphs of the text. They are meant to orient the reader in the thickets of the text, not to provide exhaustive or wholly reliable guidance. They have been found useful by my students, and may prove useful to others. Mr. Miller has further translated the text with great care and faithfulness, but no amount of either will achieve unambiguous perspicuity where the text fails to provide it.

At the end of these remarks it may be asked whether Hegel's self-justifying circular series of spiritual characterizations has done anything like show that the real must coincide with the intelligible, or that the 'truth' about anything will consist in its teleological relation to the emergence of spiritual self-consciousness. He has certainly shown up the absurdity of believing in objective arrangements which are wholly out of gear with our categories and our thought-demands, and which are not at all accommodated to our theoretical requirements or to our practical approaches and endeavours. But has he exorcised the doubt that there may be sides of the world which will remain obstinately and depressingly unintelligible, and which are without a significant teleological relation to our spiritual goals and endeavours, and which may in the end bring these all to nought? These doubts, to which the state of science and the state of the world lend some substance, are not, however, such as can be considered in this Foreword, nor is it clear by what process of reasoning, dialectical or other, they could be adequately exorcised.

Boston University

TRANSLATOR'S FOREWORD

THIS translation of Hegel's *Phenomenology of Spirit* has been made from the fifth edition (F. Meiner, Hamburg, 1952) edited by J. Hoffmeister. In attempting to convey Hegel's thought to the English reader who has no German, I have done my best to steer a course which, avoiding loose paraphrase, departs at times from a rigid consistency in rendering Hegelian locutions where this seemed to be more helpful to the reader. I have been sparing in the use of capitals and, in general, have only used them for terms which have a peculiarly Hegelian connotation. The German *Verstand* I have translated by 'the Understanding'. Where the capital is omitted, the word has the usual English meaning.

The translation was undertaken at the suggestion of Professor Findlay to whom I am greatly indebted for encouragement and advice. I also wish to thank Professor H. S. Harris of Glendon College, York University, Toronto, who saw parts of the translation and offered helpful criticism and suggestions. Responsibility for the translation rests, of course, with me. Thanks are also due to my wife Frances who typed the final draft of my manuscript.

'*Rivendell*'   A. V. MILLER
Whiteway,
Glos.
March 1976

CONTENTS

PREFACE: ON SCIENTIFIC COGNITION

1. It is customary to preface a work with an explanation of the author's aim, why he wrote the book, and the relationship in which he believes it to stand to other earlier or contemporary treatises on the same subject. In the case of a philosophical work, however, such an explanation seems not only superfluous but, in view of the nature of the subject-matter, even inappropriate and misleading. For whatever might appropriately be said about philosophy in a preface—say a historical *statement* of the main drift and the point of view, the general content and results, a string of random assertions and assurances about truth—none of this can be accepted as the way in which to expound philosophical truth. Also, since philosophy moves essentially in the element of universality, which includes within itself the particular, it might seem that here more than in any of the other sciences the subject-matter itself, and even in its complete nature, were expressed in the aim and the final results, the execution being by contrast really the unessential factor. On the other hand, in the ordinary view of anatomy, for instance (say, the knowledge of the parts of the body regarded as inanimate), we are quite sure that we do not as yet possess the subject-matter itself, the content of this science, but must in addition exert ourselves to know the particulars. Further, in the case of such an aggregate of information, which has no right to bear the name of Science, an opening talk about aim and other such generalities is usually conducted in the same historical and uncomprehending way in which the content itself (these nerves, muscles, etc.) is spoken of. In the case of philosophy, on the other hand, this would give rise to the incongruity that along with the employment of such a method its inability to grasp the truth would also be demonstrated.

2. Furthermore, the very attempt to define how a philosophical work is supposed to be connected with other efforts to deal with the same subject-matter drags in an extraneous concern, and what is really important for the cognition of the

truth is obscured. The more conventional opinion gets fixated on the antithesis of truth and falsity, the more it tends to expect a given philosophical system to be either accepted or contradicted; and hence it finds only acceptance or rejection. It does not comprehend the diversity of philosophical systems as the progressive unfolding of truth, but rather sees in it simple disagreements. The bud disappears in the bursting-forth of the blossom, and one might say that the former is refuted by the latter; similarly, when the fruit appears, the blossom is shown up in its turn as a false manifestation of the plant, and the fruit now emerges as the truth of it instead. These forms are not just distinguished from one another, they also supplant one another as mutually incompatible. Yet at the same time their fluid nature makes them moments of an organic unity in which they not only do not conflict, but in which each is as necessary as the other; and this mutual necessity alone constitutes the life of the whole. But he who rejects a philosophical system [i.e. the new philosopher] does not usually comprehend what he is doing in this way; and he who grasps the contradiction between them [i.e. the historian of philosophy] does not, as a general rule, know how to free it from its one-sidedness, or maintain it in its freedom by recognizing the reciprocally necessary moments that take shape as a conflict and seeming incompatibility.

3. Demanding and supplying these [superficial] explanations passes readily enough as a concern with what is essential. Where could the inner meaning of a philosophical work find fuller expression than in its aims and results, and how could these be more exactly known than by distinguishing them from everything else the age brings forth in this sphere? Yet when this activity is taken for more than the mere beginnings of cognition, when it is allowed to pass for actual cognition, then it should be reckoned as no more than a device for evading the real issue [*die Sache selbst*], a way of creating an impression of hard work and serious commitment to the problem, while actually sparing oneself both. For the real issue is not exhausted by stating it as an aim, but by carrying it out, nor is the result the actual whole, but rather the result together with the process through which it came about. The aim by itself is a lifeless universal, just as the guiding tendency is a mere drive that as yet

lacks an actual existence; and the bare result is the corpse which
has left the guiding tendency behind it. Similarly, the specific
difference of a thing is rather its limit; it is where the thing
stops, or it is what the thing is not. This concern with aim or
results, with differentiating and passing judgement on various
thinkers is therefore an easier task than it might seem. For instead of getting involved in the real issue, this kind of activity
is always away beyond it; instead of tarrying with it, and losing
itself in it, this kind of knowing is forever grasping at something
new; it remains essentially preoccupied with itself instead of
being preoccupied with the real issue and surrendering to it.
To judge a thing that has substance and solid worth is quite
easy, to comprehend it is much harder, and to blend judgement
and comprehension in a definitive description is the hardest
thing of all.

4. Culture and its laborious emergence from the immediacy
of substantial life must always begin by getting acquainted with
general principles and points of view, so as at first to work up
to a *general conception* [*Gedanke*] of the real issue, as well as learning to support and refute the general conception with reasons;
then to apprehend the rich and concrete abundance [of life]
by differential classification; and finally to give accurate instruction and pass serious judgement upon it. From its very beginning, culture must leave room for the earnestness of life in
its concrete richness; this leads the way to an experience of the
real issue. And even when the real issue has been penetrated
to its depths by serious speculative effort, this kind of knowing
and judging will still retain its appropriate place in ordinary
conversation.

5. The true shape in which truth exists can only be the scientific system of such truth. To help bring philosophy closer to
the form of Science, to the goal where it can lay aside the title
'*love* of knowing' and be *actual* knowing—that is what I have
set myself to do. The inner necessity that knowing should be
Science lies in its nature, and only the systematic exposition
of philosophy itself provides it. But the *external* necessity, so far
as it is grasped in a general way, setting aside accidental matters
of person and motivation, is the same as the inner, or in other
words it lies in the shape in which time sets forth the sequential
existence of its moments. To show that now is the time for philo-

sophy to be raised to the status of a Science would therefore be the only true justification of any effort that has this aim, for to do so would demonstrate the necessity of the aim, would indeed at the same time be the accomplishing of it.

6. To lay down that the true shape of truth is scientific—or, what is the same thing, to maintain that truth has only the Notion as the element of its existence—seems, I know, to contradict a view which is in our time as prevalent as it is pretentious, and to go against what that view implies. Some explanation therefore seems called for, even though it must for the present be no more than a bare assertion, like the view that it contradicts. If, namely, the True exists only in what, or better *as* what, is sometimes called intuition, sometimes immediate knowledge of the Absolute, religion or being—not at the centre of divine love but the being of the divine love itself—then what is required in the exposition of philosophy is, from this viewpoint, rather the opposite of the form of the Notion. For the Absolute is not supposed to be comprehended, it is to be felt and intuited; not the Notion of the Absolute, but the feeling and intuition of it, must govern what is said, and must be expressed by it.

7. If we apprehend a demand of this kind in its broader context, and view it as it appears at the stage which self-conscious Spirit has presently reached, it is clear that Spirit has now got beyond the substantial life it formerly led in the element of thought, that it is beyond the immediacy of faith, beyond the satisfaction and security of the certainty that consciousness then had, of its reconciliation with the essential being, and of that being's universal presence both within and without. It has not only gone beyond all this into the other extreme of an insubstantial reflection of itself into itself, but beyond that too. Spirit has not only lost its essential life; it is also conscious of this loss, and of the finitude that is its own content. Turning away from the empty husks, and confessing that it lies in wickedness, it reviles itself for so doing, and now demands from philosophy, not so much *knowledge* of what it *is*, as the recovery through its agency of that lost sense of solid and substantial being. Philosophy is to meet this need, not by opening up the fast-locked nature of substance, and raising this to self-consciousness, not by bringing consciousness out of its chaos back to an order based

on thought, nor to the simplicity of the Notion, but rather by running together what thought has put asunder, by suppressing the differentiations of the Notion and restoring the *feeling* of essential being: in short, by providing edification rather than insight. The 'beautiful', the 'holy', the 'eternal', 'religion', and 'love' are the bait required to arouse the desire to bite; not the Notion, but ecstasy, not the cold march of necessity in the thing itself, but the ferment of enthusiasm, these are supposed to be what sustains and continually extends the wealth of substance.

8. In keeping with this demand is the strenuous, almost over-zealous and frenzied effort to tear men away from their preoccupation with the sensuous, from their ordinary, private [*einzelne*] affairs, and to direct their gaze to the stars; as if they had forgotten all about the divine, and were ready like worms to content themselves with dirt and water. Formerly they had a heaven adorned with a vast wealth of thoughts and imagery. The meaning of all that is, hung on the thread of light by which it was linked to that heaven. Instead of dwelling in this world's presence, men looked beyond it, following this thread to an other-worldly presence, so to speak. The eye of the Spirit had to be forcibly turned and held fast to the things of this world; and it has taken a long time before the lucidity which only heavenly things used to have could penetrate the dullness and confusion in which the sense of worldly things was enveloped, and so make attention to the here and now as such, attention to what has been called 'experience', an interesting and valid enterprise. Now we seem to need just the opposite: sense is so fast rooted in earthly things that it requires just as much force to raise it. The Spirit shows itself as so impoverished that, like a wanderer in the desert craving for a mere mouthful of water, it seems to crave for its refreshment only the bare feeling of the divine in general. By the little which now satisfies Spirit, we can measure the extent of its loss.

9. This modest complacency in receiving, or this sparingness in giving, does not, however, befit Science. Whoever seeks mere edification, and whoever wants to shroud in a mist the manifold variety of his earthly existence and of thought, in order to pursue the indeterminate enjoyment of this indeterminate divinity, may look where he likes to find all this. He will find

ample opportunity to dream up something for himself. But philosophy must beware of the wish to be edifying.

10. Still less must this complacency which abjures Science claim that such rapturous haziness is superior to Science. This prophetic talk supposes that it is staying right in the centre and in the depths, looks disdainfully at determinateness (*Horos*), and deliberately holds aloof from Notion and Necessity as products of that reflection which is at home only in the finite. But just as there is an empty breadth, so too there is an empty depth; and just as there is an extension of substance that pours forth as a finite multiplicity without the force to hold the multiplicity together, so there is an intensity without content, one that holds itself in as a sheer force without spread, and this is in no way distinguishable from superficiality. The power of Spirit is only as great as its expression, its depth only as deep as it dares to spread out and lose itself in its exposition. Moreover, when this non-conceptual, substantial knowledge professes to have sunk the idiosyncrasy of the self in essential being, and to philosophize in a true and holy manner, it hides the truth from itself: by spurning measure and definition, instead of being devoted to God, it merely gives free rein both to the contingency of the content within it, and to its own caprice. Such minds, when they give themselves up to the uncontrolled ferment of [the divine] substance, imagine that, by drawing a veil over self-consciousness and surrendering understanding they become the beloved of God to whom He gives wisdom in sleep; and hence what they in fact receive, and bring to birth in their sleep, is nothing but dreams.

11. Besides, it is not difficult to see that ours is a birth-time and a period of transition to a new era. Spirit has broken with the world it has hitherto inhabited and imagined, and is of a mind to submerge it in the past, and in the labour of its own transformation. Spirit is indeed never at rest but always engaged in moving forward. But just as the first breath drawn by a child after its long, quiet nourishment breaks the gradualness of merely quantitative growth—there is a qualitative leap, and the child is born—so likewise the Spirit in its formation matures slowly and quietly into its new shape, dissolving bit by bit the structure of its previous world, whose tottering state is only hinted at by isolated symptoms. The frivolity and bore-

dom which unsettle the established order, the vague foreboding
of something unknown, these are the heralds of approaching
change. The gradual crumbling that left unaltered the face of
the whole is cut short by a sunburst which, in one flash, illuminates the features of the new world.

12. But this new world is no more a complete actuality than
is a new-born child; it is essential to bear this in mind. It comes
on the scene for the first time in its immediacy or its Notion.
Just as little as a building is finished when its foundation has
been laid, so little is the achieved Notion of the whole the whole
itself. When we wish to see an oak with its massive trunk and
spreading branches and foliage, we are not content to be shown
an acorn instead. So too, Science, the crown of a world of Spirit,
is not complete in its beginnings. The onset of the new spirit
is the product of a widespread upheaval in various forms of
culture, the prize at the end of a complicated, tortuous path
and of just as variegated and strenuous an effort. It is the whole
which, having traversed its content in time and space, has
returned into itself, and is the resultant *simple Notion* of the
whole. But the actuality of this simple whole consists in those
various shapes and forms which have become its moments, and
which will now develop and take shape afresh, this time in their
new element, in their newly acquired meaning.

13. While the initial appearance of the new world is, to begin
with, only the whole veiled in its *simplicity*, or the general
foundation of the whole, the wealth of previous existence is still
present to consciousness in memory. Consciousness misses in the
newly emerging shape its former range and specificity of content, and even more the articulation of form whereby distinctions are securely defined, and stand arrayed in their fixed
relations. Without such articulation, Science lacks universal intelligibility, and gives the appearance of being the esoteric possession of a few individuals: an esoteric possession, since it is
as yet present only in its Notion or in its inwardness; of a few
individuals, since its undiffused manifestation makes its existence something singular. Only what is completely determined
is at once exoteric, comprehensible, and capable of being
learned and appropriated by all. The intelligible form of
Science is the way open and equally accessible to everyone, and
consciousness as it approaches Science justly demands that it

be able to attain to rational knowledge by way of the ordinary understanding; for the understanding is thought, the pure 'I' as such; and what is intelligible is what is already familiar and common to Science and the unscientific consciousness alike, the latter through its having afforded direct access to the former.

14. Science in its early stages, when it has attained neither to completeness of detail nor perfection of form, is vulnerable to criticism. But it would be as unjust for such criticism to strike at the very heart of Science, as it is untenable to refuse to honour the demand for its further development. This polarization seems to be the Gordian knot with which scientific culture is at present struggling, and which it still does not properly understand. One side boasts of its wealth of material and intelligibility, the other side at least scorns this intelligibility, and flaunts its immediate rationality and divinity. Even if the former side is reduced to silence, whether by the force of truth alone or by the blustering of the other, and even if, in respect of fundamentals, it feels itself outmatched, it is by no means satisfied regarding the said demands; for they are justified, but not fulfilled. Its silence stems only half from the triumph of its opponent, and half from the boredom and indifference which tend to result from the continual awakening of expectations through unfulfilled promises.

15. As for content, the other side make it easy enough for themselves at times to display a great expanse of it. They appropriate a lot of already familiar and well-ordered material; by focusing on rare and exotic instances they give the impression that they have hold of everything else which scientific knowledge had already embraced in its scope, and that they are also in command of such material as is as yet unordered. It thus appears that everything has been subjected to the absolute Idea, which therefore seems to be cognized in everything and to have matured into an expanded science. But a closer inspection shows that this expansion has not come about through one and the same principle having spontaneously assumed different shapes, but rather through the shapeless repetition of one and the same formula, only externally applied to diverse materials, thereby obtaining merely a boring show of diversity. The Idea, which is of course true enough on its own account, remains in effect always in its primitive condition, if its development in-

volves nothing more than this sort of repetition of the same formula. When the knowing subject goes around applying this
single inert form to whatever it encounters, and dipping the
material into this placid element from outside, this is no more
the fulfilment of what is needed, i.e. a self-originating, self-
differentiating wealth of shapes, than any arbitrary insights into
the content. Rather it is a monochromatic formalism which
only arrives at the differentiation of its material since this has
been already provided and is by now familiar.

16. Yet this formalism maintains that such monotony and
abstract universality are the Absolute, and we are assured that
dissatisfaction with it indicates the inability to master the absolute standpoint and to keep hold of it. Time was when the bare
possibility of imagining something differently was sufficient to
refute an idea, and this bare possibility, this general thought,
also had the entire positive value of an actual cognition. Nowadays we see all value ascribed to the universal Idea in this non-
actual form, and the undoing of all distinct, determinate entities
(or rather the hurling of them all into the abyss of vacuity without further development or any justification) is allowed to pass
muster as the speculative mode of treatment. Dealing with
something from the perspective of the Absolute consists merely
in declaring that, although one has been speaking of it just now
as something definite, yet in the Absolute, the $A = A$, there is
nothing of the kind, for there all is one. To pit this single insight,
that in the Absolute everything is the same, against the full body
of articulated cognition, which at least seeks and demands such
fulfilment, to palm off its Absolute as the night in which, as
the saying goes, all cows are black—this is cognition naïvely
reduced to vacuity. The formalism which recent philosophy
denounces and despises, only to see it reappear in its midst, will
not vanish from Science, however much its inadequacy may
be recognized and felt, till the cognizing of absolute actuality
has become entirely clear as to its own nature. Since the presentation of a general idea in outline, before any attempt to
follow it out in detail, makes the latter attempt easier to grasp,
it may be useful at this point to give a rough idea of it, at the
same time taking the opportunity to get rid of certain habits
of thought which impede philosophical cognition.

17. In my view, which can be justified only by the exposition

of the system itself, everything turns on grasping and expressing the True, not only as *Substance*, but equally as *Subject*. At the same time, it is to be observed that substantiality embraces the universal, or the *immediacy of knowledge* itself, as well as that which is *being* or immediacy *for* knowledge. If the conception of God as the one Substance shocked the age in which it was proclaimed, the reason for this was on the one hand an instinctive awareness that, in this definition, self-consciousness was only submerged and not preserved. On the other hand, the opposite view, which clings to thought as thought, to *universality* as such, is the very same simplicity, is undifferentiated, unmoved substantiality. And if, thirdly, thought does unite itself with the being of Substance, and apprehends immediacy or intuition as thinking, the question is still whether this intellectual intuition does not again fall back into inert simplicity, and does not depict actuality itself in a non-actual manner.

18. Further, the living Substance is being which is in truth *Subject*, or, what is the same, is in truth actual only in so far as it is the movement of positing itself, or is the mediation of its self-othering with itself. This Substance is, as Subject, pure, *simple negativity*, and is for this very reason the bifurcation of the simple; it is the doubling which sets up opposition, and then again the negation of this indifferent diversity and of its antithesis [the immediate simplicity]. Only this self-*restoring* sameness, or this reflection in otherness within itself—not an *original* or *immediate* unity as such—is the True. It is the process of its own becoming, the circle that presupposes its end as its goal, having its end also as its beginning; and only by being worked out to its end, is it actual.

19. Thus the life of God and divine cognition may well be spoken of as a disporting of Love with itself; but this idea sinks into mere edification, and even insipidity, if it lacks the seriousness, the suffering, the patience, and the labour of the negative. *In itself*, that life is indeed one of untroubled equality and unity with itself, for which otherness and alienation, and the overcoming of alienation, are not serious matters. But this *in-itself* is abstract universality, in which the nature of the divine life *to be for itself*, and so too the self-movement of the form, are altogether left out of account. If the form is declared to be the same as the essence, then it is *ipso facto* a mistake to suppose

that cognition can be satisfied with the in-itself or the essence, but can get along without the form—that the absolute principle or absolute intuition makes the working-out of the former, or the development of the latter, superfluous. Just because the form is as essential to the essence as the essence is to itself, the divine essence is not to be conceived and expressed merely as essence, i.e. as immediate substance or pure self-contemplation of the divine, but likewise as *form*, and in the whole wealth of the developed form. Only then is it conceived and expressed as an actuality.

20. The True is the whole. But the whole is nothing other than the essence consummating itself through its development. Of the Absolute it must be said that it is essentially a *result*, that only in the *end* is it what it truly is; and that precisely in this consists its nature, viz. to be actual, subject, the spontaneous becoming of itself. Though it may seem contradictory that the Absolute should be conceived essentially as a result, it needs little pondering to set this show of contradiction in its true light. The beginning, the principle, or the Absolute, as at first immediately enunciated, is only the universal. Just as when I say '*all* animals', this expression cannot pass for a zoology, so it is equally plain that the words, 'the Divine', 'the Absolute', 'the Eternal', etc., do not express what is contained in them; and only such words, in fact, do express the intuition as something immediate. Whatever is more than such a word, even the transition to a mere proposition, contains a *becoming-other* that has to be taken back, or is a mediation. But it is just this that is rejected with horror, as if absolute cognition were being surrendered when more is made of mediation than in simply saying that it is nothing absolute, and is completely absent in the Absolute.

21. But this abhorrence in fact stems from ignorance of the nature of mediation, and of absolute cognition itself. For mediation is nothing beyond self-moving selfsameness, or is reflection into self, the moment of the 'I' which is for itself pure negativity or, when reduced to its pure abstraction, *simple becoming*. The 'I', or becoming in general, this mediation, on account of its simple nature, is just immediacy in the process of becoming, and is the immediate itself. Reason is, therefore, misunderstood when reflection is excluded from the True, and is not grasped

as a positive moment of the Absolute. It is reflection that makes the True a result, but it is equally reflection that overcomes the antithesis between the process of its becoming and the result, for this becoming is also simple, and therefore not different from the form of the True which shows itself as *simple* in its result; the process of becoming is rather just this return into simplicity. Though the embryo is indeed *in itself* a human being, it is not so *for itself*; this it only is as cultivated Reason, which has *made* itself into what it is *in itself*. And that is when it for the first time is actual. But this result is itself a simple immediacy, for it is self-conscious freedom at peace with itself, which has not set the antithesis on one side and left it lying there, but has been reconciled with it.

22. What has just been said can also be expressed by saying that Reason is *purposive activity*. The exaltation of a supposed Nature over a misconceived thinking, and especially the rejection of external teleology, has brought the form of purpose in general into discredit. Still, in the sense in which Aristotle, too, defines Nature as purposive activity, purpose is what is immediate and *at rest*, the unmoved which is also *self-moving*, and as such is Subject. Its power to move, taken abstractly, is *being-for-self* or pure negativity. The result is the same as the beginning, only because the *beginning* is the *purpose*; in other words, the actual is the same as its Notion only because the immediate, as purpose, contains the self or pure actuality within itself. The realized purpose, or the existent actuality, is movement and unfolded becoming; but it is just this unrest that is the self; and the self is like that immediacy and simplicity of the beginning because it is the result, that which has returned into itself, the latter being similarly just the self. And the self is the sameness and simplicity that relates itself to itself.

23. The need to represent the Absolute as *Subject* has found expression in the propositions: *God* is the eternal, the moral world-order, love, and so on. In such propositions the True is only posited *immediately* as Subject, but is not presented as the movement of reflecting itself into itself. In a proposition of this kind one begins with the word 'God'. This by itself is a meaningless sound, a mere name; it is only the predicate that says *what God is*, gives Him content and meaning. Only in the end of the proposition does the empty beginning become actual know-

ledge. This being so, it is not clear why one does not speak merely of the eternal, of the moral world-order, and so on, or, as the ancients did, of pure notions like 'being', 'the One', and so on, in short, of that which gives the meaning without adding the *meaningless* sound as well. But it is just this word that indicates that what is posited is not a being [i.e. something that merely *is*], or essence, or a universal in general, but rather something that is reflected into itself, a Subject. But at the same time this is only anticipated. The Subject is assumed as a fixed point to which, as their support, the predicates are affixed by a movement belonging to the knower of this Subject, and which is not regarded as belonging to the fixed point itself; yet it is only through this movement that the content could be represented as Subject. The way in which this movement has been brought about is such that it cannot belong to the fixed point; yet, after this point has been presupposed, the nature of the movement cannot really be other than what it is, it can only be external. Hence, the mere anticipation that the Absolute is Subject is not only *not* the actuality of this Notion, but it even makes the actuality impossible; for the anticipation posits the subject as an inert point, whereas the actuality is self-movement.

24. Among the various consequences that follow from what has just been said, this one in particular can be stressed, that knowledge is only actual, and can only be expounded, as Science or as *system*; and furthermore, that a so-called basic proposition or principle of philosophy, if true, is also false, just because it is *only* a principle. It is, therefore, easy to refute it. The refutation consists in pointing out its defect; and it is defective because it is only the universal or principle, is only the beginning. If the refutation is thorough, it is derived and developed from the principle itself, not accomplished by counter-assertions and random thoughts from outside. The refutation would, therefore, properly consist in the further development of the principle, and in thus remedying the defectiveness, if it did not mistakenly pay attention solely to its *negative* action, without awareness of its progress and result on their *positive* side too—The genuinely *positive* exposition of the beginning is thus also, conversely, just as much a negative attitude towards it, viz. towards its initially one-sided form of being *immediate* or *purpose*. It can therefore be taken equally well as a refutation

of the principle that constitutes the *basis* of the system, but it is more correct to regard it as a demonstration that the *basis* or principle of the system is, in fact, only its *beginning*.

25. That the True is actual only as system, or that Substance is essentially Subject, is expressed in the representation of the Absolute as *Spirit*—the most sublime Notion and the one which belongs to the modern age and its religion. The spiritual alone is the *actual*; it is essence, or that which has *being in itself*; it is that which *relates itself to itself* and is *determinate*, it is *other-being* and *being-for-self*, and in this determinateness, or in its self-externality, abides within itself; in other words, it is *in and for itself*.— But this being-in-and-for-itself is at first only for us, or *in itself*, it is spiritual *Substance*. It must also be this *for itself*, it must be the knowledge of the spiritual, and the knowledge of itself as Spirit, i.e. it must be an *object* to itself, but just as immediately a sublated object, reflected into itself. It is *for itself* only for *us*, in so far as its spiritual content is generated by itself. But in so far as it is also for itself for its own self, this self-generation, the pure Notion, is for it the objective element in which it has its existence, and it is in this way, in its existence for itself, an object reflected into itself. The Spirit that, so developed, knows itself as Spirit, is *Science*; Science is its actuality and the realm which it builds for itself in its own element.

26. *Pure* self-recognition in absolute otherness, this Aether *as such*, is the ground and soil of Science or *knowledge in general*. The beginning of philosophy presupposes or requires that consciousness should dwell in this *element*. But this element itself achieves its own perfection and transparency only through the movement of its becoming. It is pure spirituality as the *universal* that has the form of simple immediacy. This simple being in its *existential* form is the soil [of Science], it is thinking which has its being in Spirit alone. Because this element, this immediacy of Spirit, is the very substance of Spirit, it is the *transfigured essence*, reflection which is itself simple, and which is for itself immediacy as such, *being* that is reflected into itself. Science on its part requires that self-consciousness should have raised itself into this Aether in order to be able to live—and [actually] to live—with Science and in Science. Conversely, the individual has the right to demand that Science should at least provide him with the ladder to this standpoint, should show

him this standpoint within himself. His right is based on his absolute independence, which he is conscious of possessing in every phase of his knowledge; for in each one, whether recognized by Science or not, and whatever the content may be, the individual is the absolute form, i.e. he is the *immediate certainty* of himself and, if this expression be preferred, he is therefore unconditioned *being*. The standpoint of consciousness which knows objects in their antithesis to itself, and itself in antithesis to them, is for Science the antithesis of its own standpoint. The situation in which consciousness knows itself to be at home is for Science one marked by the absence of Spirit. Conversely, the element of Science is for consciousness a remote beyond in which it no longer possesses itself. Each of these two aspects [of self-conscious Spirit] appears to the other as the inversion of truth. When natural consciousness entrusts itself straightway to Science, it makes an attempt, induced by it knows not what, to walk on its head too, just this once; the compulsion to assume this unwonted posture and to go about in it is a violence it is expected to do to itself, all unprepared and seemingly without necessity. Let Science be in its own self what it may, relatively to immediate self-consciousness it presents itself in an inverted posture; or, because this self-consciousness has the principle of its actual existence in the certainty of itself, Science appears to it not to be actual, since self-consciousness exists on its own account outside of Science. Science must therefore unite this element of self-certainty with itself, or rather show *that* and *how* this element belongs to it. So long as Science lacks this *actual* dimension, it is only the content as the *in-itself*, the *purpose* that is as yet still something *inward*, not yet Spirit, but only spiritual Substance. This *in-itself* has to express itself outwardly and become *for itself*, and this means simply that it has to posit self-consciousness as one with itself.

27. It is this coming-to-be of *Science as such* or of *knowledge*, that is described in this *Phenomenology* of Spirit. Knowledge in its first phase, or *immediate Spirit*, is the non-spiritual, i.e. *sense-consciousness*. In order to become genuine knowledge, to beget the element of Science which is the pure Notion of Science itself, it must travel a long way and work its passage. This process of coming-to-be (considering the content and patterns it will display therein) will not be what is commonly understood by

an initiation of the unscientific consciousness into Science; it
will also be quite different from the 'foundation' of Science;
least of all will it be like the rapturous enthusiasm which, like
a shot from a pistol, begins straight away with absolute knowledge, and makes short work of other standpoints by declaring
that it takes no notice of them.

28. The task of leading the individual from his uneducated
standpoint to knowledge had to be seen in its universal sense,
just as it was the universal individual, self-conscious Spirit,
whose formative education had to be studied. As regards the
relation between them, every moment, as it gains concrete form
and a shape of its own, displays itself in the universal individual.
The single individual is incomplete Spirit, a concrete shape in
whose whole existence *one* determinateness predominates, the
others being present only in blurred outline. In a Spirit that
is more advanced than another, the lower concrete existence
has been reduced to an inconspicuous moment; what used to
be the important thing is now but a trace; its pattern is
shrouded to become a mere shadowy outline. The individual
whose substance is the more advanced Spirit runs through this
past just as one who takes up a higher science goes through the
preparatory studies he has long since absorbed, in order to bring
their content to mind: he recalls them to the inward eye, but
has no lasting interest in them. The single individual must also
pass through the formative stages of universal Spirit so far as
their content is concerned, but as shapes which Spirit has
already left behind, as stages on a way that has been made level
with toil. Thus, as far as factual information is concerned, we
find that what in former ages engaged the attention of men of
mature mind, has been reduced to the level of facts, exercises,
and even games for children; and, in the child's progress
through school, we shall recognize the history of the cultural
development of the world traced, as it were, in a silhouette.
This past existence is the already acquired property of universal
Spirit which constitutes the Substance of the individual, and
hence appears externally to him as his inorganic nature. In this
respect formative education, regarded from the side of the individual, consists in his acquiring what thus lies at hand,
devouring his inorganic nature, and taking possession of it for
himself. But, regarded from the side of universal Spirit as sub-

stance, this is nothing but its own acquisition of self-consciousness, the bringing-about of its own becoming and reflection into itself.

29. Science sets forth this formative process in all its detail and necessity, exposing the mature configuration of everything which has already been reduced to a moment and property of Spirit. The goal is Spirit's insight into what knowing is. Impatience demands the impossible, to wit, the attainment of the end without the means. But the *length* of this path has to be endured, because, for one thing, each moment is necessary; and further, each moment has to be *lingered* over, because each is itself a complete individual shape, and one is only viewed in absolute perspective when its determinateness is regarded as a concrete whole, or the whole is regarded as uniquely qualified by that determination. Since the Substance of the individual, the World-Spirit itself, has had the patience to pass through these shapes over the long passage of time, and to take upon itself the enormous labour of world-history, in which it embodied in each shape as much of its entire content as that shape was capable of holding, and since it could not have attained consciousness of itself by any lesser effort, the individual certainly cannot by the nature of the case comprehend his own substance more easily. Yet, at the same time, he does have less trouble, since all this has already been *implicitly* accomplished; the content is already the actuality reduced to a possibility, its immediacy overcome, and the embodied shape reduced to abbreviated, simple determinations of thought. It is no longer existence in the form of *being-in-itself*—neither still in the original form [of an abstract concept], nor submerged in existence—but is now the *recollected in-itself*, ready for conversion into the form of *being-for-self*. How this is done must now be described more precisely.

30. We take up the movement of the whole from the point where the sublation of *existence* as such is no longer necessary; what remains to be done, and what requires a higher level of cultural reorientation, is to represent and to get acquainted with these forms. The existence that has been taken back into the Substance has only been *immediately* transposed into the element of the self through that first negation. Hence this acquired property still has the same character of uncomprehended

immediacy, of passive indifference, as existence itself; existence has thus merely passed over into *figurative representation*. At the same time it is thus something *familiar*, something which the existent Spirit is finished and done with, so that it is no longer active or really interested in it. Although the activity that has finished with existence is itself only the movement of the particular Spirit, the Spirit that does not comprehend itself, [genuine] knowing, on the other hand, is directed against the representation thus formed, against this [mere] familiarity; knowing is the activity of the *universal self*, the concern of *thinking*.

31. Quite generally, the familiar, just because it is familiar, is not cognitively understood. The commonest way in which we deceive either ourselves or others about understanding is by assuming something as familiar, and accepting it on that account; with all its pros and cons, such knowing never gets anywhere, and it knows not why. Subject and object, God, Nature, Understanding, sensibility, and so on, are uncritically taken for granted as familiar, established as valid, and made into fixed points for starting and stopping. While these remain unmoved, the knowing activity goes back and forth between them, thus moving only on their surface. Apprehending and testing likewise consist in seeing whether everybody's impression of the matter coincides with what is asserted about these fixed points, whether it seems that way to him or not.

32. The *analysis* of an idea, as it used to be carried out, was, in fact, nothing else than ridding it of the form in which it had become familiar. To break an idea up into its original elements is to return to its moments, which at least do not have the form of the given idea, but rather constitute the immediate property of the self. This analysis, to be sure, only arrives at *thoughts* which are themselves familiar, fixed, and inert determinations. But what is thus *separated* and non-actual is an essential moment; for it is only because the concrete does divide itself, and make itself into something non-actual, that it is self-moving. The activity of dissolution is the power and work of the *Understanding*, the most astonishing and mightiest of powers, or rather the absolute power. The circle that remains self-enclosed and, like substance, holds its moments together, is an immediate relationship, one therefore which has nothing astonishing about it.

But that an accident as such, detached from what circumscribes it, what is bound and is actual only in its context with others, should attain an existence of its own and a separate freedom— this is the tremendous power of the negative; it is the energy of thought, of the pure 'I'. Death, if that is what we want to call this non-actuality, is of all things the most dreadful, and to hold fast what is dead requires the greatest strength. Lacking strength, Beauty hates the Understanding for asking of her what it cannot do. But the life of Spirit is not the life that shrinks from death and keeps itself untouched by devastation, but rather the life that endures it and maintains itself in it. It wins its truth only when, in utter dismemberment, it finds itself. It is this power, not as something positive, which closes its eyes to the negative, as when we say of something that it is nothing or is false, and then, having done with it, turn away and pass on to something else; on the contrary, Spirit is this power only by looking the negative in the face, and tarrying with it. This tarrying with the negative is the magical power that converts it into being. This power is identical with what we earlier called the Subject, which by giving determinateness an existence in its own element supersedes abstract immediacy, i.e. the immediacy which barely is, and thus is authentic substance: that being or immediacy whose mediation is not outside of it but which is this mediation itself.

33. The fact that the object represented becomes the property of pure self-consciousness, its elevation to universality in general, is only one aspect of formative education, not its fulfilment—The manner of study in ancient times differed from that of the modern age in that the former was the proper and complete formation of the natural consciousness. Putting itself to the test at every point of its existence, and philosophizing about everything it came across, it made itself into a universality that was active through and through. In modern times, however, the individual finds the abstract form ready-made; the effort to grasp and appropriate it is more the direct driving-forth of what is within and the truncated generation of the universal than it is the emergence of the latter from the concrete variety of existence. Hence the task nowadays consists not so much in purging the individual of an immediate, sensuous mode of apprehension, and making him into a substance that is an

object of thought and that thinks, but rather in just the opposite, in freeing determinate thoughts from their fixity so as to give actuality to the universal, and impart to it spiritual life. But it is far harder to bring fixed thoughts into a fluid state than to do so with sensuous existence. The reason for this was given above: fixed thoughts have the 'I', the power of the negative, or pure actuality, for the substance and element of their exist-ence, whereas sensuous determinations have only powerless, abstract immediacy, or being as such. Thoughts become fluid when pure thinking, this inner *immediacy*, recognizes itself as a moment, or when the pure certainty of self abstracts from itself—not by leaving itself out, or setting itself aside, but by giving up the *fixity* of its self-positing, by giving up not only the fixity of the pure concrete, which the 'I' itself is, in contrast with its differentiated content, but also the fixity of the dif-ferentiated moments which, posited in the element of pure thinking, share the unconditioned nature of the 'I'. Through this movement the pure thoughts become *Notions*, and are only now what they are in truth, self-movements, circles, spiritual essences, which is what their substance is.

34. This movement of pure essences constitutes the nature of scientific method in general. Regarded as the connectedness of their content it is the necessary expansion of that content into an organic whole. Through this movement the path by which the Notion of knowledge is reached becomes likewise a necessary and complete process of becoming; so that this pre-paratory path ceases to be a casual philosophizing that fastens on to this or that object, relationship, or thought that happens to pop up in the imperfect consciousness, or tries to base the truth on the pros and cons, the inferences and consequences, of rigidly defined thoughts. Instead, this pathway, through the movement of the Notion, will encompass the entire sphere of secular consciousness in its necessary development.

35. Further, an exposition of this kind constitutes the *first* part of Science, because the existence of Spirit *qua* primary is nothing but the immediate or the beginning—but not yet its return into itself. The *element of immediate existence* is therefore what distinguishes this part of Science from the others. The statement of this distinction leads us into a discussion of some fixed ideas which usually crop up in this connection.

36. The immediate existence of Spirit, *consciousness*, contains the two moments of knowing and the objectivity negative to knowing. Since it is in this element [of consciousness] that Spirit develops itself and explicates its moments, these moments contain that antithesis, and they all appear as shapes of consciousness. The Science of this pathway is the Science of the *experience* which consciousness goes through; the substance and its movement are viewed as the object of consciousness. Consciousness knows and comprehends only what falls within its experience; for what is contained in this is nothing but spiritual substance, and this, too, as *object* of the self. But Spirit becomes object because it is just this movement of becoming an *other to itself*, i.e. becoming an *object to itself*, and of suspending this otherness. And experience is the name we give to just this movement, in which the immediate, the unexperienced, i.e. the abstract, whether it be of sensuous [but still unsensed] being, or only thought of as simple, becomes alienated from itself and then returns to itself from this alienation, and is only then revealed for the first time in its actuality and truth, just as it then has become a property of consciousness also.

37. The disparity which exists in consciousness between the 'I' and the substance which is its object is the distinction between them, the *negative* in general. This can be regarded as the *defect* of both, though it is their soul, or that which moves them. That is why some of the ancients conceived the *void* as the principle of motion, for they rightly saw the moving principle as the *negative*, though they did not as yet grasp that the negative is the self. Now, although this negative appears at first as a disparity between the 'I' and its object, it is just as much the disparity of the substance with itself. Thus what seems to happen outside of it, to be an activity directed against it, is really its own doing, and Substance shows itself to be essentially Subject. When it has shown this completely, Spirit has made its existence identical with its essence; it has itself for its object just as it is, and the abstract element of immediacy, and of the separation of knowing and truth, is overcome. Being is then absolutely mediated; it is a substantial content which is just as immediately the property of the 'I', it is self-like or the Notion.

With this, the Phenomenology of Spirit is concluded. What

Spirit prepares for itself in it, is the element of [true] knowing. In this element the moments of Spirit now spread themselves out in that *form of simplicity* which knows its object as its own self. They no longer fall apart into the antithesis of being and knowing, but remain in the simple oneness of knowing; they are the True in the form of the True, and their difference is only the difference of content. Their movement, which organizes itself in this element into a whole, is *Logic* or *speculative philosophy*.

38. Now, because the system of the experience of Spirit embraces only the *appearance* of Spirit, the advance from this system to the Science of the *True* in its *true shape* seems to be merely negative, and one might wish to be spared the negative as something false, and demand to be led to the truth without more ado. Why bother with the false?—The view already discussed, namely, that we should begin with Science straight away, is to be answered at this point by examining the nature of the negative in general regarded as what is *false*. This is a topic regarding which established ideas notably obstruct the approach to truth. It will give us occasion to speak of mathematical cognition, which unphilosophical knowledge regards as the ideal that philosophy must strive to attain, though it has so far striven in vain.

39. 'True' and 'false' belong among those determinate notions which are held to be inert and wholly separate essences, one here and one there, each standing fixed and isolated from the other, with which it has nothing in common. Against this view it must be maintained that truth is not a minted coin that can be given and pocketed ready-made. Nor *is* there such a thing as the false, any more than there *is* something evil. The evil and the false, to be sure, are not as bad as the devil, for in the devil they are even made into a particular *subjective agent*; as the false and the evil, they are mere *universals*, though each has its own essence as against the other.

The false (for here it is only of this that we speak) would be the other, the negative of the substance, which as the content of knowledge is the True. But the substance is itself essentially the negative, partly as a distinction and determination of the content, and partly as a *simple* distinguishing, i.e. as self and knowledge in general. One can, of course, know something falsely. To know something falsely means that there is a disparity between knowledge and its Substance. But this very disparity is the process of distinguishing in general, which is an essential moment [in knowing]. Out of this distinguishing, of course, comes their identity, and this resultant identity is the truth. But it is not truth as if the disparity had been thrown away, like dross from pure metal, not even like the tool which remains separate from the finished vessel; disparity, rather, as the negative, the self, is itself still directly present in the True as such. Yet we cannot therefore say that the false is a moment of the True, let alone a component part of it. To say that in every falsehood there is a grain of truth is to treat the two like oil and water, which cannot be mixed and are only externally combined. It is precisely on account of the importance of designating the moment of *complete otherness* that the terms 'true' and 'false' must no longer be used where such otherness has been annulled. Just as to talk of the *unity* of subject and object, of finite and infinite, of being and thought, etc. is inept, since object and subject, etc. signify what they are *outside* of their unity, and since in their unity they are not meant to be what their expression says they are, just so the false is no longer *qua* false, a moment of truth.

40. *Dogmatism* as a way of thinking, whether in ordinary knowing or in the study of philosophy, is nothing else but the opinion that the True consists in a proposition which is a fixed result, or which is immediately known. To such questions as, When was Caesar born?, or How many feet were there in a stadium?, etc. a clear-cut answer ought to be given, just as it is definitely true that the square on the hypotenuse is equal to the sum of the squares on the other two sides of a right-angled triangle. But the nature of a so-called truth of that kind is different from the nature of philosophical truths.

41. As regards *historical* truths—to mention these briefly— it will be readily granted that so far as their purely historical aspect is considered, they are concerned with a particular existence, with the contingent and arbitrary aspects of a given content, which have no necessity. But even such plain truths as those just illustrated are not without the movement of self-consciousness. To cognize one of them, a good deal of comparison is called for, books must be consulted, in some way or other

inquiry has to be made. Even an immediate intuition is held to have genuine value only when it is cognized as a fact along with its reasons, although it is probably only the bare result that we are supposed to be concerned about.

42. As for *mathematical* truths, we should be even less inclined to regard anyone as a geometer who knew Euclid's theorems *outwardly* by rote, without knowing their proofs, without, as we might say, to point the contrast, knowing them *inwardly*. Similarly, if someone became aware, through measuring a number of right-angled triangles, that their sides do, in fact, have the well-known relation to one another, we should consider his [mere] awareness of the fact unsatisfactory. Yet, even in mathematical cognition, the *essentiality* of the proof does not have the significance and nature of being a moment of the result itself; when the latter is reached, the demonstration is over and has disappeared. It is, of course, as a *result* that the theorem is *something seen to be true*; but this added circumstance has no bearing on its content, but only on its relation to the knowing Subject. The movement of mathematical proof does not belong to the object, but rather is an activity external to the matter in hand. Thus the nature of the right-angled triangle does not divide itself into parts in just the way set forth in the construction necessary for the proof of the proposition that expresses its ratio. The way and the means by which the result is brought forth belong entirely to the cognitive process. In philosophical cognition, too, the way in which the [*outer*] *existence qua* existence of a thing comes about, is distinct from the way in which its *essence* or inner nature comes to be. But, to begin with, philosophical cognition includes both [existence and essence], whereas mathematical cognition sets forth only the genesis of the *existence*, i.e. the *being* of the nature of the thing in *cognition* as such. What is more, philosophical cognition also unites these two distinct processes. The inner coming-to-be or genesis of substance is an unbroken transition into outer existence, into being-for-another, and conversely, the genesis of existence is how existence is by itself taken back into essence. The movement is the twofold process and the genesis of the whole, in such wise that each side simultaneously posits the other, and each therefore has both perspectives within itself; together they thus constitute the whole by

dissolving themselves, and by making themselves into its moments.

43. In mathematical cognition, insight is an activity external to the thing; it follows that the true thing is altered by it. The means employed, construction and proof, no doubt contain true propositions, but it must none the less be said that the content is false. In the above example the triangle is dismembered, and its parts consigned to other figures, whose origin is allowed by the construction upon the triangle. Only at the end is the triangle we are actually dealing with reinstated. During the procedure it was lost to view, appearing only in fragments belonging to other figures.—Here, then, we see the negativity of the content coming in as well; this could just as much have been called a 'falsity' of the content as is the disappearance of supposedly fixed conceptions in the movement of the Notion.

44. But what is really defective in this kind of cognition concerns the cognitive process itself, as well as its material. As regards the former, we do not, in the first place, see any necessity in the construction. Such necessity does not arise from the notion of the theorem; it is rather imposed, and the instruction to draw precisely these lines when infinitely many others could be drawn must be blindly obeyed without our knowing anything beyond except that we believe that this will be to the purpose in carrying out the proof. In retrospect, this expediency also becomes evident, but it is only an external expediency, because it becomes evident only after the proof. This proof, in addition, follows a path that begins somewhere or other without indicating as yet what relation such a beginning will have to the result that will emerge. In its progress it takes up *these* particular determinations and relations, and lets others alone, without its being immediately clear what the controlling necessity is; an external purpose governs this procedure.

45. The *evident* character of this defective cognition of which mathematics is proud, and on which it plumes itself before philosophy, rests solely on the poverty of its purpose and the defectiveness of its stuff, and is therefore of a kind that philosophy must spurn. Its *purpose* or Notion is *magnitude*. It is just this relationship that is unessential, lacking the Notion. Accordingly, this process of knowing proceeds on the surface, does not touch the thing itself, its essence or Notion, and therefore fails

to comprehend it [i.e. in terms of its Notion].—The *material*, regarding which mathematics provides such a gratifying treasury of truths, is *space* and the *numerical unit*. Space is the existence in which the Notion inscribes its differences as in an empty lifeless element, in which they are just as inert and lifeless. The *actual* is not something spatial, as it is regarded in mathematics; with non-actual things like the objects of mathematics, neither concrete sense-intuition nor philosophy has the least concern. In a non-actual element like this there is only a truth of the same sort, i.e. rigid, dead propositions. We can stop at any one of them; the next one starts afresh on its own account, without the first having moved itself on to the next, and without any necessary connection arising through the nature of the thing itself.—Further, because of this principle and element—and herein consists the formalism of mathematical evidence—[this kind of] knowing moves forward along the line of *equality*. For what is lifeless, since it does not move of itself, does not get as far as the distinctions of essence, as far as essential opposition or inequality, and therefore does not make the transition of one opposite into its opposite, does not attain to qualitative, immanent motion or *self*-movement. For it is only magnitude, the unessential distinction, that mathematics deals with. It abstracts from the fact that it is the Notion which divides space into its dimensions and determines the connections between and within them. It does not, for example, consider the relationship of line to surface; and, when it compares the diameter of a circle with its circumference, it runs up against their incommensurability, i.e. a relationship of the Notion, something infinite that eludes mathematical determination.

46. Nor does the immanent, so-called pure mathematics set *time qua* time over against space, as the second material for its consideration. Applied mathematics does indeed deal with time, as well as with motion and other concrete things; but the synthetic propositions, i.e. propositions regarding relationships determined by their Notion, it takes from experience and applies its formulae only on these presuppositions. The fact that the so-called proofs of propositions, such as those regarding the equilibrium of the lever, or the relation of space and time in the motion of falling, etc., are often given and accepted as proofs itself only proves how great is the need of proof for cognition,

seeing that, where nothing better is to be had, cognition values even the hollow semblance of it, and obtains from it some measure of satisfaction. A critique of these proofs would be as noteworthy as it would be instructive,[1] partly in order to strip mathematics of these fine feathers, partly in order to point out its limitations, and thus show the necessity for a different kind of knowledge.

As for *time*, which it is to be presumed would constitute, as the counterpart of space, the material of the other part of pure mathematics, it is the existent Notion itself. The principle of *magnitude*, of difference not determined by the Notion, and the principle of *equality*, of abstract lifeless unity, cannot cope with that sheer unrest of life and its absolute distinction. It is therefore only in a paralysed form, viz. as the *numerical unit*, that this negativity becomes the second material of mathematical cognition, which, as an external activity, reduces what is self-moving to mere material, so as to possess in it an indifferent, external, lifeless content.

47. Philosophy, on the other hand, has to do, not with *unessential* determinations, but with a determination in so far as it is essential; its element and content is not the abstract or non-actual, but the *actual*, that which posits itself and is alive within itself—existence within its own Notion. It is the process which begets and traverses its own moments, and this whole movement constitutes what is positive [in it] and its truth. This truth therefore includes the negative also, what would be called the false, if it could be regarded as something from which one might abstract. The evanescent itself must, on the contrary, be regarded as essential, not as something fixed, cut off from the True, and left lying who knows where outside it, any more than the True is to be regarded as something on the other side, positive and dead. Appearance is the arising and passing away that does not itself arise and pass away, but is 'in itself' [i.e. subsists intrinsically], and constitutes the actuality and the movement of the life of truth. The True is thus the Bacchanalian revel in which no member is not drunk; yet because each member collapses as soon as he drops out, the revel is just as much transparent and simple repose. Judged in the court of this movement,

---

[1] Hoffmeister refers to *Enc.* §267 where Hegel discusses the laws of gravitation in this sense.

the single shapes of Spirit do not persist any more than determinate thoughts do, but they are as much positive and necessary moments, as they are negative and evanescent. In the *whole* of the movement, seen as a state of repose, what distinguishes itself therein, and gives itself particular existence, is preserved as something that *recollects* itself, whose existence is self-knowledge, and whose self-knowledge is just as immediately existence.

48. It might seem necessary at the outset to say more about the *method* of this movement, i.e. of Science. But its Notion is already to be found in what has been said, and its proper exposition belongs to Logic, or rather it is Logic. For the method is nothing but the structure set forth in its pure essentiality. We should realize, however, that the system of ideas concerning philosophical method is yet another set of current beliefs that belongs to a bygone culture. If this comment sounds boastful or revolutionary—and I am far from adopting such a tone—it should be noted that current opinion itself has already come to view the scientific regime bequeathed by mathematics as quite *old-fashioned*—with its explanations, divisions, axioms, sets of theorems, its proofs, principles, deductions, and conclusions from them. Even if its unfitness is not clearly understood, little or no use is any longer made of it; and though not actually condemned outright, no one likes it very much. And we should be sufficiently prejudiced in favour of what is excellent, to suppose that it will be put to use, and will find acceptance. But it is not difficult to see that the way of asserting a proposition, adducing reasons for it, and in the same way refuting its opposite by reasons, is not the form in which truth can appear. Truth is its own self-movement, whereas the method just described is the mode of cognition that remains external to its material. Hence it is peculiar to mathematics, and must be left to that science, which, as we have noted, has for its principle the relationship of magnitude, a relationship alien to the Notion, and for its material dead space and the equally lifeless numerical unit. This method, too, in a looser form, i.e. more blended with the arbitrary and the accidental, may retain its place, as in conversation, or in a piece of historical instruction designed rather to satisfy curiosity than to produce knowledge, which is about what a preface amounts to. In ordinary life, consciousness has for its content items of information, experiences, concrete

objects of sense, thoughts, basic principles,—anything will do as a content, as long as it is ready to hand, or is accepted as a fixed and stable being or essence. Sometimes consciousness follows where this leads, sometimes it breaks the chain, and deals arbitrarily with its content, behaving as if it were determining and manipulating it from outside. It refers the content back to some certainty or other, even if only to the sensation of the moment; and conviction is satisfied when a familiar resting-place is reached.

49. But we have already pointed out that, once the necessity of the Notion has banished the slipshod style of conversational discussion, and along with it the pedantry and pomposity of science, they are not to be replaced by the non-method of presentiment and inspiration, or by the arbitrariness of prophetic utterance, both of which despise not only scientific pomposity, but scientific procedure of all kinds.

50. Of course, the *triadic form* must not be regarded as scientific when it is reduced to a lifeless schema, a mere shadow, and when scientific organization is degraded into a table of terms. Kant rediscovered this triadic form by instinct, but in his work it was still lifeless and uncomprehended; since then it has, however, been raised to its absolute significance, and with it the true form in its true content has been presented, so that the Notion of Science has emerged. This formalism, of which we have already spoken generally and whose style we wish here to describe in more detail, imagines that it has comprehended and expressed the nature and life of a form when it has endowed it with some determination of the schema as a predicate. The predicate may be subjectivity or objectivity, or, say, magnetism, electricity, etc., contraction or expansion, east or west, and the like. Such predicates can be multiplied to infinity, since in this way each determination or form can again be used as a form or moment in the case of an other, and each can gratefully perform the same service for an other. In this sort of circle of reciprocity one never learns what the thing itself is, nor what the one or the other is. In such a procedure, sometimes determinations of sense are picked up from everyday intuition, and they are supposed, of course, to *mean* something different from what they say; sometimes what is in itself meaningful, e.g. pure determinations of thought like sub-

ject, Object, Substance, Cause, Universal, etc.—these are used just as thoughtlessly and uncritically as we use them in everyday life, or as we use ideas like strength and weakness, expansion and contraction; the metaphysics is in the former case as unscientific as are our sensuous representations in the latter.

51. Instead of the inner life and self-movement of its existence, this kind of simple determinateness of intuition—which means here sense-knowledge—is predicated in accordance with a superficial analogy, and this external, empty application of the formula is called a 'construction'. This formalism is just like any other. What a dullard a man must be who could not be taught in a quarter of an hour the theory that there are asthenic, sthenic, and indirectly asthenic diseases, and as many modes of treatment;[1] and, since till quite recently such instruction sufficed, who could not hope to be transformed in this short space of time from an empirical into a theoretical physician? The formalism of such a 'Philosophy of Nature' teaches, say, that the Understanding is Electricity, or the Animal is Nitrogen, or that they are the *equivalent* of the South or North Pole, etc., or represent it—whether all this is expressed as baldly as here or even concocted with more terminology—and confronted with such a power which brings together things that appear to lie far apart, and with the violence suffered by the passive things of sense through such association, and which imparts to them the Notion's semblance but saves itself the trouble of doing the main thing, viz. expressing the Notion itself or the meaning of the sensuous representation—confronted with all this, the untutored mind may be filled with admiration and astonishment, and may venerate in it the profound work of genius. It may be delighted, too, with the clarity of such characterizations, since these replace the abstract Notion with something that can be intuitively apprehended, and so made more pleasing; and it may congratulate itself on feeling a kinship of soul with such a splendid performance. The knack of this kind of wisdom is as quickly learned as it is easy to practise; once familiar, the repetition of it becomes as insufferable as the repetition of a conjuring trick already seen through. The instrument of this monotonous formalism is no more difficult to handle than a painter's palette having only two colours, say

---

[1] So-called Brownianism: John Brown, *Elementa medicinae*, 1780.

red and green, the one for colouring the surface when a historical scene is wanted, the other for landscapes. It would be hard
to decide which is greater in all this, the casual ease with which
everything in heaven and on earth and under the earth is coated
with this broth of colour, or the conceit regarding the excellence
of this universal recipe: each supports the other. What results
from this method of labelling all that is in heaven and earth
with the few determinations of the general schema, and pigeon-
holing everything in this way, is nothing less than a 'report
clear as noonday'[1] on the universe as an organism, viz. a synop-
tic table like a skeleton with scraps of paper stuck all over it,
or like the rows of closed and labelled boxes in a grocer's stall.
It is as easy to read off as either of these; and just as all the
flesh and blood has been stripped from this skeleton, and the
no longer living 'essence' [*Sache*] has been packed away in
the boxes, so in the report the living essence of the matter [*Wesen
der Sache*] has been stripped away or boxed up dead. We have
already remarked that this way of thinking at the same time
culminates in a style of painting that is absolutely monochromatic; for it is ashamed of its schematic distinctions, these products of reflection, and submerges them all in the void of the
Absolute, from which pure identity, formless whiteness, is produced. This monochromatic character of the schema and its
lifeless determinations, this absolute identity, and the transition
from one to the other, are all equally products of the lifeless
Understanding and external cognition.

52. The excellent, however, not only cannot escape the fate
of being thus deprived of life and Spirit, of being flayed and
then seeing its skin wrapped around a lifeless knowledge and
its conceit. Rather we recognize even in this fate the power that
the excellent exercises over the hearts, if not over the minds,
of men; also the constructive unfolding into universality and
determinateness of form in which its perfection consists, and
which alone makes it possible for this universality to be used
in a superficial way.

53. Science dare only organize itself by the life of the Notion
itself. The determinateness, which is taken from the schema
and externally attached to an existent thing, is, in Science, the

[1] An allusion to Fichte's *Sun-clear Report to the Public about the True Essence of the Newest
Philosophy* (1801).

self-moving soul of the realized content. The movement of a being that immediately is, consists partly in becoming an other than itself, and thus becoming its own immanent content; partly in taking back into itself this unfolding [of its content] or this existence of it, i.e. in making *itself* into a moment, and simplifying itself into something determinate. In the former movement, *negativity* is the differentiating and positing of *existence*; in this return into self, it is the becoming of the *determinate simplicity*. It is in this way that the content shows that its determinateness is not received from something else, nor externally attached to it, but that it determines itself, and ranges itself as a moment having its own place in the whole. The Understanding, in its pigeon-holing process, keeps the necessity and Notion of the content to itself—all that constitutes the concreteness, the actuality, the living movement of the reality which it arranges. Or rather, it does not keep this to itself, since it does not recognize it; for, if it had this insight, it would surely give some sign of it. It does not even recognize the need for it, else it would drop its schematizing, or at least realize that it can never hope to learn more in this fashion than one can learn from a table of contents. A table of contents is all that it offers, the content itself it does not offer at all.

Even when the specific determinateness—say one like Magnetism, for example,—is in itself concrete or real, the Understanding degrades it into something lifeless, merely predicating it of another existent thing, rather than cognizing it as the immanent life of the thing, or cognizing its native and unique way of generating and expressing itself in that thing. The formal Understanding leaves it to others to add this principal feature. Instead of entering into the immanent content of the thing, it is forever surveying the whole and standing above the particular existence of which it is speaking, i.e. it does not see it at all. Scientific cognition, on the contrary, demands surrender to the life of the object, or, what amounts to the same thing, confronting and expressing its inner necessity. Thus, absorbed in its object, scientific cognition forgets about that general survey, which is merely the reflection of the cognitive process away from the content and back into itself. Yet, immersed in the material, and advancing with its movement, scientific cognition does come back to itself, but not before its filling or content is taken back into itself, is simplified into a determinateness, and has reduced itself to *one* aspect of its own existence and passed over into its higher truth. Through this process the simple, self-surveying whole itself emerges from the wealth in which its reflection seemed to be lost.

54. In general, because, as we put it above, substance is in itself or implicitly Subject, all content is its own reflection into itself. The subsistence or substance of anything that exists is its self-identity; for a failure of self-identity would be its dissolution. Self-identity, however, is pure abstraction; but this is *thinking*. When I say 'quality', I am saying simple determinateness; it is by quality that one existence is distinguished from another, or is an existence; it is for itself, or it subsists through this simple oneness with itself. But it is thereby essentially a *thought*. Comprehended in this is the fact that Being is Thought; and this is the source of that insight which usually eludes the usual superficial [*begrifflos*] talk about the identity of Thought and Being.—Now, since the subsistence of an existent thing is a self-identity or pure abstraction, it is the abstraction of itself from itself, or it is itself its lack of self-identity and its dissolution—its own inwardness and withdrawal into itself—its own becoming. Because this is the nature of what is, and in so far as what is has this nature for [our] knowing, this knowing is not an activity that deals with the content as something alien, is not a reflection into itself away from the content. Science is not that idealism which replaced the dogmatism of assertion with a dogmatism of assurance, or a dogmatism of self-certainty. On the contrary, since [our] knowing sees the content return into its own inwardness, its activity is totally absorbed in the content, for it is the immanent self of the content; yet it has at the same time returned into itself, for it is pure self-identity in otherness. Thus it is the cunning which, while seeming to abstain from activity, looks on and watches how determinateness, with its concrete life, just where it fancies it is pursuing its own self-preservation and particular interest, is in fact doing the very opposite, is an activity that results in its own dissolution, and makes itself a moment of the whole.

55. Above we indicated the significance of the *Understanding* in reference to the self-consciousness of substance; we can now see clearly from what has been said its significance in reference

to the determination of substance as being. Existence is Quality, self-identical determinateness, or determinate simplicity, determinate thought; this is the Understanding of existence [i.e. the nature of existence from the standpoint of the Understanding]. Hence, it is *Noûs*, as Anaxagoras first recognized the essence of things to be. Those who came after him grasped the nature of existence more definitely as *Eidos* or *Idea*, determinate Universality, Species or Kind. It might seem as if the term *Species* or *Kind* is too commonplace, too inadequate, for Ideas such as the Beautiful, the Holy, and the Eternal that are currently in fashion. But as a matter of fact Idea expresses neither more nor less than Species or Kind. But nowadays an expression which exactly designates a Notion is often spurned in favour of one which, if only because it is of foreign extraction, shrouds the Notion in a fog, and hence sounds more edifying.

Precisely because existence is defined as Species, it is a simple thought; *Noûs*, simplicity, is substance. On account of its simplicity or self-identity it appears fixed and enduring. But this self-identity is no less negativity; therefore its fixed existence passes over into its dissolution. The determinateness seems at first to be due entirely to the fact that it is related to an *other*, and its movement seems imposed on it by an alien power; but having its otherness within itself, and being self-moving, is just what is involved in the *simplicity* of thinking itself; for this simple thinking is the self-moving and self-differentiating thought, it is its own inwardness, it is the pure Notion. Thus common understanding, too, is a becoming, and, as this becoming, it is *reason*ableness.

56. It is in this nature of what is to be in its being its own Notion, that *logical necessity* in general consists. This alone is the rational element and the rhythm of the organic whole; it is as much *knowledge* of the content, as the content is the Notion and essence—in other words, it alone is *speculative philosophy*. The self-moving concrete shape makes itself into a simple determinateness; in so doing it raises itself to logical form, and exists in its essentiality; its concrete existence is just this movement, and is directly a logical existence. It is for this reason unnecessary to clothe the content in an external [logical] formalism; the content is in its very nature the transition into such formal-

ism, but a formalism which ceases to be external, since the form is the innate development of the concrete content itself.

57. This nature of scientific method, which consists partly in not being separate from the content, and partly in spontaneously determining the rhythm of its movement, has, as already remarked, its proper exposition in speculative philosophy. Of course, what has been said here does express the Notion, but cannot count for more than an anticipatory assurance. Its truth does not lie in this partly narrative exposition, and is therefore just as little refuted by asserting the contrary, by calling to mind and recounting conventional ideas, as if they were established and familiar truths, or by dishing up something new with the assurance that it comes from the shrine of inner divine intuition. A reception of this kind is usually the first reaction on the part of knowing to something unfamiliar; it resists it in order to save its own freedom and its own insight, its own authority, from the alien authority (for this is the guise in which what is newly encountered first appears), and to get rid of the appearance that something has been learned and of the sort of shame this is supposed to involve. Similarly, when the unfamiliar is greeted with applause, the reaction is of the same kind, and consists in what in another sphere would take the form of ultra-revolutionary speech and action.

58. What, therefore, is important in the *study* of *Science*, is that one should take on oneself the strenuous effort of the Notion.[1] This requires attention to the Notion as such, to the simple determinations, e.g. of Being-in-itself, Being-for-itself, Self-identity, etc.; for these are pure self-movements such as could be called souls if their Notion did not designate something higher than soul. The habit of picture-thinking, when it is interrupted by the Notion, finds it just as irksome as does formalistic thinking that argues back and forth in thoughts that have no actuality. That habit should be called material thinking, a contingent consciousness that is absorbed only in material stuff, and therefore finds it hard work to lift the [thinking] self clear of such matter, and to be with itself alone. At the opposite extreme, argumentation is freedom from all content, and a sense of vanity towards it. What is looked for here is the effort

[1] i.e. the strenuous effort required to think in terms of the Notion.

to give up this freedom, and, instead of being the arbitrarily moving principle of the content, to sink this freedom in the content, letting it move spontaneously of its own nature, by the self as its own self, and then to contemplate this movement. This refusal to intrude into the immanent rhythm of the Notion, either arbitrarily or with wisdom obtained from elsewhere, constitutes a restraint which is itself an essential moment of the Notion.

59. There are two aspects of the procedure of argumentation to which speculative [*begreifende*] thinking is opposed and which call for further notice. First, such reasoning adopts a negative attitude towards the content it apprehends; it knows how to refute it and destroy it. That something is *not* the case, is a merely negative insight, a dead end which does not lead to a new content beyond itself. In order to have a content once again, something new must be taken over from elsewhere. Argumentation is reflection into the empty 'I', the vanity of its own knowing.—This vanity, however, expresses not only the vanity of this content, but also the futility of this insight itself; for this insight is the negative that fails to see the positive within itself. Because this reflection does not get its very negativity as its content, it is never at the heart of the matter, but always beyond it. For this reason it imagines that by establishing the void it is always ahead of any insight rich in content. On the other hand, in speculative [*begreifenden*] thinking, as we have already shown, the negative belongs to the content itself, and is the *positive*, both as the *immanent* movement and determination of the content, and as the whole of this process. Looked at as a result, what emerges from this process is the *determinate* negative which is consequently a positive content as well.

60. But in view of the fact that such thinking has a content, whether of picture-thoughts or abstract thoughts or a mixture of both, argumentation has another side which makes comprehension difficult for it. The remarkable nature of this other side is closely linked with the above-mentioned essence of the Idea, or rather it expresses the Idea in the way that it appears as the movement which is thinking apprehension. For whereas, in its negative behaviour, which we have just discussed, ratiocinative thinking is itself the self into which the content returns, in its positive cognition, on the other hand, the self is a *Subject* to

which the content is related as Accident and Predicate. This Subject constitutes the basis to which the content is attached, and upon which the movement runs back and forth. Speculative [*begreifendes*] thinking behaves in a different way. Since the Notion is the objects's own self, which presents itself as the *coming-to-be of the object*, it is not a passive Subject inertly supporting the Accidents; it is, on the contrary, the self-moving Notion which takes its determinations back into itself. In this movement the passive Subject itself perishes; it enters into the differences and the content, and constitutes the determinateness, i.e. the differentiated content and its movement, instead of remaining inertly over against it. The solid ground which argumentation has in the passive Subject is therefore shaken, and only this movement itself becomes the object. The Subject that fills its content ceases to go beyond it, and cannot have any further Predicates or accidental properties. Conversely, the dispersion of the content is thereby bound together under the self; it is not the universal which, free from the Subject, could belong to several others. Thus the content is, in fact, no longer a Predicate of the Subject, but is the Substance, the essence and the Notion of what is under discussion. Picture-thinking, whose nature it is to run through the Accidents or Predicates and which, because they are nothing more than Predicates and Accidents, rightly goes beyond them, is checked in its progress, since that which has the form of a Predicate in a proposition is the Substance itself. It suffers, as we might put it, a counter-thrust. Starting from the Subject as though this were a permanent ground, it finds that, since the Predicate is really the Substance, the Subject has passed over into the Predicate, and, by this very fact, has been sublated; and, since in this way what seems to be the Predicate has become the whole and the independent mass, thinking cannot roam at will, but is impeded by this weight.

Usually, the Subject is first made the basis, as the *objective*, fixed self; thence the necessary movement to the multiplicity of determinations or Predicates proceeds. Here, that Subject is replaced by the knowing 'I' itself, which links the Predicates with the Subject holding them. But, since that first Subject enters into the determinations themselves and is their soul, the second Subject, viz. the knowing 'I', still finds in the Predicate what it thought it had finished with and got away from, and from which it hoped to return into itself; and, instead of being able to function as the determining agent in the movement of predication, arguing back and forth whether to attach this or that Predicate, it is really still occupied with the self of the content, having to remain associated with it, instead of being for itself.

61. Formally, what has been said can be expressed thus: the general nature of the judgement or proposition, which involves the distinction of Subject and Predicate, is destroyed by the speculative proposition, and the proposition of identity which the former becomes contains the counter-thrust against that subject–predicate relationship.—This conflict between the general form of a proposition and the unity of the Notion which destroys it is similar to the conflict that occurs in rhythm between metre and accent. Rhythm results from the floating centre and the unification of the two. So, too, in the philosophical proposition the identification of Subject and Predicate is not meant to destroy the difference between them, which the form of the proposition expresses; their unity, rather, is meant to emerge as a harmony. The form of the proposition is the appearance of the determinate sense, or the accent that distinguishes its fulfilment; but that the predicate expresses the Substance, and that the Subject itself falls into the universal, this is the *unity* in which the accent dies away.

62. To illustrate what has been said: in the proposition 'God is being', the Predicate is 'being'; it has the significance of something substantial in which the Subject is dissolved. 'Being' is here meant to be not a Predicate, but rather the essence; it seems, consequently, that God ceases to be what he is from his position in the proposition, viz. a fixed Subject. Here thinking, instead of making progress in the transition from Subject to Predicate, in reality feels itself checked by the loss of the Subject, and, missing it, is thrown back on to the thought of the Subject. Or, since the Predicate itself has been expressed as a Subject, as *the* being or *essence* which exhausts the nature of the Subject, thinking finds the Subject immediately in the Predicate; and now, having returned into itself in the Predicate, instead of being in a position where it has freedom for argument, it is still absorbed in the content, or at least is faced with the demand

that it should be. Similarly, too, when one says: 'the *actual* is
the *universal*', the actual as subject disappears in its predicate.
The universal is not meant to have merely the significance of
a predicate, as if the proposition asserted only that the actual
is universal; on the contrary, the universal is meant to express
the essence of the actual.—Thinking therefore loses the firm
objective basis it had in the subject when, in the predicate, it
is thrown back on to the subject, and when, in the predicate,
it does not return into itself, but into the subject of the content.

63. This abnormal inhibition of thought is in large measure
the source of the complaints regarding the unintelligibility of
philosophical writings from individuals who otherwise possess
the educational requirements for understanding them. Here we
see the reason behind one particular complaint so often made
against them: that so much has to be read over and over before
it can be understood—a complaint whose burden is presumed
to be quite outrageous, and, if justified, to admit of no defence.
It is clear from the above what this amounts to. The philosophical proposition, since it *is* a proposition, leads one to believe
that the usual subject–predicate relation obtains, as well as the
usual attitude towards knowing. But the philosophical content
destroys this attitude and this opinion. We learn by experience
that we meant something other than we meant to mean; and
this correction of our meaning compels our knowing to go back
to the proposition, and understand it in some other way.

64. One difficulty which should be avoided comes from mixing up the speculative with the ratiocinative methods, so that
what is said of the Subject at one time signifies its Notion, at
another time merely its Predicate or accidental property. The
one method interferes with the other, and only a philosophical
exposition that rigidly excludes the usual way of relating the
parts of a proposition could achieve the goal of plasticity.

65. As a matter of fact, non-speculative thinking also has its
valid rights which are disregarded in the speculative way of stating a proposition. The sublation of the form of the proposition
must not happen only in an *immediate* manner, through the mere
content of the proposition. On the contrary, this opposite movement must find explicit expression; it must not just be the inward inhibition mentioned above. This return of the Notion
into itself must be *set forth*. This movement which constitutes

what formerly the proof was supposed to accomplish, is the dialectical movement of the proposition itself. This alone is the speculative *in act*, and only the expression of this movement is a
speculative exposition. As a proposition, the speculative is only
the *internal* inhibition and the non-*existential* return of the
essence into itself. Hence we often find philosophical expositions
referring us to this *inner* intuition; and in this way they evade
the systematic exposition of the dialectical movement of the
proposition which we have demanded.—The *proposition* should
express *what* the True is; but essentially the True is Subject.
As such it is merely the dialectical movement, this course that
generates itself, going forth from, and returning to, itself. In
non-speculative cognition proof constitutes this side of
expressed inwardness. But once the dialectic has been separated
from proof, the notion of philosophical demonstration has been
lost.

66. Here we should bear in mind that the dialectical movement likewise has propositions for its parts or elements; the difficulty just indicated seems, therefore, to recur perpetually, and
to be inherent in the very nature of philosophical exposition.
This is like what happens in ordinary proof, where the reasons
given are themselves in need of further reasons, and so on *ad
infinitum*. This pattern of giving reasons and stating conditions
belongs to that method of proof which differs from the dialectical movement, and belongs therefore to external cognition. As
regards the dialectical movement itself, its element is the one
Notion; it thus has a content which is, in its own self, Subject
through and through. Thus no content occurs which functions
as an underlying subject, nor receives its meaning as a predicate; the proposition as it stands is merely an empty form.

Apart from the self that is sensuously intuited or represented,
it is above all the name as name that designates the pure Subject, the empty unit without thought-content. For this reason
it may be expedient, e.g., to avoid the name 'God', since this
word is not immediately also a Notion, but rather the proper
name, the fixed point of rest of the underlying Subject; whereas,
on the other hand, e.g. 'Being' or 'the One', 'Singularity', 'the
Subject', etc. themselves at once suggest concepts. Even if speculative truths are affirmed of this subject, their content lacks
the immanent Notion, because it is present merely in the form

of a passive subject, with the result that such truths readily assume the form of mere edification. From this side, too, the habit of expressing the speculative predicate in the form of a proposition, and not as Notion and essence, creates a difficulty that can be increased or diminished through the very way in which philosophy is expounded. In keeping with our insight into the nature of speculation, the exposition should preserve the dialectical form, and should admit nothing except in so far as it is comprehended [in terms of the Notion], and is the Notion.

67. The study of philosophy is as much hindered by the conceit that will not argue, as it is by the argumentative approach. This conceit relies on truths which are taken for granted and which it sees no need to re-examine; it just lays them down, and believes it is entitled to assert them, as well as to judge and pass sentence by appealing to them. In view of this, it is especially necessary that philosophizing should again be made a serious business. In the case of all other sciences, arts, skills, and crafts, everyone is convinced that a complex and laborious programme of learning and practice is necessary for competence. Yet when it comes to philosophy, there seems to be a currently prevailing prejudice to the effect that, although not everyone who has eyes and fingers, and is given leather and last, is at once in a position to make shoes, everyone nevertheless immediately understands how to philosophize, and how to evaluate philosophy, since he possesses the criterion for doing so in his natural reason—as if he did not likewise possess the measure for a shoe in his own foot. It seems that philosophical competence consists precisely in an absence of information and study, as though philosophy left off where they began. Philosophy is frequently taken to be a purely formal kind of knowledge, void of content, and the insight is sadly lacking that, whatever truth there may be in the content of any discipline or science, it can only deserve the name if such truth has been engendered by philosophy. Let the other sciences try to argue as much as they like without philosophy—without it they can have in them neither life, Spirit, nor truth.

68. In place of the long process of culture towards genuine philosophy, a movement as rich as it is profound, through which Spirit achieves knowledge, we are offered as quite equivalent

either direct revelations from heaven, or the sound common sense that has never laboured over, or informed itself regarding, other knowledge or genuine philosophy; and we are assured that these are quite as good substitutes as some claim chicory is for coffee. It is not a pleasant experience to see ignorance, and a crudity without form or taste, which cannot focus its thought on a single abstract proposition, still less on a connected chain of them, claiming at one moment to be freedom of thought and toleration, and at the next to be even genius. Genius, we all know, was once all the rage in poetry, as it now is in philosophy; but when its productions made sense at all, such genius begat only trite prose instead of poetry, or, getting beyond that, only crazy rhetoric. So, nowadays, philosophizing by the light of nature, which regards itself as too good for the Notion, and as being an intuitive and poetic thinking in virtue of this deficiency, brings to market the arbitrary combinations of an imagination that has only been disorganized by its thoughts, an imagery that is neither fish nor flesh, neither poetry nor philosophy.

69. On the other hand, when philosophizing by the light of nature flows along the more even course of sound common sense, it offers at its very best only a rhetoric of trivial truths. And, if reproached with the insignificance of these truths, it assures us in reply that their meaning and fulfilment reside in its heart, and must surely be present in the hearts of others too, since it reckons to have said the last word once the innocence of the heart, the purity of conscience, and such like have been mentioned. These are ultimate truths to which no exception can be taken, and beyond which nothing more can be demanded. It is just the point, however, that the best should not remain in the recesses of what is inner, but should be brought out of these depths into the light of day. But it would be better by far to spare oneself the effort of bringing forth ultimate truths of that kind; for they have long since been available in catechisms or in popular sayings, etc.—It is not difficult to grasp such vague and misleading truths, or even to show that the mind in believing them is also aware of their very opposite. When it labours to extricate itself from the bewilderment this sets up, it falls into fresh contradictions, and may very well burst out with the assertion that the question is settled, that so and

so is the truth, and that the other views are sophistries. For 'sophistry' is a slogan used by ordinary common sense against educated reason, just as the expression 'visionary dreaming' sums up, once and for all, what philosophy means to those who are ignorant of it.—Since the man of common sense makes his appeal to feeling, to an oracle within his breast, he is finished and done with anyone who does not agree; he only has to explain that he has nothing more to say to anyone who does not find and feel the same in himself. In other words, he tramples underfoot the roots of humanity. For it is the nature of humanity to press onward to agreement with others; human nature only really exists in an achieved community of minds. The anti-human, the merely animal, consists in staying within the sphere of feeling, and being able to communicate only at that level.

70. Should anyone ask for a royal road to Science, there is no more easy-going way than to rely on sound common sense; and for the rest, in order to keep up with the times, and with advances in philosophy, to read reviews of philosophical works, perhaps even to read their prefaces and first paragraphs. For these preliminary pages give the general principles on which everything turns, and the reviews, as well as providing historical accounts, also provide the critical appraisal which, being a judgement, stands high above the work judged. This common road can be taken in casual dress; but the high sense for the Eternal, the Holy, the Infinite strides along in the robes of a high priest, on a road that is from the first no road, but has immediate being as its centre, the genius of profound original ideas and lofty flashes of inspiration. But just as profundity of this kind still does not reveal the source of essential being, so, too, these sky-rockets of inspiration are not yet the empyrean. True thoughts and scientific insight are only to be won through the labour of the Notion. Only the Notion can produce the universality of knowledge which is neither common vagueness nor the inadequacy of ordinary common sense, but a fully developed, perfected cognition; not the uncommon universality of a reason whose talents have been ruined by indolence and the conceit of genius, but a truth ripened to its properly matured form so as to be capable of being the property of all self-conscious Reason.

71. Since I hold that Science exists solely in the self-movement of the Notion, and since my view differs from, and is in fact wholly opposed to, current ideas regarding the nature and form of truth, both those referred to above and other peripheral aspects of them, it seems that any attempt to expound the system of Science from this point of view is unlikely to be favourably received. In the meantime, I can bear in mind that if at times the excellence of Plato's philosophy has been held to lie in his scientifically valueless myths, there have also been times, even called times of ecstatic dreaming,[1] when Aristotle's philosophy was esteemed for its speculative depth, and Plato's *Parmenides* (surely the greatest artistic achievement of the ancient dialectic) was regarded as the true disclosure and positive expression of the divine life, and times when, despite the obscurity generated by ecstasy, this misunderstood ecstasy was in fact supposed to be nothing else than the pure Notion. Furthermore, what really is excellent in the philosophy of our time takes its value to lie in its scientific quality, and even though others take a different view, it is in fact only in virtue of its scientific character that it exerts any influence. Hence, I may hope, too, that this attempt to vindicate Science for the Notion, and to expound it in this its proper element, will succeed in winning acceptance through the inner truth of the subject-matter. We must hold to the conviction that it is the nature of truth to prevail when its time has come, and that it appears only when this time has come, and therefore never appears prematurely, nor finds a public not ripe to receive it; also we must accept that the individual needs that this should be so in order to verify what is as yet a matter for himself alone, and to experience the conviction, which in the first place belongs only to a particular individual, as something universally held. But in this connection the public must often be distinguished from those who pose as its representatives and spokesmen. In many respects the attitude of the public is quite different from, even contrary to, that of these spokesmen. Whereas the public is inclined good-naturedly to blame itself when a philosophical work makes no appeal to it, these others, certain of their own competence, put all the blame on the author. The effect of such a work on the

---

[1] This was what the English Enlightment called 'enthusiasm', but the word has no religious overtones now.

public is more noiseless than the action of these dead men when they bury their dead. The general level of insight now is altogether more educated, its curiosity more awake, and its judgement more swiftly reached, so that the feet of those who will carry you out are already at the door. But from this we must often distinguish the more gradual effect which corrects the attention extorted by imposing assurances and corrects, too, contemptuous censure, and gives some writers an audience only after a time, while others after a time have no audience left.

72. For the rest, at a time when the universality of Spirit has gathered such strength, and the singular detail, as is fitting, has become correspondingly less important, when, too, that universal aspect claims and holds on to the whole range of the wealth it has developed, the share in the total work of Spirit which falls to the individual can only be very small. Because of this, the individual must all the more forget himself, as the nature of Science implies and requires. Of course, he must make of himself and achieve what he can; but less must be demanded of him, just as he in turn can expect less of himself, and may demand less for himself.

INTRODUCTION

73. It is a natural assumption that in philosophy, before we start to deal with its proper subject-matter, viz. the actual cognition of what truly is, one must first of all come to an understanding about cognition, which is regarded either as the instrument to get hold of the Absolute, or as the medium through which one discovers it. A certain uneasiness seems justified, partly because there are different types of cognition, and one of them might be more appropriate than another for the attainment of this goal, so that we could make a bad choice of means; and partly because cognition is a faculty of a definite kind and scope, and thus, without a more precise definition of its nature and limits, we might grasp clouds of error instead of the heaven of truth. This feeling of uneasiness is surely bound to be transformed into the conviction that the whole project of securing for consciousness through cognition what exists in itself is absurd, and that there is a boundary between cognition and the Absolute that completely separates them. For, if cognition is the instrument for getting hold of absolute being, it is obvious that the use of an instrument on a thing certainly does not let it be what it is for itself, but rather sets out to reshape and alter it. If, on the other hand, cognition is not an instrument of our activity but a more or less passive medium through which the light of truth reaches us, then again we do not receive the truth as it is in itself, but only as it exists through and in this medium. Either way we employ a means which immediately brings about the opposite of its own end; or rather, what is really absurd is that we should make use of a means at all.

It would seem, to be sure, that this evil could be remedied through an acquaintance with the way in which the *instrument* works; for this would enable us to eliminate from the representation of the Absolute which we have gained through it whatever is due to the instrument, and thus get the truth in its purity. But this 'improvement' would in fact only bring us back to where we were before. If we remove from a reshaped thing what the instrument has done to it, then the thing—here the Absolute—becomes for us exactly what it was before this [accordingly] superfluous effort. On the other hand, if the Absolute is supposed merely to be brought nearer to us through this instrument, without anything in it being altered, like a bird caught by a lime-twig, it would surely laugh our little ruse to scorn, if it were not with us, in and for itself, all along, and of its own volition. For a ruse is just what cognition would be in such a case, since it would, with its manifold exertions, be giving itself the air of doing something quite different from creating a merely immediate and therefore effortless relationship. Or, if by testing cognition, which we conceive of as a *medium*, we get to know the law of its refraction, it is again useless to subtract this from the end result. For it is not the refraction of the ray, but the ray itself whereby truth reaches us, that is cognition; and if this were removed, all that would be indicated would be a pure direction or a blank space.

74. Meanwhile, if the fear of falling into error sets up a mistrust of Science, which in the absence of such scruples gets on with the work itself, and actually cognizes something, it is hard to see why we should not turn round and mistrust this very mistrust. Should we not be concerned as to whether this fear of error is not just the error itself? Indeed, this fear takes something—a great deal in fact—for granted as truth, supporting its scruples and inferences on what is itself in need of prior scrutiny to see if it is true. To be specific, it takes for granted certain ideas about cognition as an *instrument* and as a *medium*, and assumes that there is a *difference between ourselves and this cognition*. Above all, it presupposes that the Absolute stands on one side and cognition on the other, independent and separated from it, and yet is something real; or in other words, it presupposes that cognition which, since it is excluded from the Absolute, is surely outside of the truth as well, is nevertheless true, an assumption whereby what calls itself fear of error reveals itself rather as fear of the truth.

75. This conclusion stems from the fact that the Absolute alone is true, or the truth alone is absolute. One may set this aside on the grounds that there is a type of cognition which, though it does not cognize the Absolute as Science aims to, is still true, and that cognition in general, though it be incapable of grasping the Absolute, is still capable of grasping other kinds

of truth. But we gradually come to see that this kind of talk which goes back and forth only leads to a hazy distinction between an absolute truth and some other kind of truth, and that words like 'absolute', 'cognition', etc. presuppose a meaning which has yet to be ascertained.

76. Instead of troubling ourselves with such useless ideas and locutions about cognition as 'an instrument for getting hold of the Absolute', or as 'a medium through which we view the truth' (relationships which surely, in the end, are what all these ideas of a cognition cut off from the Absolute, and an Absolute separated from cognition, amount to); instead of putting up with excuses which create the incapacity of Science by assuming relationships of this kind in order to be exempt from the hard work of Science, while at the same time giving the impression of working seriously and zealously; instead of bothering to refute all these ideas, we could reject them out of hand as adventitious and arbitrary, and the words associated with them like 'absolute', 'cognition', 'objective' and 'subjective', and countless others whose meaning is assumed to be generally familiar, could even be regarded as so much deception. For to give the impression that their meaning is generally well known, or that their Notion is comprehended, looks more like an attempt to avoid the main problem, which is precisely to provide this Notion. We could, with better justification, simply spare ourselves the trouble of paying any attention whatever to such ideas and locutions; for they are intended to ward off Science itself, and constitute merely an empty appearance of knowing, which vanishes immediately as soon as Science comes on the scene. But Science, just because it comes on the scene, is itself an appearance: in coming on the scene it is not yet Science in its developed and unfolded truth. In this connection it makes no difference whether we think of Science as the appearance because it comes on the scene alongside another mode of knowledge, or whether we call that other untrue knowledge its manifestation. In any case Science must liberate itself from this semblance, and it can do so only by turning against it. For, when confronted with a knowledge that is without truth, Science can neither merely reject it as an ordinary way of looking at things, while assuring us that its Science is a quite different sort of cognition for which that ordinary knowledge is of no account

whatever; nor can it appeal to the vulgar view for the intimations it gives us of something better to come. By the former *assurance*, Science would be declaring its power to lie simply in its *being*; but the untrue knowledge likewise appeals to the fact that *it is*, and *assures* us that for it Science is of no account. *One* bare assurance is worth just as much as another. Still less can Science appeal to whatever intimations of something better it may detect in the cognition that is without truth, to the signs which point in the direction of Science. For one thing, it would only be appealing again to what merely *is*; and for another, it would only be appealing to itself, and to itself in the mode in which it exists in the cognition that is without truth. In other words, it would be appealing to an inferior form of its being, to the way it appears, rather than to what it is in and for itself. It is for this reason that an exposition of how knowledge makes its appearance will here be undertaken.

77. Now, because it has only phenomenal knowledge for its object, this exposition seems not to be Science, free and self-moving in its own peculiar shape; yet from this standpoint it can be regarded as the path of the natural consciousness which presses forward to true knowledge; or as the way of the Soul which journeys through the series of its own configurations as though they were the stations appointed for it by its own nature,[1] so that it may purify itself for the life of the Spirit, and achieve finally, through a completed experience of itself, the awareness of what it really is in itself.

78. Natural consciousness will show itself to be only the Notion of knowledge, or in other words, not to be real knowledge. But since it directly takes itself to be real knowledge, this path has a negative significance for it, and what is in fact the realization of the Notion, counts for it rather as the loss of its own self; for it does lose its truth on this path. The road can therefore be regarded as the pathway of *doubt*, or more precisely as the way of despair. For what happens on it is not what is ordinarily understood when the word 'doubt' is used: shilly-shallying about this or that presumed truth, followed by a return to that truth again, after the doubt has been appropriately dispelled—so that at the end of the process the matter is taken to be what it was in the first place. On the contrary,

[1] An allusion perhaps to the Stations of the Cross.

this path is the conscious insight into the untruth of phenomenal knowledge, for which the supreme reality is what is in truth only the unrealized Notion. Therefore this thoroughgoing scepticism is also not the scepticism with which an earnest zeal for truth and Science fancies it has prepared and equipped itself in their service: the *resolve*, in Science, not to give oneself over to the thoughts of others, upon mere authority, but to examine everything for oneself and follow only one's own conviction, or better still, to produce everything oneself, and accept only one's own deed as what is true.

The series of configurations which consciousness goes through along this road is, in reality, the detailed history of the *education* of consciousness itself to the standpoint of Science. That zealous resolve represents this education simplistically as something directly over and done with in the making of the resolution; but the way of the Soul is the actual fulfilment of the resolution, in contrast to the untruth of that view. Now, following one's own conviction is, of course, more than giving oneself over to authority; but changing an opinion accepted on authority into an opinion held out of personal conviction, does not necessarily alter the content of the opinion, or replace error with truth. The only difference between being caught up in a system of opinions and prejudices based on personal conviction, and being caught up in one based on the authority of others, lies in the added conceit that is innate in the latter position. The scepticism that is directed against the whole range of phenomenal consciousness, on the other hand, renders the Spirit for the first time competent to examine what truth is. For it brings about a state of despair about all the so-called natural ideas, thoughts, and opinions, regardless of whether they are called one's own or someone else's, ideas with which the consciousness that sets about the examination [of truth] *straight away* is still filled and hampered, so that it is, in fact, incapable of carrying out what it wants to undertake.

79. The necessary progression and interconnection of the forms of the unreal consciousness will by itself bring to pass the *completion* of the series. To make this more intelligible, it may be remarked, in a preliminary and general way, that the exposition of the untrue consciousness in its untruth is not a merely *negative* procedure. The natural consciousness itself normally

takes this one-sided view of it; and a knowledge which makes this one-sidedness its very essence is itself one of the patterns of incomplete consciousness which occurs on the road itself, and will manifest itself in due course. This is just the scepticism which only ever sees pure nothingness in its result and abstracts from the fact that this nothingness is specifically the nothingness of that *from which it results*. For it is only when it is taken as the result of that from which it emerges, that it is, in fact, the true result; in that case it is itself a *determinate* nothingness, one which has a *content*. The scepticism that ends up with the bare abstraction of nothingness or emptiness cannot get any further from there, but must wait to see whether something new comes along and what it is, in order to throw it too into the same empty abyss. But when, on the other hand, the result is conceived as it is in truth, namely, as a *determinate* negation, a new form has thereby immediately arisen, and in the negation the transition is made through which the progress through the complete series of forms comes about of itself.

80. But the *goal* is as necessarily fixed for knowledge as the serial progression; it is the point where knowledge no longer needs to go beyond itself, where knowledge finds itself, where Notion corresponds to object and object to Notion. Hence the progress towards this goal is also unhalting, and short of it no satisfaction is to be found at any of the stations on the way. Whatever is confined within the limits of a natural life cannot by its own efforts go beyond its immediate existence; but it is driven beyond it by something else, and this uprooting entails its death. Consciousness, however, is explicitly the *Notion* of itself. Hence it is something that goes beyond limits, and since these limits are its own, it is something that goes beyond itself. With the positing of a single particular the beyond is also established for consciousness, even if it is only *alongside* the limited object as in the case of spatial intuition. Thus consciousness suffers this violence at its own hands: it spoils its own limited satisfaction. When consciousness feels this violence, its anxiety may well make it retreat from the truth, and strive to hold on to what it is in danger of losing. But it can find no peace. If it wishes to remain in a state of unthinking inertia, then thought troubles its thoughtlessness, and its own unrest disturbs its inertia. Or, if it entrenches itself in sentimentality, which assures

us that it finds everything to be *good in its kind*, then this
assurance likewise suffers violence at the hands of Reason, for,
precisely in so far as something is merely a kind, Reason finds
it *not* to be good. Or, again, its fear of the truth may lead consciousness to hide, from itself and others, behind the pretension
that its burning zeal for truth makes it difficult or even impossible to find any other truth but the unique truth of vanity—
that of being at any rate cleverer than any thoughts that one
gets by oneself or from others. This conceit which understands
how to belittle every truth, in order to turn back into itself and
gloat over its own understanding, which knows how to dissolve
every thought and always find the same barren Ego instead of
any content—this is a satisfaction which we must leave to itself,
for it flees from the universal, and seeks only to be for itself.

81. In addition to these preliminary general remarks about
the manner and the necessity of the progression, it may be useful
to say something about the *method of carrying out the inquiry*. If
this exposition is viewed as a way of *relating Science* to *phenomenal*
knowledge, and as an investigation and *examination of the reality
of cognition*, it would seem that it cannot take place without some
presupposition which can serve as its underlying *criterion*. For
an examination consists in applying an accepted standard, and
in determining whether something is right or wrong on the basis
of the resulting agreement or disagreement of the thing examined; thus the standard as such (and Science likewise if it were
the criterion) is accepted as the *essence* or as the *in-itself*. But
here, where Science has just begun to come on the scene, neither
Science nor anything else has yet justified itself as the essence
or the in-itself; and without something of the sort it seems that
no examination can take place.

82. This contradiction and its removal will become more
definite if we call to mind the abstract determinations of truth
and knowledge as they occur in consciousness. Consciousness
simultaneously *distinguishes* itself from something, and at the
same time *relates* itself to it, or, as it is said, this something exists
for consciousness; and the determinate aspect of this *relating*,
or of the *being* of something for a consciousness, is *knowing*.
But we distinguish this being-for-another from *being-in-itself*;
whatever is related to knowledge or knowing is also distinguished from it, and posited as existing outside of this relation-

ship; this *being-in-itself* is called *truth*. Just what might be involved in these determinations is of no further concern to us here. Since our object is phenomenal knowledge, its determinations too will at first be taken directly as they present themselves; and they do present themselves very much as we have already apprehended them.

83. Now, if we inquire into the truth of knowledge, it seems that we are asking what knowledge is *in itself*. Yet in this inquiry knowledge is *our* object, something that exists *for us*; and the *in-itself* that would supposedly result from it would rather be the being of knowledge *for us*. What we asserted to be its essence would be not so much its truth but rather just our knowledge of it. The essence or criterion would lie within ourselves, and that which was to be compared with it and about which a decision would be reached through this comparison would not necessarily have to recognize the validity of such a standard.

84. But the dissociation, or this semblance of dissociation and presupposition, is overcome by the nature of the object we are investigating. Consciousness provides its own criterion from within itself, so that the investigation becomes a comparison of consciousness with itself; for the distinction made above falls within it. In consciousness one thing exists *for* another, i.e. consciousness regularly contains the determinateness of the moment of knowledge; at the same time, this other is to consciousness not merely *for it*, but is also outside of this relationship, or exists *in itself*: the moment of truth. Thus in what consciousness affirms from within itself as *being-in-itself* or the *True* we have the standard which consciousness itself sets up by which to measure what it knows. If we designate *knowledge* as the Notion, but the essence or the *True* as what exists, or the *object*, then the examination consists in seeing whether the Notion corresponds to the object. But if we call the *essence* or in-itself of the *object* the *Notion*, and on the other hand understand by the *object* the Notion itself as *object*, viz. as it exists *for an other*, then the examination consists in seeing whether the object corresponds to its Notion. It is evident, of course, that the two procedures are the same. But the essential point to bear in mind throughout the whole investigation is that these two moments, 'Notion' and 'object', 'being-for-another' and 'being-in-itself', both fall *within* that knowledge which we are investigating.

Consequently, we do not need to import criteria, or to make use of our own bright ideas and thoughts during the course of the inquiry; it is precisely when we leave these aside that we succeed in contemplating the matter in hand as it is *in and for itself*.

85. But not only is a contribution by us superfluous, since Notion and object, the criterion and what is to be tested, are present in consciousness itself, but we are also spared the trouble of comparing the two and really *testing* them, so that, since what consciousness examines is its own self, all that is left for us to do is simply to look on. For consciousness is, on the one hand, consciousness of the object, and on the other, consciousness of itself; consciousness of what for it is the True, and consciousness of its knowledge of the truth. Since both are *for* the same consciousness, this consciousness is itself their comparison; it is for this same consciousness to know whether its knowledge of the object corresponds to the object or not. The object, it is true, seems only to be for consciousness in the way that consciousness knows it; it seems that consciousness cannot, as it were, get behind the object as it exists for consciousness so as to examine what the object is *in itself*, and hence, too, cannot test its own knowledge by that standard. But the distinction between the in-itself and knowledge is already present in the very fact that consciousness knows an object at all. Something is *for it* the *in-itself*; and knowledge, or the being of the object for consciousness, is, *for it*, another moment. Upon this distinction, which is present as a fact, the examination rests. If the comparison shows that these two moments do not correspond to one another, it would seem that consciousness must alter its knowledge to make it conform to the object. But, in fact, in the alteration of the knowledge, the object itself alters for it too, for the knowledge that was present was essentially a knowledge of the object: as the knowledge changes, so too does the object, for it essentially belonged to this knowledge. Hence it comes to pass for consciousness that what it previously took to be the *in-itself* is not an *in-itself*, or that it was only an in-itself *for consciousness*. Since consciousness thus finds that its knowledge does not correspond to its object, the object itself does not stand the test; in other words, the criterion for testing is altered when that for which it was to have been the criterion fails to pass the test;

and the testing is not only a testing of what we know, but also a testing of the criterion of what knowing is.

86. *Inasmuch as the new true object issues from it*, this *dialectical* movement which consciousness exercises on itself and which affects both its knowledge and its object, is precisely what is called *experience* [*Erfahrung*]. In this connection there is a moment in the process just mentioned which must be brought out more clearly, for through it a new light will be thrown on the exposition which follows. Consciousness knows *something*; this object is the essence or the *in-itself*; but it is also for consciousness the in-itself. This is where the ambiguity of this truth enters. We see that consciousness now has two objects: one is the first *in-itself, the second is the being-for-consciousness of this in-itself*. The latter appears at first sight to be merely the reflection of consciousness into itself, i.e. what consciousness has in mind is not an object, but only its knowledge of that first object. But, as was shown previously, the first object, in being known, is altered for consciousness; it ceases to be the in-itself, and becomes something that is the *in-itself* only *for consciousness*. And this then is the True: the being-for-consciousness of this in-itself. Or, in other words, this is the *essence*, or the *object* of consciousness. This new object contains the nothingness of the first, it is what experience has made of it.

87. This exposition of the course of experience contains a moment in virtue of which it does not seem to agree with what is ordinarily understood by experience. This is the moment of transition from the first object and the knowledge of it, to the other object, which experience is said to be about. Our account implied that our knowledge of the first object, or the being-*for*-consciousness of the first in-itself, itself becomes the second object. It usually seems to be the case, on the contrary, that our experience of the untruth of our first notion comes by way of a second object which we come upon by chance and externally, so that our part in all this is simply the pure *apprehension* of what is in and for itself. From the present viewpoint, however, the new object shows itself to have come about through a *reversal of consciousness itself*. This way of looking at the matter is something contributed by *us*, by means of which the succession of experiences through which consciousness passes is raised into a scientific progression—but it is not known to the consciousness

that we are observing. But, as a matter of fact, we have here
the same situation as the one discussed in regard to the relation
between our exposition and scepticism, viz. that in every case
the result of an untrue mode of knowledge must not be allowed
to run away into an empty nothing, but must necessarily be
grasped as the nothing *of that from which it results*—a result which
contains what was true in the preceding knowledge. It shows
up here like this: since what first appeared as the object sinks
for consciousness to the level of its way of knowing it, and since
the in-itself becomes a *being-for-consciousness* of the in-itself, the
latter is now the new object. Herewith a new pattern of consciousness comes on the scene as well, for which the essence
is something different from what it was at the preceding stage.
It is this fact that guides the entire series of the patterns of consciousness in their necessary sequence. But it is just this necessity itself, or the *origination* of the new object, that presents
itself to consciousness without its understanding how this
happens, which proceeds for us, as it were, behind the back
of consciousness. Thus in the movement of consciousness there
occurs a moment of *being-in-itself* or *being-for-us* which is not
present to the consciousness comprehended in the experience
itself. The *content*, however, of what presents itself to us does
exist *for it*; we comprehend only the formal aspect of that content, or its pure origination. *For it*, what has thus arisen exists
only as an object; *for us*, it appears at the same time as movement and a process of becoming.

88. Because of this necessity, the way to Science is itself
already *Science*, and hence, in virtue of its content, is the Science
of the *experience of consciousness*.

89. The experience of itself which consciousness goes
through can, in accordance with its Notion, comprehend nothing less than the entire system of consciousness, or the entire
realm of the truth of Spirit. For this reason, the moments of
this truth are exhibited in their own proper determinateness,
viz. as being not abstract moments, but as they are for consciousness, or as consciousness itself stands forth in its relation
to them. Thus the moments of the whole are *patterns of consciousness*. In pressing forward to its true existence, consciousness will
arrive at a point at which it gets rid of its semblance of being
burdened with something alien, with what is only for it, and

some sort of 'other', at a point where appearance becomes identical with essence, so that its exposition will coincide at just this point with the authentic Science of Spirit. And finally, when consciousness itself grasps this its own essence, it will signify the nature of absolute knowledge itself.

A. CONSCIOUSNESS

I. SENSE-CERTAINTY: OR THE 'THIS' AND 'MEANING' [*MEINEN*]

90. The knowledge or knowing which is at the start or is immediately our object cannot be anything else but immediate knowledge itself, a knowledge of the immediate or of what simply *is*. Our approach to the object must also be *immediate* or *receptive*; we must alter nothing in the object as it presents itself. In *ap*prehending it, we must refrain from trying to *com*prehend it.

91. Because of its concrete content, sense-certainty immediately appears as the *richest* kind of knowledge, indeed a knowledge of infinite wealth for which no bounds can be found, either when we *reach out* into space and time in which it is dispersed, or when we take a bit of this wealth, and by division *enter into* it. Moreover, sense-certainty appears to be the *truest* knowledge; for it has not as yet omitted anything from the object, but has the object before it in its perfect entirety. But, in the event, this very *certainty* proves itself to be the most abstract and poorest *truth*. All that it says about what it knows is just that it *is*; and its truth contains nothing but the sheer *being* of the thing [*Sache*]. Consciousness, for its part, is in this certainty only as a pure 'I'; or I am in it only as a pure 'This', and the object similarly only as a pure 'This'. I, *this* particular I, am certain of *this* particular thing, not because I, *qua* consciousness, in knowing it have developed myself or thought about it in various ways; and also not because *the thing* of which I am certain, in virtue of a host of distinct qualities, would be in its own self a rich complex of connections, or related in various ways to other things. Neither of these has anything to do with the truth of sense-certainty: here neither I nor the thing has the significance of a complex process of mediation; the 'I' does not have the significance of a manifold imagining or thinking; nor does the 'thing' signify something that has a host of qualities. On the contrary, the thing *is*, and it *is*, merely because it *is*. It *is*; this is the essential point for sense-knowledge, and this pure

being, or this simple immediacy, constitutes its *truth*. Similarly, certainty as a *connection* is an *immediate* pure connection: consciousness is '*I*', nothing more, a pure 'This'; the singular consciousness knows a pure 'This', or the single item.

92. But when we look carefully at this *pure being* which constitutes the essence of this certainty, and which this certainty pronounces to be its truth, we see that much more is involved. An actual sense-certainty is not merely this pure immediacy, but an *instance* of it. Among the countless differences cropping up here we find in every case that the crucial one is that, in sense-certainty, pure being at once splits up into what we have called the two 'Thises', one 'This' as 'I', and the other 'This' as object. When *we* reflect on this difference, we find that neither one nor the other is only *immediately* present in sense-certainty, but each is at the same time *mediated*: I have this certainty *through* something else, viz. the thing; and it, similarly, is in sense-certainty *through* something else, viz. through the 'I'.

93. It is not just we who make this distinction between essence and instance, between immediacy and mediation; on the contrary, we find it within sense-certainty itself, and it is to be taken up in the form in which it is present there, not as we have just defined it. One of the terms is posited in sense-certainty in the form of a simple, immediate being, or as the essence, the *object*; the other, however, is posited as what is unessential and mediated, something which in sense-certainty is not *in itself* but through [the mediation of] an other, the 'I', a *knowing* which knows the object only because the *object* is, while the knowing may either be or not be. But the object *is*: it is what is true, or it is the essence. It is, regardless of whether it is known or not; and it remains, even it it is not known, whereas there is no knowledge if the object is not there.

94. The question must therefore be considered whether in sense-certainty itself the object is in fact the kind of essence that sense-certainty proclaims it to be; whether this notion of it as the essence corresponds to the way it is present in sense-certainty. To this end, we have not to reflect on it and ponder what it might be in truth, but only to consider the way in which it is present in sense-certainty.

95. It is, then, sense-certainty itself that must be asked: 'What is the *This*?' If we take the 'This' in the twofold shape

of its being, as 'Now' and as 'Here', the dialectic it has in it will receive a form as intelligible as the 'This' itself is. To the question: 'What is Now?', let us answer, e.g. 'Now is Night.' In order to test the truth of this sense-certainty a simple experiment will suffice. We write down this truth; a truth cannot lose anything by being written down, any more than it can lose anything through our preserving it. If *now*, *this noon*, we look again at the written truth we shall have to say that it has become stale.

96. The Now that is Night is *preserved*, i.e. it is treated as what it professes to be, as something that *is*; but it proves itself to be, on the contrary, something that is *not*. The Now does indeed preserve itself, but as something that is *not* Night; equally, it preserves itself in face of the Day that it now is, as something that also is not Day, in other words, as a *negative* in general. This self-preserving Now is, therefore, not immediate but mediated; for it is determined as a permanent and self-preserving Now *through* the fact that something else, viz. Day and Night, is *not*. As so determined, it is still just as simply Now as before, and in this simplicity is indifferent to what happens in it; just as little as Night and Day are its being, just as much also is it Day and Night; it is not in the least affected by this its other-being. A simple thing of this kind which *is* through negation, which is neither This nor That, a *not-This*, and is with equal indifference This as well as That—such a thing we call a *universal*. So it is in fact the universal that is the true [content] of sense-certainty.

97. It is as a universal too that we *utter* what the sensuous [content] is. What we say is: 'This', i.e. the *universal* This; or, 'it is', i.e. *Being in general*. Of course, we do not *envisage* the universal This or Being in general, but we *utter* the universal; in other words, we do not strictly say what in this sense-certainty we *mean* to say. But language, as we see, is the more truthful; in it, we ourselves directly refute what we *mean* to say, and since the universal is the true [content] of sense-certainty and language expresses this true [content] alone, it is just not possible for us ever to say, or express in words, a sensuous being that we *mean*.

98. The same will be the case with the other form of the 'This', with 'Here'. 'Here' is, e.g., the tree. If I turn round,

this truth has vanished and is converted into its opposite: 'No tree is here, but a house instead'. 'Here' itself does not vanish; on the contrary, it abides constant in the vanishing of the house, the tree, etc., and is indifferently house or tree. Again, therefore, the 'This' shows itself to be a *mediated simplicity*, or a *universality*.

99. *Pure being* remains, therefore, as the essence of this sense-certainty, since sense-certainty has demonstrated in its own self that the truth of its object is the universal. But this pure being is not an immediacy, but something to which negation and mediation are essential; consequently, it is not what we *mean* by 'being', but is 'being' defined as an abstraction, or as the pure universal; and our 'meaning', for which the true [content] of sense-certainty is *not* the universal, is all that is left over in face of this empty or indifferent Now and Here.

100. When we compare the relation in which knowing and the object first came on the scene, with the relation in which they now stand in this result, we find that it is reversed. The object, which was supposed to be the essential element in sense-certainty, is now the unessential element; for the universal which the object has come to be is no longer what the object was supposed essentially to be for sense-certainty. On the contrary, the certainty is now to be found in the opposite element, viz. in knowing, which previously was the unessential element. Its truth is in the object as *my* object, or in its being *mine* [*Meinen*]; it is, because *I* know it. Sense-certainty, then, though indeed expelled from the object, is not yet thereby overcome, but only driven back into the 'I'. We have now to see what experience shows us about its reality in the 'I'.

101. The force of its truth thus lies now in the 'I', in the immediacy of my *seeing, hearing*, and so on; the vanishing of the single Now and Here that we mean is prevented by the fact that *I* hold them fast. 'Now' is day because I see it; 'Here' is a tree for the same reason. But in this relationship sense-certainty experiences the same dialectic acting upon itself as in the previous one. I, *this* 'I', see the tree and assert that 'Here' is a tree; but another 'I' sees the house and maintains that 'Here' is not a tree but a house instead. Both truths have the same authentication, viz. the immediacy of seeing, and the certainty and assurance that both have about their knowing; but the one truth vanishes in the other.

102. What does not disappear in all this is the 'I' as *universal*, whose seeing is neither a seeing of the tree nor of this house, but is a simple seeing which, though mediated by the negation of this house, etc., is all the same simple and indifferent to whatever happens in it, to the house, the tree, etc. The 'I' is merely universal like 'Now', 'Here', or 'This' in general; I do indeed *mean* a single 'I', but I can no more say what I *mean* in the case of 'I' than I can in the case of 'Now' and 'Here'. When I say 'this Here', 'this Now', or a 'single item', I am saying all Thises, Heres, Nows, all single items. Similarly, when I say 'I', this singular 'I', I say in general all 'Is'; everyone is what I say, everyone is 'I', this singular 'I'. When Science is faced with the demand—as if it were an acid test it could not pass—that it should deduce, construct, find *a priori*, or however it is put, something called 'this thing' or 'this one man', it is reasonable that the demand should *say* which 'this thing', or which 'this particular man' is *meant*; but it is impossible to say this.

103. Sense-certainty thus comes to know by experience that its essence is neither in the object nor in the 'I', and that its immediacy is neither an immediacy of the one nor of the other; for in both, what I *mean* is rather something unessential, and the object and the 'I' are universals in which that 'Now' and 'Here' and 'I' which I *mean* do not have a continuing being, or *are* not. Thus we reach the stage where we have to posit the *whole* of sense-certainty itself as its *essence*, and no longer only one of its moments, as happened in the two cases where first the object confronting the 'I', and then the 'I', were supposed to be its reality. Thus it is only sense-certainty as a *whole* which stands firm within itself as *immediacy* and by so doing excludes from itself all the opposition which has hitherto obtained.

104. This pure immediacy, therefore, no longer has any concern with the otherness of the 'Here', as a tree which passes over into a 'Here' that is not a tree, or with the otherness of the 'Now' as day which changes into a 'Now' that is night, or with another 'I' for which something else is object. Its truth preserves itself as a relation that remains self-identical, and which makes no distinction of what is essential and what is unessential, between the 'I' and the object, a relation therefore into which also no distinction whatever can penetrate. I, *this* 'I', assert then the 'Here' as a tree, and do not turn round so that

the Here would become for me *not* a tree; also, I take no notice of the fact that another 'I' sees the Here as *not* a tree, or that I myself at another time take the Here as not-tree, the Now as not-day. On the contrary, I am a pure [act of] intuiting; I, for my part, stick to the fact that the Now is day, or that the Here is a tree; also I do not compare Here and Now themselves with one another, but stick firmly to *one* immediate relation: the Now is day.

105. Since, then, this certainty will no longer come forth to *us* when we direct its attention to a Now that is night, or to an 'I' to whom it is night, we will approach *it* and let ourselves point to the Now that is asserted. We must let ourselves *point to it*; for the truth of this immediate relation is the truth of *this* 'I' which confines itself to one 'Now' or one 'Here'. Were we to examine this truth *afterwards*, or stand *at a distance* from it, it would lose its significance entirely; for that would do away with the immediacy which is essential to it. We must therefore enter the same point of time or space, point them out to ourselves, i.e. make ourselves into the same singular 'I' which is the one who knows with certainty. Let us, then, see how that immediate is constituted that is pointed out to us.

106. The Now is pointed to, *this* Now. 'Now'; it has already ceased to be in the act of pointing to it. The Now that *is*, is another Now than the one pointed to, and we see that the Now is just this: to be no more just when it iṣ. The Now, as it is pointed out to us, is Now that *has been*, and this is its truth; it has not the truth of *being*. Yet this much is true, that it has been. But what essentially *has been* [*gewesen ist*] is, in fact, not an essence that *is* [*kein Wesen*]; it is not, and it was with *being* that we were concerned.

107. In this pointing-out, then, we see merely a movement which takes the following course: (1) I point out the 'Now', and it is asserted to be the truth. I point it out, however, as something that *has been*, or as something that has been superseded; I set aside the first truth. (2) I now assert as the second truth that it *has been*, that it is superseded. (3) But what has been, *is not*; I set aside the second truth, its *having been*, its supersession, and thereby negate the negation of the 'Now', and thus return to the first assertion, that the '*Now*' *is*. The 'Now', and pointing out the 'Now', are thus so constituted that neither the

one nor the other is something immediate and simple, but a movement which contains various moments. A *This* is posited; but it is rather an *other* that is posited, or the This is superseded: and this *otherness*, or the setting-aside of the first, is itself *in turn set aside*, and so has returned into the first. However, this first, thus reflected into itself, is not exactly the same as it was to begin with, viz. something *immediate*; on the contrary, it is *something that is reflected into itself*, or a *simple* entity which, in its otherness, remains what it is: a Now which is an absolute plurality of Nows. And this is the true, the genuine Now, the Now as a simple day which contains within it many Nows—hours. A Now of this sort, an hour, similarly is many minutes, and this Now is likewise many Nows, and so on. The pointing-out of the Now is thus itself the movement which expresses what the Now is in truth, viz. a result, or a plurality of Nows all taken together; and the pointing-out is the experience of learning that Now is a *universal*.

108. The *Here pointed out*, to which I hold fast, is similarly a *this* Here which, in fact, is *not* this Here, but a Before and Behind, an Above and Below, a Right and Left. The Above is itself similarly this manifold otherness of above, below, etc. The Here, which was supposed to have been pointed out, vanishes in other Heres, but these likewise vanish. What is pointed out, held fast, and abides, is a *negative* This, which *is* negative only when the Heres are taken as they should be, but, in being so taken, they supersede themselves; what abides is a simple complex of many Heres. The Here that is *meant* would be the point; but it *is* not: on the contrary, when it is pointed out as something that *is*, the pointing-out shows itself to be not an immediate knowing [of the point], but a movement from the Here that is *meant* through many Heres into the universal Here which is a simple plurality of Heres, just as the day is a simple plurality of Nows.

109. It is clear that the dialectic of sense-certainty is nothing else but the simple history of its movement or of its experience, and sense-certainty itself is nothing else but just this history. That is why the natural consciousness, too, is always reaching this result, learning from experience what is true in it; but equally it is always forgetting it and starting the movement all over again. It is therefore astonishing when, in face of this ex-

perience, it is asserted as universal experience and put forward, too, as a philosophical proposition, even as the outcome of Scepticism, that the reality or being of external things taken as Thises or sense-objects has absolute truth for consciousness. To make such an assertion is not to know what one is saying, to be unaware that one is saying the opposite of what one wants to say. The truth for consciousness of a This of sense is supposed to be universal experience; but the very opposite is universal experience. Every consciousness itself supersedes such a truth, as e.g. Here is a tree, or, Now is noon, and proclaims the opposite: Here is *not* a tree, but a house; and similarly, it immediately again supersedes the assertion which set aside the first so far as it is also just such an assertion of a sensuous This. And what consciousness will learn from experience in all sense-certainty is, in truth, only what we have seen viz. the This as a *universal*, the very opposite of what that assertion affirmed to be universal experience.

With this appeal to universal experience we may be permitted to anticipate how the case stands in the practical sphere. In this respect we can tell those who assert the truth and certainty of the reality of sense-objects that they should go back to the most elementary school of wisdom, viz. the ancient Eleusinian Mysteries of Ceres and Bacchus, and that they have still to learn the secret meaning of the eating of bread and the drinking of wine. For he who is initiated into these Mysteries not only comes to doubt the being of sensuous things, but to despair of it; in part he brings about the nothingness of such things himself in his dealings with them, and in part he sees them reduce themselves to nothingness. Even the animals are not shut out from this wisdom but, on the contrary, show themselves to be most profoundly initiated into it; for they do not just stand idly in front of sensuous things as if these possessed intrinsic being, but, despairing of their reality, and completely assured of their nothingness, they fall to without ceremony and eat them up. And all Nature, like the animals, celebrates these open Mysteries which teach the truth about sensuous things.

110. But, just as our previous remarks would suggest, those who put forward such an assertion also themselves say the direct opposite of what they mean: a phenomenon which is perhaps best calculated to induce them to reflect on the nature of sense-

certainty. They speak of the existence of *external* objects, which can be more precisely defined as *actual*, absolutely *singular*, *wholly personal*, *individual* things, each of them absolutely unlike anything else; this existence, they say, has absolute certainty and truth. They *mean* 'this' bit of paper on which I am writing— or rather have written—'this'; but what they mean is not what they say. If they actually wanted to *say* 'this' bit of paper which they mean, if they wanted to *say* it, then this is impossible, because the sensuous This that is meant *cannot be reached* by language, which belongs to consciousness, i.e. to that which is inherently universal. In the actual attempt to say it, it would therefore crumble away; those who started to describe it would not be able to complete the description, but would be compelled to leave it to others, who would themselves finally have to admit to speaking about something which *is not*. They certainly mean, then, *this* bit of paper here which is quite different from the bit mentioned above; but they say 'actual *things*', 'external or *sensuous objects*', 'absolutely *singular entities*' [*Wesen*] and so on; i.e. they say of them only what is *universal*. Consequently, what is called the unutterable is nothing else than the untrue, the irrational, what is merely meant [but is not actually expressed].

If nothing more is said of something than that it is 'an actual thing', an 'external object', its description is only the most abstract of generalities and in fact expresses its sameness with everything rather than its distinctiveness. When I say: 'a single thing', I am really saying what it is from a wholly universal point of view, for everything is a single thing; and likewise 'this thing' is anything you like. If we describe it more exactly as 'this bit of paper', then each and every bit of paper is 'this bit of paper', and I have only uttered the universal all the time. But if I want to help out language—which has the divine nature of directly reversing the meaning of what is said, of making it into something else, and thus not letting what is meant *get into words* at all—by *pointing out* this bit of paper, experience teaches me what the truth of sense-certainty in fact is: I point it out as a 'Here', which is a Here of other Heres, or is in its own self a 'simple togetherness of many Heres'; i.e. it is a universal. I take it up then as it is in truth, and instead of knowing something immediate I take the truth of it, or *perceive* it.[1]

---

[1] The German for 'to perceive' is *wahrnehmen* which means literally 'to take truly'.

II. PERCEPTION: OR THE THING AND DECEPTION

111. Immediate certainty does not take over the truth, for its truth is the universal, whereas certainty wants to apprehend the This. Perception, on the other hand, takes what is present to it as a universal. Just as universality is its principle in general, the immediately self-differentiating moments within perception are universal: 'I' is a universal and the object is a universal. That principle has arisen for us, and therefore the way we take in perception is no longer something that just happens to us like sense-certainty; on the contrary, it is logically necessitated. With the emergence of the principle, the two moments which in their appearing merely *occur*, also come into being: one being the movement of pointing-out or the *act of perceiving*, the other being the same movement as a simple event or the *object perceived*. In essence the object is the same as the movement: the movement is the unfolding and differentiation of the two moments, and the object is the apprehended togetherness of the moments. For us, or in itself, the universal as principle is the essence of perception, and, in contrast to this abstraction, both the moments distinguished—that which perceives and that which is perceived—are the unessential. But, in fact, because both are themselves the universal or the essence, both are essential. Yet since they are related to each other as opposites, only one can be the essential moment in the relation, and the distinction of essential and unessential moment must be shared between them. One of them, the object, defined as the simple [entity], is the essence regardless of whether it is perceived or not; but the act of perceiving, as a movement, is the unessential moment, the unstable factor which can as well be as not be.

112. This object must now be defined more precisely, and the definition must be developed briefly from the result that has been reached; the more detailed development does not belong here. Since the principle of the object, the universal, is in its simplicity a *mediated* universal, the object must express this its nature in its own self. This it does by showing itself to be *the thing with many properties*. The wealth of sense-knowledge belongs to perception, not to immediate certainty, for which it was only the source of instances; for only perception contains negation, that is, difference or manifoldness, within its own essence.

113. The This is, therefore, established as *not* This, or as something superseded; and hence not as Nothing, but as a determinate Nothing, the Nothing of a content, viz. of the This. Consequently, the sense-element is still present, but not in the way it was supposed to be in [the position of] immediate certainty: not as the singular item that is 'meant', but as a universal, or as that which will be defined as a *property*. *Supersession* exhibits its true twofold meaning which we have seen in the negative: it is at once a *negating* and a *preserving*. Our Nothing, as the Nothing of the This, preserves its immediacy and is itself sensuous, but it is a universal immediacy. Being, however, is a universal in virtue of its having mediation or the negative within it; when it *expresses* this in its immediacy it is a *differentiated, determinate* property. As a result *many* such properties are established simultaneously, one being the negative of another. Since they are expressed in the simplicity of the universal, these determinacies—which are properties strictly speaking only through the addition of a further determination—are related [only] to themselves; they are indifferent to one another, each is on its own and free from the others. But the simple, self-identical universality is itself in turn distinct and free from these determinate properties it has. It is pure relating of self to self, or the *medium* in which all these determinacies are, and in which as a *simple* unity they therefore interpenetrate, but without *coming into contact* with one another; for it is precisely through participating in this universality that they exist indifferently on their own account.

This abstract universal medium, which can be called simply 'thinghood' or 'pure essence', is nothing else than what Here and Now have proved themselvess to be, viz. a *simple togetherness* of a plurality; but the many are, *in their determinateness*, simple universals themselves. This salt is a simple Here, and at the same time manifold; it is white and *also* tart, *also* cubical in shape, of a specific gravity, etc. All these many properties are in a single simple 'Here', in which, therefore, they interpenetrate; none has a different Here from the others, but each is everywhere, in the same Here in which the others are. And, at the same time, without being separated by different Heres, they do not affect each other in this interpenetration. The whiteness does not affect the cubical shape, and neither affects the tart taste, etc.; on the contrary, since each is itself a simple relating of self to self it leaves the others alone, and is connected with them only by the indifferent Also. This Also is thus the pure universal itself, or the medium, the 'thinghood', which holds them together in this way.

114. In the relationship which has thus emerged it is only the character of positive universality that is at first observed and developed; but a further side presents itself, which must also be taken into consideration. To wit, if the many determinate properties were strictly indifferent to one another, if they were simply and solely self-related, they would not be determinate; for they are only determinate in so far as they *differentiate* themselves from one another, and *relate* themselves *to others* as to their opposites. Yet; as thus opposed to one another they cannot be together in the simple unity of their medium, which is just as essential to them as negation; the differentiation of the properties, in so far as it is not an indifferent differentiation but is exclusive, each property negating the others, thus falls outside of this simple medium; and the medium, therefore, is not merely an Also, an indifferent unity, but a *One* as well, a unity which *excludes* an other. The One is the *moment of negation*; it is itself quite simply a relation of self to self and it excludes an other; and it is that by which 'thinghood' is determined as a Thing. Negation is inherent in a property as a *determinateness* which is immediately one with the immediacy of being, an immediacy which, through this unity with negation, is universality. As a One, however, the determinateness is set free from this unity with its opposite, and exists in and for itself.

115. In these moments, taken together, the Thing as the truth of perception is completed, so far as it is necessary to develop it here. It is (a) an indifferent, passive universality, the *Also* of the many properties or rather 'matters'; (b) negation, equally simply; or the *One*, which excludes opposite properties; and (c) the many *properties* themselves, the relation of the first two moments, or negation as it relates to the indifferent element, and therein expands into a host of differences; the point of singular individuality in the medium of subsistence radiating forth into plurality. In so far as these differences belong to the indifferent medium they are themselves universal, they are related only to themselves and do not affect one another. But

in so far as they belong to the negative unity they are at the same time exclusive [of other properties]; but they necessarily have this relationship of opposition to properties remote from *their* Also. The sensuous universality, or the *immediate* unity of being and the negative, is thus a *property* only when the One and the pure universality are developed from it and differentiated from each other, and when the sensuous universality unites them; it is this relation of the universality to the pure essential moments which at last completes the Thing.

116. This, then, is how the Thing of perception is constituted; and consciousness is determined as percipient in so far as this Thing is its object. It has only to *take* it, to confine itself to a pure apprehension of it, and what is thus yielded is the True. If consciousness itself did anything in taking what is given, it would by such adding or subtraction alter the truth. Since the object is the True and universal, the self-identical, while consciousness is alterable and unessential, it can happen that consciousness apprehends the object incorrectly and deceives itself. The percipient is aware of the possibility of deception; for in the universality which is the principle, *otherness* itself is immediately present for him, though present as what is *null* and superseded. His criterion of truth is therefore *self-identity*, and his behaviour consists in apprehending the object as self-identical. Since at the same time diversity is explicitly there for him, it is a connection of the diverse moments of his apprehension to one another; but if a dissimilarity makes itself felt in the course of this comparison, then this is not an untruth of the object—for this is the self-identical—but an untruth in perceiving it.

117. Let us see now what consciousness experiences in its actual perceiving. *For us*, this experience is already contained in the development of the object, and of the attitude of consciousness towards it given just now. It is only a matter of developing the contradictions that are present therein. The object which I apprehend presents itself purely as a *One*; but I also perceive in it a property which is *universal*, and which thereby transcends the singularity [of the object]. The first being of the objective essence as a One was therefore not its true being. But since the *object* is what is true, the untruth falls in me; my apprehension was not correct. On account of the *universality* of the

property, I must rather take the objective essence to be on the whole a *community*. I now further perceive the property to be *determinate, opposed* to another and excluding it. Thus I did not in fact apprehend the objective essence correctly when I defined it as a *community* with others, or as a continuity; on account of the *determinateness* of the property, I must break up the continuity and posit the objective essence as a One that excludes.

In the broken up One I find many such properties which do not affect one another but are mutually indifferent. Therefore, I did not perceive the object correctly when I apprehended it as exclusive; on the contrary, just as previouly it was only continuity in general, so now it is a universal *common medium* in which many properties are present as sensuous *universalities*, each existing on its own account and, as *determinate*, excluding the others. But this being so, what I perceive as the simple and the True is also not a universal medium, but the *single property* by itself which, however, as such, is neither a property nor a determinate being; for now it is neither in a One nor connected with others. Only when it belongs to a One is it a property, and only in relation to others is it determinate. As this pure relating of itself to itself, it remains merely *sensuous being* in general, since it no longer possesses the character of negativity; and the consciousness which takes its object to be a sensuous being is only 'my' *meaning* [*ein Meinen*], i.e. it has ceased altogether to perceive and has withdrawn into itself. But sensuous being and *my* meaning themselves pass over into perception: I am thrown back to the beginning and drawn once again into the same cycle which supersedes itself in each moment and as a whole.

118. Consciousness, therefore, necessarily runs through this cycle again, but this time not in the same way as it did the first time. For it has experienced in perception that the outcome and the truth of perception is its dissolution, or is reflection out of the True and into itself. Thus it becomes quite definite for consciousness how its perceiving is essentially constituted, viz. that it is not a simple pure apprehension, but *in its apprehension* is at the same time *reflected out of the True and into itself*. This return of consciousness into itself which is directly *mingled* with the pure apprehension [of the object]—for this return into itself

has shown itself to be essential to perception—alters the truth. Consciousness at once recognizes this aspect as its own and takes responsibility for it; by doing so it will obtain the true object in its purity. This being so, we have now in the case of perception the same as happened in the case of sense-certainty, the aspect of consciousness being driven back into itself; but not, in the first instance, in the sense in which this happened in sense-certainty, i.e. not as if the *truth* of perception fell in consciousness. On the contrary, consciousness recognizes that it is the *untruth* occurring in perception that falls within it. But by this very recognition it is able at once to supersede this untruth; it distinguishes its apprehension of the truth from the untruth of its perception, corrects this untruth, and since it undertakes to make this correction itself, the truth, *qua* truth of *perception*, *falls* of course *within consciousness*. The behaviour of consciousness which we have now to consider is thus so constituted that consciousness no longer merely perceives, but is also conscious of its reflection into itself, and separates this from simple apprehension proper.

119. At first, then, I become aware of the Thing as a *One*, and have to hold fast to it in this its true character; if, in the course of perceiving it, something turns up which contradicts it, this is to be recognized as a reflection of mine. Now, there also occur in the perception various properties which seem to be properties of the Thing; but the Thing is a One, and we are conscious that this diversity by which it would cease to be a One falls in us. So in point of fact, the Thing is white only to *our eyes*, *also* tart to *our* tongue, *also* cubical to *our* touch, and so on. We get the entire diversity of these aspects, not from the Thing, but from ourselves; and they fall asunder in this way for us, because the eye is quite distinct from the tongue, and so on. We are thus the *universal medium* in which such moments are kept apart and exist each on its own. Through the fact, then, that we regard the characteristic of being a universal medium as *our* reflection, we preserve the self-identity and truth of the Thing, its being a One.

120. But, regarded as existing each for itself in the universal medium, these *diverse aspects* for which consciousness accepts responsibility are *specifically determined*. White is white only in opposition to black, and so on, and the Thing is a One precisely

by being opposed to others. But it is not as a One that it excludes others from itself, for to be a One is the universal relating of self to self, and the fact that it is a One rather makes it like all the others; it is through its *determinateness* that the thing excludes others. Things are therefore in and for themselves determinate; they have properties by which they distinguish themselves from others. Since the property [*Eigenschaft*] is the Thing's *own* [*eigene*] property or a determinateness in the Thing itself, the Thing has a number of properties. For, in the first place, the Thing is what is true, i.e. it *possesses intrinsic being*; and what is in it, is there as the Thing's essence, and not on account of other things. Secondly, therefore, the determinate properties do not only exist on account of other things and *for* other things, but in the Thing itself; yet they are determinate properties *in it* only because they are a plurality of reciprocally self-differentiating elements. And thirdly, since this is how they are in the 'thinghood' [i.e. the essence of the *one* thing of which they are properties], they exist in and for themselves, indifferent to one another. It is in truth, then, the Thing itself that is white, and *also* cubical, *also* tart, and so on. In other words, the Thing is the *Also*, or the *universal medium* in which the many properties subsist apart from one another, without touching or cancelling one another; and when so taken, the Thing is perceived as what is true.

121. Now, in perceiving in this way, consciousness is at the same time aware that it is *also* reflected into itself, and that, in perceiving, the opposite moment to the Also turns up. But this moment is the *unity* of the Thing with itself, a unity which excludes difference from itself. Accordingly, it is this unity which consciousness has to take upon itself; for the Thing itself is the *subsistence of the many diverse and independent properties*. Thus we say of the Thing: *it is* white, *also* cubical, and *also* tart, and so on. But *in so far* as it is white, it is not cubical, and *in so far* as it is cubical and also white, it is not tart, and so on. Positing these properties as a oneness is the work of consciousness alone which, therefore, has to prevent them from collapsing into oneness in the Thing. To this end it brings in the 'in so far', in this way preserving the properties as mutually external, and the Thing as the Also. Quite rightly, consciousness makes itself responsible for the oneness, at first in such a way that what was

called a property is represented as 'free matter'. The Thing is in this way raised to the level of a genuine Also, since it becomes a collection of 'matters' and, instead of being a One, becomes merely an enclosing surface.

122. If we look back on what consciousness previously took, and now takes, responsibility for, on what it previously ascribed, and now ascribes, to the Thing, we see that consciousness alternately makes itself, as well as the Thing, into both a pure, many-less *One*, and into an *Also* that resolves itself into independent 'matters'. Consciousness thus finds through this comparison that not only *its* truthful perceiving [*Nehmen des Wahren*], contains the *distinct moments of apprehension* and *withdrawal into itself*, but rather that the truth itself, the Thing, reveals itself in this twofold way. Our experience, then, is this, that the Thing exhibits itself *for the consciousness apprehending it*, in a specific manner, but is *at the same time* reflected out of the way in which it presents itself to consciousness and back into itself; in other words, it contains in its own self an opposite truth [to that which it has for the apprehending consciousness].

123. Thus consciousness has got beyond this second type of attitude in perceiving, too, i.e. the one in which it takes the Thing as truly self-identical, and itself for what is not self-identical but returns back into itself out of identity. The object is now for consciousness this whole movement which was previously shared between the object and consciousness. The Thing is a One, reflected into itself; it is *for itself*, but it is also *for an other*; and, moreover, it is an *other* on its own account, just *because* it is for an other. Accordingly, the Thing is for itself and *also* for an other, a being that is *doubly* differentiated but *also* a One; but the oneness contradicts this diversity. Hence consciousness would again have to assume responsibility for placing [the diversity] in the One and for keeping it away from the Thing. It would have to say that *in so far* as it is for itself, the Thing is *not* for an other. But the oneness also belongs to the Thing itself as consciousness has found by experience: the Thing is essentially reflected into itself. The Also, or the indifferent difference, thus falls as much within the Thing as does the oneness; but since the two are different they do not fall within the same Thing, but in *different* Things. The contradiction which is present in the objective essence as a whole is distributed

between two objects. In and for itself the Thing is self-identical, but this unity with itself is disturbed by other Things. Thus the unity of the Thing is preserved and at the same time the otherness is preserved outside of the Thing as well as outside of consciousness.

124. Now, although it is true that the contradiction in the objective essence is in this way distributed among different Things, yet the difference will, for that reason, attach to the singular separated Thing itself. The *different Things* are thus established as existing on their own account; and the conflict between them is so far reciprocal that each is different, not from itself, but only from the other. But each is thereby determined as being itself a *different* Thing, and it has its essential difference in its own self; but all the while not as if this difference were an opposition in the Thing itself. On the contrary, for itself it is a *simple determinateness* which constitutes the Thing's essential character, and differentiates it from others. As a matter of fact, since differentness is present in it, it is of course necessarily present as an *actual* difference manfoldly constituted. But because the determinateness constitutes the essence of the Thing, by which it distinguishes itself from other Things and is for itself, this further manifold constitution is the unessential aspect. Consequently, the Thing does indeed have the twofold 'in so far' within its unity, but the aspects are unequal in value. As a result, this state of opposition does not develop into an actual opposition in the Thing itself, but in so far as the Thing through its *absolute difference* comes into a state of opposition, it is opposed to another Thing outside of it. Of course, the further manifoldness is necessarily present in the Thing too, so that it cannot be left out; but it is the unessential aspect of the Thing.

125. This determinateness, which constitutes the essential character of the Thing and distinguishes it from all others, is now defined in such a way that the Thing is thereby in opposition to other Things, but is supposed to preserve its independence in this opposition. But it is only a *Thing*, or a One that exists on its own account, in so far as it does not stand in this relation to others; for this relation establishes rather its continuity with others, and for it to be connected with others is to cease to exist on its own account. It is just through the *absolute*

character of the Thing and its opposition that it *relates* itself to *others*, and is essentially only this relating. The relation, however, is the negation of its self-subsistence, and it is really the essential property of the Thing that is its undoing.

126. The conceptual necessity of the experience through which consciousness discovers that the Thing is demolished by the very determinateness that constitutes its essence and its being-for-self, can be summarized as follows. The Thing is posited as being *for itself*, or as the absolute negation of all otherness, therefore as purely *self*-related negation; but the negation that is self-related is the suspension of *itself*; in other words, the Thing has its essential being in another Thing.

127. In fact, the definition of the object, as it has emerged, has shown itself to contain nothing else. The object is defined as having within it an essential property which constitutes its simple being-for-self; but along with this simple nature the object is also to contain diversity which, though *necessary*, is not to constitute its *essential* determinateness. This, however, is a distinction that is still only nominal; the unessential, which is none the less supposed to be necessary, cancels itself out. It is what has just been called the negation of itself.

128. With this, the last 'in so far' that separated being-for-self from being-for-another falls away; on the contrary, the object is *in one and the same respect the opposite of itself: it is for itself, so far as it is for another*, and *it is for another, so far as it is for itself*. It is for itself, reflected into itself, a One; but this 'for-itself', this reflection into itself, this being a One, is posited in a unity with its opposite, with its 'being-for-another', and hence only as cancelled; in other words, this being-for-self is just as unessential as the only aspect that was supposed to be unessential, viz. the relationship to another.

129. Thus the object in its pure determinatenesses, or in the determinatenesses which were supposed to constitute its essential being, is overcome just as surely as it was in its sensuous being. From a sensuous being it turned into a universal; but this universal, since it *originates in the sensuous*, is essentially *conditioned* by it, and hence is not truly a self-identical universality at all, but one *afflicted with an opposition*; for this reason the universality splits into the extremes of singular individuality and universality, into the One of the properties, and the Also of the

'free matters'. These pure determinatenesses seem to express the essential nature itself, but they are only a 'being-for-self' that is burdened with a 'being-for-another'. Since, however, both are essentially in a *single unity*, what we now have is *unconditioned absolute universality*, and consciousness here for the first time truly enters the realm of the Understanding.

130. Thus the singular being of sense does indeed vanish in the dialectical movement of immediate certainty and becomes universality, but it is only a *sensuous universality*. My 'meaning' has vanished, and perception takes the object as it is *in itself*, or as a universal as such. Singular being therefore emerges in the object as true singleness, as the in-itself of the One, or as a reflectedness-into-self. But this is still a *conditioned* being-for-self *alongside which* appears another being-for-self, the universality which is opposed to, and conditioned by singular being. But these two contradictory extremes are not merely *alongside each other* but in a single unity, or in other words, the defining characteristic common to both, viz. 'being-for-self', is burdened with opposition generally, i.e. it is at the same time *not* a 'being-for-self'. The sophistry of perception seeks to save these moments from their contradiction, and it seeks to lay hold on the truth, by distinguishing between the *aspects*, by sticking to the 'Also' and to the 'in so far', and finally, by distinguishing the 'unessential' aspect from an 'essence' which is opposed to it. But these expedients, instead of warding off deception in the process of apprehension, prove themselves on the contrary to be quite empty; and the truth which is supposed to be won by this logic of the perceptual process proves to be in one and the same respect the opposite [of itself] and thus to have as its essence a universality which is devoid of distinctions and determinations.

131. These empty abstractions of a 'singleness' and a 'universality' opposed to it, and of an 'essence' that is linked with something unessential—a 'non-essential' aspect which is necessary all the same—these are powers whose interplay is the perceptual understanding, often called 'sound common sense'. This 'sound common sense' which takes itself to be a solid, realistic consciousness is, in the perceptual process, only the play of these *abstractions*; generally, it is always at its poorest where it fancies itself to be the richest. Bandied about by these vacuous 'essences', thrown into the arms first of one and then of the

other, and striving by its sophistry to hold fast and affirm alternately first one of the 'essences' and then the directly opposite
one, it sets itself against the truth and holds the opinion that
philosophy is concerned only with mental entities. As a matter
of fact, philosophy does have to do with them too, recognizing
them as the pure essences, the absolute elements and powers;
but in doing so, recognizes them *in their specific determinateness*
as well, and is therefore master over them, whereas perceptual
understanding [or 'sound common sense'] takes them for the
truth and is led on by them from one error to another. It does
not itself become conscious that it is simple essentialities of this
kind that hold sway over it, but fancies that it has always to
do with wholly substantial material and content; just as sense-
certainty is unaware that the empty abstraction of pure being
is its essence. But it is, in fact, these essentialities within which
perceptual understanding runs to and fro through every kind
of material and content; they are the cohesive power and mastery over that content and they alone are what the sensuous
is *as essence* for consciousness, they are what determines the relations of the sensuous to it, and it is in them that the process
of perception and of its truth runs its course. This course, a perpetual alternation of determining what is true, and then setting
aside this determining, constitutes, strictly speaking, the steady
everyday life and activity of perceptual consciousness, a consciousness which fancies itself to be moving in the realm of truth.
It advances uninterruptedly to the outcome in which all these
essential essentialities or determinations are equally set
aside; but in each single moment it is conscious only of this *one
determinateness* as the truth, and then in turn of the opposite one.
It does indeed suspect their unessentiality, and to save them
from the danger threatening them it resorts to the sophistry of
asserting to be true what it has itself just declared to be untrue.
What the nature of these untrue essences is really trying to get
[perceptual] understanding to do is to *bring together*, and
thereby supersede, the *thoughts* of those non-entities, the
thoughts of that universality and singular being, of 'Also' and
'One', of the essentiality that is *necessarily* linked to the unessential moment, and of an unessential moment that yet is necessary. But the Understanding struggles to avoid doing this by
resorting to 'in so far as' and to the various 'aspects', or by mak-

ing itself responsible for one thought in order to keep the other one isolated as the true one. But the very nature of these abstractions brings them together of their own accord. It is 'sound common sense' that is the prey of these abstractions, which spin it round and round in their whirling circle. When common sense tries to make them true by at one time making itself responsible for their untruth, while at another time it calls their deceptiveness a semblance of the unreliability of Things, and separates what is essential from what is necessary to them yet supposedly unessential, holding the former to be their truth as against the latter—when it does this, it does not secure them *their* truth, but convicts *itself* of untruth.

III. FORCE AND THE UNDERSTANDING: APPEARANCE AND THE SUPERSENSIBLE WORLD

132. In the dialectic of sense-certainty, Seeing and Hearing have been lost to consciousness; and, as perception, consciousness has arrived at thoughts, which it brings together for the first time in the unconditioned universal. This, now, if it were taken as an inert simple essence, would itself in turn be nothing else than the one-sided extreme of *being-for-self*, for it would then be confronted by non-essence; but, if it were related to this, it would itself be unessential, and consciousness would not have escaped from the deceptions of the perceptual process. However, this universal has proved to be one which has returned into itself out of such a conditioned being-for-self. This unconditioned universal, which is now the true object of consciousness, is still just an *object* for it; consciousness has not yet grasped the Notion of the unconditioned as *Notion*. It is essential to distinguish the two: for consciousness, the object has returned into itself from its relation to an other and has thus become Notion *in principle*; but consciousness is not yet *for itself* the Notion, and consequently does not recognize itself in that reflected object. *For us*, this object has developed through the movement of consciousness in such a way that consciousness is involved in that development, and the reflection is the same on both sides, or, there is only one reflection. But since in this

movement consciousness has for its content merely the objective essence and not consciousness as such, the result must have an objective significance for consciousness; consciousness still shrinks away from what has emerged, and takes it as the essence in the *objective* sense.

133. With this, the Understanding has indeed superseded its own untruth and the untruth of the object. What has emerged for it as a result is the Notion of the True—but only as the *implicit* being of the True, which is not yet Notion, or which lacks the *bring-for-self* of consciousness, and which the Understanding, without knowing itself therein, lets go its own way. This truth follows out its own essence, so that consciousness plays no part in its free realization, but merely looks on and simply apprehends it. To begin with, therefore, *we* must step into its place and be the Notion which develops and fills out what is contained in the result. It is through awareness of this completely developed object, which presents itself to consciousness as something that immediately *is*, that consciousness first becomes explicitly a consciousness that comprehends [its object].

134. The result was the unconditioned universal, initially, in the negative and abstract sense that consciousness negated its one-sided Notions and abstracted them: in other words, it gave them up. But the result has, implicitly, a positive significance: in it, the unity of 'being-for-self' and 'being-for-another' is posited; in other words, the absolute antithesis is posited as a self-identical essence. At first sight, this seems to concern only the form of the moments in reciprocal relation; but 'being-for-self' and 'being-for-another' are the *content* itself as well, since the antithesis in its truth can have no other nature than the one yielded in the result, viz. that the content taken in perception to be true, belongs in fact only to the form, in the unity of which it is dissolved. This content is likewise universal; there can be no other content which by its particular constitution would fail to fall within this unconditioned universality. A content of this kind would be some particular way or other of being for itself and of being in relation to an other. But, in general, to be for itself and to be in relation to an other constitutes the nature and essence of the content, whose truth consists in its being unconditionally universal; and the result is simply and solely universal.

135. But because this unconditioned universal is an object for consciousness, there emerges in it the distinction of form and content; and in the shape of content the moments look like they did when they first presented themselves: on one side, a universal medium of many subsistent 'matters', and on the other side, a One reflected into itself, in which their independence is extinguished. The former is the dissolution of the Thing's independence, i.e. the passivity that is a being-for-another; the latter is being-for-self. We have to see how these moments exhibit themselves in the unconditioned universality which is their essence. It is clear at the outset that, since they exist only in this universality, they are no longer separated from one another at all but are in themselves essentially self-superseding aspects, and what is posited is only their transition into one another.

136. One moment, then, appears as the essence that has stepped to one side as a universal medium, or as the subsistence of independent 'matters'. But the independence of these 'matters' is nothing else than this medium; in other words, the [unconditioned] universal is simply and solely the *plurality* of the diverse universals of this kind. That within itself the universal is in undivided unity with this plurality means, however, that these 'matters' are each where the other is; they mutually interpenetrate, but without coming into contact with one another because, conversely, the many diverse 'matters' are equally independent. This also means that they are absolutely porous, or are sublated. This sublation in its turn, this reduction of the diversity to a pure *being-for-self*, is nothing other than the medium itself, and this is the *independence* of the different 'matters'. In oher words, the 'matters' posited as independent directly pass over into their unity, and their unity directly unfolds its diversity, and this once again reduces itself to unity. But this movement is what is called *Force*. One of its moments, the dispersal of the independent 'matters' in their [immediate] being, is the *expression* of Force; but Force, taken as that in which they have disappeared, is Force *proper*, Force which has been *driven back* into itself from its expression. First, however, the Force which is driven back into itself *must* express itself; and, secondly, it is still Force remaining *within itself* in the expression, just as much as it is expression in this self-containedness.

When *we* thus preserve the two moments in their immediate unity, the Understanding, to which the Notion of Force belongs, is strictly speaking the *Notion* which sustains the different moments *qua* different; for, *in themselves*, they are not supposed to be different. Consequently, the difference exists only in thought. That is to say, what has been posited in the foregoing is in the first instance only the Notion of Force, not its reality. In point of fact, however, Force is the unconditioned universal which is equally in its own self what it is *for an other*; or which contains the difference in its own self—for difference is nothing else than being-*for-another*. In order, then, that Force may in truth *be*, it must be completely set free from thought, it must be posited as the substance of these differences, i.e. *first* the *substance*, as this whole Force, remaining essentially *in and for itself, and then* its *differences* as possessing *substantial being*, or as moments existing on their own account. Force as such, or as driven back into itself, thus exists on its own account as an *exclusive One*, for which the unfolding of the [different] 'matters' is *another* subsisting essence; and thus two distinct independent aspects are set up. But Force is also the whole, i.e. it remains what it is according to its Notion; that is to say, these *differences* remain pure forms, superficial *vanishing* moments. At the same time there would be no difference at all between Force proper which has been driven back into itself, and Force unfolded into independent 'matters', if they had no *enduring* being, or, there would be no Force if it did not *exist* in these opposite ways. But that it does exist in these opposite ways simply means that the two moments are at the same time themselves *independent*. It is therefore this movement of the two moments in which they perpetually give themselves independence and then supersede themselves again which we are now to consider.

In general, it is clear that this movement is nothing else than the movement of perceiving, in which the two sides, the percipient and what is perceived, are indistinguishably one in the *apprehension* of the True, and yet each side is at the same time equally *reflected into itself*, or has a being of its own. Here, these two sides are moments of Force; they are just as much in a unity, as this unity, which appears as the middle term over against the independent extremes, is a perpetual diremption of itself into just these extremes which exist only through this process. Thus the movement which previously displayed itself as the self-destruction of contradictory Notions here has *objective* form and is the movement of Force, the outcome of which is the un-conditioned universal as something *not* objective, or as the *inner* being of Things.

137. Force, as thus determined, since it is conceived *as* Force or as *reflected into itself*, is one side of its Notion, but posited as a substantial extreme and, moreover, with the express character of a One. The subsistence of the unfolded 'matters' outside of Force is thus precluded and is something other than Force. Since it is necessary that *Force itself* be this *subsistence*, or that it *express* itself, its expression presents itself in this wise, that the said 'other' approaches *it* and solicits it. But, as a matter of fact, since its expression is *necessary*, what is posited as another essence is in Force itself. We must retract the assertion that Force is posited as *a One*, and that its essence is to express itself as an 'other' which approaches it externally. Force is rather itself this universal medium in which the moments subsist as 'matters'; or, in other words, Force *has expressed itself*, and what was sup-posed to be something else soliciting it is really Force itself. It exists, therefore, now as the medium of the unfolded 'matters'. But equally essentially it has the form of the supersession of the subsisting 'matters', or is essentially a *One*. Consequently, this *oneness*, since *Force* is posited as the medium of the 'matters', is *now* something *other* than Force, which has this its essence out-side of it. But, since Force must of necessity be this oneness which it is not as yet *posited* as being, this 'other' *approaches it*, soliciting it to reflect itself into itself: in other words, Force supersedes its expression. But in fact Force is *itself* this reflected-ness-into-self, or this supersession of the expression. The one-ness, in the form in which it appeared, viz. as an 'other', vanishes; Force is this 'other' itself, is Force that is driven back into itself.

138. What appears as an 'other' and solicits Force, both to expression and to a return into itself, directly proves to be *itself Force*; for the 'other' shows itself to be as much a universal medium as a One, and in such a way that each of these forms at the same time appears only as a vanishing moment. Con-sequently, Force, in that there is an 'other' for it, and it is for

an 'other', has not yet altogether emerged from its Notion. There are at the same time two Forces present; the Notion of both is no doubt the same, but it has gone forth from its unity into a duality. Instead of the antithesis remaining entirely and essentially only a moment, it seems, by its self-diremption into two wholly *independent* forces, to have withdrawn from the controlling unity. We have now to see more closely the implications of this independence.

In the first place, the second Force appears as the one that solicits and, moreover, in accordance with its content, as the universal medium in relation to the Force characterized as the one solicited. But since the second Force is essentially an alternation of these two moments and is itself Force, it is likewise the universal medium *only through its being solicited to be such*; and similarly, too, it is a negative unity, i.e. it solicits the retraction of Force [into itself], *only through its being solicited to do so*. Consequently, this distinction, too, which obtained between the two Forces, one of which was supposed to be the soliciting, the other the solicited, Force is transformed into the same reciprocal interchange of the determinatenesses.

139. The interplay of the two Forces thus consists in their being determined as mutually opposed, in their being for one another in this determination, and in the absolute, immediate alternation of the determinations—consists, i.e. in a transition through which alone these determinations *are* in which the Forces seem to make an *independent* appearance. The soliciting Force, e.g., is posited as a universal medium, and the one solicited, on the other hand, as Force driven back into itself; but the former is a universal medium only through the other being Force that is driven back into itself; or, it is really the latter that is the soliciting Force for the other and is what makes it a medium. The first Force has its determinateness only through the other, and solicits only in so far as the other solicits it to be a soliciting Force; and, just as directly, it loses the determinateness given to it, for this passes over—or rather has already passed over—to the other. The external, soliciting Force appears as a universal medium, but only through its having been solicited by the other Force to do so; but this means that the latter *gives* it that character and is really *itself essentially* a universal medium; it gives the soliciting Force this character

just because this other determination is essential to it, i.e. because *this is really its own self*.

140. To complete our insight into the Notion of this movement it may further be noticed that the differences themselves are exhibited in a twofold difference: once as a difference of *content*, one extreme being the Force reflected into itself, but the other the medium of the 'matters'; and again as a difference of *form*, since one solicits and the other is solicited, the former being active and the other passive. According to the difference of content they are distinguished [merely] in principle, or *for us*; but according to the difference of form they are independent and in their relation keep themselves separate and opposed to one another. The fact that the extremes, from the standpoint of both these sides, are thus nothing *in themselves*, that these sides in which their different essences were supposed to consist are only vanishing moments, are an immediate transition of each into its opposite, this truth becomes apparent to consciousness in its perception of the movement of Force. But *for us*, as remarked above, something more was apparent, viz. that the differences, *qua differences of content and form*, vanished in themselves; and on the side of form, the essence of the *active, soliciting* or *independent* side, was the same as that which, on the side of content, presented itself as Force driven back into itself; the side which was passive, which was *solicited* or for an *other*, was, from the side of form, the same as that which, from the side of content, presented itself as the universal medium of the many 'matters'.

141. From this we see that the Notion of Force becomes *actual* through its duplication into two Forces, and how it comes to be so. These two Forces exist as independent essences; but their existence is a movement of each towards the other, such that their being is rather a pure *positedness* or a being that is *posited by an other*, i.e. their being has really the significance of a sheer *vanishing*. They do not exist as extremes which retain for themselves something fixed and substantial, transmitting to one another in their middle term and in their contact a merely external property; on the contrary, what they are, they are, only in this middle term and in this contact. In this, there is immediately present both the repression within itself of Force, or its *being-for-self*, as well as its expression: Force that solicits

and Force that is solicited. Consequently, these moments are not divided into two independent extremes offering each other only an opposite extreme: their essence rather consists simply and solely in this, that each *is* solely through the other, and what each thus is it immediately no longer is, since it *is* the other. They have thus, in fact, no substances of their own which might support and maintain them. The *Notion* of Force rather preserves itself as the *essence* in its very *actuality*; Force, as *actual*, exists simply and solely in its *expression*, which at the same time is nothing else than a supersession of itself. This *actual* Force, when thought of as free from its expression and as being for itself, is Force driven back into itself; but in fact this determinateness, as we have found, is itself only a moment of Force's expression. Thus the truth of Force remains only the *thought* of it; the moments of its actuality, their substances and their movement, collapse unresistingly into an undifferentiated unity, a unity which is not Force driven back into itself (for this is itself only such a moment), but is its *Notion qua Notion*. Thus the realization of Force is at the same time the loss of reality; in that realization it has really become something quite different, viz. this *universality*, which the Understanding knows at the outset, or immediately, to be its essence and which also proves itself to be such in the supposed reality of Force, in the actual substances.

142. In so far as we regard the *first* universal as the Understanding's *Notion* in which Force is not yet *for itself*, the second is now Force's *essence* as it exhibits itself in and for itself. Or, conversely, if we regard the first universal as the *Immediate*, which was supposed to be an *actual* object for consciousness, then this second is determined as the *negative* of Force that is objective to sense; it is Force in the form of its true essence in which it exists only as an *object for the Understanding*. The first universal would be Force driven back into itself, or Force as Substance; the second, however, is the *inner being* of things *qua* inner, which is the same as the Notion of Force *qua* Notion.

143. This true essence of Things has now the character of not being immediately for consciousness; on the contrary, consciousness has a mediated relation to the inner being and, as the Understanding, *looks through this mediating play of Forces into the true background of Things*. The middle term which unites the

two extremes, the Understanding and the inner world, is the developed *being* of Force which, for the Understanding itself, is henceforth only a vanishing. This 'being' is therefore called *appearance*; for we call *being* that is directly and in its own self a *non-being* a surface show. But it is not merely a surface show; it is appearance, a *totality* of show. This *totality*, as totality or as a *universal*, is what constitutes the inner [of Things], the play of Forces as a reflection of the inner into itself. In it, the Things of perception are expressly present for consciousness as they are in themselves, viz. as moments which immediately and without rest or stay turn into their opposite, the One immediately into the universal, the essential immediately into the unessential, and vice versa. This play of Forces is consequently the developed negative; but its truth is the positive, viz. the *universal*, the object that, *in itself*, possesses being. The *being* of this object for consciousness is mediated by the movement of *appearance*, in which the *being of perception* and the sensuously objective in general has a merely negative significance. Consciousness, therefore, reflects itself out of this movement back into itself as the True; but, *qua* consciousness, converts this truth again into an objective *inner*, and distinguishes this reflection of Things from its own reflection into itself: just as the movement of mediation is likewise still objective for it. This inner is, therefore, for consciousness an extreme over against it; but it is for consciousness the True, since in the inner, as the in-itself, it possesses at the same time the certainty of itself, or the moment of its being-for-self. But it is not yet conscious of this ground or basis, for the *being-for-self* which the inner was supposed to possess in its own self would be nothing else but the negative movement. This, however, is for consciousness still the *objective* vanishing appearance, not yet its *own* being-for-self. Consequently, the inner is for it certainly Notion, but it does not as yet know the nature of the Notion.

144. Within this *inner truth*, as the *absolute universal* which has been purged of the *antithesis* between the universal and the individual and has become the object of the *Understanding*, there now opens up above the *sensuous* world, which is the world of *appearance*, a *supersensible* world which henceforth is the *true* world, above the vanishing *present* world there opens up a permanent *beyond*; an it-self which is the first, and therefore

imperfect, appearance of Reason, or only the pure element in which the truth has its *essence*.

145. *Our object* is thus from now on the syllogism which has for its extremes the inner being of Things and the Understanding, and for its middle term, appearance; but the movement of this syllogism yields the further determination of what the Understanding descries in this inner world through the middle term, and the experience from which Understanding learns about the close-linked unity of these terms.

146. The inner world is, for consciousness, still a *pure beyond*, because consciousness does not as yet find itself in it. It is *empty*, for it is merely the nothingness of appearance, and positively the *simple* or *unitary* universal. This mode of the inner being [of Things] finds ready acceptance by those who say that the inner being of Things is unknowable; but another reason for this would have to be given. Certainly, we have no knowledge of this inner world as it is here in its immediacy; but not because Reason is too short-sighted or is limited, or however else one likes to call it—on this point, we know nothing as yet because we have not yet gone deep enough—but because of the simple nature of the matter in hand, that is to say, because in the *void* nothing is known, or, expressed from the other side, just because this inner world is determined as the *beyond* of consciousness. The result is, of course the same if a blind man is placed amid the wealth of the supersensible world (if it has such wealth, whether it be its own peculiar content, or whether consciousness itself be this content), and if one with sight is placed in pure darkness, or if you like, in pure light, just supposing the supersensible world to be this. The man with sight sees as little in that pure light as in pure darkness, and just as much as the blind man, in the abundant wealth which lies before him. If no further significance attached to the inner world and to our close link with it through the world of appearance, then nothing would be left to us but to stop at the world of appearance, i.e. to perceive something as true which we know is not true. Or, in order that there may yet be something in the void—which, though it first came about as devoid of *objective* Things must, however, as *empty in itself*, be taken as also void of all spiritual relationships and distinctions of consciousness *qua* consciousness—in order, then, that in this *complete void*, which is even

called the *holy of holies*, there may yet be something, we must fill it up with reveries, *appearances*, produced by consciousness itself. It would have to be content with being treated so badly for it would not deserve anything better, since even reveries are better than its own emptiness.

147. The inner world, or supersensible beyond, has, however, *come into being*: it *comes from* the world of appearance which has mediated it; in other words, appearance is its essence and, in fact, its filling. The supersensible is the sensuous and the perceived posited as it is *in truth*; but the *truth* of the sensuous and the perceived is to be *appearance*. The supersensible is therefore *appearance qua appearance*. We completely misunderstand this if we think that the supersensible world is *therefore* the sensuous world, or the world as it exists for immediate sense-certainty and perception; for the world of appearance is, on the contrary, *not* the world of sense-knowledge and perception as a world that positively *is*, but this world posited as superseded, or as in truth an *inner world*. It is often said that the supersensible world is *not* appearance; but what is here understood by appearance is not appearance, but rather the *sensuous* world as itself the really actual.

148. The Understanding, which is our object, finds itself in just this position, that the inner world has come into being for it, to begin with, only as the universal, still unfilled, *in-itself*. The play of Forces has merely this negative significance of being *in itself* nothing, and its only positive significance that of being the *mediating agency*, but outside of the Understanding. The connection of the Understanding with the inner world through the mediation is, however, its own movement through which the inner world will fill itself out for the Understanding. What is *immediate* for the Understanding is the play of Forces; but what is the *True* for it, is the simple inner world. The movement of Force is therefore the True, likewise only as something altogether *simple*. We have seen, however, that this play of Forces is so constituted that the Force which is *solicited* by another Force is equally the *soliciting* Force for that other, which only thereby becomes itself a soliciting Force. What is present in this interplay is likewise merely the immediate alternation, or the absolute interchange, of the *determinateness* which constitutes the sole *content* of what appears: to be either a universal medium,

or a negative unity. It ceases immediately on its appearance in determinate form to be what it was on appearing; by appearing in determinate form, it solicits the other side to *express* itself, i.e. the latter is now immediately what the first was supposed to be. Each of these two sides, the *relation* of soliciting and the *relation* of the opposed determinate content, is *on its own account* an absolute reversal and interchange [of the determinateness]. But these two relations themselves are again one and the same; and the difference of *form*, of being the solicited and the soliciting Force, is the same as the difference of *content*, of being the solicited Force as such, viz. the passive medium on the one hand, and the soliciting Force, the active, negative unity or the One, on the other. In this way there vanishes completely all distinction of *separate*, mutually contrasted *Forces* which were supposed to be present in this movement, for they rested solely on those distinctions; and the distinction between the Forces, along with both those distinctions, likewise collapses into only one. Thus there is neither Force, nor the act of soliciting or being solicited, nor the determinateness of being a stable medium and a unity reflected into itself, there is neither something existing singly by itself, nor are there diverse antitheses; on the contrary, what there is in this absolute flux is only *difference* as a *universal* difference, or as a difference into which the many antitheses have been resolved. This difference, as a *universal* difference, is consequently the *simple element in the play of Force itself* and what is true in it. It is the *law of Force*.

149. The absolute flux of appearance becomes a *simple difference* through its relation to the simplicity of the inner world or of the Understanding. The inner being is, to begin with, only implicitly the universal; but this implicit, simple *universal* is essentially no less absolutely *universal difference*, for it is the outcome of the flux itself, or the flux is its essence; but it is a flux that is posited in the *inner* world as it is in truth, and consequently it is received in that inner world as equally an absolute universal difference that is absolutely at rest and remains selfsame. In other words, negation is an essential moment of the universal, and negation, or mediation in the universal, is therefore a *universal difference*. This difference is expressed in the *law*, which is the *stable* image of unstable appearance. Consequently, the *supersensible* world is an inert *realm of laws* which, though beyond

the perceived world—for this exhibits law only through incess-
ant change—is equally *present* in it and is its direct tranquil
image.

150. This realm of laws is indeed the truth for the Understanding, and that truth has its *content* in the law. At the same
time, however, this realm is only the *initial* truth for the Understanding and does not fill out the world of appearance. In this
the law is present, but is not the entire presence of appearance;
with every change of circumstance the law has a different actuality. Thus appearance retains *for itself* an aspect which is not
in the inner world; i.e. appearance is not yet truly posited as
appearance, as a *superseded* being-for-self. This defect in the law
must equally be made manifest in the law itself. What seems
to be defective in it is that while it does contain difference, the
difference is universal, indeterminate. However, in so far as it
is not law in general, but *a* law, it does contain determinateness;
consequently, there are indefinitely *many* laws. But this plurality
is itself rather a defect; for it contradicts the principle of the
Understanding for which, as consciousness of the simple inner
world, the True is the implicitly universal *unity*. It must therefore let the many laws collapse into *one* law, just as, e.g., the
law by which a stone falls, and the law by which the heavenly
bodies move, have been grasped as one law. But when the laws
thus coincide, they lose their specific character. The law
becomes more and more superficial, and as a result what is
found is, in fact, not the unity of *these specific* laws, but a law
which leaves out their specific character; just as the *one* law
which combines in itself the laws of falling terrestrial bodies and
of the motions of the heavenly bodies, in fact expresses neither
law. The unification of all laws in *universal attraction* expresses
no other content than just the *mere Notion of law itself*, which
is posited in that law in the form of *being*. Universal attraction
merely asserts that *everything has a constant difference in relation to
other things*. The Understanding imagines that in this unification it has found a universal law which expresses universal
reality *as such*; but in fact it has only found the *Notion* of *law
itself*, although in such a way that what it is saying is that *all*
reality is *in its own self*, conformable to law. The expression, *universal attraction*, is of great importance in so far as it is directed
against the thoughtless way in which everything is pictured as

contingent, and for which determinateness has the form of sensuous independence.

151. Thus, in contrast to specific laws, we have universal attraction, or the pure Notion of law. In so far as this pure Notion is looked on as the essence, or the true inner being, the *determinateness* of the specific law itself still belongs to appearance, or rather to sensuous being. But the pure *Notion* of law transcends not merely the law which, being itself a specific law, stands contrasted with other specific laws, but also transcends law as such. The determinateness of which we spoke is itself really only a vanishing moment which can no longer occur here as something essential, for here it is only the law that is the True; but the *Notion* of law is turned against *law* itself. That is to say, in the law the difference itself is grasped *immediately* and taken up into the universal, thereby, however, giving the moments whose relation is expressed by the law a *subsistence* in the form of indifferent and [merely] implicit essentialities. But these parts of the difference present in the law are at the same time themselves determinate sides; the pure Notion of law as universal attraction must, to get its true meaning, be grasped in such a way that in it, as what is absolutely simple or unitary, the differences present in law as such themselves return again *into the inner world as a simple unity*. This unity is the inner *necessity* of the law.

152. The law is thereby present in a twofold manner: once, as law in which the differences are expressed as independent moments; and also in the form of a *simple* withdrawal into itself which again can be called *Force*, but in the sense not of a Force that is driven back into itself, but Force as such, or the Notion of Force, an abstraction which absorbs the differences themselves of what attracts and what is attracted. In this sense, *simple* electricity, e.g., is *Force*; but the expression of difference falls within the *law*; this difference is positive and negative electricity. In the case of the motion of falling, *Force* is the simple factor, *gravity*, whose *law* is that the magnitudes of the different moments of the motion, the time elapsed and the *space* traversed, are related to one another as root and square. Electricity itself is not difference *per se*, or is not in its essence the dual essence of positive and negative electricity; hence, it is usually said that it *has* the law of this mode of *being*, and, too, that it *has the property* of

expressing itself in this way. It is true that this property is the essential and sole property of this Force, or that it belongs to it *necessarily*. But necessity here is an empty word; Force *must*, just *because* it *must*, duplicate itself in this way. Of course, given *positive* electricity, negative too is given *in principle*; for the positive *is*, only as related to a negative, or, the positive is *in its own self* the difference from itself; and similarly with the negative. But that electricity as such should divide itself in this way is not in itself a necessity. Electricity, as *simple Force*, is indifferent to its law—*to be* positive and negative; and if we call the former its Notion but the latter its being, then its Notion is indifferent to its being. It merely *has* this property, which just means that this property is not *in itself* necessary to it. This indifference is given another form when it is said that to be positive and negative belongs to the *definition* of electricity, and that this is simply *its Notion and essence*. In that case, its being would simply mean its actual existence. But that definition does not contain the *necessity of its existence*; it exists, either because we *find* it, i.e. its existence is not necessary at all, or else it exists through, or by means of, other Forces, i.e. its necessity is an external necessity. But, in basing this necessity on the determinateness of *being through another*, we relapse again into the *plurality* of specific laws which we have just left behind in order to consider *law* as law. It is only with law as law that we are to compare its *Notion* as Notion, or its necessity. But in all these forms, necessity has shown itself to be only an empty word.

153. There is still another form than that just indicated in which the indifference of law and Force, or of Notion and being, is to be found. In the law of motion, e.g., it is necessary that motion be split up into time and space, or again, into distance and velocity. Thus, since motion is only the relation of these factors, it—the universal—is certainly divided *in its own self*. But now these parts, time and space, or distance and velocity, do not in themselves express this origin in a One; they are indifferent to one another, space is thought of as able to be without time, time without space, and distance at least without velocity—just as their magnitudes are indifferent to one another, since they are not related to one another *as positive* and *negative*, and thus are not related to one another through *their own essential nature*. The necessity of the *division* is thus certainly

present here, but not the necessity of the *parts* as such for one another. But it is just for this reason that that first necessity, too, is itself only a sham, false necessity. For motion is not itself thought of as something *simple*, or as a pure essence, but as *already* divided; time and space are *in themselves* its *independent* parts or essences, or, distance and velocity are modes of being or ways of thinking, either of which can well be without the other; and motion is, therefore, only their superficial relation, not their essence. If it is thought of as a simple essence or as Force, motion is no doubt *gravity*, but this does not contain these differences at all.

154. The difference, then, in both cases is not a difference *in its own self*: either the universal, Force, is indifferent to the division which is the law, or the differences, the parts, of the law are indifferent to one another. The Understanding, how-ever, *has* the Notion of this *implicit difference* just because the law is, on the one hand, the inner, *implicit* being, but is, at the same time, inwardly differentiated. That this difference is thus an *inner* difference follows from the fact that the law is a *simple* Force or is the *Notion* of the difference, and is therefore a difference belonging to the *Notion*. But this inner difference still falls, to begin with, only within the Understanding, and is not yet posited *in the thing itself*. It is, therefore, only its *own* necessity that is asserted by the Understanding; the difference, then, is posited by the Understanding in such a way that, at the same time, it is expressly stated that the difference is not a *difference belonging to the thing itself*. This necessity, which is merely verbal, is thus a recital of the moments constituting the cycle of the necessity. The moments are indeed distinguished, but, at the same time, their difference is expressly said to be *not* a difference of the thing itself, and consequently is itself immediately can-celled again. This process is called '*explanation*'. A *law* is enunci-ated; from this, its implicitly universal element or ground is distinguished as *Force*; but it is said that this difference is no difference, rather that the ground is constituted exactly the same as the law. The single occurrence of lightning, e.g., is apprehended as a universal, and this universal is enunciated as the *law* of electricity; the 'explanation' then condenses the *law* into *Force* as the essence of the law. This Force, then, is *so constituted* that when it is expressed, opposite electricities appear,

which disappear again into one another; that is, *Force is constituted exactly the same as law*; there is said to be no difference whatever between them. The differences are the pure, universal expression of law, and pure Force; but both have the *same* content, the *same* constitution. Thus the difference *qua* difference of content, of the thing, is also again withdrawn.

155. In this tautological movement, the Understanding, as we have seen, sticks to the inert unity of its object, and the movement falls only within the Understanding itself, not within the object. It is an explanation that not only explains nothing, but is so plain that, while it pretends to say something different from what has already been said, really says nothing at all but only repeats the same thing. In the Thing itself this movement gives rise to nothing new; it comes into consideration [only] as a movement of the Understanding. In it, however, we detect the very thing that was missing in the law, viz. the absolute flux itself; for this *movement*, when we look at it more closely, is directly the opposite of itself. That is to say, it posits a difference which is not only *not* a difference for us, but one which the movement itself cancels as a difference. This is the same flux which presented itself as the play of Forces. This contained the distinction of soliciting and solicited Force, or Force expressing itself and Force repressed into itself; but these were distinctions which in reality were no distinctions, and therefore were also immediately cancelled again. What is present here is not merely bare unity in which *no difference* would be *posited*, but rather a *movement* in which *a distinction is certainly made but*, because it is no distinction, is *again cancelled*. In the process, then, of explaining, the to and fro of change which before was outside of the inner world and present only in the appearance, has penetrated into the supersensible world itself. Our consciousness, however, has passed over from the inner being as object to the other side, into the *Understanding*, and it experiences change there.

156. Thus this change is not yet a change of the thing itself, but rather presents itself as pure change by the very fact that the *content* of the moments of change remains the same. But since the *Notion*, *qua* Notion of the Understanding, is the same as the *inner being* of things, this change becomes for the Understanding the law of the inner world. The Understanding thus *learns* that

it is a *law* of *appearance itself*, that differences arise which are
no differences, or that what is *selfsame repels* itself from itself;
and similarly, that the differences are only such as are in reality
no differences and which cancel themselves; in other words,
what is *not selfsame* is *self-attractive*. And thus we have a second
law whose content is the opposite of what was previously called
law, viz. difference which remains constantly selfsame; for this
new law expresses rather that *like* becomes *unlike* and *unlike*
becomes *like*. The Notion demands of the thoughtless thinker
that he bring both laws together and become aware of their
antithesis. The second is certainly also a law, an inner self-
identical being, but a selfsameness rather of the unlike, a permanence of impermanence. In the play of Forces this law
showed itself to be precisely this absolute transition and pure
change; the selfsame, viz. Force, *splits* into an antithesis which
at first appears to be an independent difference, but which in
fact proves *to be none*; for it is the *selfsame* which repels itself from
itself, and therefore what is repelled is essentially self-attractive,
for it is the *same*; the difference created, since it is no difference,
therefore cancels itself again. Consequently, the difference
exhibits itself as difference of the *thing itself* or as absolute difference, and this difference of the *thing* is thus nothing else but
the selfsame that has repelled itself from itself, and therefore
merely posits an antithesis which is none.

157. Through this principle, the first supersensible world,
the tranquil kingdom of laws, the immediate copy of the perceived world, is changed into its opposite. The law was, in
general, like its differences, that which remains selfsame; now,
however, it is posited that each of the two worlds is really the
opposite of itself. The *selfsame* really repels itself from itself, and
what is not selfsame really posits itself as selfsame. In point of
fact, it is only when thus determined that the difference is *inner*
difference, or the difference *in its own self*, the like being unlike
itself, and the unlike, like itself. *This second supersensible world* is
in this way the *inverted* world and, moreover, since one aspect
is already present in the first supersensible world, the inversion
of the first. With this, the inner world is completed as appearance. For the first supersensible world was only the *immediate*
raising of the perceived world into the universal element; it had
its necessary counterpart in this perceived world which still

retained *for itself the principle of change and alteration.* The first kingdom of laws lacked that principle, but obtains it as an inverted world.

158. According, then, to the law of this inverted world, what is *like* in the first world is *unlike* to itself, and what is *unlike* in the first world is equally *unlike to itself*, or it becomes *like* itself. Expressed in determinate moments, this means that what in the law of the first world is sweet, in this inverted in-itself is sour, what in the former is black is, in the other, white. What in the law of the first is the north pole of the magnet is, in its other, supersensible in-itself [viz. in the earth], the south pole; but what is there south pole is here north pole. Similarly, what in the first law is the oxygen pole of electricity becomes in its other, supersensible essence, hydrogen pole; and conversely, what is there the hydrogen pole becomes here the oxygen pole. In another sphere, revenge on an enemy is, according to the *immediate law*, the supreme satisfaction of the injured individuality. This law, however, which bids me confront him as himself a person who does not treat me as such, and in fact bids me destroy him as an individuality—this law is *turned round* by the principle of the other world into its opposite: the reinstatement of myself as a person through the destruction of the alien individuality is turned into self-destruction. If, now, this inversion, which finds expression in the punishment of crime, is made into a *law*, it, too, again is only the law of one world which is confronted by an *inverted* supersensible world where what is despised in the former is honoured, and what in the former is honoured, meets with contempt. The punishment which under the law of the *first* world disgraces and destroys a man, is transformed in its *inverted* world into the pardon which preserves his essential being and brings him to honour.

159. Looked at superficially, this inverted world is the opposite of the first in the sense that it has the latter outside of it and repels that world from itself as an inverted *actual world*: that the one is appearance, but the other the in-itself; that the one is the world as it is for an other, whereas the other is the world as it is for itself. So that to use the previous examples, what tastes sweet is *really*, or *inwardly* in the thing, sour; or what is north pole in the actual magnet in the world of appearance, would be south pole in the *inner* or *essential being*; what presents

itself as oxygen pole in the phenomenon of electricity would be hydrogen pole in unmanifested electricity. Or, an action which in the world of *appearance* is a crime would, in the *inner* world, be capable of being really good (a bad action may be well-intentioned); punishment is punishment *only in the world of appearance*; *in itself*, or in another world, it may be a benefit for the criminal. But such antitheses of inner and outer, of appearance and the supersensible, as of two different kinds of actuality, we no longer find here. The repelled differences are not shared afresh between two substances such as would support them and lend them a separate subsistence: this would result in the Understanding withdrawing from the inner world and relapsing into its previous position. The one side, or substance, would be the world of perception again in which one of the two laws would be operative, and confronting it would be an inner world, *just such a sense-world* as the first, but in the *imagination*; it could not be exhibited as a sense-world, could not be seen, heard, or tasted, and yet it would be thought of as such a sense-world. But, in fact, if the one *posited world* is a perceived world, and its *in-itself*, as its inversion, is equally *thought of as sensuous*, then sourness which would be the in-itself of the sweet thing is actually a thing just as much as the latter, viz. a *sour thing*; black, which would be the in-itself of white, is an actual black; the north pole which is the in-itself of the south pole is the north pole *actually present in the same magnet*; the oxygen pole which is the in-itself of the hydrogen pole is *actually present* in the same voltaic pile. The *actual* crime, however, has *its inversion* and *its in-itself* as *possibility*, in the *intention* as such, but not in a good intention; for the truth of intention is only the act itself. But the crime, as regards its content, has its reflection-into-self, or its inversion, in the *actual* punishment; this is the reconciliation of the law with the actuality opposed to it in the crime. Finally, the *actual* punishment has its *inverted* actuality present in it in such a way that the punishment is an actualization of the law, whereby the activity exercised by the law as punishment *suspends itself*, and, from being active, the law becomes again quiescent and is vindicated, and the conflict of individuality with it, and of it with individuality, is extinguished.

160. From the idea, then, of inversion, which constitutes the essential nature of one aspect of the supersensible world, we

must eliminate the sensuous idea of fixing the differences in a different sustaining element; and this absolute Notion of the difference must be represented and understood purely as inner difference, a repulsion of the selfsame, as selfsame, from itself, and likeness of the unlike as unlike. We have to think pure change, or *think antithesis within the antithesis itself*, or *contradiction*. For in the difference which is an inner difference, the opposite is not merely *one of two*—if it were, it would simply *be*, without being an opposite—but it is the opposite of an opposite, or the other is itself immediately present in it. Certainly, I put the 'opposite' here, and the 'other' of which it is the opposite, there; the 'opposite', then, is on one side, is in and for itself without the 'other'. But just because I have the 'opposite' here in and for itself, it is the opposite of itself, or it has, in fact, the 'other' immediately present in it. Thus the supersensible world, which is the inverted world, has at the same time overarched the other world and has it within it; it is *for itself* the inverted world, i.e. the inversion of itself; it is itself and its opposite in one unity. Only thus is it difference as *inner* difference, or difference *in its own self*, or difference as an *infinity*.

161. We see that through infinity, law completes itself into an immanent necessity, and all the moments of [the world of] appearance are taken up into the inner world. That the simple character of law is infinity means, according to what we have found, (a) that it is self-*identical*, but is also in itself *different*; or it is the selfsame which repels itself from itself or sunders itself into two. What was called *simple Force duplicates* itself and through its infinity is law. (b) What is thus dirempted, which constitutes the parts thought of as in the *law*, exhibits itself as a stable existence; and if the parts are considered without the Notion of the inner difference, then space and time, or distance and velocity, which appear as moments of gravity, are just as indifferent and without a necessary relation to one another as to gravity itself, or, as this simple gravity is indifferent to them, or, again, as simple electricity is indifferent to positive and negative electricity. But (c) through the Notion of inner difference, these unlike and indifferent moments, space and time, etc. are a *difference* which is no *difference*, or only a difference of what is *selfsame*, and its essence is unity. As positive and negative they stimulate each other into activity, and their being is rather to

posit themselves as not-being and to suspend themselves in the unity. The two distinguished moments both subsist; they are *implicit* and are *opposites in themselves*, i.e. each is the opposite of itself; each has its 'other' within it and they are only one unity.

162. This simple infinity, or the absolute Notion, may be called the simple essence of life, the soul of the world, the universal blood, whose omnipresence is neither disturbed nor interrupted by any difference, but rather is itself every difference, as also their supersession; it pulsates within itself but does not move, inwardly vibrates, yet is at rest. It is self-*identical*, for the differences are tautological; they are differences that are none. This self-identical essence is therefore related only to itself; 'to itself' implies relationship to an 'other', and the *relation-to-self* is rather a *self-sundering*; or, in other words, that very self-identicalness is an inner difference. These *sundered moments* are thus *in and for themselves* each an opposite—*of an other*; thus in each moment the 'other' is at the same time expressed; or each is not the opposite of an 'other' but only a *pure opposite*; and so each is therefore in its own self the opposite of itself. In other words, it is not an opposite at all, but is purely for itself, a pure, self-identical essence that has no difference in it. Accordingly, we do not need to ask the question, still less to think that fretting over such a question is philosophy, or even that it is a question philosophy cannot answer, the question, viz. '*How*, from this pure essence, how does difference or otherness *issue forth* from it?' For the division into two moments has already taken place, difference is excluded from the self-identical and set apart from it. What was supposed to be the *self-identical* is thus already one of these two moments instead of being the absolute essence. That the self-identical divides itself into two means, therefore, just as well that it supersedes itself as *already* divided, supersedes itself as an otherness. The *unity*, of which it is usual to say that difference cannot issue from it, is in fact itself one of the two moments; it is the abstraction of the simplicity or unitary nature over against the difference. But in saying that the unity is an abstraction, that is, is only one of the opposed moments, it is already implied that it is the dividing of itself; for if the unity is a *negative*, is *opposed* to something, then it is *eo ipso* posited as that which has an antithesis within it. The different moments

of *self-sundering* and of *becoming self-identical* are therefore likewise
only this movement of *self-supersession*; for since the self-identical, which is supposed first to sunder itself or become its opposite, is an abstraction or is *already itself* a sundered moment, its
self-sundering is therefore a supersession of what it is, and therefore the supersession of its dividedness. Its *becoming self-identical*
is equally a self-sundering; what becomes identical with itself
thereby opposes itself to its self-sundering; i.e. it thereby puts
itself on one side, or rather it *becomes* a *sundered moment*.

163. Infinity, or this absolute unrest of pure self-movement,
in which whatever is determined in one way or another, e.g.
as being, is rather the opposite of this determinateness, this no
doubt has been from the start the soul of all that has gone
before; but it is in the *inner* world that it has first freely and
clearly shown itself. Appearance, or the play of Forces, already
displays it, but it is as '*explanation*' that it first freely stands forth;
and in being finally an object for consciousness, as *that which
it is*, consciousness is thus *self-consciousness*. The Understanding's
'explanation' is primarily only the description of what self-consciousness is. It supersedes the differences present in the law,
differences which have already become pure differences but are
still indifferent, and posits them in a single unity, in Force. But
this unifying of them is equally and immediately a sundering,
for it supersedes the differences and posits the oneness of Force
only by creating a new difference, that of Law and Force,
which, however, at the same time is no difference; and, moreover, from the fact that this difference is no difference, it goes
on to supersede this difference again, since it lets Force be similarly constituted to Law. But this movement, or necessity, is
thus still a necessity and a movement of the Understanding,
or, the movement *as such* is not the Understanding's *object*; on
the contrary, in this movement the Understanding has as
objects positive and negative electricity, distance, force of
attraction, and a thousand other things which constitute the
content of the moments of the movement. The reason why
'explaining' affords so much self-satisfaction is just because in
it consciousness is, so to speak, communing directly with itself,
enjoying only itself; although it seems to be busy with something else, it is in fact occupied only with itself.

164. In the contrary law, as the inversion of the first law,

or in the inner difference, it is true that infinity itself becomes the *object* of the Understanding; but once again the Understanding falls short of infinity as such, since it again apportions to two worlds, or to two substantial elements, that which is a difference in itself—the self-repulsion of the selfsame and the self-attraction of the unlike. To the Understanding, the *movement*, as it is found in experience, is here a [mere] happening, and the selfsame and the unlike are *predicates*, whose essence is an inert substrate. What is, for the Understanding, an object in a sensuous covering, is *for us* in its essential form as a pure Notion. This apprehension of the difference as it is *in truth*, or the apprehension of *infinity* as such, is *for us*, or *in itself* [i.e. is merely implicit]. The exposition of its Notion belongs to Science; but consciousness, in the way that it *immediately* has this Notion, again comes on the scene as a form belonging to consciousness itself, or as a new shape of consciousness, which does not recognize in what has gone before its own essence, but looks on it as something quite different. Since this Notion of infinity is an object for consciousness, the latter is consciousness of a difference that is no less *immediately* cancelled; consciousness is for its own self, it is a distinguishing of that which contains no difference, or *self-consciousness*. I distinguish myself from myself, and in doing so I am directly aware that what is distinguished from myself is not different [from me]. I, the selfsame being, repel myself from myself; but what is posited as distinct from me, or as unlike me, is immediately, in being so distinguished, not a distinction for me. It is true that consciousness of an 'other', of an object in general, is itself necessarily *self-consciousness*, a reflectedness-into-self, consciousness of itself in its otherness. The *necessary advance* from the previous shapes of consciousness for which their truth was a Thing, an 'other' than themselves, expresses just this, that not only is consciousness of a thing possible only for a self-consciousness, but that self-consciousness alone is the truth of those shapes. But it is only *for us* that this truth exists, not yet for consciousness. But self-consciousness has at first become [simply] *for itself*, not yet *as a unity* with consciousness in general.

165. We see that in the *inner* world of appearance, the Understanding in truth comes to know nothing else but appearance, but not in the shape of a play of Forces, but rather that play

of Forces in its absolutely universal moments and in their movement; in fact, the Understanding experiences only *itself*. Raised above perception, consciousness exhibits itself closed in a unity with the supersensible world through the mediating term of appearance, through which it gazes into this background [lying behind appearance]. The two extremes [of this syllogism], the one, of the pure inner world, the other, that of the inner being gazing into this pure inner world, have now coincided, and just as they, *qua* extremes, have vanished, so too the middle term, as something other than these extremes, has also vanished. This curtain [of appearance] hanging before the inner world is therefore drawn away, and we have the inner being [the 'I'] gazing into the inner world—the vision of the undifferentiated selfsame being, which repels itself from itself, posits itself as an inner being containing different moments, but for which equally these moments are immediately *not* different—*self-consciousness*. It is manifest that behind the so-called curtain which is supposed to conceal the inner world, there is nothing to be seen unless *we* go behind it ourselves, as much in order that we may see, as that there may be something behind there which can be seen. But at the same time it is evident that we cannot without more ado go straightway behind appearance. For this knowledge of what is the truth of appearance as ordinarily conceived, and of its inner being, is itself only a result of a complex movement whereby the modes of consciousness 'meaning', perceiving, and the Understanding, vanish; and it will be equally evident that the cognition of *what consciousness knows in knowing itself*, requires a still more complex movement, the exposition of which is contained in what follows.

B. SELF-CONSCIOUSNESS

IV. THE TRUTH OF SELF-CERTAINTY

166. In the previous modes of certainty what is true for consciousness is something other than itself. But the Notion of this truth vanishes in the experience of it. What the object immediately was *in itself*—mere being in sense-certainty, the concrete thing of perception, and for the Understanding, a Force—proves to be in truth, not this at all; instead, this *in-itself* turns out to be a mode in which the object is only for an other. The Notion of the object is superseded in the actual object, or the first, immediate presentation of the object is superseded in experience: certainty gives place to truth. But now there has arisen what did not emerge in these previous relationships, viz. a certainty which is identical with its truth; for the certainty is to itself its own object, and consciousness is to itself the truth. In this there is indeed an otherness; that is to say, consciousness makes a distinction, but one which at the same time is for consciousness *not* a distinction. If we give the name of *Notion* to the movement of knowing, and the name of *object* to knowing as a passive unity, or as the 'I', then we see that not only for *us*, but for knowing itself, the object corresponds to the Notion. Or alternatively, if we call Notion what the object is *in itself*, but call the object what *it* is *qua* object or *for an other*, then it is clear that being-*in-itself* and being-*for-an-other* are one and the same. For the *in-itself* is consciousness; but equally it is that *for which* an other (the *in-itself*) is; and it is *for* consciousness that the in-itself of the object, and the being of the object for an other, are one and the same; the 'I' is the *content* of the connection and the connecting itself. Opposed to an other, the 'I' is its own self, and at the same time it overarches this other which, for the 'I', is equally only the 'I' itself.

167. With self-consciousness, then, we have therefore entered the native realm of truth. We have now to see how the shape of self-consciousness first makes its appearance. If we consider this new shape of knowing, the knowing of itself, in rela-

tion to that which preceded, viz. the knowing of an other, then we see that though this other has indeed vanished, its moments have at the same time no less been preserved, and the loss consists in this, that here they are present as they are in themselves. The [mere] *being* of what is merely 'meant', the *singleness* and the *universality* opposed to it of perception, as also the *empty inner being* of the Understanding, these are no longer essences, but are moments of self-consciousness, i.e. abstractions or distinctions which at the same time have no reality *for* consciousness itself, and are purely vanishing essences. Thus it seems that only the principal moment itself has been lost, viz. the *simple self-subsistent existence* for consciousness. But in point of fact self-consciousness is the reflection out of the being of the world of sense and perception, and is essentially the return from *otherness*. As self-consciousness, it is movement; but since what it distinguishes from itself is *only itself as* itself, the difference, as an otherness, is *immediately superseded* for it; the difference *is not*, and *it* [self-consciousness] is only the motionless tautology of: 'I am I'; but since for it the difference does not have the form of *being*, it is *not* self-consciousness. Hence otherness is for it in the form of *a being*, or as a *distinct moment*; but there is also for consciousness the unity of itself with this difference as a *second distinct moment*. With that first moment, self-consciousness is in the form of *consciousness*, and the whole expanse of the sensuous world is preserved for it, but at the same time only as connected with the second moment, the unity of self-consciousness with itself; and hence the sensuous world is for it an enduring existence which, however, is only *appearance*, or a difference which, *in itself*, is no difference. This antithesis of its appearance and its truth has, however, for its essence only the truth, viz. the unity of self-consciousness with itself; this unity must become essential to self-consciousness, i.e. self-consciousness is *Desire* in general. Consciousness, as self-consciousness, henceforth has a double object: one is the immediate object, that of sense-certainty and perception, which however *for self-consciousness* has the character of a *negative*; and the second, viz. *itself*, which is the true *essence*, and is present in the first instance only as opposed to the first object. In this sphere, self-consciousness exhibits itself as the movement in which this antithesis is removed, and the identity of itself with itself becomes explicit for it.

168. But *for us*, or *in itself*, the object which for self-consciousness is the negative element has, on its side, returned into itself, just as on the other side consciousness has done. Through this reflection into itself the object has become Life. What self-consciousness distinguishes from itself as having *being*, also has in it, in so far as it is posited as being, not merely the character of sense-certainty and perception, but it is being that is reflected into itself, and the object of immediate desire is a *living thing*. For the *in-itself*, or the *universal* result of the relation of the Understanding to the inwardness of things, is the distinguishing of what is *not* to be distinguished, or the *unity* of what is distinguished. But this unity is, as we have seen, just as much its repulsion from itself; and this Notion sunders itself into the antithesis of self-consciousness and life: the former is the unity *for which* the infinite unity of the differences is; the latter, however, *is* only this unity itself, so that it is not at the same time *for itself*. To the extent, then, that consciousness is independent, so too is its object, but only *implicitly*. Self-consciousness which is simply *for itself* and directly characterizes its object as a negative element, or is primarily *desire*, will therefore, on the contrary, learn through experience that the object is independent.

169. The determination of Life as it has issued from the Notion, or the general result with which we enter this sphere, is sufficient to characterize it without having further to develop its nature. Its sphere is completely determined in the following moments. *Essence* is infinity as the *supersession* of all distinctions, the pure movement of axial rotation, its self-repose being an absolutely restless infinity; *independence* itself, in which the differences of the movement are resolved, the simple essence of Time which, in this equality with itself, has the stable shape of Space. The differences, however, are just as much present as *differences* in this simple universal medium; for this universal flux has its negative nature only in being the supersession of them; but it cannot supersede the different moments if they do not have an enduring existence [*Bestehen*]. It is this very flux, as a self-identical independence which is itself an *enduring existence*, in which, therefore, they are present as distinct members and parts existing on their own account. *Being* no longer has the significance of *abstract* being, nor has their pure essentiality the significance of *abstract* universality; on the contrary, their

being is precisely that simple fluid substance of pure movement within itself. The *difference*, however, *qua* difference, of these members with respect to one another consists in general in no other *determinateness* than that of the moments of infinity or of the pure movement itself.

170. The independent members are *for themselves*; but this *being-for-self* is really no less immediately their reflection into the unity than this unity is the splitting-up into independent shapes. The unity is divided within itself because it is an absolutely negative or infinite unity; and because it is what *subsists*, the difference, too, has independence only in *it*. This independence of the shape appears as something *determinate, for an other*, for the shape is divided within itself; and the supersession of this dividedness accordingly takes place through an other. But this supersession is just as much within the shape itself, for it is just that flux that is the substance of the independent shapes. This substance, however, is infinite, and hence the shape in its very subsistence is a dividedness within itself, or the supersession of its being-for-self.

171. If we distinguish more exactly the moments contained here, we see that we have, as the first moment, the subsistence of the independent shapes, or the suppression of what diremption is in itself, viz. that the shapes have no being in themselves, no enduring existence. The second moment, however is the subjection of that existence to the infinity of the difference. In the first moment there is the existent shape; as being *for itself*, or being in its determinateness infinite substance, it comes forward in antithesis to the *universal* substance, disowns this fluent continuity with it and asserts that it is not dissolved in this universal element, but on the contrary preserves itself by separating itself from this its inorganic nature, and by consuming it. Life in the universal fluid medium, a *passive* separating-out of the shapes becomes, just by so doing, a movement of those shapes or becomes Life as a *process*. The simple universal fluid medium is the *in-itself*, and the difference of the shapes is the *other*. But this fluid medium itself becomes the *other* through this difference; for now it is *for the difference* which exists in and for itself, and consequently is the ceaseless movement by which this passive medium is consumed: Life as a *living thing*.

This *inversion*, however, is for that reason again an inverted-ness *in its own self*. What is consumed is the essence: the individuality which maintains itself at the expense of the universal, and which gives itself the feeling of its unity with itself, just by so doing supersedes its antithesis to the other by means of which it exists for itself. Its self-given unity with itself is just that *fluidity* of the differences or their *general dissolution*. But, conversely, the supersession of individual existence is equally the production of it. For since the *essence* of the individual shape—universal Life—and what exists for itself is in itself simple substance, when this substance places the *other* within itself it supersedes this its *simplicity* or its essence, i.e. it divides it, and this dividedness of the differenceless fluid medium is just what establishes individuality. Thus the simple substance of Life is the splitting-up of itself into shapes and at the same time the dissolution of these existent differences; and the dissolution of the splitting-up is just as much a splitting-up and a forming of members. With this, the two sides of the whole movement which before were distinguished, viz. the passive separatedness of the shapes in the general medium of independence, and the process of Life, collapse into one another. The latter is just as much an imparting of shape as a supersession of it; and the other, the imparting of shape, is just as much a supersession as an articulation of shape. The fluid element is itself only the *abstraction* of essence, or it is *actual* only as shape; and its articulation of itself is again a splitting-up of what is articulated into form or a dissolution of it. It is the whole round of this activity that constitutes Life: not what was expressed at the outset, the immediate continuity and compactness of its essence, nor the enduring form, the discrete moment existing for itself; nor the pure process of these; nor yet the simple taking-together of these moments. Life consists rather in being the self-developing whole which dissolves its development and in this movement simply preserves itself.

172. Since we started from the first immediate unity and returned through the moments of formation and of process to the unity of both these moments, and thus back again to the original simple substance, this *reflected* unity is different from the first. Contrasted with that *immediate* unity, or that unity expressed as a [mere] *being*, this second is the *universal* unity which contains all these moments as superseded within itself. It is the simple genus which, in the movement of Life itself,

does not *exist for itself qua* this *simple* determination; on the contrary, in this *result*, Life points to something other than itself, viz. to consciousness, for which Life exists as this unity, or as genus.

173. This other Life, however, for which the genus as such exists, and which is genus on its own account, viz. self-consciousness, exists in the first instance for self-consciousness only as this simple essence, and has itself as pure 'I' for object. In the course of its experience which we are now to consider, this abstract object will enrich itself for the 'I' and undergo the unfolding which we have seen in the sphere of Life.

174. The simple 'I' is this genus or the simple universal, for which the differences are *not* differences only by its being the *negative essence* of the shaped independent moments; and self-consciousness is thus certain of itself only by superseding this other that presents itself to self-consciousness as an independent life; self-consciousness is Desire. Certain of the nothingness of this other, it explicitly affirms that this nothingness is *for it* the truth of the other; it destroys the independent object and thereby gives itself the certainty of itself as a *true* certainty, a certainty which has become explicit for self-consciousness itself *in an objective manner*.

175. In this satisfaction, however, experience makes it aware that the object has its own independence. Desire and the self-certainty obtained in its gratification, are conditioned by the object, for self-certainty comes from superseding this other: in order that this supersession can take place, there must be this other. Thus self-consciousness, by its negative relation to the object, is unable to supersede it; it is really because of that relation that it produces the object again, and the desire as well. It is in fact something other than self-consciousness that is the essence of Desire; and through this experience self-consciousness has itself realized this truth. But at the same time it is no less absolutely *for itself*, and it is so only by superseding the object; and it must experience its satisfaction, for it is the truth. On account of the independence of the object, therefore, it can achieve satisfaction only when the object itself effects the negation within itself; and it must carry out this negation of itself in itself, for it is *in itself* the negative, and must be *for* the other what it *is*. Since the object is in its own self negation, and in

being so is at the same time independent, it is consciousness. In the sphere of Life, which is the object of Desire, *negation* is present either *in an other*, viz in Desire, or as a *determinateness* opposed to another indifferent form, or as the inorganic universal nature of Life. But this universal independent nature in which negation is present as absolute negation, is the genus as such, or the genus as *self-consciousness*. *Self-consciousness achieves its satisfaction only in another self-consciousness.*

176. The notion of self-consciousness is only completed in these three moments: (a) the pure undifferentiated 'I' is its first immediate object. (b) But this immediacy is itself an absolute mediation, it *is* only as a supersession of the independent object, in other words, it is Desire. The satisfaction of Desire is, it is true, the reflection of self-consciousness into itself, or the certainty that has become truth. (c) But the truth of this certainty is really a double reflection, the duplication of self-consciousness. Consciousness has for its object one which, of its own self, posits its otherness or difference as a nothingness, and in so doing is independent. The differentiated, merely *living*, shape does indeed also supersede its independence in the process of Life, but it ceases with its distinctive difference to be what it is. The object of self-consciousness, however, is equally independent in this negativity of itself; and thus it is *for itself* a genus, a universal fluid element in the peculiarity of its own separate being; it is a living self-consciousness.

177. A self-consciousness exists *for a self-consciousness*. Only so is it in fact self-consciousness; for only in this way does the unity of itself in its otherness become explicit for it. The 'I' which is the object of its Notion is in fact not 'object'; the object of Desire, however, is only independent, for it is the universal indestructible substance, the fluid self-identical essence. A self-consciousness, in being an object, is just as much 'I' as 'object'. With this, we already have before us the Notion of *Spirit*. What still lies ahead for consciousness is the experience of what Spirit is—this absolute substance which is the unity of the different independent self-consciousnesses which, in their opposition, enjoy perfect freedom and independence: 'I' that is 'We' and 'We' that is 'I'. It is in self-consciousness, in the Notion of Spirit, that consciousness first finds its turning-point, where it leaves behind it the colourful show of the sensuous here-and-now and

the nightlike void of the supersensible beyond, and steps out into the spiritual daylight of the present.

A. INDEPENDENCE AND DEPENDENCE OF SELF-CONSCIOUSNESS: LORDSHIP AND BONDAGE

178. Self-consciousness exists in and for itself when, and by the fact that, it so exists for another; that is, it exists only in being acknowledged. The Notion of this its unity in its duplication embraces many and varied meanings. Its moments, then, must on the one hand be held strictly apart, and on the other hand must in this differentiation at the same time also be taken and known as not distinct, or in their opposite significance. The twofold significance of the distinct moments has in the nature of self-consciousness to be infinite, or directly the opposite of the determinateness in which it is posited. The detailed exposition of the Notion of this spiritual unity in its duplication will present us with the process of Recognition.

179. Self-consciousness is faced by another self-consciousness; it has come *out of itself*. This has a twofold significance: first, it has lost itself, for it finds itself as an *other* being; secondly, in doing so it has superseded the other, for it does not see the other as an essential being, but in the other sees its own self.

180. It must supersede this otherness of itself. This is the supersession of the first ambiguity, and is therefore itself a second ambiguity. First, it must proceed to supersede the *other* independent being in order thereby to become certain of *itself* as the essential being; secondly, in so doing it proceeds to supersede its *own* self, for this other is itself.

181. This ambiguous supersession of its ambiguous otherness is equally an ambiguous return *into itself*. For first, through the supersession, it receives back its own self, because, by superseding *its* otherness, it again becomes equal to itself; but secondly, the other self-consciousness equally gives it back again to itself, for it saw itself in the other, but supersedes this being of itself in the other and thus lets the other again go free.

182. Now, this movement of self-consciousness in relation to another self-consciousness has in this way been represented as the action of *one* self-consciousness, but this action of the one

has itself the double significance of being both its own action and the action of the other as well. For the other is equally independent and self-contained, and there is nothing in it of which it is not itself the origin. The first does not have the object before it merely as it exists primarily for desire, but as something that has an independent existence of its own, which, therefore, it cannot utilize for its own purposes, if that object does not of its own accord do what the first does to it. Thus the movement is simply the double movement of the two self-consciousnesses. Each sees the *other* do the same as it does; each does itself what it demands of the other, and therefore also does what it does only in so far as the other does the same. Action by one side only would be useless because what is to happen can only be brought about by both.

183. Thus the action has a double significance not only because it is directed against itself as well as against the other, but also because it is indivisibly the action of one as well as of the other.

184. In this movement we see repeated the process which presented itself as the play of Forces, but repeated now in consciousness. What in that process was *for us*, is true here of the extremes themselves. The middle term is self-consciousness which splits into the extremes; and each extreme is this exchanging of its own determinateness and an absolute transition into the opposite. Although, as consciousness, it does indeed come *out of itself*, yet, though out of itself, it is at the same time kept back within itself, is *for itself*, and the self outside it, is for *it*. It is aware that it at once is, and is not, another consciousness, and equally that this other is *for itself* only when it supersedes itself as being for itself, and is for itself only in the being-for-self of the other. Each is for the other the middle term, through which each mediates itself with itself and unites with itself; and each is for itself, and for the other, an immediate being on its own account, which at the same time is such only through this mediation. They *recognize* themselves as *mutually recognizing* one another.

185. We have now to see how the process of this pure Notion of recognition, of the duplicating of self-consciousness in its oneness, appears to self-consciousness. At first, it will exhibit the side of the inequality of the two, or the splitting-up of the

middle term into the extremes which, as extremes, are opposed to one another, one being only *recognized*, the other only *recognizing*.

186. Self-consciousness is, to begin with, simple being-for-self, self-equal through the exclusion from itself of everything else. For it, its essence and absolute object is 'I'; and in this immediacy, or in this [mere] being, of its being-for-self, it is an *individual*. What is 'other' for it is an unessential, negatively characterized object. But the 'other' is also a self-consciousness; one individual is confronted by another individual. Appearing thus immediately on the scene, they are for one another like ordinary objects, *independent* shapes, individuals submerged in the being [or immediacy] of *Life*—for the object in its immediacy is here determined as Life. They are, *for each other*, shapes of consciousness which have not yet accomplished the movement of absolute abstraction, of rooting-out all immediate being, and of being merely the purely negative being of self-identical consciousness; in other words, they have not as yet exposed themselves to each other in the form of pure being-for-self, or as self-consciousnesses. Each is indeed certain of its own self, but not of the other, and therefore its own self-certainty still has no truth. For it would have truth only if its own being-for-self had confronted it as an independent object, or, what is the same thing, if the object had presented itself as this pure self-certainty. But according to the Notion of recognition this is possible only when each is for the other what the other is for it, only when each in its own self through its own action, and again through the action of the other, achieves this pure abstraction of being-for-self.

187. The presentation of itself, however, as the pure abstraction of self-consciousness consists in showing itself as the pure negation of its objective mode, or in showing that it is not attached to any specific *existence*, not to the individuality common to existence as such, that it is not attached to life. This presentation is a twofold action: action on the part of the other, and action on its own part. In so far as it is the action of the *other*, each seeks the death of the other. But in doing so, the second kind of action, action on its own part, is also involved; for the former involves the staking of its own life. Thus the relation of the two self-conscious individuals is such that they prove

themselves and each other through a life-and-death struggle. They must engage in this struggle, for they must raise their certainty of being *for themselves* to truth, both in the case of the other and in their own case. And it is only through staking one's life that freedom is won; only thus is it proved that for self-consciousness, its essential being is not [just] being, not the *immediate* form in which it appears, not its submergence in the expanse of life, but rather that there is nothing present in it which could not be regarded as a vanishing moment, that it is only pure *being-for-self*. The individual who has not risked his life may well be recognized as a *person*, but he has not attained to the truth of this recognition as an independent self-consciousness. Similarly, just as each stakes his own life, so each must seek the other's death, for it values the other no more than itself; its essential being is present to it in the form of an 'other', it is outside of itself and must rid itself of its self-externality. The other is an *immediate* consciousness entangled in a variety of relationships, and it must regard its otherness as a pure being-for-self or as an absolute negation.

188. This trial by death, however, does away with the truth which was supposed to issue from it, and so, too, with the certainty of self generally. For just as life is the *natural* setting of consciousness, independence without absolute negativity, so death is the *natural* negation of consciousness, negation without independence, which thus remains without the required significance of recognition. Death certainly shows that each staked his life and held it of no account, both in himself and in the other; but that is not for those who survived this struggle. They put an end to their consciousness in its alien setting of natural existence, that is to say, they put an end to themselves, and are done away with as *extremes* wanting to be *for themselves*, or to have an existence of their own. But with this there vanishes from their interplay the essential moment of splitting into extremes with opposite characteristics; and the middle term collapses into a lifeless unity which is split into lifeless, merely immediate, unopposed extremes; and the two do not reciprocally give and receive one another back from each other consciously, but leave each other free only indifferently, like things. Their act is an abstract negation, not the negation coming from consciousness, which supersedes in such a way as to preserve

and maintain what is superseded, and consequently survives its own supersession.

189. In this experience, self-consciousness learns that life is as essential to it as pure self-consciousness. In immediate self-consciousness the simple 'I' is absolute mediation, and has as its essential moment lasting independence. The dissolution of that simple unity is the result of the first experience; through this there is posited a pure self-consciousness, and a consciousness which is not purely for itself but for another, i.e. is a merely *immediate* consciousness, or consciousness in the form of *thinghood*. Both moments are essential. Since to begin with they are unequal and opposed, and their reflection into a unity has not yet been achieved, they exist as two opposed shapes of consciousness; one is the independent consciousness whose essential nature is to be for itself, the other is the dependent consciousness whose essential nature is simply to live or to be for another. The former is lord, the other is bondsman.

190. The lord is the consciousness that exists *for itself*, but no longer merely the Notion of such a consciousness. Rather, it is a consciousness existing *for itself* which is mediated with itself through another consciousness, i.e. through a consciousness whose nature it is to be bound up with an existence that is independent, or thinghood in general. The lord puts himself into relation with both of these moments, to a *thing* as such, the object of desire, and to the consciousness for which thinghood is the essential characteristic. And since he is (a) *qua* the Notion of self-consciousness an immediate relation of *being-for-self*, but (b) is now at the same time mediation, or a being-for-self which is for itself only through another, he is related (a) immediately to both, and (b) mediately to each through the other. The lord relates himself mediately to the bondsman through a being [a thing] that is independent, for it is just this which holds the bondsman in bondage; it is his chain from which he could not break free in the struggle, thus proving himself to be dependent, to possess his independence in thinghood. But the lord is the power over this thing, for he proved in the struggle that it is something merely negative; since he is the power over this thing and this again is the power over the other [the bondsman], it follows that he holds the other in subjection. Equally, the lord relates himself mediately to the thing through

the bondsman; the bondsman, *qua* self-consciousness in general, also relates himself negatively to the thing, and takes away its independence; but at the same time the thing is independent *vis-à-vis* the bondsman, whose negating of it, therefore, cannot go the length of being altogether done with it to the point of annihilation; in other words, he only *works* on it. For the lord, on the other hand, the *immediate* relation becomes through this mediation the sheer negation of the thing, or the enjoyment of it. What desire failed to achieve, he succeeds in doing, viz. to have done with the thing altogether, and to achieve satisfaction in the enjoyment of it. Desire failed to do this because of the thing's independence; but the lord, who has interposed the bondsman between it and himself, takes to himself only the dependent aspect of the thing and has the pure enjoyment of it. The aspect of its independence he leaves to the bondsman, who works on it.

191. In both of these moments the lord achieves his recognition through another consciousness; for in them, that other consciousness is expressly something unessential, both by its working on the thing, and by its dependence on a specific existence. In neither case can it be lord over the being of the thing and achieve absolute negation of it. Here, therefore, is present this moment of recognition, viz. that the other consciousness sets aside its own being-for-self, and in so doing itself does what the first does to it. Similarly, the other moment too is present, that this action of the second is the first's own action; for what the bondsman does is really the action of the lord. The latter's essential nature is to exist only for himself; he is the sheer negative power for whom the thing is nothing. Thus he is the pure, essential action in this relationship, while the action of the bondsman is impure and unessential. But for recognition proper the moment is lacking, that what the lord does to the other he also does to himself, and what the bondsman does to himself he should also do to the other. The outcome is a recognition that is one-sided and unequal.

192. In this recognition the unessential consciousness is for the lord the object, which constitutes the *truth* of his certainty of himself. But it is clear that this object does not correspond to its Notion, but rather that the object in which the lord has achieved his lordship has in reality turned out to be something

quite different from an independent consciousness. What now really confronts him is not an independent consciousness, but a dependent one. He is, therefore, not certain of *being-for-self* as the truth of himself. On the contrary, his truth is in reality the unessential consciousness and its unessential action.

193. The *truth* of the independent consciousness is accordingly the servile consciousness of the bondsman. This, it is true, appears at first *outside* of itself and not as the truth of self-consciousness. But just as lordship showed that its essential nature is the reverse of what it wants to be, so too servitude in its consummation will really turn into the opposite of what it immediately is; as a consciousness forced back into itself, it will withdraw into itself and be transformed into a truly independent consciousness.

194. We have seen what servitude is only in relation to lordship. But it is a self-consciousness, and we have now to consider what as such it is in and for itself. To begin with, servitude has the lord for its essential reality; hence the *truth* for it is the independent consciousness that is *for itself*. However, servitude is not yet aware that this truth is implicit in it. But it does in fact contain within itself this truth of pure negativity and being-for-self, for it has experienced this its own essential nature. For this consciousness has been fearful, not of this or that particular thing or just at odd moments, but its whole being has been seized with dread. In that experience it has been quite unmanned, has trembled in every fibre of its being, and everything solid and stable has been shaken to its foundations. But this pure universal movement, the absolute melting-away of everything stable, is the simple, essential nature of self-consciousness, absolute negativity, *pure being-for-self*, which consequently is *implicit* in this consciousness. This moment of pure being-for-self is also *explicit* for the bondsman, for in the lord it exists for him as his *object*. Furthermore, his consciousness is not this dissolution of everything stable merely in principle; in his service he *actually* brings this about. Through his service he rids himself of his attachment to natural existence in every single detail; and gets rid of it by working on it.

195. However, the feeling of absolute power both in general, and in the particular form of service, is only implicitly this dissolution, and although the fear of the lord is indeed the begin-

ning of wisdom, consciousness is not therein aware that it is a being-for-self. Through work, however, the bondsman becomes conscious of what he truly is. In the moment which corresponds to desire in the lord's consciousness, it did seem that the aspect of unessential relation to the thing fell to the lot of the bondsman, since in that relation the thing retained its independence. Desire has reserved to itself the pure negating of the object and thereby its unalloyed feeling of self. But that is the reason why this satisfaction is itself only a fleeting one, for it lacks the side of objectivity and permanence. Work, on the other hand, is desire held in check, fleetingness staved off; in other words, work forms and shapes the thing. The negative relation to the object becomes its *form* and something *permanent*, because it is precisely for the worker that the object has independence. This *negative* middle term or the formative *activity* is at the same time the individuality or pure being-for-self of consciousness which now, in the work outside of it, acquires an element of permanence. It is in this way, therefore, that consciousness, *qua* worker, comes to see in the independent being [of the object] its *own* independence.

196. But the formative activity has not only this positive significance that in it the pure being-for-self of the servile consciousness acquires an existence; it also has, in contrast with its first moment, the negative significance of *fear*. For, in fashioning the thing, the bondsman's own negativity, his being-for-self, becomes an object for him only through his setting at nought the existing *shape* confronting him. But this objective *negative* moment is none other than the alien being before which it has trembled. Now, however, he destroys this alien negative moment, posits *himself* as a negative in the permanent order of things, and thereby becomes *for himself*, someone existing on his own account. In the lord, the being-for-self is an 'other' for the bondsman, or is only *for* him [i.e. is not his own]; in fear, the being-for-self is present in the bondsman himself; in fashioning the thing, he becomes aware that being-for-self belongs to *him*, that he himself exists essentially and actually in his own right. The shape does not become something other than himself through being made external to him; for it is precisely this shape that is his pure being-for-self, which in this externality is seen by him to be the truth. Through this rediscovery of himself by

himself, the bondsman realizes that it is precisely in his work wherein he seemed to have only an alienated existence that he acquires a mind of his own. For this reflection, the two moments of fear and service as such, as also that of formative activity, are necessary, both being at the same time in a universal mode. Without the discipline of service and obedience, fear remains at the formal stage, and does not extend to the known real world of existence. Without the formative activity, fear remains inward and mute, and consciousness does not become explicitly *for itself*. If consciousness fashions the thing without that initial absolute fear, it is only an empty self-centred attitude; for its form or negativity is not negativity *per se*, and therefore its formative activity cannot give it a consciousness of itself as essential being. If it has not experienced absolute fear but only some lesser dread, the negative being has remained for it something external, its substance has not been infected by it through and through. Since the entire contents of its natural consciousness have not been jeopardized, determinate being still *in principle* attaches to it; having a 'mind of one's own' is self-will, a freedom which is still enmeshed in servitude. Just as little as the pure form can become essential being for it, just as little is that form, regarded as extended to the particular, a universal formative activity, an absolute Notion; rather it is a skill which is master over some things, but not over the universal power and the whole of objective being.

FREEDOM OF SELF-CONSCIOUSNESS:

B. STOICISM, SCEPTICISM, AND THE UNHAPPY CONSCIOUSNESS

197. For the independent self-consciousness, it is only the pure abstraction of the 'I' that is its essential nature, and, when it does develop its own differences, this differentiation does not become a nature that is objective and intrinsic to it. Thus this self-consciousness does not become an 'I' that in its simplicity is genuinely self-differentiating, or that in this absolute differentiation remains identical with itself. On the other hand, the consciousness that is forced back into itself becomes, in its

formative activity, its own object in the form of the thing it has fashioned, and at the same time sees in the lord a consciousness that exists as a being-for-self. But for the subservient consciousness as such, these two moments—*itself* as an independent object, and this object as a mode of consciousness, and hence its own essential nature—fall apart. Since, however, the form and the being-for-self are *for us*, or *in themselves*, the same, and since in the Notion of independent consciousness the *intrinsic* being is consciousness, the moment of intrinsic being or thinghood which received its form in being fashioned is no other substance than consciousness. We are in the presence of self-consciousness in a new shape, a consciousness which, as the infinitude of consciousness or as its own pure movement, is aware of itself as essential being, a being which *thinks* or is a free self-consciousness. For *to think* does not mean to be an *abstract* 'I', but an 'I' which has at the same time the significance of *intrinsic* being, of having itself for object, or of relating itself to objective being in such a way that its significance is the *being-for-self* of the consciousness for which it is [an object]. For in *thinking*, the object does not present itself in picture-thoughts but in *Notions*, i.e. in a distinct *being-in-itself* or intrinsic being, consciousness being immediately aware that this is not anything distinct from itself. What is pictured or figuratively conceived, what *immediately is*, has, as such, the form of being something other than consciousness; but a Notion is also something that *immediately is*, and this distinction, in so far as it is present in consciousness itself, is its determinate content; but since this content is at the same time a content grasped *in thought*, consciousness remains *immediately* aware of its unity with this determinate and distinct being, not, as in the case of a picture-thought, where consciousness still has specially to bear in mind that this is *its* picture-thought; on the contrary, the Notion is for me straightway *my* Notion. In thinking, I *am free*, because I am not in an *other*, but remain simply and solely in communion with myself, and the object, which is for me the *essential* being, is in undivided unity my being-for-myself; and my activity in conceptual thinking is a movement within myself. It is essential, however, in thus characterizing this shape of self-consciousness to bear firmly in mind that it is *thinking* consciousness *in general*, that its object is an *immediate* unity of *being-in-itself* and *being-for-itself*.

The selfsame consciousness that repels itself from itself becomes aware of itself as the element of *being-in-itself*; but at first it knows itself to be this element only as a universal mode of being in general, not as it exists objectively in the development and process of its manifold being.

198. This freedom of self-consciousness when it appeared as a conscious manifestation in the history of Spirit has, as we know, been called Stoicism. Its principle is that consciousness is a being that *thinks*, and that consciousness holds something to be essentially important, or true and good only in so far as it *thinks* it to be such.

199. The manifold self-differentiating expanse of life, with all its detail and complexity, is the object on which desire and work operate. This manifold activity has now contracted into the simple positing of differences in the pure movement of thinking. Essential importance no longer attaches to the difference as a specific *thing*, or as consciousness of a specific *natural existence*, as a feeling, or as desire and its object, whether this is posited by myself or by an alien consciousness. What alone has importance is the difference posited by *thought*, or the difference which from the very first is not distinct from myself. This consciousness accordingly has a negative attitude towards the lord and bondsman relationship. As lord, it does not have its truth in the bondsman, nor as bondsman is its truth in the lord's will and in his service; on the contrary, whether on the throne or in chains, in the utter dependence of its individual existence, its aim is to be free, and to maintain that lifeless indifference which steadfastly withdraws from the bustle of existence, alike from being active as passive, into the simple essentiality of thought. Self-will is the freedom which entrenches itself in some particularity and is still in bondage, while Stoicism is the freedom which always comes directly out of bondage and returns into the pure universality of thought. As a universal form of the World-Spirit, Stoicism could only appear on the scene in a time of universal fear and bondage, but also a time of universal culture which had raised itself to the level of thought.

200. Now, it is true that for this self-consciousness the essence is neither an other than itself, nor the pure abstraction of the 'I', but an 'I' which has the otherness within itself, though in

the form of *thought*, so that in its otherness it has directly
returned into itself. Yet at the same time this its essence is only
an *abstract* essence. The freedom of self-consciousness is *indifferent* to natural existence and has therefore *let this equally go
free*: the *reflection* is a *twofold one*. Freedom in thought has only
pure thought as its truth, a truth lacking the fullness of life. Hence
freedom in thought, too, is only the Notion of freedom, not the
living reality of freedom itself. For the essence of that freedom
is at first only thinking in general, the form as such [of thought],
which has turned away from the independence of things and
returned into itself. But since individuality in its activity should
show itself to be alive, or in its thinking should grasp the living
world as a system of thought, there would have to be present
in *thought itself* a *content* for that individuality, in the one case
a content of what is good, and in the other of what is true, in
order that what is an object for consciousness should contain
no other ingredient whatever except the Notion which is the
essence. But here the Notion as an abstraction cuts itself off from
the multiplicity of things, and thus has no content *in its own
self* but one that is *given* to it. Consciousness does indeed destroy
the content as an alien *immediacy* [*Sein*] when it *thinks* it; but
the Notion is a *determinate* Notion, and this determinateness of
the Notion is the alien element which it has within it. Stoicism,
therefore, was perplexed when it was asked for what was called
a 'criterion of truth as such', i.e. strictly speaking, for a *content*
of thought itself. To the question, *What* is good and true, it again
gave for answer the *contentless* thought: The True and the Good
shall consist in reasonableness. But this self-identity of thought
is again only the pure form in which nothing is determined.
The True and the Good, wisdom and virtue, the general terms
beyond which Stoicism cannot get, are therefore in a general
way no doubt uplifting, but since they cannot in fact produce
any expansion of the content, they soon become tedious.

201. This thinking consciousness as determined in the form
of abstract freedom is thus only the incomplete negation of
otherness. *Withdrawn* from existence only into itself, it has not
there achieved its consummation as absolute negation of that
existence. The content, it is true, only counts as thought, but
also as thought that is determinate and at the same time
determinateness as such.

202. *Scepticism* is the realization of that of which Stoicism was only the Notion, and is the actual experience of what the freedom of thought is. This is *in itself* the negative and must exhibit itself as such. With the reflection of self-consciousness into the simple thought of itself, the independent existence or permanent determinateness that stood over against that reflection has, as a matter of fact, fallen outside of the infinitude of thought. In Scepticism, now, the wholly unessential and non-independent character of this 'other' becomes explicit *for consciousness*; the [abstract] thought becomes the concrete thinking which annihilates the being of the world in all its manifold determinateness, and the negativity of free self-consciousness comes to know itself in the many and varied forms of life as a real negativity.

It is clear that just as Stoicism corresponds to the *Notion* of the *independent* consciousness which appeared as the lord and bondsman relationship, so Scepticism corresponds to its *realization* as a negative attitude towards otherness, to desire and work. But although desire and work were unable to effect the negation for self-consciousness, this polemical bearing towards the manifold independence of things will, on the other hand, be successful, because it turns against them as a free self-consciousness that is already complete in its own self; more specifically, because it is *thinking*, or is in its own self infinite, and in this infinitude the independent things in their differences from one another are for it only vanishing magnitudes. The differences, which in the pure thinking of self-consciousness are only the abstraction of differences, here become the *entirety* of the differences, and the whole of differentiated being becomes a difference of self-consciousness.

203. Thus the foregoing has defined the nature of the activity of scepticism as such, and the way in which it operates. It exhibits the *dialectical movement* which Sense-certainty, Perception, and the Understanding each is; as also the unessential character of what, in the relationship of lord and bondsman, and for abstract thinking itself, is held to be a *determinate* element. That relationship at the same time embraces a *specific mode* in which ethical laws, too, are present as sovereign commands. The determinations in abstract thinking, however, are scientific Notions in which [formal] contentless thinking

spreads itself, attaching the Notion in fact in a merely external way to the being constituting its content, and which for it is independent, and holding as valid only *determinate* Notions, even though these are only pure abstractions.

204. Dialectic as a negative movement, just as it immediately *is*, at first appears to consciousness as something which has it at its mercy, and which does not have its source in consciousness itself. As Scepticism, on the other hand, it is a moment of self-consciousness, to which it does not *happen* that its truth and reality vanish without its knowing how, but which, in the certainty of its freedom, *makes* this 'other' which claims to be real, vanish. What Scepticism causes to vanish is not only objective reality as such, but its own relationship to it, in which the 'other' is held to be objective and is established as such, and hence, too, its *perceiving*, along with firmly securing what it is in danger of losing, viz. *sophistry*, and the truth it has itself determined and established. Through this self-conscious negation it procures for its own self the certainty of its freedom, generates the experience of that freedom, and thereby raises it to truth. What vanishes is the determinate element, or the moment of difference, which, whatever its mode of being and whatever its source, sets itself up as something fixed and immutable. It contains no permanent element, and must vanish before thought, because the 'different' is just this, not to be in possession of itself, but to have its essential being only in an other. Thinking, however, is the insight into this nature of the 'different', it is the negative essence, as simple.

205. The sceptical self-consciousness thus experiences in the flux of all that would stand secure before it its own freedom as given and preserved by itself. It is aware of this stoical indifference of a thinking which thinks itself, the unchanging and genuine certainty of itself. This self-certainty does not issue from something alien, whose complex development was deposited within it, a result which would leave behind it the process of its coming to be. On the contrary, consciousness itself is the *absolute dialectical unrest*, this medley of sensuous and intellectual representations whose differences coincide, and whose identity is equally again dissolved, for it is itself determinateness as contrasted with the non-identical. But it is just in this process that this consciousness, instead of being self-identical, is in fact noth-

ing but a purely casual, confused medley, the dizziness of a perpetually self-engendered disorder. It is itself aware of this; for
itself maintains and creates this restless confusion. Hence it also
admits to it, it owns to being a wholly contingent, single, and
separate consciousness—a consciousness which is *empirical*,
which takes its guidance from what has no reality for it, which
obeys what is for it not an *essential* being, which does those things
and brings to realization what it knows has no truth for it. But
equally, while it takes itself in this way to be a single and separate, contingent and, in fact, animal life, and a *lost* self-consciousness, it also, on the contrary, converts itself again into a
consciousness that is universal and self-identical; for it is the
negativity of all singularity and all difference. From this self-
identity, or within its own self, it falls back again into the former
contingency and confusion, for this same spontaneous negativity has to do solely with what is single and separate, and
occupies itself with what is contingent. This consciousness is
therefore the unconscious, thoughtless rambling which passes
back and forth from the one extreme of self-identical self-consciousness to the other extreme of the contingent consciousness
that is both bewildered and bewildering. It does not itself bring
these two thoughts of itself together. At one time it recognizes
that its freedom lies in rising above all the confusion and contingency of existence, and at another time equally admits to a
relapse into occupying itself with what is unessential. It lets the
unessential content in its thinking vanish; but just in doing so
it is the consciousness of something unessential. It pronounces
an absolute vanishing, but the pronouncement *is*, and this consciousness is the vanishing that is pronounced. It affirms the
nullity of seeing, hearing, etc., yet it is itself seeing, hearing,
etc. It affirms the nullity of ethical principles, and lets its conduct be governed by these very principles. Its deeds and its
words always belie one another and equally it has itself the
doubly contradictory consciousness of unchangeableness and
sameness, and of utter contingency and non-identity with itself.
But it keeps the poles of this its self-contradiction apart, and
adopts the same attitude to it as it does in its purely negative
activity in general. Point out likeness or identity to it, and it
will point out unlikeness or non-identity; and when it is now
confronted with what it has just asserted, it turns round and

points out likeness or identity. Its talk is in fact like the squabbling of self-willed children, one of whom says A if the other says B, and in turn says B if the other says A, and who by contradicting *themselves* buy for themselves the pleasure of continually contradicting *one another*.

206. In Scepticism, consciousness truly experiences itself as internally contradictory. From this experience emerges a *new form* of consciousness which brings together the two thoughts which Scepticism holds apart. Scepticism's lack of thought about itself must vanish, because it is in fact *one* consciousness which contains within itself these two modes. This new form is, therefore, one which *knows* that it is the dual consciousness of itself, as self-liberating, unchangeable, and self-identical, and as self-bewildering and self-perverting, and it is the awareness of this self-contradictory nature of itself.

In Stoicism, self-consciousness is the simple freedom of itself. In Scepticism, this freedom becomes a reality, negates the other side of determinate existence, but really duplicates *itself*, and now knows itself to be a duality. Consequently, the duplication which formerly was divided between two individuals, the lord and the bondsman, is now lodged in one. The duplication of self-consciousness within itself, which is essential in the Notion of Spirit, is thus here before us, but not yet in its unity: the *Unhappy Consciousness* is the consciousness of self as a dual-natured, merely contradictory being.

207. This *unhappy, inwardly disrupted* consciousness, since its essentially contradictory nature is for it a *single* consciousness, must for ever have present in the one consciousness the other also; and thus it is driven out of each in turn in the very moment when it imagines it has successfully attained to a peaceful unity with the other. Its true return into itself, or its reconciliation with itself will, however, display the Notion of Spirit that has become a living Spirit, and has achieved an actual existence, because it already possesses as a single undivided consciousness a dual nature. The Unhappy Consciousness itself *is* the gazing of one self-consciousness into another, and itself *is* both, and the unity of both is also its essential nature. But it is not as yet explicitly aware that this is its essential nature, or that it is the unity of both.

208. Since it is, to begin with, only the *immediate unity* of the

two and so takes them to be, not the same, but opposites, one
of them, viz. the simple Unchangeable, it takes to be the *essential*
Being; but the other, the protean Changeable, it takes to be
the unessential. The two are, for the Unhappy Consciousness,
alien to one another; and because it is itself the consciousness
of this contradiction, it identifies itself with the changeable consciousness, and takes itself to be the unessential Being. But as
consciousness of unchangeableness, or of simple essential Being,
it must at the same time set about freeing itself from the unessential, i.e. from itself. For though it indeed takes *itself* to be merely
the Changeable, and the Unchangeable is, for it, an alien Being,
yet it is *itself* a simple, hence unchangeable, consciousness, and
hence is aware that this consciousness is its own essence,
although in such a way that again it does not *itself* take
the essence to be its own. The attitude it assigns to both
cannot therefore be one of mutual indifference, i.e. it cannot
itself be indifferent towards the Unchangeable; rather, it
is itself directly both of them, and the relation of the two
is for it a relation of essential being to the unessential, so that
this latter has to be set aside; but since for it both are
equally essential and contradictory, it is merely the contradictory movement in which one opposite does not come to rest
in *its* opposite, but in it only produces itself afresh as an
opposite.

209. Here, then, we have a struggle against an enemy, to
vanquish whom is really to suffer defeat, where victory in one
consciousness is really lost in its opposite. Consciousness of life,
of its existence and activity, is only an agonizing over this existence and activity, for therein it is conscious that its essence is
only its opposite, is conscious only of its own nothingness. Raising itself out of this consciousness it goes over into the Unchangeable; but this elevation is itself this same consciousness.
It is, therefore, directly consciousness of the opposite, viz. of
itself as a particular individual. The Unchangeable that enters
into consciousness is through this very fact at the same time
affected by individuality, and is only present with the latter;
individuality, instead of having been extinguished in the consciousness of the Unchangeable, only continues to arise therefrom.

210. In this movement, however, consciousness experiences

just this emergence of individuality in the Unchangeable, and of the Unchangeable in individuality. Consciousness becomes aware of individuality in general in the Unchangeable, and at the same time of its *own* individuality in the latter. For the truth of this movement is just the *oneness* of this dual consciousness. This unity, however, in the first instance, becomes for it one in which the *difference* of both is still the dominant feature. Thus there exist for consciousness three different ways in which individuality is linked with the Unchangeable. Firstly, it again appears to itself as opposed to the Unchangeable, and is thrown back to the beginning of the struggle which is throughout the element in which the whole relationship subsists. Secondly, consciousness learns that individuality belongs to the Unchangeable itself, so that it assumes the form of individuality into which the entire mode of existence passes. Thirdly, it finds its own self as this particular individual in the Unchangeable. The first Unchangeable it knows only as the alien Being who passes judgement on the particular individual; since, secondly, the Unchangeable is a form of individuality like itself, consciousness becomes, thirdly, Spirit, and experiences the joy of finding itself therein, and becomes aware of the reconciliation of its individuality with the universal.

211. What is set forth here as the mode and relationship of the Unchangeable has appeared as the *experience* through which the divided self-consciousness passes in its wretchedness. Now, this experience, it is true, is not *its own one-sided* movement, for it is itself the unchangeable consciousness, and this, consequently, is at the same time a particular individual consciousness too; and the movement is just as much a movement of the unchangeable consciousness, which makes its appearance in that movement as much as the other. For the movement runs through these moments: first, the Unchangeable is opposed to individuality in general; then, being itself an individual, it is opposed to another individual; and finally, it is one with it. But this reflection, so far as it is made by us, is here premature, for what has come before for us so far is only unchangeableness as unchangeableness of *consciousness*, which for that reason is not genuine unchangeableness, but one still burdened with an antithesis, not the Unchangeable in and for itself; we do not know, therefore, how the latter will behave. Here, we know only that

for consciousness, which is our object here, the determinations indicated above appear in the Unchangeable.

212. For this reason, therefore, the unchangeable *consciousness* also retains in its very form the basic character of dividedness and being-for-self in contrast to the individual consciousness. Consequently, for the latter, the fact that the Unchangeable receives the form of individuality is only a *contingent* happening; just as it also merely *finds itself* opposed to it, so that the relation seems to result from its own nature. That, finally, it does *find itself* in the Unchangeable, appears to it to be brought about partly, no doubt, by itself, or to take place because it is itself an individual; but this unity, both as regards its origin and the fact that it *is*, appears partly due to the Unchangeable; and the antithesis persists within this unity itself. In fact, through the Unchangeable's assuming a definite form, the moment of the beyond not only persists, but really is more firmly established; for if the beyond seems to have been brought closer to the individual consciousness through the form of an actuality that is individual, it henceforth on the other hand confronts him as an opaque sensuous *unit* with all the obstinacy of what is *actual*. The hope of becoming one with it must remain a hope, i.e. without fulfilment and present fruition, for between the hope and its fulfilment there stands precisely the absolute contingency or inflexible indifference which lies in the very assumption of definite form, which was the ground of hope. By the nature of this *immediately present unit*, through the actual existence in which it has clothed itself, it necessarily follows that in the world of time it has vanished, and that in space it had a remote existence and remains utterly remote.

213. If at first the mere Notion of the divided consciousness was characterized by the effort to set aside its particular individuality and to become the unchangeable consciousness, its efforts from now on are directed rather to setting aside its relation with the pure *formless* Unchangeable, and to coming into relation only with the Unchangeable in its embodied or incarnate form. For the *oneness* of the particular individual with the Unchangeable is henceforth the essence and the object for this consciousness, just as in the mere Notion of it the formless abstract Unchangeable was the essential object; and the relation of this absolute dividedness of the Notion is now what it

has to turn away from. The initially external relation to the
incarnate Unchangeable as an alien reality has to be transformed into a relation in which it becomes absolutely one with
it.

214. The movement in which the unessential consciousness
strives to attain this oneness is itself threefold in accordance with
the threefold relation this consciousness will have with its incarnate beyond: first, as pure consciousness; second, as a particular individual who approaches the actual world in the forms
of desire and work; and third, as consciousness that is aware
of its own being-for-self. We have now to see how these three
modes of its being are present and determined in that general
relationship.

215. At first, then, this consciousness being taken as *pure consciousness*, the incarnate Unchangeable when it is an object for
pure consciousness seems to be present in its own proper nature.
But this, its own proper nature, has not yet come into existence,
as we have already remarked. In order that it should appear
in consciousness in its own proper nature, this would certainly
have to come about from *its* side, rather than from the side of
consciousness. Thus its presence here is, at first, only one-sidedly
due to consciousness, and just for that reason is not perfect and
genuine, but remains burdened with imperfection or an antithesis.

216. But although the Unhappy Consciousness does not
have the enjoyment of this presence, it has at the same time
advanced beyond pure thinking in so far as this is the abstract
thinking of Stoicism which turns its back on individuality altogether, and beyond the merely unsettled thinking of Scepticism—which is in fact only individuality in the form of an unconscious contradiction and ceaseless movement. It has
advanced beyond both of these; it brings and holds together
pure thinking and particular individuality, but has not yet risen
to that thinking where consciousness as a particular individuality is reconciled with pure thought itself. It occupies rather
this intermediate position where abstract thinking is in contact
with the individuality of consciousness *qua* individuality. The
Unhappy Consciousness *is* this contact; it is the unity of pure
thinking and individuality; also it *knows* itself to be this thinking
individuality or pure thinking, and knows the Unchangeable

itself essentially as an individuality. But what it does *not* know is that this its object, the Unchangeable, which it knows essentially in the form of individuality, is *its own self*, is itself the individuality of consciousness.

217. In this first mode, therefore, where we consider it as pure consciousness, it does not *relate* itself as a *thinking* consciousness to its object, but, though it is indeed *in itself*, or implicitly, a pure thinking individuality, and its object is just this pure thinking (although the *relation of one to the other is not itself pure thinking*), it is only a movement *towards* thinking, and so is devotion. Its thinking as such is no more than the chaotic jingling of bells, or a mist of warm incense, a musical thinking that does not get as far as the Notion, which would be the sole, immanent objective mode of thought. This infinite, pure inner feeling does indeed come into possession of its object; but this does not make its appearance in conceptual form, not as something [speculatively] comprehended, and appears therefore as something alien. What we have here, then, is the inward movement of the pure heart which *feels* itself, but itself as agonizingly self-divided, the movement of an infinite yearning which is certain that its essence is such a pure heart, a pure *thinking* which *thinks* of itself as a *particular individuality*, certain of being known and recognized by this object, precisely because the latter thinks of itself as an individuality. At the same time, however, this essence is the unattainable *beyond* which, in being laid hold of, flees, or rather has already flown. It has already flown; for it is in part the Unchangeable which thinks of itself as an individuality, and consciousness therefore directly attains in it its own self—*its own self*, but as the antithesis of the Unchangeable; instead of laying hold of the essence, it only *feels* it and has fallen back into itself. Since, in attaining itself, consciousness is unable to get away from itself as this antithesis to the Unchangeable, it has, instead of laying hold of the essence, only laid hold of what is unessential. Just as, on the one hand, when striving to find itself in the essence it takes hold only of its own separate existence, so on the other hand it cannot lay hold of the 'other' as an *individual* or as an *actual* Being. Where that 'other' is sought, it cannot be found, for it is supposed to be just a *beyond*, something that can *not* be found. When sought as a particular individual, it is not a *universal* individuality in the form of thought, not a

Notion, but an individual in the form of an object, or an *actual* individual; an object of immediate sense-certainty, and for that very reason only something that has already vanished. Consciousness, therefore, can only find as a present reality the *grave* of its life. But because this grave is itself an *actual existence* and it is contrary to the nature of what actually exists to afford a lasting possession, the presence of that grave, too, is merely the struggle of an enterprise doomed to failure. But having learned from experience that *the grave* of its *actual* unchangeable Being has *no actuality*, that the *vanished individuality*, because it has vanished, is not the true individuality, consciousness will abandon its quest for the unchangeable individuality as an *actual* existence, or will stop trying to hold on to what has vanished. Only then is it capable of finding individuality in its genuine or universal form.

218. But, in the first instance, *the return of the feeling heart into itself* is to be taken to mean that it has an *actual* existence as an *individual*. It is the *pure heart* which *for us* or *in itself* has found itself and is inwardly satiated, for although for itself in its feeling the essential Being is separated from it, yet this feeling is, in itself, a feeling of *self*; it has felt the object of its pure feeling and this object is itself. Thus it comes forward here as self-feeling, or as an actual consciousness existing on its own account. In this return into self there comes to view its second relationship, that of desire and work in which consciousness finds confirmation of that inner certainty of itself which we know it has attained, by overcoming and enjoying the existence alien to it, viz. existence in the form of independent things. But the Unhappy Consciousness merely *finds* itself *desiring* and *working*; it is not aware that to find itself active in this way implies that it is in fact certain of itself, and that its feeling of the alien existence is this self-feeling. Since it is not explicitly aware of this certainty, its inner life really remains a still incomplete self-certainty; that confirmation which it would receive through work and enjoyment is therefore equally incomplete; in other words, it must itself set at nought this confirmation so that it may indeed find in it confirmation, but only confirmation of what it is *for itself*, viz. of its dividedness.

219. The world of actuality to which desire and work are directed is no longer for this consciousness something *intrinsically*

null, something merely to be set aside and consumed, but something like that consciousness itself, an *actuality broken in two*, which is only from one aspect intrinsically null, but from another aspect is also a sanctified *world;* it is the form of the Unchangeable, for this has retained individuality, and because, as the Unchangeable, it is a Universal, its individuality has in general the significance of all actuality.

220. If consciousness were aware of being an independent consciousness, and the world of actuality were for it an absolute nullity, then in work and enjoyment it would attain to a feeling of its independence, since the world of actuality would be nullified by itself. But since this actuality is for consciousness the form of the Unchangeable, it is unable of itself to nullify it. On the contrary, since it does succeed in setting it at nought and enjoying it, this comes about through the Unchangeable's itself having *surrendered* its embodied form, and having *relinquished* it for the enjoyment of consciousness. Consciousness, on its part, *likewise* makes its appearance as an actuality, but also as divided within itself, and in its work and enjoyment this dividedness displays itself as breaking up into a *relation* to the world of *actuality* or a being which is *for itself,* and into a being that is *in itself.* That relation to actuality is the *changing* of it or *working on it,* the being-for-self which belongs to the *individual* consciousness as such. But, in this relation, it is also *in itself* or has intrinsic being; this aspect belongs to the Unchangeable beyond and consists of faculties and powers, a gift from an alien source, which the Unchangeable makes over to consciousness to make use of.

221. Accordingly, consciousness in its activity is, in the first instance, a relationship of two extremes. On one side it stands as actively present, while confronting it is a passive actuality: the two sides are in relation with one another, but both have also withdrawn into the Unchangeable and stand fast in themselves. It is, therefore, only a superficial element from each side that is involved in the moving interplay of their mutual opposition. The [passive] extreme of actuality is set aside by the active extreme; but the actuality, on its side, can only be set aside because its own unchangeable essence sets it aside, repels itself from itself, and hands over what is repelled to the active extreme. The active force appears as the *power* in which actu-

ality is dissolved; for this very reason, however, the consciousness to which the *intrinsic* or essential Being is an 'other', regards
this power which it displays in its activity to be the beyond of
itself. Instead, therefore, of returning from its activity back into
itself, and having obtained confirmation of its self-certainty,
consciousness really reflects this activity back into the other
extreme, which is thus exhibited as a pure universal, as the absolute power from which the activity started in all directions, and
which is the essence both of the self-dividing extremes as they
at first appeared, and of their interchanging relationship itself.

222. The fact that the unchangeable consciousness *renounces*
and *surrenders* its embodied form, while, on the other hand, the
particular individual consciousness *gives thanks* [for the gift], i.e.
denies itself the satisfaction of being conscious of its *independence*,
and assigns the essence of its action not to itself but to the
beyond, through these two moments of *reciprocal self-surrender*
of both parts, consciousness does, of course, gain a sense of its
unity with the Unchangeable. But this unity is at the same time
affected with division, is again broken within itself, and from
it there emerges once more the antithesis of the universal and
the individual. For though consciousness renounces the *show* of
satisfying its feeling of self, it obtains the *actual* satisfaction of
it; for it *has been* desire, work, and enjoyment; as consciousness
it has *willed*, *acted*, and *enjoyed*. Similarly, even its *giving of thanks*,
in which it acknowledges the other extreme as the essential
Being and counts itself nothing, is its *own* act which counter-
balances the action of the other extreme, and meets the self-
sacrificing beneficence with a *like* action. If the other extreme
delivers over to consciousness only the *surface* of its being, yet
consciousness *also* gives thanks; and in surrendering its own
action, i.e. its *essential* being, it really does more than the other
which only sheds a superficial element of itself. Thus the entire
movement is reflected not only in the actual desiring, working,
and enjoyment, but even in the very giving of thanks where
the reverse seems to take place, in the *extreme of individuality*.
Consciousness feels itself therein as this particular individual,
and does not let itself be deceived by its own seeming renunciation, for the truth of the matter is that it has *not* renounced itself.
What has been brought about is only the double reflection into
the two extremes; and the result is the renewed division into

the opposed consciousness of the *Unchangeable*, and the consciousness of willing, performing, and enjoying, and self-renunciation itself which *confronts* it; in other words, the consciousness of *independent individuality* in general.

223. With this appears the third relationship of the process of this consciousness, which proceeds from the second as a consciousness that has truly proved itself to be independent, by its will and its deed. In the first relationship it was merely the notion of an actual consciousness, or the inner feeling or heart which is not yet actual in action and enjoyment; the second is this actualization as an external action and enjoyment. Returned from this external activity, however, consciousness has *experienced* itself as actual and effective, or knows that it is in truth in and for itself. But here, now, is where the enemy is met with in his most characteristic form. In the struggle of the heart and emotions the individual consciousness is only a musical abstract moment. In work and enjoyment which make this unsubstantial existence a reality, it can directly forget *itself*, and the consciousness of its *own particular role* in this realization is cancelled out by the act of thankful acknowledgement. But this cancelling-out is in truth a return of consciousness into itself, and, moreover, into itself as the actuality which it knows to be true.

224. This third relationship in which this true actuality is one of the terms is the *relation* of that actuality, as a nothingness, to the universal Being. The process of this relation we have yet to consider.

225. To begin with, as regards the contradictory relation in which consciousness takes its own *reality* to be *immediately a nothingness*, its actual doing thus becomes a doing of nothing, its enjoyment a feeling of its wretchedness. Work and enjoyment thus lose all *universal content* and *significance*, for if they had any, they would have an absolute being of their own. Both withdraw into their mere particularity, which consciousness is set upon reducing to nothingness. Consciousness is aware of itself as *this actual individual* in the animal functions. These are no longer performed naturally and without embarrassment, as matters trifling in themselves which cannot possess any importance or essential significance for Spirit; instead, since it is in them that the enemy reveals himself in his characteristic shape, they are

rather the object of serious endeavour, and become precisely matters of the utmost importance. This enemy, however, renews himself in his defeat, and consciousness, in fixing its attention on him, far from freeing itself from him, really remains for ever in contact with him, and for ever sees itself as defiled; and, since at the same time this object of its efforts, instead of being something essential, is of the meanest character, instead of being a universal, is the merest particular, we have here only a personality confined to its own self and its own petty actions, a personality brooding over itself, as wretched as it is impoverished.

226. But to both of these moments, the feeling of its wretchedness and the poverty of its actions, is linked the consciousness of its unity with the Unchangeable. For the attempted direct destruction of what it actually is is *mediated* by the thought of the Unchangeable, and takes place in this *relation* to it. The *mediated* relation constitutes the essence of the negative movement in which consciousness turns against its particular individuality, but which, *qua relation*, is *in itself positive*, and will bring consciousness itself to an awareness of its *unity* with the Unchangeable.

227. This mediated relation is thus a syllogism in which the individuality, initially fixed in its antithesis to the *in-itself*, is united with this other extreme only through a third term. Through this middle term the one extreme, the Unchangeable, is brought into relation with the unessential consciousness, which equally is brought into relation with the Unchangeable only through this middle term; thus this middle term is one which presents the two extremes to one another, and ministers to each in its dealings with the other. This middle term is itself a conscious Being [the mediator], for it is an action which mediates consciousness as such; the content of this action is the extinction of its particular individuality which consciousness is undertaking.

228. In the mediator, then, this consciousness frees itself from action and enjoyment so far as they are regarded as its own. As a separate, independent extreme, it rejects the essence of its will, and casts upon the mediator or minister [priest] its own freedom of decision, and herewith the responsibility for its own action. This mediator, having a direct relationship with the un-

changeable Being, ministers by giving advice on what is right. The action, since it follows upon the decision of someone else, ceases, as regards the doing or the *willing* of it, to be its own. But there is still left to the unessential consciousness the *objective* aspect, viz. the fruit of its labour, and its enjoyment. These, therefore, it rejects as well, and just as it renounces its *will*, so it renounces the *actuality* it received in work and enjoyment. It renounces them, partly as identified with the truth it has attained regarding its own self-conscious *independence*—inasmuch as what it does is foreign to it, a thinking and speaking of what is meaningless to it; partly, as identified with *external possessions*—when it gives away part of what it has acquired through work; and partly, also, as identified with the enjoyment it has had—when, in its fastings and mortifications, it once more completely denies itself that enjoyment.

229. Through these moments of surrender, first of its right to decide for itself, then of its property and enjoyment, and finally through the positive moment of practising what it does not understand, it truly and completely deprives itself of the consciousness of inner and outer freedom, of the actuality in which consciousness exists *for itself*. It has the certainty of having truly divested itself of its '*I*', and of having turned its immediate self-consciousness into a *Thing*, into an *objective* existence. Only through this *actual* sacrifice could it demonstrate this self-renunciation. For only therein does the *deception* vanish which lies in the inner acknowledgement of gratitude through heart, sentiment, and tongue, an acknowledgement which indeed disclaims all power pertaining to its own independent existence, ascribing it all to a gift from above, but which in this very disclaimer, holds on to its own particular existence, does so outwardly in the possessions it does not surrender, inwardly in the consciousness of the decision it has itself made, and in the consciousness of its content which it has itself determined, which it has not exchanged for one coming from outside, which last would fill it up with what is meaningless for it.

230. But in the sacrifice actually carried out, consciousness, having nullified the *action* as its own doing, has also *in principle* obtained relief from its *misery*. That this relief has been obtained *in principle* is, however, the action of the other extreme of the syllogism, which is the essence possessed of *intrinsic being*. But

that sacrifice made by the unessential extreme was at the same time not a one-sided action, but contained within itself the action of the other. For the surrender of one's own will is only from one aspect negative; in principle, however, or in itself, it is at the same time positive, viz. the positing of will as the will of an 'other', and specifically of will, not as a particular, but as a universal will. This positive meaning of the negatively posited particular is taken by this consciousness to be the will of the other extreme, the will which, precisely because it is an 'other' for consciousness, becomes actual for it, not through the Unhappy Consciousness itself, but through a Third, the mediator as counsellor. Hence, for consciousness, its will does indeed become universal and essential will, but consciousness itself does not take itself to be this essential will. The surrender of its own will, as a *particular* will, is not taken by it to be in principle the positive aspect of universal will. Similarly, its giving up of possessions and enjoyment has only the same negative meaning, and the universal which thereby comes to be for it, is not regarded as its *own doing*. This *unity* of objectivity and being-for-self, which lies in the Notion of action, and which therefore becomes for consciousness essence and *object*—this unity is not the principle of its action, and so too it does not become an object *for consciousness*, directly and through itself. Rather, it lets the mediating minister express this certainty, a certainty which is itself still incomplete, that its misery is only *in principle* the reverse, i.e. that its action brings it only *in principle* self-satisfaction or blessed enjoyment; that its pitiable action too is only *in principle* the reverse, viz. an absolute action; that in principle, action is only really action when it is the action of a particular individual. But *for itself*, action and its own actual doing remain pitiable, its enjoyment remains pain, and the overcoming of these in a positive sense remains a *beyond*. But in this object, in which it finds that its own action and being, as being that of this *particular* consciousness, are being and action *in themselves*, there has arisen for consciousness the idea of *Reason*, of the certainty that, in its particular individuality, it has being absolutely *in itself*, or is all reality.

C. (AA.) REASON

V. THE CERTAINTY AND TRUTH OF REASON

231. In grasping the thought that the *single* individual consciousness is *in itself* Absolute Essence, consciousness has returned into itself. For the Unhappy Consciousness the in-itself is the beyond of itself. But its movement has resulted in positing the completely developed single individual, or the single individual that is an *actual* consciousness, as the *negative* of itself, viz. as the *objective* extreme; in other words, it has successfully struggled to divest itself of its being-for-self and has turned it into [mere] being. In this movement it has also become aware of its *unity* with this universal, a unity which, for us, no longer falls outside of it since the superseded single individual is the universal, and which, since consciousness maintains itself in this its negativity, is present in consciousness as such as its essence. Its truth is that which appears in the syllogism whose extremes appeared as held absolutely asunder, as the middle term which proclaims to the unchangeable consciousness that the single individual has renounced itself, and, to the individual, that the Unchangeable is for it no longer an extreme, but is reconciled with it. This middle term is the unity directly aware of both and connecting them, and is the consciousness of their unity, which it proclaims to consciousness and thereby to itself, the consciousness of the certainty of being all truth.

232. Now that self-consciousness is Reason, its hitherto negative relation to otherness turns round into a positive relation. Up till now it has been concerned only with its independence and freedom, concerned to save and maintain itself for itself at the expense of the *world*, or of its own actuality, both of which appeared to it as the negative of its essence. But as Reason, assured of itself, it is at peace with them, and can endure them; for it is certain that it is itself reality, or that everything actual is none other than itself; its thinking is itself directly actuality, and thus its relationship to the latter is that of idealism. Apprehending itself in this way, it is as if the world had for it only

now come into being; previously it did not understand the world; it desired it and worked on it, withdrew from it into itself and abolished it as an existence on its own account, and its own self *qua* consciousness—both as consciousness of the world as essence and as consciousness of its nothingness. In thus apprehending itself, after losing the grave of its truth, after the abolition of its actuality is itself abolished, and after the singleness of consciousness is for it in itself Absolute Essence, it discovers the world as *its* new real world, which in its permanence holds an interest for it which previously lay only in its transiency; for the *existence* of the world becomes for self-consciousness its own *truth* and *presence*; it is certain of experiencing only itself therein.

233. Reason is the certainty of consciousness that it is all reality; thus does idealism express its Notion. Just as consciousness, that comes on the scene as Reason, possesses that certainty *directly* in itself, so too does idealism give direct expression to that certainty: 'I am I', in the sense that the 'I' which is an object for me is the sole object, is all reality and all that is present. Here, the 'I' that is object for me, is not merely an *empty* object in general, as it is for self-consciousness as such, nor is it, as in free self-consciousness, merely an object that withdraws itself from other objects which retain their worth *alongside* it; on the contrary, it is for self-consciousness an object such that any other object whatever is a *non-being*. But self-consciousness is all reality, not merely *for itself* but also *in itself*, only through *becoming* this reality, or rather through *demonstrating* itself to be such. It demonstrates itself to be this *along the path* in which first, in the dialectic movement of 'meaning', perceiving and understanding, otherness as an *intrinsic being* vanishes. Then, in the movement through the independence of consciousness in lordship and bondage, through the conception of freedom, through the liberation that comes from Scepticism and the struggle for absolute liberation by the consciousness divided against itself, otherness, in so far as it is only *for consciousness*, vanishes for *consciousness itself*. There appeared two aspects, one after the other: one in which the essence or the True had for consciousness the determinateness of *being*, the other in which it had the determinateness of being only *for consciousness*. But the two reduced themselves to a single truth, viz. that what *is*,

or the in-itself, only *is* in so far as it is *for* consciousness, and what is *for* consciousness is also *in itself* or has *intrinsic* being. The consciousness which is this truth has this path behind it and has forgotten it, and comes on the scene *immediately* as Reason; in other words, this Reason which comes immediately on the scene appears only as the *certainty* of that truth. Thus it merely *asserts* that it is all reality, but does not itself comprehend this; for it is along that forgotten path that this immediately expressed assertion is comprehended. And equally, anyone who has not trodden this path finds this assertion incomprehensible when he hears it in this pure form— although he does as a matter of fact make the assertion himself in a concrete shape [i.e. the assertion is implicit in his behaviour].

234. The idealism that does not demonstrate that path but starts off with this assertion is therefore, too, a pure *assertion* which does not comprehend its own self, nor can it make itself comprehensible to others. It proclaims an *immediate certainty* which is confronted by other immediate certainties, which have, however, been lost on that same path. With equal right, therefore, the assertions of these other certainties, too, take their place alongside the assertion of that certainty. Reason appeals to the *self*-consciousness of each and every consciousness: '*I am I*, my object and my essence is *I*'; and no one will deny Reason this truth. But in basing itself on this appeal, Reason sanctions the truth of the other certainty, viz. that there is for me an 'other'; that an other than 'I' is object and essence for me, or, in that I am object and essence to myself, I am only so by drawing back from the 'other' altogether, and taking my place as an actuality *alongside* it. Not until Reason comes on the scene as a *reflection* from this opposite certainty does its affirmation about itself present itself not merely as a certainty and an assertion, but as truth; and not merely alongside other truths but as the sole truth. Its *immediate appearance* on the scene is the abstraction of its *actual presence*, the essence and the *in-itself* of which is the absolute Notion, i.e. *the movement which has brought it into being*. Consciousness will determine its relationship to otherness or its object in various ways, according to the precise stage it has reached in the development of the World-Spirit into self-consciousness. How it *immediately* finds and determines itself

and its object at any time, or the way in which it is *for itself*, depends on what it has already *become*, or what it already is *in itself*.

235. Reason is the certainty of being all *reality*. This *in-itself* or this *reality* is, however, a universal pure and simple, the pure *abstraction* of reality. It is the first *positivity* in which self-consciousness is *in its own self* explicitly *for itself*, and '*I*' is therefore only the *pure essentiality* of the existent, or is the simple *category*. The category, which formerly had the meaning of being the essentiality of the existent—and it was *undetermined* whether of the existent as such, or of the existent contrasted with consciousness—is now the essentiality or simple *unity* of the existent only as a reality that thinks; in other words, the category means this, that self-consciousness and being are the same essence, the same, not through comparison, but in and for themselves. It is only the one-sided, spurious idealism that lets this unity again come on the scene as consciousness, on one side, confronted by an *in-itself*, on the other. But now this category or *simple* unity of self-consciousness and being possesses difference *in itself*; for its essence is just this, to be immediately one and selfsame in *otherness*, or in absolute difference. The difference therefore *is*, but is perfectly transparent, and a difference that is at the same time none. It appears as a *plurality* of categories. Since idealism proclaims the simple unity of self-consciousness to be all reality, and *immediately* makes it the essence without having grasped it as the absolutely negative essence—only this has negation, determinateness, or difference within it—this second assertion is even more incomprehensible than the first, viz. that in the category there are *differences* or *species* of categories. The assertion as such, as also the assertion as to any *specific number* of species of categories, is a new assertion which, however, itself implies that we no longer have to accept it as an assertion. For since the difference originates in the pure '*I*', in the pure Understanding itself, it is thereby made explicit that the *immediacy*, the making of assertions and [mere] finding of differences, is here given, and we begin to *comprehend*. But to pick up the plurality of categories again in some way or other as a welcome find, taking them, e.g., from the various judgements, and complacently accepting them so, is in fact to be regarded as an outrage on Science. Where else should the Understanding be

able to demonstrate a necessity, if it is unable to do so in its own self, which is pure necessity?

236. Now, because, in this way, the pure essentiality of things, like their difference, belongs to Reason, we can, strictly speaking, no longer talk of *things* at all, i.e. of something which would be for consciousness merely the negative of itself. For to say that the many categories are *species* of the pure category means that this latter is still their *genus* or *essence*, and is not opposed to them. But ambiguity already attaches to them, since in their *plurality* they possess otherness in contrast to the pure category. In fact, they contradict the pure category by such plurality, and the pure unity must supersede them in itself, thereby constituting itself a *negative unity* of the differences. But, as *negative* unity, it excludes from itself both the differences as such, as well as that first *immediate* pure unity as such, and is a *singular individual*; a new category which is consciousness as exclusive, i.e. consciousness for which there is an 'other'. The singular individual is the transition of the category from its Notion to an *external* reality, the pure *schema* which is both consciousness, and, since it is a singular individual and an exclusive unit, the pointing to an 'other'. But this 'other' of the category is merely the other first-mentioned categories, viz. *pure essentiality* and *pure difference*; and in this category, i.e. just in the positedness of the 'other', or in this 'other' itself, consciousness is equally itself. Each of these different moments points or refers to another; but at the same time they do not attain to otherness. The pure category points to the *species*, which pass over into the negative category or singular individual; this latter, however, points back to them. It is itself pure consciousness which is aware in each of them of being always this clear unity with itself, but a unity which equally is referred to an 'other', which in being, has vanished, and in vanishing also comes into being again.

237. Here we see pure consciousness posited in a twofold manner: once as the restless movement to and fro through all its moments, aware in them of an otherness which is superseded in the act of grasping it; and again, rather as the *tranquil unity* certain of its [own] truth. For this unity that movement is the 'other', while for this movement that tranquil unity is the 'other'; and consciousness and object alternate within these

reciprocal determinations. Thus on the one hand consciousness finds itself moving about searching here and there, its object being the *pure in-itself* and essence; on the other hand, it knows itself to be the simple category, and the object is the movement of the different moments. Consciousness, however, as essence is this whole process itself, of passing out of itself as simple category into a singular individual, into the object, and of contemplating this process in the object, nullifying the object as distinct [from it], *appropriating* it as its own, and proclaiming itself as this certainty of being all reality, of being both itself and its object.

238. Its first declaration is only this abstract empty phrase that everything is *its own*. For the certainty of being all reality is at first [only] the pure category. This Reason which first recognizes itself in the object finds expression in the empty idealism which grasps Reason only as it first comes on the scene; and fancies that by pointing out this pure 'mine' of consciousness in all being, and by declaring all things to be sensations or ideas, it has demonstrated this 'mine' of consciousness to be complete reality. It is bound, therefore, to be at the same time absolute empiricism, for in order to give filling to the empty 'mine', i.e. to get hold of *difference* with all its developed formations, its Reason requires an extraneous impulse, in which first is to be found the *multiplicity* of sensations and ideas. This idealism therefore becomes the same kind of self-contradictory ambiguity as Scepticism, except that, while this expresses itself negatively, the former does so positively; but it fails equally with Scepticism to bring together its contradictory thoughts of pure consciousness being all reality, while the extraneous impulse or sensations and ideas are equally reality. Instead of bringing them together, it shifts from one to the other, and is caught up in the spurious, i.e. the sensuous, infinite. Since Reason is all reality in the sense of the abstract 'mine', and the 'other' is for it something indifferent and extraneous, what is here made explicit is that kind of knowing of an 'other' by Reason, which we met with in the form of 'meaning', 'perceiving' and the 'Understanding', which apprehends what is 'meant' and what is 'perceived'. Such a knowing is at the same time pronounced by the very principle of this idealism not to be a true knowing, for only in the unity of apperception lies

the truth of knowing. The pure Reason of this idealism, in order to reach this 'other' which is *essential* to it, and thus is the *in-itself*, but which it does not have within it, is therefore thrown back by its own self on to that knowing which is *not* a knowing of what is true; in this way, it condemns itself of its own knowledge and volition to being an untrue kind of knowing, and cannot get away from 'meaning' and 'perceiving', which for it have no truth. It is involved in a direct contradiction; it asserts essence to be a duality of opposed factors, the *unity of apperception* and equally a *Thing*; whether the Thing is called an extraneous impulse, or an empirical or sensuous entity, or the Thing-in-itself, it still remains in principle the same, i.e. extraneous to that unity.

239. This idealism is involved in this contradiction because it asserts the *abstract Notion* of Reason to be the True; consequently, reality directly comes to be for it a reality that is just as much *not* that of Reason, while Reason is at the same time supposed to be all reality. This Reason remains a restless searching and in its very searching declares that the satisfaction of *finding* is a sheer impossibility. Actual Reason, however, is not so inconsistent as that; on the contrary, being at first only the *certainty* that it is all reality, it is aware in this *Notion* that *qua certainty*, qua '*I*', it is not yet in truth reality, and it is impelled to raise its certainty to truth and to give filling to the empty 'mine'.

A. OBSERVING REASON

240. It is true that we now see this consciousness, for which Being [*Sein*] means what is its own [*Seinen*], revert to the standpoint of 'meaning' and 'perceiving'; but not in the sense that it is certain of what is merely an 'other'. Previously, its perception and *experience* of various aspects of the Thing were something that only *happened to* consciousness; but here, consciousness *makes its own* observations and experiments. 'Meaning' and 'perceiving', which previously were superseded *for us*, are now superseded by and for consciousness itself. Reason sets to work to *know* the truth, to find in the form of a Notion that which, for 'meaning' and 'perceiving', is a Thing; i.e. it seeks to possess in thinghood the consciousness only of itself. Reason now has,

therefore, a universal *interest* in the world, because it is certain
of its presence in the world, or that the world present to it is
rational. It seeks its 'other', knowing that therein it possesses
nothing else but itself: it seeks only its own infinitude.

241. While at first it is only dimly aware of its presence in
the actual world, or only knows quite simply that this world
is its own, it strides forward in this belief to a general appropriation of its own assured possessions, and plants the symbol of
its sovereignty on every height and in every depth. But this
superficial '[it is] mine', is not its ultimate interest; the joy of
this general appropriation finds still in its possessions the alien
'other' which abstract Reason does not contain within itself.
Reason is dimly aware of itself as a profounder essence than
the pure 'I' *is*, and must demand that difference, that being,
in its manifold variety, become its very own, that it behold itself
as the *actual* world and find itself present as an [outer] shape
and Thing. But even if Reason digs into the very entrails of
things and opens every vein in them so that it may gush forth
to meet itself, it will not attain this joy; it must have completed
itself inwardly before it can experience the consummation of
itself.

242. Consciousness *observes*; i.e. Reason wants to find and to
have itself as existent object, as an object that is actually and
sensuously present. The consciousness that observes in this way
means, and indeed says, that it wants to learn, not about itself
but, on the contrary, about the essence of things *qua* things.
That this consciousness means and says this, is implied in the
fact that it *is* Reason; but Reason as such is not as yet object
for this consciousness. If it knew that *Reason* is equally the
essence of things and of consciousness itself, and that it is only
in consciousness that Reason can be present in its own proper
shape, it would go down into the depths of its own being, and
seek Reason there rather than in things. If it did find it there,
it would be directed to the actual world outside again, in order
to behold therein Reason's sensuous expression, but at the same
time to take it essentially as Notion. Reason, as it *immediately*
comes before us as the certainty of consciousness that it is all
reality, takes its reality in the sense of the *immediacy of being*,
and similarly, the unity of the 'I' with this objective being in
the sense of an *immediate unity*, in which it has not yet divided

and reunited the moments of being and the 'I', or which has not yet discerned them. Reason, therefore, in its observational activity, approaches things in the belief that it truly apprehends them as sensuous things opposite to the 'I'; but what it actually does, contradicts this belief, for it apprehends them *intellectually*, it transforms their sensuous being into *Notions*, i.e. into just that kind of being which is at the same time 'I', hence transforms thought into the form of being, or being into the form of thought; it maintains, in fact, that it is only as Notions that things have truth. Consciousness, in this observational activity, comes to know what *things* are; but *we* come to know what *consciousness itself* is. The outcome of its movement will be that what consciousness is *in itself* will become *explicit* for it.

243. This *action* of Reason in its observational role we have to consider in the moments of its movement: how it looks upon Nature and Spirit, and, lastly, upon the relationship of both in the form of sensuous being, and how it seeks itself as actuality in the form of immediate being.

a. *Observation of Nature*

244. When the unthinking consciousness declares observation and experience to be the source of truth, what it says may well sound as if only tasting, smelling, feeling, hearing, and seeing were involved. It forgets, in the zeal with which it recommends tasting, smelling, etc., to say that it has no less essentially determined the object of this sensuous apprehension, and this determination is at least as valid for the object as is the sensuous apprehension. It will also readily admit that its concern is not wholly and solely with perception, and will not let, e.g., the perception that this penknife lies alongside this snuff-box, pass for an observation. What is perceived should at least have the significance of a *universal*, not of a *sensuous particular*.

245. This universal is thus, to begin with, only what remains *identical with itself*; its movement is only the uniform recurrence of the same action. Consciousness, which thus far finds in the object only *universality*, or the abstract '*it is mine*', must take upon itself the movement proper to the object and, since it is not yet the understanding of the object, must at least be the remembrance of it, which expresses in a universal way what in actuality is present only as a single item. This superficial raising

out of singularity, and the equally superficial form of universality into which the sensuous object is merely taken up, without becoming in its own self a universal, this activity of *describing* things, is not as yet a movement in the object itself; the movement is really only in the describing of the object. The object, as described, has lost its interest; when one has been described, then another must be started on, and continually looked for, in order that the activity of describing shall not come to an end. If it is no longer easy to find new *whole* things, then we must go back to those already found, divide and analyse them further, and bring to light fresh aspects of thinghood in them. This restless, insatiable instinct can never run out of material; to discover a new genus of major importance, or even a new planet which, although an individual, possesses the nature of a universal, can be the lot of only a lucky few. But the line of demarcation of what is *distinctive* of, say, elephant, oak, gold, of what is *genus* and what *species*, passes through many stages into the endless particularization of the chaos of animals and plants, of rocks, or the metals, earths, etc., that only force and skill can bring to view. In this realm where the universal is undetermined, where particularization approximates again to *singleness*, and again, here and there, descends to it entirely, there is opened up an inexhaustible supply of material for observation and description. But here, at the boundary-line of the universal where an immense field is opened up for that instinct, it can have found not an immeasurable wealth, but instead merely the bounds of Nature and of its own activity. It can no longer know whether what appears to possess intrinsic being is not really something contingent. What bears in itself the impress of a confused or immature feeble structure, barely developing out of rudimentary indeterminateness, cannot claim even to be described.

246. While this searching and describing seems to be concerned only with things, we see that in fact it does not run away into sense-perception. On the contrary, what enables things to be intelligently apprehended is more important to it than the rest of the complex of sensuous properties which, of course, the thing itself cannot dispense with, but which consciousness can do without. Through this distinction into what is essential and what is unessential, the Notion rises above the dispersion of the

sensuous, and cognition thus makes it clear that it is just as essentially concerned with its own self as with things. This duplication of what is essential gives rise to hesitation on the part of cognition as to whether what is essential and necessary for cognition is so also in respect of things. On the one hand, the *differentiae* enable cognition to distinguish one thing from another; but, on the other hand, it is not the unessential aspect of things that has to be known, but that characteristic whereby the things themselves *break loose* from the general continuity of being as such, *separate* themselves from others, and are explicitly *for themselves*. *Differentiae* are supposed, not merely to have an essential connection with cognition, but also to accord with the essential characteristics of things, and our artificial system is supposed to accord with Nature's own system and to express only this. This follows necessarily from the Notion of Reason; and the instinct of Reason—for, in this observational activity, Reason operates only instinctively—has also in its systems achieved this unity, viz. its objects are themselves so constituted that they contain in themselves an essentiality or a *being-for-self*, and are not merely the accident of a particular moment or a particular place. The distinguishing marks of animals, e.g., are taken from their claws and teeth; for in point of fact it is not only cognition that thereby distinguishes one animal from another, but each animal itself *separates* itself from others thereby; by means of these weapons it maintains itself in its independence and in its detachment from the generality. The plant, on the other hand, does not attain to a *being-for-self* but merely touches the boundary-line of individuality. It is at this boundary, therefore, where there is a show of *division* into sexes, that plants have been studied and distinguished from one another. What, however, stands on a still lower level cannot itself any longer distinguish itself from another, but in being contrasted with it gets lost. Being that is at rest, and being that is in a relation, come into conflict with each other; a Thing in the latter case is something different from what it is in the former state, whereas the single individual maintains itself in its relation to something else. What, however, is unable to do this and, *qua chemical* object, becomes something else than it is *empirically*, confuses cognition, and gives rise to the same conflicting views as to whether it ought to keep to one side or the other, since the thing itself does not remain identical with itself, and in it the two sides fall apart.

247. In those systems, therefore, which are characterized by a fixed, general selfsameness, this means that both the cognitive side and the things themselves remain selfsame. But this expansion of the self-identical determinatenesses, each of which describes the course of its progress unhindered and with scope for free play, leads of necessity equally to its opposite, to the confusion of these determinatenesses; for the *differentia*, the general characteristic, is the unity of opposites, of what is determinate and what is in itself universal; it must therefore split up into this antithesis. If, now, on the one side, the determinateness gains the ascendancy over the universal in which it has its essence, on the other side again, this universal equally maintains its control over that determinateness, pushes it to its boundary and there mixes up its distinctions and essentialities. Observation, which kept them properly apart and believed that in them it had something firm and settled, sees principles overlapping one another, transitions and confusions developing; what it at first took to be absolutely separate, it sees combined with something else, and what it reckoned to be in combination, it sees apart and separate. So it is that observation which clings to passive, unbroken selfsameness of being, inevitably sees itself tormented just in its most general determinations—e.g. of what are the *differentiae* of an animal or a plant—by instances which rob it of every determination, invalidate the universality to which it had risen, and reduce it to an observation and description which is devoid of thought.

248. Observation which confines itself in this way to what is simple, or restrains the scattered sensuous elements by the universal, thus finds in its object the confusion of its principle, because what is determinate must, through its own nature, lose itself in its opposite. Reason must therefore move on from the inert determinateness which had a show of permanence, to observing it as it is in truth, viz. as relating itself to its opposite. What are called *differentiae* are *passive* determinatenesses which, when expressed and apprehended as *simple*, do not represent their nature, which is to be vanishing *moments* of a movement which returns back into itself. Since Reason now reaches the stage of looking for the determinateness as some-

thing which essentially is *not* for itself, but which passes over into its opposite, it seeks for the *law* and the *Notion* of the determinateness. True, it seeks for them equally as an actuality in the form of *immediate being*, but this will, in fact, vanish for it, and the aspects of the law become pure moments or abstractions, so that the law comes to light in the nature of the Notion, which has destroyed within itself the indifferent subsistence of sensuous reality.

249. To the observing consciousness, the *truth of the law* is found in *experience*, in the same way that sensuous being is [an object] for consciousness; is not in and for itself. But if the law does not have its truth in the Notion, it is a contingency, not a necessity, not, in fact, a law. But the fact that it is essentially in the form of Notion, not only does not conflict with its being accessible to observation, but rather for that very reason gives it a necessary *existence*, and makes it [an object] for observation. The universal, in the *sense of the universality of Reason*, is also universal in the sense implied in the above Notion, viz. that it is *for* consciousness, that it displays itself as something present and actual. In other words, the Notion displays itself in the form of thinghood and sensuous being; but it does not on that account lose its nature, nor relapse into an inert subsistence or an indifferent succession. What is universally valid is also universally effective; what *ought* to be, in fact also *is*, and what only *ought* to be without [actually] being, has no truth. The instinct of Reason, for its part, rightly holds firmly to this standpoint, and refuses to be led astray by figments of thought which only *ought* to be and, as 'oughts', are credited with truth, although they are nowhere met with in experience; or by hypotheses as little as by all the other invisible entities of a perennial 'ought'. For Reason is just this certainty of possessing reality; and what is not present for consciousness as something existing in its own right [*Selbstwesen*], i.e. what does not appear, is for consciousness nothing at all.

250. That the truth of a law is essentially *reality* no doubt again becomes for that consciousness which remains at the level of observation an antithesis to the Notion and to what is intrinsically universal; in other words, it does not regard an object such as its law, as having the nature of Reason, but fancies that it is something alien. But it contradicts its own belief in the fact

that it does not itself take its universality to mean that *every single* sensuous thing must have provided evidence of the law, in order to enable the truth of the law to be asserted. The assertion that stones fall when raised above the ground and dropped certainly does not require us to make this experiment with every stone; it does perhaps mean that the experiment must have been made with at least a great number, and from this we can then *by analogy* draw an inference about the rest with the greatest probability or with perfect right. But analogy not only does not give a perfect right, but on account of its nature contradicts itself so often that the inference to be drawn from analogy itself is rather that analogy does not permit an inference to be made. *Probability*, which is what the result would amount to, loses, in face of *truth*, every distinction of lesser and greater probability; let it be as great as it may, it is nothing as against truth. But the instinct of Reason does in fact take such laws for truth, and it is when it does not discern necessity in them that it comes to make this distinction, and reduces the truth of the matter itself to the level of probability, in order to indicate the imperfect way in which truth presents itself to the consciousness which has not yet attained to insight into the pure Notion; for universality is present only as a *simple immediate* universality. But, at the same time, on account of this universality, the law has truth for consciousness. That a stone falls, is true for consciousness because in its heaviness the stone has in and for itself that essential relation to the earth which is expressed in falling. Consciousness thus has in experience the *being* of the law, but it has, too, the law in the form of a *Notion*; and it is only because of the two aspects together that the law is true for consciousness. The law is valid as a law because it is manifested in the world of appearance, and is also in its own self a Notion.

251. Because the law is at the same time *in itself* a Notion, the instinct of Reason in this consciousness proceeds to *refine* the law and its moments into a Notion; it does this of necessity, but without knowing that this is what it aims to do. It puts the law to the test of experiment. The law as it first appears exhibits itself in an impure form, enveloped in single, sensuous forms of being, and the Notion constituting its nature is immersed in empirical material. In its experiments the instinct

of Reason sets out to find what happens in such and such circumstances. The result is that the law seems only to be all the more immersed in sensuous being. The inner significance of this investigation is to find the *pure conditions* of the law; and this means nothing else (even if the consciousness expressing its meaning in this way were to think it meant something different) than to raise the law into the form of Notion, and to free its moments completely from being tied to a specific being. For example, negative electricity, which at first comes to be known, say, as resin-electricity, and positive electricity as glass-electricity, these, as a result of experiments, lose altogether such a significance and become purely positive and negative electricity, neither of which is any longer attached to a particular kind of thing; and we can no longer say that there are bodies which are positively electrical and others which are negatively electrical. In the same way, the relationship of acid and base and their reaction constitute a law in which these opposite sides appear as bodies. But these separated detached things have no actuality; the power which forces them apart cannot prevent them from at once entering again into a process, for they are only this relation. They cannot, like a tooth or a claw, remain apart on their own and as such be pointed out. This essential nature of theirs, to pass over immediately into a neutral product, makes their *being* into a being which is implicitly superseded or universal; and acid and base have truth only as *universals*. Therefore, just as glass and resin can just as well be positively as negatively electrical, in the same way acid and base are not tied as properties to this or that *actuality*; each thing is only *relatively* acid or base: what seems to be an absolute base or acid gets in the so-called synsomaties[1] the opposite significance in relation to something else.—The result of the experiments is in this way to cancel the moments or activated sides as properties of specific things, and to free the predicates from their subjects. These predicates are found only as universals, as in truth they are; because of this self-subsistence they get the name of 'matters', which are neither bodies nor properties;

---

[1] A term coined by a chemist, Winterl, at the beginning of the nineteenth century. These synsomaties are combinations formed directly without any intermediary which would produce and itself undergo change; they are still, in consequence, not strictly chemical processes.

and certainly no one would call oxygen, positive and negative electricity, heat, etc., bodies.

252. *Matter*, on the contrary, is not an *existent thing*, but is being in the form of a *universal*, or in the form of a Notion. Reason which is still instinctive makes this correct distinction, without being aware that just by testing the law on all sensuous being, it gets rid of the merely sensuous being of the law, and when it interprets the moments of the law as 'matters', their essential nature has become for Reason a universal, and as such is expressed as a non-sensuous thing of sense, as an incorporeal and yet objective being.

253. We have now to see what turn its result takes for it, and what new shape its observational activity assumes in consequence. We find, as the truth of this experimenting consciousness, *pure law*, which is freed from sensuous being; we see it as a *Notion* which, while present in sensuous being, operates there independently and unrestrained, and, while immersed in it, is free of it, and a *simple* Notion. This which is in truth the result and essence [of its activity], is now present to this consciousness itself, but as an *object*; further, since *for it* the object is not a *result*, and is not connected with the preceding activity, it presents itself to consciousness as a *particular kind* of object, and the relation of consciousness to it appears as another kind of observation.

254. Such an object, in which the process is present in the *simplicity* of the Notion, is the *organism*. It is this absolute fluidity in which the determinateness, through which it would be only *for an other*, is dissolved. The inorganic thing has determinateness for its essential nature, and for that reason constitutes the moments of the Notion in their completeness only together with another thing, and therefore is lost when it enters into the process; in the organic being, on the contrary, every determinateness through which it is open to an other is controlled by the organic simple unity. None of them shows itself as essential, as free to enter into relation with an other, and consequently what is organic maintains itself in its relation.

255. The *aspects of law* which the instinct of Reason here proceeds to observe are, as follows from the above characterization, in the first instance, *organic* Nature and *inorganic* Nature in their relation to one another. The latter is, for organic Nature, no

more than the freedom—a freedom opposed to the *simple Notion*
of organic Nature—of the *loosely connected* determinatenesses in
which the individual forms of Nature are *dissolved* and which,
at the same time, breaking away from their continuity, exist
on their own account. Air, water, earth, zones, and climate are
universal elements of this sort, which constitute the indeterminate simple essence of [natural] individualities, and in which
these are at the same time reflected into themselves. Neither
the individuality, nor the universal element, is absolutely in and
for itself; on the contrary, though they appear to observation
as free and independent, they behave at the same time as *essentially connected*, but in such a way that their independence and
mutual indifference are the predominant feature, and only in
part become abstractions. Here, then, we have law as the connection of a [universal] element with the formative process of
the organism which, on the one hand, has the elementary being
over against it, and, on the other hand, exhibits it within its
organic reflection. But laws of this kind: animals belonging to
the air have the nature of birds, those belonging to water have
the nature of fish, animals in northern latitudes have thick,
hairy pelts, and so on—such laws are seen at a glance to display
a poverty which does not do justice to the manifold variety of
organic Nature. Besides the fact that organic Nature in its freedom can divest its forms of these characteristics, and of necessity
everywhere presents exceptions to such laws, or rules as we
might call them, the characterization of the creatures to which
they do apply is so superficial that even the necessity of the laws
cannot be other than superficial, and amounts to no more than
the *great influence* of environment; and this does not tell us what
does and what does not strictly belong to this influence. Such
relations of organisms to the elements [they live in] cannot
therefore in fact be called *laws*. For, firstly, the *content* of such
a relation, as we saw, does not exhaust the range of the organisms concerned, and secondly, the sides of the relation itself are
mutually indifferent, and express no necessity. In the Notion
of acid lies the *Notion* of base, just as the Notion of positive electricity *implies* that of negative; but often as we may find a thick,
hairy pelt associated with northern latitudes, or the structure
of a fish associated with water, or that of birds with air, the
Notion of north does not imply the Notion of a thick, hairy pelt,

the Notion of sea does not imply the Notion of the structure
of fish, or the Notion of air that of the structure of birds. Because
of the freedom of the two sides in relation to each other, *there
are* also land animals which have the essential characteristics
of a bird, of a fish, and so on. The necessity, just because it
cannot be grasped as an inner necessity of the creature, ceases
to have a sensuous existence, and can no longer be observed
in the world of reality, but has withdrawn from it. Finding thus
no place in the actual creature, it is what is called a teleological
relation, a relation which is *external* to the related terms, and
therefore really the antithesis of a law. It is a conception completely freed from the necessity of Nature, a conception which
leaves that necessity behind and operates spontaneously above
it.

256. If the relation, referred to above, of the organism to the
natural elements does not express its essence, the notion of End,
on the other hand, does contain it. It is true that, for the observing consciousness, this Notion is not the organism's own *essence*,
but something falling outside of it, and is then only the above-
mentioned external *teleological* relation. Yet the organism, as it
has been characterized above, is, in fact, the real End itself;
for since it preserves *itself* in the relation to an other, it is just
that kind of natural existence in which Nature reflects itself into
the Notion, and the two moments of cause and effect, of active
and passive moments, which were the result of a necessary
separating-out, are brought together into a unity, so that here
something does not appear merely as a *result* of necessity. But,
because it has returned into itself, the last, or the result, is just
as much the *first* which initiated the movement, and is to itself
the realized *End*. The organism does not produce something
but only preserves itself; or, what is produced, is as much
already present as produced.

257. We must examine more closely this determination of
End, both as it is in itself, and as it is for the instinct of Reason,
in order to see how the latter finds itself therein, but does not
recognize itself in what it finds. The notion of End, then, to
which Reason in its role of observer rises, is a *Notion* of which
it is *aware*; but it is also no less present as something *actual*, and
is not an *external relation* of the latter, but its *essence*. This actuality, which is itself an End, is related purposively to an other:

which means that its relation is a contingent one with respect to what both *immediately* are; immediately, both are independent and mutually indifferent. But the essence of their relation is something different from what they thus appear to be, and their action has a different meaning from the one sense-perception at first finds in it. The necessity in what takes place is hidden, and shows itself only in the End, but in such a way that this very End shows that the necessity has also been there from the beginning. The End, however, shows this priority of itself in the fact that nothing else issues from the alteration resulting from the action than what was already there. Or, if we start from what is first, then this in its End, or in the outcome of its action, returns only to itself; and through this very fact it demonstrates itself to be something that has its own self for its End, and thus, as a *prius*, has already returned to itself or is *in and for itself*. Therefore, what it arrives at through the process of its action is *itself*; and in arriving only at itself, it obtains its feeling of self. We have here, it is true, the distinction between what it *is* and what it *seeks*, but this is merely the show of a distinction, and consequently it is in its own self a Notion.

258. But this is just how *self-consciousness* is constituted; it likewise distinguishes itself from itself without producing any distinction. Hence it finds in the observation of organic Nature nothing else than a being of this kind; it finds itself as a thing, *as a life*, but makes a distinction between what it is itself and what it has found, a distinction, however, which is none. Just as the instinct of the animal seeks and consumes food, but thereby brings forth nothing other than itself, so too the instinct of Reason in its quest finds only Reason itself. The animal finishes up with the feeling of self. The instinct of Reason, on the other hand, is at the same time self-consciousness; but because it is only instinct it is put on one side over against consciousness, in which it has its antithesis. Its satisfaction is, therefore, shattered by this antithesis; it does indeed find itself, viz. the End, and likewise this End as a Thing. But firstly, the End is for that instinct *outside* of the thing presenting itself as End. Secondly, this End, *qua* End, is also *objective*, and therefore does not fall within the observing consciousness itself, but in another intelligence.

259. Examined more closely, this determination of End lies

just as much in the Notion of the thing, that of being in its own self an End. That is to say, it preserves *itself*; i.e. it is at one and the same time its nature to conceal the necessity, and to exhibit it in the form of a *contingent* relation. For its freedom or its *being-for-self* is just this, to treat the necessity [of the relation] as of no importance. Thus it presents itself as something whose Notion falls outside of its being. Similarly, Reason has of necessity to look on its own Notion as falling outside of it, hence as a Thing, as something towards which it is indifferent and which is therefore reciprocally *indifferent* towards Reason and its Notion. As instinct, Reason also remains at the level of [mere] *being* and a state of *indifference*, and the Thing expressing the Notion remains for it something other than this Notion, and the Notion other than the Thing. Thus, for Reason, the organic thing is in its own self an End only in the sense that the necessity which presents itself as hidden in the action of the thing—for this behaves as an indifferent being-for-self—falls outside of the organism itself. Since, however, the organism as an End in its own self cannot behave in any other way than as an organism, the fact that it is an End in itself is also manifest and present in sensuous fashion, and it is as such that it is observed. The organism shows itself to be a being that *preserves* itself, that *returns* and *has returned* into itself. But this observing consciousness does not recognize in this being the Notion of End, or that the Notion of End exists just here and in the form of a Thing, and not elsewhere in some other intelligence. It makes a distinction between the Notion of End and being-for-self and self-preservation, a distinction which is none. That it is in fact no distinction is something of which this consciousness is not aware; on the contrary, the making of the distinction appears to it as a contingent act having no essential connection with what is brought about by that act; and the unity which links the two together, viz. the said act and the End, falls asunder for this consciousness.

260. On this view, what belongs to the organism itself is the action lying in the middle between its first and last stage, so far as this action bears within it the character of singleness. So far, however, as the action has the character of universality and the agent of the action is equated with the outcome of that action, purposive action as such would not belong to the organ-

ism. That single action which is only a means comes through its singleness under the category of an altogether single·or contingent necessity. What an organism does to preserve itself as an individual or as a genus is, therefore, as regards this immediate content, quite uncontrolled by any law, for the universal and the Notion fall outside of it. Accordingly, its activity would be an empty activity devoid of any content of its own; it would not be even the activity of a machine, for this has a purpose, and its activity therefore a specific content. Deserted in this way by the universal, it would be the activity merely of something immediate *qua immediate*, i.e. an activity like that of an acid or base which is not at the same time reflected into itself; an activity which could not separate itself from its immediate existence, nor give up this existence (which gets lost in the relation to its opposite), and still preserve itself. But the thing whose activity is under consideration here is posited as a thing that *preserves itself* in its relation to its opposite. The *activity* as such is nothing but the pure essenceless form of its being-for-self, and its substance, which is not merely a determinate being but the universal, or its *End*, does not fall outside of it. It is an activity which spontaneously returns into itself, and is not turned back into itself by anything alien to it.

261. However, this unity of universality and the activity does not exist for this *observing* consciousness, because that unity is essentially the inner movement of the organism and can only be grasped as Notion; but observation seeks the moments in the form of being, of enduring being; and because the nature of what is organically a whole is such that the moments are not contained in it nor can be found in it in that form, consciousness converts the antithesis into one that conforms to its point of view.

262. In this way, the organism appears to the observing consciousness as a relation of two *fixed* moments in the form of *immediate* being—of an antithesis whose two sides, on the one hand, appear to be given to it in observation, and on the other hand, as regards their content, express the antithesis of the organic *Notion* of *End* and actuality; but because the Notion as such is effaced therein, the antithesis is expressed in an obscure and superficial way, in which thought has sunk to the level of picture-thinking. Thus we see the Notion taken to mean

roughly the *inner*, and actuality the *outer*; and their relation produces the law that *the outer is the expression of the inner*.

263. When we consider more closely this inner with its opposite and their relation, we find that, in the first place, the sides
of the law no longer have the same import as in the case of
previous laws, in which they appeared as self-subsistent *things*,
each as a particular body; nor, in the second place, do we find
that the universal is supposed to have its existence elsewhere,
outside of the two sides. On the contrary, the organic being in its
absolute undividedness is made the foundation, as the content
of inner and outer, and is the same for both. Consequently, the
antithesis is still only a purely formal one, whose real sides have
the same in-itself for their essence; but, at the same time, since
inner and outer are opposite realities, and each is a distinct
being for observation, they each seem to observation to have
a peculiar content of their own. However, this peculiar content,
since it is the same substance or organic unity, can in fact only
be a different form of that substance, of that unity; and this
is implied by the observing consciousness when it says that
the outer is merely the *expression* of the inner. We have seen in
the Notion of End the same determinations of the relation, viz.
the indifferent independence of the different sides and their
unity in that independence, a unity in which they vanish.

264. We have now to see what *shape* the being of inner and
outer each has. The inner as such must have an outer being
and a shape, just as much as the outer as such; for it is an object,
or is itself posited in the form of being, and as present for
observation.

265. The organic substance as *inner* is the *simple*, *unitary* soul,
the pure *Notion of End* or the universal, which in its partition
equally remains a universal fluidity, and therefore appears in
its *being* as the *action* or *movement* of the vanishing actuality;
whereas the *outer*, opposed to that existent inner, subsists in the
quiescent being of the organism. The law, as the relation of that
inner to this outer, thus expresses its content, once by setting
forth universal *moments* or *simple essentialities*, and again by setting forth the actualized essentiality or *shape*. Those first simple,
organic *properties*, to call them such, are Sensibility, Irritability,
and Reproduction. These properties, at least the first two, seem
indeed to refer not to the organism in general, but only to the

animal organism. As a matter of fact the vegetable organism expresses only the simple Notion of the organism, which does *not develop* its moments. Consequently, in regard to those moments, so far as observation has to take account of them, we must confine ourselves to the organism which exhibits them in their developed existence.

266. Now, as regards these moments themselves, they are directly derived from the notion of 'end-in-itself', of a being whose end is its own self. For Sensibility expresses in general the simple Notion of organic reflection-into-self, or the universal fluidity of this Notion. Irritability, though, expresses organic elasticity, the capacity of the organism to react at the same time that it is reflected into itself, the actualization which is opposed to the initial quiescent *being-within-self*, an actualization in which that abstract being-for-self is a being-*for-another*. Reproduction, however, is the action of this *whole* introreflected organism, its activity as in itself an End, or as *genus*, in which the individual repels itself from itself, and in the procreative act reproduces either its organic members or the whole individual. Reproduction, taken in the sense of *self-preservation in general*, expresses the formal Notion of the organism, or Sensibility; but it is, strictly speaking, the real organic Notion or the *whole*, which returns into itself, either *qua* individual by producing single parts of itself, or, *qua* genus, by bringing forth individuals.

267. The other significance of these organic elements, viz. as *outer*, is their particular *shape*, according to which they are present as [outwardly] *actual*, but at the same time, *universal* parts, or organic *systems*: Sensibility, let us say, as a nervous system, Irritability as a muscular system, Reproduction as a visceral system, for the preservation of the individual and the species.

268. The laws peculiar to organisms accordingly concern a relationship of the organic moments in their twofold significance, once as being a *part* of the organic structure, and again as being a *universal fluid* determinateness which pervades all those systems. Thus, in formulating such a law, a specific sensibility, e.g., would find its expression, *qua* moment of the *whole* organism, in a specifically formed nervous system, or it would also be linked up with a specific *reproduction* of the organic parts

of the individual or with the propagation of the whole, and so on. Both aspects of such a law can be *observed*. The *outer*, in accordance with its Notion is *being-for-another*; sensibility, e.g., has its immediately actualized mode in the *system* of sensibility; and, as a *universal property*, it is in its outer expressions an objective existence as well. The aspect which is called the *inner* has its *own outer* aspect, which is distinct from what in general is called the *outer*.

269. Both aspects of an organic law would thus no doubt be observable, but not the law connecting them; and observation is unable to perceive these laws, not because, *qua observation*, it is too short-sighted and ought not to proceed empirically but ought to start from the Idea—for such laws, if they were something real, must in fact actually exist and therefore be observable; but rather because the conception of laws of this kind proves to have no truth.

270. We found that a law existed when the relation was such that the universal organic *property* in an organic *system* had made itself into a Thing, and in this Thing had a structured copy of itself, so that both were the same being, present in the one case as a universal moment, and in the other, as a Thing. But, in addition, the aspect of the inner is, on its own account, also a relationship of several aspects; and we are therefore presented, to begin with, with the conception of a law as an inter-relationship of the universal organic activities or properties. Whether such a law is possible must be decided from the nature of such a property. This, however, as a universal fluid is, on the one hand, not something restricted like a Thing, keeping itself to the restricted form which is supposed to constitute its shape: sensibility extends beyond the nervous system and permeates all the other systems of the organism. On the other hand, such a property is a *universal* moment, which is essentially not divorced or separated from reaction or irritability, and reproduction. For, as reflection-into-self, it *eo ipso* contains reaction. Mere reflectedness-into-self is passivity or a dead being, not sensibility; just as action—which is the same as reaction—when not reflected into itself, is not irritability. It is precisely the unity of reflection in action or reaction, and action or reaction in reflection, that constitutes the organism, a unity which is synonymous with organic reproduction. It follows from this that, in

every mode of the organism's actuality, there must be present the same *quantity* of sensibility—since to begin with we are considering the relation of sensibility and irritability to one another—as of irritability, and that an organic phenomenon can be apprehended and determined or, if you like, explained, just as much in terms of the one as of the other. What one person takes, say, for high sensibility, another may equally well take for high irritability, and irritability of the *same degree*. If they are called *factors*, and this word is not to be meaningless, they are thereby declared to be *moments* of the Notion; thus the real object whose essence is constituted by this Notion, contains them both equally within it, and if the object is characterized according to the one moment as very sensitive, it must also be stated, according to the other moment, to be just as irritable.

271. If they are distinguished, as they necessarily are, this is in accordance with the Notion, and their opposition is *qualitative*. But when, apart from this true difference, they are also posited as they immediately are, and for ordinary thought, as they might be as aspects of the law, then they appear as *quantitatively* distinct. Their peculiar qualitative antithesis thus becomes one of *magnitude*, and there arise laws of this kind, for example, that sensibility and irritability stand in an inverse ratio of their magnitude, so that as the one increases the other decreases; or better, taking directly the magnitude itself as the content, as its smallness decreases. Should, however, a specific content be given to this law, say, that the size of a hole *increases*, the more what it is filled with *decreases*, then this inverse relation can equally be changed into a direct relation and expressed in this way, that the size of the hole *increases* in direct ratio to the amount taken away—a *tautological* proposition, whether expressed as a direct or an inverse ratio. As so expressed, the proposition means simply this, that a quantity increases as this quantity increases. Just as the hole and what fills it and is taken away are qualitatively opposed, but what is real in them, and its specific quantity, is one and the same in both, and similarly, increase of magnitude and decrease of smallness are the same, and their meaningless antithesis amounts to a tautology: so are the organic moments alike indivisible in their real content, and in their magnitude, which is the magnitude of that being; the

one decreases only with the other and increases only with it; or rather, it is a matter of indifference whether an organic phenomenon is considered as irritability or as sensibility; this is so in general and equally when its magnitude is under discussion. Similarly, it is a matter of indifference whether we speak of the increase of a hole as an increase of the hole *qua* emptiness, or as an increase of the filling removed from it. Or again, a number, e.g. *three*, remains the same quantity whether it is taken positively or negatively, and if I increase the three to four, then both the positive and the negative have become four; just as the south pole of a magnet is exactly as strong as its north pole, or a positive electricity, or an acid, is exactly as strong as its negative, or the base on which it acts. An organic *existence* is just such a magnitude as the said 'three', or a magnet, etc. It is that which is increased or diminished, and when it is increased *both* of its factors are increased, just as both poles of the magnet or both kinds of electricity increase if the potential of a magnet or of one of the electric currents is raised. That both can vary just as little in intension and extension, that the one cannot decrease in extension but increase in intension, while the other, conversely, is supposed to decrease its intension but increase its extension—this stems from the same notion of an empty antithesis; the real intension is absolutely as great as the extension, and vice versa.

272. It is evident that what really happens in formulating this kind of law is that at the outset irritability and sensibility constitute the organic antithesis; but this content gets lost sight of and the antithesis deteriorates into a formal one of quantitative increase and decrease, or of varying intension and extension—an antithesis which no longer has anything to do with the nature of sensibility and irritability, and no longer expresses it. Hence this empty play of formulating laws is not confined to organic moments but can be practised everywhere and with everything, and rests in general on a lack of acquaintance with the logical nature of these antitheses.

273. Lastly, if instead of sensibility and irritability, reproduction is brought into relation with one or the other of them, there is no longer even the occasion for making laws of this kind; for reproduction does not stand in an antithetical relation to those moments as they do to one another; and since this law-

making is based on such an antithesis, here even the show of its being practised is absent.

274. The law-making just considered contains the differences of the organism in their significance as moments of its *Notion*, and strictly speaking should be an *a priori* formulation of the law. But it essentially involves this thought, that those differences have the significance of being *already given*, and the consciousness that merely observes has, moreover, to confine itself only to their outer existence. The actual organism necessarily contains such an antithesis as is expressed by its Notion, and such as can be determined as irritability and sensibility, as these in turn appear distinct from reproduction. The *externality* in which the moments of the Notion of organism are here considered is the inner's *own immediate* externality, not the *outer* which is the outer of the whole organism and its *shape*; the inner in its relation to this is to be considered later on.

275. If, however, the antithesis of the moments is understood in the way it is present in outer existence, then sensibility, irritability, reproduction, sink to the level of common properties, which are universalities equally indifferent towards one another as are specific gravity, colour, hardness, etc. In this sense it may well be observed that the organism is more sensitive or more irritable, or has a greater reproductive capacity than another, just as we may observe that the sensibility of one is different in kind from that of another, that one reacts differently to a given stimulus than another, e.g. a horse reacts differently to oats than to hay, and a dog again differently to both, differences as readily observable as that one body is harder than another, and so on. But these sensuous properties, hardness, colour, etc., as also the phenomena of response to the stimulus of oats, of irritable response to loads, or of the number and kind of young produced, when they are related to one another and compared among themselves, essentially conflict with any conformity to a law. For what characterizes their *sensuous being* is just this, that they exist in complete mutual indifference, and manifest the freedom of Nature released from the control of the Notion rather than the unity of a relation, irrationally playing up and down on the scale of contingent magnitude between the moments of the Notion, rather than exhibiting these moments themselves.

276. It is the other aspect, where the simple moments of the Notion of organism are compared with the moments of the *outer structure*, that would first furnish the genuine law expressing the true *outer* as a copy of the *inner*. Now, because those simple moments are pervasive fluid properties, they do not have in the organic thing such a separate, real expression as what is called an individual system of the shape. Or, again, if the abstract Idea of the organism is truly expressed in those three moments, merely because they are not static and are only moments of the Notion and of movement, the organism, on the other hand, as a structured shape, is not exhaustively dealt with in the three specific systems into which it is analysed by anatomy. In so far as such systems are supposed to be found actually existing, and to be authenticated by being so found, it must also be borne in mind that anatomy presents us not only with three such systems but with a good many more. Furthermore, apart from this, the system of sensibility as a whole must mean something quite different from what is called the nervous system, the irritable system something different from the muscular system, the reproductive system something different from the intestinal mechanism of reproduction. In the systems of *shape* as such, the organism is apprehended from the abstract aspect of a dead existence; its moments so taken pertain to anatomy and the corpse, not to cognition and the living organism. In such parts, the moments have really ceased *to be*, for they cease to be processes. Since the *being* of the organism is essentially a universality or a reflection-into-self, the *being* of its totality, like its moments, cannot consist in an anatomical system; on the contrary, the actual expression of the whole, and the externalization of its moments, are really found only as a movement which runs its course through the various parts of the structure, a movement in which what is forcibly detached and fixed as an individual system essentially displays itself as a fluid moment. Consequently, that actual existence as it is found by anatomy must not be reckoned as its real being, but only that existence taken as a process, in which alone even the anatomical parts have a meaning.

277. We see, then, that the moments of the organic *inner*, taken by themselves, are incapable of furnishing the aspects of a law of being, since in such a law they are asserted of an outer

existence, are distinguished from one another, and neither aspect could be equally named in place of the other; further, that, placed on one side, they do not find in the other side their realization in a fixed system; for this latter would as little possess any organic truth [i.e. the truth of organic being] as it would be the expression of those moments of the [organic] inner. The essential nature of organic being, since it is in itself the universal, rather consists in general in its moments being equally universal in actual existence, i.e. in their being pervasive processes, but not in giving an image of the universal in an isolated thing.

278. In this way the idea of a *law* in the case of organic being is altogether lost. The law wants to grasp and express the antithesis as inert aspects, and in them the determinateness which is their relation to one another. The *inner*, to which the manifested universality belongs, and the *outer*, to which belong the parts of the inert shape, were supposed to constitute the corresponding aspects of the law, but as thus held apart, they lose their organic significance; and what lies at the base of the idea of law is precisely this, that each of its two aspects should have an independent, indifferent subsistence of its own, the relation of the aspects being shared between them as a twofold determinateness corresponding to that relation. The fact is that each aspect of the organism is in its own self just this: to be a simple universality in which all determinations are dissolved, and to be the movement of this process.

279. An insight into the difference between this way of formulating a law and previous forms will make its nature perfectly clear. If, namely, we look back to the movement of perceiving and to that of the Understanding, in which the latter reflects itself into itself, and thereby determines its object, we see that the Understanding does not, in that movement, have before itself in its object the *relation* of these abstract determinations of universal and individual, essential and external: it is itself the transition, which does not become objective to it. Here, on the contrary, the organic unity, which is just the relation of those opposites, this relation being a pure transition, is itself the *object*. This transition in its simplicity is immediately *universality*; and since this universality explicates the different moments whose relation is to express the law, its moments are *universal* objects of this consciousness, and the law runs, 'the

outer is the expression of the inner'. Here, the Understanding has grasped the *thought* of the law itself, whereas previously it only looked for laws generally, and their moments were only vaguely present to it as a specific content, but not as the thoughts of the laws. As regards content, the laws obtained here ought not to be such as are merely a passive taking-up into the form of universality of simply *inert* differences, but laws which directly possess in these differences the unrest of the Notion, and consequently at the same time possess the necessity of the relation between the aspects. But just because the object, the organic unity, directly unites the infinite supersession, or absolute negation, of being with inert being, and because the moments are essentially a *pure transition*, there are no such *inert* aspects as are required for the law.

280. In order to obtain such aspects, the Understanding must keep to the other moment of the organic relationship, viz. to the *reflectedness* of organic existence into itself. But this being is so completely reflected into itself that there is no determinateness related to something else left over for it. *Immediate* sensuous being is immediately one with the determinateness as such, and therefore expresses a qualitative difference in that being, e.g. blue as against red, acid as against alkali, and so on. But organic being that has returned into itself is completely indifferent towards an other, its existence is a simple universality, and it denies to observation any lasting sensuous differences or, what is the same thing, displays its essential determinateness only as the *flux* of *inert* determinatenesses. Consequently, the way in which difference, *qua* inert, expresses itself is just this, that it is an *indifferent* difference, i.e. difference as *magnitude*. In this, however, the Notion is extinguished and necessity has vanished. But then the content and filling of this indifferent being, the flux of sensuous determinations gathered up into an organic determination, expresses also this, that the content really does not have that determinateness, viz. that of the immediate property, and the qualitative element falls solely in [the determination of] magnitude, as we saw above.

281. Although, then, the objective aspect which is apprehended as an organic determinateness itself contains the Notion and is thereby distinguished from the object as it presents itself to the Understanding which, in apprehending the content of

its laws, behaves purely as perception, yet apprehension in the
first case relapses completely into the principle and the manner
of the Understanding that merely perceives. For by so doing,
what is apprehended receives the character of a fixed determinateness, the form of an immediate property or of an inert
phenomenon; furthermore, it is subsumed under the category
of quantity and the nature of the Notion is suppressed. The
exchange of an object that is merely perceived for one reflected
into itself, of a merely sensuous determinateness for an organic
one, thus loses once more its value and does so by the fact that
the Understanding has not yet put behind it the formulating
of laws.

282. To illustrate this exchange by some examples, we may
find perhaps that something which perception takes to be an
'animal with strong muscles' is defined as an 'animal organism
of high irritability', or what perception takes to be a 'condition
of great weakness' is defined as a 'condition of high sensibility',
or, if we prefer it, as an 'abnormal affection' and, moreover,
a 'raising of it to a higher potency'—expressions which translate
sensuous facts into Latin, and a bad Latin at that, instead of
into the Notion. That an animal has strong muscles may also
be expressed by the Understanding by saying that the animal
'possesses a great muscular force'—great weakness meaning similarly a 'slight force'. Determination in terms of irritability has
this advantage over determination in terms of force, that the
latter expresses indeterminate, but the former determinate, reflection-into-self; for the force peculiar to muscle is precisely
irritability; and irritability is a preferable determination to
'strong muscles', since, as in 'force', reflection-into-self is
already directly implied in it. Similarly, weakness or slight
force, *organic passivity*, is given determinate expression in terms
of sensibility. But when this sensibility is so taken by itself and
fixed and, in addition, is bound up with *quantitative* determinations and, *qua* greater or less sensibility, is opposed to a greater
or less irritability, each is wholly in the element of sense and
is reduced to the ordinary form of a property; what connects
them is not the Notion but, on the contrary, a quantitative antithesis, which becomes a difference lacking any thought-content. Though the indefiniteness of the expressions 'force',
'strength', and 'weakness' was thereby eliminated, there now

arises the equally futile, vague floundering-about between the antitheses of higher and lower sensibility and irritability as they increase and decrease relatively to one another. The determinations of greater or lesser sensibility or irritability are no less the unthinking apprehension and expression of a sensuous phenomenon than are the wholly sensuous determinations of strength and weakness which are devoid of any thought-content. Those thoughtless expressions have not been replaced by the Notion; instead, 'strength' and 'weakness' have been given a determination which, taken solely by itself, is based on the Notion, which it has for its content, but loses completely this origin and character. On account of the form of simplicity and immediacy in which this content is made into the aspect of a law, and because quantity constitutes the element of difference in such determinations, the essence of the content, which originally is the Notion and is posited as such, retains the mode of sense-perception, and remains as far removed from being cognized as when determined in terms of strength and weakness or by immediate sense-properties.

283. Now, there still remains to be considered, *solely on its own account*, what the *outer* aspect of organic being is, and how in it the antithesis of *its* inner and outer is determined; just as at first the *inner* of the whole in relation to its *own* outer was considered.

284. The *outer*, considered by itself, is the *structured shape* in general, the system of life articulating itself in the *element* of being, and at the same time essentially the being *for an other* of the organism—objective being in its *being-for-self*. This *other* appears, in the first instance, as its outer inorganic nature. If these two are considered in relation to a law, the inorganic nature cannot, as we saw above, constitute the aspect of a law over against the organism, because the latter is at the same time absolutely for itself, and has a universal and free relation to inorganic nature.

285. To define more precisely, however, the relationship of these two aspects in the organic shape, this shape is, in one aspect, turned against its inorganic nature, while in the other it is *for itself* and reflected into itself. The *actual* organism is the middle term which unites the *being-for-self* of life, with the *outer* in general, or with *being-in-itself*. The extreme of being-for-self

is, however, the inner as an infinite One which takes back into itself, out of their subsistence and connection with outer Nature, the moments of shape itself; it is that which, without a content of its own, gives itself a content in its shape and appears in shape as its *process*. In this extreme where it is a simple negativity or a *pure singular*, the organism possesses its absolute freedom in virtue of which it is indifferent towards, and secured against, being-for-other, and the determinateness of the moments of shape. This freedom is at the same time freedom of the moments themselves, it is their possibility of appearing as an *outer existence*, and of being apprehended as such; and just as, in this freedom, they are free and indifferent towards this outer existence, so, too, are they in relation to one another; for the *simplicity* of this freedom is *being*, or is their simple substance. This Notion, or pure freedom, is one and the same life, no matter how many and varied its shapes or its being-for-other; it is a matter of in-difference to this stream of life what kind of mills its drives. Now, in the first place it is to be noted that this Notion is not to be understood here as it was formerly, when we were considering the properly inner in its form of *process*, or the development of its moments, but in its form of a *simple inner*, which constitutes the purely universal aspect in contrast to the *actual* living being, or as the *element* in which the existent members of the [organic] shape have their *subsistence*. For it is this shape that we are con-sidering here, and in it the essence of life is present as the sim-plicity of subsistence. In the next place, the being-for-other, or the determinateness of the actual structured shape, is taken up into this simple universality which is its essence, a determinate-ness which is equally simple, universal, and non-sensuous, and can only be that which is expressed in *number*. This determinate-ness is the middle term of the shape which links indeterminate life with the actual life, simple like the former and determinate like the latter. That which in the former, the *inner*, would be expressed *numerically*, the outer would have to express in accord-ance with *its* mode as a multiform actuality, viz. as its manner of life, colour, etc., in general, as the entire host of differences which are developed in the world of appearance.

286. If the two aspects of the organic whole—the one being the inner, while the other is the outer, in such a way that each again has in its own self an inner and an outer—are compared

with reference to the inner which each aspect has, then the inner
of the first aspect was the Notion as the unrest of *abstraction*;
the second, however, has for its inner a quiescent universality
which also involves a quiescent determinateness, number. If,
therefore, the first inner, because the Notion develops its
moments in it, made a deceptive promise of laws on account
of the show of necessity in the relationship, the second directly
disclaims doing so, since number shows itself to be the determination of one aspect of its laws. For number is just that completely quiescent, lifeless, and indifferent determinateness in
which all movement and relation is extinguished, and which
has broken the bridge to the living element of instincts, manner
of life, and other aspects of sensuous existence.

287. But to consider the *shape* of the organism as such, and
the inner, *qua* inner, merely of the shape, is in fact no longer
to consider organic being. For the two aspects which were supposed to be related are posited as merely indifferent towards
each other, with the result that the reflection-into-self which
constitutes the essence of the organism is done away with. What
really happens here is that the attempted comparison of inner
and outer is transferred to inorganic Nature. Here the infinite
Notion is only the *essence* which is concealed within, or falls without in self-consciousness, and no longer, as in the organism, is
objectively present. This relation of inner and outer has thus
still to be considered in its own proper sphere.

288. In the first place, that inner aspect of shape as the simple
singularity of an inorganic thing is *specific gravity*. As a simple
being, it can be observed just as well as the determinateness
of number, of which alone it is capable, or, strictly speaking,
it can be found by comparing observations; and it seems in this
way to give one aspect of the law. Shape, colour, hardness,
toughness, and a countless host of other properties would
together constitute the *outer* aspect, and would have to give
expression to the determinateness of the inner, viz. number, so
that the one would have its counterpart in the other.

289. Now, because negativity is understood here not as a
movement of the process, but as a unity *brought to rest*, or as
a *simple being-for-self*, it appears rather as that by which the thing
resists the process and inwardly preserves itself, as indifferent
towards it. But, in virtue of the fact that this simple being-for-

self is a tranquil indifference towards an other, specific gravity appears as one *property alongside* others; and with that, all necessary relation of it to this plurality, in other words, all conformity to law, ceases. Specific gravity, as this simple inner, does not have [the moment of] difference *within itself*, in other words, the difference it has is only unessential; for it is just its *pure simplicity* that effaces all essential distinction. This unessential difference, *magnitude*, must therefore have its counterpart or *other* in the other aspect, viz. the plurality of properties, since it is only through this that it is difference at all. If this plurality itself is concentrated into the simplicity of the antithesis, and determined, say, as *cohesion*, so that this cohesion is a *being-for-self in otherness* (just as specific gravity is a *pure being-for-self*), then this cohesion is in the first place pure determinateness posited in the Notion in contrast to that other determinateness; and the way of formulating the law would be that which we considered above, in connection with the relation of sensibility to irritability. In the next place, cohesion, *qua Notion* of being-for-self in otherness, is further only the *abstraction* of the aspect standing over against specific gravity, and as such has no existence. For being-for-self in otherness is the process in which the inorganic would have to express its being-for-self as a *self-preservation*, which would secure it from emerging from the process as moment of a product. But just this is contrary to its nature, which has no purpose or universality in it. Its process, rather, is merely the specific activity in which its being-for-self, i.e. its specific gravity, is suspended. But this specific activity itself in which its cohesion would exist in its true Notion, and the specific quantity of its specific gravity, are Notions completely indifferent towards each other. If the way in which they react to each other is left out of account, and attention is confined to the idea of quantity, we could perhaps think of the determination like this, that a greater specific weight, as a more intensive being-within-self, would resist involvement in the process more than would a smaller specific weight. But, conversely, the freedom of being-for-self only proves itself in the ease with which it enters into relation with everything, and preserves itself in this multiplicity. The said intensity without extension of relations is an empty abstraction, for extension constitutes the *outer* existence of intension. But the self-preservation of the inorganic in its relation falls, as we have noted, outside of its nature, since the inorganic does not contain within itself the principle of movement, or, in other words, because its being is not absolute negativity and Notion.

290. This other aspect of the inorganic, on the other hand, when considered not as process but as a quiescent being, is ordinary cohesion, a *simple* sensuous property standing over against the liberated moment of *otherness* which is separated into a number of mutually indifferent properties and which, like specific gravity, is one of these properties. The multiplicity of properties together, then, constitutes the other aspect of cohesion. In this, however, as in the other properties, *number* is the sole determinateness, and this not only does not express a relation between these properties and a transition from one to another, but is essentially just the absence of any necessary relation and it represents rather the abolition of all conformity to law; for it is the expression of a determinateness that is *unessential*. This being so, then a series of bodies in which the difference is expressed as a numerical difference of their specific gravities by no means runs parallel to a series in which the difference is that of the other properties, even if, to facilitate the comparison, only one or some of them are taken. For, as a matter of fact, only the entire bundle of properties could constitute the other series in such a parallel. To bring this into order and bind it into a whole, observation has at its disposal, on the one hand, the quantitative determinatenesses of these various properties; on the other hand, however, their differences are manifest as qualitative. Now in this heap of properties, what would have to be characterized as positive or negative and as mutually cancelling each other—in general, the internal arrangement and exposition of the formula, which would be a very complicated matter—this would be for the Notion to determine; but the Notion is excluded by the very manner in which the properties are *immediately* there and taken up. In this [mere] being [of the properties], none displays the character of a negative over against the other; on the contrary, one *is* just as well as the other is, nor does it indicate in any other way its place in the arrangement of the whole. In the case of a series which progresses with parallel differences—whether the relation is meant to be one of simultaneous increase on both sides, or of increase

only on one and decrease on the other—what is of interest is only the *final* simple expression of this combined whole, which was supposed to constitute one aspect of the law over against specific gravity; but this one aspect, as a *given result*, is precisely nothing else than what has already been mentioned, viz. a single property, say, like ordinary cohesion, alongside which the indifferent others, specific gravity among them, are found, and each of the others can with equal right, i.e. with equal incorrectness, be taken as representative of the entire other side; the one, like the other, would merely represent [*repräsentieren*], in German, *vorstellen*, the essential nature, but would not itself be that essential nature. So that the attempt to find series of bodies which would run simply parallel to each other and would express the essential nature of the bodies according to a law of these two series must be regarded as a conception that is ignorant of its task and of the means whereby it should be carried out.

291. Previously, the connection of inner and outer in the organic shape, which is supposed to be present to observation, was straightway transferred to the sphere of the inorganic. The determination which produced this transfer can now be more precisely indicated, and resulting therefrom we have still another form and connection of this relationship. Namely, what in the case of the inorganic seems to offer the possibility of such a comparison of inner and outer, in the case of the organism is altogether absent. The inorganic inner is a simple inner which presents itself to perception as a property that merely *is*; its determinateness is therefore essentially magnitude, and, as a property that merely *is*, it appears indifferent towards the outer, or the various other sensuous properties. But the being-for-self of the living organism does not stand on one side in this way over against its outer; on the contrary, it has in its own self the principle of *otherness*. If we define being-for-self as *simple, self-preserving relation-to-self*, then its otherness is simple *negativity*; and organic unity is the unity of a self-identical relating-to-self and pure negativity. This unity is, *qua* unity, the inwardness of the organism; this is thereby in itself universal, or it is *genus*. But the freedom of the genus, in relation to its actual existence, is different from the freedom of specific *gravity* in relation to shape. That of the latter is a freedom that merely *is*, in other

words, specific gravity as a particular property stands on one side. But because it is a freedom that merely *is*, it is also only a *determinateness* which *essentially* belongs to this shape, or whereby this shape, *qua essential* being, is something determinate. The freedom of the genus, however, is a universal freedom and is indifferent towards this shape or towards its actuality. The *determinateness* which attaches to the *being-for-self* of the inorganic *as such* falls therefore in the case of organic being *under its* being-for-self, just as, in the case of the inorganic, it falls only under the *being* of the latter. Hence, although determinateness in the inorganic is at the same time present only as a *property*, yet it acquires the dignity of *essential* being because, as a simple negative, it stands over against outer existence which is a being-for-another; and this simple negative is, in its ultimate single determinateness, a number. The organic being, however, is a singular individual, which is itself pure negativity, and therefore destroys within itself the fixed determinateness which attaches to *indifferent being*. In so far, therefore, as it has within it the moment of indifferent being, and so, too, of number, this latter can be taken as merely a by-product, but not as the essence of its vitality.

292. But now, though pure negativity, the principle of the process, does not fall outside of the organism, which therefore does not have it in its *essence* as a determinateness, the single individual being itself intrinsically universal, yet in the organism the moments of this pure individual are not developed and actual as moments which are themselves *abstract* or *universal*. On the contrary, this their expression appears outside of that universality, which falls back into the *inwardness* of the organism; and between the actual existence or shape, i.e. the self-developing individual, and the organic universal or the genus, there comes the *determinate* universal, the *species*. The concrete existence attained by the negativity of the universal or the genus is only the developed movement of a process which runs its course in the *parts of the [inert] existence of the shape*. If the genus, as a quiescent unitary being, had within it the differentiated parts, and if, too, its *simple negativity* as such were at the same time a movement which ran through parts which were equally simple and immediately universal in themselves, parts which here were actual as such moments, then the organic genus

would be consciousness. But, as it is, the *simple determinateness*, *qua* determinateness of the species, is present in the genus in a non-spiritual manner; actuality starts from the genus, or, what enters into actual existence is not the genus as such, i.e. in general, not the thought of it. The genus as an actual organism is merely represented by a surrogate, by number. This latter, number, seems to mark the transition from the genus into the individual structured shape, and to provide observation with the two necessary aspects of the latter, one as a simple determinateness, and the other as a shape whose manifold nature is fully developed. This number, however, really indicates the indifference and freedom of the universal and the individual in relation to one another; the genus puts the individual at the mercy of the non-essential quantitative difference, but the individual itself, *qua* living individual, equally shows itself to be free. True universality, as we have defined it, is here only an *inner essence*; as *determinateness of the species* it is a formal universality, and, over against this, the true universality takes its stand on the side of the single individual, which is thereby a living individual, and in virtue of its *inner being* takes no account of its *determinateness as species*. But this individual is not at the same time a universal individual, i.e. one in which the universality would have an outer actual existence as well; the universal individual falls outside of the living organism. This *universal* individual, however, as *immediately* the individual of natural structured shapes, is not consciousness itself; its existence as a *single organic living individual* must not fall outside of it if it is to be consciousness.

293. Consequently, we have a syllogism in which one extreme is the *universal life as a universal* or as genus, the other extreme, however, being the same *universal as a single individual*, or as a universal individual; but the middle term is composed of both: the first seems to fit itself into it as a *determinate* universality or as *species*, the other, however, as *individuality proper* or as a single individual. And since this syllogism pertains wholly to the aspect of the structured shape, it equally embraces within its scope what is distinguished as inorganic Nature.

294. Now, since the universal life, *qua* the *simple essence of the genus*, develops from its side the differences of the Notion, and must exhibit them as a series of simple determinatenesses, this

series is a system of differences posited as [mutually] indifferent, or is a *numerical series*. Whereas previously the organism in the form of a single individual was set over against this essenceless difference, which neither expresses nor contains its living nature; and whereas just the same must be said in respect of the inorganic, taking it as an existence in which the whole of its properties are developed: it is now the universal individual we have to consider, and not merely as free from any systematization of the genus, but also as the power controlling the genus. The genus, which divides itself into species on the basis of the *general determinateness* of number, or which may adopt as its principle of division particular features of its existence, e.g. shape, colour, etc., while peacefully engaged in this activity, suffers violence from the universal individual, *the Earth*, which as the universal negativity preserves the differences as they exist within itself—their nature, on account of the substance to which they belong, being different from the nature of those of the genus—and in face of the systematization of the genus. This action of the genus comes to be a quite restricted affair which it is permitted to carry on only inside those powerful elements, and which is interrupted, incomplete and curtailed on all sides by their unchecked violence.

295. It follows from this that in existence in its structured shape, observation can encounter Reason only as *life in general*, which, however, in its differentiating process does not actually possess any rational ordering and arrangement of parts, and is not an immanently grounded system of shapes. If, in the syllogism of organic structured shapes, the middle term, which contains the species and its actuality as a single individuality, had in its own self the extremes of inner universality and of universal individuality, then this middle term would have in the *movement* of its actuality the expression and the nature of universality, and would be a self-systematizing development. It is thus that *consciousness*, as the middle term between universal Spirit and its individuality or sense-consciousness, has for middle term the system of structured shapes assumed by consciousness as a self-systematizing whole of the life of Spirit— the system that we are considering here, and which has its objective existence as world-history. But organic Nature has no history; it falls from its universal, from life, directly into the single-

ness of existence, and the moments of simple determinateness, and the single organic life united in this actuality, produce the process of Becoming merely as a contingent movement, in which each is active in its own part and the whole is preserved; but this activity is restricted, so far as *itself* is concerned, merely to its centre, because the whole is not present in it, and is not present in it because here it is not *qua* whole *for itself*.

296. Apart, then, from the fact that Reason, in observing organic Nature, attains only to a contemplation of itself as universal life as such, it comes to see its development and realization merely in the form of systems distinguished quite generally, whose essential character lies not in the organic as such, but in the universal individual [the Earth]; and it sees that development and realization *among* these differences belonging to the Earth in the form of arrangements which the genus attempts to achieve.

297. Since, then, the *universality of organic life* falls, in its actuality, directly into the extreme of singleness without a genuine mediation of its own, the thing before the observing Reason is only something 'meant'; and if Reason can take an idle interest in observing this 'meant' thing, it is restricted to the description and narration of the 'meanings' and fanciful conceits it finds in Nature. This unspiritual freedom of 'meaning' will, it is true, offer on all sides the beginnings of laws, traces of necessity, allusions to order and system, ingenious and plausible connections. But, as regards law and necessity, when observation connects the organic with the merely given differences of the inorganic, the elements, zones, and climates, it does not get beyond the idea of a 'great influence'. So, too, on the other side, where individuality has the significance, not of the Earth, but of the *oneness immanent* in life, and where this, in immediate unity with the universal, does indeed constitute the genus, the simple unity of which, however, is just for that reason determined only as number, and therefore sets free the qualitative manifestation; here observation cannot do more than to make clever remarks, indicate interesting connections, and make a friendly approach to the Notion. But clever *remarks* are not a knowledge of necessity, *interesting* connections go no further than being 'of interest', while the interest is still nothing more than a subjective opinion about Reason; and the *friendliness* with which the

individual alludes to a Notion is a childlike friendliness which
is childish if it wants to be, or is supposed to be, valid in and
for itself.

b. *Observation of self-consciousness in its purity and in its relation to
external actuality. Logical and psychological laws*

298. Observation of Nature finds the Notion realized in inorganic Nature, laws whose moments are things which, at the
same time, have the character of abstractions; but this Notion
is not a simplicity that is reflected into itself. The life of organic
Nature, on the other hand, is only this introreflected simplicity;
the antithesis within it of universal and individual does not
sunder itself in the essence of this life itself. The essence is not
the genus which, in its undifferentiated element, would be self-
sundered and self-moved, and at the same time would be, for
itself, undifferentiated in its antithesis. Observation finds this
free Notion, whose universality contains just as absolutely
within it developed individuality, only in the Notion which
itself *exists* at Notion, i.e. in self-consciousness.

299. When observation now turns in upon itself and directs
its attention to the Notion existing as free Notion, it finds, to
begin with, the *Laws of Thought*. This individuality which
Thought is in its own self is the abstract movement of the negative, a movement wholly retracted into simplicity; and the
Laws are outside of reality. To say that they have no *reality*,
means, in general, nothing else than that they lack truth. They
are indeed, not supposed to be the *entire* truth, but still *formal*
truth. But what is purely formal without any reality is a mere
figment of thought, or pure abstraction without that internal
division which would be nothing else but the content.—On the
other hand, however, since they are Laws of pure thought, and
pure thought is intrinsically universal, and therefore a knowledge which immediately contains being, and therein all reality,
these Laws are absolute Notions, and are inseparably the essential principles both of form and of things. Since immanent self-
moving universality is the *sundered* simple Notion, the latter thus
has in itself a *content*, and one which is all content, only not a
sensuous being. It is a content which is neither in contradiction
with the form nor is separated at all from it; rather, it is essenti-

ally the form itself, for the latter is nothing else but the universal dividing itself into its pure moments.

300. But the way in which this form or content *presents itself to observation qua* observation gives it the character of something *found*, something that is *given*, i.e. a content that merely *is*. It becomes a *quiescent being* of relations, a multitude of detached necessities which, as in and for themselves a *fixed* content, are supposed to have truth *in their determinateness*, and thus are, in fact, withdrawn from the form. This absolute truth of fixed determinatenesses, or of a number of different Laws, contradicts, however, the unity of self-consciousness, or of thought and form in general. What is asserted to be a fixed Law that is in itself constant can only be a moment of the unity which is reflected into itself, can only appear as a vanishing magnitude. But, torn out of this context of movement in the course of considering them, and represented separately, it is not content that they lack, for they possess a definite content, but rather form which is their essence. In point of fact, these Laws are not the truth of thought, not because they are supposed to be merely formal, and to possess no content, but rather for the opposite reason, viz. that they are supposed in their determinateness, or just *as a content* from which form has been removed, to rank as something absolute. In their truth, as vanishing moments in the unity of thought, they would have to be taken as a knowing, or as a movement of thought, but not as *Laws* of being. But *observing* is not *knowing* itself, and is ignorant of it; it converts its own nature into the form of *being*, i.e. it grasps its negativity only as *laws* of knowing. It is sufficient here to have pointed out the invalidity of the so-called Laws of Thought from the general nature of the case. The more precise development belongs to speculative philosophy in which they show themselves to be what they are in truth, viz. single vanishing moments whose truth is only the whole movement of thought, *knowing* itself.

301. This negative unity of thought is *for itself*, or rather it is *being-for-its-own-self*, the principle of individuality, and in its actuality is *active consciousness*. Consequently, the observing consciousness will, by the nature of the case, be led towards this as the actuality of those laws. Since this connection is not explicit for the observing consciousness, it supposes that

thought, in its Laws, remains over on one side, and that, on the other side, it obtains another being in what is now an object for it, viz. the active consciousness, which is *for itself* in such a way that it supersedes otherness and, in this intuition of itself as the negative, has its actuality.

302. A new field thus opens up for observation in the *behaviour of consciousness in its actuality*. Psychology contains the collection of laws in accordance with which Spirit relates itself in various ways to the various modes of its actuality as an *otherness already given*. On the one hand, Spirit receives these modes into itself, conforming to the habits, customs, and way of thinking already to hand, as being that in which it is an actuality or an object to itself; and, on the other hand, Spirit knows itself as spontaneously active in face of them, and in singling out from them something for itself, it follows its own inclinations and desires, making the object conform to *it*: in the first case it behaves negatively towards itself as an individuality; in the second case, negatively towards itself as a universal being. According to the first aspect, independence gives to what is already there merely the *form* of self-conscious individuality as such and, as regards the content, remains within the general actuality already given; according to the second aspect, it gives the actuality at least a peculiar modification which does not contradict its essential content, or one even whereby the individual, *qua* particular actuality with a peculiar content, sets itself in opposition to the general actuality, an opposition which becomes wrongdoing or crime when it sets aside that actuality in a merely individual manner, or when it does this in a general way and thus for all, putting another world, another right, law, and customs in place of those already existing.

303. Observational psychology, which in the first instance records its perceptions of the *general modes* coming to its notice in the active consciousness, comes across all sorts of faculties, inclinations, and passions; and since, while recounting the details of this collection it cannot help recalling the unity of self-consciousness, it must at least go so far as to be astonished that such a contingent medley of heterogeneous beings can be together in the mind like things in a bag, more especially since they show themselves to be not dead, inert things but restless movements.

keeping to the universal aspect; the unity of these manifold capacities is the opposite aspect to this universality, the *actual* individuality. However, to take up again in this way the distinctive actual individualities, and to recount that one man has more inclination for this, another for that, that one has more intelligence than another, all this is much less interesting even than enumerating the species of insects, mosses, etc.; for these give observation the right to take them thus singly and uncomprehendingly, because they belong essentially to the element of contingent particularization. On the other hand, to take conscious individuality unintelligently, as a manifestation that is single and separate, involves a contradiction, since its essential nature is the universal of Spirit. But, since observation in apprehending it, endows it with the form of universality, it finds *its law*, and seems now to have a rational aim and to be engaged in a necessary activity.

305. The moments constituting the content of the law are, on the one hand, the individuality itself, on the other hand, its universal inorganic nature, viz. the given circumstances, situation, habits, customs, religion, and so on; from these the specific individuality is to be comprehended. They embrace specific as well as universal elements, and are at the same time something *given*, something which provides material for observation and which, on the other hand, expresses itself in the form of individuality.

306. Now, the law of this relation of the two sides would have to state the kind of effect and influence exerted on the individuality by these specific circumstances. But this individuality consists precisely both in being the *universal*, and hence directly and unresistingly coalescing with the *given* universal, the customs, habits, etc., and becoming conformed to them; and in setting itself in opposition to them and in fact transforming them; and again, in behaving towards them in its individuality with complete indifference, neither letting them exert an influence on it, nor being active against them. Therefore, *what* is to have an influence on the individuality, and what *kind* of influence it is to have—which really mean the same thing—depend solely on the individuality itself; to say that by such and such an influence this individuality has become *this specific individuality* means nothing else than that it has been this all along. Circumstances,

situation, customs, etc., which on the one hand are shown as *already there*, and on the other hand as present in *this specific indivi-duality*, express only the indeterminate nature of the individu-ality, which is not the point under consideration. If these cir-cumstances, way of thinking, customs, in general the state of the world, had not been, then of course the individual would not have become what he is; for all those elements present in this 'state of the world' *are* this universal substance. The fact, however, that the state of the world has particularized itself in this *particular* individual—and it is such an individual that is to be comprehended—implies that it must also have particu-larized itself on its own account and have operated on an indivi-dual in this specific character which it has given itself; only in this way would it have made itself into this specific individual that he is. If the constitution which the external world has spon-taneously given itself is that which is manifest in the individu-ality, the latter would be comprehended from the former. We should have a double gallery of pictures, one of which would be the reflection of the other: the one, the gallery of external circumstances which completely determine and circumscribe the individual, the other, the same gallery translated into the form in which those circumstances are present in the conscious individual: the former the spherical surface, the latter the centre which represents that surface within it.

307. But the spherical surface, the world of the individual, has at once an ambiguous meaning: it is the actual state of the world as it is in and for itself, and it is the world of the indivi-dual; it is the latter either in so far as the individual has merely coalesced with that world, has let it, just as it is, enter into him, behaving towards it as a merely formal consciousness; or, on the other hand, it is the world of the individual, in the sense that the actual world as given has been *transformed* by the indivi-dual. Since, on account of this freedom, the actual world is capable of having this twofold meaning, the world of the indivi-dual is to be comprehended only from the individual himself; and the *influence* on the individual of the actual world, conceived as *existing* in and for itself, receives through the individual the absolutely opposite significance, viz. that the individual either *allows* free play to the stream of the actual world flowing in upon it, or else breaks it off and transforms it. The result of this, how-

ever, is that 'psychological necessity' becomes an empty phrase, so empty that there exists the absolute possibility that what is supposed to have had this influence could just as well not have had it.

308. Thus there is no question of a *being* which would be *in and for itself* and was supposed to constitute one aspect, and the universal aspect at that, of a law. Individuality is what *its* world is, the world that is its *own*. Individuality is itself the cycle of its action in which it has exhibited itself as an actual world, and as simply and solely the unity of the world as *given* and the world it has *made*; a unity whose sides do not fall apart, as in the conception of psychological law, into a world that *in itself* is already given, and an individuality existing *on its own account*. Or, if those sides are thus considered each by itself, there exists no necessity and no law of their connection with one another.

c. *Observation of the relation of self-consciousness to its immediate actuality. Physiognomy and Phrenology*

309. Psychological observation discovers no law for the relation of self-consciousness to actuality, or to the world over against it; and, through the mutual indifference of both, it is forced to fall back on the *peculiar determinateness* of real individuality which exists *in and for itself*, or contains the antithesis of being *for itself* and being *in itself* effaced within its own absolute mediation. Individuality has now become the object for observation, or the object to which observation now turns.

310. The individual exists in and for himself: he is *for himself* or is a free activity; but he has also an *intrinsic* being or has an *original* determinate being of his own—a determinateness which is in principle the same as what psychology thought to find outside of him. In his own self, therefore, there emerges the antithesis, this duality of being the movement of consciousness, and the fixed being of an appearing actuality, an actuality which in the individual is immediately his *own*. This *being*, the *body* of the specific individuality, is the latter's *original* aspect, that aspect in the making of which it has not itself played a part. But since the individual is at the same time only what he has done, his body is also the expression of himself which

he has himself *produced*; it is at the same time a *sign*, which has
not remained an *immediate* fact, but something through which
the individual only makes known what he really is, when he
sets his original nature to work.

311. If we consider the moments here before us in relation to
the previous view, we have here a general human shape, or at
least the general character of a climate, a continent, a people,
just as previously we had the same general customs and culture.
In addition, there are the particular circumstances and situation within the general sphere of actuality; here this particular
actuality is present as a particular formation of the shape of
the individual. On the other side, just as previously the free
activity of the individual was made explicit, as also the fact
of his *own* actuality in the face of the actuality already given, here
the shape stands for the expression of his *own* actualization
established by the individual himself, the lineaments and
forms of his spontaneously active being. But the actuality,
both general and particular, which observation previously
found given outside of the individual, is here the actuality of
the individual, his inherited body, and it is precisely in this that
the 'expression' originating from his activity appears. From the
psychological point of view, actuality in and for itself and the
specific individuality were supposed to be brought into relation
to one another; here, however, the *whole* specific *individuality*
is the object of observation; and each side of the antithesis is
itself the whole. To the outer whole, therefore, belongs not only
the *original being*, the inherited body, but equally the formation
of the body resulting from the activity of the inner being; the
body is the unity of the unshaped and of the shaped being, and
is the individual's actuality permeated by his being-for-self.
This whole, which contains within it the specific original fixed
parts and the lineaments arising solely from the activity, *is*, and
this *being* is the *expression* of the inner being, of the individual
posited as consciousness and movement. This *inner* being is, too,
no longer a formal, spontaneous activity, devoid of content or
indeterminate, an activity whose content and determinateness,
as before was the case, lay in external circumstances; on the
contrary, it is an intrinsically determined original character,
whose form is merely the activity. We have then to consider
here how to determine the relation between these two sides and

what is to be understood by this 'expression' of the inner in the outer.

312. This outer, in the first place, acts only as an *organ* in making the inner visible or, in general, a being-for-another; for the inner, in so far as it is in the organ, is the *activity* itself. The speaking mouth, the working hand, and, if you like, the legs too are the organs of performance and actualization which have within them the action *qua* action, or the inner as such. But the externality which the inner obtains through them is the action as a reality separated from the individual. Speech and work are outer expressions in which the individual no longer keeps and possesses himself within himself, but lets the inner get completely outside of him, leaving it to the mercy of something other than himself. For that reason we can say with equal truth that these expressions express the inner too much, as that they do so too little: too much, because the inner itself breaks out in them and there remains no antithesis between them and it; they give not merely an *expression* of the inner, but directly the inner itself; too little, because in speech and action the inner turns itself into something else, thus putting itself at the mercy of the element of change, which twists the spoken word and the accomplished act into meaning something else than they are in and for themselves, as actions of this particular individual. Not only do the results of the actions, through this externality of the influences of others, lose the character of being something constant in face of other individualities, but since, in their relationship to the inner which they contain, they behave as a separated, indifferent externality, they can, *qua* inner, *through the individual himself*, be something other than they appear to be: either the individual intentionally makes them appear to be other than what they are in truth; or else he is too clumsy to give himself the outer aspect he really wanted, and to establish it so firmly that his work cannot be misconstrued by others. The action, then, as a completed work, has the double and opposite meaning of being either the *inner* individuality and *not* its *expression*, or, *qua* external, a reality *free from* the inner, a reality which is something quite different from the inner. On account of this ambiguity, we must look around for the inner as it still is within the individual himself, but in a visible or external shape. In the organ, however, it is present

only as the immediate activity itself, which attains its externalization in the deed, which either does, or again does not,
represent the inner. The organ, regarded in the light of this
antithesis, does not therefore provide the expression which is
sought.

313. If now the outer shape could express the inner individuality only in so far as that shape is neither an organ nor an
action, hence only in so far as it is a *passive* whole, it would
behave as an existent Thing, which passively received the inner
as an alien element into its passive existence, and thereby
became a sign of it—an external contingent expression whose
actual aspect lacked any meaning of its own—a language whose
sounds and sound-combinations are not the real thing itself, but
are linked with it by sheer caprice and are contingent in relation
to it.

314. Such an arbitrary combination of factors that are
external for one another yields no law. Physiognomy, however, is supposed to differ from other questionable arts and per-
nicious studies because it considers specific individuality in the
necessary antithesis of an inner and an outer, of character as a
conscious disposition, and this again as an existent shape, and
the way it relates these factors to each other is the way they
are related by their Notion; hence these factors must constitute
the content of a law. In astrology, palmistry, and similar
sciences, on the other hand, what seems to be related is only
an outer to an outer, something or other to an element alien
to it. *This* particular constellation at birth, and, when this
external element is brought closer to the body, *these* particular
lines on the hand, are *external* factors indicating a longer or
shorter life, and the fate in general of the particular individual.
Being externalities, they are indifferent towards each other, and
lack the necessity for one another that ought to lie in the relation
of an outer to an inner.

315. Admittedly the hand does not seem to be such a very
external factor for fate; it seems rather to be related to it as
something inner. For fate itself is also only the manifestation
of what the particular individuality is *in itself* as an inner original specific character. Now, to find out what this particular individuality is in itself, the palmist, like the physiognomist, takes
a shorter cut than, e.g., Solon, who thought he could only know

this from and after the course of the whole life; *he* examined the manifestation, but the former examines the [unexplicated] *in-itself*. That the hand, however, must represent the in-itself of the individuality in respect of its fate is easy to see from the fact that, next to the organ of speech, it is the hand most of all by which a man manifests and actualizes himself. It is the living artificer of his fortune. We may say of the hand that it *is* what a man *does*, for in it, as the active organ of his self-fulfilment, he is present as the animating soul; and since he is primarily his own fate, his hand will thus express this in-itself.

316. From this nature of the *organ* of activity, to be a [passive] *being* as well as the *action* within it, or from the fact that the *in-itself*-ness is itself *present* in it, and has a *being for* others, we obtain another view of it than the preceding. Namely, if the organs in general showed themselves to be incapable of being taken as *expressions* of the inner, because in them the action *qua action* is present, but the action *qua* [completed] deed is merely external, and inner and outer in this way fall apart and are or can be alien to each other, then the organ must now, in accordance with its nature, be taken again as also a *middle term* of both. This very fact that the action is *present* in it constitutes an *externality* of it, and, moreover, one that is other than the deed; for the organ remains with and in the individual. Now, this middle term and unity of inner and outer is in the first place itself external too. But then this externality is at the same time taken up into the inner; as *simple* externality it stands over against the dispersed externality, which either is merely a *single* deed or condition contingent for the individuality as a whole, or else, as a *total* externality, is fate split up into a multiplicity of deeds and conditions. Thus the simple lines of the hand, the timbre and compass of the voice as the individual characteristic of speech—this too again as expressed in writing, where the hand gives it a more durable existence than the voice does, especially in the particular style of handwriting—all this is an expression of the inner, so that, as a *simple externality*, the expression again stands over against the *manifold externality* of action and fate, stands in relation to them as an *inner*. Thus, if at first the specific nature and innate peculiarity of the individual, together with what these have become as a result of cultivation

and education, are taken as the inner, as the essence of his action
and his fate, then this essence has its appearance and externality
to begin with in his mouth, hand, voice, handwriting, and the
other organs and their permanent characteristics. *Thereafter*,
and not till then, does it give itself *further* outward expression
in its actual existence in the world.

317. Now, because this middle term gives itself the form of
an outer expression, which is at the same time taken back into
the inner, its existence is not restricted to the immediate organ
of the action; the middle term is rather the movement and form
of countenance and figure in general, which take no part in
the action. These lineaments and their movements are, according to this notion, the action which is held back and which
remains in the individual, and as regards the individual's relation to the action really performed, they constitute his own control and observation of the action, *expression* in the sense of a
reflection on the actual expression. The individual is therefore not
dumb as regards his external action, because he is thereby at
once reflected into himself, and gives expression to this reflectedness-into-self. This theoretical action, or the individual's
speech with himself about the external action, is also perceptible to others, for this speech is itself an expression.

318. In this inner, therefore, which in its expression remains
an inner, there is observed the individual as reflected out of
his actual being; and we have to see what is the significance
of this necessity which is posited in this unity. This reflectedness
is in the first place different from the deed itself and therefore
can be something other than the deed, and can be taken for
something other. We see from a man's face whether he is *in
earnest* about what he is saying or doing. Conversely, however,
what is here supposed to be the expression of the inner is at
the same time an expression in the form of *immediate* being, and
hence is itself degraded to the level of [mere] being, which is
absolutely contingent for the self-conscious being. It is therefore
indeed an expression, but at the same time only in the sense
of a *sign*, so that the particular way in which the content is
expressed is a matter of complete indifference so far as the content itself is concerned. In this appearance, the inner is no doubt
a *visible* invisible, but it is not tied to this appearance: it can
be manifested just as well in another way, just as another inner

can be manifested in the same appearance. Lichtenberg[1] therefore rightly says: 'Suppose the physiognomist ever did take the
measure of a man, it would only require a courageous resolve
on the part of the man to make himself incomprehensible again
for a thousand years.'

Just as, in the previous relationship, the given circumstances
were a [passive] being from which the individuality took what
it could and wanted, either submitting to or transforming that
being, for which reason it did not contain the necessity and
essential nature of the individuality; so here, the manifest immediate being of the individuality is one which either expresses
the fact of its being reflected out of its actual existence and its
being within itself, or which is for the individuality merely a
sign indifferent to what is signified, therefore truly signifying
nothing; for the individuality, it is as much its countenance as
its mask which it can lay aside. The individuality permeates
its shape, moves and speaks in it; but this existence in its entirety
equally turns into a being that is indifferent to the will and the
deed. Individuality effaces from it the significance it formerly
had, viz. of being that in which the individuality is reflected
into itself or has its true essence; instead it places its essence
rather in the will and the deed.

319. Individuality gives up that *reflectedness-into-self* which is
expressed in *lines* and *lineaments*, and *places its essence in the work
it has done*. Herein it contradicts the relationship established by
the instinct of Reason, which is engaged in observing the self-
conscious individuality, ascertaining what its *inner* and *outer* are
supposed to be. This point of view leads us to the thought which
really lies at the base of the 'science'—if one wishes to call it
such—of physiognomy. The antithesis which this observation
encounters has the form of the antithesis of the practical and
the theoretical, both falling within the practical aspect itself—
the antithesis of individuality making itself actual in its 'doing'
('doing' in its most general sense), and individuality as being
at the same time reflected out of this 'doing' into itself and making this its object. Observation accepts this antithesis in the
same inverted relationship which characterizes it in the sphere
of appearance. It regards as the *unessential outer* the *deed* itself
and the performance, whether it be that of speech or a more

[1] *Über Physiognomik*, 2nd edn., Göttingen, 1778, p. 35.

durable reality; but it is the being-within-self of the individuality which is for it the *essential inner*. Of the two aspects possessed
by the practical consciousness, intention and deed (what is
'meant' or intended by the deed and the deed itself), observation selects the former as the true inner; the intention is supposed to have its more or less *unessential* expression in the deed,
but it has its true expression in the shape of the individuality.
The latter expression is the immediate sensuous presence of the
individual spirit; the inwardness which is supposed to be the
true inner is the particularity of the intention and the singleness
of the being-for-self; both together are the spirit as only 'meant'
or intended. What observation has for its objects is thus an existence which is only 'meant', and it looks for laws between such
existences.

320.   The forming of opinions prima facie about the presumed
[outward] presence of Spirit is natural or everyday physiognomy, the over-hasty judgement formed at first sight about the
inner nature and character of its outer shape. The object of this
opinion is of such a kind that its essence involves its being in
truth something else than merely sensuous immediate being.
True, it is also just this reflectedness into itself, out of sense,
in sensuous form, and this which is visibly present as visibility
of the invisible, is the object of observation. But just this sensuous immediate presence is the *reality* of Spirit only for mere
opinion; and observation, in keeping with this aspect, busies
itself with this presumed existence of Spirit, with physiognomy,
handwriting, sound of voice, etc. It connects such existence with
just such a *presumed* inner. It is not the murderer, the thief, who
is to be recognized, but the *capacity to be one*. The fixed abstract
quality thereby gets lost in the concrete, infinitely determinate,
character of the *particular* individual, which now demands more
skilfully contrived delineations than those qualifications are.
Such ingenious delineations certainly say more than the qualifi-
cation, 'murderer', 'thief', or 'good-natured', 'unspoiled', and
so on; but they are far from being adequate for their purpose,
which is to express the *presumed* being or the particular individuality; as inadequate as the delineations of the bodily shape
which go [no][1] further than a 'flat forehead', a 'long nose', etc.
For the individual shape, like the individual self-consciousness,

[1] The sense seems to require a 'no' here.

is, *qua* a being that is 'meant', inexpressible. The 'science of knowing men',[1] which deals with the supposed human being, like the 'science' of physiognomy which deals with his presumed reality, and aims at raising the unconscious judging of everyday physiognomy to the level of knowledge, is therefore something which lacks both foundation and finality; it can never succeed in saying what it means because it *merely* 'means' and its content is something merely 'meant'.

321. The *laws* which this 'science' sets out to find are relations between these two supposed aspects, and hence can themselves be nothing more than empty subjective opinions. Also, since the object of this supposed way of knowing, which takes it upon itself to deal with the reality of Spirit, is just the reflection of Spirit out of its sensuous existence back into itself, and a particular [physical] existence is for Spirit something indifferent and contingent, this kind of knowing must be directly aware that the laws it has discovered tell us nothing, that, strictly speaking, it is idle chatter, or merely the *voicing of one's own opinion* (an expression which contains the truth about itself, viz. that it is one's *own* opinion that is put forward, hence not the matter itself but merely an opinion of *one's own*). As regards their content, however, these observations are on a par with these: 'It always rains when we have our annual fair,' says the dealer; 'and every time, too,' says the housewife, 'when I am drying my washing'.

322. Lichtenberg, who characterizes physiognomic observation in this way, also says this: 'If anyone said, "You certainly act like an honest man, but I see from your face that you are forcing yourself to do so and are a rogue at heart"; without a doubt, every honest fellow to the end of time, when thus addressed, will retort with a box on the ear.' This retort is to the point, because it refutes the primary assumption of such a 'science' of mere subjective opinion, viz. that the reality of a man is his face, etc. The *true being* of a man is rather his deed; in this the individual is *actual*, and it is the deed that does away with both aspects of what is [merely] 'meant' to be: in the one aspect where what is 'meant' has the form of a corporeal passive

---

[1] This refers to the claims put forward by Lavater, whose work was entitled *Physiognomische Fragmente zur Beförderung der Menschenkenntniss und Menschenliebe*, Leipzig, 1775-8 (Baillie's note).

being, the individuality, in the deed, exhibits itself rather as the *negative* essence, which only *is* in so far as it supersedes [mere] *being*. Then, too, the deed equally does away with the inexpressibility of what is 'meant', in respect of the self-conscious individuality. In such mere opinion the individuality is infinitely determined and determinable. In the accomplished deed this spurious infinity is destroyed. The deed is something *simply* determined, universal, to be grasped in an abstraction; it is murder, theft, or a good action, a brave deed, and so on, and what it *is* can be *said* of it. It *is* this, and its being is not merely a sign, but the fact itself. It *is* this, and the individual human being *is* what the *deed is*. In the simplicity of *this being*, the individual is for others a universal being who really is, and who ceases to be something only 'meant'. It is true that, in the deed, he is not explicitly present as Spirit; but when it is a question of his being *qûa being*, and, on the one hand, the twofold being of bodily shape and deed are contrasted, each purporting to be what he actually is, then it is the deed alone that must be affirmed as his *genuine being*—not his face or outward appearance, which is supposed to express what he 'means' by his deeds, or what anyone might suppose he merely *could* do. Similarly, on the other hand, when his *performance* and his inner *possibility*, capacity or intention are contrasted, it is the former alone which is to be regarded as his true actuality, even if he deceives himself on the point, and, turning away from his action into himself, fancies that in this inner self he is something else than what he is in the deed. Individuality, when it commits itself to the objective element in putting itself into a deed, does of course risk being altered and perverted. But what settles the character of the deed is just this: whether the deed is an *actual* being that endures, or whether it is merely a fancied performance, that in itself is nothing at all, and passes away. The analysis of this being into intentions and subtleties of that sort, whereby the *actual* man, i.e. his deed, is to be explained away again in terms of a being that is only 'meant', just as the individual himself even may create for himself special intentions concerning his actuality, all this must be left to the laziness of mere conjecture. Should this idle thinking want to set its sterile wisdom to work, with the aim of denying the doer the character of Reason, and so ill-using him as to declare that not his deed, but his face and lineaments are his real being, then it may expect to get the retort spoken of above, a retort which demonstrates that the face or outward appearance is not the individual's *in-itself* but, on the contrary, can be an object for handling.

323. If we look now at the range of relationships as a whole, in which the self-conscious individuality can be observed to stand towards its outer aspect, there will be one left which has still to be made an object for observation. In psychology it is the *external reality of things* which is supposed to have its self-conscious *counterpart* in Spirit and to make Spirit intelligible. In physiognomy, on the other hand, Spirit is supposed to be known in its *own* outer aspect, as in a being which is the *utterance* of Spirit—the visible invisibility of its essence. There remains the further determination of the aspect of reality, viz. that the individuality expresses its essence in its immediate, firmly established, and purely existent actuality. This last relation is thus distinguished from the physiognomic by the fact that this is the *speaking* presence of the individual who, in expressing himself in *action*, at the same time exhibits himself as inwardly *reflecting* and *contemplating* himself, an expression which is itself a movement, features in repose which are themselves essentially a mediated being. In the determination yet to be considered, however, the outer aspect is lastly a wholly *immobile* reality which is not in its own self a speaking sign but, separated from self-conscious movement, presents itself on its own account and is a mere Thing.

324. In the first place, in regard to the relation of the inner to this its outer, it seems clear that that relation must be grasped as a *causal connection*, since the relation of one being-in-itself to another being-in-itself, *qua* a *necessary* relation, is a causal connection.

325. Now, for spiritual individuality to have an effect on the body it must, *qua* cause, be itself corporeal. The corporeal element, however, in which it acts as cause is the organ, but the organ not of action against external reality, but of the internal action of the self-conscious being operating outwards only against its own body. It is not at once clear which organs these can be. If we were thinking only of organs in general, the organ for work as such would be quite obvious, similarly the organ of sex, and so on. Organs of that sort, however, are to be

considered as instruments or parts which Spirit, as one extreme, possesses as a middle term against the other extreme, which is the external *object*. Here, however, is to be understood an organ in which the self-conscious individual, as an extreme, preserves himself *for himself* against his own [corporeal] actuality which is opposed to him, the individual at the same time not being turned to the outer world but reflected in his action, and in which is an organ in which the aspect of *being* is not a *being-for-another*. It is true that in the physiognomic relation the organ is also considered as an existence reflected into itself and reviewing the action; but this being is an objective being, and the result of the physiognomic observation is this, that self-consciousness confronts this its actuality as something to which it is indifferent. This indifference vanishes in the fact that this very reflectedness-into-self is productive of an effect; thereby that objective existence receives a necessary relation to it. But to act on that existence the reflectedness-into-self must itself have a being, though not, strictly speaking, an objective being, and as such an organ it must be pointed out.

326. Now, in ordinary life, anger, e.g., as such an internal action, is located in the liver. Plato[1] even assigns the liver something still higher, something which is even regarded by some as the highest function of all, viz. prophesying, or the gift of speaking of holy and eternal things in a non-rational manner. But the movement which the individual has in his liver, heart, and so on, cannot be regarded as wholly reflected into itself; rather it is present in such a manner that it has already taken on a corporeal aspect in him and has an animal existence turning outwards to external reality.

327. The *nervous system*, on the other hand, is the immediate repose of the organism in its movement. The *nerves* themselves, it is true, are again the organs of that consciousness which is already immersed in its outward-directed activity; brain and spinal cord, however, may be considered as the immediate presence of self-consciousness, a presence which abides within itself, is not objective and also does not look outwards. In so far as the moment of being which this organ has is a *being-for-another*, i.e. is an outer existence, it is a dead thing and no longer the presence of self-consciousness. This *being-within-itself*, however,

[1] *Timaeus*, 71, 72.

is by its very nature a fluid system, in which the circles cast
into it immediately dissolve, and in which no *lasting* distinction
is expressed. Meanwhile, as Spirit itself is not abstractly simple,
but a system of movements in which it differentiates itself into
moments, but in this very differentiation remains free; and as
Spirit articulates its body into a variety of functions, and allots
one particular part for only one function: so too, the fluid *being*
of its being-*within-self* can be thought of as articulated into parts.
And it seems that it must be thought of in this way, because
the *being* of Spirit which, in the brain, is reflected into itself,
is itself again only a middle term between Spirit's pure essence
and its corporeal articulation, a middle term which therefore
must partake of the nature of both; the corporeal aspect must
therefore also be present in the middle term in the form of *immediate* being.

328. The spiritually organic being has at the same time the
necessary aspect of an *inert, enduring* existence; the former, *qua*
the extreme of being-for-self, must step back, and have this latter as the other extreme over against it, which is then the object
on which the spiritually organic being acts as cause. If now the
brain and spinal cord together constitute that corporeal *being-
for-self* of Spirit, the skull and vertebral column form the other
extreme to it, an extreme which is separated off, viz. the solid,
inert Thing. When, however, anyone thinks of the proper location of Spirit's outer existence, it is not the back that comes
to mind but only the head. Therefore, in examining a way of
knowing like the one we are now dealing with, we can be
satisfied with this reason—not a very bad reason in this case—
in order to confine this existence to the skull. Should it occur
to anyone to think of the back as the location of Spirit in so
far as by it, too, knowing and doing are no doubt sometimes
partly driven *in* and partly driven *out*, this would be no proof
at all that the spinal cord must be taken as included in the indwelling seat of Spirit, because this proves too much. For one
may equally recall that there are other popular external ways,
too, for getting at the activity of Spirit in order to stimulate
or inhibit it. The vertebral column is, then, *rightly* ruled out,
if you like; that the skull alone does *not* contain the *organs* of
Spirit is as well 'explained' as many another doctrine of 'philosophy of Nature'. For this was previously excluded from the

Notion of this relation, and for this reason the skull was taken for the aspect of outer existence; or, if we are not to be allowed to recall the *Notion* of the relation, then certainly experience teaches that, as it is with the eye *qua* organ that we see, so it is *not* with the skull that we murder, steal, write poetry, etc. That is the reason why we must also refrain from using the expression 'organ' for that *significance* of the skull which has still to be mentioned. For although it is commonly said that reasonable men pay attention not to the word but to the thing itself, yet this does not give us permission to describe a thing in terms inappropriate to it. For this is at once incompetence and deceit, to fancy and to pretend that one merely has not the right *word*, and to hide from oneself that really one has failed to get hold of the thing itself, i.e. the Notion. If one had the Notion, then one would also have the right word. What has been determined here in the first instance is only that just as the brain is the living head, the skull is the *caput mortuum*.

329. It is in this dead being, then, that the mental processes and specific functions of the brain would have to display their outer reality, a reality, however, which is still in the individual himself. For the relation of those processes and functions to the skull, which as a dead being does not have Spirit dwelling within it, there presents itself, in the first instance, the external mechanical relation established above, so that the organs proper—and these are in the brain—*here* press the skull out around, *there* widen or flatten it, or in whatever other way one cares to represent this action on it. Being itself a part of the organism, it must indeed be credited, as in the case of every bone, with a living spontaneous formative activity so that, from this point of view, it is rather the skull that on its part presses on the brain, and fixes its outer boundary; and it is better able to do this, being the harder. But in that case the same relation would still obtain in the determination of their reciprocal activity; for whether the skull is the determining factor or the factor determined, this would produce no alteration at all in the causal connection, except that the skull would then be made the immediate organ of self-consciousness because in it, *qua cause*, would be found the aspect of *being-for-self*. But in point of fact, since being-for-self, as an organic spontaneity, is equally present in both, any causal connection between them is ruled

out. This development of the two, however, would be inwardly connected, and would be an organic pre-established harmony, which would leave the two interrelated aspects free in respect of each other, each with its own shape to which the shape of the other need not correspond; and still more so as regards the relation between the shape and the quality, just as the shape of the grape and the taste of the wine are mutually independent. But since the determination of *being-for-self* falls on the side of the brain, but that of *existence* on the side of the skull, there is *also* to be established a causal connection between them within the organic unity—a necessary relation between them as external for one another, i.e. a relation itself external through which, therefore, the *shape* of each would be determined by the other.

330. However, as regards the determination in which the organ of self-consciousness would act causally on the opposite aspect, all sorts of things can be said. For what is in question is the constitution of a cause which is considered in regard to its *indifferent* outer existence, its shape and size, a cause whose inner being and being-for-self are to be precisely of a kind which does not conern the immediate or outer existence. The organic spontaneous formation of the skull is in the first place indifferent to any mechanical influence exerted on it, and the relationship of these two relations, since the former is a relating of itself to itself, is just this very indefiniteness and unboundedness. Furthermore, even if the brain received into itself the distinctions of Spirit as existential distinctions and were a plurality of internal organs each occupying a different space, it would be left undetermined whether a spiritual feature would, according as it was originally stronger or weaker, be bound to possess in the first case a more expanded brain-organ, or in the latter case a more contracted brain-organ, or even the other way about. But it is contradictory to Nature for the brain to be such a plurality of internal organs, for Nature gives the moments of the Notion an existence of their own, and therefore puts the fluid simplicity of organic life clearly on one side, and its articulation and division with its distinctions clearly on the other, so that in the way they are to be grasped here, they display themselves as particular anatomical things. Similarly with the question whether the development of the brain would enlarge or

diminish the organ, whether it would make it coarser and thicker or finer. From the fact that it remains undetermined how the cause is constituted, it is equally left undetermined how the effect is produced in the skull, whether it is an enlarging or a narrowing and falling-in of the latter. When this influence is defined, as it were, more imposingly as a 'stimulation', it is still undetermined whether this takes place by swelling, like the effect of a cantharides plaster, or by shrivelling, like the effect of vinegar. All views of this kind can be supported by plausible grounds, for the organic relation which just as much plays a part accommodates one view as readily as another, and is indifferent to all this cleverness.

331. However, it is not the function of observation to seek to determine this relation, for in any case it is not the brain, *qua* a *physical* part, which stands on the one side, but the brain *qua* the *being* of the *self-conscious* individuality. This latter as a lasting character and spontaneous conscious activity exists *for* itself and *within* itself. Over against this being-for-and-within-itself stand its actuality and its existence-for-another. The being-for-and-within-itself is the essence and the subject which has a being in the brain; this being is *subsumed under the subject*, and gets its value only through its indwelling significance. But the other aspect of self-conscious individuality, the aspect of its outer existence, is *being qua* independent and subject, or *qua* a 'thing', viz. a bone: the *actuality and existence of man is his skull-bone*. This is how the relationship and the two sides of this relation are understood by the consciousness observing them.

332. Observation has now to deal with the more determinate relation of these aspects. The skull-bone does have in general the significance of being the immediate actuality of Spirit. But the many-sidedness of Spirit gives its existence a corresponding variety of meanings. What we have to obtain is the specific meaning of the particular areas into which this existence is divided; and we have to see how these areas contain an indication of that specific meaning.

333. The skull-bone is not an organ of activity, nor even a 'speaking' movement. We neither commit theft, murder, etc. with the skull-bone, nor does it in the least betray such deeds by a change of countenance, so that the skull-bone would become a speaking gesture. Nor has this *immediate* being the

value even of a *sign*. Look and gesture, tone of voice, even a pillar or post erected on a desert island, directly proclaim that they mean something else than what they *simply are* at first sight. They at once profess to be signs, since they have in them a peculiarity which points to something else, by the fact that it does not properly belong to them. A variety of ideas may well occur to us in connection with a skull, like those of Hamlet over Yorick's skull; but the skull-bone just by itself is such an indifferent, natural thing that nothing else is to be directly seen in it, or fancied about it, than simply the bone itself. It does indeed remind us of the brain and its specific nature, and of skulls of a different formation, but not of a conscious movement, since there is impressed on it neither a look nor a gesture, nor anything that proclaims itself to have come from a conscious action; for it is an actuality whose role it is to exhibit another sort of aspect of the individuality, one that would no longer be a self-reflected, but a purely *immediate* being.

334. Further, while the skull-bone does not itself feel, it seems that perhaps a more specific significance could still be found for it in the fact that specific feelings, through their proximity to the skull, might enable us to ascertain what it is that the skull means to convey; and when a conscious mode of Spirit has its feeling in a specific area of the skull, the shape of this part of the skull might perhaps indicate what that mode is, and what is its special nature. Just as, e.g., some people complain of feeling a painful tension somewhere in the head when they are thinking hard, or even when thinking at all, so too could stealing, committing murder, writing poetry, and so on, each be accompanied by its own feeling, which besides would necessarily be localized in its own special place. This area of the brain which would in this way be more moved and activated would probably also develop the adjacent area of the skull-bone; or again this particular area would, from sympathy or consensus, not be inert, but would enlarge or diminish itself or modify its shape in some way or other. What, however, makes this hypothesis improbable is this, that feeling as such is something indeterminate, and feeling in the head as the centre might be a general sympathetic feeling accompanying all forms of suffering, so that mixed up with the thief's, murderer's, poet's, head-itching or headache are other feelings which could as little be

distinguished from one another and also from those we can call
merely bodily feelings, as an illness can be diagnosed from the
symptom of headache, if we restrict its significance merely to
the bodily aspect.

335. In fact, from whatever side we look at the matter, there
is no necessary reciprocal relation at all between them, nor any
direct indication of such a relation. If, all the same, the relation
is still to exist, what remains and is necessary to form it is an
irrational, free, pre-established harmony of the corresponding
determination of the two aspects; for one of the two aspects is
to be a non-spiritual reality, a mere thing.—On the one side,
then, we have a multitude of inert areas of the skull, on the
other, a multitude of mental properties, whose number and
character will depend on the state of psychology. The more
paltry the conception of Spirit, the easier becomes the task from
this side; for partly, the mental properties become fewer, and
partly, they become more detached, rigid, and ossified, and
therefore more akin to characteristics of the bone, and more
comparable with them. But, although the task is made much
easier by the paltry conception of Spirit, yet there still remains
a very great deal to be done on both sides: there remains for
observation the entire contingency of their relation. If the children of Israel, who were likened in number to the sands of the
sea-shore, should each take unto himself the grain of sand
which stood for him, the indifference and arbitrariness of such
a procedure would be no more glaring than that which assigns
to every faculty of soul, to every passion, and—what must
equally be considered here—to each nuance of character which
the more refined psychology and 'knowledge of human nature'
likes to talk about, its particular area of skull and shape of skull-
bone. The skull of a murderer has—not this organ or even
sign—but this bump. But this murderer has as well a multitude
of other properties, just as he has other bumps, and along with
the bumps also hollows; one has a choice of bumps and hollows.
And again, his murderous disposition can be related to any
bump or hollow, and this in turn to any mental property; for
the murderer is neither merely this abstraction of a murderer,
nor does he have only one bump and one hollow. The observations indulged in on this point must, just for that reason, sound
as sensible as those of the dealer and of the housewife about

rain at the annual fair and on wash-day. Dealer and housewife might as well make the observation that it always rains when a particular neighbour goes by, or when they eat roast pork. Just as rain is indifferent to circumstances like these, so too, from the standpoint of observation, a *particular* determinateness of Spirit is indifferent to a *particular* formation of the skull. For of the two objects of this observation, one is a dry, sapless *being-for-itself*, an ossified property of Spirit, the other is an equally sapless *being-in-itself*; such an ossified thing as both are is completely indifferent to everything else. It is just as much a matter of indifference to the high bump whether a murderer is in its vicinity, as it is to the murderer whether flatness is close by him.

336. It is of course undeniable that there remains the *possibility* that a bump at some place or other is connected with a particular property, passion, etc. One *can imagine* the murderer with a high bump here at this place on the skull, and the thief with one there. From this aspect phrenology is capable of still greater expansion; for in the first instance it seems to confine itself to connecting a bump with a property in the *same individual*, that is, the individual possesses both. But natural or everyday phrenology—for there must be such a 'science' as well as a natural physiognomy—already goes beyond this restriction. It not only declares that a cheating fellow has a bump as big as your fist behind his ear, but also asserts that, not the unfaithful wife herself, but the other conjugal party, has a bump on the forehead. Similarly, one can *imagine* the man who is living under the same roof as the murderer, or even his neighbour, or, going further afield, imagine his fellow-citizens, etc. with high bumps on some part or other of the skull, just as well as one can *imagine* the flying cow, that first was caressed by the crab, that was riding on the donkey, etc. etc. But if *possibility* is taken, not in the sense of the possibility of *imagining*, but in the sense of *inner* possibility, or the possibility of the *Notion*, then the object is a reality of the kind which is a pure 'thing', and is, and should be, without a significance of this sort, and can therefore have it only in imagination or picture-thinking.

337. The observer, ignoring the mutual indifference of the two aspects, may nevertheless set to work to determine their relations, partly encouraged by the general rational principle that the *outer* is the *expression of the inner*, and partly supported

by the analogy of the skulls of animals—which indeed may well
have a simpler character than human beings, but of which at
the same time it will be all the harder to say what character
they do have, since it cannot be easy for anyone really to enter
in imagination into the nature of an animal. Should, however,
the observer do so, he will find, in assuring us of the certainty
of the laws he claims to have discovered, an *excellent aid* in a
distinction which must necessarily occur to us here too. The
being of Spirit cannot in any case be taken as something fixed
and immovable. Man is free; it is admitted that the *original*
being consists merely of *dispositions*, about which a man is free
to do much as he wishes, or which require favourable circumstances for their development; i.e. an *original* being of Spirit is
equally well to be spoken of as a being that does not exist *qua
being*. Were observations therefore to conflict with what someone happens to maintain is a law, should it happen to be fine
weather at the annual fair or on wash-day—then dealer and
housewife might say that *really* it *ought* to rain, and that the *tendency* to rain is certainly *present*. So too when observing the skull,
it might be said that this individual *really ought* to be what,
according to the law, his skull proclaims him to be, and that
he has an *original disposition*, but one that has not been developed: this quality is not *present*, but it *ought to be present*. The
'law' and the 'ought' are based on observation of actual rainfall,
and on the actual significance in the case of this particular
characteristic feature of the skull; but if the *reality* is not present,
the *empty possibility* serves equally well. This possibility, i.e. non-
actuality, of the stated law, and hence the observations conflicting with the law, inevitably result from the fact that the freedom
of the individual, and the developing circumstances, are indifferent to *being* as such [or to what merely *is*], indifferent to
being, both as an original inner and as an outer osseous form,
and this also from the fact that the individual can be something
else than he is by inner disposition, and still more than what
he is as a bone.

338. We get then the possibility that this bump or this hollow
on the skull may denote something actual, as well as merely
a disposition, one, moreover, that is so ill-defined as to denote
something that is *not* actual; we see what happens, as always,
to a bad subterfuge, viz. that it is itself ready to be used against

what it is supposed to support. We see mere subjective imagining brought by the very nature of the fact to say—but *unthinkingly*—the opposite of what it affirms; to say that by this particular bone something or other is indicated, but equally too, is *not* indicated.

339. What such imagining vaguely has in mind in the case of this subterfuge is the true thought which, in fact, abolishes that imagining, viz. that *being* as such is not the truth of Spirit at all. Just as the disposition is itself an *original being*, which has no part in the activity of Spirit, just such a being is the bone on *its* side. What merely *is*, without any spiritual activity is, for consciousness, a Thing, and, far from being the essence of consciousness, is rather its opposite; and consciousness is only *actual* to itself through the negation and abolition of such a being. From this point of view it must be regarded as a complete denial of Reason to pass off a bone as the *actual existence* of consciousness; and it is passed off as such when it is regarded as the outer being of Spirit, for the outer is just that reality which merely *is*. It is no use saying that the inner is only being inferred from the outer, and is *something different*, nor that the outer is not the inner itself, but only its *expression*. For in the relation of the two to one another the determination of the reality that *thinks* itself, and is in the form of *thought*, does fall on the side of the inner; but on the side of the outer, falls the determination of the reality which *merely is*. When, therefore, a man is told 'You (your inner being) are this kind of person because your skull-bone is constituted in such and such a way,' this means nothing else than, 'I regard a bone as *your reality*'. To reply to such a judgement with a box on the ear, as in the case of a similar judgement in physiognomy mentioned above, at first takes away from the *soft* parts their importance and position, and proves only that these are no true *in-itself*, are not the reality of Spirit; the retort here would, strictly speaking, have to go the length of beating in the skull of anyone making such a judgement, in order to demonstrate in a manner just as palpable as his wisdom, that for a man, a bone is nothing *in itself*, much less *his* true reality.

340. The crude instinct of self-conscious Reason will reject out of hand such a 'science' of phrenology—this other observational instinct of self-conscious Reason which, having

attained to a glimpse of the cognitive process, has grasped it
unintelligently in a way that takes the outer to be the expression
of the inner. But the worse the conception, the less sometimes
does it occur to one wherein its badness specifically lies, and
the harder it is to analyse it. For a conception is said to be worse,
the purer and emptier the abstraction which is taken to be its
essence. But the antithesis we are here concerned with has for
its sides the individuality that is conscious of itself, and the
abstraction of externality that has become wholly a *Thing*—
that inner being of Spirit grasped as a fixed non-spiritual being,
opposed to just such a being. But Reason, in its role of observer,
having reached thus far, seems also to have reached its peak,
at which point it must abandon itself and do a right-about turn;
for only what is wholly bad is implicitly charged with the immediate necessity of changing round into its opposite. Just so, it
may be said of the Jewish people that it is precisely because
they stand before the portal of salvation that they are, and have
been, the most reprobate and rejected: what that people should
be in and for it self, this essential nature of its own self, is not
explicitly present to it; on the contrary, it places it beyond itself.
By this alienation it creates for itself the *possibility* of a higher
existence, if only it could take back again into itself its alienated
object, than if it had remained undisturbed within the immediacy of being—because Spirit is all the greater, the greater the
opposition from which it has returned into itself; but it creates
this opposition for itself by setting aside its immediate unity,
and by alienating its being-for-self. However, if such a consciousness does not reflect on itself, the intermediate position,
or middle term, which it occupies is an unhappy void, since
what should fill and fulfil it has been turned into a fixed
extreme. Thus it is that this final stage of Reason in its observational role is its worst; and that is why its reversal becomes
a necessity.

341. For a survey of the series of relations considered so far
which constitute the content and object of observation shows
that in their first form, i.e. in the observation of the relations
of inorganic Nature, sensuous being is already lost to view; the
moments of the relations present themselves as pure abstractions and as simple Notions which should be firmly tied to the
existence of things, an existence, however, which gets lost, so

that the moment demonstrates itself to be a pure movement
and a universal. This free process which is complete within itself
retains the significance of something objective, but now appears
as a unitary being; in the process of the inorganic, this unitary
being is the non-existent inner; but the process existing as a unitary being is the organism. The unitary being, *qua* a being-for-
self or negative being, stands in antithesis to the universal,
draws away from it, and remains free for itself, so that the
Notion, being realized only in the element of absolute singleness
and isolation, does not find in organic existence its true expression, viz. to be present as a *universal*, but remains an outer or,
what is the same thing, an *inner* of organic Nature. The organic
process is only *implicitly* free, but is not *explicitly* free *for itself;*
the being-for-self of its freedom appears in *purpose* and *exists* as
another being, as a wisdom that is conscious of itself and is outside
of the process. Reason in the role of observer thus turns to this
wisdom, turns to Spirit, to the Notion existing as a universality,
or to purpose existing as purpose; and henceforth the object
before it is its own essence.

342. It turns its attention at first to its purity [i.e. its abstract
form]; but since Reason *qua* observer apprehends the object,
which moves among its own distinct moments, as an inert being,
its Laws of Thought become connections of one constant
moment to another constant moment. But the content of these
laws being only moments, these run together into the single unit
of self-consciousness. This new object, similarly taken as an *inert
being*, is the *single, contingent* self-consciousness. Observation
stands, therefore, within what it imagines to be Spirit, and
within the contingent relation of conscious reality to a reality
that is not conscious. Spirit alone is in its own self the necessity
of this relation. Observation therefore looks more closely at this
object, and compares its reality which wills and acts with its
reality which ponders and is reflected into itself, a reality which
is itself objective. This outer aspect, although a language of the
individual which he possesses within himself, is at the same
time, *qua* sign, something indifferent to the content it is supposed to denote, just as that which posits for itself the sign is
indifferent to it.

343. For this reason, observation finally goes back again
from this inconstant language to the *fixed being*, and declares,

in accordance with its Notion, that externality is the outer and immediate reality of Spirit, not as an organ, and not as a language or a sign, but as a *dead* Thing. What was ruled out by the very first observation of inorganic Nature, viz. the idea that the Notion ought to be present in the form of a Thing, is reinstated by this last form of observation in such a way that it turns the reality of Spirit itself into a Thing or, expressing it the other way round, gives to lifeless being the significance of Spirit. Observation has here reached the point where it openly declares what *our* Notion of it was, viz. that the certainty of Reason seeks its own self as an objective reality. Of course, the intention here is not to state that Spirit, which is represented by a skull, is a Thing; there is not meant to be any materialism, as it is called, in this idea; rather Spirit must be something more and other than these bones. But to say that Spirit [merely] *is*, means nothing else than that it is a Thing. When *being* as such, or thinghood, is predicated of Spirit, the true expression of this is that Spirit is, therefore, the same kind of being that a *bone is*. It must therefore be regarded as extremely important that the true expression has been found for the bare statement about Spirit—that it *is*. When in other respects it is said of Spirit that it *is*, that it has *being*, is a *Thing*, a single, separate *reality*, this is not *intended* to mean that it is something we can see or take in our hands or touch, and so on, but that is what is *said*; and what *really* is said is expressed by saying that the *being of Spirit is a bone*.

344. Now this result has a twofold significance. One is its true meaning, in so far as it is a completion of the outcome of the preceding movement of self-consciousness. The Unhappy Self-consciousness renounced its independence, and struggled to make its *being-for-self* into a *Thing*. It thereby reverted from self-consciousness to consciousness, i.e. to the consciousness for which the object is something which merely *is*, a Thing; but here, what is a Thing is self-consciousness; the Thing is, therefore, the unity of the 'I' and being—the *category*. The object being determined thus for consciousness, the latter *possesses* Reason. Consciousness, as well as self-consciousness, is *in itself* Reason; but only that consciousness for which the object is determined as the category can be said to *have* Reason. From this, however, we must still distinguish the knowledge of what Reason is. The

category, which is the *immediate* unity of *being* and *self*,[1] must pass through both forms, and it is precisely for consciousness *qua* observer that the category presents itself in the form of *being*. This consciousness, in its result, enunciates as a proposition that of which it is the unconscious certainty—the proposition that is implicit in the Notion of Reason. This proposition is the *infinite judgement* that the self is a Thing, a judgement that suspends itself. Through this result, then, the category is further determined as being this self-superseding antithesis. The *pure* category, which is present for consciousness in the form of *being* or *immediacy*, is the object as still *unmediated*, as merely *given*, and consciousness is equally unmediated in its relation to it. The moment of that infinite judgement is the transition of *immediacy* into mediation, or *negativity*. The given object is consequently determined as a negative object; consciousness, however, is determined as *self*-consciousness over against it; in other words, the category which, in the course of observation, has run through the form of *being* is now posited in the form of being-for-self: consciousness no longer aims to *find* itself *immediately*, but to produce itself by its own activity. It is *itself* the End at which its action aims, whereas in its role of observer it was concerned only with things.

345. The other significance of the result is the one already considered, viz. the significance of an observational activity that dispenses with the Notion. This knows no other way of understanding and expressing itself than naïvely asserting the *reality* of self-consciousness to lie in the bone just as it exists as a sensuous thing, and which at the same time does not lose its objectivity for consciousness. It has no clear consciousness, however, of what is implied in its assertion, and does not grasp the specific character of the subject and predicate, and their relation in its proposition, still less in the sense of the infinite, self-suspending judgement and of the Notion. Rather, out of a profounder self-consciousness of Spirit, which here appears as a natural honesty, it conceals from itself the disgracefulness of the irrational, crude thought which takes a bone for the reality of self-consciousness; and it whitewashes that thought by unthinkingly mixing up with it all sorts of relationships of cause and effect, of 'sign', 'organ', etc. which are meaningless here, and

[1] Einheit des *Seins* und des *Seinen*.

it hides the crudity of the proposition by distinctions derived from them.

346. Brain fibres and the like, when regarded as the being of Spirit, are no more than a merely hypothetical reality existing only in one's head, not the true reality which has an *outer* existence, and which can be felt and seen; when they exist *out there*, when they are seen, they are dead objects, and then no longer pass for the being of Spirit. But objectivity proper must be an *immediate*, *sensuous* objectivity, so that in this dead objectivity—for the bone is a dead thing, so far as what is dead is present in the living being itself—Spirit is explicitly present as actual. The Notion underlying this idea is that Reason takes itself to be *all thinghood*, even *purely objective* thinghood itself; but it is this only *in the Notion*, or, only the Notion is the truth of this idea; and the purer the Notion itself is, the sillier an idea it becomes when its content is in the form, not of the Notion, but of picture-thinking, i.e. if the self-suspending judgement is not taken with the consciousness of this its infinitude, but as a fixed proposition the subject and predicate of which are valid each on its own account, the self fixed as self, the thing fixed as thing, and yet each is supposed to be the other. Reason, essentially the Notion, is directly sundered into itself and its opposite, an antithesis which for that very reason is equally immediately resolved. But when Reason is presented as its own self and its opposite, and is held fast in the entirely separate moment of this asunderness, it is apprehended irrationally; and the purer the moments of this asunderness, the cruder is the appearance of this content which is either only for consciousness, or only ingenuously expressed by it. The *depth* which Spirit brings forth from within—but only as far as its picture-thinking consciousness where it lets it remain—and the *ignorance* of this consciousness about what it really is saying, are the same conjunction of the high and the low which, in the living being, Nature naïvely expresses when it combines the organ of its highest fulfilment, the organ of generation, with the organ of urination. The infinite judgement, *qua* infinite, would be the fulfilment of life that comprehends itself; the consciousness of the infinite judgement that remains at the level of picture-thinking behaves as urination.[1]

[1] Cf. *Philosophy of Nature*, p. 404 (Miller's translation): 'In many animals the organs

B. THE ACTUALIZATION OF RATIONAL SELF-CONSCIOUSNESS THROUGH ITS OWN ACTIVITY

347. Self-consciousness found the Thing to be like itself, and itself to be like a Thing; i.e. it is aware that it is *in itself* the objectively real world. It is no longer the *immediate* certainty of being all reality, but a certainty for which the immediate in general has the form of something superseded, so that the *objectivity* of the immediate still has only the value of something superficial, its inner being and essence being self-consciousness itself. The object, to which it is positively related, is therefore a self-consciousness. It is in the form of thinghood, i.e. it is *independent*; but it is certain that this independent object is for it not something alien, and thus it knows that it is *in principle* recognized by the object. It is Spirit which, in the duplication of its self-consciousness and in the independence of both, has the certainty of its unity with itself. This certainty has now to be raised to the level of truth; what holds good for it *in principle*, and in its inner certainty, has to enter into its consciousness and become *explicit* for it.

348. What the general stages of this actualization will be is readily apparent in a general way from a comparison with the path hitherto followed. Just as Reason, in the role of observer, repeated, in the element of the category, the movement of *consciousness*, viz. sense-certainty, perception, and the Understanding, so will Reason again run through the double movement of self-consciousness, and pass over from independence into its freedom. To begin with, this active Reason is aware of itself merely as an individual and as such must demand and produce its reality in an 'other'. Then, however, its consciousness having raised itself into universality, it becomes *universal* Reason, and is conscious of itself as Reason, as a consciousness that is already recognized in and for itself, which in its pure consciousness unites all self-consciousness. It is the simple, spiritual essence which, in attaining consciousness, is at the same time *real Substance*, into which the earlier forms return as into their ground,

---

of excretion and the genitals, the highest and lowest parts in the animal organization, are intimately connected: just as speech and kissing, on the one hand, and eating, drinking and spitting, on the other, are all done with the mouth.'

so that, in comparison with the latter, they are merely particular moments of its Becoming, moments which do indeed break
loose and appear as independent forms, but in fact have existence and reality only as grounded in that Becoming, and possess
their truth only in so far as they are and remain in it.

349. If we take this goal—and this is the *Notion* which *for
us* has already appeared on the scene—in its reality, viz. the
self-consciousness that is recognized and acknowledged, and
which has its own self-certainty in the other free self-consciousness, and possesses its truth precisely in that 'other'; in other
words, if we look on this still *inner* Spirit as Substance that has
already advanced to the stage of having an *outer* existence, then
in this Notion there is disclosed the *realm of ethical life.* For this
is nothing else than the absolute spiritual *unity* of the essence
of individuals in their independent *actual existence*; it is an intrinsically universal self-consciousness that takes itself to be
actual in another consciousness, in such wise that this has complete independence, or is looked on as a Thing, and it is precisely therein that the universal self-consciousness is aware of
its *unity* with it, and only in this unity with this objective being
is it self-consciousness. This ethical *Substance*, taken in its
abstract universality, is only law in the form of *thought*; but it
is no less immediately actual *self-consciousness*, or it is *custom.* The
single individual consciousness, conversely, is only this existent
unit in so far as it is aware of the universal consciousness in
its individuality as its *own* being, since what it does and is, is
the universal custom.

350. It is in fact in the life of a people or nation that the
Notion of self-conscious Reason's actualization—of beholding,
in the independence of the 'other', complete *unity* with it, or
having for my object the free thinghood of an 'other' which
confronts me and is the negative of myself, as my own being-
for-*myself*—that the Notion has its complete reality. Reason is
present here as the fluid universal *Substance*, as unchangeable
simple thinghood, which yet bursts asunder into many completely independent beings, just as light bursts asunder into
stars as countless self-luminous points, which in their absolute
being-for-self are dissolved, not merely *implicitly* in the simple
independent Substance, but *explicitly for themselves.* They are
conscious of being these separate independent beings through

the sacrifice of their particularity, and by having this universal Substance as their soul and essence, just as this universal again is their own doing as particular individuals, or is the work that they have produced.

351. The purely particular activity and occupation of the individual refers to the needs which he has as a natural creature, i.e. as a *merely immediate* individuality. That even these, its commonest functions, are not frustrated, but enjoy an actual existence, is due to the universal sustaining medium, to the *might* of the entire nation. But, in the universal Substance, the individual has this *form* of subsistence not only for his activity as such, but no less also for the *content* of that activity; what he does *is* the skill and customary practice of all. This content, in so far as it is completely particularized, is, in its actual existence, confined within the framework of the activity of all. The *labour* of the individual for his own needs is just as much a satisfaction of the needs of others as of his own, and the satisfaction of his own needs he obtains only through the labour of others. As the individual in his *individual* work already *unconsciously* performs a *universal* work, so again he also performs the universal work as his *conscious* object; the whole becomes, as *a* whole, his own work, for which he sacrifices himself and precisely in so doing receives back from it his own self. There is nothing here which would not be reciprocal, nothing in relation to which the independence of the individual would not, in the dissolution of its being-for-self in the *negation* of itself, give itself its *positive* significance of being *for itself*. This unity of being-for-another or making oneself a Thing, and of being-for-self, this universal Substance, speaks its *universal language* in the customs and laws of its nation. But this existent unchangeable essence is the expression of the very individuality which seems opposed to it; the laws proclaim what each individual is and does; the individual knows them not only as his universal objective thinghood, but equally knows himself in them, or knows them as *particularized* in his own individuality, and in each of his fellow citizens. In the universal Spirit, therefore, each has only the certainty of himself, of finding in the actual world nothing but himself; he is as certain of the others as he is of himself. I perceive in all of them the fact that they know themselves to be only these independent beings, just as I am. I perceive in them the free

unity with others in such wise that, just as this unity exists through me, so it exists through the others too—I regard them as myself and myself as them.

352. In a free nation, therefore, Reason is in truth realized. It is a present living Spirit in which the individual not only finds his essential character, i.e. his universal and particular nature, expressed, and present to him in the form of thinghood, but is himself this essence, and also has realized that essential character. The wisest men of antiquity have therefore declared that wisdom and virtue consist in living in accordance with the customs of one's nation.

353. But from this happy state of having realized its essential character and of living in it, self-consciousness, which at first is Spirit only *immediately* and in *principle*, has withdrawn, or else has not yet realized it; for both may equally well be said.

354. Reason *must* withdraw from this happy state; for the life of a free people is only in principle or immediately the *reality* of an ethical order. In other words, the ethical order exists merely as something *given*; therefore this universal Spirit itself is a separate, individual spirit, and the customs and laws in their entirety are a *specific* ethical substance, which only in the higher stage, viz. in Spirit's consciousness of its essence, sheds this limitation and in this knowledge alone has its absolute truth, not directly as it *immediately* is. In the latter form it is a *limited* ethical substance, and absolute limitation is just this, that Spirit is in the form of [mere] *being*.

355. Further, therefore, the single, individual consciousness as it exists immediately in the real ethical order, or in the nation, is a solid unshaken trust in which Spirit has not, for the individual, resolved itself into its *abstract* moments, and therefore he is not aware of himself as being a pure individuality on his own account. But once he has arrived at this idea, as he must, then this *immediate* unity with Spirit, the [mere] *being* of himself in Spirit, his trust, is lost. Isolated and on his own, it is he who is now the essence, no longer universal Spirit. This individuality of self-consciousness is, it is true, a moment in universal Spirit itself, but only as a vanishing quantity which, appearing on its own, is at once resolved within universal Spirit, and enters consciousness merely as trust. In thus establishing himself—and each moment, because it is a moment of the essence, must suc-

ceed in exhibiting itself as the essence—the individual has
thereby placed himself in opposition to the laws and customs.
These are regarded as mere ideas having no absolute essentiality, an abstract theory without any reality, while he as this
particular 'I' is his own living truth.

356. Or, self-consciousness has *not yet* attained *this happy state*
of being the ethical substance, the Spirit of a people. For having
turned back from its role of observer, Spirit, at first, is not yet
as such realized through itself; it is established only as an *inner*
essence or as an abstraction. In other words, Spirit is, at first,
immediate; but existing immediately, it is separate and individual. It is the *practical* consciousness, which steps into its world
which it finds already *given*, with the aim of duplicating itself
in this distinct form of something separate and individual, of
producing itself as *this* individual, as this existent counterpart
of itself, and of becoming conscious of this unity of its own actuality with the objective being of the world. Self-consciousness
has the *certainty* of this unity; it holds that the unity is *implicitly*
already present, or that this agreement of itself with thinghood
already exists, and has only to become so *for it* through its own
agency; or that the production of that unity is equally the finding of it. Since this unity means happiness, the individual is
sent out into the world by his own spirit to seek his happiness.

357. If, then, *for us* the truth of this rational self-consciousness
is the ethical substance, here, *for that self-consciousness*, it is the
beginning of its ethical experience of the world. In so far as
it has not yet become the ethical substance, this movement
presses forward to it, and what is superseded in the movement
are the individual moments which for self-consciousness are
valid in their isolation. They have the form of an immediate
will or *natural impulse* which obtains its satisfaction, which is itself
the content of a fresh impulse. If, however, self-consciousness
has lost the happiness of being in the substance, these natural
impulses are bound up with an awareness that their goal is the
true character and essential nature of self-consciousness. The
ethical substance has sunk to the level of a predicate devoid
of self, whose living subjects are individuals who themselves
have to provide the filling for their universality and to fulfil
their essential nature through their own efforts. Taken in the
former sense, then, those forms are the coming-to-be of the

ethical substance and precede it; in the latter, they succeed it and reveal to self-consciousness what its essential nature is. In the former case, the immediacy or rawness of the impulses gets lost in the process of getting to know what their truth is, and their content takes on a higher form. In the latter case, what is lost is the false idea of the consciousness which places its essential nature in those impulses. In the former case, the goal they attain is the ethical Substance, while, in the latter, it is the consciousness of that Substance, a consciousness which knows the Substance to be its own essence; and to that extent this process would be the coming into existence of morality, of a higher form than the ethical Substance. But these forms, at the same time, constitute only one side of morality's entry into existence, that, namely, which belongs to *being-for-self*, or in which consciousness sets aside *its* Ends—not the side where morality arises from the [ethical] substance itself. Since these moments cannot as yet carry the significance of being made into Ends opposed to the lost ethical order, they signify here, it is true, no more than what they immediately are, and the goal which they strive to attain is the ethical Substance; but since in our times that form of these moments is more familiar in which they appear after consciousness has lost its ethical life and, in the search for it, repeats those forms, they may be represented more in terms of this sort.

358. Self-consciousness which is at first only the Notion of Spirit, enters on this path with the characteristic of holding itself to be, as a particular spirit, essential being; and its aim, therefore, is to give itself as a particular individual an actual existence and to enjoy itself as an individual in it.

359. In holding itself to be, *qua being-for-self*, essential being, it is the *negativity* of the 'other'. In its consciousness, therefore, it appears as the Positive in contrast to something which certainly *is*, but which has for it the significance of something without intrinsic being; consciousness appears split into this *given* actuality and the *End* which it realizes by superseding that actuality, an End which, in fact, it makes an actuality in place of that which was *given*. Its primary End, however, is its *immediate* abstract *being-for-self*; in other words, seeing itself as *this particular individual* in another, or seeing another self-consciousness as itself. The experience of what the truth of this End

is raises self-consciousness to a higher level, and from now on it is itself its own End, in so far as it is at the same time universal and has the law directly within it. In carrying out this law of its heart, however, it learns that the individual, in doing so, cannot preserve himself, but rather tht the good can only be accomplished through the sacrifice of the individual: and self-consciousness becomes *virtue*. What virtue learns from experience can only be this, that its End is already attained in principle, that happiness is found directly in the action itself, and that action itself is the good. The Notion or principle of this entire sphere, viz. that thinghood is Spirit's very *being-for-itself*, becomes in the course of this experience a truth *for* self-consciousness. Having discovered this, self-consciousness thus knows itself to be reality in the form of an individuality that directly expresses *itself*, an individuality which no longer encounters resistance from an actual world opposed to it, and whose aim and object are only this expressing of itself.

a. *Pleasure and Necessity*

360. Self-consciousness which, on the whole, knows itself to be *reality*, has its object in its own self, but as an object which initially is merely *for self-consciousness*, and does not as yet possess [objective] being which confronts it as a reality other than its own; and self-consciousness, by behaving as a being-for-self, aims to see itself as another independent being. This *primary* End is to become aware of itself as an individual in the other self-consciousness, or to make this other into itself; it is certain that this other is *in principle* already itself. In so far as it has lifted itself out of the ethical Substance and the tranquil being of thought to its being-*for-self*, it has left behind the law of custom and existence, the knowledge acquired through observation, and theory, as a grey shadow which is in the act of passing out of sight. For the latter is rather a knowledge of something whose being-for-self and actuality are other than those of this self-consciousness. Instead of the heavenly-seeming Spirit of the universality of knowledge and action in which the feeling and enjoyment of individuality are stilled, there has entered into it the Spirit of the earth, for which true actuality is merely that being which is the actuality of the *individual* consciousness.

It despises intellect and science
The supreme gifts of man
It has given itself to the devil
And must perish[1]

361. It plunges therefore into life and indulges to the full the pure individuality in which it appears. It does not so much make its own happiness as straightway take it and enjoy it. The shadowy existence of science, laws and principles, which alone stand between it and its own reality, vanishes like a lifeless mist which cannot compare with the certainty of its own reality. It takes hold of life much as a ripe fruit is plucked, which readily offers itself to the hand that takes it.

362. Its action is only in one respect an action of *desire*. It does not aim at the destruction of objective being in its entirety, but only at the form of its otherness or its independence, which is a show devoid of essence; for it holds this objectivity to be *in principle* the same essence as itself, or its selfhood. The element in which desire and its object subsist, as mutually indifferent and independent, is animate existence; the enjoyment of desire puts an end to this existence so far as it belongs to the object of desire. But here this element which gives to both a separate actuality is rather the category, a being which is essentially in the form of *thought*. It is therefore the *consciousness* of independence—let it be natural consciousness, or consciousness developed into a system of laws—which preserves the individuals each for himself. This separation is not in itself a *fact* for self-consciousness, which knows the other as its own selfhood. It attains therefore to the enjoyment of *pleasure*, to the consciousness of its actualization in a consciousness which appears as independent, or to the vision of the unity of the two independent self-consciousnesses. It attains its End, but only to learn there what the truth of that End is. It comprehends itself as this particular individual who exists *for himself*, but the realization of this End is itself the setting-aside of the latter. For it is not as *this particular* individual that it becomes an object to itself, but rather as the *unity* of itself and the other self-consciousness, hence as an individual that is only a moment, or a *universal*.

363. The pleasure enjoyed has indeed the positive signifi-

[1] *Faust*, Part I (adapted).

cance that self-consciousness has become objective *to itself*; but equally it has the negative one of having reduced *itself* to a moment. And since it grasped its realization in the former sense only, its experience is of a contradiction in which the attained reality of its individuality sees itself destroyed by the negative *essence* confronting it, which is devoid of reality and content, and which yet is the power which destroys it. This essence is nothing else than the *Notion* of what this individuality in itself is. It is, however, as yet the poorest form of self-realizing Spirit; for it is aware of itself at first only as the *abstraction* of Reason, or is the *immediacy* of the unity of being-*for-itself* and being-*in-itself*; its essence is, therefore, only the *abstract* category. Nevertheless it no longer has the form of *immediate simple* being, as it has for Reason in its observational role where it is abstract *being* or, posited in the form of an alien being, is *thinghood* in general. Here in *this* thinghood there has entered being-for-self and mediation. It therefore makes its appearance as a *circle* whose content is the developed pure relation of the simple essentialities. The realization attained by this individuality consists therefore in nothing more than this, viz. that it has cast forth this circle of abstractions from its confinement *within* simple self-consciousness, into the element where they are *for* self-consciousness, in other words, are expanded into an objective existence. The *object*, then, that is for self-consciousness as it takes its pleasure its essence is the expansion of those empty essentialities of pure unity, of pure difference, and their relation; beyond this, the object which the individuality experiences as its *essence*, has no content. It is what is called *necessity*; for necessity, fate, and the like, is just that about which we cannot say *what* it does, what its specific laws and positive content are, because it is the absolute pure Notion itself viewed as [mere] *being*, a *relation* that is simple and empty, but also irresistible and imperturbable, whose work is merely the nothingness of individuality. It is this *fixed* relation, because what is related is the pure essentialities or empty abstractions. Unity, difference, and relation are categories each of which is nothing in and for itself, but only in relation to its opposite, and they cannot therefore be separated from one another. They are related to one another through their *Notion*, for they are pure Notions themselves; and this *absolute relation* and abstract movement constitutes necessity. The

merely single individuality which, in the first instance, has only
the pure Notion of Reason for its content, instead of having
taken the plunge from dead Theory into Life, has therefore really only plunged into the consciousness of its own lifelessness and has as its lot only empty and alien necessity, a *dead*
actuality.

364. The transition is made from the form of the *one* or unit
into that of *universality*, from one absolute abstraction into the
other, from the purpose of pure *being-for-self* which has thrown
off all community with others, into the sheer opposite which
is thus equally abstract *being-in-itself*. Consequently, the form
in which this appears is that the individual has simply perished,
and the absolute unyieldingness of individual existence is pul-
verized on the equally unrelenting but continuous world of actuality. Since it is, as consciousness, the unity of itself and its
opposite, this downfall is still for it its goal and realization, as
also the contradiction of what was *for it* essence and what is
in itself essence. It experiences the double meaning implicit in
what it did, viz. when it took hold of life and possessed it; but
in doing so it really laid hold of death.

365. This *transition* of its living being into a lifeless necessity
therefore appears to it as an inversion which is not mediated by
anything at all. The mediating agency would have to be that in
which both sides would be one, where, therefore, consciousness
recognized one moment in the other: its purpose and action
in fate, and its fate in its purpose and action, that is, would
recognize its *own essence* in this *necessity*. But this unity is, for
this consciousness, just pleasure itself, or the simple single feeling, and the transition from the moment of this its purpose into
the moment of its true essence is for it a sheer leap into its antithesis. For these moments are not contained and linked together
in feeling, but only in the pure self, which is a universal or
thought. Consciousness, therefore, through its experience in
which it should have found its truth, has really become a riddle
to itself, the consequences of its deeds are for it not the deeds
themselves. What befalls it is, *for it*, not the experience of what
it is *in itself*, the transition is not a mere alteration of the form
of the same content and essence, presented now as the content
and essence, and again as object or [outwardly] beheld essence
of itself. The *abstract necessity* therefore has the character of the

merely negative, uncomprehended power of universality, on which individuality is smashed to pieces.

366. This is as far as the manifestation of this form of self-consciousness goes. The final moment of its existence is the thought of the loss of itself in necessity, or the thought of itself as a being that is absolutely *alien* to it. However, self-consciousness has *in itself* survived this loss; for this necessity or pure universality is *its own* essence. This reflection of consciousness into itself, the knowledge that necessity is *itself*, is a new form of consciousness.

b. *The law of the heart and the frenzy of self-conceit*

367. What necessity truly is in self-consciousness, it is for this new form of self-consciousness, in which it knows its own self to be the principle of necessity. It knows that it has the universal of law *immediately* within itself, and because the law is *immediately* present in the being-for-*self* of consciousness, it is called the *law* of the *heart*. This form takes *itself* to be, *qua* individuality, essence like the previous form; but the new form is richer because its *being-for-self* has for it the character of necessity or universality.

368. The law, therefore, which is immediately self-consciousness's own law, or a heart which, however, has within it a law, is the *End* which self-consciousness proceeds to realize. We have to see whether its realization corresponds to this Notion and whether in that realization it will find that this its law is its essential nature.

369. This heart is confronted by a real world; for in the heart the law is, in the first place, only for its own self, it is not yet realised, and is therefore at the same time something other than what the Notion is. This other is thereby characterized as a reality which is the opposite of what is to be realized, and consequently is the contradiction of the law and the individuality. This reality is, therefore, on the one hand a law by which the particular individuality is oppressed, a violent ordering of the world which contradicts the law of the heart, and, on the other hand, a humanity suffering under that ordering, a humanity that does not follow the law of the heart, but is subjected to an alien necessity. It is evident that this real world which appears over against the present form of consciousness is

nothing else but the foregoing discordant relationship of individuality and its truth, the relationship of a cruel necessity by which the former is oppressed. *For us*, the preceding movement appears to stand over against the new form, because the latter in itself has resulted from it, and the moment from which it has come is therefore necessary for it; but to the new form that moment appears as something *already given*, since it is not conscious of its *origin*, and it holds that its essential nature is rather to be for its own self, or the negative element relatively to this positive *in-itself*.

370. This individuality therefore directs its energies to getting rid of this necessity which contradicts the law of the heart, and also the suffering caused by it. And so it is no longer characterized by the levity of the previous form of self-consciousness, which only wanted the particular pleasure of the individual; on the contrary, it is the earnestness of a high purpose which seeks its pleasure in displaying the *excellence* of its own nature, and in promoting the welfare of mankind. What it realizes is itself the law, and its pleasure is therefore at the same time the universal pleasure of all hearts. To it the two are undivided; its pleasure is what conforms to the law, and the realization of the law of universal humanity procures for it its own particular pleasure. For within its own self, individuality and the necessary are *immediately* one; the law is the law of the heart. Individuality is not as yet dislodged from its seat, and the unity of both has not been brought about by the mediating agency of the individuality itself, has not yet been achieved by discipline. The realization of the immediate *undisciplined* nature passes for a display of its excellence and as productive of the welfare of humanity.

371. The law, on the other hand, which confronts the law of the heart is separated from the heart, and exists in its own right. Humanity which is bound by this law does not live in the blessed unity of the law with the heart; but either lives in their cruel separation and in suffering, or at least dispenses with the enjoyment *of itself* in obeying the law, and lacks the consciousness of its own excellence in *transgressing* it. Because that authoritative divine and human ordinance is separated from the heart, it is for the latter a mere show which ought to lose what is still associated with it, viz. the power of authority and reality. In

its *content* it may well by chance agree with the law of the heart, and then the latter can submit to it; but for the heart, what is essential is not the bare conformity to law as such, but that in the law it has the consciousness of *itself*, that therein it has satisfied *itself*. Where, however, the content of universal necessity does not agree with the heart then necessity, even as regards its content, is in itself nothing and must give way before the law of the heart.

372. The individual, then, *carries out* the law of his heart. This becomes a *universal* ordinance, and pleasure becomes a reality which absolutely conforms to law. But, in this realization, the law has in fact escaped the individual; it directly becomes merely the relation which was supposed to be got rid of. The law of the heart, through its very realization, ceases to be a law of the *heart*. For in its realization it receives the form of an [affirmative] *being*, and is now a *universal* power for which this particular heart is a matter of indifference, so that the individual, by setting up his own ordinance, no longer finds it to be his own. Consequently, what the individual brings into being through the realization of his law, is not *his* law; on the contrary, since the realization is in principle his own, but actually is for him an alien affair, what he brings about is merely the entanglement of himself in the actual ordinance, an entanglement in it, moreover, not as a superior power which is only alien to him, but one which is hostile. By his act he places himself in, or rather posits himself as, the universal element of existent reality, and his act is supposed to have, even according to his own interpretation, the value of a universal ordinance. But he has thereby *freed* himself from himself; he goes on growing *qua* universality, on his own account and purges himself of his particularity. The individual who wants to recognize universality only in the form of his immediate being-for-self does not therefore recognize himself in this free universality, while at the same time he belongs to it, for it is his doing. This doing, therefore, has the reverse significance; it contradicts the universal ordinance. For the individual's act is supposed to be the act of *his* particular heart, not a free universal reality; and at the same time he has in fact *recognized* the latter, for his action has the significance of positing his essential being as a free reality, i.e. of acknowledging the real world to be his own essential being.

373. The individual has, by the principle of his action, determined the more precise way in which the actual universality,
to which he has attached himself, turns against him. His deed,
qua actuality, belongs to the universal; but its content is his own
individuality which, as this particular individuality, wants to
preserve itself in opposition to the universal. It is not any specific
law the setting-up of which would be in question; on the contrary, the immediate unity of the *individual* heart with universality is the thought, elevated into a supposedly valid law,
that, in what is law, *every* heart must recognize its own self. But
only the heart of *this* individual has placed its reality in its deed,
which expresses for him *his being-for-self* or *his pleasure*. The deed
is *supposed* to have immediately the status of a universal; that
is to say, it is in truth something particular, and has merely
the form of universality; the *particular* content of the heart *as
such* is supposed to have the status of a universal. Consequently,
others do not find in this content the fulfilment of the law of
their hearts, but rather that of someone else; and, precisely in
accordance with the universal law that each shall find in what
is law *his* own heart, they turn against the reality *he* set up, just
as he turned against theirs. Thus, just as the individual at first
finds only the rigid law, now he finds the hearts of men themselves, opposed to his excellent intentions and detestable.

374. Because this consciousness at first knows universality
only as *immediate*, and necessity as necessity of the *heart*, the
nature of the realization and the activity is unknown to it; it
does not know that this realization as what *affirmatively is*, is in
truth rather the *implicit universal* in which the individuality of
consciousness, which entrusts itself to it in order to *be* this particular immediate individuality, really perishes; instead of
acquiring a being of its own, it therefore attains to being the
alienation of itself. But that in which it does not recognize itself
is no longer a dead necessity, but a necessity animated by the
universal individuality. It took this divine and human ordinance which it found as an accepted authority to be a dead
authority in which not only its own self—to which it clings as
this particular independent heart opposed to the universal—
but also those subject to that ordinance would have no consciousness of themselves; but it finds that this ordinance is really
animated by the consciousness of all, that it is the law of every

heart. It learns from experience that the reality is a vivified ordinance, and it learns this in fact precisely in realizing the law of its own heart; for this means nothing else than that individuality becomes an object to itself in the form of universality in which, however, it does not recognize itself.

375. Thus what emerges from the experience of this shape of self-consciousness as the true, *contradicts* what this consciousness is *for itself*. But what it is for itself, has itself the form of absolute universality for it, and it is the law of the heart which is immediately one with the consciousness of *self*. At the same time, the established living order is equally its *own essential* being and work; it produces nothing else but that; that order is in equally immediate unity with self-consciousness. In this way self-consciousness is related to a twofold antithetic essence; it is in its own self a contradiction, and is distraught in its inmost being. The law of *this* particular heart is alone that in which self-consciousness recognizes itself; but the universally valid order has, through the realizing of that law, equally become for self-consciousness its own essential being and its own reality. Thus what contradicts itself in its consciousness has for it in each case the form of essence and of its own reality.

376. In giving expression to this moment of its self-conscious downfall as the result of its experience, it reveals itself to be this inner perversion of itself, to be a deranged consciousness which finds that its essential being is immediately non-essential, its reality immediately an unreality. The derangement cannot be taken to mean that in general something devoid of essence is regarded as essential, something unreal as real, so that what for one person is essential or real would not be so for another, and that the consciousness of reality and unreality, or of essentiality and unessentiality, would thus fall apart. If something is in fact real and essential for consciousness in general, but is not so for me, then in the consciousness of its nothingness I have at the same time—since I am consciousness in general—the consciousness of its reality; and since they are both fixed [in my consciousness], this is a unity which is madness in general. But in this state only an *object* is deranged for consciousness, not consciousness as such within and for itself. But in the outcome of experience which here has come to view, consciousness, in its law, is *aware of being* itself this reality; and at the same

time, since the very same essentiality, the same reality, is *alienated* from it, it is, *qua* self-consciousness, *qua* absolute reality, aware of its own unreality. In other words, it holds the two sides in their contradiction to be immediately its essential being, which is thus in its inmost being distraught.

377. The heart-throb for the welfare of humanity therefore passes into the ravings of an insane self-conceit, into the fury of consciousness to preserve itself from destruction; and it does this by expelling from itself the perversion which it is itself, and by striving to look on it and express it as something else. It therefore speaks of the universal order as a perversion of the law of the heart and of its happiness, a perversion invented by fanatical priests, gluttonous despots and their minions, who compensate themselves for their own degradation by degrading and oppressing others, a perversion which has led to the nameless misery of deluded humanity. In this its derangement, consciousness declares individuality to be the source of this derangement and perversion, but one that is alien and accidental. It is the heart, however, or the individuality of consciousness that would be immediately universal, that is itself the source of this derangement and perversion, and the outcome of its action is merely that *its* consciousness becomes aware of this contradiction. For the True is for it the law of the heart—something merely *intended* which, unlike the established order, has not stood the test of time, but rather when thus tested is overthrown. This its law ought to have reality; the law, then, is for it *qua* reality, *qua* valid ordinance, its own aim and essential nature; but reality, that very law *qua valid ordinance*, is on the contrary immediately for it something which is not valid. Similarly, its *own* reality, the heart itself as a particular individual consciousness, is for it its essence; but its purpose is to establish that particular individuality as an [objective] being. Thus it is rather its self as *not* a particular individual that is immediately for it its essence, or its purpose has the form of a law, hence the form of a universality, which it is for its own consciousness. This its Notion becomes by its own action its object; thus the heart learns rather that its self is not real, and that its reality is an unreality. It is therefore not an accidental and alien individuality, but just *this* particular heart, which in all its aspects is, in its own self, perverted and perverting.

378. While, however, the *immediately* universal individuality is perverted and the source of perversion, this universal ordinance, since it is the law of all *hearts*, i.e. of what is perverted, is no less itself essentially perverted, as the ravings of the deranged consciousness declared. On the one hand, this ordinance proves itself to be a law of all hearts, by the resistance which the law of one individual heart encounters from other individuals. The established laws are defended against the law of an individual, because they are not an unconscious, empty, and dead necessity, but a spiritual universality and Substance, in which those in whom this spiritual substance has its actuality live as individuals, and are conscious of themselves; so that even when they complain about this ordinance as if it went against their own inner law, and maintain against it the opinions of the heart, they cling to it with their hearts, as being their essential being; and, if this ordinance is taken from them, or they place themselves outside it, they lose everything. Since it is precisely in this that the reality and power of public order consist, the latter thus appears as the self-identical essence alive in everyone, and individuality appears as its form. But this ordinance is equally a perversion.

379. The fact that it is the law of all hearts, that all individuals are immediately this universal, means that the ordinance is a reality which is only that of the individuality that is *for itself*, or as only the reality of the heart. The consciousness which sets up the law of *its* heart therefore meets with resistance from others, because it contradicts the equally *individual* laws of their hearts; and these others in their resistance are doing nothing else but setting up and claiming validity for their own law. The universal that we have here is, then, only a universal resistance and struggle of all against one another, in which each claims validity for his own individuality, but at the same time does not succeed in his efforts, because each meets with the same resistance from the others, and is nullified by their reciprocal resistance. What seems to be public *order*, then, is this universal state of war, in which each wrests what he can for himself, executes justice on the individuality of others and establishes his own, which is equally nullified through the action of the others. It is the 'way of the world', the show of an unchanging course that is only *meant* to be a universality, and whose content is

rather the essenceless play of establishing and nullifying individualities.

380. If we contrast the two sides of the universal ordinance, we see that this latter universality has for its content the restless individuality which regards [mere] opinion or individuality as law, what is real as unreal, and what is unreal as real. But it is at the same time the side of the reality of the ordinance, for to it belongs the individuality's *being-for-self*. The other side is the universal in the form of a tranquil essence; but it is for that very reason only something inner which, though not absolutely non-existent, still has no reality and can itself become a reality only by getting rid of the individuality which has arrogated reality to itself. This shape of consciousness which, in the law, is aware of *itself*, which knows itself in what is *intrinsically* true and good, not as an individuality but only as it becomes an *essential* being; and which knows individuality to be perverted and the source of perversion, and therefore knows it must sacrifice the individuality of consciousness—this shape of consciousness is Virtue.

c. *Virtue and the way of the world*

381. In the first shape of active Reason, self-consciousness took itself to be pure individuality, and it was confronted by an empty universality. In the second, the two sides of the antithesis each had both moments within them, law *and* individuality; but one side, the heart, was their immediate unity, the other their antithesis. Here, in the relationship of virtue and the 'way of the world', the two members are each severally the unity and antithesis of these moments, or are each a movement of law and individuality towards one another, but a movement of opposition. For the virtuous consciousness law is the essential moment, and individuality the one to be nullified, and therefore both in its own consciousness as well as in the 'way of the world'. In the former case, one's own individuality is to be brought under the discipline of the universal, the intrinsically true and good; but under that discipline it still remains a personal consciousness. True discipline requires nothing less than the sacrifice of the entire personality as proof that individual peculiarities are in fact no longer insisted on. In this individual sacrifice, the individuality in the 'way of the world' is at the same time

eradicated, for it too is a simple moment common to both. In the 'way of the world', individuality behaves in a way which is the reverse of its behaviour in the virtuous consciousness, viz. it makes itself the essential moment, whereas what is *intrinsically* good and true it subordinates to itself. Further, the 'way of the world', too, is for virtue not merely this universal which is *perverted by individuality*; on the contrary, the absolute *order* is likewise a common moment, only one that is not present for consciousness as an *existent reality*, but as the *inner* essence of the 'way of the world'. That order, strictly speaking, has not first to be brought into existence by virtue, for to bring into existence is, *qua* action, a consciousness of individuality, and individuality is really what has to be nullified; but this nullifying of individuality merely makes room, as it were, for the *in-itself* of the 'way of the world' to enter into existence on its own account.

382. The general *content* of the actual 'way of the world' we already know; looked at more closely, it is again nothing else but the two preceding movements of self-consciousness. From them has issued the shape of virtue; since they are its origin, they are antecedent to it; but virtue proceeds to nullify its origin, and to realize itself, in other words, to become *for itself*. The 'way of the world' is thus, on the one hand, the single individuality which seeks its [own] pleasure and enjoyment. It is true that in doing so it destroys itself, and thus satisfies the universal, but this very satisfaction, like the rest of the moments of this relationship, is a perverted form and movement of the universal. The reality is only the individuality of the pleasure and enjoyment to which, however, the universal is opposed, a necessity which is merely the empty form of the universal, a merely negative reaction and an action devoid of content. The other moment of the 'way of the world' is the individuality which claims to be law in its own right, and in its own conceit disturbs the existing order. The universal law, it is true, preserves itself in face of this conceit, and no longer makes its appearance as something opposed to consciousness and empty of content, as a blind necessity, but as a necessity *within consciousness itself*. But, when it exists as the *conscious* relation of an absolutely contradictory reality, it is madness; as an *objective* reality, however, it is perversion in general. The universal, then, does display itself in both aspects as the might which moves

them, but the *existence* of this might is merely a universal perversion.

383. It is from virtue now that the universal is to receive its true reality by nullifying individuality, the principle of the perversion. Virtue's purpose is, by so doing, to reverse again the perverted 'way of the world' and to make manifest its true essence. This true essence is at first only implicit in the 'way of the world', only its *in-itself*; it is not yet actual, and consequently virtue only *believes* it. This faith virtue proceeds to raise to sight, without, however, enjoying the fruits of its labour and sacrifice. For in so far as it is an *individuality*, it is the *activity* of the conflict it wages with the 'way of the world'; but its aim and true nature is to conquer the reality of the 'way of the world'. The bringing into existence of the good thus effected is thus the cessation of its *activity* or of the *consciousness* of individuality. What will be the outcome of this conflict itself, what virtue learns from it, whether, by the sacrifice it makes of itself, the 'way of the world' succumbs while virtue triumphs—this must be decided by the nature of the living weapons borne by the combatants. For the weapons are nothing else but the *nature* of the combatants themselves, a nature which only makes its appearance for both of them reciprocally. What their weapons are is already evident from what is implicitly present in this conflict.

384. The universal is true for the virtuous consciousness in its *faith*, or is *implicitly* true; it is not yet an actual, but an *abstract*, universality; in this consciousness itself it is present as a *purpose*, in the 'way of the world' as an *inner* principle. It is precisely in this determination that the universal is present in virtue, too, in relation to the 'way of the world'. For virtue as yet only *wills* to accomplish the good, and does not, to begin with, claim that it is a reality. This characteristic can also be looked at in this way: the good, in making its appearance in the conflict with the 'way of the world', thereby presents itself as being for an *other*, as something that does not have a being of its own, for otherwise it would not want to make itself true by conquering its opposite. That it is, to begin with, only for an *other*, means the same as was shown in the opposite way of looking at it, viz. that it is, to begin with, an *abstraction* which has reality, not in its own right, but only in its relation to the 'way of the world'.

385. The good or the universal, then, as it comes to view there, is what are called gifts, capacities, powers. It is a mode of the spiritual, in which it is represented as a universal, which requires the principle of individuality to give it life and movement, and in this principle has an *actual* existence. This universal is put to *good* use by the principle of individuality, in so far as this principle lives in the virtuous consciousness, but is *misused* in so far as it clings to the 'way of the world'—a passive instrument which, controlled by a free individuality which is indifferent to the use it makes of it, can also be misused for the production of an actual existence which destroys it: a lifeless material lacking an independence of its own, which can be formed this way or that, or even to its own ruin.

386. Since this universal is equally at the disposal of the virtuous consciousness and the 'way of the world', it is not apparent whether virtue thus armed will conquer vice. The weapons are the same; they are these capacities and powers. Virtue has, it is true, held in reserve its belief in the original unity of its own purpose and the essential nature of the 'way of the world', a reserve that is intended to fall on the enemy from the rear during the fight, and *in principle* to achieve that aim. As a matter of fact, therefore, the knight of virtue's own part in the fighting is, strictly speaking, a sham-fight which he *cannot* take seriously—because he knows that his true strength lies in the fact that the good exists absolutely in its own right, i.e. brings itself to fulfilment—a sham-fight which he also *dare* not allow to become serious. For what he turns against the enemy and finds turned against himself, and what he runs the risk of wasting and damaging both in his own case as well as that of the enemy, is not to be the good itself; for he fights to preserve and accomplish that. What are risked in the fight are only the gifts and capacities which are not themselves at issue. But these are, in fact, nothing else but just that very universal in which individuality has been nullified, which is supposed to be preserved and realized by the conflict. But, at the same time, this universal is *already realized* directly by the very notion of the conflict, it is the in-itself, the universal, and its realization means merely this, that it is at the same time for an 'other'. The two aspects specified above, in accordance with each of which it became an abstraction, are no longer separated; it is

especially in and through the conflict that the good is established in both modes. The virtuous consciousness, however,
enters into conflict with the 'way of the world', as if this were
something opposed to the good; what the conflict offers to it
is the universal, not merely as an abstract universal, but as a
universal animated by individuality and existing for an other,
in other words, the *actual good*. Therefore, wherever virtue
comes to grips with the 'way of the world', it always hits upon
places which are the actual existence of the good itself which,
as the *in-itself* of the 'way of the world', is inextricably inter-
woven in every manifestation of the 'way of the world'. And
in the actuality of that in-itself, virtue has its own existence,
too; for virtue, therefore, the 'way of the world' is invulnerable.
All the moments which in virtue itself were supposed to be
risked and sacrificed, are just such existences of the good, and
hence are inviolable relationships. Consequently, the conflict
can only be an oscillation between preserving and sacrificing;
or rather there can be neither a sacrifice of what is one's own,
nor a violation of what is alien. Virtue is not merely like the
combatant who, in the conflict, is only concerned with keeping
his sword bright, but it has even started the fight in order to
preserve the weapons. And not only can it not use its own
weapons, it must also preserve intact those of the enemy and
protect them against its own attack, for all are noble parts of
the good, on behalf of which it went into battle.

387. For this enemy, on the other hand, what is the essence
is not the *in-itself*, the implicit universal, but *individuality*; its
power, therefore, is the negative principle for which nothing
is established or absolutely sacred, but which can risk and
endure the loss of anything and everything. In doing so, it is
just as certain of victory through its own resources, as through
the contradiction in which its opponent gets entangled. What
virtue holds to be an *intrinsic being*, the 'way of the world' regards
as merely an [indifferent] object; it is free from every principle
that virtue holds to be established, and by which it is bound.
Such a principle the 'way of the world' has in its power, since
it regards it as something it can either set aside or let be, as
it can also the virtuous knight who is fast-bound by it. The latter
cannot disentangle himself from it, as if it were a cloak thrown
round him from which he could free himself by leaving it

behind; for to him it is something essential which he must not give up.

388. Finally, as regards the ambush from which the intrinsically good is to attack the 'way of the world' cunningly from the rear, this is essentially a vain hope. The 'way of the world' is the alert, self-assured consciousness that cannot be got at from behind, but faces in every direction; for its nature is that everything is [merely] an object for it, that everything stands in front of it. But when the intrinsically good is an [indifferent] object for the enemy, then it is involved in the conflict we have seen; but in so far as it is not such an object but possesses intrinsic being, it is the passive instrument of gifts and capacities, a material lacking reality. If represented as a real being, it would be a dormant consciousness, one remaining in the background, no one knows where.

389. Virtue, therefore, is conquered by the 'way of the world' because its purpose is, in fact, the abstract, unreal *essence*, and because its action as regards reality rests on distinctions which are purely nominal. It wanted to consist in bringing the good into actual existence by the sacrifice of individuality, but the side of reality is itself nothing else but the side of individuality. The good was supposed to be that which has an *implicit* being, and to be opposed to what *is*; but the in-itself, taken in its real and true sense, is rather *being itself*. The *in-itself* is, in the first instance, the *abstraction of essence* in contrast to reality; but an abstraction is precisely what is not true, but exists only *for consciousness*, which means, however, that it is itself what is called *real*; for the real is that which is essentially *for an other*, or is *being*. But the consciousness of virtue rests on this distinction between the *in-itself* and *being*, a distinction which has no truth. The 'way of the world' was supposed to be the perversion of the good because it had individuality for its principle; only, individuality is the principle of the *real* world; for it is precisely individuality that is consciousness, whereby what exists *in itself* exists equally *for an other*; it does pervert the Unchangeable, but it perverts it in fact from the *nothing of abstraction into the being of reality*.

390. Thus the 'way of the world' triumphs over what, in opposition to it, constitutes virtue, triumphs over that which is the essenceless abstraction of essence. However, it does not

triumph over something real but over the creation of distinctions that are no distinctions; it glories in this pompous talk
about doing what is best for humanity, about the oppression
of humanity, about making sacrifices for the sake of the good,
and the misuse of gifts. Ideal entities and purposes of this kind
are empty, ineffectual words which lift up the heart but leave
reason unsatisfied, which edify, but raise no edifice; declama-
tions which specifically declare merely this: that the individual
who professes to act for such noble ends and who deals in such
fine phrases is in his own eyes an excellent creature—a puffing-
up which inflates him with a sense of importance in his own
eyes and in the eyes of others, whereas he is, in fact, inflated
with his own conceit.

Virtue in the ancient world had its own definite sure meaning, for it had in the *spiritual substance* of the nation a foundation
full of meaning, and for its purpose an actual good already in
existence. Consequently, too, it was not directed against the
actual world as against something *generally perverted*, and against
a 'way of the world'. But the virtue we are considering has its
being outside of the spiritual substance, it is an unreal virtue,
a virtue in imagination and name only, which lacks that substantial content. The emptiness of this rhetoric which
denounces the 'way of the world' would be at once revealed
if the meaning of its fine phrases had to be stated. These, therefore, are assumed to be something the meaning of which is familiar. The request to say what this familiar meaning is would
be met either by a fresh flood of phrases or by an appeal to
the heart, which *inwardly* says what they mean—which amounts
to admitting that it is *in fact* unable to say what the meaning
is. The fatuousness of this rhetoric seems, too, in an unconscious
way to have come to be a certainty for the culture of our time,
since all interest in the whole mass of such rhetoric, and the
way it is used to boost one's ego, has vanished—a loss of interest
which is expressed in the fact that it produces only a feeling
of boredom.

391. The result, then, which issues from this antithesis consists in the fact that consciousness drops like a discarded cloak
its idea of a good that exists [only] in principle, but has as yet
no actual existence. In its conflict it has learnt by experience
that the 'way of the world' is not as bad as it looked; for its

reality is the reality of the universal. With this lesson in mind, the idea of bringing the good into existence by means of the sacrifice of individuality is abandoned; for individuality is precisely the actualizing of what exists only in principle, and the perversion ceases to be regarded as a perversion of the good, for it is in fact really the conversion of the good, as a mere End, into an actual existence: the movement of individuality is the reality of the universal.

392. However, with this result, that which as the 'way of the world' stood opposed to the consciousness of what existed [only] in principle, has in fact likewise been conquered and has vanished. In that antithesis, individuality's *being-for-self* was opposed to essence or the universal, and appeared as a reality separated from what exists [only] *in itself* or in principle. But, since reality has shown itself to be in undivided unity with the universal, then, just as the *in-itself* of virtue is merely an aspect, so does the being-for-self of the 'way of the world' also prove to be no more than that. The individuality of the 'way of the world' may well imagine that it acts only for *itself* or in its own interest. It is better than it thinks, for its action is at the same time an implicitly universal action. When it acts in its own interest, it simply does not know what it is doing; and when it avers that everyone acts in his own interest, it is merely asserting that no one knows what action is. When it acts *for itself*, it simply gives reality to what, to begin with, exists only *in itself*. The purpose of its being-for-self, which it imagines is opposed to what virtue is in itself, its shallow cunning, as also its finespun explanations which know how to demonstrate the presence of self-interest in every action—all these have vanished, just as the purpose of virtue that exists only *in itself*, along with its rhetoric, have vanished.

393. Thus the activity of individuality, all that it does, is in its own self an End; the employment of its powers, the play of these powers in action, is what gives them life; otherwise they would be a lifeless in-itself. But the in-itself is not an unrealized abstract universal that lacks an existence, but rather is itself immediately the present, real existence of the process of individuality.

C. INDIVIDUALITY WHICH TAKES ITSELF TO BE REAL IN
AND FOR ITSELF

394. Self-consciousness has now grasped the Notion of itself which, to begin with, was only *our* Notion of it, viz. that in its certainty of itself it is all reality; and End and essence are for it henceforth the spontaneous interfusion of the universal—of gifts and capacities—and individuality. The individual moments of this fulfilling and interfusion, *prior* to the unity in which they have coalesced, are the Ends hitherto considered. These have vanished, being abstractions and chimeras belonging to those first shallow shapes of spiritual self-consciousness, and having their truth only in the imaginary being of the heart, in imagination and rhetoric, not in Reason. This, being now absolutely certain of its reality, no longer seeks only to realize itself as End in an antithesis to the reality which immediately confronts it but, on the contrary, has the category as such for the object of its consciousness.

In other words, self-consciousness determined as being for *itself*, or as the *negative* self-consciousness in which Reason at first made its appearance, is set aside; this self-consciousness came face to face with a reality supposedly the negative of it, and only by overcoming it did it realize its End. But since *End* and *intrinsic being* have proved to be the same as *being-for-another* and the *reality* confronting it, truth is no longer separated from certainty, no matter whether the proposed End is taken as certainty of self and the realization of it as truth, or whether the End is taken for truth and the reality for certainty. On the contrary, intrinsic being and End in and for itself are the certainty of immediate reality itself, the interfusion of *being-in-itself* and *being-for-itself*, of the universal and individuality. Action is in its own self its truth and reality, and individuality in its setting-forth or expression is, in relation to action, the End in and for itself.

395. With this Notion of itself, therefore, self-consciousness has returned into itself out of those opposed determinations which the category had for it, and which characterized the relation of self-consciousness to the category in its observational and also active roles. It has for its object the pure category itself, or it is the category which has become aware of itself.

Its account with its previous shapes is thereby closed; they lie forgotten behind it, and no longer confront it as a world *given* to it, but are developed solely within itself as transparent moments. Yet they still fall apart within its consciousness as a *movement* of distinct moments, a movement which has not yet brought them together into their substantial unity. But in all these moments self-consciousness holds fast to the simple unity of [objective] being and the self, a unity which is its *genus*.

396. In so doing, consciousness has cast away all opposition and every condition affecting its action; it starts afresh from *itself*, and is occupied not with an *other*, but with *itself*. Since individuality is in its own self actuality, the material of its efforts and the aim of action lie in the action itself. Action has, therefore, the appearance of the movement of a circle which moves freely within itself in a void, which, unimpeded, now expands, now contracts, and is perfectly content to operate in and with its own self. The element in which individuality sets forth its shape has the significance solely of putting on the shape of individuality; it is the daylight in which consciousness wants to display itself. Action alters nothing and opposes nothing. It is the pure form of a transition from a state of not being seen to one of being seen, and the content which is brought out into the daylight and displayed, is nothing else but what this action already is in itself. It is *implicit*: this is its form as a unity in *thought*; and it is *actual*—this is its form as an *existent* unity. Action itself is a *content* only when, in this determination of simplicity, it is contrasted with its character as a transition and movement.

a. *The spiritual animal kingdom and deceit, or the 'matter in hand' itself*

397. This intrinsically real individuality is at first again a *single* and *specific* one. The absolute reality which it knows itself to be is, therefore, as it will become aware, an *abstract, universal* reality lacking filling and content, merely the empty thought of this category. We have to see how this Notion of intrinsically real individuality characterizes itself in its moments, and how its Notion of itself enters into its consciousness.

398. The Notion of this individuality, which as such knows itself to be all reality, is to begin with a *result*: it has not yet set forth its movement and reality, and is posited here *immediately* as a simple in-itself or *implicit* being. Negativity, however,

which is the same as that which is manifested as movement, is present in the simple in-itself as a determinateness; and
[mere] *being*, or the simple in-itself, becomes a definite range
of being. Accordingly, individuality appears on the scene as an
original determinate nature: *original*, for it is implicit; originally
determinate, for the negative moment is present in the in-itself
and this latter is thus a quality. This limitation of being, however, cannot limit the *action* of consciousness, for here consciousness is a relation purely of itself to itself: relation to an *other*,
which would be a limitation of it, has been eliminated. The
original determinateness of the nature is, therefore, only a
simple principle, a transparent universal element, in which the
individuality remains as free and self-identical as it is unimpeded in unfolding its different moments, and in its realization is simply in a reciprocal relation with itself; just as in the
case of indeterminate animal life, which breathes the breath
of life, let us say, into the element of water, or air or earth, and
within these again into more specific principles, steeping its
entire nature in them, and yet keeping that nature under its
own control, and preserving itself as a unity, in spite of the limitation imposed by the element, and remaining in the form of
this particular organization the same general animal life.

399. This determinate original *nature* of consciousness which
remains free and entire in it appears as the immediate and
sole proper *content* of that which for the individual is its End.
Admittedly, it is a *determinate* content, but it is only a *content*
at all in so far as we consider the *in-itself* in isolation. In truth,
however, it is the reality that is permeated by individuality,
actuality as it is present in consciousness *qua* individual, and
it is, in the first instance, posited as [merely] *being*, not yet as
acting. But as regards action, that determinateness is, on the one
hand, not a limitation it would want to overcome, for, regarded
as an existent quality, it is the simple colour of the element in
which it moves; on the other hand, however, negativity is a
determinateness only in being; but *action* is itself nothing else but
negativity. Therefore, when individuality acts, determinateness
is dissolved in the general process of negativity or in the sum
total of every determinateness.

400. In *action* and the consciousness of action, the simple
original nature now splits up into the distinction which action

implies. Action is present at first in the form of *object*, an object, too, as pertaining to consciousness, as *End*, and hence opposed to a reality already given. The second moment is the *movement* of the End conceived as passive, and realization conceived as the relation of the End to the wholly formal actuality, hence the idea of the transition itself, or the *means*. The third moment is, finally, the object, which is no longer in the form of an End directly known by the agent to be *his own*, but as brought out into the light of day and having *for him* the form of an 'other'. The Notion of this sphere requires that these various aspects be grasped in such a way that the content in them remains the same without any distinction, whether between individuality and being in general, or between End as against individuality as an original nature, or between End and the given reality; or between the means and that reality as an absolute End, or between the reality brought about by the agent as against the End, or the original nature, or the means.

401. First of all, then, the *originally* determinate nature [or natural predisposition] of individuality, its *immediate* essence, is not as yet posited as active, and as such is called *special* capacity, talent, character, and so on. This peculiar tinge of Spirit is to be looked on as the sole content of the End itself and as the sole reality. If we thought of consciousness as going beyond that, and as wanting to give reality to a different content, then we should be thinking of it as a Nothing working towards Nothing. Further, this original essence is not merely the content of the End, but is in itself the *reality* as well, which otherwise has the appearance of being a *given* material of the action, of being a reality *found to begin with*, which is to be shaped by the action. That is to say, action simply translates an initially implicit being into a being that is made explicit; the being-in-itself of the reality opposed to consciousness is reduced to a mere empty show. This consciousness, then, when bringing itself to act, does not let itself be led astray by what is merely the show of a *given* reality, and equally it has to avoid floundering about in empty thoughts and Ends, and has to hold on to the original content of its essence. True, this original content is only explicit *for* consciousness when the latter has made it into a reality; but the distinction between a content, which is explicit *for* consciousness only *within consciousness itself*, and an intrinsic reality outside it,

no longer exists. Consciousness must act merely in order that what it is *in itself* may become explicit *for it*; in other words, action is simply the coming-to-be of Spirit as *consciousness*. What the latter is *in itself*, it knows therefore from what it *actually* is. Accordingly, an individual cannot know what he [really] is until he has made himself a reality through action. However, this seems to imply that he cannot determine the *End* of his action until he has carried it out; but at the same time, since he is a *conscious* individual, he must have the action in front of him beforehand as *entirely his own*, i.e. as an *End*. The individual who is going to act seems, therefore, to find himself in a circle in which each moment already presupposes the other, and thus he seems unable to find a beginning, because he only gets to know his original nature, which must be his End, *from the deed*, while, in order to act, he must have that End beforehand. But for that very reason he has to start immediately, and, whatever the circumstances, without further scruples about beginning, means, or End, proceed to action; for his essence and *intrinsic* nature is beginning, means, and End, all in one. As *beginning*, this nature is present in the circumstances of the action; and the *interest* which the individual finds in something is the answer already given to the question, 'whether he should act, and what should be done in a given case'. For what seems to be a *given* reality is in itself his own original nature, which has merely the illusory appearance of an [objective] being—an appearance implied in the Notion of action with its twofold aspect, but which shows itself to be his own original nature by the interest he takes in it. Similarly, the 'how' or the means is determined in and for itself. *Talent* is likewise nothing else but the determinate, original individuality considered as an *inner means*, or as a *transition* from End to an achieved reality. But the *actual* means and the real transition are the unity of talent with the nature of the matter in hand, present in that interest: talent represents in the means the side of action, interest the side of content; both are individuality itself, as an interfusion of being and action. What we have, therefore, is a set of given *circumstances* which are *in themselves* the individual's own original nature; next, the interest which treats them as *its own* or as its End; and finally, the union [of these] and the abolition of the antithesis in the *means*. This union itself still falls within consciousness and the whole just considered is one side of an antithesis. This illusory appearance of an antithesis which still remains, is removed by the transition or the means; for the means is a *unity* of inner and outer, the antithesis of the specific character it has as an *inner* means. It therefore rids itself of that character and posits itself—this unity of action and being—equally as an *outer*, as an individuality that has itself become a reality, i.e. an individuality which is posited for individuality itself as [objectively] existent. In this way, the entire action does not go outside itself, either as circumstances, or as End, or means, or as a work done.

402. But with 'work done' the difference of the original natures seems to enter; the work, like the individual's original nature which it expresses, is something specific; for the negativity implicit in action, being freely discharged by it as an existent reality, is present in the action as a quality. Consciousness, however, as against the work, is determined as that in which the quality is present as negativity *in general*, i.e. as action; it is thus the universal as against the specific character of the work done. It can therefore compare one work with another, and by so doing grasp individualities themselves as *different*; it can regard an individual whose work is more wide-ranging as possessing greater energy of will or a richer nature, i.e. a nature whose native quality is less limited; and another, on the other hand, as a weaker and poorer nature.

403. In contrast with this unessential *quantitative* difference, 'good' and 'bad' would express an absolute difference; but here this is not in place. Whether something is held to be good or bad, it is in either case an action and an activity in which an individuality exhibits and expresses itself, and for that reason it is all good; and it would, strictly speaking, be impossible to say what 'badness' was supposed to be. What would be called a bad work is the individual life of a specific nature, which therein gives itself reality. It would only be put down as a bad work by a comparing reflection, which, however, is an idle affair, since it goes beyond the essential nature of the work, which is to be a self-expression of the individuality, and in it looks for and demands something else, no one knows what. The comparison could only have regard to the above-mentioned difference. But this, being a quantitative difference, is in itself not an essential one; and here, specifically, because the things

compared would be different works or individualities. But these
have no connection with one another; each is purely self-
related. The original nature is alone the *in-itself*, or what could
be laid down as a standard for judging the work, and conversely. Both, however, correspond to each other: there is
nothing *for* individuality which has not been made so *by* it, or
there is no reality which is not individuality's own nature and
doing, and no action nor in-itself of individuality that is not
real; and only these moments are to be compared.

404. Therefore, feelings of exaltation, or lamentation, or
repentance are altogether out of place. For all that sort of thing
stems from a mind which imagines a *content* and an *in-itself*
which are different from the original nature of the individual
and the actual carrying-out of it in the real world. Whatever
it is that the individual does, and whatever happens to him,
that he has done himself, and he *is* that himself. He can have
only the consciousness of the simple transference *of himself* from
the night of possibility into the daylight of the present, from
the *abstract in-itself* into the significance of *actual* being, and can
have only the certainty that what happens to him in the latter
is nothing else but what lay dormant in the former. It is true
that the consciousness of this unity is likewise a comparison,
but what is compared is merely an illusory appearance of an
antithesis, an appearance of the form [of antithesis] which, for
self-conscious Reason that is aware that individuality in its own
self is reality, is nothing more than an illusory show. The individual, therefore, knowing that in his actual world he can find
nothing else but its unity with himself, or only the certainty
of himself in the truth of that world, *can experience only joy in
himself*.

405. This is the Notion which consciousness forms of itself,
of itself as an absolute interfusion of individuality and being.
Let us see whether this Notion is confirmed by experience, and
whether its reality corresponds to it. The work produced is the
reality which consciousness gives itself; it is that in which the
individual is explicitly for himself what he is implicitly or in
himself, and in such a manner that the consciousness, for which
the individual becomes explicit in the work, is not the particular, but the universal, consciousness. In his work, he has placed
himself altogether in the element of universality, in the quality-

less void of being. The consciousness which withdraws from its work is, in fact, the universal consciousness in contrast to its work, which is *determinate* or *particular*—and it is universal because it is absolute negativity or action in this antithesis. It thus goes beyond itself in the work, and is itself the quality-less void which is left unfilled by its work. But if their unity before was preserved in the Notion, this happened simply because the work *qua existent* was sublated. But it is supposed to *exist*, and we have to see how in its existence the individuality will preserve its universality, and will know how to satisfy itself.

In the first place, we have to consider by itself the work produced. It has received into itself the whole nature of the individuality. Its *being* is therefore itself an action in which all differences interpenetrate and are dissolved. The work is thus expelled into an existence in which the quality of the original nature in fact turns against other determinate natures, encroaches on them, and gets lost as a vanishing element in this general process. Although *within the Notion* of the objectively real individuality all the moments—circumstances, end, means, and realization—have the same value, and the original specific nature has the value of no more than a universal element, on the other hand, when this element becomes an objective being, its *specific character* as such comes to light in the work done, and obtains its truth in its dissolution. More precisely, the form which this dissolution takes is that, in this specific character, the individual, *qua* this particular individual, has become aware of himself as actual; but the specific character is not only the content of the reality, but equally its form; in other words, the reality simply as such is just this quality of being opposed to self-consciousness. Looked at from this aspect, the reality is revealed as a reality that has vanished from the Notion, and is merely an alien reality that is found given. The work *is*, i.e. it exists for other individualities, and is for them an alien reality, which they must replace by their own in order to obtain through *their* action the consciousness of *their* unity with reality; in other words, *their* interest in the work which stems from *their* original nature, is something different from this work's *own* peculiar interest, which is thereby converted into something different. Thus the work, is, in general, something perishable, which is obliterated by the counter-action of other forces and interests, and really exhibits the reality of the individuality as vanishing rather than as achieved.

406. Consciousness, then, in doing its work, is aware of the antithesis of doing and being, which in the earlier shapes of consciousness was at the same time the *beginning* of action, while here it is only a *result*. But in fact this antithesis was likewise the foundation, in that consciousness proceeded to act as an *implicitly* real individuality; for the action presupposed the specific original nature as the *in-itself* of the individuality, and the *content* of that nature was achievement simply for the sake of achievement. Pure action, however, is a *self-identical* form with which, therefore, the *specific character* of the original nature is not in agreement. Here, as elsewhere, it is a matter of indifference which of the two is called Notion and which reality. The original nature has only an ideal existence, or is the in-itself in contrast to the action in which it first becomes a reality; or in other words, the original nature is the *being* both of the individuality as such and of the individuality in the form of work, while action is the original Notion as an absolute transition, or as the coming-to-be [of the reality]. This *disparity* between Notion and reality which lies in its essence, is learnt by consciousness from experience in its work; in work, therefore, consciousness becomes what it is in truth, and its empty Notion of itself vanishes.

407. In this fundamental contradiction inherent in work—which is the truth of this essentially real individuality—all the aspects of the individuality thus appear again as contradictory; that is to say, the work, *qua* the content of the whole individuality, when transferred from the *doing* of it, which is the negative unity holding captive all the moments of that content, now lets the moments go free; and in the element of existence they become indifferent to one another. Notion and reality are thus separated into purpose, and that which is the original essentiality. It is accidental if the purpose has a truly essential nature, or if the in-itself is made the purpose. Even so, Notion and reality again fall apart as a *transition* to reality and as *purpose*; in other words, it is accidental if a *means* is chosen which expresses the purpose. And finally the entirety of these inner moments (whether they possess an inner unity or not), i.e. the *action* of the individual, is again in an accidental relationship

to *reality* in general; fortune decides as well in favour of an ill-disposed purpose and an ill-chosen means, as against them.

408. If, now, consciousness is thus made aware in its work of the *antithesis* of willing and achieving, between end and means, and, again, between this inner nature in its entirety and reality itself, an antithesis which in general includes within it the contingency of its action, yet the unity and necessity of the action are no less present, too. The latter aspect overlaps the former, and the experience of the contingency of the action is itself only a contingent experience. The necessity of the action consists in the fact that *purpose* is related simply to *actuality*, and this unity is the Notion of action; action takes place because action is in and for itself the essence of actuality. In the work, it is true, there is revealed the contingency possessed by achievement when contrasted with willing and doing; and this experience, which seems as if it must be accepted as truth, contradicts that Notion of action. If, however, we consider the content of this experience in its completeness, it is seen to be the vanishing work. What is preserved is not the vanishing: the vanishing is itself actual and is bound up with the work and vanishes with it; the negative itself perishes along with the positive whose negative it is.

409. This vanishing of the vanishing lies in the Notion of the intrinsically real individuality itself; for that in which the work vanishes or what vanishes in the work, and what was supposed to give experience, as it was called, its supremacy over individuality's own Notion of itself, is the *objective reality*. Objective reality, however, is a moment which itself no longer possesses any truth on its own account in this consciousness; that truth consists solely in the unity of this consciousness with the action, and the true work is only that unity of *doing* and *being*, of willing and achieving. Consciousness, then, because of the fundamental certainty of its actions, holds the reality opposed to that certainty to be for it alone; for self-consciousness which has returned into itself, and for which all antithesis has vanished, antithesis can no longer take this form of being *for itself* in antithesis to reality. On the contrary, then, the antithesis and the negativity manifested in work affect not merely the content of the work *or* the content of consciousness as well, but affect the reality as such, and hence affect the antithesis present in that

reality, and present only in virtue of it, and the vanishing of the work. In this way, then, consciousness is reflected out of its perishable work into itself, and preserves its Notion and its certainty as what objectively exists and endures in face of the experience of the *contingency* of action. It experiences in point of fact its Notion, in which reality is only a moment, i.e. something *for consciousness*, not something which exists in its own right; it experiences it as a vanishing moment, and reality therefore has for consciousness only the value of *being* as such, whose universality is one with action. This unity is the true work; it is the very heart of the matter [*die Sache selbst*] which completely holds its own and is experienced as that which *endures*, independently of what is merely the *contingent* result of an individual action, the result of contingent circumstances, means, and reality.

410. The 'heart of the matter' is only opposed to these moments in so far as they are supposed to be isolated, but as an interfusion of the reality and the individuality it is essentially their unity. It is equally an action and, *qua* action, pure action in general, hence just as much an action of this particular individual; and this action as still *his* in antithesis to reality, is a purpose. Equally, it is the transition from this determinateness into the opposite, and lastly it is a reality which is explicitly present *for* consciousness. The 'heart of the matter' thus expresses the *spiritual* essentiality in which all these moments have lost all validity of their own, and are valid therefore only as universal, and in which the certainty consciousness has of itself is an objective entity, an objective fact for it, an object born of self-consciousness as its own, without ceasing to be a free object in the proper sense. The Thing of sense-certainty and perception now acquires its significance through self-consciousness and through it alone; on this rests the distinction between a Thing and a cause or a 'matter in hand'. A movement corresponding to that from [sense-] certainty to perception will run its course here.

411. In the 'matter in hand', then, in which the interfusion of individuality and objectivity has itself become objective, self-consciousness has come into possession of its true Notion, or has attained to a consciousness of its substance. At the same time, this consciousness as it exists here is one that has just now come into being, and hence is an immediate consciousness of its sub-

stance; and this is the specific way in which spiritual being is present here; it has not yet developed into a truly real substance. The 'matter in hand' has, in this immediate consciousness of its substance, the form of simple essence which, as a universal, contains within itself all its various moments and belongs to them, but, again, is also indifferent to them as specific moments, and is free and independent, and as this free, *simple, abstract* 'matter in hand' has the value of essential being. The various moments of the original determinateness or of the 'matter in hand' of *this* particular individual, the moments of his End, of the means, of the action itself, and of the reality, all these are, on the one hand, single particular moments for this consciousness, which, in comparison with the 'matter in hand', it can abandon and surrender. On the other hand, however, they all have this 'matter in hand' as their essence but only in such a way that it, being their *abstract* universal, can be found in each of these various moments, and can be a *predicate* of them. The 'matter in hand' is not yet a subject; but those moments count as subject because they fall on the side of *individuality* in general, whereas the 'matter in hand' is at first only the simple universal. It is the *genus* which is found in all these moments as *species* of itself, and is equally free and independent of them.

412. Consciousness is called *honest* when it has on the one hand attained to the idealism which the 'matter in hand' expresses, and on the other hand possesses the truth in it *qua* this formal universality; a consciousness which is concerned solely with the 'matter in hand' and therefore busies itself solely with the various moments or species of it; and when it does not attain the 'matter in hand' in one of these moments or in one meaning, it for that very reason gets hold of it in another. Consequently, it does in fact always obtain the satisfaction which it should enjoy in virtue of its Notion. Whichever way things turn out, it has accomplished and attained the 'matter in hand', for this being the *universal* genus of those moments is the predicate of them all.

413. If this consciousness does not convert its purpose into a reality, it has at least *willed* it, i.e. it makes the purpose *qua* purpose, the mere doing which does nothing, the 'heart of the matter', and can therefore explain and console itself with the fact that all the same something was taken in hand and done.

Since the universal itself contains subsumed under it the negative moment or the vanishing, the fact that the work annihilates itself, this too is *its* doing. It has incited the others to do this, and in the vanishing of its reality still finds satisfaction, just like naughty boys who enjoy *themselves* when they get their ears boxed because *they* are the cause of its being done. Or, again, suppose it has not even attempted to carry out the 'matter in hand', and has done absolutely nothing, then it has not *been able* to; the 'matter in hand' is for it just the unity of its resolve and the reality; it asserts that the reality would be nothing else but what it was possible for it to do. Finally, suppose something of interest to him has come his way without any effort on his part, then for him this *reality* is the 'matter in hand' just because of the interest he finds in it, even though that reality has not been produced by him. If it is a piece of good fortune that has befallen him personally, then he is sure that it is his own doing and his own desert; if, on the other hand, it should be an event of historical importance which does not really concern him, he makes it likewise his own; and an interest for which he has done nothing is, in his own eyes, a party interest which *he* has favoured or opposed, and even combated or supported.

414. The *integrity* of this consciousness, as well as the satisfaction it experiences in all its relationships, obviously consists in the fact that it does not bring together its *thoughts* about the 'matter in hand'. For it, the 'matter in hand' is as much its *own* affair as not a work at all, or is a mere action and an empty purpose, or even a reality involving no action at all; it makes one meaning after another the subject of this predicate, and forgets them one after another. Now, the 'matter in hand' in being merely willed, or even in being incapable of realization, has the meaning of an empty purpose and of a unity of willing and achievement only *in thought*. The consolation for the failure of the purpose which at least was *willed*, or at least *simply done*, as well as the satisfaction of having given others something to do, makes simple doing, or thoroughly bad work, the essence of the whole affair; for that work is to be called bad which is no work at all. Finally, in the lucky event of finding the reality already in being, this 'being' becomes without any effort the 'matter in hand' itself.

415. The truth about this integrity, however, is that it is not

as honest as it seems. For it cannot be so unthinking as to let these various moments actually fall apart in that way; it must be directly aware of their antithesis because they are absolutely interrelated. The *pure* action is essentially the action of this particular individual, and this action is equally essentially a *reality* or a 'matter in hand'. Conversely, the reality is essentially only as *his* doing and as action in general as well; and *his* action is at the same time only as action in general and so, too, as reality in general. While, then, it seems to him that his concern is only with the 'matter in hand' as an *abstract* reality, it is also a fact that he is concerned with it as his own doing. But just because he is concerned merely with being active and busy, he is not really in earnest about it; he has only to do with some objective matter and with one that is his own. Since, finally, he seems to will only *his own* affair or his own action, it is again a matter of dealing with an *affair in general* or with a reality that endures in its own right.

416. Just as the 'matter in hand' itself and its moments appear here as *content*, they are equally necessary, too, as *forms* in consciousness. They appear as content only to vanish, each making room for the other. They must therefore be present in the character of superseded forms; but as such they are aspects of consciousness itself. The 'matter in hand' is present as the in-itself or the reflection into itself of consciousness; the supplanting of the moments by one another finds expression there, however, in their being established in consciousness, not as they are in themselves but only as existing for another consciousness. One of the moments of the content is exposed by it to the light of day and made manifest to others; but consciousness is at the same time reflected back from it into itself and the opposite is equally present within consciousness which retains it for itself as its own. At the same time what occurs is not that one or other of the moments is *merely* exposed, and another merely retained; on the contrary, consciousness operates alternately with them, for it must make one as well as another essential for itself and for the others. The *whole* is the spontaneous interfusion of individuality and the universal; but because this whole is present for consciousness only as the *simple* essence, and thus as the abstraction, of the 'matter in hand' its separate moments fall apart outside of that 'matter in hand' and of one another. As a *whole*,

it is only exhaustively exhibited by alternately exposing its moments and retaining them for itself. Since in this alternation consciousness keeps, in its reflection, one moment for itself and as essential, while another is only externally present in *it*, or is for *others*, there thus enters a play of individualities with one another in which each and all find themselves both deceiving and deceived.

417. An individuality sets about carrying out something; by so doing it seems to have made something *its own* affair; it acts, and in acting becomes involved with others and seems to itself to be having to do with *reality*. The others therefore take its action for a sign of its interest in the 'matter in hand' as such, and its purpose to be the carrying-out of the matter *per se*, regardless whether this is done by the first individuality or by them. Accordingly, when they point out that this matter has already been accomplished by them, or, if it has not, offer and furnish their assistance, then this consciousness has really left the position they believe it to occupy; it is its *own* action and its *own* effort that constitute its interest in the 'matter in hand', and when the others become aware that this was really the 'matter in hand,' then they feel they have been deceived. But actually their eagerness to come and help was itself nothing else but a desire to see and exhibit *their* own action, not the matter in hand itself; that is, they wanted to deceive the others in just the same way that they complain of having been deceived. Since it now turns out that its *own* action and effort, the play of its *own* powers, is the 'heart of the matter', it seems that consciousness is occupied with its own interest, not with that of others, and is anxious only about action as its own action, not about action as the action of others, and hence seems to allow the others to do as they like about the matter *they* have in hand. But again they are mistaken; that consciousness has already left the position they thought it occupied. It is not concerned with the 'matter in hand' as its *own* particular affair, but simply as a 'matter in hand', as a universal, which is for everyone. It interferes, therefore in the action and work of others, and, if it can no longer take the work out of their hands, it at least shows an interest in it by passing judgement on it; if it gives it the stamp of its approval and praise, this is meant to imply that, in the work, it praises not only the work itself, but also *its own*

generosity and moderation in not having damaged the work as work, nor damaged it by *its* censure. In showing an interest in the work, it is enjoying its own self; and the work which it censures is equally welcome to it for just this enjoyment of its own action which its censure provides. Those, however, who think or pretend to think that they have been deceived by this interference, wanted really themselves to practise the same kind of deceit. They pretend that their action and efforts are something for themselves alone in which they have only themselves and their own essential nature in mind. However, in doing something, and thus bringing themselves out into the light of day, they directly contradict by their deed their pretence of wanting to exclude the glare of publicity and participation by all and sundry. Actualization is, on the contrary, a display of what is one's own in the element of universality whereby it becomes, and should become, the affair of everyone.

418. It is, then, equally a deception of oneself and of others if it is pretended that what one is concerned with is the '*matter in hand*' *alone*. A consciousness that opens up a subject-matter soon learns that others hurry along like flies to freshly poured-out milk, and want to busy themselves with it; and they learn about that individual that he, too, is concerned with the subject-matter, not as an *object*, but as his *own* affair. On the other hand, if what is supposed to be essential is merely the doing of it, the employment of powers and capacities, or the expression of this particular individuality, then equally it is learned by all parties that they all regard themselves as affected and invited to participate, and instead of a mere 'doing', or separate action, peculiar to the individual who opened up the subject-matter, something has been opened up that is for others as well, or is a subject-matter on its own account. In both cases the same thing happens and only has a different significance by contrast with what was assumed and was supposed to be accepted. Consciousness experiences both sides as equally essential moments, and in doing so learns what the *nature of the 'matter in hand'* really is, viz. that it is neither merely something which stands opposed to action in general, and to individual action, nor action which stands opposed to a continuing being and which would be the free *genus* of these moments as its *species*. Rather is its nature such that its *being* is the *action* of the *single* individual and of

all individuals and whose action is immediately *for others*, or
is a 'matter in hand' and is such only as the action of *each* and
everyone: the essence which is the essence of all beings, viz. *spiri-*
tual essence. Consciousness learns that no one of these moments
is *subject*, but rather gets dissolved in the *universal 'matter in hand'*;
the moments of the individuality which this unthinking consciousness regarded as subject, one after the other, coalesce into
simple individuality, which, as this particular individuality, is
no less immediately universal. Thus the 'matter in hand' no
longer has the character of a predicate, and loses the characteristic of lifeless abstract universality. It is rather substance permeated by individuality, *subject* in which there is individuality
just as much *qua* individual, or *qua this particular* individual, as
qua all individuals; and it is the universal which has being only
as this action of all and each, and a *reality* in the fact that *this*
particular consciousness knows it to be its own individual reality
and the reality of all. The pure 'matter in hand' itself is what
was defined above as 'the category', being that is the 'I' or
the 'I' that is being, but in the form of *thought* which is still distinguished from *actual self-consciousness*. Here, however, the
moments of actual self-consciousness in so far as we call them
its content (purpose, action, and reality), and also in so far as
we call them its form (being-for-self and being-for-another), are
posited as one with the simple category itself, and the category
is thereby at the same time the entire content.

b. *Reason as lawgiver*

419. Spiritual essence is, in its simple being, *pure consciousness*,
and *this self*-consciousness. The originally *determinate* nature of
the individual has lost its positive meaning of being *in itself* the
element and the purpose of its activity; it is merely a superseded
moment, and the individual is a *self* in the form of a universal
self. Conversely, the *formal* 'matter in hand' gets its filling from
the active, self-differentiating individuality; for the differences
within the latter constitute the *content* of that universal. The
category is *in itself*, or implicit, as the universal of *pure conscious-*
ness; it is equally *for itself* or explicit, for the *self* of consciousness
is equally a moment of it. It is absolute being, for that universality is the simple *self-identity* of being.

420. Thus what is object for consciousness has the signifi-

cance of being the True; *it is* and it is *authoritative*, in the sense that it exists and is authoritative in and for itself. It is the *absolute* 'matter in hand', which no longer suffers from the antithesis of certainty and its truth, between universal and individual, between purpose and its reality, but whose existence is the *reality* and *action* of self-consciousness. This 'matter in hand' is therefore the *ethical substance*; and consciousness of it is the *ethical* consciousness. Its object is likewise for it the True, for it combines self-consciousness and being in a single unity. It has the value of the *Absolute*, for self-consciousness cannot and does not want any more to go beyond this object, for in it, it is in communion with itself: it *cannot*, for it is all being and all power; it does not *want* to, for it is the *self* or the will of this self. The object is in its own self *real* as object, for it contains within itself the distinction characteristic of consciousness; it divides itself into 'masses' [*Massen*] or spheres which are the *determinate laws* of the absolute essence. These 'masses', however, do not obscure the Notion, for the moments of being and pure consciousness and of the self remain enclosed within it—a unity which constitutes the essence of these 'masses' and which, in this distinction, no longer lets these moments fall apart from one another.

421. These laws or 'masses' of the ethical substance are immediately acknowledged. We cannot ask for their origin and justification, nor can we look for any other warrant; for something other than essence that is in and for itself could only be self-consciousness itself. But self-consciousness is nothing but this essence, for it is itself the being-for self of this essence which is the truth, just because it is as much the *self* of consciousness as it is its *in-itself* or pure consciousness.

422. Since self-consciousness knows itself to be a moment of the *being-for-self* of this substance, it expresses the existence of the law within itself as follows: sound Reason knows immediately what is right and good. Just as it knows the law immediately, so too the law is valid for it immediately, and it says directly: 'this is right and good'—and, moreover, this particular law. The laws are *determinate*; the law is the 'matter in hand' itself filled with a significant content.

423. What is thus given immediately must likewise be accepted and considered immediately. Just as in the case of

sense-certainty, we had to examine the nature of what it immediately expressed as *being*, so here, too, we have to see how the
being expressed by this immediate ethical certainty, or by the
immediately existing 'masses' of the ethical substance, is constituted. Examples of some such laws will show us this; and since
we take them in the form of declarations of the sound Reason
which *knows* them, *we* do not have first to introduce the moment
which has to be made valid in them, considered as *immediate*
ethical laws.

424. 'Everyone ought to speak the truth.' In this duty as
expressed unconditionally, the condition will at once be
admitted: *if* he knows the truth. The commandment, then, will
now run: everyone ought to speak the truth at all times, according to his knowledge and conviction. Sound Reason, this ethical
Substance precisely, which knows immediately what is right
and good, will also explain that this condition was already so
much part and parcel of that universal maxim that this is how
it *meant* that commandment to be understood. But, with this
admission, it in fact admits that already, in the very act of
saying the commandment, it really violates it. It *said*: everyone
ought to speak the truth; but it *meant*: he ought to speak it
according to his knowledge and conviction; that is to say, what
it said was different from what it meant; and to speak otherwise
than one means, means not speaking the truth. The untruth
or inapt expression in its improved form now runs: everyone
ought to speak the truth according to his knowledge and conviction at the time. But with this correction, what the proposition wanted to enunciate as universally necessary and intrinsically valid, has really turned round into something completely
contingent. For speaking the truth is made contingent on
whether I can know it, and can convince myself of it; and the
proposition says nothing more than that a confused muddle of
truth and falsehood ought to be spoken just as anyone happens
to know, mean, and understand it. This contingency of the content has universality merely in the *propositional form* in which
it is expressed; but as an ethical proposition it promises a universal and necessary *content*, and thus contradicts itself by the
content being contingent. Finally, if the proposition were recti-
fied by saying that the contingency of the knowledge and conviction of the truth ought to be dropped, and that the truth ought

also to be *known*, then this would be a commandment which directly contradicts the one we started from. Sound Reason was at first supposed to possess *immediately* the capacity to speak the truth; now, however, it is said that it *ought to know*, that is to say, that it does not *immediately* know what is true. Looking at this from the side of the content, then this has dropped out in the demand that we should *know* the truth; for this refers to *knowing in general*: we ought to *know*. What is demanded is, therefore, really something free of all specific content. But here the point in question was about a *specific* content, a *distinction* in the ethical substance. Yet this *immediate* determination of the substance is a content which showed itself to be really completely contingent and which, when raised into universality and necessity by making the law refer to *knowing* [instead of to *content*], in fact vanishes.

425. Another celebrated commandment is: 'Love thy neighbour as thyself.' It is directed to the individual in his relationship with other individuals and asserts the commandment as a relationship between two individuals, or as a relationship of feeling. Active love—for love that does not act has no existence and is therefore hardly intended here—aims at removing an evil from someone and being good to him. For this purpose I have to distinguish what is bad for him, what is the appropriate good to counter this evil, and what in general is good for him; i.e. I must love him *intelligently*. Unintelligent love will perhaps do him more harm than hatred. Intelligent, substantial beneficence is, however, in its richest and most important form the intelligent universal action of the state—an action compared with which the action of a single individual, as an individual, is so insignificant that it is hardly worth talking about. The action of the state is, moreover, of so great a power that, if the action of the individual were to oppose it, and either were intended to be a downright, explicitly criminal act, or the individual out of love for someone else wanted to cheat the universal out of its right, and its share in the action, such an action would be altogether useless and inevitably frustrated. The only significance left for beneficence, which is a *sentiment*, is that of an action which is quite single and isolated, of help in [a situation of] need, which is as contingent as it is transitory. Chance determines not only the occasion of the action but also whether it

is a 'work' at all, whether it is not immediately undone and even perverted into something bad. Thus this acting for the good of others which is said to be *necessary*, is of such kind that it may, or may not, exist; is such that, if by chance the occasion offers, the action is perhaps a 'work' and is good, but also perhaps not. This law, therefore, as little has a universal content as the one we first considered, and does not express, as an absolute ethical law should, something that is valid in and for itself. In other words, such laws stop short at Ought, they have no actuality; they are not laws, but merely commandments.

426. It is evident, however, from the very nature of the case, that we must give up all idea of a universal, absolute content. For any determinateness placed in the simple substance (whose nature is to be simple) is inadequate to it. The commandment in its simple absoluteness itself expresses an *immediate ethical being*; the distinction appearing in it is a determinateness, and therefore a content subsumed under the absolute universality of this simple being. Since, then, all idea of an absolute content must be given up, it can only claim a formal universality, or that it is not self-contradictory. For universality that lacks a content is [merely] formal, and an *absolute* content itself is tantamount to a distinction which is no distinction, i.e. to absence of content.

427. All that is left, then, for the making of a law is the mere form of universality, or, in fact, the tautology of consciousness which stands over against the content, and the knowledge, not of an *existing* or a real content, but only of the essence or self-identity of a content.

428. The ethical nature, therefore, is not itself simply as such a content, but only a standard for deciding whether a content is capable of being a law or not, i.e. whether it is or is not self-contradictory. Reason as the giver of laws is reduced to a Reason which merely *critically examines* them.

c. *Reason as testing laws*

429. A distinction within the simple ethical substance is for it an accident which appeared, as we saw in specific commandments, as the contingency of the knowledge [of the circumstances], of the circumstances themselves, and of the action. The *comparison* of that simple being with the determinateness

corresponding to it was made by us; and in that comparison the simple substance has shown itself to be a formal universality, or pure *consciousness* which is free from the content and stands over against it, and is a *knowing* of it as something determinate. This universality in this way remains the same as what the 'matter in hand' itself was. But in consciousness it is something else; it is, namely, no longer the unthinking, inert genus, but is related to the particular and regarded as the power over it and as its truth. This consciousness seems at first to be the same process of testing which formerly *we* carried out, and it seems that its action cannot be anything other than what has already happened, viz. a comparison of the universal with the determinate particular which, as previously, would reveal their disparity. Here, however, the relationship of the content to the universal is different, since the latter has acquired a different significance; it is a *formal* universality of which the determinate content is capable, for in that universality the content is considered only in relation to itself. When *we* were testing, the universal pure substance stood over against the determinateness, which displayed itself as a contingency of the consciousness into which the substance entered. Here, one term of the comparison has vanished; the universal is no longer the affirmatively present and authoritative substance, or that which is right in and for itself, but a simple knowing or a form, which compares a content only with itself, and considers whether it is a tautology. Laws are no longer given, but *tested*; and for the consciousness which tests them they are *already* given. It takes up their *content* simply as it is, without concerning itself, as we did, with the particularity and contingency inherent in its reality; it is concerned with the commandment simply as commandment, and its attitude towards it is just as uncomplicated as is its being a criterion for testing it.

430. But that is the reason why this testing does not get very far. Just because the criterion is a tautology, and indifferent to the content, one content is just as acceptable to it as its opposite. Suppose the question is: Ought it to be an absolute law that there should be property? Absolute, and not on grounds of utility for other ends: the essence of ethics consists just in law being identical with itself and through this self-identity, i.e. through having its ground in itself, it is unconditioned.

Property, simply as such, does not contradict itself; it is an *iso-lated* determinateness, or is posited as merely self-identical. Non-property, the non-ownership of things, or a common ownership of goods, is just as little self-contradictory. That something belongs to nobody, or to the first-comer who takes possession of it, or to all together, to each according to his need or in equal portions—that is a *simple* determinateness, a *formal* thought, like its opposite, property. Admittedly, if a thing that belongs to no one is considered as a *necessary object of a need*, then it is necessary that it become the property of some particular individual; and the contradiction would stem rather from the freedom of the thing being made into a law. But by non-ownership of the thing is not meant absolute non-ownership, but that it shall come into someone's possession according to the individual's need, and, moreover, not in order to be kept, but to be used immediately. But to provide for the need in such a completely arbitrary way is contradictory to the nature of the conscious individual who alone is under discussion. For such an individual must think of his need in the form of *universality*, must provide for the whole of his existence, and acquire a lasting possession. This being so, the idea of a thing being arbitrarily allotted to the first self-conscious individual who comes along and needs it, does not accord with itself. In a society based on a common ownership of goods, in which provision would be made in accordance with a universal fixed rule, either each receives as much as he *needs*—in which case there is a contradiction between this inequality and the essential nature of that consciousness whose principle is the equality of individuals—or, in accordance with that principle, goods will be *equally* distributed, and in this case the share is not related to the need, although such a relationship alone constitutes the very notion of 'sharing'.

431. Still, if in this way [the notion of] non-property appears contradictory, this is only because it has not been left as a *simple* determinateness. The same applies to [the notion of] property, if this is resolved into its moments. The single thing that is my property is held as such to be something universal, solidly established, and permanent; but this contradicts its nature, which consists in its being used and in *vanishing*. At the same time, it is held to be *mine*, something which everyone else acknowledges,

and lets alone. The fact, however, that I am acknowledged implies rather my equality, my identity, with everyone, and that is the opposite of exclusiveness. What I possess is a Thing, i.e. something which is for others in general and is only for *me* in a quite general, undefined way; that *I* possess it, contradicts its universal thinghood. Consequently, property is just as much an all-round contradiction as non-property; each contains within it these two opposed, self-contradictory moments of individuality and universality. But each of these determinatenesses when thought of as *simple*, as property or non-property, without explicating them further, is as *simple* as the other, i.e. is not self-contradictory. The criterion of law which Reason possesses within itself fits every case equally well, and is thus in fact no criterion at all. It would be strange, too, if tautology, the maxim of contradiction, which is admitted to be only a formal criterion for the cognition of theoretical truth, i.e. something which is quite indifferent to truth and falsehood, were supposed to be more than this for the cognition of practical truth.

432. In both the above moments, which fill the former emptiness of spiritual being, the process of placing immediate determinatenesses in the ethical substance, and then getting to know whether they are laws, has been eliminated. The result therefore seems to be that neither specific laws nor a knowledge of them is admissible. But the substance is the *consciousness* of itself as absolutely essential being, which, therefore, can give up neither the *distinction* within it nor the *knowledge* of that distinction. That law-giving and the testing of laws have proved to be futile, means that both, when taken singly and in isolation, are merely unstable moments of the ethical consciousness; and the movement in which they appear has the formal meaning that the ethical substance thereby exhibits itself as consciousness.

433. In so far as these two moments are more precise determinations of consciousness of the '*matter in hand*', they can be regarded as forms of the *honest* consciousness which, as previously in the case of its formal moments, now busies itself with a supposed content of the good and the right, and with testing such established truth, and fancies that in sound Reason and intelligent insight it possesses that which gives force and validity to commandments.

434. However, without this honesty, laws do not have validity as the *essence* of consciousness, nor, similarly, does the testing of them count as an action *within* consciousness. On the contrary, these moments, appearing each by itself *immediately* as a *reality*, express in the one case an invalid establishing and existence of actual laws, and in the other case an equally invalid immunity from them. The law, as a specific law, has a contingent content; this means here that it is the law of a single consciousness and has an arbitrary content. To legislate immediately in that way is thus the tyrannical insolence which makes caprice into a law and ethical behaviour into obedience to such caprice—obedience to laws which are *merely* laws and not at the same time *commandments*, So, too, the second moment, in so far as it is isolated, means testing the laws, moving the immovable, means the insolence of a knowledge which argues itself into a freedom from absolute laws, treating them as an alien caprice.

435. In both forms, these moments are a negative relation to substance or real spiritual being; or we may say that in them substance does not as yet possess its reality, but rather that consciousness contains them still in the form of its own immediacy, and that substance is at first only a *willing* and *knowing* by this particular individual, or the 'ought to be' of an unreal commandment and a knowledge of formal universality. But since these modes have been superseded, consciousness has returned into the universal and those antitheses have vanished. Spiritual being is actual substance through these modes being valid, not in isolation, but only as superseded [moments]; and the unity in which they are merely moments is the self of consciousness which, being from now on posited in the spiritual being, makes that being actual, full-filled, and self-conscious.

436. The spiritual being thus exists first of all for self-consciousness as law which has an *intrinsic* being; the universality associated with testing the law, a merely formal, not an *essential* universality, is now behind us. The law is equally an eternal law which is grounded not in the will of a particular individual, but is valid in and for itself; it is the absolute *pure will of all* which has the form of immediate being. Also, it is not a *commandment*, which only *ought* to be: it *is* and is *valid*; it is the universal 'I' of the category, the 'I' which is immediately a reality,

and the world *is* only this reality. But since this existent law is valid unconditionally, the obedience of self-consciousness is not the serving of a master whose commands were arbitrary, and in which it would not recognize itself. On the contrary, laws are the thoughts of its own absolute consciousness, thoughts which are immediately its *own*. Also, it does not *believe* in them, for although belief does perceive essential being it perceives it as something alien to itself. Ethical *self*-consciousness is *immediately* one with essential being through the *universality* of its *self*; belief, on the other hand, starts from the *individual* consciousness; it is the movement of that consciousness always towards this unity, but without attaining to the presence of its essential being. The above consciousness, on the other hand, has put its merely individual aspect behind it, this mediation is finished and complete, and only because this is so, is this consciousness immediate self-consciousness of the ethical substance.

437. The difference between self-consciousness and essence, is therefore, perfectly transparent. Because of this, the distinctions in essence itself are not accidental determinatenesses; on the contrary, in virtue of the unity of essence and self-consciousness (this latter being the only possible source of disparity), they are 'masses' articulated into groups by the life of the unity which permeates them, unalienated spirits transparent to themselves, stainless celestial figures that preserve in all their differences the undefiled innocence and harmony of their essential nature. The *relationship* of self-consciousness to them is equally simple and clear. They *are*, and nothing more; this is what constitutes the awareness of its relationship to them. Thus, Sophocles' *Antigone*[1] acknowledges them as the unwritten and infallible law of the gods.

> They are not of yesterday or today, but everlasting,
> Though where they came from, none of us can tell.

They *are*. If I inquire after their origin and confine them to the point whence they arose, then I have transcended them; for now it is I who am the universal, and *they* are the conditioned and limited. If they are supposed to be validated by *my* insight, then I have already denied their unshakeable, intrinsic being,

[1] Sophocles, *Antigone*, ll. 456–7.

and regard them as something which, for me, is perhaps true, but also is perhaps not true. Ethical disposition consists just in sticking steadfastly to what is right, and abstaining from all attempts to move or shake it, or derive it. Suppose something has been entrusted to me; it *is* the property of someone else and I acknowledge this *because* it *is so*, and I keep myself unfalteringly in this relationship. If I should keep for myself what is entrusted to me, then according to the principle I follow in testing laws, which is a tautology, I am not in the least guilty of contradiction; for then I no longer look upon it as the property of someone else: to hold on to something which I do not regard as belonging to someone else is perfectly consistent. Alteration of the *point of view* is not contradiction; for what we are concerned with is not the point of view, but the object and content, which ought not to be self-contradictory. Just as I can—as I do when I give something away—alter the view that it is my property into the view that it belongs to someone else, without becoming guilty of a contradiction, so I can equally pursue the reverse course. It is not, therefore, because I find something is not self-contradictory that it is right; on the contrary, it is right because it is what is right. That something *is* the property of another, this is fundamental; I have not to argue about it, or hunt around for or entertain thoughts, connections, aspects, of various kinds; I have to think neither of making laws nor of testing them. All such thinking on my part would upset that relation, since, if I liked, I could in fact just as well make the opposite conform to my indeterminate tautological knowledge and make *that* the law. But whether this or the opposite determination is the right, that is determined *in* and *for itself*. I could make whichever of them I liked the law, and just as well neither of them, and as soon as I start to test them I have already begun to tread an unethical path. By acknowledging the *absoluteness* of the right, I am within the ethical substance; and this substance is thus the *essence* of self-consciousness. But this self-consciousness is the *actuality* and *existence* of the substance, its *self* and its *will*.

(BB.) SPIRIT

VI. SPIRIT

438. Reason is Spirit when its certainty of being all reality has been raised to truth, and it is conscious of itself as its own world, and of the world as itself. The coming-to-be of Spirit was indicated in the immediately preceding movement in which the object of consciousness, the pure category, rose to be the Notion of Reason. In Reason as *observer*, this pure unity of the *I* and *being*, of being *for itself* and being *in itself*, is determined as the *in-itself* or as *being*, and the consciousness of Reason *finds* itself. But the truth of observation is rather that it leaves behind it this immediate instinct which merely finds Reason, this unconscious existence of Reason. The *intuited category*, the *found Thing*, enters consciousness as the *being-for-self* of the 'I', which is now aware of itself as the *self* in objective being. But this determination of the category, of being-for-self opposed to being-in-itself, is equally one-sided and is a moment that supersedes itself. The category is therefore determined for consciousness as it is in its universal truth, as a being that is *in* and *for itself*. This still *abstract* determination which constitutes the 'matter in hand' itself is at first only spiritual essence, and its consciousness [only] a formal knowing of it, which busies itself with all kinds of content of the essence. This consciousness, as a particular individual, is still in fact distinct from substance, and either makes arbitrary laws or fancies that in simply knowing laws it possesses them in their own absolute nature. Or, looked at from the side of substance, this is spiritual essence that is in and for itself, but which is not yet *consciousness* of itself. But essence that is *in* and *for itself*, and which is at the same time actual as consciousness and aware of itself, this is *Spirit*.

439. Its spiritual *essence* has already been designated as ethical *substance*; but Spirit is the *actuality* of that substance. It is the *self* of actual consciousness to which it stands opposed, or rather which it opposes to itself as an objective, actual *world*, but a world which has completely lost the meaning for the self

of something alien to it, just as the self has completely lost the meaning of a being-for-self separated from the world, whether dependent on it or not. Spirit, being the *substance* and the universal, self-identical, and abiding essence, is the unmoved solid *ground* and *starting-point* for the action of all, and it is their purpose and goal, the in-itself of every self-consciousness expressed in thought. This substance is equally the universal *work* produced by the action of all and each as their unity and identity, for it is the *being-for-self*, the self, action. As *substance*, Spirit is unshaken righteous self-identity; but as *being-for-self* it is a fragmented being, self-sacrificing and benevolent, in which each accomplishes his own work, rends asunder the universal being, and takes from it his own share. This resolving of the essence into individuals is precisely the *moment* of the action and the self of all; it is the movement and soul of substance and the resultant universal being. Just because it is a being that is resolved in the self, it is not a dead essence, but is *actual* and *alive*.

440. Spirit is thus self-supporting, absolute, real being. All previous shapes of consciousness are abstract forms of it. They result from Spirit analysing itself, distinguishing its moments, and dwelling for a while with each. This isolating of those moments *presupposes* Spirit itself and subsists therein; in other words, the isolation exists only in Spirit which is a concrete existence. In this isolation they have the appearance of really existing as such; but that they are only moments or vanishing quantities is shown by their advance and retreat into their ground and essence; and this essence is just this movement and resolution of these moments. Here, where Spirit, or Spirit's reflection into itself, is posited, we may briefly recall this aspect of them in our own reflection: they were consciousness, self-consciousness, and Reason. Spirit, then is consciousness in general which embraces sense-certainty, perception, and the Understanding, in so far as in its self-analysis Spirit holds fast to the moment of being an objectively existent actuality to itself, and ignores the fact that this actuality is its own being-for-self. If, on the contrary, it holds fast to the other moment of the analysis, viz. that its object is its own *being-for-self*, then it is self-consciousness. But as immediate consciousness of the being that is *in and for itself*, as unity of consciousness and self-con-

sciousness, Spirit is consciousness that *has Reason*; it is consciousness which, as the word 'has' indicates, has the object in a shape which is *implicitly* determined by Reason or by the value of the category, but in such a way that it does not as yet have for consciousness the value of the category. Spirit is that consciousness which we were considering immediately prior to the present stage. Finally, when this Reason which Spirit *has* is intuited by Spirit as Reason that *exists*, or as Reason that is *actual* in Spirit and is its world, then Spirit exists in its truth; it *is* Spirit, the *ethical* essence that has an *actual* existence.

441. Spirit is the *ethical life* of a nation in so far as it is the *immediate truth*—the individual that is a world. It must advance to the consciousness of what it is immediately, must leave behind it the beauty of ethical life, and by passing through a series of shapes attain to a knowledge of itself. These shapes, however, are distinguished from the previous ones by the fact that they are real Spirits, actualities in the strict meaning of the word, and instead of being shapes merely of consciousness, are shapes of a world.

442. The *living ethical* world is Spirit in its *truth*. When Spirit first arrives at an abstract knowledge of its essence, ethical life is submerged in the formal universality of legality or law. Spirit, which henceforth is divided within itself, traces one of its worlds, the *realm of culture*, in the harsh reality of its objective element; over against this realm, it traces in the element of thought the *world of belief or faith*, the *realm of essential being*. Both worlds, however, when grasped by Spirit—which, after this loss of itself, withdraws into itself—when grasped by the *Notion*, are confounded and revolutionized by the *insight* [of the individual] and the diffusion of that insight, known as the Enlightenment; and the realm which was divided and expanded into *this world* and the *beyond*, returns into self-consciousness which now, in the form of morality, grasps itself as the essentiality and essence as the actual self; it no longer places its *world* and its *ground* outside of itself, but lets everything fade into itself, and, as *conscience*, is Spirit that is certain of itself.

443. The ethical world, the world which is rent asunder into this world and a beyond, and the moral view of the world, are thus the Spirits whose process and return into the simple *self*-consciousness of Spirit are now to be developed. The goal

and outcome of that process will appear on the scene as the actual self-consciousness of absolute Spirit.

A. THE TRUE SPIRIT. THE ETHICAL ORDER

444. Spirit is, in its simple truth, consciousness, and forces its moments apart. *Action* divides it into substance, and consciousness of the substance; and divides the substance as well as consciousness. Substance, as the universal essence and End, stands over against the *individualized* reality; the infinite middle term is self-consciousness which, being the implicit unity of itself and substance, now becomes that unity explicitly and unites the universal essence and its individualized reality. The latter it raises to the former and acts *ethically*, the former it brings down to the latter and realizes the End, the substance which had an existence only in thought. It brings into existence the unity of its self and substance as its own work, and thus as an actual existence.

445. In this separation of the moments of consciousness, the simple substance has, on the one hand, preserved the antithesis to self-consciousness, and on the other, it equally exhibits in its own self the nature of consciousness, viz. to create distinctions within itself, exhibiting itself as a world articulated into its [separate] spheres. It thus splits itself up into distinct ethical substances, into a human and a divine law. Similarly, the self-consciousness confronting the substance assigns to itself according to its nature one of these powers, and as a knowing, is on the one hand ignorant of what it does, and on the other knows what it does, a knowledge which for that reason is a deceptive knowledge. It learns through its own act the contradiction of those powers into which the substance divided itself and their mutual downfall, as well as the contradiction between *its* knowledge of the ethical character of its action, and what is in its own proper nature ethical, and thus finds its own downfall. In point of fact, however, the ethical substance has developed through this process into actual self-consciousness; in other words, this particular self has become the actuality of what it is in essence; but precisely in this development the ethical order has been destroyed.

a. *The ethical world. Human and Divine Law: Man and Woman*

446. The simple substance of Spirit, as consciousness, is divided. In other words, just as the consciousness of abstract sensuous being passes over into perception, so also does the immediate certainty of a real ethical situation; and just as for sense-perception simple being becomes a Thing of many properties, so for ethical perception a given action is an actual situation with many ethical connections. For the former, however, the superfluous plurality of properties concentrates itself into the essential antithesis of individuality and universality; and still more for ethical perception, which is the purified substantial consciousness, does the plurality of ethical moments become the duality of a law of individuality and a law of universality. But each of these divisions of substance remains Spirit in its entirety; if in sense-perception things have no other substance than the two determinations of individuality and universality, here these determinations express only the superficial antithesis of the two sides.

447. In the essence we are considering here, individuality has the meaning of *self-consciousness* in general, not of a particular, contingent consciousness. In this determination, therefore, the ethical substance is *actual* substance, absolute Spirit realized in the plurality of existent consciousnesses; this spirit is the community which, when we entered the sphere of Reason in its practical embodiment, was *for us* absolute essence, and here has emerged *on its own account* in its truth as conscious ethical essence, and as essence *for* the consciousness which here is our object. It is Spirit which is *for itself* in that it preserves itself in its reflection in individuals; and it is *implicitly* Spirit, or substance, in that it preserves them within itself. As *actual substance*, it is a nation, as *actual consciousness*, it is the citizens of that nation. This consciousness has its essence in simple Spirit, and the certainty of itself in the *actuality* of this Spirit, in the nation as a whole; it has its truth, therefore, not in something that is not actual, but in a Spirit that exists and prevails.

448. This Spirit can be called the human law, because it is essentially in the form of a reality that is conscious of itself. In the form of universality it is the *known* law, and the prevailing custom; in the form of individuality it is the actual certainty

of itself in the individual as such, and the certainty of itself as a simple individuality is that Spirit as government. Its truth is the authority which is openly accepted and manifest to all; a *concrete existence* which appears for immediate certainty in the form an existence that has freely issued forth.

449. Confronting this clearly manifest ethical power there is, however, another power, the Divine Law. For the ethical power of the state, being the movement of self-conscious action, finds its antithesis in the simple and immediate essence of the ethical sphere; as *actual* universality it is a force actively opposed to individual being-for-self; and as actuality in general it finds in that *inner* essence something other than the ethical power of the state.

450. It has already been mentioned that each of the opposites in which the ethical substance exists contains the entire substance, and all the moments of its content. If, then, the community is that substance conscious of what it actually does, the other side has the form of immediate substance or substance that simply is. The latter is thus on the one hand the inner Notion or general possibility of the ethical sphere in general, but on the other hand equally contains within it the moment of self-consciousness. This moment which expresses the ethical sphere in this element of immediacy or [simple] being, or which is an *immediate* consciousness of itself, both as essence and as this particular self, in an 'other', i.e. as a *natural* ethical community—this is the Family. The Family, as the *unconscious*, still inner Notion [of the ethical order], stands opposed to its actual, self-conscious existence; as the *element* of the nation's actual existence, it stands opposed to the nation itself; as the *immediate* being of the ethical order, it stands over against that order which shapes and maintains itself by working for the universal; the Penates stand opposed to the universal Spirit.

451. However, although the Family is *immediately* determined as an ethical being, it is within itself an *ethical* entity only so far as it is not the *natural* relationship of its members, or so far as their connection is an *immediate* connection of separate, actual individuals; for the ethical principle is intrinsically universal, and this natural relationship is just as much a spiritual one, and it is only as a spiritual entity that it is ethical. We have to see what constitutes its peculiar ethical character. In

the first place, because the ethical principle is intrinsically universal, the ethical connection between the members of the Family is not that of feeling, or the relationship of love. It seems, then, that the ethical principle must be placed in the relation of the *individual* member of the Family to the *whole* Family as the Substance, so that the End and content of what he does and actually is, is solely the Family. But the conscious End motivating the action of this whole, so far as it is directed towards that whole, is itself the individual. The acquisition and maintenance of power and wealth is in part concerned only with needs and belongs to the sphere of appetite; in part, they become in their higher determination something that is only mediated. This determination does not fall within the Family itself, but bears on what is truly universal, the community; it has, rather, a negative relation to the Family, and consists in expelling the individual from the Family, subduing the natural aspect and separateness of his existence, and training him to be virtuous, to a life in and for the universal. The *positive* End peculiar to the Family is the individual as such. Now, in order that this relationship be ethical, neither he who performs the action, nor he to whom the action refers, can be in an *accidental* relationship as happens perhaps in rendering some assistance or service in a particular case. The content of the ethical action must be substantial or whole and universal; therefore it can only be related to the *whole* individual or to the individual *qua* universal. And this, again, must not be understood as if it were only *imagined* that doing him a service would promote his total happiness, whereas the service, being an immediate and actual deed, produces only a particular effect on him. Nor must we imagine that service in the form of education, i.e. in a *series* of efforts, really has him in his entirety for object, and produces him as a 'work'; for apart from the purpose which is negatively connected with the Family, the actual deed has only a limited content. Finally, just as little should we understand the service as a help in time of need by which in truth the individual in his entirety is rescued; for such help is itself a completely contingent act, the occasion of which is an ordinary reality which can either be or not be. The deed, then, which embraces the entire existence of the blood-relation, does not concern the citizen, for he does not belong to the Family, nor the individual who is to

become a citizen and will cease to count as this particular individual; it has as its object and content this particular individual who belongs to the Family, but is taken as a *universal* being
freed from his sensuous, i.e. individual, reality. The deed no
longer concerns the living but the dead, the individual who,
after a long succession of separate disconnected experiences, concentrates himself into a single completed shape, and has raised
himself out of the unrest of the accidents of life into the calm
of simple universality. But because it is only as a citizen that
he is actual and substantial, the individual, so far as he is not
a citizen but belongs to the Family, is only an unreal impotent
shadow.

452. This universality which the individual *as such* attains
is *pure being, death*; it is a state which has been reached *immediately*, in the *course of Nature*, not the result of an action *consciously done*. The duty of the member of a Family is on that
account to add this aspect, in order that the individual's ultimate being, too, shall not belong solely to Nature and remain
something irrational, but shall be something *done*, and the right
of consciousness be asserted in it. Or rather, the meaning of
the action is that because in truth the calm and universality
of a self-conscious being do not belong to Nature, the illusory
appearance that the death of the individual results from a *conscious* action on the part of Nature may be dispelled, and the
truth established. What Nature did in the individual is that
aspect in which his development into a universal is exhibited
as the movement of an [immediate] existent. This movement
falls, it is true, within the ethical community, and has this for
its End; death is the fulfilment and the supreme 'work'
which the individual as such undertakes on its behalf. But in
so far as he is essentially a *particular* individual, it is an accident
that his death was directly connected with his 'work' for the
universal and was the result of it; partly because, if his death
was such a result, it is the *natural* negativity and movement of
the individual as a [mere] existent, in which consciousness does
not return into itself and become self-consciousness; or partly
because, since the movement of what [merely] exists consists
in its being superseded and becoming a being-for-self, death
is the side of diremption in which the attained being-for-self
is something other than the mere existent which began the

movement. Because the ethical order is Spirit in its *immediate* truth, the sides into which its consciousness sunders itself also fall into this form of *immediacy*, and individuality passes over into this *abstract* negativity which, being *in its own self* without consolation and reconciliation, must receive them essentially through a *real* and *external act*. Blood-relationship supplements, then, the abstract natural process by adding to it the movement of consciousness, interrupting the work of Nature and rescuing the blood-relation from destruction; or better, because destruction is necessary, the passage of the blood-relation into mere being, it takes on itself the act of destruction. Through this it comes about that the *dead*, the universal *being*, becomes a being that has returned into itself, a being-for-self, or, the powerless, simply isolated individual has been raised to universal individuality. The dead individual, by having liberated his *being* from his *action* or his negative unity, is an empty singular, merely a passive being-for-another, at the mercy of every lower irrational individuality and the forces of abstract material elements, all of which are now more powerful than himself: the former on account of the life they possess, the latter on account of their negative nature. The Family keeps away from the dead this dishonouring of him by unconscious appetites and abstract entities, and puts its own action in their place, and weds the blood-relation to the bosom of the earth, to the elemental imperishable individuality. The Family thereby makes him a member of a community which prevails over and holds under control the forces of particular material elements and the lower forms of life, which sought to unloose themselves against him and to destroy him.

453. This last duty thus constitutes the perfect *divine* law, or the positive *ethical* action towards the individual. Every other relationship to him which does not remain one simply of love but is ethical, belongs to human law and has the negative significance of raising the individual above his confinement within the natural community to which he in his [natural] existence belongs. Now, although human right has for its content and power the actual ethical substance that is conscious of itself, i.e. the entire nation, while the *divine* right and law has for *its* content and power the individual who is beyond the real world, yet he is not without power. *His* power is the *abstract*, pure

universal, the *elemental* individual which equally draws back into
the pure abstraction which is its essence the individuality that
breaks loose from the element, and constitutes the self-conscious
reality of the nation—draws it back into the essence which is
its ground. How this power is manifested in the Notion itself,
we shall see in the ensuing development.

454. Now, in the one law as in the other there are also differences and gradations. For since both laws have within them
the moment of consciousness, difference is developed within the
laws themselves, and this constitutes their movement and their
own peculiar life. Consideration of these differences reveals the
way in which they operate, and the mode of self-consciousness
of the two universal essential natures of the ethical world, and
also their connection and transition into one another.

455. The *community*, the superior law whose validity is openly
apparent, has its real vitality in the government as that in which
it has an individual form. Government is the reality of Spirit
that is reflected into itself, the simple *self* of the entire ethical
substance. This simple power does indeed allow the Family to
expand into its constituent members, and to give to each part
an enduring being and a being-for-self of its own. Spirit has
in this its reality or its objective existence, and the Family is
the *element* of this reality. But Spirit is at the same time the power
of the whole, which brings these parts together again into a
negative unity, giving them the feeling of their lack of independence, and keeping them aware that they have their life only
in the whole. The community may, on the one hand, organize
itself into systems of personal independence and property, of
laws relating to persons and things; and, on the other hand,
the various ways of working for Ends which are in the first instance particular Ends—those of gain and enjoyment—it may
articulate into their own special and independent associations.
The Spirit of universal assembly and association is the simple
and negative essence of those systems which tend to isolate
themselves. In order not to let them become rooted and set in
this isolation, thereby breaking up the whole and letting the
[communal] spirit evaporate, government has from time to
time to shake them to their core by war. By this means the
government upsets their established order, and violates their
right to independence, while the individuals who, absorbed in

their own way of life, break loose from the whole and strive after the inviolable independence and security of the person, are made to feel in the task laid on them their lord and master, death. Spirit, by thus throwing into the melting-pot the stable existence of these systems, checks their tendency to fall away from the ethical order, and to be submerged in a [merely] natural existence; and it preserves and raises conscious self into freedom and its own power. The negative essence shows itself to be the real power of the community and the force of its self-preservation. The community therefore possesses the truth and the confirmation of its power in the essence of the Divine Law and in the realm of the nether world.

456. The Divine Law which governs the family has likewise on its side differences within itself whose interrelationships constitute the living process of its actuality. But among the three relationships, of husband and wife, parents and children, brothers and sisters, the relationship of husband and wife is in the first place the one in which one consciousness immediately recognizes itself in another, and in which there is knowledge of this mutual recognition. Because this self-recognition is a natural and not an ethical one, it is only a representation, an image of Spirit, not actually Spirit itself. A representation or image, however, has its actual existence in something other than itself. This relationship therefore has its actual existence not in itself but in the child—an 'other', whose coming into existence is the relationship, and is also that in which the relationship itself gradually passes away; and this alternation of successive generations has its enduring basis in the nation. The dutiful reverence of husband and wife towards each other is thus mixed with a natural relation and with feeling, and the return-into-self of the relationship does not take place within the relationship itself; similarly with the second relationship, the dutiful reverence of parents and children towards one another. That of parents towards their children is emotionally affected by the fact that the objective reality of the relationship does not exist in them, but in the children, and by their witnessing the development in the children of an independent existence which they are unable to take back again; the independent existence of the children remains an alien reality, a reality all its own. That of children towards parents is emotionally affected,

conversely, by the fact that they derive their existence from, or have their essential being in, what is other than themselves, and passes away, and by their attaining independence and a self-consciousness of their own only by being separated from their source—a separation in which the source dries up.

457. Both these relationships are confined within the transition and the disparity of the sides which are assigned to them. The relationship in its unmixed form is found, however, in that between brother and sister. They are the same blood which has, however, in them reached a state of rest and equilibrium. Therefore, they do not desire one another, nor have they given to, or received from, one another this independent being-for-self; on the contrary, they are free individualities in regard to each other. Consequently, the feminine, in the form of the sister, has the highest *intuitive* awareness of what is ethical. She does not attain to *consciousness* of it, or to the objective existence of it, because the law of the Family is an implicit, inner essence which is not exposed to the daylight of consciousness, but remains an inner feeling and the divine element that is exempt from an existence in the real world. The woman is associated with these household gods [Penates] and beholds in them both her universal substance and her particular individuality, yet in such a way that this relation of her individuality to them is at the same time not the natural one of desire. As a daughter, the woman must now see her parents pass away with a natural emotion and ethical resignation, for it is only at the cost of this relationship that she can achieve that existence of her own of which she is capable. Thus in the parents, she does not behold her own being-for-self in a positive form. The relationships of mother and wife, however, are those of particular individuals, partly in the form of something natural pertaining to desire, partly in the form of something negative which sees in those relationships only something evanescent and also, again, the particular individual is for that very reason a contingent element which can be replaced by another individual. In the ethical household, it is not a question of *this* particular husband, *this* particular child, but simply of husband and children generally; the relationships of the woman are based, not on feeling, but on the universal. The difference between the ethical life of the woman and that of the man consists just in this, that in

her vocation as an individual and in her pleasure, her interest is centred on the universal and remains alien to the particularity of desire; whereas in the husband these two sides are separated; and since he possesses as a citizen the self-conscious power of universality, he thereby acquires the right of desire and, at the same time, preserves his freedom in regard to it. Since, then, in this relationship of the wife there is an admixture of particularity, her ethical life is not pure; but in so far as it *is* ethical, the particularity is a matter of indifference, and the wife is without the moment of knowing herself as *this* particular self in the other partner. The brother, however, is for the sister a passive, similar being in general; the recognition of herself in him is pure and unmixed with any natural desire. In this relationship, therefore, the indifference of the particularity, and the ethical contingency of the latter, are not present; but the moment of the individual self, recognizing and being recognized, can here assert its right, because it is linked to the equilibrium of the blood and is a relation devoid of desire. The loss of the brother is therefore irreparable to the sister and her duty towards him is the highest.[1]

458. This relationship is at the same time the limit at which the self-contained life of the Family breaks up and goes beyond itself. The brother is the member of the Family in whom its Spirit becomes an individuality which turns towards another sphere, and passes over into the consciousness of universality. The brother leaves this immediate, elemental, and therefore, strictly speaking, negative ethical life of the Family, in order to acquire and produce the ethical life that is conscious of itself and actual.

459. He passes from the divine law, within whose sphere he lived, over to human law. But the sister becomes, or the wife remains, the head of the household and the guardian of the divine law. In this way, the two sexes overcome their [merely] natural being and appear in their ethical significance, as diverse beings who share between them the two distinctions belonging to the ethical substance. These two *universal* beings of the ethical world have, therefore, their *specific* individuality in *naturally* distinct self-consciousnesses, because the ethical Spirit is the *immediate* unity of the substance with self-consciousness—an *imme-*

[1] Cf. *Antigone*, l. 910.

diacy which appears, therefore, both from the side of reality and of difference, as the existence of a natural difference. It is that side which, in the shape of individuality that is real to itself, showed itself in the Notion of spiritual being as an *originally determinate nature*. This moment loses the indeterminateness which it still has there, and the contingent diversity of dispositions and capacities. It is now the specific antithesis of the two sexes whose natural existence acquires at the same time the significance of their ethical determination.

460. The difference of the sexes and their ethical content remains, however, in the unity of the substance, and its movement is just the constant becoming of that substance. The husband is sent out by the Spirit of the Family into the community in which he finds his self-conscious being. Just as the Family in this way possesses in the community its substance and enduring being, so, conversely, the community possesses in the Family the formal element of its actual existence, and in the divine law its power and authentication. Neither of the two is by itself absolutely valid; human law proceeds in its living process from the divine, the law valid on earth from that of the nether world, the conscious from the unconscious, mediation from immediacy—and equally returns whence it came. The power of the nether world, on the other hand, has its actual existence on earth; through consciousness, it becomes existence and activity.

461. The universal ethical beings are, then, the substance *qua* universal, and the substance *qua* an individual consciousness. Their universal actuality is the nation and the Family; while they have their natural self and operative individuality in man and woman. In this content of the ethical world we see achieved those ends which the previous insubstantial forms of consciousness set themselves; what reason apprehended only as object has become self-consciousness, and what the latter possessed only within itself is now present as a true, objective reality. What observation knew as a *given* object in which the self had no part, is here a given custom, but a reality which is at the same time the deed and the work of the subject finding it. The individual who seeks the pleasure of *enjoying his individuality*, finds it in the Family, and the necessity in which that pleasure passes away is his own self-consciousness as a citizen

of his nation. Or, again, it is in knowing that the law of his own heart is the law of all hearts, in knowing the consciousness of the self as the acknowledged universal order; it is virtue, which enjoys the fruits of its sacrifice, which brings about what it sets out to do, viz. to bring forth the essence into the light of day, and its enjoyment is this universal life. Finally, consciousness of the 'matter in hand' itself finds satisfaction in the real substance which contains and preserves in a positive manner the abstract moments of that empty category. That substance has, in the ethical powers, a genuine content that takes the place of the insubstantial commandments which sound Reason wanted to give and to know; and thus it gets an intrinsically determinate standard for testing, not the laws, but what is done.

462. The whole is a stable equilibrium of all the parts, and each part is a Spirit at home in this whole, a Spirit which does not seek its satisfaction outside of itself but finds it within itself, because it is itself in this equilibrium with the whole. This equilibrium can, it is true, only be a living one by inequality arising in it, and being brought back to equilibrium by Justice. Justice, however, is neither an alien entity remote from this whole, nor the reality (unworthy of the name of Justice) of mutual malice, treachery, ingratitude, etc. which would execute judgement in an unreasoning, arbitrary manner, by misunderstanding the context of the action, and by unconscious acts of omission and commission. On the contrary, it is the Justice of *human* law which brings back into the universal the element of being-for-self which has broken away from the balanced whole, viz. the independent classes and individuals; it is the government of the nation, which is the self-affirming individuality of the universal essence and the self-conscious will of all. The Justice, however, which brings back to equilibrium the universal in its ascendancy over the individual is equally the simple Spirit of the individual who has suffered wrong; it is not split up into two, the one who has suffered the wrong and an entity in a remote beyond. The individual himself is the power of the nether world, and it is *his* Erinys, *his* 'fury', which wreaks vengeance. For his individuality, his blood, still lives on in the household, his substance has an enduring reality. The wrong which can be inflicted on the individual in the ethical realm is simply this,

that something merely *happens* to him. The power which inflicts this wrong on the conscious individual of making him into a mere Thing, is Nature; it is the universality not of the *community*, but the *abstract* universality of *mere being*; and the individual, in avenging the wrong he has suffered, does not turn against the former, for it is not at its hands that he has suffered, but against the latter. As we saw, the consciousness of [those who share] the blood of the individual repair this wrong in such a way that what has simply *happened* becomes rather a *work deliberately done*, in order that the mere being of the wrong, its ultimate form, may also be something *willed* and thus something agreeable.

463.   The ethical realm is in this way in its enduring existence an immaculate world, a world unsullied by any internal dissension. Similarly, its process is a tranquil transition of one of its powers into the other, in such a way that each preserves and brings forth the other. We do indeed see it divide itself into two essences and their reality; but their antithesis is rather the authentication of one through the other, and where they come into direct contact with each other as real opposites, their middle term and common element is their immediate interpenetration. The one extreme, the universal self-conscious Spirit, becomes, through the individuality of the man, united with its other extreme, its force and element, with *unconscious* Spirit. On the other hand, the divine law has its individualization—or the *unconscious* Spirit of the individual its real existence—in the woman, through whom, as the *middle term*, the unconscious Spirit rises out of its unreality into actual existence, out of a state in which it is unknowing and unconscious into the realm of conscious Spirit. The union of man and woman constitutes the active middle term of the whole and the element which sunders itself into these extremes of divine and human law. It is equally their immediate union which converts those first two syllogisms into one and the same syllogism, and unites into one process the opposite movements: one from actuality down to unreality, the downward movement of human law, organized into independent members, to the danger and trial of death; and the other, the upward movement of the law of the nether world to the actuality of the light of day and to conscious existence. Of these movements, the former falls to man, the latter to woman.

b. *Ethical action. Human and Divine knowledge. Guilt and Destiny*

464. The way in which the antithesis is constituted in this ethical realm is such that self-consciousness has not yet received its due as a particular individuality. There it has the value, on the one hand, merely of the universal will, and on the other, of consanguinity. *This* particular individual counts only as a shadowy unreality. As yet, no deed has been committed; but the deed is the *actual self*. It disturbs the peaceful organization and movement of the ethical world. What there appears as order and harmony of its two essences, each of which authenticates and completes the other, becomes through the deed a transition of opposites in which each proves itself to be the non-reality, rather than the authentication, of itself and the other. It becomes the negative movement, or the eternal necessity, of a dreadful fate which engulfs in the abyss of its single nature divine and human law alike, as well as the two self-consciousnesses in which these powers have their existence—and for us passes over into the absolute being-for-self of the purely individual self-consciousness.

465. The ground from which this movement starts and on which it takes place, is the ethical realm; what is active in this movement, however, is self-consciousness. *Qua* ethical consciousness, it is the simple, pure direction of activity towards the essentiality of ethical life, i.e. duty. In it there is no caprice and equally no struggle, no indecision, since the making and testing of law has been given up; on the contrary, the essence of ethical life is for this consciousness immediate, unwavering, without contradiction. Consequently, we are not faced with the sorry spectacle of a collision between passion and duty, nor with the comic spectacle of a collision between duty and duty—a collision which, as regards its content, is the same as that between passion and duty; for passion is equally capable of being seen as a duty, because when consciousness separates itself from its immediate, substantial essence and withdraws into itself, it becomes the merely formal universal into which one content as well as another fits equally well as we found before. But the collision of duties is comic because it expresses a contradiction, viz. the contradiction of an Absolute that is opposed to itself: an Absolute, and then the nothingness of this so-called

Absolute or duty. The ethical consciousness, however, knows what it has to do, and has already decided whether to belong to the divine or the human law. This immediate firmness of decision is something implicit, and therefore has at the same time the significance of a natural being as we have seen. Nature, not the accident of circumstances or choice, assigns one sex to one law, the other to the other law; or conversely, the two ethical powers themselves give themselves an individual existence and actualize themselves in the two sexes.

466. Now, because, on the one hand, the ethical order essentially consists in this immediate firmness of decision, and for that reason there is for consciousness essentially only one law, while, on the other hand, the ethical powers are real and effective in the *self* of consciousness, these powers acquire the significance of excluding and opposing one another: in self-consciousness they exist explicitly, whereas in the ethical order they are only implicit. The ethical consciousness, because it is *decisively* for one of the two powers, is essentially character; it does not accept that both have the same *essential* nature. For this reason, the opposition between them appears as an *unfortunate* collision of duty merely with a reality which possesses no rights of its own. The ethical consciousness is, *qua* self-consciousness, in this opposition and as such it at once proceeds to force into subjection to the law which it accepts, the reality which is opposed to it, or else to outwit it. Since it sees right only on one side and wrong on the other, that consciousness which belongs to the divine law sees in the other side only the violence of human caprice, while that which holds to human law sees in the other only the self-will and disobedience of the individual who insists on being his own authority. For the commands of government have a universal, public meaning open to the light of day; the will of the other law, however, is locked up in the darkness of the nether regions, and in its outer existence manifests as the will of an isolated individual which, as contradicting the first, is a wanton outrage.

467. In this way there arises in consciousness the antithesis of the known and the unknown, just as in substance there was an antithesis of the conscious and the unconscious; and the absolute right of ethical self-consciousness comes into conflict with the divine right of essential being. For self-consciousness, *qua*

consciousness, the world of objective reality as such has an essential being; but according to its substance it is the unity of itself and this opposite; and ethical self-consciousness is the consciousness of that substance; therefore the object, in its opposition to the subject, has lost entirely the significance of having an essential being of its own. Just as those spheres in which it is only a Thing have long since vanished, so too have these spheres in which consciousness gives a fixed existence to something from out of itself and converts an isolated moment into essence. Against such one-sidedness, the actual world has a power of its own; it stands leagued with truth against consciousness, and itself shows the latter what truth is. The ethical consciousness, however, has drunk from the cup of substance and has forgotten all the one-sidedness of being-for-self, of its ends and peculiar notions, and has, therefore, at the same time drowned in this Stygian water all essentiality of its own, and all independence of the objective, actual world. Its absolute right is, therefore, that when it acts in accordance with ethical law, it shall find in this actualization nothing else but the fulfilment of this law itself, and the deed shall manifest only ethical action. What is ethical, being at once absolute *essence* and absolute *power*, cannot suffer any perversion of its content. If it were only absolute essence without power, it could suffer perversion by the individuality; but this, as an ethical consciousness, when it gave up its one-sided being-for-self, renounced its right to pervert the content; just as, conversely, mere power would be perverted by essence if it were a one-sided being-for-self. On account of this unity, the individuality is the pure form of substance which is the content, and the action is the transition from thought to actuality merely as the movement of an insubstantial antithesis whose moments have no particular, distinctive content and no essentiality of their own. Consequently, the absolute right of the ethical consciousness is that the deed, the *shape* in which it *actualizes* itself, shall be nothing else but what it *knows*.

468. But the ethical essence has split itself into two laws, and consciousness, as an undivided attitude towards law, is assigned only to one. Just as this simple, unitary consciousness insists, as its absolute right, that the essence has *appeared* to it, *qua* ethical, as the essence is *in itself*, so too this essence insists on the right belonging to its *reality*, or on its own right to be a twofold

essence. But at the same time this right of the essence does not stand over against self-consciousness, as if the essence existed somewhere else; on the contrary, it is self-consciousness's own essence; it has its existence and its power in self-consciousness alone, and its antithesis is the act of self-consciousness itself. For this latter, just because it is a self to itself and advances to action, raises itself out of simple immediacy, and spontaneously splits itself into two. By this act it gives up the specific quality of the ethical life, of being the simple certainty of immediate truth, and initiates the division of itself into itself as the active principle, and into the reality over against it, a reality which, for it, is negative. By the deed, therefore, it becomes guilt. For the deed is its own doing, and 'doing' is its inmost nature. And the guilt also acquires the meaning of *crime*; for as simple, ethical consciousness, it has turned towards one law, but turned its back on the other and violates the latter by its deed. Guilt is not an indifferent, ambiguous affair, as if the deed as actually seen in the light of day could, or perhaps could not, be the action of the self, as if with the doing of it there could be linked something external and accidental that did not belong to it, from which aspect, therefore, the action would be innocent. On the contrary, the action is itself this splitting into two, this explicit self-affirmation and the establishing over against itself of an alien external reality; that there is such a reality, this stems from the action itself and results from it. Innocence, therefore, is merely non-action, like the mere being of a stone, not even that of a child. As regards content, however, the ethical action contains the moment of crime, because it does not do away with the *natural* allocation of the two laws to the two sexes, but rather, being an undivided attitude towards the law, remains within the sphere of natural immediacy, and, *qua* action, turns this one-sidedness into guilt by seizing on only one side of the essence, and adopting a negative attitude towards the other, i.e. violating it. The place in the universal ethical life of guilt and crime, of deeds and actions, will find more definite expression later; but this much is immediately evident, that it is not *this* particular individual who acts and is guilty; for as *this* self he is only the unreal shadow, or he exists merely as a universal self, and individuality is purely the *formal* moment of the action as such, the content being the laws and customs which, for the individual, are those of his class and station. He is the Substance *qua* genus, which by its determinateness, becomes indeed a species, though the species remains at the same time the universal of the genus. Self-consciousness within the nation descends from the universal only as far down as mere particularity, and not down to the single individuality which posits an exclusive self, an actual existence which in its action is negative towards itself. On the contrary, its action rests on secure confidence in the whole, unmixed with any alien element, neither with fear nor hostility.

469. Ethical self-consciousness now learns from its deed the developed nature of what it *actually* did, as much when it obeyed divine law as when it followed human law. The law that is manifest to it is linked in the essence with its opposite; the essence is the unity of both; but the deed has only carried out one law in contrast to the other. But the two laws being linked in the essence, the fulfilment of the one evokes the other and—the deed having made it so—calls it forth as a violated and now hostile entity demanding revenge. In the action, only one aspect of the resolve as such is clearly manifest. The resolve, however, is *in itself* the negative aspect which confronts the resolve with an 'other', with something alien to the resolve which knows what it does. Actuality therefore holds concealed within it the other aspect which is alien to this knowledge, and does not reveal the whole truth about itself to consciousness: the son does not recognize his father in the man who has wronged him and whom he slays, nor his mother in the queen whom he makes his wife. In this way, a power which shuns the light of day ensnares the ethical self-consciousness, a power which breaks forth only after the deed is done, and seizes the doer in the act. For the accomplished deed is the removal of the antithesis between the knowing self and the actuality confronting it. The doer cannot deny the crime or his guilt: the significance of the deed is that what was unmoved has been set in motion, and that what was locked up in mere possibility has been brought out into the open, hence to link together the unconscious and the conscious, non-being with being. In this truth, therefore, the deed is brought out into the light of day, as something in which the conscious is bound up with the unconscious, what is one's own with what is alien to it, as an entity

divided within itself, whose other aspect consciousness experiences and also finds to be its own, but as the power it has violated and roused to hostility.

470. It can be that the right which lay in wait is not present in its own proper shape to the *consciousness* of the doer, but is present only *implicitly* in the inner guilt of the resolve and the action. But the ethical consciousness is more complete, its guilt more inexcusable, if it knows *beforehand* the law and the power which it opposes, if it takes them to be violence and wrong, to be ethical merely by accident, and, like Antigone, knowingly commits the crime. The accomplished deed completely alters its point of view; the very performance of it declares that what is *ethical* must be *actual*; for the *realization* of the purpose is the purpose of the action. Doing directly expresses the unity of actuality and substance; it declares that actuality is not an accident of essence, but that, in union with essence, it is not granted to any right that is not a true right. The ethical consciousness must, on account of this actuality and on account of its deed, acknowledge its opposite as its own actuality, must acknowledge its guilt.

Because we suffer we acknowledge we have erred.[1]

471. With this acknowledgement there is no longer any conflict between ethical purpose and actuality; it signifies the return to an ethical frame of mind, which knows that nothing counts but right. But the doer thereby surrenders his own *character* and the *reality* of his self, and has been ruined. His *being* consists in his belonging to his ethical law, as his substance; in acknowledging the opposite law, the other ceases to be for him his substance, and instead of attaining actuality it has become an unreality, a sentiment or disposition. The substance does appear, it is true, *in* the individuality as his 'pathos', and the individuality appears as that which animates the substance and hence stands above it; but the substance is a 'pathos' that is at the same time his character. The ethical individuality is directly and intrinsically one with this his universal aspect, exists in it alone, and is incapable of surviving the destruction of this ethical power by its opposite.

472. But at the same time, this individuality has the certainty that that individuality whose 'pathos' is this opposing power

[1] *Antigone*, l. 926.

suffers no more injury than it has inflicted. The movement of the ethical powers against each other and of the individualities calling them into life and action have attained their true end only in so far as both sides suffer the same destruction. For neither power has any advantage over the other that would make it a more essential moment of the substance. The equal essentiality of both and their indifferent existence alongside each other means that they are without a self. In the *deed* they exist as beings with a self, but with a diverse self; and this contradicts the unity of the self, and constitutes their unrighteousness and necessary destruction. Character likewise, in respect of its 'pathos' or substance, in part belongs to one only; in part, from the aspect of knowing, the one character like the other is split up into a conscious and an unconscious part; and since each itself calls forth this opposition and its not-knowing is, through the deed, its own affair, each is responsible for the guilt which destroys it. The victory of one power and its character, and the defeat of the other, would thus be only the part and the incomplete work which irresistibly advances to the equilibrium of the two. Only in the downfall of both sides alike is absolute right accomplished, and the ethical substance as the negative power which engulfs both sides, that is, omnipotent and righteous Destiny, steps on the scene.

473. If both powers are taken according to their specific content and its individualization, we are presented with the picture of the conflict between them in their individual forms. On its formal side, it is the conflict of the ethical order and self-consciousness with unconscious Nature and the contingency stemming from Nature. The latter has a right against the former, because this is only *true* Spirit, is only in an *immediate* unity with its substance. On the side of content, it is the clash between divine and human law. The youth comes away from the unconscious Spirit of the Family, and becomes the individuality of the community. But that he still belongs to the Nature from which he wrenched himself free is evidenced by the fact that he emerges in the contingent form of two brothers, each of whom with equal right takes possession of the community; the inequality of the earlier and later birth, an inequality which is a natural difference, has no importance for them when they enter the ethical life of the community. But the government,

as the unitary soul or the self of the national Spirit, does not tolerate a duality of individuality; and the ethical necessity of this unity is confronted by the natural accident of there being more than one. These two brothers therefore fall into dispute and their equal right to the power of the state destroys them both, for they were equally wrong. Looked at from the human point of view, the one who has committed the crime is the one who, not being in actual possession, attacks the community at the head of which the other stood, while, on the other hand, *he* has right on his side who knew how to apprehend the other merely as an isolated individual, detached from the community, and, taking advantage of his powerlessness, banished him; he has struck only at the individual as such, not the community, not at the essence of human right. The community, attacked and defended by what is merely particular, and so without a substantial content, preserves itself, and the brothers bring about their own destruction through their reciprocal action. For individuality, which for the sake of its being-for-self, puts the whole in peril, has expelled itself from the community, and is the source of its own destruction. The community, however, will honour the one who was found on its side; but the government, the restored unitary self of the community, will punish him who already proclaimed its devastation on the walls of the city, by depriving him of the last honour. He who wantonly attacked the Spirit's highest form of consciousness, the Spirit of the community, must be stripped of the honour of his entire and finished being, the honour due to the Spirit of the departed.

474. But if the universal thus easily knocks off the very tip of the pyramid and, indeed, carries off the victory over the rebellious principle of pure individuality, viz. the Family, it has thereby merely entered on a conflict with the divine law, a conflict of self-conscious Spirit with what is unconscious. For the latter is the other essential power, and is therefore not destroyed, but merely wronged, by the conscious Spirit. But it has only the bloodless shade to help it in actually carrying out *its* law in face of the power and authority of that other, publicly manifest law. Being the law of weakness and darkness it therefore at first succumbs to the powerful law of the upper world, for the power of the former is effective in the underworld, not

on earth. But the outwardly actual which has taken away from the inner world its honour and power has in so doing consumed its own essence. The publicly manifest Spirit has the root of its power in the nether world. The self-certainty and self-assurance of a nation possesses the *truth* of its oath, which binds all into one, solely in the mute unconscious substance of all, in the waters of forgetfulness. Thus it is that the fulfilment of the Spirit of the upper world is transformed into its opposite, and it learns that its supreme right is a supreme wrong, that its victory is rather its own downfall. The dead, whose right is denied, knows therefore how to find instruments of vengeance, which are equally effective and powerful as the power which has injured it. These powers are other communities whose altars the dogs or birds defiled with the corpse, which is not raised into unconscious universality by being given back, as is its due, to the elemental individuality [the earth], but remains above ground in the realm of outer reality, and has now acquired as a force of divine law a self-conscious, real universality. They rise up in hostility and destroy the community which has dishonoured and shattered its own power, the sacred claims of the Family.

475. In this representation, the movement of human and divine law finds its necessity expressed in individuals in whom the universal appears as a 'pathos', and the activity of the movement appears as the action of individuals, which gives the appearance of contingency to the necessity of the activity. But individuality and action constitute the principle of individuality as such, a principle which in its pure universality was called inner divine law. As a moment of the visible community its activity is not confined merely to the underworld, or to its outer existence, but it has an equally visible existence and movement in the actual nation. Taken in this form, what was represented as a simple movement of the individualized 'pathos' acquires a different look, and the crime and consequent destruction of the community acquire the proper and characteristic form of their existence. Human law in its universal existence is the community, in its activity in general is the manhood of the community, in its real and effective activity is the government. It *is*, *moves*, and *maintains* itself by consuming and absorbing into itself the separatism of the Penates, or the separation into

independent families presided over by womankind, and by keeping them dissolved in the fluid continuity of its own nature. But
the Family is, at the same time, in general its element, the individual consciousness the basis of its general activity. Since the
community only gets an existence through its interference with
the happiness of the Family, and by dissolving [individual] self-
consciousness into the universal, it creates for itself in what it
suppresses and what is at the same time essential to it an internal
enemy—womankind in general. Womankind—the everlasting
irony [in the life] of the community—changes by intrigue the
universal end of the government into a private end, transforms
its universal activity into a work of some particular individual,
and perverts the universal property of the state into a possession
and ornament for the Family. Woman in this way turns to ridicule the earnest wisdom of mature age which, indifferent to
purely private pleasures and enjoyments, as well as to playing
an active part, only thinks of and cares for the universal. She
makes this wisdom an object of derision for raw and irrespon-
sible youth and unworthy of their enthusiasm. In general, she
maintains that it is the power of youth that really counts: the
worth of the son lies in his being the lord and master of the
mother who bore him, that of the brother as being one in whom
the sister finds man on a level of equality, that of the youth
as being one through whom the daughter, freed from her dependence [on the family] obtains the enjoyment and dignity of
wifehood. The community, however, can only maintain itself
by suppressing this spirit of individualism, and, because it is
an essential moment, all the same creates it and, moreover, creates it by its repressive attitude towards it as a hostile principle.
However, this principle, being merely evil and futile in its
separation from the universal end, would be quite ineffectual
if the community itself did not recognize the power of youth
(the manhood which, while immature, still stands within the
sphere of individuality), as the *power* of the whole. For the community is a nation, is itself an individuality, and essentially is
only such for *itself* by other individualities being *for it*, by
excluding them from itself and knowing itself to be independent
of them. The negative side of the community, suppressing the
isolation of individuals *within it*, but spontaneously active in an
outward direction, finds its weapons in individuality. War is the

Spirit and the form in which the essential moment of the ethical substance, the absolute freedom of the ethical *self* from every existential form, is present in its actual and authentic existence. While, on the one hand, war makes the individual *systems* of property and personal independence, as well as the *personality* of the individual himself, feel the power of the negative, on the other hand, this negativity is prominent in war as that which preserves the whole. The brave youth in whom woman finds her pleasure, the suppressed principle of corruption, now has his day and his worth is openly acknowledged. Now, it is physical strength and what appears as a matter of luck, that decides on the existence of ethical life and spiritual necessity. Because the existence of ethical life rests on strength and luck, the *decision is already made* that its downfall has come. Just as previously only the Penates succumbed to the national Spirit, so now the *living* Spirits of the nation succumb through their own individuality and perish in a *universal* community, whose simple universality is soulless and dead, and is alive only in the *single* individual, *qua* single. The ethical shape of Spirit has vanished and another takes its place.

476. This ruin of the ethical Substance and its passage into another form is thus determined by the fact that the ethical consciousness is directed on to the law in a way that is essentially *immediate*. This determination of immediacy means that Nature as such enters into the ethical act, the reality of which simply reveals the contradiction and the germ of destruction inherent in the beautiful harmony and tranquil equilibrium of the ethical Spirit itself. For this immediacy has the contradictory meaning of being the unconscious tranquillity of Nature, and also the self-conscious restless tranquillity of Spirit. On account of this natural aspect, this ethical nation is, in general, an individuality determined by Nature and therefore limited, and thus meets its downfall at the hands of another. But with the vanishing of this determinateness—which in the form of a real existence is a limitation, but equally the negative element in general and the self of the individuality—the life of Spirit and this Substance, which is self-conscious in everyone, is lost. The substance emerges as a formal universality in them, no longer dwelling in them as a living Spirit; on the contrary, the simple compactness of their individuality has been shattered into a multitude of separate atoms.

c. *Legal status*

477. The universal unity into which the living immediate unity of individuality and substance withdraws is the soulless community which has ceased to be the substance—itself unconscious—of individuals, and in which they now have the value of selves and substances, possessing a separate being-for-self. The universal being thus split up into a mere multiplicity of individuals, this lifeless Spirit is an equality, in which all count the same, i.e. as *persons*. What in the world of the ethical order was called the hidden divine law, has in fact emerged from its inward state into actuality; in the former state the individual was actual, and counted as such, merely as a blood-relation of the family. As *this* particular individual, he was the departed spirit devoid of a self; now, however, he has emerged from his unreal existence. Because the ethical substance is only the *true* Spirit, the individual therefore withdraws into the *certainty* of his own self; he is that substance as the *positive* universal, but his actuality consists in his being a *negative* universal self. We saw the powers and shapes of the ethical world swallowed up in the simple necessity of a blank Destiny. This power of the ethical world is the substance reflected into its simple unitary nature; but that being which is reflected back into itself, that very necessity of blank Destiny, is nothing else but the 'I' of self-consciousness.

478. This, therefore, counts henceforth as a being that is in and for itself. To be so acknowledged is its substantiality. But it is an *abstract* universality because its content is this rigid unyielding self, not the self that is dissolved in the substance.

479. Personality, then, has stepped out of the life of the ethical substance. It is the independence of consciousness, an independence which has *actual* validity. The non-actual thought of it which came from renouncing the *actual* world appeared earlier as the *Stoical* self-consciousness. Just as this proceeded from lordship and bondage, as the immediate existence of self-consciousness, so personality has proceeded from the immediate life of Spirit, which is the universal dominating will of all, and equally their service of obedience. What was for Stoicism only the *abstraction* of an *intrinsic* reality is now an *actual* world. Stoi-

cism is nothing else but the consciousness which reduces to its abstract form the principle of legal status, an independence that lacks the life of Spirit. By its flight from the actual world it attained only to the *thought* of independence; it is absolutely for *itself*, in that it does not attach its being to anything that exists, but claims to give up everything that exists and places its essence solely in the unity of pure thought. In the same way, the right of a person is not tied to a richer or more powerful existence of the individual as such, nor again to a universal living Spirit, but rather to the pure One of its abstract actuality, or to that One *qua* self-consciousness in general.

480. Now, just as the *abstract* independence of Stoicism exhibited [the process of] its actualization, so too will this last form of independence [= personality] recapitulate the process of the first form. The former passes over into the sceptical confusion of consciousness, into a negative rambling which, lacking any stable form, strays fortuitously from one form of being and thought to another, dissolving them, it is true, in [its] absolute independence but no less recreating them; it is, in fact, merely the contradiction of a consciousness which is at once independent and dependent. Personal independence in the sphere of *legal right* is really a similar general confusion and reciprocal dissolution of this kind. For what counts as absolute, essential being is self-consciousness as the sheer *empty unit* of the person. In contrast to this empty universality, substance has the form of *fulness* and *content*, and this content is now set free and is unorganized; for the Spirit that subdued it and held it together in its unity is no longer present. This empty unit of the person is, therefore, in its *reality* a contingent existence, and essentially a process and an action that comes to no lasting result. Like Scepticism, the formalism of legal right is thus by its very nature without a peculiar content of its own; it finds before it a manifold existence in the form of 'possession' and, as Scepticism did, stamps it with the same abstract universality, whereby it is called 'property'. But whereas in Scepticism the reality so determined is called an *illusory appearance* and has only a negative value, in legal right it has a positive value. That negative value consists in the actual having the significance of the self *qua* thought, *qua* the *implicit* universal; the positive value in the case

of legal right, however, consists in its being *mine* in the sense
of the category, as something whose validity is *recognized* and
actual. Both are the same *abstract* universal. The actual content
or the specific character of what is mine—whether it be an
external possession, or also the inner riches or poverty of spirit
and character—is not contained in this empty form, and does
not concern it. The content belongs, therefore, to an autono-
mous power, which is something different from the formal universal, to a power which is arbitrary and capricious. Consciousness of right, therefore, in the very fact of being recognized as
having validity, experiences rather the loss of its reality and its
complete inessentiality; and to describe an individual as a 'person' is an expression of contempt.

481. The free power of the content determines itself in such
a way that the dispersion of the content into a sheer multiplicity
of personal atoms is, by the nature of this determinateness, at
the same time gathered into a single point, alien to them and
soulless as well. This single point is, on the one hand, like the
unyielding rigidity of their personality, a merely single personality; but in contrast to their empty singleness, it has at the
same time the significance for them of the whole content, hence
of real essence, and as against their presumedly absolute, but
intrinsically essenceless, reality it is absolute power and absolute
actuality. This lord and master of the world holds himself in
this way to be the absolute person, at the same time embracing
within himself the whole of existence, the person for whom there
exists no superior Spirit. He is a person, but the solitary person
who stands over against all the rest. These constitute the real
authoritative universality of that person; for the single individual as such is true only as a universal multiplicity of single
individuals. Cut off from this multiplicity, the solitary self is,
in fact, an unreal, impotent self. At the same time it is the consciousness of the content which has placed itself in antithesis
to that universal personality. But this content, liberated from
the negative power controlling it, is the chaos of spiritual powers
which, in their unfettered freedom, become elemental beings
raging madly against one another in a frenzy of destructive
activity. Their impotent self-consciousness is the defenceless
enclosed arena of their tumult. In this knowledge of himself as
the sum and substance of all actual powers, this lord and master

of the world is the titanic self-consciousness that thinks of itself as being an actual living god. But since he is only the *formal* self which is unable to tame those powers, his activities and self-enjoyment are equally monstrous excesses.

482. The lord of the world becomes really conscious of what he is, viz. the universal power of the actual world, in the destructive power he exercises against the self of his subjects, the self which stands over against him. For his power is not the *union* and *harmony* of Spirit in which persons would recognize their own self-consciousness. Rather they exist, as persons, on their own account, and exclude any continuity with others from the rigid unyieldingness of their atomicity. They exist, therefore, in a merely negative relationship, both to one another and to him who is their bond of connection or continuity. As this continuity, he is the essence and the content of their merely formal self, but a content alien to them, and a hostile being which in reality deprives them of that very thing which they regard as their essential nature, viz. the completely empty form of being-for-self; and, again, as the continuity of their personality, he destroys this very personality itself. Legal personality thus learns rather that it is without any substance, since the alien content makes itself authoritative in it, and does so because that content is the reality of such personality. On the other hand, by indulging in this destructive activity in this insubstantial arena, the lord of the world obtains for himself the consciousness of his complete supremacy. However, this self is a mere laying-waste of everything and therefore merely beside itself, and is really the abandonment of its own self-consciousness.

483. Such, then, is the constitution of that aspect in which self-consciousness, *qua* absolute Being, is *actual*. But the consciousness that is *driven back into itself* from this actuality ponders this its inessential nature. Earlier we saw the Stoical independence of pure thought pass through Scepticism and find its truth in the Unhappy Consciousness—the truth about what constitutes its own true being. If this knowledge appeared then merely as the one-sided view of consciousness as consciousness, here the *actual* truth of that view has become apparent. This truth consists in the fact that this *universally acknowledged authority* of self-consciousness is the reality from which it is alienated. This acknowledgement of its authority is the universal actuality

of the self; but this actuality is directly the perversion of the self as well; it is the loss of its essence. The actuality of the self that did not exist in the ethical world has been won by its return into the 'person'; what in the former was harmoniously one now emerges in a developed form, but as alienated from itself.

B. SELF-ALIENATED SPIRIT. CULTURE

484. The ethical Substance kept the antithesis confined within its simply unitary consciousness, and preserved this consciousness in an immediate unity with its essence. Essence has, therefore, the simple determinateness of mere being for consciousness, which is directed *immediately* upon it, and is the essence in the form of custom. Consciousness neither thinks of itself as *this particular exclusive self*, nor has substance the significance of an existence excluded from it, with which it would have to become united only by alienating itself from itself and at the same time producing the substance itself. But the Spirit whose self is an absolutely discrete unit has its content confronting it as an equally hard unyielding reality, and here the world has the character of being something external, the negative of self-consciousness. This world is, however, a spiritual entity, it is in itself the interfusion of being and individuality; this its existence is the *work* of self-consciousness, but it is also an alien reality already present and given, a reality which has a being of its own and in which it does not recognize itself. This real world is the external essence and the free content of legal right. But this external world, which the lord of the world of legal right takes to himself, is not merely this elemental being confronting the self as something contingently given; on the contrary, it *is* his work, but not in a positive, rather in a negative, sense. It obtains its existence through self-consciousness's *own* externalization and separation of itself from its essence which, in the ruin and devastation which prevail in the world of legal right, seems to inflict on self-consciousness from without, the violence of the liberated elements. These by themselves are sheer ruin and devastation and the dissolution of themselves. This dissolution, however, this negative nature of theirs, is just the self; it is their subject, their activity, and their process. But this activity and process whereby the substance becomes *actual*

is the alienation of the personality, for the self that has an absolute significance in its *immediate* existence, i.e. without having
alienated itself from itself, is without substance, and is the
plaything of those raging elements. *Its* substance, therefore, is
its externalization, and the externalization is the substance, i.e.
the spiritual powers ordering themselves into a world and
thereby preserving themselves.

485. Substance is in this way *Spirit*, the self-conscious unity
of the self and essence; each has for the other the significance
of alienation. Spirit is the *consciousness* of an objective real world
freely existing on its own account; but this consciousness is confronted by the unity of the self and essence, *actual* consciousness
by *pure* consciousness. On the one side, actual self-consciousness,
through its externalization, passes over into the actual world,
and the latter back into actual self-consciousness. On the other
side, this same actuality—both person and objectivity—is
superseded; they are purely universal. This their alienation is
pure consciousness or *essence*. The *present* actual world has its antithesis directly in its *beyond*, which is both the thinking of it and
its thought-form, just as the beyond has in the present world
its actuality, but an actuality alienated from it.

486. Consequently, this Spirit constructs for itself not merely
a world, but a world that is double, divided and self-opposed.
The world of the ethical Spirit is its own *present* world; and
therefore each of its powers exists in this unity, and in so far
as they are distinct from one another they are in equilibrium
with the whole. Nothing has the significance of being the negative of self-consciousness; even the departed spirit is present in
his *blood*-relationship, in the *self* of the family, and the universal
power of the government is the *will*, the self of the nation. Here,
however, what is *present* has the significance only of an objective
reality, the consciousness of which exists in a beyond; each
single moment *qua* essence receives this, and with it actuality,
from an 'other', and so far as it is actual, its essence is something
other than its own actuality. Nothing has a Spirit that is
grounded within itself and indwells it, but each has its being
in something outside of and alien to it. The equilibrium of the
whole is not the unity which remains with itself, nor the con-
tentment that comes from having returned into itself, but rests
on the alienation of opposites. The whole, therefore, like each

single moment, is a self-alienated actuality; it falls apart into a realm in which *self-consciousness* as well as its object is *actual*, and into another, the realm of *pure* consciousness which, lying beyond the first, is not a present actuality but exists only for Faith. Now, just as the ethical world which is separated into divine and human law in their various forms, and its consciousness which is separated into knowing and not-knowing, returns from that dividedness into its destiny, into the *self* as the *negative power* of this antithesis, so these two realms of the self-alienated Spirit will also return into the *self*; but if the former was the first, merely *immediately* valid self, the single *person*, this second realm, which returns out of its externalization into itself, will be the *universal self*, the consciousness which has grasped its *Notion*, and these spiritual worlds, all of whose moments insist on a fixed actuality and non-spiritual existence of their own, will dissolve in *pure intellectual insight*. This insight, as the self that *apprehends* itself, completes [the stage of] culture; it apprehends nothing but self and everything as self, i.e. it *comprehends* everything, wipes out the objectivity of things and converts all *intrinsic* being into a being for *itself*. In its hostility to Faith as the alien realm of *essence* lying in the beyond, it is the Enlightenment. This Enlightenment completes the alienation of Spirit in this realm, too, in which that Spirit takes refuge and where it is conscious of an unruffled peace. It upsets the housekeeping of Spirit in the household of Faith by bringing into that household the tools and utensils of *this* world, a world which that Spirit cannot deny is its own, because its consciousness likewise belongs to it. In this negative activity pure insight at the same time realizes itself, and produces its own object, the unknowable *absolute Being* and the principle of *utility*. Since in this way actuality has lost all substantiality and nothing in it has *intrinsic* being, not only the realm of Faith, but also the realm of the actual world, is overthrown. This revolution gives birth to *absolute freedom*, and with this freedom the previously alienated Spirit has completely returned into itself, has abandoned this region of culture and passes on to another region, the region of the *moral consciousness*.

I. THE WORLD OF SELF-ALIENATED SPIRIT

487. The world of this Spirit breaks up into two. The first

is the world of reality or of its self-alienation; but the other is
that which Spirit, rising above the first, constructs for itself in
the Aether of pure consciousness. This second world, standing
in antithesis to that alienation, is for that very reason not free
from it; on the contrary, it is really only the other form of that
alienation which consists precisely in being conscious of two different worlds, and which embraces both. Therefore, it is not
the self-consciousness of absolute being as it is *in* and *for itself*,
not religion, that is here dealt with but Faith, so far as this is
a *flight* from the real world and thus is not *in* and *for itself*. This
flight from the realm of the present is, therefore, in its own self
dual-natured. Pure consciousness is the element into which
Spirit raises itself, but it is not only the element of Faith, but
equally of the *Notion*. Consequently, both together make their
appearance at the same time, and the former comes into consideration only in its antithesis to the latter.

a. *Culture and its realm of actuality*

488. The Spirit of this world is a spiritual *essence* that is permeated by a *self*-consciousness which knows itself, and knows
the essence as an actuality confronting it. But the existence of
this world, as also the actuality of self-consciousness, rests on
the process in which the latter divests itself of its personality,
thereby creating its world. This world it looks on as something
alien, a world, therefore, of which it must now take possession.
But the renunciation of its being-for-self is itself the product of
the actual world, and by this renunciation, therefore, self-consciousness directly takes possession of this world. Or we may
say that self-consciousness is merely a 'something', it has *actuality* only in so far as it alienates itself from itself; by so doing,
it gives itself the character of a universal, and this its universality
is its authentication and actuality. This *equality* with everyone
is, therefore, not the equality of the sphere of legal right, not
that immediate recognition and validity of self-consciousness
simply because it *is*; on the contrary, to be valid it must have
conformed itself to the universal by the mediating process of
alienation. The non-spiritual universality of the sphere of legal
right accepts every natural form of character as well as of existence and justifies them. The universality which counts here,

however, is one that has made itself what it is and for that reason
is *actual*.

489. It is therefore through culture that the individual
acquires standing and actuality. His true *original nature* and substance is the alienation of himself as Spirit from his *natural* being.
This externalization is, therefore, both the purpose and the existence of the individual; it is at once the *means*, or the *transition*,
both of the [mere] *thought-form of substance* into *actuality*, and,
conversely, of the *specific individuality* into *essentiality*. This individuality *moulds* itself by culture into what it intrinsically is, and
only by so doing is it an intrinsic being that has an actual existence; the measure of its culture is the measure of its actuality
and power. Although here the self knows itself as *this* self, yet
its actuality consists solely in the setting-aside of its natural self.
Consequently, the originally *specific* nature is reduced to the *unessential* difference of quantity, to a greater or lesser energy of
will. But the purpose and content of the will belong solely to
the universal substance itself and can only be a universal. The
particularity of a nature which becomes purpose and content is
something powerless and unreal; it is a *'kind'* of being which
vainly and ridiculously strains every nerve to get going; it is
the contradiction of giving to what is particular an actuality
which is immediately a universal. If, therefore, individuality
is erroneously supposed to be rooted in the *particularity* of nature
and character, then in the actual world there are no individualities and no characters, but everyone is like everyone else; but
this presumed individuality really only exists in someone's
mind, an *imaginary* existence which has no abiding place in this
world, where only that which externalizes itself, and, therefore,
only the universal, obtains an actual existence. That is why such
an imagined existence is esteemed for what it is, for a *kind* of
being. 'Kind' is not quite the same as *espèce*, 'the most horrid
of all nicknames; for it denotes mediocrity and expresses the
highest degree of contempt'.[1] 'Kind' and 'good of its kind' are,
however, German expressions which add an air of honesty to
this meaning, as if it were not really meant so badly; or, again,
consciousness is, in fact, not yet aware what 'kind', and what
'culture' and 'reality' are.

490. What, in relation to the single *individual*, appears as his

[1] Diderot, *Nephew of Rameau*.

culture, is the essential moment of the *substance* itself, viz. the
immediate passage of the [mere] thought-form of its universality into actuality; or, culture is the simple soul of the
substance by means of which, what is *implicit* in the substance,
acquires an *acknowledged, real existence*. The process in which the
individuality moulds itself by culture is, therefore, at the same
time the development of it as the universal, objective essence,
i.e. the development of the actual world. Although this world
has come into being through individuality, it is for self-consciousness immediately an alienated world which has the form
of a fixed and solid reality over against it. But at the same time,
certain that this world is its substance, it sets about making it
its own. It gains this power over it through culture which,
looked at from this aspect, has the appearance of self-consciousness making itself conform to reality, and doing so to the extent
that the energy of its original character and talent permits.
What appears here as the power and authority of the individual
exercised over the substance, which is thereby superseded, is
the same thing as the actualization of the substance. For the
power of the individual consists in conforming itself to that substance, i.e. in externalizing its own self and thus establishing
itself as substance that has an objective existence. Its culture
and its own actuality are, therefore, the actualization of the substance itself.

491. The self knows itself as actual only as a *transcended* self.
Therefore, it is not constituted by the unity of *consciousness* of
itself and the object; on the contrary, the object is, for the self,
its negative. Thus, by means of the self as soul of the process,
substance is so moulded and developed in its moments that one
opposite stirs the other into life, each by its alienation from the
other gives it an existence and equally receives from it an existence of its own. At the same time, each moment possesses its
own specific nature as something unchallengeably valid and as
a firm reality *vis-à-vis* the other. Thinking fixes this difference
in the most general way by the absolute antithesis of *good* and
bad which, shunning each other, cannot in any way become
one and the same. The soul of this fixed being, however, is the
immediate transition into its opposite; existence is really the
perversion of every determinateness into its opposite, and it is
only this alienation that is the essential nature and support of

the whole. We have now to consider this process in which the moments are stirred into life and given an existence of their own; the alienation will alienate itself, and the whole will, through this alienation, return into its Notion.

492. We have first to consider the simple unitary substance itself in the immediate organization of its moments, which are present in the substance but as yet have not been stirred into life. In the same way that Nature displays itself in the universal elements of Air, Water, Fire, and Earth: Air is the enduring, purely universal, and transparent element; Water, the element that is perpetually sacrificed; Fire, the unity which energizes them into opposition while at the same time it perpetually resolves the opposition; lastly, Earth, which is the firm and solid knot of this articulated whole, the *subject* of these elements and of their process, that from which they start and to which they return; so in the same way, the inner *essence* or simple Spirit of self-conscious actuality displays itself in similar such uni-versal—but here spiritual—'masses' or spheres, displays itself as a world. In the first sphere it is an implicitly universal, self-identical spiritual being; in the second it is explicitly for itself and has become inwardly divided against itself, sacrificing and abandoning itself; in the third, which as self-consciousness is Subject, it possesses directly in its own self the force of Fire. In the first it is conscious of itself as an intrinsic being; but in the second it develops an explicit being of its own by sacrificing the universal. Spirit, however, is itself at once the essence and the actuality of the whole, which sunders itself into a substance which endures, and a substance which sacrifices itself, and which at the same time also takes them back into its unity; it is both the outburst of flaming Fire which consumes the sub-stance, and also the abiding form of that substance. We see that these spheres correspond to the community and the family in the ethical world, without, however, possessing the native Spirit peculiar to the latter. On the other hand, while Destiny is alien to this Spirit, here self-consciousness is and knows itself to be the real power of these spheres.

493. We have to consider how, in the first instance, these two members are represented within pure consciousness as thoughts, or as having only an *implicit* being; and also how they are represented in actual consciousness as having an *objective*

existence. In the simple form of thoughts, the first is the Good—
the self-accordant, immediate, and unchangeable essence of
every consciousness, the independent spiritual power of the *in-
itself*, alongside which the activity of *actual* consciousness is
something merely incidental. Its other, on the contrary, is the
passive spiritual essence, or the universal in so far as it surrenders
itself and allows individuals to get in it the consciousness of their
separate existence; it is the essence that is null and invalid, the
Bad. This absolute break-up of the essence is itself permanent.
While the first essence is the foundation, starting-point, and
result of individuals who in it are purely universal, the second,
on the other hand, is partly their self-sacrificing being-for-
another, and partly, for that very reason, their perpetual
return-to-self as separate individuals and the perpetual process
in which they develop a being of their own.

494. But [secondly], these simple *thoughts* of Good and Bad
are likewise immediately self-alienated; they are *actual* and are
present in actual consciousness as *objective* moments. Thus the
first essence is *state power*, the other is *wealth*. As state power is
the simple *substance*, so too is it the universal '*work*'—the absolute
'heart of the matter' itself in which individuals find their *essential*
nature expressed, and where their separate individuality is
merely a consciousness of their *universality*. It is also the 'work'
and the simple *result* from which the sense that it results from
their doing has vanished; it remains the absolute foundation and
subsistence of all that they do. This *simple*, ethereal substance
of their life is, in virtue of this determination of their unchangeable self-identity, [mere] *being* and, in addition, merely a being-
for-another. It is thus directly the opposite of itself, *wealth*.
Although this is indeed something passive, something devoid
of inner worth, it is equally the perpetually produced result of
the labour and activity of all, just as it is dissipated again in
the enjoyment of all. It is true that in the enjoyment, the individuality develops an awareness of himself as a particular individual, but this enjoyment itself is the result of the general
activity, just as reciprocally, wealth produces universal labour
and enjoyment for all. The actual has simply the spiritual significance of being immediately universal. Each individual is
quite sure that he is acting in his own interest when seeking
this enjoyment; for it is in this that he becomes conscious of

his own independent existence and for that reason does not take it to be something spiritual. Yet, even when looked at from an external point of view, it is evident that each in his own enjoyment provides enjoyment for all, just as in working for himself he is at the same time working for all and all are working for him. His being for *himself* is therefore in itself *universal* and his self-interest is something merely in his mind, something that cannot get as far as making a reality of what it *means* to do, viz. to do something that would not benefit all.

495. In these two spiritual powers, then, self-consciousness recognizes its substance, content, and purpose; in them it beholds its dual nature: in one it sees what it implicitly is, in the other what it is explicitly for itself. But it is at the same time, *qua* Spirit, the negative *unity* of their subsistence and of the separation of individuality from the universal, or of actuality and the self. Dominion and wealth therefore confront the individual as objects, i.e. as things from which he knows himself to be free, and between which he believes he can choose, or even choose neither. As this free and *pure* consciousness he confronts the essence as something which is merely *for him*. He has, then, the essence, *qua* essence, within himself. In this pure consciousness the moments of substance are for him not state power and wealth, but the *thoughts* of Good and Bad. But further, self-consciousness is the relation of its pure consciousness to its actual consciousness, of what is in the form of thought to what exists objectively: it is essentially *judgement*. It is true that the immediate determinations of the two sides of objective reality have already made clear which is Good and which is Bad; the Good is state power, the Bad is wealth. But this first judgement cannot be regarded as a spiritual judgement; for in it one side has been determined only as a being-*in-itself*, or as the positive, the other only as a being-*for-itself*, and as the negative. But as spiritual essences each is the interfusion of both moments, and is therefore not exhausted in those determinations; and self-consciousness which is self-related is both *in* and *for* itself. It must therefore be related to each determination in a twofold manner, with the result that their nature, which consists in being self-alienated determinations, will be brought to light.

496. Now, self-consciousness holds that object to be good, and to possess intrinsic being, in which it finds itself; and that

to be bad in which it finds the opposite of itself. Goodness is the likeness of objective reality to it, Badness, however, their unlikeness. At the same time, what for self-consciousness is good and bad, is *intrinsically* good and bad; for it is just that in which these two moments of *intrinsic* being, and of being *for it*, are the same. It is the *actual* Spirit of the objective realities, and the judgement is the proof of its power within them, a power which *makes* them into what they are *in themselves*. It is not how they are like or unlike directly in themselves, i.e. not abstract being-in-itself or being-for-itself, that is their criterion and their truth, but how they are in the relation of Spirit to them: their likeness or unlikeness to Spirit. Spirit's *relation* to them, in virtue of which they lose their initial status of *objects* and develop their own *in-itself* or *intrinsic* nature, becomes at the same time their *reflection into themselves*, through which they acquire an actual spiritual being; and what their Spirit is, comes to view. But just as their first *immediate determination* is distinct from the *relation* of Spirit to them, so also will the third moment, their own proper Spirit, be distinct from the second. First of all, their second *in-itself*, which stems from the relation of Spirit to them, must, of course, turn out to be different from the *immediate* in-itself; for this *mediation* of Spirit rather acts on the *immediate* determinateness and makes it into something else.

497. It follows, then, that the consciousness that is in and for itself does find in the state power its simple essence and subsistence in general, but not its individuality as such; it does find there its *intrinsic* being, but not what it explicitly is *for itself*. Rather, it finds that the state power disowns action *qua* individual action and subdues it into obedience. The individual, therefore, faced with this power reflects himself into himself; it is for him an oppressor and the Bad; for, instead of being of like nature to himself, its nature is essentially different from that of individuality. Wealth, on the other hand, is the Good; it leads to the general enjoyment, is there to be made use of, and procures for everyone the consciousness of his particular self. It is *implicitly* universal beneficence; if it refuses a particular benefit and does not choose to satisfy every need, this is accidental and does not detract from its universal and necessary nature of imparting itself to all and being a universal provider.

498. These two judgements give the thoughts of Good and Bad a content which is the opposite of what they had for us. But self-consciousness was at first only incompletely related to its objects, viz. only according to the criterion of being-for-self. Consciousness has equally, however, an *intrinsic nature* of its own and must likewise make this aspect a criterion, and only when it has done this is the spiritual judgement complete. According to this aspect, the state power expresses its *essence*; this power is in part the established law, and in part government and command, which regulates the particular activities within the action of the whole. The one is the simple Substance itself, the other is its action which animates and sustains itself and everyone. The individual thus finds therein his ground and essence expressed, organized, and manifested. On the other hand, the individual, through the enjoyment of wealth, gains no experience of his universal nature, but only gets a *transitory* consciousness and enjoyment of himself *qua* single and independent individual, and of the disparity between himself and his essence. The Notions of Good and Bad thus receive here a content which is the opposite of what they had before.

499. Each of these two ways of judging finds a likeness and a disparity; in the first case consciousness judges the state power to be essentially different from it, and the enjoyment of wealth to accord with its own nature; while in the second case it judges the state power to accord with its nature and the enjoyment of wealth to be essentially different from it. We have before us a twofold finding of likeness and a twofold finding of disparity, an antithetical relation between the two real essentialities. We must ourselves judge these different judgements and apply to them the criterion set up. According to this, the conscious relation which finds likeness is the Good; that which finds disparity is the Bad; and these two forms of the relation we are henceforth to hold fast as diverse shapes of consciousness. By forming diverse relationships, consciousness itself comes to be determined as diverse, as being good or bad; not because it had for its principle either being-for-itself or pure being-in-itself, for both are equally essential moments. In the twofold judging considered above, the principles were thought of as separate, and therefore contained merely *abstract* ways of judging. *Actual* consciousness has within it both principles, and the distinction

between them falls solely within its own *essence*, viz. in the relation of itself to the actual.

500. There are two antithetical forms of this relation: one is a relationship to the state power and wealth as to something of like nature to itself; the other as to something disparate from it. The consciousness which finds them of like nature to itself is *noble*. It sees in public authority what is in accord with itself, sees in it its own simple *essence* and the factual evidence of it, and in the service of that authority its attitude towards it is one of actual obedience and respect. Similarly, in the case of wealth, it sees that this procures for it awareness of its other essential side, the consciousness of being *for itself*; it therefore looks upon wealth likewise as *essential* in relation to itself, and acknowledges the source of its enjoyment as a benefactor to whom it lies under an obligation.

501. The consciousness which adopts the other relation is, on the contrary, *ignoble*. It clings to the disparity between the two essentialities, thus sees in the sovereign power a fetter and a suppression of its own *being-for-self*, and therefore hates the ruler, obeys only with a secret malice, and is always on the point of revolt. It sees, too, in wealth, by which it attains to the enjoyment of its own self-centred existence, only the disparity with its permanent *essence*; since through wealth it becomes conscious of itself merely as an isolated individual, conscious only of a transitory enjoyment, loving yet hating wealth, and with the passing of the enjoyment, of something that is essentially evanescent, it regards its relation to the rich as also having vanished.

502. Now, these relations express, in the first instance, the *judgement*, the determination, of what these two essential realities are as *objects* for consciousness, not as yet what they are in and for themselves. The reflection which is presented in the judgement is partly an affirmation of the one as of the other only *for us*, and is therefore an equal annulling of both; it is not yet the reflection of them for consciousness itself. Partly, at first, they simply *are essences*, they have not *become* such, nor do they possess *self*-consciousness: that for which they are is not that which animates them, they are predicates which are not yet themselves subject. On account of this separation, the whole of the spiritual judgement falls apart into two consciousnesses,

each of which is subject to a one-sided determination. Now, just as at first the *indifference* of the two sides of the alienation—one of which was the *in-itself* of pure consciousness, viz. the specific *thoughts* of Good and Bad, the other their *existence* as state power and wealth—was raised into a relation between them, into a judgement, so must this external relation be raised to an inner unity, or to a relation of thought to actuality, and the Spirit of both forms of the judgement must make its appearance. This happens when the judgement becomes a syllogism, i.e. becomes the mediating process in which the necessity and the middle term of both sides of the judgement come to view.

503. The noble consciousness thus finds itself, in the judgement, confronting the state power in such a way that the latter is, indeed, not yet a self, but only the universal substance; it is, however, conscious of being the *essence* of that substance, its end and absolute content. Being so positively related to it, it adopts a negative attitude to its own ends, to its particular content and existence, and lets them vanish. This consciousness is the heroism of *service*, the *virtue* which sacrifices the single individual to the universal, thereby bringing this into existence—the *person*, one who voluntarily renounces possessions and enjoyment and acts and is effective in the interests of the ruling power.

504. Through this process the universal becomes united with existence in general, just as the [merely] existent consciousness through this renunciation develops into an *essential* existence. That from which this consciousness alienates itself in serving the universal is the consciousness that is immersed in [mere] existence; but the being that is alienated from itself is the *in-itself*. Through this development, therefore, it wins self-respect and the respect of others. The state power, however, which was at first only the universal *in thought*, the *in-itself*, becomes through this very process the universal *in existence*, actual power. This it actually is only in the actual obedience which it gets through self-consciousness *judging* the state power to be the *essence*, and through the free sacrifice of self-consciousness to it. This action which unites the essence with the self produces the *twofold* actuality: the self that has a *true* actuality, and the state power as the True which is acknowledged as such.

505. Through this alienation, however, the state power is not

a self-consciousness that knows itself as state power. It is only its *law*, or its *in-itself*, that has authority; it has as yet no *particular will*. For the self-consciousness that serves the state power has not as yet renounced its own pure self and made it the active principle of the state power; it has only given that power its mere being, has only sacrificed its *outer existence* to it, not its *intrinsic being*. This self-consciousness is deemed to be in conformity with the *essence* and is acknowledged on account of what it *intrinsically* is. In it the others find their own essence exemplified, but not their own being-for-self—find their thought, or pure consciousness, fulfilled, but not their individuality. It therefore possesses authority in their *thoughts* and enjoys *honour*. It is the *haughty* vassal who is active on behalf of the state power in so far as the latter is not a personal will, but an *essential* will; the vassal who knows himself to be esteemed only in that *honour*, only in the *essential* representation of him in general opinion, not in the *gratitude* shown to him by an individuality, for he has not helped this individuality to gratify his *being-for-self*. His language, were he to stand in relation to the state power which has not yet come into being, would take the form of *counsel*, imparted for the general good.

506. State power, therefore, still lacks a will with which to oppose counsel, and the power to decide which of the different opinions is best for the general good. It is not yet a *government*, and therefore not yet in truth an actual state power. The *being-for-self*, the *will*, which, as will is not sacrificed, is the inner, separated Spirit of the various classes and 'estates', and this, in spite of its chatter about the *general* good, reserves to itself what suits its *own* best interest, and is inclined to make this chatter about the general good a substitute for action. The sacrifice of existence which happens in the service of the state is indeed complete when it has gone as far as death; but the hazard of death which the individual survives leaves him with a definite existence and hence with a *particular self-interest*, and this makes his counsel about what is best for the general good ambiguous and open to suspicion. It means that he has in fact reserved his own opinion and his own particular will in face of the power of the state. His conduct, therefore, conflicts with the interests of the state and is characteristic of the ignoble consciousness which is always on the point of revolt.

507. This contradiction which being-for-self must resolve, that of the disparity between its *being-for-self* and the state power, is at the same time present in the following form. That renunciation of existence, when it is complete, as it is in death, is simply a renunciation; it does not return into consciousness; consciousness does not survive the renunciation, is not *in and for itself*, but merely passes over into its unreconciled opposite. Consequently, the true sacrifice of *being-for-self* is solely that in which it surrenders itself as completely as in death, yet in this renunciation no less preserves itself. It thereby becomes in actuality what it is in itself, becomes the identical unity of itself and of its opposed self. The separated inner Spirit, the self as such, having come forward and renounced itself, the state power is at the same time raised to the position of having a self of its own. Without this renunciation of self, the deeds of honour, the deeds of the noble consciousness, and the counsels based on its insight would retain the ambiguity possessed by that private reserve of particular intention and self-will.

508. But this alienation takes place solely in *language*, which here appears in its characteristic significance. In the world of ethical order, in *law* and *command*, and in the actual world, in *counsel* only, language has the *essence* for its content and is the form of that content; but here it has for its content the form itself, the form which language itself is, and is authoritative as *language*. It is the power of speech, as that which performs what has to be performed. For it is the *real existence* of the pure self as self; in speech, self-consciousness, *qua independent separate individuality*, comes as such into existence, so that it exists *for others*. Otherwise the 'I', this *pure* 'I', is non-existent, is not *there*; in every other expression it is immersed in a reality, and is in a shape from which it can withdraw itself; it is reflected back into itself from its action, as well as from its physiognomic expression, and dissociates itself from such an imperfect existence, in which there is always at once too much as too little, letting it remain lifeless behind. Language, however, contains it in its purity, it alone expresses the 'I', the 'I' itself. This *real* existence of the 'I' is, *qua* real existence, an objectivity which has in it the true nature of the 'I'. The 'I' is this particular 'I'—but equally the *universal* 'I'; its manifesting is also at once the externalization and vanishing of *this* particular 'I', and as a result

the 'I' remains in its universality. The 'I' that utters itself is *heard* or *perceived*; it is an infection in which it has immediately passed into unity with those for whom it is a real existence, and is a universal self-consciousness. That it is *perceived* or *heard* means that its *real existence dies away*; this its otherness has been taken back into itself; and its real existence is just this: that as a self-conscious Now, as a real existence, it is *not* a real existence, and through this vanishing it *is* a real existence. This vanishing is thus itself at once its abiding; it is its own knowing of itself, and its knowing itself as a self that has passed over into another self that has been perceived and is universal.

509. Spirit obtains this actuality here because the extremes, of which it is the *unity*, are also directly determined as being actualities on their own account. Their unity is broken up into two rigid, unyielding sides, each of which is for the other an actual object excluded from it. Consequently, the unity appears as a *middle term*, which is excluded and distinct from the separated, actual existence of the sides; it has, therefore, itself an actual objective existence distinct from its sides, and has reality *for them*, i.e. is something that exists. The spiritual substance enters as such into existence only when it has gained for its two sides self-consciousnesses which know this pure self as an actual existence having *immediate validity*, and in knowing this are also immediately aware that they are such actual existences only through the *mediation* of their self-alienation. Through that pure self, the moments of substance are so far purified as to be the self-knowing category, and thus to be moments of Spirit; through this mediation Spirit comes to exist *qua* Spirit as a reality. It is thus the middle term which presupposes those extremes and is created by their existence—but equally it is the spiritual whole issuing forth between them, which sunders itself into them and only by means of this contact creates each into the whole in terms of its own principle. The fact that both extremes are already *implicitly* reduced to moments and set apart produces their unity, and this is the process which brings both into a unity, interchanges their determinations, and unites them in *each extreme*. This mediation thus posits the *Notion* of each of the two extremes in its actuality, or makes what each is *in itself* into its *Spirit*.

510. The two extremes, the state power and the noble

consciousness, are split up by the latter: the state power into the abstract universal which is obeyed, and into the self-centred will which, however, does not yet conform to the universal; and the noble consciousness into the obedience rendered by the existence which is not self-centred, or the *intrinsic being* of self-respect and honour, and into the still unsurrendered being-for-self, the will that still reserves its independence. The two moments into which both sides are purified and which, therefore, are moments of language, are the *abstract universal*, called 'the general good', and the *pure self* which, in serving the state, renounced its own many and various interests. Both are essentially the same; for pure self is just the abstract universal, and consequently their unity is expressed as their middle term. But the *self* is at first actual only in consciousness, in the one extreme, while the *in-itself* is actual only in the state power, the other extreme. What consciousness lacks is the *actual* transference to it of the state power, not merely in the form of *honour*; and what is lacking in the state power is that it should be obeyed, not merely as the so-called 'general good', but as will, or that it should endow the self with the power of decision. The unity of the Notion in which the state power still stands and into which consciousness has been purified becomes actual in this process of *mediation*, the simple existence of which as *middle term* is language. However, the sides of the unity are not yet selves which exist as selves; for the state power has yet to be energized into a self. This language is, therefore, not yet Spirit that completely knows and expresses itself.

511. The noble consciousness, being the extreme which is the self, appears as the source of the language by which the sides of the relation are shaped into animated wholes. The heroism of silent service becomes the heroism of flattery. This vocal reflection of service constitutes the spiritual self-separating middle term and reflects back into itself not only its own extreme, but also reflects back into this self the extreme of universal power, making that power, which is at first only implicit, into a power that is explicit with an existence of its own, makes it into a self-conscious individuality. The result is that the Spirit of this power is now an *unlimited monarch*: *unlimited*, because the language of flattery raises this power into its purified *universality*; this moment being the product of language, of an existence which

has been purified into Spirit, is a purified self-identity; a *monarch*, for such language likewise raises individuality to its extreme point; what the noble consciousness divests itself of as regards this aspect of the simple spiritual unity is the pure *intrinsic being of its thinking*, its very 'I'. Expressed more definitely, it raises the individuality, which otherwise is only a presumed existence, into the existence of its pure form, by giving the monarch his own proper *name*; for it is in the name alone that the *difference* of the individual from everyone else is not *presumed*, but is made *actual* by all. In the name, the individual *counts* as a pure individual, no longer only in his own consciousness, but in the consciousness of everyone. By his name, then, the monarch is absolutely separated off from everyone else, exclusive and solitary; as monarch, he is a unique atom that cannot impart any of its essential nature. This name is thus the reflection-into-self, or the *actuality* which the universal power has *in its own* self; through the name the power is the monarch. Conversely, he, this particular individual, thereby knows himself, *this* individual, to be the universal power, knows that the nobles not only are ready and prepared for the service of the state power, but that they group themselves round the throne as an *ornamental setting*, and that they are continually *telling* him who sits on it what he *is*.

512. The language of their praise is in this way the Spirit that in the *state power itself* unites the two extremes. It reflects the abstract power into itself and gives it the moment of the other extreme, the *being-for-self* that wills and decides, and by so doing gives it a self-conscious existence; or otherwise expressed, this individual, actual self-consciousness attains to the *certain knowledge* of itself as the power of the state. It is the point of the self into which the many points or selves through renouncing their own *inner certainty*, are fused into one. Since, however, this Spirit proper of state power consists in its obtaining actuality and nourishment from the sacrifice of action and thought by the noble consciousness, it is an *independence that is self-alienated*; the noble consciousness, the extreme of *being-for-self*, receives back the other extreme, that of *actual universality*, in return for the universality of thought which it relinquished; the power of the state *has passed* to the noble consciousness. In it, that power is first made truly effective; in the *being-for-self* of the noble

consciousness it ceases to be the *inert entity* which it appeared to be as the extreme of abstract being-in-itself. Considered as it is *in itself*, state power that is reflected into itself, or has become Spirit, simply means that it has become a moment of self-consciousness, i.e. it exists only as *superseded*. Consequently, it is now essence in the form of something, the Spirit of which is that it is to be sacrified and surrendered, i.e. it exists as wealth. It does, indeed, at the same time have a continuing existence as a reality *vis-à-vis* wealth, into which it is ever changing in accordance with its Notion; but it is a reality whose Notion is just this process of passing over—by way of the service and honour done to it and from which it derives its existence—into its opposite, into the relinquishment of power. Thus the peculiar *self* that is its will knows that through the debasement of the noble consciousness it has become a universality that renounces itself, has become a completely separate and contingent individuality which is at the mercy of every more powerful will. What remains to it of *universally* acknowledged and incommunicable independence is the empty name.

513. While, therefore, the noble consciousness behaves as if it were *conforming* to the universal power, the truth about it is rather that in its service it retains its own being-for-self, and that in the genuine renunciation of its personality, it actually sets aside and rends in pieces the universal Substance. Its Spirit is a completely disparate relationship: on the one hand, in its position of honour it retains its own will; on the other hand, it gives up its will, but in so doing it in part alienates itself from its own inner nature and becomes utterly at variance with itself, and in part subjects to itself the universal substance and makes *it* completely at variance with itself. It is clear that, as a result, the specific character which it was judged to have in comparison with what was called the ignoble consciousness has disappeared and with it the latter too. The ignoble consciousness has achieved its purpose, viz. to bring the universal power under the control of being-for-self.

514. Self-consciousness, thus enriched by the universal power, exists as universal beneficence, or is *wealth* which is itself in turn an object for consciousness. For although wealth is, for consciousness, the deposed universal, the latter has not yet by this first subjection returned absolutely into the self. The self

has not yet for object itself *qua* self, but the subordinated universal essence. Since this object has only just come into being,
consciousness has formed an *immediate* relation with it and thus
has not yet exhibited its disparity with it; we have here the
noble consciousness which preserves its being-for-self in the universal which has become unessential, and therefore acknowledges the object and is grateful to the benefactor.

515. Wealth already contains within it the moment of being-
for-self. It is not the self-less universal of state power, or the
naïve inorganic nature of Spirit; it is state power which wills
to hold its own against those who would take possession of it
for their own enjoyment. But since wealth has merely the form
of essence, this one-sided being-for-self which has no intrinsic
being of its own, but is rather the cancelling of it, is in its
enjoyment the essenceless return of the individual into himself.
It therefore itself requires to be ensouled; and the movement
of its reflection consists in this, that wealth which is only for itself,
develops an *intrinsic being of its own*, that, instead of being a cancelled essence, it develops an essential being. It thus receives
within itself a Spirit of its own. Since the form of this movement
has already been set forth in detail, it is sufficient here to characterize its content.

516. The noble consciousness, then, is not related here to the
object as an essence in general; on the contrary, what is alien
to it is its own *being-for-self*. It *finds* confronting it its own, but
alienated, self as such, in the shape of an objective fixed reality
which it has to receive from another fixed being-for-self. Its
object is a being-for-self, i.e. its *own* being-for-self; but, because
it is an object, it is at the same time *ipso facto* an alien reality
which has its own being-for-self, which has a will of its own;
i.e. it sees self in the power of an alien will on which it is dependent for possession of its own self.

517. Self-consciousness can make abstraction from every
particular aspect, and for that reason, even when it is tied to
one of them, it retains the recognition and *intrinsic validity* of
itself as an independent being. Here, however, as regards the
aspect of that pure *actuality* which is its very own, viz. its own
'I', it finds that it is outside of itself and belongs to another,
finds its *personality* as such dependent on the contingent personality of another, on the accident of a moment, on a caprice,

or some other utterly unimportant circumstance. In the sphere
of law, what is in the power of an objective being appears as
a *contingent content* from which it is possible to make abstraction,
and the controlling power does not affect the *self as such*; on
the contrary, the self is acknowledged. Here, however, the self
sees its self-certainty as such to be completely devoid of essence,
sees that its pure personality is absolutely not a personality. The
spirit of its gratitude is, therefore, the feeling of the most profound dejection as well as of extreme rebellion. When the pure
'I' beholds itself outside of itself and rent asunder, then everything that has continuity and universality, everything that is
called law, good, and right, is at the same time rent asunder
and is destroyed. All identity dissolves away, for the utmost disparity now occupies the scene; what is absolutely essential is
now absolutely unessential, being-for-self is now external to
itself: the pure 'I' itself is absolutely disrupted.

518. Therefore, although this consciousness receives back
from riches the objectivity of its being-for-self and supersedes
it, it is not only, like the preceding reflection, incomplete in
principle, but is *conscious* of not being satisfied; the reflection,
in which the self receives itself as something objective to it, is
thus a direct contradiction lodged in the pure 'I' itself. *Qua* self,
however, it stands at the same time directly above this contradiction ; it is absolutely elastic and therefore again supersedes this supersession of its self, rejects this disowning of itself
which would make its being-for-self into something alien, and
rebels against this reception of itself, and in this very *reception*
is conscious of *itself*.

519. Since, then, the condition of this consciousness is linked
with this absolute disruption, the distinction within its Spirit
of being noble, as opposed to ignoble, falls away and both are
the same. The beneficent Spirit of wealth can, further, be distinguished from that of the consciousness receiving the benefit, and
has to be considered separately. The Spirit of wealth was an
essenceless being-for-self, something to be sacrificed for others.
But by imparting itself it becomes *intrinsic being*; in fulfilling its
destiny, which is to sacrifice itself, it rids itself of the singleness
which characterizes its merely self-centred enjoyment, and as
such subordinated individuality it is *universality* or *essence*. What
it imparts, what it gives to others, is being-for-self. It does not.

however, give itself over as a nature that has no self, as the un-controlled surrender of the condition of life, but as a self-con-scious being in control of itself; it is not the inorganic power of the element that is known by the consciousness receiving it to be essentially transitory, but is the power over the self, the power that knows itself to be *independent* and *arbitrary*, and at the same time knows that what it dispenses is the self of another. Wealth thus shares its dejection with the recipient; but in place of rebellion appears arrogance. For in one respect it knows as well as the recipient that *being-for-self* is a contingent Thing; but it is itself this contingency in the power of which personality stands. In this arrogance which fancies it has, by the gift of a meal, acquired the self of another's 'I' and thereby gained for itself the submission of that other's inmost being, it overlooks the inner rebellion of the other; it overlooks the fact that all restraints have been cast off, overlooks this state of sheer dis-ruption in which, the *self-identity* of being-for-self having become divided against itself, all identity, all existence, is dis-rupted, and in which the sentiment and view-point of the bene-factor suffer most distortion. It stands on the very edge of this innermost abyss, of this bottomless depth, in which all stability and Substance have vanished; and in this depth it sees nothing but a common thing, a plaything of its whims, an accident of its caprice. Its Spirit is a subjective opinion wholly devoid of essentiality, a superficiality from which Spirit has fled.

520. Just as self-consciousness had its own language with state power, in other words, just as Spirit emerged as actively mediating between these extremes, so also has self-consciousness its own language in dealing with wealth; but still more so when it rebels. The language that gives wealth a sense of its essential significance, and thereby gains possession of it, is likewise the language of flattery, but of base flattery; for what it pronounces to be an essence, it knows to be expendable, to be without any *intrinsic* being. The language of flattery, however, as we have already observed, is Spirit that is still one-sided. For although its moments are indeed the *self* which has been refined by the discipline of service into a pure existence, and the *intrinsic being* of power, yet the pure Notion in which the simple, unitary *self* and the *in-itself*, the former a pure 'I' and the latter this pure essence or thought, are the same—this unity of the two sides

which are in reciprocal relation is not present in the consciousness that uses this language. The object is still for consciousness an *intrinsic* being in contrast to the self, that is, the *object* is not for consciousness at the same time consciousness's own *self* as such. The language of this disrupted consciousness is, however, the perfect language and the authentic existent Spirit of this entire world of culture. This self-consciousness which rebels against this rejection of itself is *eo ipso* absolutely self-identical in its absolute disruption, the pure mediation of pure self-consciousness with itself. It is the sameness of the identical judgement in which one and the same personality is both subject and predicate. But this identical judgement is at the same time the infinite judgement; for this personality is absolutely dirempted, and subject and predicate are utterly indifferent, immediate beings which have nothing to do with one another, which have no necessary unity, so much so that each is the power of a separate independent personality. The being-for-self [of this consciousness] has its own being-for-self for object as an out-and-out 'other', and yet, at the same time, directly as its own self—itself as an 'other'; not as if this had a different content, for the content is the same self in the form of an absolute antithesis and a completely indifferent existence of its own. Here, then, we have the Spirit of this real world of culture, Spirit that is *conscious* of itself in its truth and in its Notion.

521. It is this absolute and universal inversion and alienation of the actual world and of thought; it is *pure culture*. What is learnt in this world is that neither the *actuality* of power and wealth, nor their specific *Notions*, 'good' and 'bad', or the consciousness of 'good' and 'bad' (the noble and the ignoble consciousness), possess truth; on the contrary, all these moments become inverted, one changing into the other, and each is the opposite of itself. The universal power, which is the *Substance*, when it acquires a spiritual nature of its own through the principle of individuality, receives its own self merely as a name, and though it is the *actuality* of power, is really the powerless being that sacrifices its own self. But this expendable, self-less being, or the self that has become a Thing, is rather the return of that being into itself; it is being-for-self that is explicitly for itself, the concrete existence of Spirit. The *thoughts* of these two essences, of 'good' and 'bad', are similarly inverted in this move-

ment; what is characterized as good is bad, and vice versa. The
consciousness of each of these moments, the consciousnesses
judged as noble and ignoble, are rather in their truth just as
much the reverse of what these characterizations are supposed
to be; the noble consciousness is ignoble and repudiated, just
as the repudiated consciousness changes round into the nobility
which characterizes the most highly developed freedom of self-
consciousness. From a formal standpoint, everything is *outwardly* the reverse of what it is *for itself*; and, again, it is not
in truth what it is for itself, but something else than it wants
to be; being-for-self is rather the loss of itself, and its self-alienation rather the preservation of itself. What we have here, then,
is that all the moments execute a universal justice on one
another, each just as much alienates its own self, as it forms
itself into its opposite and in this way inverts it. True Spirit,
however, is just this unity of the absolutely separate moments,
and, indeed, it is just through the free actuality of these self-
less extremes that, as their middle term, it achieves a concrete
existence. It exists in the universal talk and destructive judgement which strips of their significance all those moments which
are supposed to count as the true being and as actual members
of the whole, and is equally this nihilistic game which it plays
with itself. This judging and talking is, therefore, what is true
and invincible, while *it* overpowers everything; it is solely with
this alone that one has truly to do with in this actual world.
In this world, the Spirit of each part finds expression, or is
wittily talked about, and finds said about it what it is. The honest
individual takes each moment to be an abiding essentiality, and
is the uneducated thoughtlessness of not knowing that it is
equally doing the reverse. The disrupted consciousness, however, is consciousness of the perversion, and, moreover, of the
absolute perversion. What prevails in it is the Notion, which
brings together in a unity the thoughts which, in the honest
individual, lie far apart, and its language is therefore clever and
witty.

522. The content of what Spirit says about itself is thus the
perversion of every Notion and reality, the universal deception
of itself and others; and the shamelessness which gives utterance
to this deception is just for that reason the greatest truth. This
kind of talk is the madness of the musician 'who heaped up and

mixed together thirty arias, Italian, French, tragic, comic, of every sort; now with a deep bass he descended into hell, then, contracting his throat, he rent the vaults of heaven with a falsetto tone, frantic and soothed, imperious and mocking, by turns'.[1] To the tranquil consciousnes which, in its honest way, takes the melody of the Good and the True to consist in the evenness of the notes, i.e. in unison, this talk appears as a 'rigmarole of wisdom and folly, as a medley of as much skill as baseness, of as many correct as false ideas, a mixture compounded of a complete perversion of sentiment, of absolute shamefulness, and of perfect frankness and truth. It will be unable to refrain from entering into all these tones and running up and down the entire scale of feelings from the profoundest contempt and dejection to the highest pitch of admiration and emotion; but blended with the latter will be a tinge of ridicule which spoils them.'[2] The former, however, will find in their very frankness a strain of reconciliation, will find in their subversive depths the all-powerful note which restores Spirit to itself.

523. If we contrast with the speech of this mind which is fully aware of its confused state, the speech of that simple consciousness of the true and the good, we find that in face of the frank and self-conscious eloquence of the educated mind, it can be no more than taciturn; for to the latter it can say nothing that it does not already know and say. If it gets beyond speaking in monosyllables, it says, therefore, the same thing that is said by the educated mind, but in doing so also commits the folly of imagining it is saying something new and different. Its very words 'shameful', 'ignoble' are already this folly, for the other says them about itself. This latter mind perverts in its speech all that is unequivocal, because what is self-identical is only an abstraction, but in its actual existence is in its own self a perversion. The plain mind, on the other hand, takes under its protection the good and noble i.e. what retains its self-identity in its utterance, in the only way here possible—that is to say, the 'good' does not lose its value because it may be associated or mixed with the 'bad', for this is its condition and necessity, and in this fact lies the wisdom of Nature. Yet this plain mind, while

[1] Diderot, *Nephew of Rameau.*
[2] ibid.

it imagined it was contradicting what was said, has, in doing so, merely condensed into a trivial form the content of Spirit's utterance; in making the *opposite* of the noble and good into the *condition* and *necessity* of the noble and good, it thoughtlessly supposes itself to be saying something else than that what is called noble and good is in its essence the reverse of itself, or that, conversely, the 'bad' is the 'excellent'.

524. If the simple consciousness compensates for this dull, uninspired *thought* by the *actuality* of the excellent, by adducing an *example* of the latter, either in the form of a fictitious case or a true story, thus showing that it is no empty name but actually exists, the *universal* actuality of the perverted action stands opposed to the whole of the real world in which the said example constitutes something quite single and separate, an *espèce*, a mere 'sort' of thing; and to represent the existence of the good and noble as an isolated anecdote, whether fictitious or true, is the most disparaging thing that can be said about it. Finally, should the plain mind demand the dissolution of this whole world of perversion, it cannot demand of the *individual* that he remove himself from it, for even Diogenes in his tub is conditioned by it, and to make this demand of the individual is just what is reckoned to be bad, viz. to care for *himself qua* individual. But if the demand for this removal is directed to the universal *individuality*, it cannot mean that Reason should give up again the spiritually developed consciousness it has acquired, should submerge the widespread wealth of its moments again in the simplicity of the natural heart, and relapse into the wilderness of the nearly animal consciousness, which is also called Nature or innocence. On the contrary, the demand for this dissolution can only be directed to the *Spirit* of culture itself, in order that it return out of its confusion to itself as *Spirit*, and win for itself a still higher consciousness.

525. But in point of fact, Spirit has already accomplished this in principle. The consciousness that is aware of its disruption and openly declares it, derides existence and the universal confusion, and derides its own self as well; it is at the same time the fading, but still audible, sound of all this confusion. This vanity of all reality and every definite Notion, vanity which knows itself to be such, is the double reflection

of the real world into itself: once in *this particular self* of consciousness *qua* particular, and again in the pure *universality* of
consciousness, or in thought. In the first case, Spirit that has
come to itself has directed its gaze to the world of actuality and
still has there its purpose and immediate content; but, in the
other case, its gaze is in part turned only inward and negatively
against it, and in part is turned away from that world towards
heaven, and its object is the beyond of this world.

526. In that aspect of the return into the self, the vanity of
all *things* is its *own* vanity, it is *itself* vain. It is the self-centred
self that knows, not only how to pass judgement on and chatter
about everything, but how to give witty expression to the *contradiction* that is present in the solid elements of the *actual* world,
as also in the fixed determinations posited by judgement; and
this contradiction is their truth. Looked at from the point of
view of form, it knows everything to be self-alienated, being-
for-self is separated from being-in-itself; what is meant, and
purpose, are separated from truth; and from both again, the
being-for-another, the ostensible meaning from the real meaning, from the true thing and intention. Thus it knows how to
give correct expression to each moment in relation to its opposite, in general, how to express accurately the perversion of
everything; it knows better than each what each is, no matter
what its specific nature is. Since it knows the substantial from
the side of the disunion and conflict which are united within
the substantial itself, but not from the side of this union, it
understands very well how to pass judgement on it, but has lost
the ability to *comprehend* it. This vanity at the same time needs
the vanity of all things in order to get from them the consciousness of self; it therefore creates this vanity itself and is the soul
that supports it. Power and wealth are the supreme ends of its
exertions, it knows that through renunciation and sacrifice it
forms itself into the universal, attains to the possession of it, and
in this possession is universally recognized and accepted: state
power and wealth are the real and acknowledged powers. However, this recognition and acceptance is itself vain; and just by
taking possession of power and wealth it knows them to be without a self of their own, knows rather that *it* is the power over
them, while they are vain things. The fact that in possessing
them it is itself apart from and beyond them, is exhibited in

its witty talk which is, therefore, its supreme interest and the truth of the whole relationship. In such talk, this particular self, *qua* this pure self, determined neither by reality nor by thought, develops into a spiritual self that is of truly universal worth. It *is* the self-disruptive nature of all relationships and the conscious disruption of them; but only as self-consciousness in revolt is it aware of its own disrupted state, and in thus knowing it has immediately risen above it. In that vanity, all content is turned into something negative which can no longer be grasped as having a positive significance. The positive object is merely the *pure 'I' itself*, and the disrupted consciousness *in itself* this pure self-identity of self-consciousness that has returned to itself.

b. *Faith and pure insight*

527. The Spirit of self-alienation has its existence in the world of culture. But since this whole has become alienated from itself, there stands beyond that world the unreal world of *pure consciousness*, or of *thought*. Its content is in the form of pure thought, and thought is its absolute element. Since, however, thought is in the first instance [only] the *element* of this world, consciousness only *has* these thoughts, but as yet it does not *think* them, or is unaware that they are thoughts; they exist for consciousness in the form of *picture-thoughts*. For it steps out of its actual world into pure consciousness, yet is itself generally still in the sphere of the actual world and its determinateness. The disrupted consciousness is only *in itself*, or implicitly, the *self-identity* of pure consciousness, a fact that is known to *us*, but not to *itself*. Thus, it is only the *immediate* elevation of itself, an elevation it has not yet accomplished within itself, and it still has within it its opposite principle by which it is conditioned, without having become master of it through the movement of mediation. Consequently, the essence of its thought has for it the value of *essence*, not merely in the form of the abstract *in-itself*, but in the form of a *common actuality*, of an actuality that has merely been raised into another element without having lost therein the specific character of an actuality that does not exist merely in thought. It is essential to distinguish it from the *in-itself* which is the essence of the Stoic consciousness. What counted for the latter was merely the *form of thought* as such

which, besides, has any alien content taken from the actual world. What counts, however, for the consciousness we are dealing with is not the *form of thought*. This, too, is essentially distinct from the *in-itself* of the virtuous consciousness for which essence, though it stands in a relationship to the actual world and is the essence of the actual world itself, yet is initially a non-actual essence. In the consciousness under discussion essence, although lying beyond the actual world, none the less counts as an actual essence. In the same way, what is intrinsically right and good in the sphere of legislative Reason, and the universal that is adopted by consciousness in testing laws, these also do not possess the character of actuality. Therefore, while pure thought fell within the world of culture itself as an aspect of the alienation, viz. as the standard for judging Good and Bad in the abstract, through having passed through the process of the whole, it has become enriched with the moment of actuality and thereby with content. But this actuality of the essence is at the same time only an actuality of *pure*, not of *actual*, consciousness; although it is raised into the element of thought it does not yet count as a thought for this actual consciousness; rather it lies for the latter beyond its own actuality, for it is the flight from this actuality.

528. *Religion*—for it is obviously religion that we are speaking about—in the form in which it appears here as the faith belonging to the world of culture, does not yet appear as it is in and for itself. We have already seen it in other characteristic forms, viz. as the Unhappy Consciousness, as a shape of the insubstantial process of consciousness itself. It made its appearance, too, in the ethical Substance as faith in the underworld, though consciousness of the departed spirit is, strictly speaking, not *faith*, not essence posited in the element of pure consciousness beyond the actual world, but has itself an immediate presence; its element is the family. Here, however, religion in part has proceeded from the *Substance* and is the pure consciousness of it; in part, this pure consciousness is alienated from its actual consciousness the *essence* from its *existence*. True, it is thus no longer the insubstantial process of consciousness, but it still has the characteristic of an antithesis to actuality as *this* actuality in general, and of an antithesis to self-consciousness in particular. It is therefore essentially merely a *belief*.

529. This *pure consciousness* of absolute Being is an *alienated* consciousness. We have now to look more closely at the specific nature of that of which it is the 'other', and we must consider it only in connection with this 'other'. To begin with, this pure consciousness seems to have over against it only the *world* of actuality; but since it is the flight from this world and therefore has the character of an *antithesis* to it, it bears this world within itself; pure consciousness is therefore in its own self alienated from itself, and faith constitutes only one aspect of it. At the same time, the other aspect has already come to view. Pure consciousness, namely, is reflection out of the world of culture in such a way that the Substance of that world, and also the 'masses' or groups into which it is articulated, are shown to be what they are in themselves, *spiritual* essentialities, absolutely restless processes or determinations which are directly cancelled in their opposite. Their essence, simple consciousness, is thus the simplicity of *absolute difference* which is at once no difference. Consequently, it is pure *being-for-self*, not as this *single* self but as the immanently *universal* self in the form of a restless process which attacks and pervades the passive essence of the 'matter in hand'. In it is thus to be found the certainty that at once knows itself to be the truth, pure thought as the *absolute Notion* in the might of its *negativity*, which eliminates everything objective that supposedly stands over against consciousness, and makes it into a being which has its origin in consciousness. This pure consciousness is at the same time equally *simple*, just because its difference is no difference. But as this form of simple reflection-into-self, it is the element of faith in which Spirit has the determinateness of *positive universality*, of *being-in-itself* in contrast to that being-for-self of self-consciousness. Forced back into itself out of the essenceless, merely dissolving world, Spirit, in accordance with its truth, is in an undivided unity, at once the *absolute movement* and *negativity* of its process of manifestation, as well as its inwardly *satisfied* essence and its positive *repose*. But coming generally under the determinateness of *alienation*, these two moments fall apart into a dual consciousness. The former is *pure insight* as the spiritual *process* which focuses itself in *self*-consciousness, a process which is confronted by consciousness of what is positive, the form of objectivity or of picture-thinking, and which turns against it; but pure

insight's own object is only the *pure 'I'*. The simple consciousness of the positive, or of tranquil self-identity, on the other hand, has for its object the inner *essence qua* essence. Pure insight has, therefore, in the first instance, no content of its own, because it is negative being-for-self; to faith, on the other hand, there belongs a content, but without insight. If the former does not step outside self-consciousness, the latter certainly has its content in the element of pure self-consciousness, but in *thought*, not in *Notions, in pure consciousness, not in pure self-consciousness.* Hence faith is certainly pure consciousness of essence, i.e. of the *simple inner being*, and thus *is* thought—the cardinal factor in the nature of faith, which is usually overlooked. The *immediacy* of the presence of essence in it is due to the fact that its object is *essence*, i.e. *pure thought*. This *immediacy*, however, so far as *thought* enters into *consciousness*, or pure consciousness enters into self-consciousness, acquires the significance of an objective *being* which lies beyond the consciousness of the self. It is through this significance which the immediacy and simplicity of *pure* thought obtains in *consciousness*, that the essence of faith is no longer a [pure] thought, but is reduced to the level of something imagined, and becomes a supersensible world which is essentially an '*other*' in relation to self-consciousness. In pure insight, on the other hand, the transition of pure thought into consciousness has the opposite determination; objectivity has the significance of a merely negative content, a content which is reduced to a moment and returns into the self; that is to say, only the self is really the object of the self, or the object only has truth so far as it has the form of the self.

530. Just as faith and pure insight belong in common to the element of pure consciousness, so also are they in common the return from the actual world of culture. Consequently, they present themselves according to three aspects. First, each is an *intrinsic being on its own account*, apart from all relationships; second, each stands in relationship with the *actual* world in an antithesis to pure consciousness; and third, each is related within pure consciousness to the other.

531. In the consciousness of the *believer*, the aspect of *being in and for itself* is its absolute object whose content and determination we already know. For according to the Notion of faith it is nothing else but the actual world raised into the universality

of pure consciousness. The articulation of this world, therefore, constitutes the organization of the world of faith, except that in the latter the parts do not alienate themselves in their spiritualization, but are Beings, each with an existence of its own, Spirits which have returned into themselves and abide with themselves. The movement of their transition [into one another] is therefore only *for us* an alienation of the specific character in which they exist in their distinctiveness, and is only *for us* a *necessary* series; for faith, however, their difference is a tranquil diversity and their movement a [real] *happening*.

532. To name them briefly according to the external determination of their form: just as in the world of culture state power, or the Good, was primary, so here, too, the first is the *Absolute Being*, Spirit that is in and for itself in so far as it is the simple eternal *substance*. But in the actualization of its Notion, in being Spirit, it passes over into *being-for-another*, its self-identity becomes an *actual*, self-*sacrificing* absolute Being; it becomes a *self*, but a mortal, perishable self. Consequently, the third moment is the return of this alienated self and of the humiliated substance into their original simplicity; only in this way is substance represented as Spirit.

533. These distinct Beings, when brought back to themselves by thought, out of the flux of the actual world, are immutable eternal Spirits, whose being lies in thinking the unity which they constitute. Removed thus from self-consciousness, these Beings are nevertheless actively present in it; for if the absolute Being were to remain unmoved in the form of the first simple substance, it would remain alien to self-consciousness. But the externalization of this substance, and then its Spirit, involves the moment of actuality and thereby makes itself a participant in the self-consciousness of the believer, or the believing consciousness belongs to the actual world.

534. According to this second relationship, the believing consciousness partly has its actuality in the real world of culture, and constitutes the Spirit and the existence of that world which we have already considered; partly, however, the believing consciousness confronts this its own actuality as something worthless, and is the process of overcoming it. This process does not consist in the believing consciousness making brilliant remarks about the perversion of its real world; for it is the simple

naïve consciousness which reckons such brilliance as vanity, since it still has the real world for its purpose. On the contrary, contrasted with the tranquil realm of its thought, the real world is a soulless existence, which therefore has to be overcome in an external manner. This obedience of service and praise, by setting aside sense-knowledge and action, produces the consciousness of unity with the absolute Being, though not as a unity that is actually perceived; on the contrary, this service is only the perpetual process of producing that unity, a process which does not completely attain its goal in the present. The [religious] community, it is true, does so, for it is universal self-consciousness; but for the individual self-consciousness, the realm of pure thought necessarily remains a beyond of its actual world, or since this beyond, through the externalization of the eternal Being, has entered the actual world, the actuality is an uncomprehended, sensuous actuality. But one sensuous actuality remains indifferent to the other, and the beyond has only received the further character of remoteness in space and time. The Notion, however, the actuality of Spirit present to itself, remains in the consciousness of the believer the *inner being*, which is everything and which acts, but does not itself come forth.

535. In *pure Insight*, however, the Notion is alone the actual; and this third aspect of Faith, that of being an object for pure Insight, is really the true relation in which Faith here appears. Pure Insight itself, like Faith, is to be considered partly in and for itself, and partly in its relationship to the actual world so far as this is still present in a positive form, viz. as a vain consciousness, and lastly, in that relation to faith mentioned above.

536. We have seen what pure insight is in and for itself. As faith is the tranquil pure *consciousness* of Spirit as *essence*, so is pure insight the *self*-consciousness of Spirit as essence; it therefore knows essence, not as *essence*, but as absolute *self*. It therefore seeks to abolish every kind of independence other than that of self-consciousness, whether it be the independence of what is actual, or of what possesses *intrinsic* being, and to give it the form of *Notion*. Pure insight is not only the certainty of self-conscious Reason that it is all truth: it *knows* that it is.

537. However, in the form in which the Notion of pure insight first makes its appearance, it is not yet *realized*. Accordingly, its consciousness still appears as *contingent*, as *single* and

separate, and its essence appears for it in the form of an *end* which it has to realize. It has, to begin with, the *intention* of making *pure insight universal*, i.e. of making everything that is actual into a Notion, and into one and the same Notion in every self-consciousness. The intention is *pure*, for it has pure insight for its content; and this insight is likewise *pure*, for its content is solely the absolute Notion, which meets with no opposition in an object, nor is it restricted in its own self. In the unrestricted Notion there are directly found the two aspects: that everything objective has only the significance of *being-for-self*, of self-consciousness, and that this has the significance of a *universal*, that pure insight is to become the property of every self-consciousness. This second aspect of the intention is a result of culture in so far as in this culture, the difference of objective Spirit, the parts and the determinations which its judgement imposed on the world, as well as the differences which appear as natural predispositions, have all been upset. Genius, talent, special capacities generally, belong to the world of actuality, in so far as this world still contains the aspect of being a spiritual animal kingdom in which individuals, amid confusion and mutual violence, cheat and struggle over the essence of the actual world. These differences, it is true, have no place in this world as honest *espèces*; individuality neither is contented with the unreal 'matter in hand' itself nor has it a *particular* content and ends of its own. On the contrary, it counts merely as something universally acknowledged, viz. as an educated individuality; and the difference is reduced to one of less or more energy, a *quantitative* difference, i.e. a non-essential difference. This last difference, however, has been effaced by the fact that in the completely disrupted state of consciousness difference changed round into an absolutely qualitative difference. There, what is for the 'I' an 'other' is only the 'I' itself. In this infinite judgement all one-sidedness and peculiarity of the original being-for-self has been eradicated; the self knows itself *qua* pure self to be its own object; and this absolute identity of the two sides is the element of pure insight. Pure insight is, therefore, the simple, immanently differentiated *essence*, and equally the universal *work* or achievement and a universal possession. In this *simple* spiritual substance, self-consciousness gives itself and preserves for itself in every object the consciousness of this its own *particular being* or of its own *action*, just as conversely, the individuality of self-consciousness is therein *self-identical* and universal. This pure insight is thus the Spirit that calls to *every* consciousness: *be for yourselves* what you all are *in yourselves—reasonable*.

II. THE ENLIGHTENMENT

538. The peculiar object against which pure insight directs the power of the Notion is faith, which is the form of pure consciousness confronting it in the same element. But it also has a relation to the actual world for, like faith, it is the return from the actual world into pure consciousness. We have, first of all, to see the nature of its activity as it is directed against the impure intentions and perverse insights of the actual world.

539. We have already mentioned the tranquil consciousness that stands opposed to this turmoil which, having once settled down starts up all over again; it constitutes the side of pure insight and intention. This tranquil consciousness, however, as we saw, has no *special insight* into the world of culture; this latter has itself rather the most painful feeling and the truest insight about itself: the feeling that all its defences have broken down, that every part of its being has been tortured on the rack and every bone broken; it is also the language of this feeling and the brilliant talk which pronounces judgement on every aspect of its condition. Here, therefore, pure insight can have no activity and content of its own and thus can only behave as the formal and faithful *apprehension* of its own brilliant insight into the world and of its own peculiar language. Since this language is that of a distracted mind, and the pronouncement only some twaddle uttered on the spur of the moment, which is again quickly forgotten, and exists as a whole only for a third consciousness, this latter can only be distinguished as *pure* insight if it brings these scattered traits into a general picture and then makes them into an insight for everyone.

540. By this simple means it will clear up the confusion of this world. For we have found that it is not the groups [Massen] and the specific Notions and individualities that are the essence of this actuality, but that this has its substance and support solely in the Spirit which exists *qua* judging and discussing, and

that the interest of having a content for this argumentation and chatter alone preserves the whole and the groups into which it is articulated. In this language of insight, its self-consciousness is for it still a being *existing on its own account, this single individual*; but the vanity of the content is at the same time the vanity of the self that knows itself to be vain. When the placidly apprehending consciousness makes a collection of the most telling and penetrating versions of all this brilliant talk, the soul that still preserves the whole, then the vanity of witty judgements perishes with that other vanity, the vanity of existence. The collection shows to most people a better wit, or to everyone at least a more varied wit, than their own, and shows that 'knowing better' and 'judging' are in general something universal and now universally known. With this, the sole remaining interest is eradicated, and the individual judgement is resolved into the universal insight. However, the knowledge of essence is still firmly established as superior to empty knowledge, and pure insight only manifests its own peculiar activity in so far as it opposes itself to faith.

a. *The struggle of the Enlightenment with Superstition*

541. The various modes of the negative attitude of consciousness, the attitude of scepticism and that of theoretical and practical idealism, are inferior shapes compared with that *of pure insight* and its diffusion, of the *Enlightenment*; for pure insight is born of the substance [of Spirit], knows the pure *self* of consciousness to be absolute, and enters into dispute with the pure consciousness of the absolute essence of all reality. Since faith and insight are the same pure consciousness, but as regards form are opposed—the essence is for faith [mere] *thought*, not *Notion*, and is therefore the sheer opposite of *self*-consciousness, whereas for pure insight the essence is the *self*—their nature is such that each is for the other the sheer negative of it. In their appearance as mutually opposed, all *content* falls to faith, for each moment, in its tranquil element of thought, obtains an enduring being. Pure insight, however, is in the first instance devoid of content and is rather the pure vanishing of it; but by the negative movement towards what is negative to *it*, it will realize itself and give itself a content.

542. It knows that faith is opposed to pure insight, opposed

to Reason and truth. Just as it sees faith in general to be a tissue of superstitions, prejudices, and errors, so it further sees the consciousness of this content organized into a realm of error in which false insight, common to the mass of people, is immediate, naïve, and unreflective; but also it has within it the moment of reflection-into-self, or of self-consciousness, separated from its naïvety, in the shape of an insight which remains independently in the background, and an evil intention by which the general mass of the people is befooled. The masses are the victims of the deception of a *priesthood* which, in its envious conceit, holds itself to be the sole possessor of insight and pursues its other selfish ends as well. At the same time it conspires with *despotism* which, as the synthetic, non-notional unity of the real and this ideal realm—a curiously inconsistent entity—stands above the bad insight of the multitude and the bad intentions of the priests, and yet unites both within itself. From the stupidity and confusion of the people brought about by the trickery of priestcraft, despotism, which despises both, draws for itself the advantage of undisturbed domination and the fulfilment of its desires and caprices, but is itself at the same time this same dullness of insight, the same superstition and error.

543. The Enlightenment does not attack these three aspects of the enemy without making a distinction. For since its essence is pure insight, what is *universal* in and for itself, its true relation to the other extreme is that in which it concerns itself with the *common* and *identical element* in both. The aspect of *individuality*, isolating itself from the general naïve consciousness, is its antithesis which it cannot directly affect. The will of the deceiving priesthood and of the oppressive despot is, therefore, not directly the object of its activity; its object is the insight devoid of will which has no separable individuality of its own, the *Notion* of rational self-consciousness which has its existence in the general mass but is not yet present there *qua* Notion. Pure insight, however, in delivering this honest insight and its essentially naïve nature from prejudices and errors, wrests from the hands of the bad intention the reality and power of its deceit, for whose realm the naïve consciousness of the general mass of the people provides its basis and material—i.e. the being-for-self [of that realm] has its *substance* in the *simple*, naïve consciousness as such.

544. The relation of pure insight to the naïve consciousness of absolute Being now has a twofold aspect. On the one hand, pure insight is *itself* the same as that consciousness. On the other hand, this naïve consciousness gives complete liberty to absolute Being, as well as to its parts, in the simple element of its thought, and allows them to subsist there and to be valid only as its *implicit being*, and hence to be objectively valid; but in this implicit being it renounces its own *being-for-self*. In so far as, according to the first aspect, this faith is for pure insight *in itself* pure *self*-consciousness and has only to become this explicitly *for itself*, pure insight has, in this Notion of self-consciousness, the element in which, instead of false insight, it realizes itself.

545. Since from this aspect both are essentially the same and the relation of pure insight takes place through and in the same element, the communication between them is direct and their giving and receiving is an unimpeded flow of each into the other. Whatever wedges of any sort may be driven into consciousness, it is *in itself* this simplicity in which everything is dissolved, forgotten, and unbiased, and which therefore is absolutely receptive to the Notion. It is on this account that the communication of pure insight is comparable to a silent expansion or to the *diffusion*, say, of a perfume in the unresisting atmosphere. It is a penetrating infection which does not make itself noticeable beforehand as something opposed to the indifferent element into which it insinuates itself, and therefore cannot be warded off. Only when the infection has become widespread is that consciousness, which unheedingly yielded to its influence, *aware of it*. For though the nature of what consciousness received into itself was simple and homogeneous with it, yet it was also the simplicity of an introreflected *negativity* which subsequently also develops, in keeping with its nature, into something opposed to it and thereby reminds consciousness of its previous state. This simplicity is the Notion, which is the simple knowing that knows itself and also its opposite, but knows this opposite to be reduced to a moment within it. Consequently, when consciousness does become aware of pure insight, the latter is already widespread; the struggle against it betrays the fact that infection has occurred. The struggle is too late, and every remedy adopted only aggravates the disease, for it has laid hold of the marrow of spiritual life, viz. the Notion

of consciousness, or the pure essence itself of consciousness. Therefore, too, there is no power in consciousness which could overcome the disease. Because this is present in the essence itself, its manifestations, while still isolated, can be suppressed and the superficial symptoms smothered. This is greatly to its advantage, for it does not now squander its power or show itself unworthy of its real nature, which is the case when it breaks out in symptoms and single eruptions antagonistic to the content of faith and to its connection with the reality of the world outside of it. Rather, being now an invisible and imperceptible Spirit, it infiltrates the noble parts through and through and soon has taken complete possession of all the vitals and members of the unconscious idol; then 'one fine morning it gives its comrade a shove with the elbow, and bang! crash! the idol lies on the floor'.[1] On 'one fine morning' whose noon is bloodless if the infection has penetrated to every organ of spiritual life. Memory alone then still preserves the dead form of the Spirit's previous shape as a vanished history, vanished one knows not how. And the new serpent of wisdom raised on high for adoration has in this way painlessly cast merely a withered skin.

546. But this silent, ceaseless weaving of the Spirit in the simple inwardness of its substance, Spirit concealing its action from itself, is only one side of the realization of pure insight. Its diffusion consists not merely in the fact that like goes together with like, nor is its actualization merely an expansion in which there is no antithesis. On the contrary, the action of the negative essence is no less essentially a developed, self-differenting movement which, being a conscious act, must give its moments a definite manifest existence and must appear on the scene as a sheer uproar and a violent struggle with its antithesis.

547. We have therefore to see how *pure insight* and *intention* behaves in its *negative* attitude to that 'other' which it finds confronting it. Pure insight and intention which takes up a negative attitude can only be—since its Notion is all essentiality and there is nothing outside of it—the negative of itself. As insight, therefore, it becomes the negative of pure insight, becomes untruth and unreason, and, as intention, it becomes the negative of pure intention, becomes a lie and insincerity of purpose.

[1] Diderot's *Nephew of Rameau*.

548. It entangles itself in this contradiction through engaging in dispute, and imagines that what it is attacking is something other than itself. It only *imagines* this, for its essence as absolute negativity implies that it contains that otherness within itself. The absolute Notion is the category; in that Notion, knowing and the *object* known are the same. Consequently, what pure insight pronounces to be its other, what it asserts to be an error or a lie, can be nothing else but its own self; it can condemn only what it is itself. What is not rational has no *truth*, or, what is not grasped conceptually, *is not*. When, therefore, Reason speaks of something *other* than itself, it speaks in fact only of itself; so doing, it does not go outside of itself. This struggle with its antithesis, therefore, also has the significance of being the *actualization* of insight. For this consists precisely in the process of developing the moments and taking them back into itself. One part of this process is the differentiation in which intellectual insight confronts its own self as *object*; so long as it persists in this relationship it is alienated from itself. As pure insight it is devoid of all *content*; the process of its realization consists in its making *itself* its content; for nothing else can become its content because it is the self-consciousness of the category. But since in confronting the content, pure insight at first knows it only as a *content* and not yet as its own self, it does not recognize itself in it. Complete insight is therefore attained when the content, which to begin with was objective to it, is recognized as its own. Its result, however, will thus be neither the re-establishment of the errors it struggles against, nor merely its original Notion, but an insight which recognizes the absolute negation of itself to be its own actual existence, to be its own self, or an insight whose Notion recognizes its own self. This nature of the struggle of the Enlightenment with errors, that of fighting itself in them, and of condemning in them what it itself asserts, is explicit *for us*, or what Enlightenment and its struggle is *in itself*. It is the first aspect of this struggle, however, the defilement of Enlightenment through the adoption by its self-identical *purity* of a negative attitude, that is an object for faith, which therefore comes to know it as falsehood, unreason, and as ill-intentioned, just as Enlightenment regards faith as error and prejudice. As regards its content, it is in the first instance an empty insight whose content appears to it to be some-

thing other than itself; consequently, it *finds* it given in the shape
of a content which is not yet its own, as something that exists
quite independently of it, finds it given in faith.

549. The way, therefore, in which Enlightenment apprehends its object in the first instance and generally, is that it takes
it as *pure insight*, and, not recognizing itself therein, declares it
to be error. In *insight* as such, consciousness apprehends an
object in such a way that it becomes the essence of consciousness, or becomes an object which consciousness permeates, in
which consciousness preserves itself, abides with itself, and
remains present to itself, and since it is thus the movement of
the object, brings it into existence. It is just this that Enlightenment rightly declares faith to be, when it says that what is
for faith the absolute Being, is a Being of its own consciousness,
is its own thought, something that is a creation of consciousness
itself. Thus what Enlightenment declares to be an error and
a fiction is the very same thing as Enlightenment itself is.
Enlightenment that wants to teach faith the new wisdom does
not tell it anything new; for its object is also for it just this,
viz. a pure essence of its own consciousness, so that this consciousness does not take itself to be lost and negated in that
object, but rather puts its trust in it, i.e. it finds itself as *this
particular* consciousness, or as *self*-consciousness, precisely *in the
object*. Whomsoever I trust, his *certainty of himself* is for me the
certainty of myself; I recognize in him my own being-for-self,
know that he acknowledges it and that it is for him purpose
and essence. Trust, however, is faith, because the consciousness
of the believer is *directly related* to its object and is thus also intuitively aware that it is *one* with it and in it. Further, since
what is object for me is that in which I recognize myself, I am
for myself at the same time in that object in the form of *another*
self-consciousness, i.e. one which has become in that object
alienated from its particular individuality, viz. from its natural
and contingent existence, but which partly remains therein self-
consciousness, partly, in that object, is an *essential* consciousness
just as pure insight is. The Notion of pure insight implies not
merely that consciousness recognizes itself in the object of its
insight and is *immediately* present in it without first leaving the
element of thought and returning into itself; it also implies that
consciousness is aware of itself as being also the *mediating* move-

ment, aware of itself as being the activity of producing the object. This unity of itself as unity of *self* and object is thereby explicit for it in thought. Faith, too, is just this consciousness. Obedience and action form a necessary moment, through which the certainty that absolute Being *is* comes about. This action of faith does not indeed make it appear as if absolute Being itself is produced by it. But the absolute Being of faith is essentially not the *abstract* essence that would exist beyond the consciousness of the believer; on the contrary, it is the Spirit of the [religious] community, the unity of the abstract essence and self-consciousness. That it be the Spirit of the community, this requires as a necessary moment the action of the community. It is this Spirit, *only by being produced* by consciousness; or rather, it does *not* exist as the Spirit of the community *without* having been produced by consciousness. For essential as is the producing of it, this is equally essentially not the sole ground of absolute Being, but only a moment. Absolute Being is at the same time in and for itself.

550. On the other side, the Notion of pure insight is something *other* to itself than its own object; for it is just this negative determination that constitutes the object. Thus, from the other side, it also declares the essence of faith to be something *alien* to consciousness, to be not *its* essence but a changeling foisted on it. But here Enlightenment is foolish; faith regards it as not knowing what it is saying, and as not understanding the real facts when it talks about priestly deception and deluding the people. It talks about this as if by some hocus-pocus of conjuring priests consciousness had been palmed off with something absolutely *alien* and '*other*' to it in place of its own essence; and at the same time it says that this is an essence of consciousness, that consciousness believes in it, puts its trust in it, and seeks to make it favourably disposed towards itself, i.e. consciousness beholds in it *its pure* essence just as much as its own single and universal *individuality*, and through this action produces this unity of itself with its essence. Thus what it asserts to be *alien* to consciousness, it directly declares to be the *inmost nature of consciousness itself*. How then can it possibly talk about deception and delusion? Since, in the same voice, it asserts the very opposite of what it maintains regarding faith, it really reveals itself to faith as the conscious *lie*. How are delusion and deception

to take place where consciousness in its truth has directly the *certainty of itself*, where in its object it possesses *its own self*, since it just as much finds as produces itself in it? The distinction no longer exists even in words. If the general question has been propounded, whether it is permissible to delude a people,[1] the answer would in fact have to be that the question is pointless, because it is impossible to deceive a people in this matter. Brass instead of gold, counterfeit instead of genuine money, may well be passed off in isolated cases; many may be persuaded to believe that a battle lost was a battle won, and other lies about things of sense and isolated happenings may be made credible for a time; but in the knowledge of that essential being in which consciousness has the immediate *certainty of itself*, the idea of delusion is quite out of the question.

551. Let us see further how faith experiences the Enlightenment in the *different* moments of its own consciousness, to which the view mentioned above referred to only generally. These moments are: pure thought or, as object, *absolute Being* in and for itself; then its relation—as a knowing—to absolute Being, the *ground of its belief*; and lastly, its relation to absolute Being in its acts, or its *worship* and *service*. Just as pure insight has failed to recognize itself and has denied itself in belief generally, so too in these moments it will behave in an equally perverse manner.

552. Pure insight adopts a negative attitude to the absolute Being of the believing consciousness. This Being is pure *thought*, and pure thought posited within itself as an object or as *essence*; in the believing consciousness, this *intrinsic being* of thought acquires at the same time for consciousness that is *for itself*, the form—but only the empty form—of objectivity; it has the character of something presented to consciousness. To pure insight, however, since it is pure consciousness from the side of the *self that is for itself*, the 'other' appears as something *negative of self-consciousness*. This could still be taken either as the pure *intrinsic being* of thought, or also as the *being* of *sense-certainty*. But since it is at the same time for the *self*, and this self, *qua* self that has an object, is an actual consciousness, the object proper as such is for pure insight an ordinary Thing of sense-certainty that merely *is*. This its object is manifest to it in the *picture-thought*

[1] The subject of a prize essay proposed by Frederick the Great in 1778.

of faith. It condemns this picture-thought, and in it its own object. But in apprehending the object of faith as insight's own object, it already does faith a wrong. For it is saying that the absolute Being of faith is a piece of stone, a block of wood, which has eyes and sees not, or again, a piece of dough which, having come from the field is transformed by man and returned to earth again; or in whatever other ways faith anthropomorphizes absolute Being, making it into an object that it can represent to itself.

553. Enlightenment, which professes to be pure, here converts what is for Spirit eternal life and Holy Spirit into an actual, *perishable thing*, and defiles it with sense-certainty's view of it, a viewpoint which is essentially trivial and definitely absent from faith in its worship, so that Enlightenment is completely in the wrong when it imputes this view to faith. What faith reveres, it certainly does not regard as stone or wood or dough, nor any other kind of temporal, sensuous thing. If Enlightenment has a mind to say that, all the same, its object is *also* this, or even that it is essentially and in truth this, then firstly, faith is equally well aware of that '*also*' which, however, lies outside of its worship; secondly, however, faith does not regard such things as stones, etc. as possessing *intrinsic* being; on the contrary, what has intrinsic being for faith is solely the essential being of pure thought.

554. The second moment is the relation of faith to this absolute Being as a consciousness that *knows* it. For faith, as a thinking, pure consciousness, this Being is *immediately* present; but pure consciousness is just as much a *mediated* relation of certainty to truth, a relation which constitutes the *ground* of faith. For Enlightenment, this ground becomes equally a fortuitous *knowledge of fortuitous* events. But the ground of knowledge is the *conscious* universal, and in its truth is absolute *Spirit* which, in abstract pure consciousness, or in thought as such, is merely absolute Being, but, *qua* self-consciousness, is *knowledge* of itself. Pure insight characterizes this conscious universal, the *simple, self-knowing Spirit*, equally as a negative of self-consciousness. It is true that pure insight is itself *pure mediated*, i.e. self-mediated thought, is a pure knowing; but since it is a *pure insight*, a *pure knowing*, that does not as yet know itself, i.e. is not aware that it *is* this pure, mediating movement, the mediation seems to

insight, as does everything that is itself insight, to be an 'other'. In its realization, therefore, it develops this moment which is essential to it; but this moment seems to it to belong to faith and to have the character of something external to pure insight, to be a fortuitous knowledge of narratives of real events, real in the ordinary sense of the word. Here, therefore, it falsely charges religious belief with basing its certainty on some *particular historical evidences* which, considered as historical evidences, would certainly not guarantee the degree of certainty about their content which is given by newspaper accounts of any happening—further, that its certainty rests on the accidental *preservation* of these evidences; on the one hand, the preservation by means of paper, and on the other hand, by the skill and honesty of their transference from one piece of paper to another, and lastly, on the *correct interpretation* of the meaning of dead words and letters. In fact, however, it does not occur to faith to fasten its certainty to such evidences and such fortuitous circumstances. Faith, in its certainty, is an unsophisticated relationship to its absolute object, a pure knowing of it which does not mix up letters, paper, and copyists in its consciousness of absolute Being, and does not bring itself into relation with it by means of things of that kind. On the contrary, this consciousness is the self-mediating ground of its knowledge; it is Spirit itself which bears witness to itself, both in the *inwardness* of the *individual* consciousness and through the *universal presence* in everyone of faith in it. If faith wants to appeal to historical evidences in order to get that kind of foundation, or at least confirmation, of its content that Enlightenment talks about, and seriously thinks and acts as if that were a matter of importance, then it has already let itself be corrupted by the Enlightenment; and its efforts to establish and consolidate itself in such a way are merely evidence it gives of its corruption by the Enlightenment.

555. There still remains the third side, *the relation to absolute Being of consciousness* as *action*. This action is the setting-aside of the particularity of the individual, or of the natural mode of its being-for-self, whence proceeds its certainty of being pure self-consciousness, of being, in accordance with its action, i.e. as an *independent* individual, one with absolute Being. Since, in action, *purposiveness* and *End* are distinguished, and pure insight

in relation to this action equally adopts a *negative attitude* and, as in the other moments, denies its own self, it must, as regards *purposiveness*, exhibit itself as lacking in intelligence, since insight united with intention, i.e. the harmony of End and Means, appears to it as an 'other', or rather as the opposite of insight; as regards the End itself, however, it has to make badness, enjoyment, and possession its End and so prove itself to be the impurest kind of intention, since pure intention, *qua* 'other', is equally impure intention.

556. Accordingly, we see that as regards *purposiveness*, Enlightenment finds it foolish when the believer gives himself the superior consciousness of not being in bondage to natural enjoyment and pleasure by *actually* denying himself natural enjoyment and pleasure, and demonstrating *by his actions* that his contempt for them is no lie but is genuine. Similarly, Enlightenment finds it foolish that the individual absolves itself of its quality of being absolutely individual, excluding all others and of possessing property of its own, by itself giving up its property; for thereby it shows *in truth* that it is not in earnest with this isolation of itself, but is raised above the natural necessity of isolating itself, and in this absolute isolation of being-for-self denying that others are the *same as itself*. Pure insight finds both to be of no purpose as well as wrong: the purpose of showing oneself to be free of pleasure and possession is not served by denying oneself pleasure and giving away a possession; in the opposite case, therefore, it will declare the man a fool who, in order to eat, has recourse to actually eating. Insight also finds it *wrong* to deny oneself a meal and to give away butter and eggs, not for money, nor money for butter and eggs, but simply to give them away without receiving anything in return; it declares a meal or the possession of things of that sort to be an End in itself, and hence in fact declares itself to be a very *impure* intention, which treats such enjoyment and possession as something wholly essential. Again, it also affirms as a pure intention the necessity of rising above natural existence, above acquisitiveness about the means of existence; only it finds it foolish and wrong that this elevation should be demonstrated *by deeds*; in other words, this pure insight is in truth a deception, which feigns and demands an *inner* elevation, but declares that it is superfluous, foolish, and even wrong to be *in earnest* about it,

to put this elevation into *actual practice* and *demonstrate its truth*. Pure insight thus denies itself both as pure insight—for it denies directly purposive action—and as pure intention—for it denies the intention of proving itself freed from the Ends of a separate individual existence.

557. It is thus that Enlightenment lets itself be understood by faith. It presents itself in this bad light because, just by being in relation to an 'other', it gives itself a *negative reality*, or exhibits itself as the opposite of itself; but pure insight and intention must enter into this relationship, for it is their realization. This at first appeared as a negative reality. Perhaps its *positive reality* is better constituted. Let us see how things stand with this. If all prejudice and superstition have been banished, the question arises, *What next? What is the truth Enlightenment has propagated in their stead?* It has already declared that this positive content is in its extirpation of error, for that alienation of itself is just as much its positive reality. In its approach to what, for faith, is absolute Spirit, it interprets any *determinateness* it discovers there as wood, stone, etc., as particular, real things. Since in this way it grasps in general *every determinateness*, i.e. all content and filling, as something *finite*, as a *human entity* and [*mere*] *idea*, absolute Being becomes for it a *vacuum* to which no determinations, no predicates, can be attributed. The attribution of predicates to such a vacuum would be in itself reprehensible; and it is just in such a union that the monstrosities of superstition have been produced. Reason, *pure insight*, is certainly not empty itself, since the negative of itself is *for it*, and is its content; on the contrary, it is rich, but rich only in particularity and limitations. To let nothing of that sort appertain to absolute Being or be attributed to it, this is the prudent behaviour of Reason, of pure insight, which knows how to put itself and its finite riches in their proper place, and how to deal with the Absolute in a worthy manner.

558. In contrast to this empty Being there stands, as the second moment of the positive truth of Enlightenment, the *singleness* in general of consciousness and of all being, a singleness excluded from absolute Being and in the form of *absolute being-in-and-for-itself*. Consciousness, which in its very first reality is sense-certainty and mere 'meaning', returns here to this from the whole course of its experience and is again a knowledge of what is *purely negative of itself*, or of *things of sense*, i.e. of things

which *immediately* and indifferently confront its *being-for-self*. Here, however, it is not an *immediate*, natural consciousness; on the contrary, it has *become* such for itself. Whereas at first it was at the mercy of every sort of entanglement into which it was plunged by its unfolding, and now has been led back by pure insight to its first shape, it has experienced that shape as *result*. Being *based* on the nothingness of all the other shapes of consciousness, and hence of everything beyond sense-certainty, this sense-certainty is no longer mere 'meaning', but rather absolute truth. This nothingness of everything that lies beyond sense-certainty is no doubt merely a negative proof of this truth; but it is not susceptible of any other. For the positive truth of sense-certainty is in its own self the *immediate* being-for-self of the Notion itself *qua* object, and that too in the form of otherness— the positive truth that every consciousness is *absolutely certain* that it *is*, and that there are other real things outside of it, and that in its *natural* being it, like these things, is *in and for itself* or *absolute*.

559. Lastly, the third moment of the *truth of Enlightenment* is the relation of the individual being to absolute Being, is the relation between the first two moments. Insight, *qua* pure insight of what is *identical* or *unrestricted*, also *goes beyond* what is *not* identical, viz. beyond finite reality, or beyond itself as mere otherness. For the beyond of this otherness it has the *void* to which, therefore, it relates the sensuous reality. In the determination of this *relation*, both of the sides do not enter as *content*; for one of them is the void, and it is only through the other, the sensuous reality, that a content is present. But the *form* of the relation, to the determination of which the side of the *in-itself* contributes, can be a matter of choice; for the form is something *intrinsically negative*, and therefore self-opposed: being as well as nothing, the *in-self* as well as its *opposite*; or, what is the same thing, the relation of the *actual world* to the *in-itself qua* a *beyond*, is as much a *negating* as a *positing* of that actual world. Finite reality can therefore, properly speaking, be taken just as one needs. The sensuous is therefore now related *positively* to the Absolute as to the *in-itself*, and sensuous reality is itself an *intrinsic being*; the Absolute makes it, fosters and cherishes it. Then, again, it is related to the Absolute as an opposite, as to its own *non-being*; in this relationship it is not anything in

itself, but exists only for an 'other'. Whereas in the preceding shape of consciousness, the *Notions* of the antithesis were determined as Good and Bad, in the case of pure insight, on the other hand, they become the purer abstractions of *being-in-itself* and *being-for-another*.

560. Both ways of viewing the positive and the negative relations of the finite to the in-itself are, however, in fact equally necessary, and everything is thus as much something *in itself* as it is *for an 'other'*; in other words, everything is *useful*. Everything is at the mercy of everything else, now lets itself be used by others and is *for them*, and now, so to speak, stands again on its hind legs, is stand-offish towards the other, is for itself, and uses the other in its turn. From this, we see what is the essence and what is the place of man regarded as a Thing that is *conscious* of this relation. As he immediately is, as a natural consciousness *per se*, man is *good*, as an individual he is *absolute* and all else exists for him; and moreover, since the moments have for him, *qua* self-conscious animal, the significance of universality, *everything* exists for his pleasure and delight and, as one who has come from the hand of God, he walks the earth as in a garden planted for him. He must also have plucked the fruit of the tree of the knowledge of Good and Evil. He possesses in this an advantage which distinguishes him from all other creatures, for it happens that his intrinsically good nature is *also* so constituted that an excess of pleasure does it harm, or rather his individuality has *also its beyond* within it, can go beyond itself and destroy itself. To counter this, Reason is for him a useful instrument for keeping this excess within bounds, or rather for preserving himself when he oversteps his limit; for this is the power of consciousness. Enjoyment on the part of the conscious, intrinsically *universal* being, must not itself be something determinate as regards variety and duration, but universal. 'Measure' or proportion has therefore the function of preventing pleasure in its variety and duration from being cut short; i.e. the function of 'measure' is immoderation. Just as everything is useful to man, so man is useful too, and his vocation is to make himself a member of the group, of use for the common good and serviceable to all. The extent to which he looks after his own interests must also be matched by the extent to which he serves others, and so far as he serves others,

so far is he taking care of himself: one hand washes the other. But wherever he finds himself, there he is in his right place; he makes use of others and is himself made use of.

561. Different things are useful to one another in different ways; but all things are mutually serviceable through their own nature, viz. through being related to the Absolute in two ways, the one positive, whereby they exist entirely on their own account, the other negative, whereby they exist for others. The *relation* to absolute Being, or religion, is therefore of all useful things the supremely useful; for it is pure utility itself, it is this enduring being of all things, or their *being-in-and-for-themselves*, and it is their downfall, or their *being-for-another*.

562. To faith, of course, this positive outcome of Enlightenment is as much an abomination as its negative attitude towards belief. This [enlightened] insight into absolute Being which sees nothing in it but just *absolute* Being, the *Être suprême*, or the void—this *intention* to regard everything in its immediate existence as having *intrinsic being* or as good, and finally, to regard the *relation* of the individual conscious being to absolute Being, *religion*, as exhaustively expressed in the Notion of utility—all this is for faith utterly detestable. This *wisdom*, peculiar to Enlightenment, at the same time necessarily seems to faith to be undiluted *platitude*, and the *confession* of platitude; because it consists of knowing nothing of absolute Being or, what amounts to the same thing, in knowing this quite flat truism about it, just that it is only *absolute* Being; and, on the other hand, in knowing only what is finite and, moreover, knowing it as truth, and thinking that this knowledge of the finite as true is the highest knowledge attainable.

563. Faith has the divine right, the right of absolute *self-identity* or of pure thought, as against Enlightenment, and receives at its hands nothing but wrong; for Enlightenment distorts all the moments of faith, changing them into something different from what they are in it. But Enlightenment has only a human right as against faith and for the support of its own truth; for the wrong it commits is the right to be *non-identical*, and consists in perverting and altering, a right which belongs to the nature of *self-consciousness* as against simple essential being or *thought*. But since the right of Enlightenment is the right of self-consciousness, it will not only *also* retain its own

right, so that two equal rights of Spirit could be left confronting each other, neither being capable of satisfying the other: it will maintain its absolute right because self-consciousness is the negativity of the Notion, a negativity which is active not only on its own account, but which also takes within its grasp its opposite. And because faith itself is a consciousness it will not be able to deny Enlightenment its right.

564. For Enlightenment does not employ principles peculiar to itself in its attack on faith, but principles which are implicit in faith itself. Enlightenment merely presents faith with its *own* thoughts which faith unconsciously lets fall apart, but which Enlightenment brings together; it merely reminds faith when one of its own modes is present to it, of the others which it also has, but which it always forgets when the other one is present. Enlightenment shows itself to faith to be pure insight by the fact that, in a *specific* moment, it sees the whole, brings forward the other moment which is opposed to it, and, converting one into the other, brings to notice the negative essence of both thoughts, the Notion. To faith, it seems to be a perversion and a lie because it points out the *otherness* of its moments; in doing so, it seems directly to make something else out of them than they are in their separateness; but this 'other' is equally essential and, in truth, is present in the believing consciousness itself, only this does not think about it, but puts it away somewhere. Consequently, it is neither alien to faith, nor can faith disavow it.

565. Enlightenment itself, however, which reminds faith of the opposite aspect of its separated moments, is just as little enlightened about itself. It has a purely *negative* attitude to faith so far as it excludes its own content from its purity and takes that content to be the *negative* of itself. It therefore neither recognizes itself in this negative, in the content of faith, nor for this reason does it bring the two thoughts together, the one which it puts forward itself, and the one to which it opposes the first. Since it does not recognize that what it condemns in faith is directly its own thought, it is itself in the antithesis of the two moments, only one of which—viz. in every case the one opposed to faith—it acknowledges, but separates the other from the first, just as faith does. Consequently, Enlightenment does not produce the unity of both *as* their unity, i.e. the Notion; but the Notion *comes into being* for it of its own accord, in other words,

Enlightenment *finds* the Notion there merely as something *given*. For, in itself, the realization of pure insight is just this, that insight, whose essence is the Notion, at first becomes for itself an absolute 'other' and repudiates itself—for the antithesis of the Notion is an absolute antithesis—and then out of this otherness it comes to itself, or to its Notion. But Enlightenment *is* only this movement, it is the still unconscious activity of the pure Notion, an activity which, though it does arrive at its object, takes it to be an *other*, and, too, does not know the nature of the Notion, viz. that it is the undifferentiated which absolutely sunders itself. As against faith, then, insight is the might of the Notion in so far as it is the movement and the relating of the moments lying asunder in its consciousness, a relating in which their contradiction comes to light. Herein lies the absolute *right* of the authority which insight exercises over faith; but the *reality* on which it exercises this authority lies just in the fact that the believing consciousness is itself the Notion, and therefore itself acknowledges the opposite [aspect] which insight puts before it. Insight therefore retains its right as against faith because it makes valid in faith what is necessary to faith itself and what faith possesses in itself.

566. At first, Enlightenment affirms this moment of the Notion, that it is an *act of consciousness*; opposing faith, it maintains that the absolute Being of faith is a Being of the believer's own consciousness *qua* a self, or that this absolute Being is a *product* of consciousness. To faith, its absolute Being, while it is possessed of *intrinsic being* for the believer, is also at the same time not like an alien thing which is just *found* in him, no one knowing how and whence it came. On the contrary, the faith of the believer consists just in his *finding* himself as *this* particular personal consciousness in the absolute Being, and his obedience and service consist in producing, through his own *activity*, that Being as *his own* absolute Being. Enlightenment, strictly speaking, only reminds faith of this, if faith roundly asserts that the *in-itself* of absolute Being is beyond the activity of consciousness. But while Enlightenment, it is true, corrects the one-sidedness of faith by bringing to its notice the opposite moment of *action* in contrast to *being*—and it is *being* which faith is alone thinking of here—and yet does not itself bring its own thoughts together, it isolates the pure moment of *action* and asserts that the *in-itself*

of faith is *only* a *product* of consciousness. This action, taken in isolation and opposed to the *in-itself*, is, however, a contingent action and, *qua* an activity of picture-thinking, is a creating of fictions—picture-thoughts which possess no *intrinsic* being; and this is how Enlightenment regards the content of faith. But, conversely, pure insight equally says the reverse. In maintaining the moment of *otherness* which the Notion has within it, it pronounces [absolute] Being to be for faith something which in no way concerns consciousness, lies beyond it, is alien to it and unknown. The case is similar with faith. On the one hand, it puts its trust in absolute Being, and in doing so obtains the certainty of itself; on the other hand, for faith, absolute Being is unsearchable in all its ways and in its Being unattainable.

567. Further, Enlightenment maintains against the believer a right which the latter himself concedes, when Enlightenment regards the object of the believer's veneration as stone and wood, or else as something finite and anthropomorphic. For since this consciousness is divided within itself, having a *beyond* of the real world and a world that is altogether *this side* of the *world beyond*, there is, as a matter of fact, also present in it this view of the thing of sense according to which it counts as a being that is in and for itself; but faith does not bring together these two thoughts of absolute Being, which is for it at one time *pure essence* and at another time an ordinary *thing of sense*. Even its pure consciousness is affected by the latter view; for the differences of the supersensible world, because this is without the Notion, are a series of independent shapes and their movement is a *happening*, i.e. they exist only in *picture-thinking* and have within them the marks of sensuous existence. Enlightenment, on its side, equally isolates the actual world as an entity forsaken by Spirit, isolates determinateness as unmoved finitude, as if it were not even a *moment* in the spiritual movement of essential being, not nothing, but also not something that absolutely *is*, but something that is evanescent.

568. It is clear that the same is the case with the *ground* of knowledge. Faith itself acknowledges a contingent knowledge; for it has a relationship to contingent things, and absolute Being itself exists for faith in the form of a pictorial representation of a common reality. Consequently, the believing consciousness, too, is a certainty which does not possess the truth within

itself, and it confesses itself to be such an unessential consciousness, to be of *this* world and separated from the Spirit that is certain of itself and self-authenticated. But it forgets this moment in its immediate spiritual knowledge of absolute Being. Enlightenment, however, which reminds it of this, in its turn thinks *only* of contingent being and forgets the other—thinks only of the mediation which takes place through an *alien* third term, not of the mediation in which the immediate is itself the third term through which it mediates itself with the other, viz. with its *own self*.

569. Finally, Enlightenment in its view of the *action* of faith finds the rejection of enjoyment and possessions wrong and purposeless. As to the rejection being wrong, Enlightenment is in agreement with faith on this point; for faith itself acknowledges this reality of possessing, holding on to, and enjoying, property. In holding on to property its behaviour is all the more self-centred and stubborn, and in its enjoyment it is all the more crudely self-abandoned, since its religious act of *giving up* possessions and enjoyment falls on the far side of this reality and purchases freedom for itself on that side. This service of sacrifice of natural impulses and enjoyments has, in fact, owing to this antithesis, no truth. Retention occurs *along with* sacrifice; the latter is merely a *symbol* which performs real sacrifice on only a small portion, and is therefore in point of fact only a sacrifice in *imagination*.

570. As regards *purposiveness*, Enlightenment finds it inept to throw away *one* possession in order to know and to prove that one is liberated from *all* possessions, to deny oneself *one* enjoyment in order to know and to prove that one is liberated from all enjoyment. Faith itself apprehends the absolute action as a *universal* action; not only is the action of its absolute Being as its object a universal action for faith, but the individual consciousness, too, has to show that it is liberated entirely and generally from its sensual nature. But throwing away a single possession, or renouncing a single enjoyment, is not this universal action; and since in the action the purpose, which is a universal purpose, and the performance, which is a single performance, would be bound to present themselves to consciousness as essentially incompatible, that action shows itself to be one in which consciousness has no part, and thus this kind of

action is seen to be really too naïve to be an action at all. It is too naïve to fast, in order to prove that one is liberated from the pleasures of the table; too naïve to rid the *body* of another pleasure, as Origen did, in order to show that that pleasure is finished and done with. The action itself proves to be an *external* and *single* operation; but desire is rooted *inwardly* and is a *universal*. Its pleasure disappears neither with the instrument nor by abstention from particular pleasures.

571. But Enlightenment on its side here isolates the *inward*, the *unreal*, as opposed to reality, just as it held fast to the externality of the Thing as opposed to the inwardness of faith in the latter's contemplation and devotion. It places the essential factor in the *intention*, in the *thought*, and thereby saves itself the trouble of actually accomplishing the liberation from natural aims. On the contrary, this inwardness is itself the formal element which has its filling in the natural impulses, which are justified simply by the fact that they are inward, that they belong to *universal being*, to Nature.

572. Enlightenment, then, holds an irresistible authority over faith because, in the believer's own consciousness, are found the very moments which Enlightenment has established as valid. Examining the effect of this authority more closely, its behaviour towards faith seems to rend asunder the *beautiful* unity of *trust* and immediate *certainty*, to pollute its *spiritual* consciousness with mean thoughts of *sensuous* reality, to destroy the soul which is *composed* and *secure* in its submission, by the vanity of the Understanding and of self-will and self-fulfilment. But as a matter of fact, the result of the Enlightenment is rather to do away with the *thoughtless*, or rather *non-notional*, separation which is present in faith. The believing consciousness weighs and measures by a twofold standard; it has two sorts of eyes, two sorts of ears, speaks with two voices, has duplicated all ideas without comparing the twofold meanings. In other words, faith lives in two sorts of non-*notional* perceptions, the one the perceptions of the *slumbering* consciousness which lives purely in non-notional thoughts, the other those of the *waking* consciousness which lives solely in the world of sense; and in each of them it has its own separate housekeeping. The enlightenment illuminates that heavenly world with ideas belonging to the world of sense, and points out this finitude which

faith cannot deny, because it is self-consciousness and hence is the unity to which both kinds of ideas belong and in which they do not fall apart; for they belong to the same indivisible *unitary* self into which faith has passed.

573. As a result, faith has lost the content which filled its element, and collapses into a state in which it moves listlessly to and fro within itself. It has been expelled from its kingdom; or, this kingdom has been ransacked, since the waking consciousness has monopolized every distinction and expansion of it and has vindicated earth's ownership of every portion of it and given them back to earth. Yet faith is not on that account satisfied, for this illumination has everywhere brought to light only single, separate entities, so that what speaks to Spirit is only a reality without any substance, and a finitude forsaken by Spirit. Since faith is without any content and it cannot remain in this void, or since, in going beyond the finite which is the sole content, it finds only the void, it is a *sheer yearning*, its truth an empty beyond, for which a fitting content can no longer be found, for everything is bestowed elsewhere. Faith has, in fact, become the same as Enlightenment, viz. the consciousness of the relation of what is in itself finite to an Absolute without predicates, an Absolute unknown and unknowable; but there is this difference, the latter is *satisfied* Enlightenment, but faith is *unsatisfied* Enlightenment. However, we shall see whether Enlightenment can remain satisfied; that yearning of the troubled Spirit which mourns over the loss of its spiritual world lurks in the background. Enlightenment itself bears within it this blemish of an unsatisfied yearning: as *pure object*, in its *empty* absolute Being; as *action* and *movement*, in *going beyond* its individual self to an empty and unfulfilled beyond; as an object *with a content*, in the *lack of selfhood* in the thing that is 'useful'. Enlightenment will rid itself of this blemish; a closer examination of the positive result which is its truth will show that in that result the blemish is in principle already removed.

b. *The truth of Enlightenment*

574. The listless movement of Spirit which no longer creates a distinction within itself has thus entered into its own self beyond consciousness, which, on the other hand, sees itself clearly. The first moment of this clarity is determined in its

necessity and condition by the fact that pure insight, or insight that is *implicitly* Notion, actualizes itself; it does so when it posits otherness or determinateness within itself. In this way it is negative pure insight, i.e. a negation of the Notion; this negation is equally pure; and thus there has come into being the *pure Thing*, the absolute Being, that has no further determination whatever. Characterized more precisely, pure insight, *qua* absolute Notion, is a distinguishing of differences which are no longer differences, of abstractions or pure Notions which are no longer self-supporting, but are supported and distinguished only by the *movement as a whole*. This distinguishing of what contains no difference consists simply in the fact that the absolute Notion makes itself into its *object* and posits itself as the essence over against that *movement*. This results in the essence being without that side wherein abstractions or differences are *held apart*, and therefore becomes *pure thought* in the form of a *pure Thing*. This, then, is just the listless, unconscious movement to and fro within itself of Spirit to which faith was reduced when it lost a content that contained a difference; it is at the same time that *movement* of pure self-consciousness for which the essence is supposed to be the absolutely alien beyond. For because this pure self-consciousness moves about in pure Notions, in differences that are not differences, it collapses in fact into the unconscious movement to and fro of Spirit, i.e. into pure *feeling*, or pure *thinghood*. The self-alienated Notion—for the Notion here is still standing at the stage of this alienation—does not, however, recognize this *identical* essence of the two sides—the movement of self-consciousness and of its absolute Being—does not recognize their *identical* essence which is, in fact, their substance and enduring being. Since the Notion is unconscious of this unity, absolute Being has value for it only in the form of a beyond standing over against it, while the consciousness making these distinctiions and in this way having the in-itself outside of it, is held to be a finite consciousness.

575. In regard to that absolute Being, Enlightenment is caught up in the same internal conflict that it formerly experienced in connection with faith, and it divides itself into two parties. One party proves itself to be victorious by breaking up into two parties; for in so doing, it shows that it contains

within itself the principle it is attacking, and thus has rid itself of the one-sidedness in which it previously appeared. The interest which was divided between itself and the other party now falls entirely within itself, and the other party is forgotten, because that interest finds within itself the antithesis which occupies its attention. At the same time, however, it has been raised into the higher victorious element in which it exhibits itself in a clarified form. So that the schism that arises in one of the parties and seems to be a misfortune, demonstrates rather that party's good fortune.

576. The pure essence itself has no difference in it; consequently, the way in which it does obtain a difference is that two such pure essences exhibit themselves for consciousness, or there is a twofold consciousness of the essence. Pure absolute Being is only in pure thought, or rather it is pure thought itself, and therefore utterly *beyond* the finite, *beyond self*-consciousness, and is only Being in a negative sense. But in this way, it is just [mere] *being*, the negative of self-consciousness. As the *negative* of self-consciousness it is *also* related to it; it is an *external being* which, related to self-consciousness within which differences and determination fall, receives within it the differences of being tasted, seen, etc.; and the relationship is that of *sense*-certainty and perception.

577. If we start from this *sensuous* being into which that negative beyond necessarily passes, but abstract from these specific ways in which consciousness is related to it, then what remains is pure *matter* as a listless, aimless movement to and fro within itself. In this connection, it is important to bear in mind that *pure matter* is merely what is *left over* when we *abstract* from seeing, feeling, tasting, etc., i.e. it is not matter that is seen, tasted, felt, etc.; what is seen, felt, tasted, is not *matter*, but colour, a stone, a salt, etc. Matter is rather a *pure abstraction*; and so what we are presented with here is the *pure essence of thought*, or pure thought itself as the Absolute, which contains no differences, is indeterminate and devoid of predicates.

578. One party of the Enlightenment calls absolute Being that predicateless Absolute which exists in thought beyond the actual consciousness which formed the starting-point; the other calls it *matter*. If these were to be distinguished as *Nature* and Spirit, or *God*, then the unconscious and aimless inner

movement to and fro would lack the wealth of developed life which would make it Nature, and the self-differentiated consciousness which would make it Spirit or God. The two, as we saw, are absolutely the same Notion; the difference lies not in what they actually are, but simply and solely in the different starting-points of the two developments, and in the fact that each sticks to its own point in the movement of thought. If they could disregard their own starting-points they would meet and would recognize that what to the one is, so it pretends, an abomination, and to the other, a folly, is the same thing. For to the one, absolute Being is in its pure thinking, or is immediately for pure consciousness, is outside finite consciousness, the *negative* beyond of it. If it would reflect, firstly, that the simple immediacy of thought is nothing else but *pure being*, and secondly, that what is *negative* for consciousness is at the same time related to it, that in the negative judgement the '*is*' (copula) holds together as well as separates the terms, it would come to see that this beyond, characterized as something existing *externally*, stands in a relation to consciousness and is thus the same as what is called *pure matter*: the missing moment of *presence* would be gained. The other Enlightenment starts from sensuous being, then *abstracts* from the sensuous relation of tasting, seeing, etc., and makes that being into a pure *in-itself*, into an *absolute matter*, into what is neither felt nor tasted. This being has in this way become something simple without predicates, the essence of *pure consciousness*; it is the pure Notion as *implicitly* existent, or *pure thought within itself*. This insight does not consciously take the reverse step from what *is*, what *simply* is, to what is thought, which is the same as what *simply* is, does not take the step from the pure positive to the pure negative; although, after all, the positive is pure solely through negation, while the *pure* negative, as pure, is in its own self self-identical and just for that reason positive. Or again, they have not arrived at the Notion found in Descartes's metaphysics, that being and thought are, *in themselves*, the same; they have not arrived at the thought that being, *pure* being, is not something *concretely real* but a *pure abstraction*, and conversely, pure thought, self-identity or essence, partly is the *negative* of self-consciousness and therefore *being*, partly, as immediately simple, is likewise nothing else but being; *thought* is *thinghood*, or *thinghood* is *thought*.

579. Essence, here, is split into two in such a way that, to begin with, two different ways of considering it are involved. In part, essence must contain difference within itself; in part, just because of this, the two ways of considering it merge into one; for the abstract moments of pure being and the negative, by which they are distinguished, are then united in the object so considered. The universal common to both is the abstraction of a pure, inward oscillation, or of pure self-thinking. This simple rotatory motion must become more complex because it is itself only motion by distinguishing its moments. This distinguishing of the moments leaves their unmoved [unity] behind as the empty husk of pure *being*, which is no longer actual thought, no longer has any life within it; for this process of differentiation is, *qua* difference, all the content. This process, however, which places itself *outside* of that *unity*, is an alternation—an alternation which *does not return into itself*, of being-*for-an-other*, and of being-*for-self*; it is reality in the way this is an object for the actual consciousness of pure insight—Utility.

580. Bad as Utility may look to faith or sentimentality, or even to the abstract thought that calls itself speculation, which clings to the *in-itself*, yet it is in Utility that pure insight achieves its realization and has itself for its *object*, an object which it now no longer repudiates and which, too, no longer has for it the value of the void or the pure beyond. For pure insight is, as we saw, the existent Notion itself, or pure self-identical personality distinguishing itself within itself in such a way that each of the distinguished moments is itself pure Notion, i.e. is at the same time not distinguished; pure insight is simple, pure self-consciousness which is *for itself* as well as *in itself* in an immediate unity. Its *being-in-itself* is therefore not an enduring *being*, but in its difference immediately ceases to be something; such a being, however, that is immediately without support is not an *intrinsic* being, but is essentially *for an other* which is the power that absorbs it. But this second moment which is opposed to the first, to the being-*in-itself*, equally vanishes immediately like the first; or, as a being which is only *for an other*, it is rather the *vanishing* itself, and there is posited the accomplished *return into itself*, *being-for-self*. This simple being-for-self, however, as self-identity, is rather *a* [mere] *being*, or is thereby *for an other*. This nature of pure insight in the unfolding of its moments,

or insight *qua object*, is expressed in the Useful. What is useful, is something with an enduring being in itself, or a Thing; this being-in-itself is at the same time only a pure moment; hence it is absolutely *for an other*, but equally is for an 'other' merely what it is in itself; these opposed moments have returned into the indivisible unity of being-for-self. While the Useful does express the Notion of pure insight, it is not pure insight as such but insight *conceived* by it in the form of *object*; it is merely the restless alternation of those moments, of which one indeed is itself the accomplished return into itself, but only as a *being-for-self*, i.e. as an abstract moment appearing on one side over against the others. The Useful itself is not a negative essence, having in itself these moments in their antithesis and, at the same time as *undivided* in *one and the same respect*, or as *thought*, as they are *qua* pure insight; the moment of *being-for-self* is certainly present in the Useful, but not in such a way that it overarches the other moments, the *in-itself* and the *being-for-an other*, in which case it would be the *self*. Pure insight has, therefore, in the Useful its own Notion in its *pure* moments for *object*; it is the awareness of this *metaphysics*, but not as yet the comprehension of it; consciousness has not yet reached the *unity* of *Being* and *Notion* itself. Since the Useful still has the form of an object for pure insight, it does have a *world*, one which, it is true, is no longer in and for itself, but yet a world which it distinguishes from itself. Only, since the antitheses have emerged at the summit of the Notion, the next stage will see them come into collision, and the Enlightenment will taste the fruits of its deeds.

581. Looking at the object obtained, in relation to this whole sphere, we see that the actual world of culture was summed up in the *vanity* of self-consciousness, into a being-for-self whose content is still that confused world of culture and which is still the *single, individual* Notion, not yet the explicitly *universal* Notion. But returned into itself, that Notion is *pure insight*—pure consciousness as pure *self*, or negativity, just as faith is precisely the same as *pure thought*, or positivity. In that self, faith has the moment that makes it complete; but perishing through being thus completed, it is in pure insight that we now see the two moments: as absolute Being, which is simply *thought* or the negative, and as *matter*, which has positive *being*. This completeness still lacks that *actual* world of self-consciousness which belongs

to the *vain* consciousness—the world out of which thought raised itself to itself. What is thus lacking is obtained in Utility in so far as pure insight there acquires positive objectivity; pure insight is thereby an actual consciousness satisfied within itself. This objectivity now constitutes its *world*; it has become the truth of the entire preceding world, of the ideal, as well as of the real, world. The first world of Spirit is the widespread realm of its self-dispersed existence and of the self-*certainty* of its individual forms, just as Nature disperses its life into infinitely various forms without the *genus* of those forms having an actual existence. The second world contains the *genus* and is the realm of *intrinsic being* or *truth* over against that certainty. The third world, however, that of the Useful, is the *truth* which is equally the *certainty* of itself. The realm of the truth of *faith* lacks the principle of *actuality*, or the certainty of self as this particular individual. But the actuality or the certainty of self as this particular individual lacks *intrinsic being*. In the object of pure insight both worlds are united. The Useful is the object in so far as self-consciousness penetrates it and has in it the *certainty* of its *individual self*, its enjoyment (its *being-for-self*); self-consciousness sees right into the object, and this insight contains the *true* essence of the object (which is to be something that is penetrated [by consciousness], or to be *for an 'other'*). This insight is thus itself a *true knowing*, and self-consciousness has equally directly the universal certainty of itself, its *pure consciousness*, in this relationship in which, therefore, *truth* as well as presence and *actuality* are united. The two worlds are reconciled and heaven is transplanted to earth below.

III. ABSOLUTE FREEDOM AND TERROR

582. Consciousness has found its Notion in Utility. But it is partly still an *object*, and partly, for that very reason, still an *End* to be attained, which consciousness does not find itself to possess immediately. Utility is still a predicate of the object, not itself a subject or the immediate and sole *actuality* of the object. It is the same thing that appeared before, when being-for-self had not yet shown itself to be the substance of the other moments, a demonstration which would have meant that the Useful was directly nothing else but the self of consciousness and that this latter was thereby in possession of it. This

withdrawal from the form of objectivity of the Useful has, however, already taken place in principle and from this inner revolution there emerges the actual revolution of the actual world,
the new shape of consciousness, *absolute freedom*.

583. In fact, what we have here is no more than an empty
show of objectivity separating self-consciousness from possession. For, partly, all existence and validity of the specific
members of the organization of the actual world and the world
of faith have, in general, returned into this simple determination as into their ground and spiritual principle; partly, however, this simple determination no longer possesses anything of
its own, it is rather pure metaphysic, pure Notion, or a pure
knowing by self-consciousness. That is to say, of the *being-in-
and-for-itself* of the Useful *qua* object, consciousness recognizes
that its *being-in-itself* is essentially a *being-for-an-other*; being-in-
itself, as *devoid of self*, is in truth a passive self, or that which
is a self for another self. The object, however, exists for consciousness in this abstract form of pure being-in-itself, for consciousness is pure *insight* whose distinctions are in the pure form
of Notions. But the *being-for-self* into which being-for-an-other
returns, i.e. the self, is not a self belonging exclusively to what
is called object and distinct from the 'I'; for consciousness, *qua*
pure insight, is not a *single* self which could be confronted by
the object as equally having a self of its own, but is pure Notion,
the gazing of the self into the self, the absolute seeing of *itself*
doubled; the certainty of itself is the universal Subject, and its
conscious Notion is the essence of all actuality. If, then, the Useful was merely the alternation of the moments, an alternation
which did not return into its own *unity*, and hence was still an
object for knowing, it now ceases to be this. For knowing is itself
the movement of those abstract moments, it is the universal self,
the self of itself as well as of the object and, as universal, is the
self-returning unity of this movement.

584. Spirit thus comes before us as *absolute freedom*. It is self-
consciousness which grasps the fact that its certainty of itself
is the essence of all the spiritual 'masses', or spheres, of the real
as well as of the supersensible world, or conversely, that essence
and actuality are consciousness's knowledge of *itself*. It is conscious of its pure personality and therein of all spiritual reality,
and all reality is solely spiritual; the world is for it simply its

own will, and this is a general will. And what is more, this will is not the empty thought of will which consists in silent assent, or assent by a representative, but a real general will, the will of all *individuals* as such. For will is in itself the consciousness of personality, or of each, and it is as this genuine actual will that it ought to be, as the *self*-conscious essence of each and every personality, so that each, undivided from the whole, always does everything, and what appears as done by the whole is the direct and conscious deed of each.

585. This undivided Substance of absolute freedom ascends the throne of the world without any power being able to resist it. For since, in truth, consciousness alone is the element in which the spiritual beings or powers have their substance, their entire system which is organized and maintained by division into 'masses' or spheres has collapsed, now that the individual consciousness conceives the object as having no other essence than self-consciousness itself, or as being absolutely Notion. What made the Notion into an existent *object* was its diremption into separate *subsistent* spheres, but when the object becomes a Notion, there is no longer anything in it with a continuing existence; negativity has permeated all its moments. It comes into existence in such a way that each individual consciousness raises itself out of its allotted sphere, no longer finds its essence and its work in this particular sphere, but grasps itself as the *Notion* of will, grasps all spheres as the essence of this will, and therefore can only realize itself in a work which is a work of the whole. In this absolute freedom, therefore, all social groups or classes which are the spiritual spheres into which the whole is articulated are abolished; the individual consciousness that belonged to any such sphere, and willed and fulfilled itself in it, has put aside its limitation; its purpose is the general purpose, its language universal law, its work the universal work.

586. The object and the [moment of] *difference* have here lost the meaning of *utility*, which was the predicate of all real being; consciousness does not begin its movement in the object as if this were something *alien* from which it first had to return into itself; on the contrary, the object is for it consciousness itself. The antithesis, consists, therefore, solely in the difference between the *individual* and the *universal* consciousness; but the individual consciousness itself is directly in its own eyes that

which had only the *semblance* of an antithesis; it is universal consciousness and will. The *beyond* of this its actual existence hovers over the corpse of the vanished independence of real being, or the being of faith, merely as the exhalation of a stale gas, of the vacuous *Être suprême*.

587. After the various spiritual spheres and the restricted life of the individual have been done away with, as well as his two worlds, all that remains, therefore, is the immanent movement of universal self-consciousness as a reciprocity of self-consciousness in the form of *universality* and of *personal* consciousness: the universal will goes *into itself* and is a *single, individual* will to which universal law and work stand opposed. But this *individual* consciousness is no less directly conscious of itself as universal will; it is aware that its object is a law given by that will and a work accomplished by it; therefore, in passing over into action and in creating objectivity, it is doing nothing individual, but carrying out the laws and functions of the state.

588. This movement is thus the interaction of consciousness with itself in which it lets nothing break loose to become a *free object* standing over against it. It follows from this that it cannot achieve anything positive, either universal works of language or of reality, either of laws and general institutions of *conscious* freedom, or of deeds and works of a freedom that *wills* them. The work which *conscious* freedom might accomplish would consist in that freedom, *qua universal* substance, making itself into an *object* and into an *enduring being*. This otherness would be the moment of difference in it whereby it divided itself into stable spiritual 'masses' or spheres and into the members of various powers. These spheres would be partly the 'thought-things' of a *power* that is separated into legislative, judicial, and executive powers; but partly, they would be the *real essences* we found in the real world of culture, and, looking more closely at the content of universal action, they would be the particular spheres of labour which would be further distinguished as more specific 'estates' or classes. Universal freedom, which would have separated itself in this way into its constituent parts and by the very fact of doing so would have made itself into an *existent* Substance, would thereby be free from *particular* individuality, and would apportion the *plurality* of individuals to its various constituent parts. This, however, would restrict the activity and

the being of the personality to a branch of the whole, to one kind of activity and being; when placed in the element of *being*, personality would have the significance of a specific personality; it would cease to be in truth universal self-consciousness. Neither by the mere idea of obedience to *self-given* laws which would assign to it only a part of the whole, nor by its being *represented* in law-making and universal action, does self-consciousness let itself be cheated out of *reality*, the reality of *itself* making the law and accomplishing, not a particular work, but the universal work itself. For where the self is merely *represented* and is present only as an idea, there it is not *actual*; where it is represented by proxy, it *is not*.

589. Just as the individual self-consciousness does not find itself in this *universal work* of absolute freedom *qua* existent Substance, so little does it find itself in the *deeds* proper and *individual* actions of the will of this freedom. Before the universal can perform a deed it must concentrate itself into the One of individuality and put at the head an individual self-consciousness; for the universal will is only an *actual* will in a self, which is a One. But thereby all other individuals are excluded from the entirety of this deed and have only a limited share in it, so that the deed would not be a deed of the *actual universal* self-consciousness. Universal freedom, therefore, can produce neither a positive work nor a deed; there is left for it only *negative* action; it is merely the *fury* of destruction.

590. But the supreme reality and the reality which stands in the greatest antithesis to universal freedom, or rather the sole object that will still exist for that freedom, is the freedom and individuality of actual self-consciousness itself. For that universality which does not let itself advance to the reality of an organic articulation, and whose aim is to maintain itself in an unbroken continuity, at the same time creates a distinction within itself, because it is movement or consciousness in general. And, moreover, by virtue of its own abstraction, it divides itself into extremes equally abstract, into a simple, inflexible cold universality, and into the discrete, absolute hard rigidity and self-willed atomism of actual self-consciousness. Now that it has completed the destruction of the actual organization of the world, and exists now just for itself, this is its sole object, an object that no longer has any content, possession, existence, or

outer extension, but is merely this knowledge of itself as an absolutely pure and free individual self. All that remains of the
object by which it can be laid hold of is solely its *abstract* existence as such. The relation, then, of these two, since each exists
indivisibly and absolutely for itself, and thus cannot dispose of
a middle term which would link them together, is one of wholly
unmediated pure negation, a negation, moreover, of the individual as a being *existing* in the universal. The sole work and deed
of universal freedom is therefore *death*, a death too which has
no inner significance or filling, for what is negated is the empty
point of the absolutely free self. It is thus the coldest and
meanest of all deaths, with no more significance than cutting
off a head of cabbage or swallowing a mouthful of water.

591. In this flat, commonplace monosyllable is contained the
wisdom of the government, the abstract intelligence of the universal will, in the fulfilling of itself. The government is itself
nothing else but the self-established focus, or the individuality,
of the universal will. The government, which wills and executes
its will from a single point, at the same time wills and executes
a specific order and action. On the one hand, it excludes all
other individuals from its act, and on the other hand, it thereby
constitutes itself a government that is a specific will, and so
stands opposed to the universal will; consequently, it is absolutely
impossible for it to exhibit itself as anything else but a *faction*.
What is called government is merely the *victorious* faction, and
in the very fact of its being a faction lies the direct necessity
of its overthrow; and its being government makes it, conversely,
into a faction, and [so] guilty. When the universal will maintains that what the government has actually done is a crime
committed against it, the government, for its part, has nothing
specific and outwardly apparent by which the guilt of the will
opposed to it could be demonstrated; for what stands opposed
to it as the *actual* universal will is only an unreal pure will, *intention*. *Being suspected*, therefore, takes the place, or has the significance and effect, of *being guilty*; and the external reaction
against this reality that lies in the simple inwardness of intention, consists in the cold, matter-of-fact annihilation of this
existent self, from which nothing else can be taken away but
its mere being.

592. In this its characteristic *work*, absolute freedom becomes

explicitly objective to itself, and self-consciousness learns what absolute freedom in effect is. *In itself*, it is just this *abstract self-consciousness*, which effaces all distinction and all continuance of distinction within it. It is as such that it is objective to itself; the *terror* of death is the vision of this negative nature of itself. But absolutely free self-consciousness finds this its reality quite different from what its own Notion of itself was, viz. that the universal will is merely the *positive* essence of personality, and that this latter knows itself in it only positively, or as preserved therein. Here, however, this self-consciousness which, as pure insight, completely separates its positive and its negative nature—completely separates the predicateless Absolute as pure *Thought* and as pure *Matter*—is confronted with the absolute *transition* of the one into the other as a present reality. The universal will, *qua* absolutely *positive*, actual self-consciousness, because it is this self-conscious reality heightened to the level of *pure* thought or of *abstract* matter, changes round into its negative nature and shows itself to be equally that which *puts an end to the thinking of oneself*, or to self-consciousness.

593. Absolute freedom as *pure* self-identity of the universal will thus has within it *negation*; but this means that it contains *difference* in general, and this again it develops as an *actual* difference. For pure *negativity* has in the self-identical universal will the element of subsistence, or the *Substance* in which its moments are realized; it has the matter which it can utilize in accordance with its own determinateness; and in so far as this Substance has shown itself to be the negative element for the individual consciousness, the organization of spiritual 'masses' or spheres to which the plurality of individual consciousnesses are assigned thus takes shape once more. These individuals who have felt the fear of death, of their absolute master, again submit to negation and distinctions, arrange themselves in the various spheres, and return to an apportioned and limited task, but thereby to their substantial reality.

594. Out of this tumult, Spirit would be thrown back to its starting-point, to the ethical and real world of culture, which would have been merely refreshed and rejuvenated by the fear of the lord and master which has again entered men's hearts. Spirit would have to traverse anew and continually repeat this cycle of necessity if the result were only the complete interpene-

tration of self-consciousness and Substance—an interpenetration in which self-consciousness, which has experienced the negative power of its universal essence acting on it, would desire to know and find itself, not as this particular individual, but only as a universal, and therefore, too, would be able to endure the objective reality of universal Spirit, a reality excluding self-consciousness *qua* particular. But in absolute freedom there was no reciprocal action between a consciousness that is immersed in the complexities of existence, or that sets itself specific aims and thoughts, and a valid *external* world, whether of reality or thought; instead, the world was absolutely in the form of consciousness as a universal will, and equally self-consciousness was drawn together out of the whole expanse of existence or manifested aims and judgements, and concentrated into the simple self. The culture to which it attains in interaction with that essence is, therefore, the grandest and the last, is that of seeing its pure, simple reality immediately vanish and pass away into empty nothingness. In the world of culture itself it does not get as far as to behold its negation or alienation in this form of pure abstraction; on the contrary, its negation is filled with a content, either honour or wealth, which it gains in place of the self that it has alienated from itself; or the language of Spirit and insight which the disrupted consciousness acquires; or it is the heaven of faith, or the Utility of the Enlightenment. All these determinations have vanished in the loss suffered by the self in absolute freedom; its negation is the death that is without meaning, the sheer terror of the negative that contains nothing positive, nothing that fills it with a content. At the same time, however, this negation in its real existence is not something alien; it is neither the universal inaccessible *necessity* in which the ethical world perishes, nor the particular accident of private possession, nor the whim of the owner on which the disrupted consciousness sees itself dependent; on the contrary, it is the *universal will* which in this its ultimate abstraction has nothing positive and therefore can give nothing in return for the sacrifice. But for that very reason it is immediately one with self-consciousness, or it is the pure positive, because it is the pure negative; and the meaningless death, the unfilled negativity of the self, changes round in its inner Notion into absolute positivity. For consciousness, the immediate unity of itself with the universal will, its demand to know itself as this specific point in the universal will, is changed round into the absolutely opposite experience. What vanishes for it in that experience is abstract *being* or the immediacy of that insubstantial point, and this vanished immediacy is the universal will itself which it now knows itself to be in so far as it is a pure knowing or pure will. Consequently, it knows that will to be itself, and knows itself to be essential being; but not essential being as an *immediate existence*, not will as revolutionary government or anarchy striving to establish anarchy, nor itself as the centre of this faction or the opposite faction; on the contrary, the *universal will* is its *pure knowing and willing* and *it* is the universal will *qua* this pure knowing and willing. It does not lose *itself* in that will, for pure knowing and willing is much more *it* than is that atomic point of consciousness. It is thus the interaction of pure knowing with itself; pure *knowing qua essential being* is the universal will; but this essential being is abolutely nothing else but pure knowing. Self-consciousness is, therefore, the pure knowing of essential being *qua* pure knowing. Further, as an *individual self*, it is only the form of the subject or of real action, a form which is known by it as *form*. Similarly, *objective* reality, *being*, is for it simply a selfless form; for that reality would be something that is not known. This knowing, however, knows knowing to be essential being.

595. Absolute freedom has thus removed the antithesis between the universal and the individual will. The self-alienated Spirit, driven to the extreme of its antithesis in which pure willing and the agent of that pure willing are still distinct, reduces the antithesis to a transparent form and therein finds itself. Just as the realm of the real world passes over into the realm of faith and insight, so does absolute freedom leave its self-destroying reality and pass over into another land of self-conscious Spirit where, in this unreal world, freedom has the value of truth. In the thought of this truth Spirit refreshes itself, in so far as *it is* and remains *thought*, and knows this being which is enclosed within self-consciousness to be essential being in its perfection and completeness. There has arisen the new shape of Spirit, that of the *moral* Spirit.

596.   The ethical world showed its fate and its truth to be the Spirit that had merely passed away in it, the *individual self*. This *legal person*, however, has its Substance and fulfilment outside of that world. The movement of the world of culture and faith does away with this abstraction of the person, and, through the completed alienation, through the ultimate abstraction, Substance becomes for Spirit at first the universal will, and finally Spirit's own possession. Here, then, knowledge appears at last to have become completely identical with its truth; for its truth is this very knowledge and any antithesis between the two sides has vanished, vanished not only *for us* or *in itself*, but for self-consciousness itself. In other words, self-consciousness has gained the mastery over the antithesis within consciousness itself. This antithesis rests on the antithesis of the certainty of self and of the object. Now, however, the object is for consciousness itself the certainty of itself, viz. knowledge—just as the certainty of itself as such no longer has ends of its own, is therefore no longer [contained] within a determinateness, but is pure knowledge.

597.   Thus for self-consciousness, its knowledge is the *Substance* itself. This Substance is for it just as *immediate* as it is absolutely *mediated* in an indivisible unity. It is *immediate*, like the ethical consciousness which knows its duty and does it, and is bound up with it as with its own nature; but it is not *character*, as that ethical consciousness is which, on account of its immediacy, is a specifically determined Spirit, belongs only to one of the ethical essentialities, and has the characteristic of *not* knowing. It is *absolute mediation*, like the consciousness which cultivates itself, and the consciousness which believes; for it is essentially the movement of the self to set aside the abstraction of *immediate existence*, and to become conscious of itself as a universal—and yet to do so neither by the pure alienation and disruption of itself and of actuality, nor by fleeing from it. Rather, it is *immediately present* to itself in its substance, for this is its knowledge, is the intuited pure certainty of itself; and just *this immediacy* which is its own reality, is all reality, for the immediate is *being* itself, and, as pure immediacy purified by absolute negativity, it is *being* in general, or *all* being.

598. Absolute essential being is, therefore, not exhausted when determined as the simple *essence* of *thought*; it is all *reality*, and this reality *is* only as knowledge. What consciousness did not know would have no significance for consciousness and can have no power over it. Into its conscious will all objectivity, the whole world, has withdrawn. It is absolutely free in that it knows its freedom, and just this knowledge is its substance and purpose and its sole content.

a. *The moral view of the world*

599. Self-consciousness knows duty to be the absolute essence. It is bound only by duty, and this substance is its own pure consciousness, for which duty cannot receive the form of something alien. However, as thus locked up within itself, moral self-consciousness is not yet posited and considered as *consciousness*. The object is immediate knowledge, and, being thus permeated purely by the self is *not* an object. But because self-consciousness is essentially a mediation and negativity, its Notion implies relation to an *otherness* and [thus] is consciousness. This otherness, because duty constitutes the sole aim and object of consciousness, is, on the one hand, a reality completely without significance for consciousness. But because this consciousness is so completely locked up within itself, it behaves with perfect freedom and indifference towards this otherness; and therefore the existence of this otherness, on the other hand, is left completely free by self-consciousness, an existence that similarly is related only to itself. The freer self-consciousness becomes, the freer also is the negative object of its consciousness. The object has thus become a complete world within itself with an individuality of its own, a self-subsistent whole of laws peculiar to itself, as well as an independent operation of those laws, and a free realization of them—in general, a *Nature* whose laws like its actions belong to itself as a being which is indifferent to moral self-consciousness, just as the latter is indifferent to it.

600. From this determination is developed a moral view of the world which consists in the relation between the absoluteness of morality and the absoluteness of Nature. This relation is based, on the one hand, on the complete *indifference* and independence of Nature towards moral purposes and activity, and, on the other hand, on the consciousness of duty alone as

the essential fact, and of Nature as completely devoid of independence and essential being. The moral view of the world contains the development of the moments which are present in this relation of such completely conflicting presuppositions.

601. To begin with, then, the moral consciousness as such is presupposed; duty is the essence for this consciousness which is actual and active, and in its actuality and action fulfils its duty. But this moral consciousness is at the same time faced with the presupposed freedom of Nature; in other words, it learns from experience that Nature is not concerned with giving the moral consciousness a sense of the unity of its reality with that of Nature, and hence that Nature perhaps may let it become happy, or perhaps may not. The non-moral consciousness, on the other hand, finds, perhaps by chance, its realization where the moral consciousness sees only an *occasion* for acting, but does not see itself obtaining, through its action, the happiness of performance and the enjoyment of achievement. Therefore, it finds rather cause for complaint about such a state of incompatibility between itself and existence, and about the injustice which restricts it to having its object merely as a *pure duty*, but refuses to let it see the object and *itself* realized.

602. The moral consciousness cannot forego happiness and leave this element out of its absolute purpose. The purpose, which is expressed as *pure duty*, essentially implies this *individual* self-consciousness; *individual conviction* and the knowledge of it constitute an absolute element in morality. This element in the *objectified* purpose, in the *fulfilled* duty, is the *individual* consciousness that beholds itself as realized; in other words, it is enjoyment, which is thus implied in the Notion of morality, not indeed immediately, in morality regarded as sentiment or disposition, but only in the Notion of its actualization. This, however, means that enjoyment is also implied in morality as disposition, for this does not remain disposition in contrast to action, but proceeds to act or to realize itself. Thus the purpose, expressed as the whole with the consciousness of its moments, is that the fulfilled duty is just as much a moral action as a realized *individuality*, and that Nature, the aspect of individuality in contrast to the abstract purpose, is one with this purpose. Necessary as is the experience of the disharmony of the two sides, because Nature is free, even so, what is essential is duty

alone, and Nature contrasted with it is devoid of a self. That purpose in its *entirety* which the harmony of the two constitutes, contains within it actuality itself. It is at the same time the *thought* of actuality. The harmony of morality and Nature—or, since Nature comes into account only in so far as consciousness experiences its unity with it—the harmony of morality and happiness, is *thought of* as something that necessarily *is*, i.e. it is *postulated*. For to say that something is *demanded*, means that something is thought of in the form of *being* that is not yet actual—a necessity not of the *Notion qua* Notion, but of *being*. But necessity is at the same time essentially relation based on the Notion. The *being* that is demanded, then, is not the imagined being of a contingent consciousness, but is implied in the Notion of morality itself, whose true content is the *unity* of the pure and the individual consciousness; it is for the latter to see that this unity be, *for it*, an actuality: in the *content* of the purpose this is happiness, but in its *form*, is existence in general. The existence thus demanded, i.e. the unity of both, is therefore not a wish nor, regarded as purpose, one whose attainment were still uncertain; it is rather a demand of Reason, or an immediate certainty and presupposition of Reason.

603. That first experience and this postulate are not the sole postulates, but a whole circle of postulates opens up. Nature, that is to say, is not merely this wholly free, *external* mode of being in which, as a pure object, consciousness had to realize its purpose. This consciousness is, *in its own self*, essentially one *for which* this other free actual existence is, i.e. it is itself a contingent and natural existence. This Nature, which is for consciousness its own nature, is sensuousness, which in the shape of volition, as instincts and inclinations, possesses a *specific* essentiality of its own, or has its own *individual* purposes, and thus is opposed to the pure will and its pure purpose. However, in contrast with this opposition, pure consciousness has rather the relation of sensuousness to it, the absolute unity of the latter with it, for its essence. Both of these, pure thought and the sensuous aspect of consciousness, are *in themselves a single consciousness*, and it is precisely pure thought for which and in which this pure unity is. But *qua* consciousness, what is explicit for it is the antithesis of itself and impulses and instincts. In this conflict between Reason and sensuousness, the essential thing for Reason is that

the conflict be resolved, the result being the emergence of the unity of both, a unity which is not the former *original* [i.e. immediate] unity of both in a single individual, but a unity which proceeds from the *known* antithesis of both. Only such a unity is *actual* morality, for in it is contained the antithesis whereby the self is consciousness, or first is an actual self in fact, and at the same time a universal. In other words, in that unity there is expressed that *mediation* which, as we see, is essential to morality. Since, of the two moments of the antithesis, sensuousness is sheer *otherness*, or the negative, while, on the other hand, the pure thought of duty is the essence, no element of which can be given up, it seems that the resultant unity can only be brought about by getting rid of sensuousness. But since sensuousness is itself a moment of the process producing the unity, viz. the moment of *actuality*, we have to be content, in the first instance, with expressing the unity by saying that sensuousness should be *in conformity with* morality. This unity is likewise a *postulated being*; it is not actually *there*; for what *is* there is consciousness, or the antithesis of sensuousness and pure consciousness. But at the same time, the unity is not an in-itself or merely implicit like the first postulate in which free Nature constitutes an element of the unity, and in consequence the harmony of Nature with the moral consciousness falls outside of the latter. On the contrary, Nature here is that which is an element of consciousness itself, and we have here to deal with morality as such, with a morality that is the active self's very own. Consciousness has, therefore, itself to bring about this harmony and continually to be making progress in morality. But the consummation of this progress has to be projected into a future infinitely remote; for if it actually came about, this would do away with the moral consciousness. For morality is only moral *consciousness* as negative essence, for whose pure duty sensuousness has only a *negative* significance, is only *not* in conformity with duty. But, in that harmony, *morality qua* consciousness, i.e. its *actuality*, vanishes, just as in the moral consciousness, or in the *actuality* of morality, the *harmony* vanishes. The consummation, therefore, cannot be attained, but is to be thought of merely as an *absolute* task, i.e. one which simply remains a task. Yet at the same time its content has to be thought of as something which simply must *be*, and must not remain a task:

whether we imagine the [moral] consciousness to be altogether done away with in this goal, or not. Which of these really is the case can no longer clearly be determined in the dim remoteness of infinity, to which for that very reason the attainment of the goal is postponed. Strictly speaking, we shall have to say that a definite idea on this point ought not to interest us, and ought not to be looked for, because it leads to contradictions— the contradiction of a task which is to remain a task and yet ought to be fulfilled, and the contradiction of a morality which is no longer to be [a moral] *consciousness*, i.e. not actual. However, the idea that a perfected morality would involve a contradiction would do harm to the sanctity of the very essence of morality, and absolute duty would appear as something unreal.

604. The first postulate was the harmony of morality and objective Nature, the final purpose of the *world*; the other, the harmony of morality and the sensuous will, the final purpose of *self-consciousness* as such. The first, then, is harmony in the form of an *implicit* being, the other, in the form of *being-for-self*. But what connects, as middle term, these postulated two extreme final purposes is the movement of *actual* conduct itself. They are harmonies whose moments, in their abstract distinctiveness, have not yet developed into objects [for consciousness]. This occurs in the actuality in which the sides appear in consciousness proper, each as the *other* of the *other*. The postulates arising from this now contain the harmonies both in and for themselves, whereas previously they were postulated only as separate, one being *in itself* or implicit and the other being *for itself* or explicit.

605. The moral consciousness as the *simple knowing* and *willing* of pure duty is, in the doing of it, brought into relation with the object which stands in contrast to its simplicity, into relation with the actuality of the complex case, and thereby has a complex moral *relationship* with it. Here arise, in relation to content, the *many* laws generally, and in relation to form, the contradictory powers of the knowing consciousness and of the non-conscious.

In the first place, as regards the *many* duties, the moral consciousness in general heeds only the *pure duty* in them; the many duties *qua* manifold are *specific* and therefore as such have nothing sacred about them for the moral consciousness. At the same time, however, being *necessary*, since the Notion of 'doing' implies a complex actuality and therefore a complex moral relation to it, these many duties must be regarded as possessing an intrinsic being of their own. Further, since they can exist only in a moral *consciousness*, they exist at the same time in another consciousness than that for which only pure duty *qua* pure duty possesses an intrinsic being of its own and is sacred.

606. Thus it is postulated that it is *another* consciousness which makes them sacred, or which knows and wills them as duties. The first holds to pure duty, indifferent to all *specific* content, and duty is only this indifference towards such content. The other, however, contains the equally essential relation to 'doing', and to the necessity of the *specific* content: since for this other, duties mean *specific* duties, the content as such is equally essential as the form which makes the content a duty. This consciousness is consequently one in which universal and particular are simply one, and its Notion is, therefore, the same as the Notion of the harmony of morality and happiness. For this antithesis equally expresses the separation of the *self-equal* moral consciousness from that actuality which, as *manifold* being, conflicts with the simple essential nature of duty. While, however, the first postulate expresses the harmony of morality and Nature, as a harmony that simply *is*, because in it Nature is this negative aspect of self-consciousness, is the moment of *being*, this *implicit* harmony, on the other hand, is now essentially posited as consciousness. For what simply *is*, now has the form of the *content* of duty, or is the *determinateness* in the *determinate duty*. The implicit harmony is thus the unity of what are *simple essentialities*, essentialities of thought, and are therefore only in a consciousness. This is then henceforth a master and ruler of the world, who brings about the harmony of morality and happiness, and at the same time sanctifies duties in their multiplicity. This last means this much, that for the consciousness of *pure duty*, the determinate or specific duty cannot straightway be sacred; but because a specific duty, on account of the actual 'doing' which is a *specific* action, is likewise *necessary*, its necessity falls outside of that consciousness into another consciousness, which thus mediates or brings together the specific and the pure duty and is the reason why the former also has validity.

607. In the actual 'doing', however, consciousness behaves as this particular self, as completely individual; it is directed towards reality as such, and has this for its purpose, for it wills to achieve something. Duty in general thus falls outside of it into another being, which is consciousness and the sacred law-giver of pure duty. For the consciousness which acts, and just because it acts, the validity of the other consciousness, that of pure duty, is directly acknowledged; this pure duty is thus the content of another consciousness, and is sacred for the consciousness that acts only mediately, viz. through the agency of this other consciousness.

608. Because it is in this way posited that the validation of duty, as something *absolutely* sacred, falls outside of actual consciousness, this latter accordingly stands altogether on one side as the *imperfect* moral consciousness. Just as, in regard to its *knowledge*, it knows itself then as a consciousness whose knowledge and conviction are imperfect and contingent; similarly, in regard to its *willing*, it knows itself as a consciousness whose purposes are affected with sensuousness. On account of its unworthiness, therefore, it cannot look on happiness as necessary, but as something contingent, and can expect it only as a gift of Grace.

609. But though its actuality is imperfect, all the same its *pure* will and knowledge hold duty to be what is essential. In the Notion, therefore, so far as the Notion is contrasted with reality, or in thought, it *is* perfect. But the absolute Being is just this being that is *thought*, a being that is postulated *beyond* reality. It is, therefore, the thought in which morally imperfect knowledge and willing are held to be perfect, and the absolute Being, since it gives full weight to this imperfection, bestows happiness according to worthiness, i.e. according to the *merit ascribed to* the imperfect moral consciousness.

610. In this, the moral view of the world is completed. For in the Notion of the moral self-consciousness the two aspects, pure duty and actuality, are explicitly joined in a single unity, and consequently the one, like the other, is expressly without a being of its own, but is only a *moment*, or is superseded. This becomes explicit for consciousness in the last phase of the moral view of the world. That is to say, it places pure duty in a being other than itself, i.e. it posits pure duty partly as something

existing only in *thought*, partly as something that is not valid in and for itself; rather it is the non-moral [consciousness] that is held to be perfect. Equally, it gives itself the character of a consciousness whose actuality, not being in conformity with duty, is superseded and, *qua* superseded, or in the idea of absolute Being, no longer contradicts morality.

611. For the moral consciousness itself, however, its moral view of the world does not mean that consciousness develops therein its own Notion, and makes this its object. It is not conscious of this antithesis either as regards the form or the content; it does not relate and compare the sides of this antithesis with one another, but, in its development, rolls onward, without being the *Notion* which holds the moments together. For it knows only the *pure essence*, or the object so far as it is *duty*, so far as it is an *abstract* object of its pure consciousness, as a pure knowing, or as its own self. It thinks, therefore, only in abstractions, and does not comprehend [i.e. in terms of the Notion]. Consequently, the object of its *actual* consciousness is not yet transparent to it; it is not the absolute Notion, which alone grasps *otherness* as such, or its absolute opposite, as its own self. It does indeed hold its own reality, like all objective reality, to be *unessential*; but its freedom is the freedom of pure thought, in contrast to which, therefore, Nature likewise has arisen as an existence that is equally free. Because both are equally present in it, i.e. the *freedom* of [mere] *being*, and the inclusion of this being within consciousness, its object becomes one that has *being*, but at the same time exists only in *thought*; in the last stage of the moral view of the world, the content is explicitly such that its *being* is given to it by *thought*, and this conjunction of being and thought is pronounced to be what in fact it is— *imagining*.

612. When we consider the moral view of the world in such a way that this objective mode is nothing else than the very Notion of moral self-consciousness which it makes objective to itself, this awareness of the form of its origin gives rise to its exposition in another shape. The first stage which forms the starting-point is the *actual* moral self-consciousness, or the fact that *there is such* a moral self-consciousness. For the Notion gives it this explicit character, viz. that all reality in general has essential being for it only so far as it is in conformity with duty; and

this essential being it characterizes as knowledge, i.e. as in immediate unity with the actual self. Hence this unity is itself actual, it *is* a moral, actual consciousness. This now, *qua* consciousness, pictures its content to itself as an object, viz. as the final purpose of the world, as harmony of morality and all reality. But since it thinks of this unity as *object*, and is not the Notion which has mastery over the object as such, the unity is a negative of self-consciousness for it, or it falls outside of it, as something beyond its actual existence, and yet at the same time is something that *also* has *being*, but a being existing only in thought.

613. This self-consciousness which, *qua* self-consciousness, is *other* than the object, is thus left with the lack of harmony between the consciousness of duty and reality, and that, too, its own reality. Accordingly, the proposition now runs as follows: 'There is no *moral, perfect, actual* self-consciousness'; and, since the moral sphere is at all, only in so far as it is perfect, for duty is the *pure* unadulterated *intrinsic being* or in-itself, and morality consists only in conformity to this pure in-itself—the second proposition simply runs: 'There is no moral existence in reality.'

614. Since, however, in the third place, it is a single self, it is *in itself* or implicitly the unity of duty and reality. This unity therefore becomes an object for it as perfect morality—but as a *beyond* of its reality, yet a beyond that ought to be actual.

615. In this goal of the synthetic unity of the first two propositions, the self-conscious reality [i.e. actual self-consciousness] as well as duty, is posited as only a superseded moment. For neither of these two is single and separate; on the contrary, each of them, whose essential determination lies in their being *free from one another*, is thus in the unity no longer free from the other, and each therefore is superseded. Hence, as regards content, they become as such, objects each of which counts as object for the other, and as regards form, in such a way that this interchange is at the same time only *imagined* [i.e. occurs only *in thought*], Or, again, the *actually non-moral* sphere, because it is equally pure thought, and is raised above its actual existence, is yet, in imagination, moral, and is taken to be completely valid. In this way, the first proposition, that there *is* a moral self-consciousness, is reinstated, but is bound up with the second,

that there is *none*, i.e. that there *is* one, but only in imagination; or, in other words, it is true that there is none, yet, all the same, it is allowed by another consciousness to pass for one.

b. *Dissemblance or duplicity*

616. In the moral view of the world we see, on the one hand, consciousness itself *consciously* produce its object; we see that it neither encounters the object as something alien to it, nor does the object come before it in an unconscious manner. On the contrary, it proceeds in every case in accordance with a principle on the basis of which it posits *objective* being. It thus knows this latter to be its own self, for it knows itself to be the *active* agent that produces it. It seems, therefore, to attain here its peace and satisfaction, for this can only be found where it no longer needs to go beyond its object, because this no longer goes beyond *it*. On the other hand, however, consciousness itself really places the object *outside* itself as a beyond of itself. But this object with an intrinsic being of its own is equally posited as being, not free from self-consciousness, but as existing in the interest of, and by means of, it.

617. The moral world-view is, therefore, in fact nothing other than the elaboration of this fundamental contradiction in its various aspects. It is, to employ here a Kantian expression where it is most appropriate, a 'whole nest' of thoughtless contradictions. The way in which consciousness proceeds in this development, is to establish one moment and to pass directly from it to another, setting aside the first; but now, as soon as it has *set up* this second moment, it also *sets it aside* again, and really makes the opposite moment the essential one. At the same time, it is *also* aware of its contradiction and *shiftiness*, for it passes from one moment, *immediately* in its relation to this very moment, over to the opposite. *Because* a moment has no reality for it, it posits that very same moment as *real*: or, what comes to the same thing, in order to assert one moment as possessing being in itself, it asserts the *opposite* as the one that possesses being in itself. In so doing it confesses that, as a matter of fact, it is in earnest with neither of them. We must examine more closely the moments of this insincere shuffling.

618. Let us, to begin with, not question the assumption that there is an actual moral consciousness, because the assumption

is made directly and not in connection with something preceding; and let us turn to the harmony of morality and Nature, the first postulate. It is supposed to be an *implicit* harmony, not explicitly for actual consciousness, not present; on the contrary, what is present is rather only the contradiction of the two. In the present, morality is assumed as *already in existence*, and actuality is so placed that it is not in harmony with it. The *actual* moral consciousness, however, is one that *acts*; it is precisely therein that the actuality of its morality consists. But in the very doing or acting, the place [given to actuality] is *dis*placed; for the action is nothing other than the actualization of the inner moral purpose, nothing other than the production of an *actuality determined by the purpose*, or of the harmony of the moral purpose and actuality itself. At the same time, the performance of the action is a fact of which consciousness is aware, it is the *presence* of this unity of actuality and purpose, and because, in the accomplished deed, consciousness knows itself to be actualized as this particular consciousness, or beholds existence returned into itself—and enjoyment consists in this—there is also contained in the actuality of the moral purpose that form of actuality which is called enjoyment and happiness. Action, therefore, in fact directly fulfils what was asserted could not take place, what was supposed to be merely a postulate, merely a beyond. Consciousness thus proclaims through its deed that it is not in earnest in making its postulate, because the meaning of the action is really this, to make into a present reality what was not supposed to exist in the present. And, since the harmony is postulated for the sake of the action—that is to say, what is to to become *actual* through action, must be so *in itself*, otherwise actuality would not be *possible*—the connection of action and postulate is so constituted that, for the sake of the action, i.e. for the sake of the *actual* harmony of purpose and actuality, this harmony is postulated as *not* actual, as a beyond.

619. Since action *does* take place, the lack of fitness between purpose and reality is not taken seriously at all. On the other hand, action itself does seem to be taken seriously. In point of fact, however, the actual deed is only a deed of the *individual* consciousness, and therefore itself only something individual, and the result contingent. But the purpose of Reason as the universal, all-embracing purpose, is nothing less than the whole

world; a final purpose going far beyond the content of this individual deed, and therefore to be placed altogether beyond anything actually done. Because the universal *best* ought to be carried out, nothing *good* is done. In fact, however, the *nullity* of what is actually done, and the *reality* of the *whole* purpose alone, which are now postulated—these, too, are in every respect again 'displaced'. The moral action is not something contingent and restricted, for it has as its essence pure *duty*. This constitutes the sole entire purpose; and thus the deed, no matter in what other way its content is limited, is, *qua* actualization of that purpose, the accomplishment of the entire absolute purpose. Or, again, if reality is taken to be Nature, which has its own laws and stands in contrast to pure duty, so that duty cannot realize its law within Nature, then, since it is duty as such that essentially matters, what we are in fact concerned with is *not* the fulfilment of pure duty, which is the whole purpose; for the fulfilment would really have as its purpose, not pure duty, but its antithesis, reality. But there is again a shift from the position that it is not reality with which we are concerned; for according to the Notion of moral action, pure duty is essentially an active consciousness. Thus there certainly ought to be action, absolute duty ought to be expressed in the whole of Nature, and moral law to become natural law.

620. If then we allow that it is this highest good that essentially matters, then consciousness is not in earnest with morality at all. For in this highest good, Nature does not have a different law from that of morality. Hence moral action itself is ruled out, for action takes place only on the assumption of a negative which is to be set aside by the action. But if Nature is in conformity with the moral law, the latter would in fact be violated by the setting-aside of what is in existence. In the assumption that the highest good is what essentially matters, there is admitted a situation in which moral action is superfluous, and does not take place at all. The postulate of the harmony of morality and reality—a harmony posited by the Notion of moral action, which implies bringing the two into agreement—is expressed from this point of view, too, in the form: 'Because moral action is the absolute purpose, the absolute purpose is, that there should be no such thing as moral action.'

621. When we put together these moments, which conscious-

ness has traversed in its ideas of morality, it is clear that each one in turn is superseded in its opposite. Consciousness starts from the idea that, *for it*, morality and reality do not harmonize; but it is not in earnest about this, for in the deed the presence of this harmony becomes *explicit for it*. But it is not in earnest even about this deed, since the deed is something individual; for it has such a high purpose, the *highest good*. But this again is only a dissemblance of the facts, for such dissemblance would do away with all action and all morality. In other words, consciousness is not, strictly speaking, in earnest with *moral* action: what it really holds to be most desirable, to be the Absolute, is that the highest good be accomplished, and that moral action be superfluous.

622. From this result consciousness must go on still further in its contradictory movement, and of necessity again dissemble this *suppression* of moral action. Morality is the 'in-itself', the merely *implicit* element; if it is to be *actual*, the final purpose of the world cannot be fulfilled; rather the moral consciousness must exist on its own account and find itself confronted by a Nature *opposed* to it. But it must be perfected in its own self. This leads to the second postulate of the harmony of itself and the Nature which is immediately an element in it, i.e. the sense-nature. Moral self-consciousness asserts that its purpose is pure, is independent of inclinations and impulses, which implies that it has eliminated within itself sensuous purposes. But this alleged elimination of the element of sense it dissembles again. It acts, brings its purpose into actual existence, and the self-conscious sense-nature which is supposed to be eliminated is precisely this middle term or mediating element between pure consciousness and actual existence—it is the instrument or organ of the former for its realization, and what is called impulse, inclination. Moral self-consciousness is not, therefore, in earnest with the elimination of inclinations and impulses, for it is just these that are the *self-realizing self-consciousness*. But also they ought not to be *suppressed*, but only to be *in conformity with* Reason. And they *are* in conformity with Reason, for moral *action* is nothing else but consciousness realizing itself, thus giving itself the shape of an *impulse*, i.e. it is immediately the *present* harmony of impulse and morality. But impulse is not in fact merely this empty shape which could have within it a spring

of action other than the one it is, and be impelled by it. For sense-nature is one which contains within itself its own laws and springs of action; consequently, morality cannot therefore be in earnest about being itself the mainspring of impulses, the angle of inclination for inclinations. For since these have their own fixed quality and peculiar content, the consciousness to which *they* were to conform would be rather in conformity with *them*—a conformity with which moral self-consciousness refuses to comply. The harmony of the two is thus merely *implicit*, merely *postulated*.

In moral action the actually present harmony of morality and the sense-nature was just now asserted, but *now* is 'displaced'; the harmony is beyond consciousness in a nebulous remoteness where nothing can any more be accurately distinguished or comprehended; for our attempt just now to comprehend this unity failed. In this [merely] implicit harmony, however, consciousness surrenders itself altogether. This implicit harmony is its moral perfection, where the struggle of morality and the sense-nature has ceased, and the latter is in conformity with morality in a way that is beyond our comprehension. For that reason this perfection is again only a dissemblance, a falsification of the situation, since as a matter of fact it would be rather *morality* itself that was given up in that perfection, because it is only consciousness of absolute purpose as *pure* purpose, one therefore *opposed* to all other purposes. Morality is both the *activity* of this pure purpose, and also the consciousness of rising above sense-nature, of being mixed up with sense-nature and struggling against it. That consciousness is not in earnest about the perfection of morality is indicated by the fact that consciousness itself shifts it away into *infinity*, i.e. asserts that the perfection is never perfected.

623. What consciousness really holds to be the truth of the matter is only this intermediate state of imperfection, a state nevertheless which at least is supposed to be a *progress towards* perfection. But it cannot even be that; for to advance in morality would really be to move towards its disappearance. That is to say, the goal would be the nothingness or the abolition, mentioned above, of morality and consciousness itself; but to approach ever nearer to nothingness means to diminish. Besides, 'advancing' as such, like 'diminishing', would assume

quantitative differences in morality; but there can be no question of these in it. In morality, as in consciousness, for which the moral purpose is *pure* duty, there cannot be any thought at all of difference, least of all of the superficial one of quantity; there is only one virtue, only one pure duty, only one morality.

624. Since, then, it is not moral perfection that is taken seriously, but rather the intermediate state, i.e. as just argued, nonmorality, we thus return, from another aspect, to the content of the first postulate: viz. we cannot understand how happiness is to be demanded for this moral consciousness on the ground of its *worthiness*. It is aware of its imperfection and cannot, therefore, in point of fact demand happiness as a desert, as something of which it is worthy. It can only ask for happiness to be granted as a free act of grace, i.e. it can only ask for happiness *as such*, as something existing in and for itself, and can expect it, not on the absolute ground mentioned above, but as coming to it by chance and caprice. Here, then, non-morality declares just what it is—that it is concerned not about morality, but solely about happiness as such without reference to morality.

625. By this second aspect of the moral view of the world, the other assertion of the first aspect, in which the disharmony of morality and happiness is assumed, is also nullified. It is claimed that experience shows that in this present world the moral individual often fares badly, while the immoral individual often flourishes. But the intermediate state of an imperfect morality, which has shown itself to be the essential one, clearly shows that this observation, this supposed experience, is merely a dissemblance of the true state of the case. For since morality is imperfect, i.e. morality in fact is *not*, what can there be in the experience that morality fares badly? Since, at the same time, it has turned out that it is happiness simply as such that is involved, it is evident that in making the judgement that the immoral individual flourishes, it was not intended to imply that an injustice occurred here. The designation of an individual as immoral *necessarily* falls away when morality in general is imperfect, and has therefore only an arbitrary basis. Therefore, the sense and content of the judgement of experience is solely this, that happiness simply as such should not have been the lot of some individuals, i.e. the judgement is an expression of *envy* which covers itself with the cloak of morality. The reason,

however, why so-called good luck should fall to the lot of others, is good friendship, which *grants* and *wishes* them, and itself, too, this lucky chance.

626. Morality, then, in the moral consciousness is imperfect; this is now what is put forward. But it is the essence of morality to be only the *perfectly pure*; imperfect morality is therefore impure, or is immorality. Morality itself thus exists in another being than the actual consciousness. This other being is a *holy moral lawgiver*. The *imperfect* morality in consciousness, which is the reason for making these postulates, means, *in the first instance*, that morality, when it is posited in consciousness as *actual*, stands in relation to an 'other', to an existence, and therefore itself receives within it otherness or difference, giving rise to a whole variety of moral laws. The moral self-consciousness at the same time, however, holds these *many* duties to be unessential; for it is concerned only with the one pure duty, and the *many* have no truth *for it* in so far as they are *specific* duties. They can therefore have their truth only in another being and are made sacred—which they are *not* for the moral consciousness— by a holy lawgiver. But this again is only a dissemblance of the real position. For the moral self-consciousness is its own Absolute, and duty is absolutely only what *it knows* as duty. But duty it knows only as pure duty; what is not sacred for it is not sacred in itself, and what is not in itself sacred, cannot be made sacred by the holy being. The moral consciousness, too, is not really in earnest about letting something be made sacred *by another consciousness* than itself; for that alone it holds to be sacred which it has itself made sacred, and is sacred *in it*. It is, therefore, just as little in earnest about the holiness of this other being, for in this something was supposed to obtain an essentiality which for the moral consciousness, i.e. in itself, it did not possess.

627. If the holy being was postulated in order that in it duty might have its validity, not as pure duty, but as a multiplicity of *specific* duties, then this again must be dissembled, and the other being alone must be holy in so far as only *pure* duty has validity in it. Pure duty has also in point of fact validity only in another being, not in the moral consciousness. Although in the latter it seems that pure morality alone has validity, the position must be put in another way, for it is at the same time a natural consciousness. In it, morality is affected and con-

ditioned by the sense-nature, and is therefore not free and independent, but contingent on free *will*; in it, however, as pure *will*, morality is contingent on knowledge. Morality, therefore, in and for itself is in another being.

628. This other being, then, is here the purely perfect morality, for in it morality does not stand in a relation to Nature and sense. But the *reality* of pure duty is its *realization* in Nature and sense. The moral consciousness attributes its imperfection to the fact that in it morality has a *positive* relation to Nature and sense, because it holds that an essential moment in morality is that it should have a *negative*, and *only* a negative, relation to them. The pure moral being, on the other hand, because it is above the *struggle* with Nature and sense, does not stand in a *negative* relation to them. Therefore, in fact, there remains for it only the *positive* relation to them, i.e. just what a moment ago was, *qua* imperfect, held to be immoral. But a pure morality that was completely separated from reality, and so likewise was without any positive relation to it, would be an unconscious, unreal abstraction in which the concept of morality, which involves thinking of pure duty, willing, and doing it, would be done away with. Such a purely moral being is therefore again a dissemblance of the facts, and has to be given up.

629. In this purely moral being, however, the moments of the contradiction, in which this synthetic presentation of them flounders about, are brought closer together; and consciousness lets these opposites follow one after the other, one always being replaced by the other, without bringing its *thoughts* together, so that in the end it is forced to give up its moral view of the world and seek refuge within itself.

630. It knows its morality to be imperfect because it is affected by the sense-nature and Nature opposed to it, which in part adulterate morality itself as such, and in part give rise to a host of duties by which in concrete cases of real action it is embarrassed. For each case is the concrescence of many moral relations, just as an object of perception in general is a thing of many properties; and since the *specific* duty is a purpose, it has a content, and its *content* is part of the purpose, and morality is not pure. This latter therefore has its *reality* in another being. This reality, however, means nothing else than that the being of morality here is both *intrinsic* and *explicit*: explicit, i.e. it is

the morality of a *conscious* being, and intrinsic, i.e. it has an *existence* and a *reality*. In that first, imperfect consciousness morality is not realized. There, it is the 'in-itself', or merely implicit being in the sense of a mere 'thought-thing'; for it is associated with Nature and sense, with the *reality* of being and consciousness which constitutes its content, and Nature and sense are morally nothing. In the second consciousness morality exists as *perfect* and not as an unrealized 'thought-thing'. But this perfection consists precisely in morality having *reality* in a *consciousness*, as well as a *free* reality, an existence in general, in being something not empty but full-filled, full of content; i.e. the perfection of morality is placed in the fact that what has just been characterized as morally nothing is present in it and intrinsic to it. On one hand it is supposed to have validity simply and solely as the unreal 'thought-thing' of pure abstraction, and then again equally to have no validity in that mode; its truth is supposed to consist in its being opposed to reality, and to be entirely free and empty of it, and then again, to consist in its being reality.

631. The syncretism of these contradictions which is set forth at length in the moral view of the world, collapses internally, since the distinction on which it rests, the distinction between what *must* be thought and postulated, and yet is at the same time *not* essential, becomes a distinction which no longer exists even in words. What finally is posited as diverse, both as a nothing and also as a reality, is one and the very same thing, viz. existence and reality; and what is supposed to be absolute, only as the *beyond* of real being and consciousness, and yet equally to be absolute only in them, and so as a beyond to be nothing— this Absolute is pure duty, and the knowledge of duty as essence. The consciousness which makes this distinction that is no distinction, which asserts that actual existence has no validity, and at the same time that it is real, that pure morality is both truly essential, and also devoid of essence—such a consciousness expresses in one and the same breath the thoughts which it previously separated, and itself proclaims that it is not in earnest about this determination and separation of the moments of *self* and *in-itself* or intrinsic being; but that on the contrary, what it asserts as having absolute *being* outside of consciousness, it really keeps enclosed within the self of self-consciousness, and

that what it asserts to have absolute being in *thought*, or to be absolutely *intrinsic* being, it for that very reason takes to be something that has no truth. Consciousness comes to see that the placing-apart of these moments is a '*dis*placing' of them, a dissemblance, and that it would be *hypocrisy* if, nevertheless, it were to keep them separate. But as moral pure self-consciousness, it flees from this disparity between the way it thinks [of these moments] and its own essential nature, flees from this untruth which asserts that to be true which it holds to be untrue, flees from this with abhorrence back into itself. It is a pure conscience which rejects with scorn such a moral idea of the world; it is in its own self the simple Spirit that, certain of itself, acts conscientiously regardless of such ideas, and in this immediacy possesses its truth. While, however, this world of dissemblance is nothing else but the development of moral self-consciousness in its moments, and hence is its *reality*, its essential nature, by retreating into itself, will not become anything different. Its retreat into itself means rather that consciousness has realized that its truth is a pretended truth. It would always have to be giving out this pretended truth as *its* truth, for it would have to express and present itself as an objective idea, but would be aware that all this is merely a dissemblance. It would therefore be, in fact, hypocrisy, and the scornful rejection of that dissemblance would be itself the first expression of hypocrisy.

c. *Conscience. The 'beautiful soul', evil and its forgiveness*

632. The antinomy of the moral view of the world, viz. that there is a moral consciousness, and that there is none, or that the validation of duty lies beyond consciousness, and conversely, takes place *in* it—these contradications were gathered up in the idea in which the *non*-moral consciousness has moral validity, its contingent knowing and willing are assumed to have full weight, and happiness is granted to it as an act of grace. Moral self-consciousness did not accept responsibility for this self-contradictory idea, but shifted it on to a being other than itself. But this placing outside of itself what it must think of as necessary is as much a contradiction as regards form, as the other was as regards content. Because, however, what appear as contradictory propositions, which the moral consciousness makes clumsy efforts first to separate and then to

reconcile, are intrinsically the same, since pure duty, viz. as *pure knowing*, is nothing else than the *self* of consciousness, and the self of consciousness is *being* and *actuality*: and similarly, because what is supposed to lie beyond *actual* consciousness is nothing else than pure thought, and thus is, in fact, the self—because this is so, self-consciousness, *for us* or *in itself*, retreats into itself, and is aware that that being is its own self, in which what is actual is at the same time pure knowing and pure duty. It is itself in its contingency completely valid in its own sight, and knows its immediate individuality to be pure knowing and doing, to be the true reality and harmony.

633. This self of conscience, Spirit that is directly aware of itself as absolute truth and being, is the *third* self. We have reached it as the outcome of the third world of Spirit and we shall briefly compare it with the two preceding selves. The totality or actuality which shows itself to be the truth of the ethical world is the self of the [legal] person; its existence consists in its being acknowledged by others. Just as this person is the self that is devoid of substance, so is its existence an abstract reality too. The person *counts*, and that simply as a person: the self is the point immediately at rest in the element of its being. That point is not separated off from its universality, and therefore the two are not actively related to one another: the universal is in it without any distinction, and is neither the content of the self, nor is the self filled by itself. The second self is the world of culture which has attained its truth, or it is Spirit that has recovered itself from its dividedness—absolute freedom. In this self, that first, immediate unity of individuality and universality is sundered; the universal which all the same remains a purely spiritual entity, the state of being acknowledged or a universal willing and knowing, is *object* and content of the self and its universal reality. But it does not have the form of an existence free from the self; in this self, therefore, it obtains no filling and no positive content, no world. Moral self-consciousness does indeed let its universality go free so that it becomes a nature of its own, and equally it holds fast to it within itself as a superseded moment. It is, however, merely an insincere play of alternating these two determinations. It is as conscience that it first has, in its *self-certainty*, a *content* for the previously empty duty, as also for the right and the universal will

that were empty of content. And because this self-assurance is at the same time an *immediacy*, conscience *exists*.

634. Moral self-consciousness having attained its truth, it therefore abandons, or rather supersedes, the internal division which gave rise to the dissemblance, the division between the in-itself and the self, between pure duty *qua* pure purpose, and reality *qua* a Nature and sense opposed to pure purpose. It is, when thus returned into itself, *concrete* moral Spirit which, in the consciousness of pure duty, does not give itself an empty criterion to be used against actual consciousness; on the contrary, pure duty, as also the Nature opposed to it, are superseded moments. Spirit is, in an immediate unity, a *self-actualizing* being, and the action is immediately something *concretely* moral.

635. Suppose a case of moral action; it is an objective reality for the knowing consciousness. This, *qua* conscience, knows it in an immediate, concrete manner; and at the same time it *is* only as conscience knows it. Knowing is contingent in so far as it is something other than the object; but Spirit that is self-certain is no longer such a contingent knower, and a producer of thoughts divorced from reality. On the contrary, since the separation of the in-itself and the self has been done away with, a case of moral action is, in the sense-*certainty* of knowing, directly as it is *in itself*, and it is *in itself* only in the way that it is in this [kind of] knowing. Action *qua* actualization is thus the pure form of will—the simple conversion of a reality that merely *is* into a reality that results from *action*, the conversion of the bare mode of *objective* knowing [i.e. knowing an object] into one of knowing *reality* as something produced by consciousness. Just as sense-certainty is immediately taken up, or rather converted, into the in-itself of Spirit, so this conversion, too, is simple and unmediated, a transition effected by the pure Notion without alteration of the content, the content being determined by the interest of the consciousness knowing it. Further, conscience does not split up the circumstances of the case into a variety of duties. It does not behave as a *positive universal medium*, wherein the many duties would acquire, each for itself, a fixed substantial nature. If it did, then *either* no action could take place at all, because each concrete case involves an antithesis in general, and, in a case of morality, a clash of

duties—and therefore by the very nature of action one side
would be injured, one duty violated: *or else*, if action did take
place, there would be an actual violation of one of the conflicting duties. Conscience is rather the negative One, or absolute
self, which does away with these various moral substances; it
is simple action in accordance with duty, which fulfills not this
or that duty, but knows and does what is concretely right. It
is, therefore, first of all moral *action qua* action into which the
previous moral consciousness that did not act has passed. The
concrete shape of the deed may be analysed by the consciousness looking for distinctions into various properties, i.e. here,
into various moral relations; and each of these may either be
asserted as absolutely valid (as it must be if it is supposed to
be duty), or else compared and tested. In the simple moral
action of conscience, duties are lumped together in such a way
that all these single entities are straightway *demolished*, and the
sifting of them in the steadfast certainty of conscience to ascertain what our duty is, simply does not take place.

636. Just as little is there present in conscience that fluctuating uncertainty of consciousness which now places so-called
pure morality outside of itself into another, holy being and takes
itself to be unholy, but then again places so-called pure morality
within itself, and the connection of the sensuous with the moral
in that other being.

637. It renounces all these attitudes and dissemblances, connected with the moral view of the world, when it renounces
that consciousness which thinks of duty and reality as contradictory. According to this latter view, I act morally when I am
conscious of performing only pure duty and nothing else but that;
this means, in fact, when I do *not* act. But when I really act,
I am conscious of an 'other', of a reality which is already in
existence, and of a reality I wish to produce; I have a *specific*
purpose and fulfil a *specific* duty in which there is something
else than the pure duty which alone should be intended. Conscience, on the other hand, is awareness of the fact that, when
the moral consciousness declares *pure duty* to be the essence of
its action, this pure purpose is a dissemblance of the truth of
the matter; for the fact is that pure duty consists in the empty
abstraction of pure thought, and has its reality and its content
only in a specific reality, in a reality which is the reality of con-

sciousness itself, and consciousness not as a mere 'thought-thing' but as an individual. As for conscience itself, this knows that it has its truth in the *immediate certainty* of itself. This *immediate* concrete self-certainty is the essence [of the action]; looking at this certainty from the point of view of the antithesis of consciousness, the content of the moral action is the doer's own immediate *individuality*; and the *form* of that content is just this self as a pure movement, viz. as [the individual's] knowing or his *own conviction*.

638. Looking more closely at the unity of the moral consciousness and at the significance of its moments, we see that it regards itself as the *in-itself* or *essence*; but as conscience, it apprehends its *being-for-self* or its self. The contradiction of the moral consciousness *resolves itself*, i.e. the difference which lies at its base proves to be none, and it runs away into pure negativity; but this precisely is the self, a simple *self* which is both a *pure* knowing and a knowledge of itself as this *individual* consciousness. Consequently, this self constitutes the content of what was previously the empty essence; for it is *actual*, a self which no longer has the significance of being a nature alien to the essence and, with laws of its own, independent of it. As the negative, it is the *difference* within pure essence, a content, and one, too, which is valid in and for itself.

639. Further, this self, *qua* a pure self-identical knowing, is the *absolute universal*, so that just this knowing, as *its own* knowing, as conviction, is *duty*. Duty is no longer the universal that stands over against the self; on the contrary, it is known to have no validity when thus separated. It is now the law that exists for the sake of the self, not the self that exists for the sake of the law. Law and duty, however, have for that reason the significance not only of *being-for-self* but also of *intrinsic being*; for this knowing, because it is self-identical, is precisely the in-itself. In consciousness, too, this in-itself separates itself from that immediate unity with being-for-self; as thus standing over against the latter it is *being*, a *being-for-another*. Duty itself, as duty forsaken by the self, is now known to be only a *moment*; from signifying the *absolute essence*, it has fallen to the level of mere *being*, which is not self, is not *for itself*, and is therefore a *being-for-another*. But the *being-for-another* remains an essential moment just because the self, *qua* consciousness, constitutes the antithesis

of being-for-self and being-for-another; and now duty is present in consciousness as something directly *actual*, is no longer merely abstract pure consciousness.

640. This *being-for-another* is, therefore, the substance which remains *in itself* or unexplicated, which is distinct from the self. Conscience has not given up pure duty or the *abstract in-itself*; duty is the essential moment of relating itself, *qua universality*, to another. Conscience is the common element of the two self-consciousnesses, and this element is the substance in which the deed has an *enduring reality*, the moment of being *recognized* and *acknowledged* by others. The moral consciousness does not possess this moment of recognition by others, of *pure consciousness* which has a *real existence*; and consequently does not act, or actualize anything at all. Its *in-itself* is for it either abstract, *unreal* essence, or being as a *reality* which is not spiritual. The *existent reality* of conscience, however, is one which is a *self*, an existence which is conscious of itself, the spiritual element of being recognized and acknowledged. The action is thus only the translation of its *individual* content into the *objective* element, in which it is universal and recognized, and it is just the fact that it is recognized that makes the deed a reality. The deed is recognized and thereby made real because the existent reality is directly linked with conviction or knowledge; or, in other words, knowing one's purpose is directly the element of existence, is universal recognition. For the *essence* of the action, duty, consists in conscience's *conviction* about it; it is just this conviction that is the *in-itself*; it is the *implicitly universal* self-*consciousness*, or the state of *being recognized*, and hence a reality. What is done with the conviction of duty is, therefore, at once something that has standing and a real existence. There is, then, no more talk of good intentions coming to nothing, or of the good man faring badly; on the contrary, the duty that is known to be such is fulfilled and becomes a reality, just because what is essentially a duty is the universal for all self-consciousnesses, is that which is recognized and acknowledged and thus positively *is*. But, taken separately and alone, without the content of self, duty is a *being-for-another*, something transparent which has merely the significance of an essentiality in general, lacking all content.

641. If we look back on the sphere where spiritual reality first made its appearance, we find that the Notion involved was

that the utterance of individuality is that which is both in and for itself. But the shape which immediately expressed this Notion was the *honest consciousness* which busied itself with the *abstract thing itself* [*Sache selbst*]. This 'thing itself' was there a *predicate*; but it is in conscience that it is for the first time a *subject* which has made explicit all the moments of consciousness within it, and for which all these moments, substantiality in general, external existence, and the essential nature of thought, are contained in this certainty of itself. The 'thing itself' has substantiality in general in the ethical sphere, external existence in culture, the self-knowing essentiality of thought in morality; and in conscience it is the *subject* that knows these moments within it. While the 'honest consciousness' always seizes merely the empty thing itself, conscience, on the other hand, wins the thing in its fullness, a fullness given to it by conscience itself. Conscience is this power because it knows the moments of consciousness as *moments*, dominating them as their negative essence.

642. When conscience is considered in relation to the single determinations of the antithesis manifest in action and its awareness of the nature of those determinations, its relation to the *actual* case in which it has to act is, in the first instance, that of *knower*. In so far as this knowing has in it the moment of *universality*, conscientious action requires that the actual case before it should be viewed unrestrictedly in all its bearings, and therefore that all the circumstances of the case should be accurately known and taken into consideration. But this knowing, since it *knows* the universality as a *moment*, is at the same time aware that it does not know all the circumstances, or, in other words, that it does not act conscientiously. The genuinely universal and pure relation of knowing would be a relation to something not containing an *antithesis*, a relation to itself; but *action*, in virtue of the antithesis it essentially contains, is related to a negative of consciousness, to a reality possessing *intrinsic* being. Contrasted with the simplicity of pure consciousness, with the absolute *other* or *implicit* manifoldness, this reality is a plurality of circumstances which breaks up and spreads out endlessly in all directions, backwards into their conditions, sideways into their connections, forwards in their consequences. The conscientious mind is aware of this nature of the thing and of its

relation to it, and knows that, in the case in which it acts, it does not possess that full acquaintance with *all* the attendant circumstances which is required, and that its pretence of conscientiously weighing all the circumstances is vain. However, this acquaintance with, and weighing of, all the circumstances are not altogether lacking; but they exist only as a *moment*, as something which is only for *others*; and this *incomplete* knowledge is held by the conscientious mind to be sufficient and complete, because it is its *own* knowledge.

643. Similarly with the universality of the *essence*, that is, with the determination of the content by pure consciousness. Conscience, when it proceeds to action, enters into relation with the many aspects of the case. The case breaks up into its various separate parts and so, too, does the relation of pure consciousness to it, with the result that the manifold nature of the case becomes a multiplicity of duties. Conscience knows that it has to choose between them, and to make a decision; for none of them, in its specific character or in its content, is absolute; only pure duty is that. But this abstraction [of pure duty] has attained in its reality the significance of the self-conscious 'I'. The self-certain Spirit rests, *qua* conscience, within itself, and its *real* universality or its duty lies in its pure *conviction* of duty. This *pure* conviction is, as such, as empty as pure *duty*, is pure in the sense that there is nothing in it, no specific content that is a duty. But action is called for, something must be *determined* by the individual, and the self-certain Spirit in which the in-itself has attained the significance of the self-conscious 'I', knows that it has this determination and content in the immediate *certainty* of itself. This, as a determination and content, is the *natural* consciousness, i.e. impulses and inclinations. Conscience does not recognize the absoluteness of any content, for it is the absolute negativity of everything determinate. It determines from *its own self*; but the sphere of the self into which falls the determinateness as such is the so-called sense-nature; to have a content taken from the immediate certainty of itself means that it has nothing to draw on but sense-nature. Everything that in previous forms of experience presented itself as good or bad, as law and right, is something *other* than the immediate certainty of self; it is a *universal* which is now a being-for-another. Or, looked at from another aspect, it is an object which, while

mediating consciousness with itself, comes between consciousness and its own truth, so that instead of the object being the immediacy of consciousness, it rather cuts consciousness off from itself. For conscience, however, self-certainty is the pure, immediate truth; and this truth is thus its immediate certainty of self, conceived as *content*, i.e. this truth is in general the caprice of the individual, and the contingency of his unconscious natural being [his sense-nature].

644. This content at the same time counts as a moral *essentiality* or as *duty*. For pure duty, as was found when testing laws, is utterly indifferent to any content and tolerates any content. Here it has, at the same time, the essential form of *being-for-self*, and this form of individual conviction is nothing else but consciousness of the emptiness of pure duty and of the fact that pure duty is only a moment, that its substantiality is a predicate which has its subject in the individual, whose caprice gives it its content and can associate every content with this form and attach its conscientiousness to the content. An individual increases his property in a certain way; it is everyone's duty to provide for the support of himself and his family, and no less to have regard to the *possibility* of being useful to his fellow men, and of doing good to those in need. The individual is aware that this is a duty, for this content is directly contained in his certainty of himself; furthermore, he perceives that he fulfils this duty in this particular case. Others, perhaps, hold this specific way of behaving to be humbug; *they* hold to other aspects of the concrete case, *he*, however, holds firmly to this aspect, because he is conscious of the increase of property as a pure duty. Thus, what others call violence and wrongdoing, is the fulfilment of the individual's duty to maintain his independence in face of others; what they call cowardice, is the duty of supporting life and the possibility of being useful to others; but what they call courage violates both duties. But cowardice cannot be so inept as not to know that the preservation of life and the possibility of being useful to others are duties—so inept as not to be *convinced* of the moral obligatoriness of its action, and not to know that this obligatoriness consists in *knowing* it to be such. Otherwise it would be guilty of ineptitude, of being immoral. Since morality lies in the consciousness of having fulfilled one's duty, this will not be lacking when the action is

called cowardice any more than when it is called courage. The abstraction called duty, being capable of any content, is also capable of cowardice. The doer, then, knows what he does to be a duty, and since he knows this, and the conviction of duty is the very essence of moral obligation, he is thus recognized and acknowledged by others. The action is thereby validated and has an actual existence.

645. It is of no use to object to this freedom, which places any and every kind of content in the universal passive medium of 'duty' and 'knowing', by maintaning that another content ought to have been placed in it; for whatever content it be, it contains the *blemish of determinateness* from which pure knowing is free, determinateness which pure knowing can disdainfully reject, or equally can accept. Every content, because it is determinate, stands on the same level as any other, even if it does seem to be characterized by the elimination in it of the element of particularity. It may seem that, since, in the actual case, duty in general is sundered into an antithesis and thereby into the antithesis of individuality and universality, the duty whose content is the universal itself directly contains the nature of pure duty, and form and content are thus completely in accord. It might seem, then, that action for the general good is to be preferred to action for the good of the individual; but this universal duty is simply what *already exists* as absolute substance, as law and right, and is valid on its own account independently of the individual's knowledge and conviction, not to mention his own immediate interest. It is, therefore, precisely against the *form* of that duty that morality in general is directed. But as regards its *content*, that too is a *determinate* content, in so far as the general good is *opposed* to the good of the individual. Consequently, its law is one from which conscience knows itself to be absolutely free, and it gives itself the authority to add to and take from, to neglect as well as fulfil it. Then, again, the above distinction between duty to the individual and duty to the universal is, in accordance with the nature of the antithesis as such, not something definitely fixed. The truth is rather that what the individual does for himself also contributes to the general good; the more he has made provision for himself, not only is there a greater *possibility* of his being of service to others, but his *actual* existence itself consists only in his being and living

in contact with others. His individual enjoyment essentially has the meaning of putting what is his own at the disposal of others and of helping them to obtain *their* enjoyment. Therefore, in the fulfilment of duty to individuals and so to oneself, the duty to the universal is also fulfilled. Any weighing and comparing of duties which might be made here would be tantamount to calculating the advantage accruing to the universal from an action. But firstly, the result would be that morality would be made dependent on the necessary *contingency* of *insight*, and secondly, it is precisely the essence of conscience to have no truck with this calculating and weighing of duties, and to make its *own* decision without reference to any such reasons.

646. In this way, then, conscience acts and preserves itself in the unity of its *essential* and *actual* being, in the unity of pure thought and individuality: it is the self-assured Spirit which has its truth within *itself*, in *its* knowledge, and therein as knowledge of duty. It maintains itself therein by the very fact that what is *positive* in the action—the content as well as the form of duty and the knowledge of it—belongs to the self, to the certainty of itself; but what seeks to *confront* the self with an *essential being of its own* is held to be something not true, something stripped of its self-subsistence and only a moment. Consequently, what counts is not simply knowing in general, but conscience's knowledge of the circumstances. It places in duty, as the universal in-itselfness, the content which it takes from its natural individuality; for the content is one that is present within itself. This content, in virtue of the universal medium in which it exists, becomes the *duty* which it carries out, and empty pure duty, just through this action, becomes established as something *not* self-subsistent, as only a moment; this content is the cancelled emptiness of pure duty, or its fulfilment. But even so, conscience is free from any content whatever; it absolves itself from any specific duty which is supposed to have the validity of law. In the strength of its own self-assurance it possesses the majesty of absolute autarky, to bind and to loose. This *self-determination* is therefore without more ado absolutely in conformity with duty. Duty is the knowing itself; this simple selfhood, however, is the in-itself; for the *in-itself* is pure self-identity, and this is in this consciousness.

647. This pure knowing is immediately a being-for-another;

for, as pure self-identity, it is *immediacy*, or being. But this being is at the same time the pure universal, the selfhood of all: in other words, the action is acknowledged and therefore actual. This being is the element whereby conscience stands directly in a relation of equality with every self-consciousness; and the meaning of this relation is not an impersonal law, but the self of conscience.

648. However, in that this right thing which conscience does is at the same time a *being-for-another*, it seems that a disparity attaches to conscience. The duty which it fulfils is a *specific* content; it is true that this content is the *self* of consciousness, and so consciousness's *knowledge* of itself, its *identity* with itself. But once fulfilled, set in the medium of *being*, this identity is no longer knowing, no longer this process of differentiation in which its differences are at the same time immediately superseded; on the contrary, in *being*, the difference is established as an *enduring* difference, and the action is a *specific* action, not identical with the element of everyone's self-consciousness, and therefore not necessarily acknowledged. Both sides, the conscience that acts and the universal consciousness that acknowledges this action as duty, are equally free from the specificity of this action. On account of this freedom, their relationship in the common medium of their connection is really a relation of complete disparity, as a result of which the consciousness which is explicitly aware of the action finds itself in a state of complete *uncertainty* about the Spirit which does the action and is certain of itself. The latter acts, it gives being to a specific content; others hold to this *being* as this Spirit's truth, and are therein certain of this Spirit; it has declared therein *what* it holds to be duty. But it is free from any *specific* duty; it is not present at that point where others imagine it actually to be; and this very medium of being, and duty as something possessing *intrinsic* being, count for it only as a moment. What, therefore, it places before them it also 'displaces' again, or rather has straightway 'displaced' or dissembled. For its *actual* being is for it not this duty and determinate character it has put forward, but the actuality which it has in the absolute certainty of itself.

649. Others, therefore, do not know whether this conscience is morally good or evil, or rather they not only cannot know, but they must also take it to be evil. For, just as *it* is free from

the *specificity* of duty, and from duty as possessing an *intrinsic* being, so likewise are they. What conscience places before them, they themselves know how to 'displace' or dissemble; it is something expressing only the self of another, not their own self: not only do they know themselves to be free from it, but they must dispose of it in their own consciousness, nullify it by judging and explaining it in order to preserve their own self.

650. But the action of conscience is not only this *determination* of being which is forsaken by the pure self. What is to be valid, and to be recognized as duty, is so only through the knowledge and conviction that it *is* duty, through the knowledge of oneself in the deed. If the deed ceases to have this self within it, it ceases to be that which alone is its essence. Its existence, forsaken by this consciousness, would be an ordinary reality, and the action would appear to us to be the fulfilling of one's pleasure and desire. What ought to *be there*, is here an essentiality solely by its *being known* to be the self-expression of an individuality; and it is this *being known* that is acknowledged by others, and which *as such* ought to have an *existence*.

651. The self enters into existence *as self*; the self-assured Spirit exists as such for others. Its *immediate* action is not that which has validity and is actual; what is acknowledged is not the *determinate* aspect of the action, not its *intrinsic* being, but solely the self-knowing *self* as such. The element of lasting being is the universal self-consciousness; what enters into this element cannot be the *effect* of the action: the effect cannot endure in it, and acquires no permanence; it is only self-consciousness that is acknowledged and that obtains an actual existence.

652. Here again, then, we see language as the existence of Spirit. Language is self-consciousness existing *for others*, self-consciousness which *as such* is immediately *present*, and as *this* self-consciousness is universal. It is the self that separates itself from itself, which as pure 'I' = 'I' becomes objective to itself, which in this objectivity equally preserves itself as *this* self, just as it coalesces directly with other selves and is *their* self-consciousness. It perceives itself just as it is perceived by others, and the perceiving is just *existence which has become a self*.

653. The content which language has here acquired is no longer the perverted, and perverting and distracted, self of the world of culture; on the contrary, it is the Spirit that has

returned into itself, is certain of itself, and certain in itself of its truth, or of its own recognition [of that truth], and which is acknowledged as knowing it. The language of the ethical Spirit is law and simple command, and complaint, which is more the shedding of a tear about necessity. Moral consciousness, on the other hand, is still *dumb*, shut up with itself within its inner life, for there the self does not as yet have an existence: existence and the *self* stand as yet only in an external relation to each other. Language, however, only emerges as the middle term, mediating between independent and acknowledged self-consciousnesses; and the *existent self* is immediately universal acknowledgement, an acknowledgement on the part of many, and in this manifoldness a simple acknowledgement. The content of the language of conscience is the *self that knows itself as essential being*. This alone is what it declares, and this declaration is the true actuality of the act, and the validating of the action. Consciousness declares its *conviction*; it is in this conviction alone that the action is a duty; also it is valid as duty solely through the conviction being *declared*. For universal self-consciousness is free from the *specific* action that merely *is*; what is valid for that self-consciousness is not the *action* as an *existence*, but the *conviction* that it is a duty; and this is made actual in language. To make the deed a reality does not mean here translating its content from the form of *purpose* or *being-for-self* into the form of an *abstract* reality: it means translating it from the form of immediate self-*certainty*, which knows its knowledge or being-for-self to be essential being, into the form of an *assurance* that consciousness is convinced of its duty and, as conscience, knows *in its own mind* what duty is. This assurance thus affirms that consciousness is convinced that its conviction is the essence of the matter.

654. Whether the assurance of acting from a conviction of duty is *true*, whether what is done is actually a *duty*—these questions or doubts have no meaning when addressed to conscience. To ask whether the assurance is true would presuppose that the inner intention is different from the one put forward, i.e. that what the individual self wills, can be separated from duty, from the will of the universal and pure consciousness; the latter would be put into words, but the former would be strictly the true motive of the action. But this distinction between the universal consciousness and the individual self is just what has been

superseded, and the supersession of it *is* conscience. The self's immediate knowing that is certain of itself is law and duty. Its intention, through being its own intention, is what is right; all that is required is that it should know this, and should state its conviction that its knowing and willing are right. The declaration of this assurance in itself rids the form of its particularity. It thereby acknowledges the *necessary universality of the self*. In calling itself *conscience*, it calls itself pure knowledge of itself and pure abstract willing, i.e. it calls itself a universal knowing and willing which recognizes and acknowledges others, is the same as them—for they are just this pure self-knowing and willing—and which for that reason is also recognized and acknowledged by *them*. In the will of the self that is certain of itself, in this knowledge that the self is essential being, lies the essence of what is right. Therefore, whoever says he acts in such and such a way from conscience, speaks the truth, for his conscience is the self that knows and wills. But it is essential that he should *say* so, for this self must be at the same time the *universal* self. It is not universal in the *content* of the act, for this, on account of its specificity, is intrinsically an indifferent affair: it is in the form of the act that the universality lies. It is this form which is to be established as actual: it is the *self* which as such is actual in language, which declares itself to be the truth, and just by so doing acknowledges all other selves and is acknowledged by them.

655. Conscience, then, in the majesty of its elevation above specific law and every content of duty, puts whatever content it pleases into its knowing and willing. It is the moral genius which knows the inner voice of what it immediately knows to be a divine voice; and since, in knowing this, it has an equally immediate knowledge of existence, it is the divine creative power which in its Notion possesses the spontaneity of life. Equally, it is in its own self divine worship, for its action is the contemplation of its own divinity.

656. This solitary divine worship is at the same time essentially the divine worship of a *community*, and the pure inner *knowing* and perceiving of itself advances to the moment of *consciousness*. The contemplation of itself is its *objective* existence and this objective element is the declaration of its knowing and willing as something *universal*. Through this declaration the self

acquires moral validity and the act becomes an effective deed. The actuality and lasting existence of what it does is universal self-consciousness; but the declaration of conscience affirms the certainty of itself to be pure self, and thereby to be a universal self. On account of this utterance in which the self is expressed and acknowledged as essential being, the validity of the act is acknowledged by others. The spirit and substance of their association are thus the mutual assurance of their conscientiousness, good intentions, the rejoicing over this mutual purity, and the refreshing of themselves in the glory of knowing and uttering, of cherishing and fostering, such an excellent state of affairs. In so far as this conscience still distinguishes its *abstract* consciousness from its *self-consciousness*, it has only a *hidden* life in God; it is true that God is *immediately* present in its mind and heart, in its self; but what is manifest, its actual consciousness and the mediating movement of that consciousness, is for it something other than that hidden inner life and the immediacy of God's presence. It is only in the completed form of conscience that the distinction between its abstract consciousness and its self-consciousness is eliminated. Conscience knows that the *abstract* consciousness is just *this self*, this being-for-itself that is certain of itself, knows that it is precisely in the *immediacy* of the *relation* of the self to the *in-itself*—which when posited outside the self is an abstract God and hidden from it—that the difference is eliminated. For that relation is a *mediating* one in which the related terms are not one and the same, but each is an other for the other, and only in a third term are they one. The *immediate* relation, however, means in fact nothing else but the unity of the terms. The consciousness that has risen above the thoughtlessness that still holds these differences—which are none—to be differences, knows the immediacy of the presence within it of the absolute Being as the unity of that Being and its own self: it thus knows itself as the living in-itself, and knows that this knowledge is religion, which as knowledge that has a perceived or outer existence is the utterance of the community concerning its own Spirit.

657. Here, then, we see self-consciousness withdrawn into its innermost being, for which all externality as such has vanished—withdrawn into the contemplation of the 'I' = 'I', in which this 'I' is the whole of essentiality and existence. It is

submerged in this Notion of itself, for it has been driven to the limit of its extremes, and, moreover, in such a way, that the moments distinguished whereby it is real, or is still *consciousness*, are not only *for us* these pure extremes; on the contrary, what it is *for itself*, and what is for it *intrinsic* and what is for it *existence*, have evaporated into abstractions which no longer have any stability, any substance, for this consciousness itself; and all that before was essential being for consciousness has reverted into these abstractions. Refined into this purity, consciousness exists in its poorest form, and the poverty which constitutes its sole possession is itself a vanishing. This absolute *certainty* into which substance has resolved itself is the absolute *untruth* which collapses internally; it is the absolute *self-consciousness* in which *consciousness* is submerged.

658. Looking at this submergence of consciousness within itself, we see that the *unexplicated substance* is, for consciousness, *knowledge* as *its* knowledge. As consciousness, it is divided into the antithesis of itself and its object which is, for it, essence; but it is just this object that is perfectly transparent, is its own *self*, and its consciousness is only this knowledge of itself. All life, all spiritual essentiality, has withdrawn into this self and has lost its difference from the *I* itself. The moments of consciousness are, therefore, these extreme abstractions, none of which endures but each of which loses itself in the other and produces it. It is the fluctuating attitude to itself of the Unhappy Consciousness; but here this fluctuation takes place explicitly for consciousness within itself, and is conscious of being the Notion of Reason, whereas the Unhappy Consciousness is only *implicitly* that Notion. The absolute certainty of itself thus finds itself, *qua* consciousness, changed immediately into a sound that dies away, into an objectification of its being-for-self; but this created world is its *speech*, which likewise it has immediately heard and only the echo of which returns to it. This return, therefore, does not mean that the self is in essence and actuality present in its speech; for essence is not for it an *it-self* or merely *implicit* being, but its very self. Just as little has consciousness an *outer existence*, for the objective aspect does not get as far as being a negative of the actual self, in the same way that this self does not attain to an actual existence. It lacks the power to externalize itself, the power to make itself into a Thing, and

to endure [mere] being. It lives in dread of besmirching the splendour of its inner being by action and an existence; and, in order to preserve the purity of its heart, it flees from contact with the actual world, and persists in its self-willed impotence to renounce its self which is reduced to the extreme of ultimate abstraction, and to give itself a substantial existence, or to transform its thought into being and put its trust in the absolute difference [between thought and being]. The hollow object which it has produced for itself now fills it, therefore, with a sense of emptiness. Its activity is a yearning which merely loses itself as consciousness becomes an object devoid of substance, and, rising above this loss, and falling back on itself, finds itself only as a lost soul. In this transparent purity of its moments, an unhappy, so-called 'beautiful soul', its light dies away within it, and it vanishes like a shapeless vapour that dissolves into thin air.

659. This silent fusion of the pithless essentialities of the evaporated life has, however, still to be taken in the other meaning of the *actuality* of conscience, and in the *manifestation* of its movement: conscience has to be considered as acting. The *objective* moment in this consciousness acquired above the determination of a universal consciousness. The knowledge that knows itself is, *qua this* particular self, distinct from other selves; the language in which all reciprocally acknowledge each other as acting conscientiously, this universal identity, falls apart into the non-identity of individual being-for-self: each consciousness is just as much simply reflected out of its universality into itself. As a result, the antithesis of individuality to other individuals, and to the universal, inevitably comes on the scene, and we have to consider this relationship and its movement. In other words, this universality and duty have the very opposite significance of the specific *individuality* that exempts itself from the universal, for which pure duty is only a universality that appears on the surface, and is turned outwards: duty is only a matter of words, and counts as a being-for-another. Conscience, which in the first instance is only *negatively* directed against duty as *this given specific* duty, knows itself to be free from it; but since it fills the empty duty with a *specific* content *from itself*, it is positively aware that it, as *this particular* self, makes the content. Its pure self, as an empty knowing, is something

devoid of content and determination. The content which it gives to that knowing is taken from its own self, as *this specific* self, is taken from itself as a natural individuality. And, in speaking of the conscientiousness of its action, it may well be aware of its pure self, but in the *purpose* of its action, a purpose with an actual content, it is aware of itself as this particular individual, and is conscious of the antithesis between what it is for itself and what it is for others, of the antithesis of universality or duty and its reflection out of universality into itself.

660. While in this way the antithesis, into which conscience enters when it *acts*, expresses itself in its inner being, the antithesis is at the same time a disparity on its outer side in the element of existence, the disparity of its particular individuality in relation to another individual. Its particularity consists in the fact that the two moments constituting its consciousness, the self and the in-itself, are held to be unequal in value within it, a disparity in which they are so determined that the certainty of itself is the essential being in face of the in-itself or the universal, which counts only as a moment. In contrast to this internal determination there thus stands the element of existence or universal consciousness, for which the essential being is rather universality, duty; while individuality, on the other hand, which in contrast to the universal is for itself, counts only as a superseded moment. For the consciousness which holds firmly to duty, the first consciousness counts as *evil*, because of the disparity between its *inner being* and the universal; and since, at the same time, this first consciousness declares its action to be in conformity with itself, to be duty and conscientiousness, it is held by the universal consciousness to be *hypocrisy*.

661. The *movement* of this antithesis is in the first instance the formal production of an identity of what the evil consciousness is in its own self and what it declares itself to be; it must be made apparent that it *is* evil, and thus its existence made to correspond to its essence; the hypocrisy must be unmasked. This return of the disparity present in hypocrisy into a correspondence is not already an accomplished fact because hypocrisy, as is commonly said, demonstrates its respect for duty and virtue just by making a show of them, and using them as a mask to hide itself from its own consciousness, no less than from others; as if in this acknowledgement of the antithesis within

itself, identity and correspondence were implied. Only, it is at the same time just as much reflected out of this spoken acknowledgement and into itself; and the fact that it uses what is an essence as a *being-for-another* implies rather its own contempt for that essence, and the exposure to everyone of its own lack of any substantial being. For what lets itself be used as an external instrument shows itself to be a thing which possesses no importance of its own.

662. Also, this identity is not brought about either by the one-sided persistence of the evil consciousness in its own attitude, or by the judgement of the universal consciousness. If the former denies itself in face of the consciousness of duty, and declares that what this asserts to be wickedness, to be absolutely non-identical with the universal, is an action in accordance with inner law and conscience, then in this one-sided assurance of an identity there still remains its non-identity with the other, since this other does not believe it or acknowledge it. In other words, since the one-sided persistence in one extreme cancels itself out, evil would, it is true, thereby confess to being evil, but in so doing it would *directly* abolish itself and cease to be hypocrisy, and would not, as such, unmask itself. It admits, in fact, to being evil by asserting that it acts, in opposition to the acknowledged universal, according to its *own* inner law and conscience. For if this law and conscience were not the law of its single individuality and caprice, it would not be something inner or peculiar to it, but what is universally acknowledged. Therefore, when anyone says that he is acting according to his *own* law and conscience against others, he is saying, in fact, that he is wronging them. But *actual* conscience is not this persistence in a knowing and willing that opposes itself to the universal; on the contrary, the universal is the element of its existence, and its language declares its action to be an *acknowledged* duty.

663. Just as little is the persistence of the universal consciousness in its judgement an unmasking and abolition of hypocrisy. In denouncing hypocrisy as base, vile, and so on, it is appealing in such judgement to its *own* law, just as the evil consciousness appeals to *its* law. For the former comes forward in opposition to the latter and thereby as a *particular* law. It has, therefore, no superiority over the other law, rather it legitimizes it. And this zeal does the very opposite of what it means to do; for it

shows that what it calls true or genuine duty and which ought to be *universally* acknowledged, is something *not* acknowledged; in so doing it concedes to the other an equal right to be *for itself.*

664. This judgement has, however, at the same time another aspect from which it becomes the way to a resolution of the antithesis confronting it. The consciousness of the *universal*, in its relation to the first [evil] consciousness, does not behave as one that is *actual* and *acts*—for the latter is rather the actual consciousness—but in its antithesis to it, is a consciousness that is not entangled in the antithesis of individuality and universality, which occurs when action is entered upon. It remains in the universality of *thought*, behaves as a consciousness that *apprehends*, and its first action is merely one of judgement. Now, through this judgement, it places itself, as we have just remarked, *alongside* the first consciousness, and the latter, *through this likeness*, comes to see its own self in this other consciousness. For the consciousness of duty maintains an attitude of *passive* apprehension; but it is thereby in contradiction with itself as the absolute will of duty, as a consciousness whose determining comes solely from itself. It does well to preserve itself in its purity, for it *does not act*; it is the hypocrisy which wants its judging to be taken for an *actual* deed, and instead of proving its rectitude by actions, does so by uttering fine sentiments. Its nature, then, is altogether the same as that which is reproached with making duty a mere matter of words. In both alike, the side of reality is distinct from the words uttered: in the one, through the selfish purpose of the action, in the other, through the failure to act at all, although the necessity to act is involved in the very talk of duty, for duty without deeds is utterly meaningless.

665. Judging, however, is also to be looked at as a positive act of thought and has a positive content. Through this aspect, the contradiction present in the apprehending consciousness, and its identity with the first consciousness, become still more complete. The consciousness that acts declares its specific action to be a duty, and the consciousness that judges it cannot deny this; for duty itself is the form which lacks all content but is capable of any. In other words, the concrete action which in its many-sidedness is in its own self diverse, contains the universal aspect—that which is taken as duty—just as much as the

particular aspect which constitutes the share and interest of the individual in the action. Now, the judging consciousness does not stop short at the former aspect of duty, at the doer's knowledge of it, that this is his duty, and at the fact that the doer knows it to be his duty, the condition and status of his reality. On the contrary, it holds to the other aspect, looks at what the action is in itself, and explains it as resulting from an *intention* different from the action itself, and from selfish *motives*. Just as every action is capable of being looked at from the point of view of conformity to duty, so too can it be considered from the point of view of the particularity [of the doer]; for, *qua* action, it is the actuality of the individual. This judging of the action thus takes it out of its outer existence and reflects it into its inner aspect, or into the form of its own particularity. If the action is accompanied by fame, then it knows this inner aspect to be a *desire* for fame. If it is altogether in keeping with the station of the individual, without going beyond this station, and of such a nature that the individuality does not possess its station as a character externally attached to it, but through its own self gives filling to this universality, thereby showing itself capable of a higher station, then the inner aspect of the action is judged to be ambition, and so on. Since, in the action as such, the doer attains to a vision of *himself* in objectivity, or to a feeling of self in his existence, and thus to enjoyment, the inner aspect is judged to be an urge to secure his own happiness, even though this were to consist merely in an inner moral conceit, in the enjoyment of being conscious of his own superiority and in the foretaste of a hope of future happiness. No action can escape such judgement, for duty for duty's sake, this pure purpose, is an unreality; it becomes a reality in the deed of an individuality, and the action is thereby charged with the aspect of particularity. No man is a hero to his valet; not, however, because the man is not a hero, but because the valet—is a valet, whose dealings are with the man, not as a hero, but as one who eats, drinks, and wears clothes, in general, with his individual wants and fancies. Thus, for the judging consciousness, there is no action in which it could not oppose to the universal aspect of the action, the personal aspect of the individuality, and play the part of the *moral* valet towards the agent.[1]

[1] Cf *Lectures on Philosophy of World History* (H. B. Nisbet's transl. p. 87).

666. The consciousness that judges in this way is itself base, because it divides up the action, producing and holding fast to the disparity of the action with itself. Further, it is hypocrisy, because it passes off such judging, not as another manner of being wicked, but as the correct consciousness of the action, setting itself up in this unreality and conceit of knowing well and better above the deeds it discredits, and wanting its words without deeds to be taken for a superior kind of *reality*. By putting itself, then, in this way on a level with the doer on whom it passes judgement, it is recognized by the latter as the same as himself. This latter does not merely find himself apprehended by the other as something alien and disparate from it, but rather finds that other, according to its own nature and disposition, identical with himself. Perceiving this identity and giving utterance to it, he confesses this to the other, and equally expects that the other, having in fact put himself on the same level, will also respond in words in which he will give utterance to this identity with him, and expects that this mutual recognition will now exist in fact. His confession is not an abasement, a humiliation, a throwing-away of himself in relation to the other; for this utterance is not a one-sided affair, which would establish his disparity with the other: on the contrary, he gives himself utterance solely on account of his having seen his identity with the other; he, on his side, gives expression to their common identity in his confession, and gives utterance to it for the reason that language is the *existence* of Spirit as an immediate self. He therefore expects that the other will contribute his part to this existence.

667. But the confession of the one who is wicked, 'I am so', is not followed by a reciprocal similar confession. This was not what the judging consciousness meant: quite the contrary. It repels this community of nature, and is the hard heart that is *for itself*, and which rejects any continuity with the other. As a result, the situation is reversed. The one who made the confession sees himself repulsed, and sees the *other* to be in the wrong when he refuses to let his own *inner* being come forth into the *outer* existence of speech, when the other contrasts the beauty of his own soul with the penitent's wickedness, yet confronts the confession of the penitent with his own stiff-necked unrepentant character, mutely keeping himself to himself and

refusing to throw himself away for someone else. There is here expressed in its extreme form the rebellion of the Spirit that is certain of itself; for it beholds itself, as this simple self-knowledge, in someone else, and, too, in such a way that even the outer shape of this other is not, as in the case of material wealth, something without substantial being, is not a Thing; on the contrary, what is held opposed to this other is Thought, simply knowledge itself, this absolutely fluid continuity of pure *knowing* which refuses to put itself into communication with the other which, in its confession, had *ipso facto* renounced its *separate being-for-self*, and thereby expressly superseded its particularity, and in so doing posited itself in continuity with the other as a universal. The other, however, retains *within itself* and for itself its uncommunicative being-for-self; and it retains, in face of the individual who did confess, just the same uncommunicative being-for-self, although the latter has already thrown this away. It thereby reveals itself as a consciousness which is forsaken by and which itself denies Spirit; for it does not know that Spirit, in the absolute certainty of itself, is lord and master over every deed and actuality, and can cast them off, and make them as if they had never happened. At the same time, it does not recognize the contradiction it falls into in not letting the rejection which has taken place in *words*, be validated as a genuine rejection, while itself has the certainty of its Spirit, not in an actual deed, but in its inner being, and finds the outer existence of this inner being in the *utterance* of its judgement. It is thus its own self which hinders that other's return from the deed into the spiritual existence of speech and into the identity of Spirit, and by this hardness of heart produces the disparity which still exists.

668. Now, in so far as the self-certain Spirit, as a 'beautiful soul', does not possess the power to renounce the knowledge of itself which it keeps to itself, it cannot attain to an identity with the consciousness it has repulsed, nor therefore to a vision of the unity of itself in the other, cannot attain to an objective existence. Consequently, the identity comes about only negatively, as a being devoid of Spirit. The 'beautiful soul', lacking an *actual* existence, entangled in the contradiction between its pure self and the necessity of that self to externalize itself and change itself into an actual existence, and dwelling in the *imme-*

diacy of this firmly held antithesis—an immediacy which alone
is the middle term reconciling the antithesis, which has been
intensified to its pure abstraction, and is pure being or empty
nothingness—this 'beautiful soul', then, being conscious of this
contradiction in its unreconciled immediacy, is disordered to
the point of madness, wastes itself in yearning and pines away
in consumption. Thereby it does in fact surrender the *being-for-
self* to which it so stubbornly clings; but what it brings forth
is only the non-spiritual unity of [mere] being.

669. The true, i.e. the *self-conscious* and *existent*, equalization
of the two sides is necessitated by and already contained in the
foregoing. The breaking of the hard heart, and the raising of
it to universality, is the same movement which was expressed
in the consciousness that made confession of itself. The wounds
of the Spirit heal, and leave no scars behind. The deed is not
imperishable; it is taken back by Spirit into itself, and the aspect
of individuality present in it, whether as intention or as an
existent negativity and limitation, straightway vanishes. The
self that carries out the action, the form of its act, is only a *moment*
of the whole, and so likewise is the knowledge, that by its judgement determines and establishes the distinction between the individual and universal aspects of the action. The evil consciousness, referred to above, posits this externalization of itself, or
posits itself, as a moment, being enticed into openly confessing
itself by the vision of itself in the other. But just as the former
has to surrender its one-sided, unacknowledged existence of its
particular being-for-self, so too must this other set aside its one-
sided, unacknowledged judgement. And just as the former
exhibits the power of Spirit over its actual existence, so does
this other exhibit the power of Spirit over the specific Notion
of itself.

670. The latter, however, renounces the divisive thought,
and the hard-heartedness of the being-for-self which clings to
it, because it has in fact seen itself in the first. This first consciousness which turns its back on its actual existence, and
makes itself into a superseded *particular* consciousness, thereby
displays itself as in fact a universal. It returns from its external
actual existence back into itself as essential being, and therein
the universal consciousness thus recognizes itself. The forgiveness which it extends to the other is the renunciation of itself,

of its *unreal* essential being which it put on a level with that
other which was a *real* action, and acknowledges that what
thought characterized as bad, viz. action, is good; or rather
it abandons this distinction of the specific thought and its *subjec-*
tively determined judgement, just as the other abandons its *sub-*
jective characterization of action. The word of reconciliation is
the *objectively* existent Spirit, which beholds the pure knowledge
of itself *qua universal* essence, in its opposite, in the pure knowledge of itself *qua* absolutely self-contained and exclusive *indivi-*
duality—a reciprocal recognition which is *absolute* Spirit.

671. It enters into existence only at that point where its pure
knowledge about itself is the antithesis and alternation [of its
dual aspect]. Aware that its pure knowledge is an abstract
essence, absolute Spirit is this conscious duty in absolute antithesis to the knowledge that is conscious of itself, *qua* absolute
individuality of self, as *essence*. The former is the pure continuity
of the universal, which is aware that the individuality which
is conscious of itself as essence, is intrinsically a nullity, is evil.
This, however, is the absolute discreteness which is conscious
of *itself* in its pure oneness as absolute, and of the *universal* as
something unreal, which exists only for *someone else*. Both aspects
are purified into the unity in which there is no longer in them
any existence devoid of self, any negative of consciousness,
where, on the contrary, *duty* is the unchanging identical character of its self-knowledge, and *evil* equally has its purpose in its
being-within-itself, and its actuality in its utterance. The content
of this utterance is the substance of its enduring existence; it
is the assurance of Spirit's immanent self-certainty. Each of
these two self-certain Spirits has no other purpose than its own
pure self, and no other reality and existence than just this pure
self. But yet they are different; and the difference is absolute
because it is set in this element of the pure Notion. It is also
absolute, not only for us, but for the Notions themselves which
stand in this antithesis. For these Notions, though *specific* in relation to one another, are at the same time in themselves universal, so that they fill out the whole range of the self, and this
self has no other content than this its own determinateness,
which neither goes beyond the self nor is more restricted than
it; for one of them, the absolute universal, is equally the pure
knowledge of itself, as the other is the absolute discreteness of

individuality, and both are only this pure self-knowledge. Both determinatenesses are thus pure conscious Notions, whose determinatenness is itself immediately a knowing, or whose *relationship* and antithesis is the 'I'. Consequently, they are these sheer opposites *for one another*; it is the completely *inner* being which thus confronts its own self and enters into outer existence. They constitute *pure knowledge* which, through this antithesis, is posited as *consciousness*. But it is still not yet *self-consciousness*. It becomes actually such in the movement of this antithesis. For this antithesis is rather itself the *indiscrete continuity* and *identity* of 'I' = 'I'; and each, through the very contradiction of its pure universality, which at the same time still strives against its identity with the other, and cuts itself off from it, *explicitly* supersedes itself within its own self. Through this externalization, this knowledge which in its existence is self-discordant returns into the unity of the *self*. It is the *actual* 'I', the universal knowledge *of itself* in its *absolute opposite*, in the knowledge which remains *internal*, and which, on account of the purity of its separated *being-within-self*, is itself completely universal. The reconciling *Yea*, in which the two 'I's let go their antithetical *existence*, is the *existence* of the 'I' which has expanded into a duality, and therein remains identical with itself, and, in its complete externalization and opposite, possesses the certainty of itself: it is God manifested in the midst of those who know themselves in the form of pure knowledge.

(CC.) RELIGION

VII. RELIGION

672. In the structured forms hitherto considered which are distinguished in general as Consciousness, Self-consciousness, Reason, and Spirit, religion, too, as consciousness of *absolute Being* as such, has indeed made its appearance, although only from the *standpoint of the consciousness* that is conscious of absolute Being; but absolute Being in and for itself, the self-consciousness of Spirit, has not appeared in those 'shapes'.

673. Even Consciousness, in so far as it is the Understanding, is consciousness of the *supersensible* or the *inner side* of objective existence. But the supersensible, the eternal, or whatever else it may be called, is devoid of self; it is only, to begin with, the universal, which is a long way yet from being Spirit that knows itself as Spirit. Then there was the self-consciousness that reached its final 'shape' in the *Unhappy* Consciousness, that was only the *pain* of the Spirit that wrestled, but without success, to reach out into objectivity. The unity of the *individual* self-consciousness and its changeless *essence*, to which the former attains, remains, therefore, a *beyond* for self-consciousness. The immediate existence of *Reason* which, for us, issued from that pain, and its peculiar shapes, have no religion, because the self-consciousness of them knows or seeks *itself* in the *immediate* present.

674. On the other hand, in the ethical world we did see a religion, namely, the religion of the *underworld*. It is the belief in the terrible, unknown night of Fate and in the Eumenides of the *departed spirit*: the former is pure negativity in the form of universality, the latter the same negativity in the form of individuality. Absolute Being is, in the latter form, indeed the *self* and *present*, since other than present the self cannot *be*. But the individual self is *this* individual shade which has separated from itself the universality which Fate is. True, it is a shade, a superseded particular self, and thus a universal self; but the negative significance of the shade has still not changed round

into the positive significance of the universal self, and therefore the superseded self still has, at the same time, the immediate significance of this particular and essenceless being. But Fate devoid of self remains the unconscious night which does not attain to an immanent differentiation, nor to the clarity of self-knowledge.

675. This belief in the nothingness of necessity and in the underworld becomes belief in Heaven, because the departed self must unite with its universality, must explicate in this universality what it contains and thus become clear to itself. This *kingdom* of faith, however, we saw unfold its content only in the element of thought without the [concrete] Notion, and for that reason perish in its fate, viz. in the religion of the Enlightenment. In this religion, the supersensible beyond of the Understanding is reinstated, but in such a way that self-consciousness remains satisfied in *this* world; and the supersensible, *empty* beyond which is neither to be known nor feared it knows neither as a self nor as a power.

676. In the religion of morality, the fact that absolute Being is a positive content is at last again recognized; but the content is bound up with the negativity of the Enlightenment. It is a *being* that is at the same time taken back into the self, in which it remains shut up, and a *differentiated content* whose parts are just as immediately negated as they are produced. The Fate, however, which engulfs this contradictory movement is the self which is conscious of itself as the Fate of what is *essential* and *actual*.

677. The self-knowing Spirit is, in religion, immediately its own pure self-consciousness. Those forms of it which have been considered, viz. the true Spirit, the self-alienated Spirit, and the Spirit that is certain of itself, together constitute Spirit in its *consciousness* which, confronting its *world*, does not recognize itself therein. But in conscience it brings itself, as well as its objective world in general, into subjection, as also its picture-thinking and its specific Notions, and is now a self-consciousness that communes with its own self. In this, Spirit conceived as object, has for itself the significance of being the universal Spirit that contains within itself all essence and all actuality; yet it is not in the form of free actuality or the apparent independence of Nature. True, it has '*shape*' or the form of being, in that it

is the *object* of its consciousness; but because in religion consciousness is posited essentially in the determination of *self*-consciousness, the shape is perfectly transparent to itself; and the reality it contains is shut up in it and superseded in it in just the same way as when we speak of 'all reality'; it is universal reality as *thought*.

678. Since, then, in religion the determination of the consciousness proper of Spirit does not have the form of free *otherness*, Spirit's *existence* is distinct from its *self-consciousness*, and its reality proper falls outside of religion. There is indeed one Spirit of both, but its consciousness does not embrace both together, and religion appears as a part of existence, of conduct and activity, whose other part is the life lived in its real world. As we now know that Spirit in its own world and Spirit conscious of itself as Spirit, or Spirit in religion, are the same, the perfection of religion consists in the two becoming identical with each other: not only that religion concerns itself with Spirit's reality but, conversely, that Spirit, as self-conscious Spirit, becomes actual to itself and *object of its consciousness*. So far as Spirit in religion *pictures* itself to itself, it is indeed consciousness, and the reality enclosed within religion is the shape and the guise of its picture-thinking. But, in this picture-thinking, reality does not receive its perfect due, viz. to be not merely a guise but an independent free existence; and, conversely, because it lacks perfection within itself it is a *specific* shape which does not attain to what it ought to show forth, viz. Spirit that is conscious of itself. If its shape is to express Spirit itself, it must be nothing else than Spirit, and Spirit must appear to itself, or be in actuality, what it is in its essence. Only by so doing would that also be obtained which may seem to be the demand for the opposite, viz. that the *object* of its consciousness have at the same time the form of free actuality; but only Spirit that is object to itself as absolute Spirit is conscious of itself as a free actuality to the extent that it is and remains conscious of itself therein.

679. When self-consciousness and consciousness proper, *religion* and Spirit in its world, or Spirit's *existence*, are in the first instance distinguished from each other, the latter consists in the totality of Spirit so far as its moments exhibit themselves in separation, each on its own account. But the moments are *consciousness, self-consciousness, Reason*, and *Spirit*—Spirit, that is, as

immediate Spirit, which is not yet consciousness of Spirit. Their totality, *taken together*, constitutes Spirit in its mundane existence generally; Spirit as such contains the previous structured shapes in universal determinations, in the moments just named. Religion presupposes that these have run their full course and is their *simple* totality or absolute self. The course traversed by these moments is, moreover, in relation to religion, not to be represented as occurring in Time. Only the totality of Spirit is in Time, and the 'shapes', which are 'shapes' of the totality of *Spirit*, display themselves in a temporal succession; for only the whole has true actuality and therefore the form of pure freedom in face of an 'other', a form which expresses itself as Time. But the *moments* of the whole, consciousness, self-consciousness, Reason, and Spirit, just because they are moments, have no existence in separation from one another. Just as Spirit was distinguished from its moments, so we have further, in the third place, to distinguish from these moments themselves their individual determination. We saw that each of those moments was differentiated again in its own self into a process of its own, and assumed different 'shapes': as, e.g., in consciousness, sense-certainty and perception were distinct from each other. These latter shapes fall apart in Time and belong to a *particular totality*. For Spirit descends from its universality to individuality through determination. The determination, or middle term, is consciousness, self-consciousness, and so on. But *individuality* is constituted by the shapes assumed by these moments. These, therefore, exhibit Spirit in its individuality or *actuality*, and are distinguished from one another in Time, though in such a way that the later moment retains within it the preceding one.

680. If, therefore, religion is the perfection of Spirit into which its individual moments—consciousness, self-consciousness, Reason, and Spirit—return and have returned as into their ground, they together constitute the *existent* actuality of the totality of Spirit, which *is* only as the differentiating and self-returning movement of these its aspects. The genesis of religion *in general* is contained in the movement of the universal moments. But since each of these attributes was exhibited, not merely as it determines itself in general, but as it is in and for itself, i.e. as it runs its course as a totality within itself, therefore, what has come to be is not merely the genesis of religion *in*

general: those complete processes of the *individual* aspects at the same time contain the *specific forms* of religion itself. The totality of Spirit, the Spirit of religion, is again the movement away from its immediacy towards the attainment of the *knowledge* of what it is *in itself* or immediately, the movement in which, finally, the '*shape*' in which it appears for its consciousness will be perfectly identical with its essence, and it will behold itself as it is. In this genesis of religion, Spirit itself therefore assumes *specific* 'shapes' which constitute the different moments of this movement; at the same time, the specific religion has likewise a specific actual Spirit. Thus, if consciousness, self-consciousness, Reason, and Spirit, belong to self-knowing Spirit in general, similarly the specific 'shapes' which were specially developed within consciousness, self-consciousness, Reason, and Spirit, belong to the specific 'shapes' of self-knowing Spirit. From the 'shapes' belonging to each of its moments, the *specific* 'shape' of religion picks out the one appropriate to it for its actual Spirit. The one distinctive feature which characterizes the religion penetrates every aspect of its actual existence and stamps them with this common character.

681. In this way, the arrangement of the 'shapes' which have hitherto appeared differs from the way they appeared in their own order. On this point we shall observe briefly at the start what is necessary. In the series we considered, each moment, exploring its own depths, formed itself into a totality within its own peculiar principle; and cognition was the depth, or the Spirit, wherein the moments which have no other subsistence of their own possessed their substance. But this substance is now manifest; it is the depth of Spirit that is certain of itself, which does not allow the principle of each individual moment to become isolated and to make itself a totality within itself; on the contrary, gathering and holding together all these moments within itself, it advances within this total wealth of its actual Spirit, and all its particular moments take and receive in common into themselves the like determinateness of the whole. This self-certain Spirit and its movement is their true actuality and the *being-in-and-for-self* which belongs to each moment. Thus while the previous single series in its advance marked the retrogressive steps in it by nodes, but continued itself again from them in a single line, it is now, as it were, broken at these nodes,

at these universal moments, and falls apart into many lines which, gathered up into a single bundle, at the same time combine symmetrically so that the similar differences in which each particular moment took shape within itself meet together.

However, it is self-evident from the whole exposition how this co-ordination of the general directions here represented is to be understood; so that it is superfluous to remark that these differences are to be grasped essentially only as moments of the development, not as parts. In actual Spirit, they are attributes of its substance, but in religion, on the other hand, they are only predicates of the Subject. Similarly, all forms in general are certainly *in themselves* or *for us* contained in Spirit and in each Spirit, but as regards Spirit's actuality, the main point is solely which determinateness is explicit for it in its *consciousness*, in which determinateness it has expressed its self, or in which 'shape' it knows its essence.

682. The distinction which was made between *actual* Spirit and Spirit that knows itself as Spirit, or between itself, *qua* consciousness, and *qua* self-consciousness, is superseded in the Spirit that knows itself in its truth; its consciousness and its self-consciousness are on the same level. But, as religion here is, to begin with, *immediate*, this distinction has not yet returned into Spirit. What is posited is only the *Notion* of religion; in this the essence is self-consciousness, which is conscious of being all truth and contains all reality within that truth. This self-consciousness has, as consciousness, itself for object. Spirit which, to begin with, has an *immediate* knowledge of itself is thus to itself Spirit in the *form* of *immediacy*, and the determinateness of the form in which it appears to itself is that of [mere] *being*. This being, it is true, is *filled* neither with sensation nor a manifold material, nor with any other kind of one-sided moments, purposes, and determinations: it is filled with Spirit and is known by itself to be all truth and reality. Such *filling* is not identical with its *shape*, Spirit *qua* essence is not identical with its consciousness. Spirit is actual as absolute Spirit only when it is also for itself in its *truth* as it is in its *certainty of itself*, or when the extremes into which, as consciousness, it parts itself are explicitly for each other in the shape of Spirit. The shape which Spirit assumes as object of its consciousness remains filled by the certainty of Spirit as by its substance; through this content, the object is

saved from being degraded to pure objectivity, to the form of negativity of self-consciousness. Spirit's immediate unity with itself is the basis, or pure consciousness, *within* which consciousness parts asunder [into the duality of subject and object]. In this way Spirit, shut up within its pure self-consciousness, does not exist in religion as the creator of a *Nature* in general; what it does create in this movement are its shapes *qua* Spirits, which together constitute the completeness of its manifestation. And this movement itself is the genesis of its complete reality through its individual aspects, or through its incomplete shapes.

683. The first reality of Spirit is the Notion of religion itself, or religion as *immediate*, and therefore Natural Religion. In this, Spirit knows itself as its object in a natural or immediate shape. The second reality, however, is necessarily that in which Spirit knows itself in the shape of a *superseded* natural existence, or of the self. This, therefore, is the Religion of Art; for the shape raises itself to the form of the self through the creative activity of consciousness whereby this beholds in its object its act or the self. Finally, the third reality overcomes the one-sidedness of the first two; the self is just as much an immediacy, as the immediacy is the self. If, in the first reality, Spirit in general is in the form of consciousness, and in the second, in that of self-consciousness, in the third it is in the form of the unity of both. It has the shape of being-in-and-for-itself; and when it is thus conceived as it is in and for itself, this is the Revealed Religion. But although in this, Spirit has indeed attained its true *shape*, yet the shape itself and the picture-thought are still the unvanquished aspect from which Spirit must pass over into the Notion, in order wholly to resolve therein the form of objectivity, in the Notion which equally embraces within itself its own opposite. It is then that Spirit has grasped the Notion of itself, just as we now have first grasped it; and its shape or the element of its existence, being the Notion, is Spirit itself.

A. NATURAL RELIGION

684. The Spirit that knows Spirit is consciousness of itself and is present to itself in objective form; it *is*; and is at the same time being that is *for itself*. *It is for itself*, it is the aspect of *self*-consciousness, and that too, in contrast to the aspect of its con-

sciousness, or of the relating of itself to itself as *object*. In its consciousness there is antithesis, and in consequence the *specific character* of the 'shape' in which it appears to itself and knows itself. It is solely with this that we are concerned in this treatment of religion; for we have already considered its unembodied essence, or its pure Notion. But at the same time the difference of consciousness and self-consciousness falls within the latter; the 'shape' of religion contains, not the existence of Spirit as Nature that is free from thought, nor as a thought that is free from existence; but it is an existence that is preserved in thinking, and also something thought that is objectively present to it. It is in accordance with the specific character of this 'shape' in which Spirit knows itself that one religion is distinguished from another; but we have at the same time to note that the exposition of this knowledge of itself within the framework of this *single* specific character does not in fact exhaust the totality of an actual religion. The series of different religions which will come to view, just as much sets forth again only the different aspects of a *single* religion, and, moreover, of every single religion, and the ideas which seem to distinguish one actual religion from another occur in each one. At the same time, however, the difference must also be viewed as a difference of religion. For since Spirit lives in the difference of its consciousness and its self-consciousness, the aim of the movement is to supersede this cardinal distinction and to give the form of self-consciousness to the 'shape' that is the object of consciousness. But this difference is not superseded simply by the fact that the 'shapes' contained by self-consciousness have within them the moment of self, and that God is *thought of* as self-consciousness. The self that is *thought of* is not the *actual* self; in order that the self, like any other more precise determination of 'shape', may in truth belong to this 'shape', it must, on the one hand, be posited in the 'shape' by the act of self-consciousness, and, on the other hand, the lower determination must show itself to be reduced to a moment of the higher and to be comprehended by it. For what is *thought of*, ceases to be something [merely] thought of, something alien to the self's knowledge, only when the self has produced it, and therefore beholds the determination of the object as its *own*, consequently beholds *itself* in the object. Through this activity, the lower determination has at the same time vanished; for the act is the negative that is realized at the expense of something else. In so far as the lower determination is still present, it has retreated into an unessential aspect; just as, on the other hand, where the lower is still dominant but the higher is also present, the one determination devoid of self has its place alongside the other. Accordingly, if the various ideas within a particular religion do indeed exhibit the entire movement of its 'shapes', the character of each idea is determined by the particular unity of consciousness and self-consciousness [in that religion], i.e. by the fact that self-consciousness embraces within itself the determination of the object of consciousness, by its act has completely appropriated it and knows it as the essential determination in face of the other. The truth of the belief in a determination of the religious Spirit is revealed in the fact that the constitution of the *actual* Spirit is similar to that of the 'shape' in which Spirit beholds itself in the religion—as, e.g., the incarnation of God which occurs in oriental religion has no truth, because the actual Spirit of that religion is without this reconciliation. It is inappropriate here to return from the totality of determinations to the individual ones, and to show in which 'shape' within the totality and its particular religion the others are contained in their completeness. The higher form being placed under a lower has lost its significance for self-consciousness, belongs to it only superficially and to its picture-thought. It is to be considered in its proper significance only where it is the principle of this particular religion and is upheld by its actual Spirit.

a. *God as Light*

685. Spirit as the essence that is *self-consciousness*—or the self-conscious Being that is all truth and knows all reality as its own self—is, to begin with, only its *Notion* in contrast to the actuality which it gives itself in the movement of its consciousness. And this Notion is, as contrasted with the daylight of this explicit development, the night of its essence; as contrasted with the outer existence of its moments as independent shapes, it is the creative secret of its birth. This secret has its revelation within itself; for the existence of its moments has its necessity in this Notion, because this Notion is self-knowing Spirit and

therefore has in its essence the moment of being consciousness, and of presenting itself objectively.—This is the pure 'I', which in its externalization has within itself as *universal object* the certainty of its own self, or, in other words, this object is for the 'I' the penetration of all thought and all reality.

686. In the immediate, first diremption of self-knowing absolute Spirit its 'shape' has the determination which belongs to *immediate consciousness* or to *sense*-certainty. Spirit beholds itself in the form of *being*, though not of the non-spiritual being that is filled with the contingent determinations of sensation, the being that belongs to sense-certainty; on the contrary, it is being that is filled with Spirit. It also includes the form which appeared in immediate *self-consciousness*, the form of *lord and master* over against the self-consciousness that retreats from its object. This being which is filled with the Notion of Spirit is, then, the *'shape'* of the *simple* relation of Spirit to itself, or the 'shape' of 'shapelessness'. In virtue of this determination, this 'shape' is the pure, all-embracing and all-pervading *essential light* of sunrise, which preserves itself in its formless substantiality. Its otherness is the equally simple negative, *darkness*. The movements of its own externalization, its creations in the unresisting element of its otherness, are torrents of light; in their simplicity, they are at the same time the genesis of its being-for-self and the return from the existence [of its moments], streams of fire destructive of [all] structured form. The [moment of] difference which it gives itself does, it is true, proliferate unchecked in the substance of existence and shapes itself to the forms of Nature; yet the essential simplicity of its thought moves aimlessly about in it without stability or intelligence, enlarges its bounds to the measureless, and its beauty, heightened to splendour, is dissolved in its sublimity.

687. The content developed by this pure *being*, or the activity of its perceiving, is, therefore, an essenceless by-play in this substance which merely *ascends*, without *descending* into its depths to become a subject and through the self to consolidate its distinct moments. The determinations of this substance are only attributes which do not attain to self-subsistence, but remain merely names of the many-named One. This One is clothed with the manifold powers of existence and with the 'shapes' of reality as with an adornment that lacks a self; they are merely

messengers, having no will of their own, messengers of its might, visions of its glory, voices in its praise.

688. However, this reeling, unconstrained Life must determine itself as being-for-self and endow its vanishing 'shapes' with an enduring subsistence. The *immediate being* in which it stands in antithesis to its consciousness is itself the *negative* power which dissolves its distinctions. It is thus in truth the Self; and Spirit therefore passes on to know itself in the form of self. Pure Light disperses its unitary nature into an infinity of forms, and offers up itself as a sacrifice to being-for-self, so that from its substance the individual may take an enduring existence for itself.

b. *Plant and animal*

689. Self-conscious Spirit that has withdrawn into itself from the shapeless essence, or has raised its immediacy to self in general, determines its unitary nature as a manifoldness of being-for-self, and is the religion of spiritual *perception*. In this it falls apart into the numberless multiplicity of weaker and stronger, richer and poorer Spirits. This pantheism which, to begin with, is the passive subsistence of these spiritual atoms develops into a hostile movement within itself. The innocence of the *flower religion*, which is merely the self-less idea of self, gives place to the earnestness of warring life, to the guilt of *animal religions*; the passivity and impotence of contemplative individuality pass into destructive being-for-self. It is of no use to have taken from the things of perception the deadness of abstraction, and to have raised them to beings of spiritual perception; the ensoulment of this kingdom of Spirits bears this death within it owing to the determinateness and the negativity which encroach upon the innocent indifference of plant life. Through this negativity, the dispersion into the multiplicity of passive plant forms becomes a hostile movement in which the hatred which stems from being-for-self is aroused. The *actual* self-consciousness of this dispersed Spirit is a host of separate, antagonistic national Spirits who hate and fight each other to the death and become conscious of specific forms of animals as their essence; for they are nothing else than animal spirits, animal lives which separate themselves off from one another and are unconscious of their universality.

690. In this hatred, however, the determinateness of purely negative being-for-self consumes itself, and through this movement of the Notion Spirit enters into another shape. *Superseded being-for-self* is the *form of the object*, a form produced by the self, or rather is the produced self, the self-consuming self, i.e. the self that becomes a Thing. The artificer therefore retains the upper hand over these mutually destructive animal spirits, and his action is not merely negative, but tranquil and positive. Spirit's consciousness is thus now the movement which is above and beyond the immediate in-itself as it is above and beyond the abstract being-for-self. Since the in-itself is reduced, through opposition, to being a determinateness, it is no longer the proper form of absolute Spirit, but a reality which its consciousness *finds* confronting it as an ordinary existent thing, and which it supersedes; at the same time, this consciousness is not only this being-for-self which supersedes its object, but it also produces its own idea, the being-for-self that is put forth in the form of an object. This productive activity, however, is not a perfect, but a conditioned, activity, the fashioning of a material already to hand.

c. *The artificer*

691. Spirit, therefore, here appears, as an *artificer*, and its action whereby it produces itself as object but without having yet grasped the thought of itself is an instinctive operation, like the building of a honeycomb by bees.

692. The first form, because it is immediate, is the abstract form of the Understanding, and the work is not yet in its own self filled with Spirit. The crystals of pyramids and obelisks, simple combinations of straight lines with plane surfaces and equal proportions of parts, in which the incommensurability of the round is destroyed, these are the works of this artificer of rigid form. On account of the merely *abstract* intelligibleness of the form, the significance of the work is not in the work itself, is not the spiritual self. Thus either the works receive Spirit into them only as an alien, departed spirit that has forsaken its living saturation with reality and, being itself dead, takes up its abode in this lifeless crystal; or they have an external relation to Spirit as something which is itself there externally and not as Spirit—

they are related to it as to the dawning light, which casts its significance on them.

693. The division from which the artificer-spirit starts—the *in-itself* which becomes the material it fashions, and the being-for-self which is the aspect of self-consciousness at work—this division has become objective to it in its work. Its further efforts must aim at getting rid of this division of soul and body: to clothe and give shape to soul in its own self, and to endow body with soul. The two aspects, in being brought closer to each other, retain the specific character of Spirit as ideally conceived and as its enveloping husk; Spirit's unity with itself contains this antithesis of individuality and universality. Since the work, in the coming-together of its aspects, comes closer to itself, this at the same time produces another result, viz. that the work comes closer to the self-consciousness performing it and that the latter, in the work, comes to know itself as it is in its truth. But in this way, the work at first constitutes only the abstract aspect of the *activity* of Spirit, which does not yet know the content of this activity within itself, but in its work, which is a Thing. The artificer himself, Spirit in its entirety, has not yet appeared, but is the still inner, hidden essence which, as an entirety, is present only as divided into active self-consciousness and the object it has produced.

694. The surrounding habitation, then, the outer reality which has been raised at first only into the abstract form of the Understanding, is fashioned by the artificer into a more lifelike form. For this purpose he employs plant-life, which is no longer sacred as it was to the earlier, impotent pantheism; on the contrary, the artificer who grasps *himself* as the being that is *for itself*, takes that plant life as something to be used and reduces it to an outer aspect, to a mere ornament. But it is not used unaltered; for the artificer of the self-conscious form at the same time destroys the transitoriness inherent in the immediate existence of this life and brings its organic forms nearer to the more rigid and more universal forms of thought. The organic form which, left to itself, proliferates unchecked in particularity, being itself subjugated by the form of thought, in turn raises these rectilinear flat shapes into a roundness more typical of the organic form—a blending which becomes the root of free architecture.

695. This dwelling, the aspect of the *universal element* or inorganic nature of Spirit, now also includes within it a shape of individuality which brings nearer to actuality the Spirit that previously was separated from existence, and was external or internal to it, and thereby makes the work more in harmony with active self-consciousness. The artificer lays hold first of all of the form of being-for-self in general, of the animal shape. That he is no longer conscious of himself *immediately* in animal life, he proves by constituting himself the productive power in relation to it, and knows himself in it as in *his* work, whereby the animal shape at the same time becomes superseded and the hieroglyph of another meaning, of a thought. Consequently, the shape, too, is no longer solely and entirely used by the artificer, but is blended with the shape of thought, with the human form. But the work still lacks the shape and outer reality in which the self exists as self; it still does not in its own self proclaim that it includes within it an inner meaning, it lacks speech, the element in which the meaning filling it is itself present. Therefore the work, even when it is wholly purged of the animal element and wears only the shape of self-consciousness, is still the soundless shape which needs the rays of the rising sun in order to have sound which, generated by light, is even then merely noise and not speech, and reveals only an outer, not the inner, self.

696. Over against this outer shape of the self stands the other shape which proclaims its possession of an *inner being*. Nature, withdrawing into its essence, deposes its living, self-particularizing, self-entangling manifold existence to the level of an unessential husk, which is the *covering for the inner being*; and this inner being is, in the first instance, still simple darkness, the unmoved, the black, formless stone. [The Black Stone in the Kaaba at Mecca.]

697. Both representations contain inwardness and outer existence—the two moments of Spirit; and both representations contain the two moments at once in an antithetical relation, the self both as inner and as outer. The two have to be united. The soul of the statue in human shape does not yet come forth from the inner being, is not yet speech, the outer existence that is in its own self inward; and the inner being of multiform existence is still soundless, is not immanently differentiated and is

still separated from its outer existence to which all differences belong. The artificer therefore unites the two by blending the natural and the self-conscious shape, and this ambiguous being which is a riddle to itself, the conscious wrestling with the non-conscious, the simple inner with the multiform outer, the darkness of thought mating with the clarity of utterance, these break out into the language of a profound, but scarcely intelligible wisdom.

698. In this work, there is an end of the instinctive effort which produced the work that, in contrast to self-consciousness, lacked consciousness; for in it, the activity of the artificer, which constitutes self-consciousness, comes face to face with an equally self-conscious, self-expressive inner being. In it he has worked himself up to the point where his consciousness is divided against itself, where Spirit meets Spirit. In this unity of self-conscious Spirit with itself, in so far as it is the shape and the object of its consciousness, its blendings with the unconscious shapes are purged of the immediate shapes of Nature. These monsters in shape, word, and deed are dissolved into spiritual shape: into an outer that has retreated into itself, and an inner that utters or expresses itself out of itself and in its own self; into thought which begets itself, which preserves its shape in harmony with itself and is a lucid, intelligible existence. Spirit is *Artist*.

B. RELIGION IN THE FORM OF ART

699. Spirit has raised the shape in which it is present to its own consciousness into the form of consciousness itself and it produces such a shape for itself. The artificer has given up the *synthetic* effort to blend the heterogeneous forms of thought and natural objects; now that the shape has gained the form of self-conscious activity, he has become a spiritual worker.

700. If we ask, which is the *actual* Spirit which has the consciousness of its absolute essence in the religion of art, we find that it is the *ethical* or the *true* Spirit. This is not merely the universal substance of all individuals; on the contrary, since this substance has for *actual* consciousness the shape of consciousness and it is individualized, it follows that the substance is known by the individuals as their own essence and their own work.

It is for them neither the divine, essential Light in whose unity the being-for-self of self-consciousness is contained only negatively, only transitorily, and in which it beholds the lord and master of its actual world; nor is it the restless destruction of hostile peoples, nor their subjection to a caste-system which gives the semblance of organization of a completed whole, but in which the universal freedom of the individuals is lacking. On the contrary, this Spirit is the free nation in which hallowed custom constitutes the substance of all, whose actuality and existence each and everyone knows to be his own will and deed.

701. The religion of the ethical Spirit is, however, its elevation above its real world, the withdrawal from its truth into the pure knowledge of itself. Since the ethical nation lives in immediate unity with its substance and lacks the principle of the pure individuality of self-consciousness, the complete form of its religion first appears as *divorced* from its existential shape [Bestehen]. For the reality of the ethical substance rests partly on its passive unchangeableness as contrasted with the absolute movement of self-consciousness, and consequently on the fact that this self-consciousness has not yet withdrawn into itself from its contented acceptance of custom and its firm trust therein. Partly, too, on its organization into a multiplicity of rights and duties, as also on its distribution into the spheres of the various classes and their particular activities which co-operate to form the whole; and hence on the fact that the individual is content with the limitation of his existence and has not yet grasped the unrestricted thought of his free self. But that tranquil *immediate* trust in the substance turns back into trust in oneself and into the certainty of oneself; and the multiplicity of rights and duties, like the restricted activity, is the same dialectical movement of the ethical sphere as the multiplicity of things and their specific natures—a movement which finds its rest and stability only in the simplicity of the Spirit that is certain of itself. The consummation of the ethical sphere in free self-consciousness, and the fate of the ethical world, are therefore the individuality that has withdrawn into itself, the absolute levity of the ethical Spirit which has dissolved within itself all the firmly established distinctions of its stable existence and the spheres of its organically ordered world and, being perfectly sure of itself, has attained to unrestrained joyfulness and the

freest enjoyment of itself. This simple certainty of Spirit within itself has a twofold meaning: it is a serene, stable existence and settled truth, and also absolute unrest and the passing-away of the ethical order. But it changes round into the latter; for the truth of the ethical Spirit is, in the first instance, still only this substantial essence and trust in it, in which the self does not know itself as a free individuality, and which, therefore, in this inwardness, or in the liberation of the self, perishes. Since, then, its trust is broken, and the substance of the nation bruised, Spirit, which hitherto mediated the unstable extremes, has now stepped forth as an extreme, that of self-consciousness grasping itself as essence. This is Spirit, inwardly sure of itself, which mourns over the loss of its world, and now out of the purity of self creates its own essence which is raised above the real world.

702. In such an epoch, absolute art makes its appearance. Prior to this it is an instinctive fashioning of material; submerged in the world of determinate being, it works its way out of it and into it; it does not possess its substance in the free ethical sphere, and therefore does not have the character of free spiritual activity for the self at work. Later on, Spirit transcends art in order to gain a higher representation of itself, viz. to be not merely the *substance* born of the self, but to be, in its representation as object, *this self*, not only to give birth to itself from its Notion, but to have its very Notion for its shape, so that the Notion and the work of art produced know each other as one and the same.

703. The ethical substance having withdrawn from its outer existence back into its pure self-consciousness, this is the aspect of the Notion or of the *activity* with which Spirit brings itself forth as object. This activity is pure form, because the individual, in ethical obedience and service, has worked off every unconscious existence and fixed determination in the same way that substance itself has become this fluid essence. This form is the night in which substance was betrayed and made itself into Subject. It is out of this night of pure certainty of self that the ethical Spirit is resurrected as a shape freed from Nature and its own immediate existence.

704. The concrete existence of the pure Notion into which Spirit has fled from its body is an individual which Spirit selects

to be the vessel of its sorrow. Spirit is present in this individual as his universal and as the power over him from which he suffers violence, as his 'pathos', by giving himself over to which his self-consciousness loses its freedom. But that positive power of universality is subdued by the pure self of the individual, the negative power. This pure activity, conscious of its inalienable strength, wrestles with the shapeless essence. Becoming its master, it has made the 'pathos' into its material and given itself its content, and this unity emerges as a work, universal Spirit individualized and set before us.

a. *The abstract work of art*

705. The first work of art, as immediate, is abstract and individual. As for itself, it has to move away from this immediate and objective mode towards self-consciousness, while self-consciousness, on the other hand, in the cult aims at getting rid of the distinction by which it distinguishes itself at first from its Spirit, and by so doing to produce a work of art which is in its own self animate.

706. The first mode in which the artistic spirit keeps its shape and its active consciousness farthest apart is the immediate mode, viz. the shape *is there* or is *immediately* present simply as a *thing*. In this mode, the shape is broken up into the distinction of individuality, which bears within it the shape of the self, and of universality, which represents the inorganic essence in reference to the shape, its environment and habitation. This shape, through the raising of the whole into the pure Notion, acquires its pure, spiritually appropriate form. It is neither the crystal, the form characteristic of the Understanding, which houses the dead or is illumined by a soul outside of it, nor is it that blending of the forms of Nature and of thought which first emerged from the plant, thought's activity in this being still an *imitation*. On the contrary, the Notion strips off the traces of root, branches, and leaves still adhering to the forms and purifies the latter into shapes in which the crystal's straight lines and flat surfaces are raised into incommensurable ratios, so that the ensoulment of the organic is taken up into the abstract form of the Understanding and, at the same time, its essential nature—incommensurability—is preserved for the Understanding.

707. But the indwelling god is the Black Stone drawn forth from its animal covering and pervaded with the light of consciousness. The human form strips off the animal shape with which it was blended; the animal is for the god merely an accidental guise; it steps alongside its true shape and no longer has any worth on its own account, but is reduced to signifying something else and has sunk to the level of a mere symbol. By this very fact, the shape of the god in its own self strips off also the poverty of the natural conditions of animal existence, and hints at the internal dispositions of animal life melted into its surface and belonging only to this surface. The *essential* being of the god is, however, the unity of the universal existence of Nature and of self-conscious Spirit which, in its actuality, confronts the former. At the same time, being in the first instance an *individual* shape, its existence is one of the elements of Nature, just as its self-conscious actuality is an individual national Spirit. But the former is, in this unity, that element reflected into Spirit, Nature transfigured by thought and united with self-conscious life. The form of the gods has, therefore, its Nature-element within it as a transcended moment, as a dim memory. The chaotic being and confused strife of the freely existing elements, the unethical realm of the Titans, is conquered and banished to the fringes of an actuality that has become transparent to itself, to the obscure boundaries of the world which finds itself in [the sphere of] Spirit and is there at peace. These ancient gods, first-born children of the union of Light with Darkness, Heaven, Earth, Ocean, Sun, the Earth's blind typhonic Fire, and so on, are supplanted by shapes which only dimly recall those Titans, and which are no longer creatures of Nature, but lucid, ethical Spirits of self-conscious nations.

708. This simple shape has thus rid itself of the unrest of endless individuation, both of its Nature-element which, only *qua* universal essence, is ruled by necessity, but in its existence and activity is open to contingency; and of the nation which, dispersed into particular spheres of activity and individual centres of self-consciousness, has an existence which is manifold in meaning and activity. All this individuation has been got rid of by this simple form and brought together into an individuality that is at rest. This individuality is, therefore, confronted by the moment of unrest, it—the *essence*—is confronted by *self-*

consciousness for which, as the birthplace of that unrest, nothing remains except to be *pure activity*. What belongs to the substance, the artist gave entirely to his work, but to himself as a particular individuality he gave in his work no actual existence: he could impart perfection to his work only by emptying himself of his particularity, depersonalizing himself and rising to the abstraction of pure action. In this first immediate production, the separation of the work from his self-conscious activity is not yet restored to their unity. The work by itself is not, therefore, actually an inspired work; it is a *whole* only together with its genesis. The common element in a work of art, viz. that it is produced in consciousness and is made by human hands, is the moment of the Notion existing *qua* Notion, which stands in contrast to the work. And if this Notion, whether in the shape of artist or spectator, is unselfish enough to declare the work of art to be in its own self absolutely inspired, and to forget himself as performer or as spectator, then against this we must stick to the Notion of Spirit which cannot dispense with the moment of being conscious of itself. This moment, however, stands contrasted with the work because in this initial duality of itself Spirit gives the two sides their abstract, contrasted characters of *action* and of being a Thing, and their return into the unity from which they proceeded has not yet come about.

709. The artist, then, learns in his work that he did not produce a being *like himself*. From it, it is true, there comes back to him a consciousness in the sense that an admiring crowd reveres it as the Spirit which is their own essence. But this inspiration, since it returns to him his self-consciousness only as admiration, is rather a confession to the artist that the inspired work is not on the same level as himself. Since his work comes back to him simply as joyfulness, he does not find therein the painful labour of making himself into an artist, and of creation, nor the strain and effort of his work. Furthermore, the crowd may judge the work or bring it offerings, endue it with their own consciousness in whatever way it may be: if they with their knowledge set themselves above it, he knows how much more his *act* is than what they understand and say; if they put themselves *below* it and recognize in it the essence which dominates them, he knows himself as the master of this being.

710. The work of art therefore demands another element of

its existence, the god another mode of coming forth than this, in which, out of the depths of his creative night, he descends into the opposite, into externality, into the determination of the Thing which lacks self-consciousness. This higher element is Language—an outer reality that is immediately self-conscious existence. Just as the *individual* self-consciousness is *immediately* present in language, so it is also immediately present as a *universal* infection; the complete separation into independent selves is at the same time the fluidity and the universally communicated unity of the many selves; language is the soul existing as soul. The god, therefore, who has language for the element of his shape is the work of art that is in its own self inspired, that possesses immediately in its outer existence the pure activity which, when it existed as a Thing, was in contrast to it. In other words, self-consciousness, in the objectification of its essence, abides immediately with itself. Abiding thus with itself in its essence, it is *pure thought*, or the devotion whose *inwardness* in the hymn has at the same time an *outer* existence. It retains within itself the individuality of self-consciousness, and this individuality is at the same time heard as a universal individuality that is immediately present. Devotion, kindled in the manifold units of self-consciousness, is conscious of its act as the act of all alike and as *simple being*. Spirit, as this universal self-consciousness of all, has its pure inwardness, no less than the being-for-others and the being-for-self of the individuals, in a single unity.

711. This language is distinct from another language of the god which is not that of universal self-consciousness. The *Oracle*, both of the god of the religions of art and of the preceding religions, is the necessary, first form of the god's utterance; for the *Notion* of the god implies that he is the essence of both Nature and Spirit, and therefore has not only natural but spiritual existence as well. In so far as this moment is at first merely implied in his *Notion* and not yet realized in religion, the language is, for the religious self-consciousness, the language of an *alien* self-consciousness. The self-consciousness that is still alien to its community is not yet *immediately present* in the manner demanded by its Notion. The self is simple or unitary, and thereby absolutely *universal being-for-self*; but the self that is separated from the self-consciousness of the community is at first only an *indivi-*

dual self. The content of this its own and individual language stems from the universal determinateness in which absolute Spirit in general is posited in its religion. Thus the universal Spirit of the Sunrise which has not yet particularized its existence utters equally simple and universal statements about the divine Being, the substantial content of which is sublime in its simple truth, but on account of this universality at the same time appears trivial to the progressively developing self-consciousness.

712. The further developed self which rises to become a *being-for-self* is master over the pure 'pathos' of substance, over the objectivity of the Light of Sunrise, and knows that simplicity of truth as *essential being* which does not have the form of contingent existence through an alien speech, knows it as the *sure and unwritten law of the gods, a law that is 'everlasting and no one knows whence it came'*.[1] Just as the universal truth which was revealed by the divine Light has here withdrawn into the inner or nether world of being, and is thus freed from the form of contingent existence, so, on the other hand, in the religion of art because the shape of the god has taken on consciousness and hence individuality in general, the utterance peculiar to the god who is the Spirit of an ethical nation is the Oracle, which knows its particular affairs and what is advantageous concerning them. The universal truths, however, because they are known as that which possesses essential being are claimed by *conscious thought* for itself, and their speech is no longer alien to it but is its own. Just as that wise man of old[2] searched in his own thought for what was good and beautiful, but left it to his 'daemon' to know the petty contingent content of what he wanted to know—whether it would be good for him to keep company with this or that person, or good for one of his acquaintances to go on a journey, and similar unimportant things; in the same way the universal consciousness draws knowledge of the contingent from birds, or trees, or the yeasty earth, the vapour from which deprives self-consciousness of its self-possession. For the contingent is something that is not self-possessed and is alien, and therefore the ethical consciousness lets itself settle such matters too, as by a throw of the dice, in an unthinking and alien

[1] Sophocles, *Antigone*.
[2] Socrates.

manner. When the individual, by using his understanding, makes up his mind, and after deliberation chooses what is advantageous for him, this self-determination is based on the specific nature of his particular character. This latter is itself contingent, and therefore knowledge supplied by the understanding as to what is advantageous for the individual is just such a knowledge as that of the oracles or of the 'lot'; only that he who questions the oracle or 'lot' thereby expresses the ethical sentiment of indifference to what is contingent, while the former, on the other hand, treats what is intrinsically contingent as an important concern of his thinking and knowing. What is higher than both, however, is not only to make deliberation the Oracle for a contingent action but, in addition, to know that this deliberate action is itself something contingent on account of its connection with the particular aspect of the action and of its advantageousness.

713. The true self-conscious existence which Spirit receives in speech which is not the utterance of an alien, and therefore contingent, not universal, self-consciousness, is the work of art we met with before. It stands in contrast to the Thing-like character of the statue. Whereas this exists at rest, speech is a vanishing existence; and whereas in the statue the liberated objectivity lacks an immediate self of its own, in speech, on the other hand, objectivity remains too much shut up within the self, falls short of attaining a lasting shape and is, like Time, no longer immediately present in the very moment of its being present.

714. The movement of the two sides constitutes the Cult: a movement in which the divine shape *in motion* in the pure feeling element of self-consciousness, and the divine shape *at rest* in the element of thinghood, mutually surrender their distinctive characters, and the unity which is the Notion of their essence achieves an existence. In the Cult, the self gives itself the consciousness of the divine Being descending to it from its remoteness, and this divine Being, which formerly was not actual but only an object over against it, through this act receives the actuality proper to self-consciousness.

715. This Notion of the Cult is already implicitly contained and present in the stream of sacred song. This devotion is the immediate, pure satisfaction of the self by and within itself. It

is the purified soul which, in this purity, is directly only essence and is one with essence. The soul, because of its abstract character, is not consciousness which distinguishes its object from itself; it is thus only the night of its existence and the place prepared for its [outer] shape. The abstract Cult therefore raises the self into being this pure divine element. The soul perfects this purification with consciousness. Yet it is still not the self that has descended into its depths and knows itself as evil; but it is something that only *immediately* is, a soul that cleanses its exterior by washing it, and puts on white robes, while its inward being traverses the imaginatively conceived path of works, punishments, and rewards, the path of spiritual training in general, i.e. of ridding itself of its particularity, as a result of which it reaches the dwellings and the community of the blest.

716. This Cult is, at first, only a *secret* fulfilment, i.e. a fulfilment only in imagination, not in actuality. It must be an *actual* deed, for a deed that is not actual is self-contradictory. Consciousness proper thereby raises itself into its *pure* self-consciousness. The divine Being has in this the meaning of a free object; through the actual Cult, this object returns into the self; and in so far as it has, in pure consciousness, the meaning of the pure divine Being dwelling beyond reality, this Being descends from its universality, through the mediation of the Cult, into individuality, and thus unites itself with reality.

717. The way the two sides enter into the act is determined as follows: for the self-conscious aspect, so far as it is *actual* consciousness, the divine Being presents itself as *actual Nature*; on the one hand, Nature belongs to consciousness as its possession and property, and has the value of an existence that has no being *of its own*. On the other hand, Nature is consciousness's *own* immediate actuality and individuality, which equally is regarded as a non-essential being and is stripped of its apparent independence. But for its *pure* consciousness, this external Nature has at the same time the *opposite* meaning, viz. of being the *implicitly* divine Being, for which the self sacrifices its unessential being, just as, conversely, it sacrifices the unessential aspect of Nature to itself. This makes the act a spiritual movement, because it is this twofold process, on the one hand, of superseding the *abstraction* of the divine Being (which is how devotion determines its object) and making it actual, and, on

the other hand, of superseding the actual (which is how the
doer determines the object and himself) and raising it into a
universality.

718. The act of the Cult itself begins, therefore, with the pure
surrender of a possession which the owner, apparently without
any profit whatever to himself, pours away or lets rise up in
smoke. In so doing, he renounces before the essence of his pure
consciousness all possession and right of the property, and
enjoyment thereof, renounces [his] personality and the return
of his act into himself; and he reflects the act into the universal,
or into the divine Being, rather than into himself. Conversely,
however, the divine Being in its *immediacy* also perishes in this
act. The animal sacrificed is the *symbol* of a god; the fruits consumed are the *living* Ceres and Bacchus themselves. In the
former, die the powers of the upper law which has blood and
actual life, in the latter, the powers of the lower law that possesses in bloodless form secret and cunning power. The sacrifice
of the divine substance, in so far as it is an *act*, belongs to the
self-conscious aspect; that this actual deed be possible, the
divine Being must already have sacrificed itself *in principle*. This
it has done by giving itself an [outer] existence and has made
itself into an individual animal and into fruit. This renunciation, therefore, which the divine Being has already
accomplished *in principle*, is shown forth by the self who performs
the sacrifice as an existent fact and for his own consciousness,
thus replacing that *immediate* actuality of the divine Being by
the higher actuality, viz. that of himself. For the unity which
has resulted from overcoming the singleness and separation of
the two sides is not merely a negative fate, but has a positive
significance. It is only to the abstract being of the underworld
that the sacrificial offering is wholly surrendered, and thus the
reflection of possessions and being-for-self into the universal is
distinguished from the self as such. At the same time, however,
this is only a small part, and the other act of sacrifice is merely
the destruction of what cannot be used, and is really the preparation of the offering for a meal, the feast that cheats the act
out of its negative significance. At that first sacrifice, the person
making the offering reserves the greatest share for his own
enjoyment, and from the latter sacrifice, what is useful, for the
same purpose. This enjoyment is the negative power which puts

an end both to the divine Being and to the singleness, and it is at the same time the positive actuality in which the *objective* existence of the divine Being is transformed into *self-conscious* existence, and the self has consciousness of its unity with the divine Being.

719. For the rest, though this Cult is in fact an act, its meaning yet lies mostly in devotion. What belongs to devotion is not objectively produced, just as the result, in the enjoyment [of the feast], is itself robbed of its outer existence. The Cult, therefore, goes further and replaces this defect, in the first instance by giving its devotion an enduring objective existence, since the Cult is the common task—or the individual task for each and all to do—which produces a dwelling and adornments for the glory of the god. By so doing, in part the objectivity of the statue is transcended; for by this dedication of his gifts and labours the labourer inclines the god to look favourably upon him, and contemplates his self as belonging to the god. In part, too, this action is not the individual labour of the artist, this particular aspect of it being dissolved in universality. But it is not only the glory of the god that is accomplished, and the blessing of his favour shed on the labourer only ideally and in imagination: the work has also a meaning the reverse of the first, which was that of alienating and glorifying something alien. The dwellings and halls of the god are for the use of man, the treasures preserved therein are his own in case of need; the honour and glory enjoyed by the god in his adornment are the honour and glory of the nation, great in soul and in artistic achievement. At the festival, this people adorns its own dwellings and garments, no less than the things of the god, with graceful decorations. In this way, they receive from the grateful god a return for their gifts and proofs of his favour, in which through their work they became united with him, not as a hope and in a future realization, but rather, in witnessing to his glory and in bringing him gifts, the nation has the immediate enjoyment of its own wealth and adornment.

b. *The living work of art*

720. The nation that approaches its god in the Cult of the religion of art is the ethical nation that knows its state and the actions of the state to be the will and the achievement of its

own self. This Spirit, confronting the self-conscious nation is, therefore, not the divine Light which, being devoid of a self, does not contain within it the self-certainty of the individuals, but is only their universal essence and the lordly power in which they disappear. The Cult of the religion of this simple, amorphous essence gives back to its votaries, therefore, in general merely this: that they are the people of their god, who secures for them only their enduring existence and their substance as such; not, however, their actual self which, on the contrary, is rejected. For they reverence their god as the empty Depth, not as Spirit. But the Cult of the religion of art, on the other hand, is without that abstract *simplicity* of the essence and therefore of its *depth*. That essence, however, which is *immediately united* with the self is *in itself* Spirit and the truth that is a *knowing*, though still not the truth that is known, or the truth that knows itself in the depths of its nature. Because, then, the essence here contains a self, its manifestation is well disposed towards consciousness; and, in the Cult, consciousness receives not only the general sanction of its enduring existence, but also its conscious existence in the Cult itself; just as, conversely, the essence does not have an actuality devoid of self, in a rejected people whose substance merely is acknowledged, but in the people whose *self* is acknowledged in its substance.

721. Self-consciousness, then, comes forth from the Cult satisfied in its essence, and the god enters into it as into its habitation. This habitation is, by itself, the night of Substance or its pure individuality, but no longer the tense individuality of the artist, an individuality which has not yet reconciled itself with its essence that is in process of becoming *objective*; it is the satisfied night [of substance] which has its 'pathos' within it and is not in need of anything, because it returns from intuition, from the objectivity that has been superseded.

This 'pathos' is, by itself, the Being of the risen Sun, but a Being which has now 'set' within itself, and has its 'setting' or going-down, i.e. self-consciousness—and hence existence and actuality—within itself. It has here traversed the movement of its actualization. Coming down from its pure essential nature and becoming an objective force of Nature and the expressions of that force, it is an outer existence for the 'other', for the self by which it is consumed. The silent essence of self-less Nature in its fruits attains to that stage where, self-prepared and digested, it offers itself to life that has a self-like nature. In its usefulness as food and drink it reaches its highest perfection; for in this it is the possibility of a higher existence and comes into contact with spiritual reality. In its metamorphosis, the Earth-Spirit has developed, partly into a silently energizing Substance, partly into a spiritual fermentation: in the first case it is the feminine principle of nourishment, in the other the masculine principle, the self-impelling force of self-conscious existence.

722. In this enjoyment, then, is revealed what that divine risen Light really is; enjoyment is the mystery of its being. For the mystical is not concealment of a secret, or ignorance, but consists in the self knowing itself to be one with the divine Being and that this, therefore, is revealed. Only the self is manifest to itself; or what is manifest is so, only in the immediate certainty of itself. But it is in this immediate certainty that the simple divine Being has been placed by the Cult; as a thing that can be used it not only has an existence that is seen, felt, smelt, tasted, but it is also an object of desire, and by being actually enjoyed becomes one with the self and thereby completely revealed to the self and manifest to it. That which is said to be manifest to Reason, to the heart, is in fact still secret, for it still lacks the actual certainty of immediate existence, both the certainty of objectivity and the certainty belonging to enjoyment, a certainty which in religion, however, is not merely immediate and unthinking, but is at the same time purely the certainty that is known by the self.

723. What has thus, through the Cult, become manifest to self-conscious Spirit within itself, is *simple* essence as the movement, partly out of its dark night of concealment up into consciousness, there to be its silently nourishing substance; but no less, however, the movement of again losing itself in the nether darkness, and lingering above only with a silent maternal yearning. The moving impulse is, however, nothing but the many-named divine Light of the risen Sun and its undisciplined tumultuous life which, similarly let go from its [merely] abstract Being, at first enters into the objective existence of the fruit, and then, surrendering itself to self-consciousness, in it attains to genuine reality—and now roams about as a crowd of frenzied

females, the untamed revelry of Nature in self-conscious form.

724. But what is disclosed to consciousness is still only absolute [i.e. abstract] Spirit, which is this simple essence, not Spirit as it is in its own self; in other words, it is only *immediate* Spirit, the Spirit of Nature. Consequently, its self-conscious life is only the mystery of bread and wine, of Ceres and of Bacchus, not of the other, the strictly higher, gods whose individuality includes as an essential moment self-consciousness as such. Therefore, Spirit has not yet sacrificed itself as *self-conscious* Spirit to self-consciousness, and the mystery of bread and wine is not yet the mystery of flesh and blood.

725. This undisciplined revelry of the god must bring itself to rest as an *object*, and the enthusiasm which did not attain to consciousness must produce a work that confronts it, as in the previous case the statue confronts the artist; as a work, moreover, that is equally complete, but not, however, as an intrinsically lifeless, but as a *living*, self. Such a Cult is the festival which man celebrates in his own honour, though not yet imparting to that Cult the significance of the absolute Being; for it is *essence* that is manifest to him at first, not yet Spirit; not as something that *essentially* takes on human form. But this Cult lays the foundation for this revelation and unfolds its moments separately. Thus here we have the *abstract* moment of the living *corporeality* of essence, just as previously we had the unity of both in an unconscious revelry. Man thus puts himself in the place of the statue as the shape that has been raised and fashioned for perfectly free *movement*, just as the statue is perfectly free *repose*. Although each individual knows how to play the part of at least a torch-bearer, one of them comes forward who is the patterned movement, the smooth elaboration and fluent energy of all the participants. He is an inspired and living work of art that matches strength with its beauty; and on him is bestowed, as a reward for his strength, the decoration with which the statue was honoured, and the honour of being, in place of the god in stone, the highest bodily representation among his people of their essence.

726. In both representations which have just come before us there is present the unity of self-consciousness and spiritual essence; but they are still not equally balanced against each

other. In the Bacchic enthusiasm it is the self that is beside itself, but in corporeal beauty it is spiritual essence. The stupor of consciousness and its wild stammering utterance in the former case must be taken up into the clear existence of the latter, and the non-spiritual clarity of the latter into the inwardness of the former. The perfect element in which inwardness is just as external as externality is inward is once again speech; but it is neither the speech of the Oracle, wholly contingent and individual as regards its content, nor the emotional hymn sung in praise of the individual god, nor again is it the meaningless stammer of Bacchic frenzy. On the contrary, it has gained a lucid and universal content: a content that is *lucid*, because the artist has worked his way out of the initial enthusiasm, originating wholly from substance, into a [definite] shape. This shape is his *own* existence which, in all its stirrings and impulses, is permeated and accompanied by self-conscious soul; and the content is universal, for in this festival which honours man there vanishes the one-sidedness of the statues which contain only a national Spirit, a specific character of the divine nature. The handsome warrior is indeed the glory of his particular nation, but he is a corporeal individuality in which are swallowed up the fulness and seriousness of meaning and the inner character of the Spirit which bears the particular life, the demands, the needs, and customs of his nation. In this kenosis, this externalization of itself, into complete corporeality, Spirit has laid aside the special influences and sympathies of Nature which, as the Spirit of the nation, it contained shut up within it. Its nation is, therefore, no longer conscious in this Spirit of its particularity but rather of having laid this aside, and is conscious of the universality of its human existence.

c. *The spiritual work of art*

727. The national Spirits which become conscious of their essence in the shape of a particular animal coalesce into a single Spirit. Thus it is that the separate beautiful national Spirits unite into a single pantheon, the element and habitation of which is language. The pure intuition of itself as *universal humanity* has, in the actuality of the national Spirit, this form: the national Spirit combines with the others with which it constitutes through Nature a single nation, in a common undertak-

ing, and for this task forms a collective nation and therewith a collective Heaven. This universality to which Spirit in its existence attains, is, however, only this first universality which first issues from the individuality of the ethical sphere, which has not yet overcome its immediacy, has not yet formed a single State out of its peoples. The ethical life of the actual national Spirit rests partly on the immediate trust of the individuals in their nation as a whole, partly on the direct share which all, regardless of differences of class, take in the decisions and actions of the government. In the union which, to begin with, is not a permanent arrangement but only for the purpose of a common action, that freedom of participation by each and all is, *for the time being*, put on one side. This first alliance is, therefore, more an assembly of individualities than their domination by an abstract thought which would rob the individuals of their self-conscious participation in the will and deed of the State.

728. The assembly of national Spirits constitutes a circle of shapes which now embraces the whole of Nature as well as the whole ethical world. They stand, too, under the supreme *command* of the one, rather than under his *sovereignty*. By themselves, they are the universal substances of what the *self-conscious* essence *in itself* is and does. This, however, constitutes the power and, in the first instance, the centre at least with which those universal beings are concerned, and which at first seems to merge their affairs only contingently. But it is the return of the divine Being into self-consciousness that already contains the reason why self-consciousness forms the centre for those divine powers and conceals their unity, to begin with, under the form of a friendly, external connection of the two worlds.

729. The same universality which belongs to this content attaches necessarily also to the form of consciousness in which the content appears. It is no longer the actual practice of the Cult, but a practice that is raised, not yet indeed into the Notion, but at first into *picture-thinking*, into the synthetic linking-together of self-conscious and external existence. The external existence of this picture-thinking, *language*, is the earliest language, the Epic as such, which contains the universal content of the world, universal at least in the sense of *completeness*, though not indeed as the universality of *thought*. The Minstrel is the individual and actual Spirit from whom, as a

subject of this world, it [the world] is produced and by whom it is borne. His 'pathos' is not the stupefying power of Nature but Mnemosyne, recollection and a gradually developed inwardness, the remembrance of essence that formerly was directly present. He is the organ that vanishes in its content; what counts is not his own self but his Muse, his universal song. What, however, is in fact present is the syllogism in which the extreme of universality, the world of the gods, is linked with individuality, with the Minstrel, through the middle term of particularity. The middle term is the nation in its heroes, who are individual men like the Minstrel, but presented only in idea, and are thereby at the same time *universal*, like the free extreme of universality, the gods.

730. In this Epic, then, there is in general *presented* to consciousness what is *implicitly* accomplished in the Cult, the relation of the divine to the human. The content is an *action* of the self-conscious essence. The *acting* disturbs the tranquillity of the Substance and excites the essence so that its simple, unitary nature is divided and opened up into the manifold world of natural and ethical powers. The action is the violation of the peaceful earth, the trench which, animated by blood, evokes the departed spirits and these, thirsting for life, receive it in the action of self-consciousness. The business which is the object of these general exertions has two sides: the side of the *self*, by which the business is accomplished by a totality of actual nations and the individualities standing at their head; and the side of the *universal*, by which it is accomplished by their substantial powers. Formerly, however, the relation of the two bore the character of a synthetic combination of the universal and the individual, i.e. of picture-thinking. On this specific character depends the appraisal of this world. The relation of the two is thus a mingling of them which inconsistently divides and apportions the unity of the action, and superfluously throws the action over from one side to the other. The universal powers have the form of individuality and hence the principle of action in them; what they effect appears, therefore, to proceed entirely from them and to be as free an action as that of men. Consequently, both gods and men have done one and the same thing. The earnestness of those divine powers is a ridiculous superfluity, since they are in fact the power or strength of the

individuality performing the action; while the exertions and labour of the latter is an equally useless effort, since it is rather the gods who manage everything. Ephemeral mortals who are as nothing are at the same time the mighty *self* that brings into subjection the universal Beings, offends the gods, and, in general, procures for them an actual existence and an interest in acting. Just as, conversely, these impotent universal Beings who nourish themselves on the gifts of men and through them alone get something to do, are the natural substance and the material of all events, and are equally the ethical matter and the 'pathos' of action. If their elemental natures are first brought into actual existence and into an active relationship by the free self of individuality, they are no less the universal that withdraws itself from this connection, that remains unrestricted in its own specific character, and through the invincible elasticity of its unity effaces the atomistic singleness of the doer and his constructions, preserves itself in its purity and dissolves everything individual in its fluid nature.

731. Just as the gods fall into a contradictory relation with the self-like nature opposed to them, so too their universality comes into conflict with their own specific character and its relationship to others. They are the eternal, beautiful individuals who, serene in their own existence, are exempt from transitoriness and the influence of alien powers. But they are at the same time *specific* elements, *particular* gods, which therefore stand in relation to others. But that relation to others which, in virtue of the opposition involved in it, is a conflict with them, is a comical self-forgetfulness of their eternal nature. Determinateness is rooted in their divine existence and possesses in its limitation the independence of the whole individuality; through this their characters at once lose the sharpness of their peculiar disposition and blend together in their ambiguity. One purpose of the activity—and their activity itself—since it is directed against an 'other', and hence against an invincible divine power, is an arbitrary showing-off which at once melts away and transforms the apparent earnestness of the action into a harmless, self-confident play, without result or outcome. If, however, in the nature of their divinity, the negative element or the specific determinateness of that nature appears merely as the inconsistency of their activity and as the contradiction between purpose

and result, and if that independent assurance retains the pre-
ponderance over the element of determinateness, then by that
very fact the pure power of the negative confronts it, and, moreover, as the ultimate power over it and against which it can
do nothing. They are the universal, and the positive, over
against the *individual self* of mortals which cannot hold out
against their might; but the universal self, for that reason,
hovers over them and over this whole world of picture-thinking
to which the entire content belongs, as the irrational void of
Necessity—a mere happening which they must face as beings
without a self and sorrowfully, for these *determinate* natures cannot find themselves in this purity.

732. This Necessity, however, is the *unity* of the Notion which
brings under control the contradictory substantial being of the
separate moments, a unity in which the inconsistency and arbitrariness of their action is orderly disposed, and the play of their
actions receives its earnestness and worth in the actions themselves. The content of the world of pictorial thought freely unfolds itself in the *middle term* on its own account, gathering itself
round the individuality of a hero who, however, in his strength
and beauty feels his life is broken and sorrowfully awaits an
early death. For the individuality that is in itself firmly established and actual is banished to its extreme and split into its
moments which have not yet found and united themselves. The
one individual moment, the *abstract* non-actual one, is
Necessity, which shares in the life of the middle term just as
little as does the other, the *actual* individual, the Minstrel, who
keeps himself outside of it and is lost in his performance. Both
extremes must draw nearer to the content; one of them,
Necessity, has to fill itself with the content, the other, the language of the Minstrel, must participate in it; and the content
formerly left to itself must receive within it the certainty and
the fixed character of the negative.

733. This higher language, that of Tragedy, gathers closer
together the dispersed moments of the inner essential world and
the world of action: the substance of the divine, in accordance
with the nature of the Notion, sunders itself into its shapes, and
their movement is likewise in conformity with the Notion. In
regard to form, the language ceases to be narrative because it
enters into the content, just as the content ceases to be one that

is imaginatively presented. The hero is himself the speaker, and the performance displays to the audience—who are also spectators—*self-conscious* human beings who *know* their rights and purposes, the power and the will of their specific nature and know how to *assert* them. They are artists, who do not express with unconscious naturalness and naivety the *external* aspect of their resolves and enterprises, as happens in the language accompanying ordinary actions in actual life; on the contrary, they give utterance to the inner essence, they prove the rightness of their action, and the 'pathos' which moves them is soberly asserted and definitely expressed in its universal individuality, free from the accidents of circumstance and personal idiosyncrasies. Lastly, these characters *exist* as actual human beings who impersonate the heroes and portray them, not in the form of a narrative, but in the actual speech of the actors themselves. Just as it is essential for the statue to be the work of human hands, so is the actor essential to his mask—not as an external condition from which artistically considered we must abstract; or, so far as we do have to make abstraction from it, we admit just this, that Art does not yet contain in it the true and proper self.

734. The *general ground* on which the movement of these shapes produced from the Notion takes place, is the consciousness expressed in the first imaginative language [that of the Epic] where the content, devoid of a self, is left disunited. It is the commonalty as such whose wisdom finds utterance in the Chorus of the Elders; in the powerlessness of this chorus the commonalty has its representative, because the common people themselves constitute merely the positive and passive material of the individuality of the government confronting it. Lacking the power of the negative, it is unable to hold together and to subdue the riches and varied abundance of the divine life, but lets it all go its own separate ways, and in its reverential hymns it extols each individual moment as an independent god, first one and then another. But where it does detect the earnestness of the Notion in its onward march dashing these figures to pieces, and comes to see how ill it fares with its venerated gods who dare to trespass on ground where the Notion holds sway, then it is not itself the negative power which actively interferes; on the contrary, it clings to the self-less thought of such power,

clings to the consciousness of an *alien fate* and produces the empty desire for ease and comfort, and feeble talk of appeasement. In its fear of the higher powers which are the immediate instruments of the Substance, *fearful* of their struggles among themselves, and *fearful* of the simple self of Necessity which crushes them as well as the living beings linked with them; in its *compassion* for these living beings which it also knows to be the same as itself—it is conscious only of a paralysing terror of this movement, of equally helpless pity, and as the end of it all, the empty repose of submission to Necessity, whose work is understood neither as the necessary deed of the character, nor as the action of the absolute Being within itself.

735. At the level of this spectator-consciousness [the Chorus], the indifferent ground on which the performance takes place, Spirit does not appear in its scattered multiplicity, but in the simple diremption of the Notion. Its Substance, therefore, shows itself torn asunder merely into its two extreme powers. These elementary *universal* beings are at the same time self-conscious *individualities*—heroes, who place their consciousness into one of these powers, find in it determinateness of character and constitute the effective activity and actuality of these powers. This universal individuation descends again, as will be remembered, to the immediate reality of existence and presents itself to a crowd of spectators who have in the Chorus their counterpart, or rather their own thought expressing itself.

736. The content and movement of Spirit which here is object to itself has already been considered as the nature and realization of the ethical substance. In its religion, it attains to a consciousness of itself, or exhibits itself to consciousness in its purer form and its simpler embodiment. If, then, the ethical substance, in virtue of its Notion, split itself as regards its *content* into powers which were defined as divine and human law, or law of the nether and of the upper world—the one the Family, the other the State power, the first being the feminine and the second the masculine character—similarly, now, the previously multiform circle of gods with its fluctuating characteristics confines itself to these powers which are thereby brought closer to genuine individuality. For the previous dispersion of the whole into manifold and abstract forces, which appear hypostatized,

is the dissolution of the Subject, which comprehends them only as *moments* within its self, so that individuality is merely the superficial form of these entities. Conversely, a further distinction of characters than that just named is to be attributed to contingent and intrinsically external personality.

737. At the same time, the [ethical] substance is divided with respect to its *form* or to *knowing*. Spirit when *acting* appears *qua* consciousness over against the object to which its activity is directed and which, consequently, is determined as the *negative* of the knower; the doer finds himself thereby in the antithesis of knowing and not-knowing. He takes his purpose from his character and knows it as an ethical essentiality; but on account of the determinateness of his character he knows only the *one* power of substance, the other remaining for him concealed. The present reality is, therefore, one thing *in itself*, and another thing for consciousness; the upper and the nether law come to signify in this connection the power that knows and reveals itself to consciousness, and the power that conceals itself and lies in ambush. The one is the aspect of Light, the god of the Oracle who, in accordance with its natural moment, has sprung from the all-illuminating Sun, knows all and reveals all—Phoebus, and Zeus who is his father. But the commands of this truth-speaking god and his announcements of what *is*, are really deceptive. For this knowing is, in its principle, immediately a not-knowing, because *consciousness*, in its action, is in its own self this antithesis. He[1] who was able to unlock the riddle of the Sphinx, and he who trusted with childlike confidence,[2] are, therefore both sent to destruction through what the god revealed to them. This priestess through whom the beautiful god speaks[3] is in no way different from the equivocating sisters of Fate[4] who, by their promises, drive to crime [those who listen to them], and who by the double-tongued character of what they announced as a certainty deceive him[5] who relied on the obvious meaning. The consciousness,[6] therefore, that is purer than the latter[5] which believes witches, and is more prudent,

[1] Oedipus.
[2] Orestes.
[3] The Delphic Oracle.
[4] The witches in *Macbeth*.
[5] Macbeth.
[6] Hamlet.

more solid, and thorough than the former which trusts the priestess and the beautiful god, tarries with his revenge, even though
the very spirit of his father reveals to him the crime by which
he was murdered, and institutes still other proofs—for the
reason that this revelatory spirit could also be the devil.

738. The grounds of this mistrust are that the knowing consciousness is caught up in the antithesis of the certainty of itself
and objective essence. Ethical rightness, which holds that what
actually is, is *in itself* nothing when opposed to absolute law,
learns that its knowing is one-sided, its law only a law of its
own character, and that it has seized on only one of the powers
of the substance. The action itself is this inversion of the *known*
into its opposite, into *being*, is the changing-round of the rightness based on character and knowing into the rightness of the
very opposite with which the former is bound up in the essential
nature of the Substance—converts it into the Furies [Erinnyes]
who embody the other power and character aroused into hostility. This *nether* right sits with Zeus on the throne and enjoys
equal honour with the god who is revealed and known.

739. To these three beings, the world of the gods of the
Chorus is restricted by the acting individuality. One of them
is the Substance, the power presiding over the hearth and the
spirit of family piety, as well as the universal power of state and
government. Since this distinction belongs to the substance as
such, when it is pictorially represented it is not individualized
in two distinct figures, but has in actuality the two persons of
its characters. On the other hand, the distinction between
knowing and not-knowing falls within each of the self-consciousnesses—and only in abstraction, in the element of universality, is it divided into two individual shapes. For the self
of the hero has an existence only as a whole consciousness and
is therefore essentially the *whole* of the distinction belonging to
the form; but its substance is determinate and only one side
of the distinguished content belongs to him. Therefore, the two
sides of consciousness which have in actuality no separate individuality peculiar to each receive, when *pictorially represented*,
each its own particular shape: the one, that of the revelatory
god, the other, that of the Furies who keep themselves concealed. In part, both enjoy equal honour, but again, the *shape*
assumed by the *substance*, Zeus, is the necessity of the *relation*

of the two to each other. The substance is the relation [a] that the knowing is *for itself*, but has its truth in what is simple; [b] that the distinction through and in which actual consciousness exists has its basis in that inner being which destroys it; [c] that the clear conscious *assurance* of *certainty* has its confirmation in *forgetfulness*.

740. Consciousness disclosed this antithesis through action; acting in accordance with the knowledge revealed it finds out that that knowledge is deceptive; and being committed as regards the content of that knowledge to one of the attributes of substance, it violated the other and so gave it the right as against itself. In following the god that knows, it really got hold of what was not revealed, and pays the penalty of trusting a knowledge whose ambiguity, for such is its nature, also becomes explicit *for* consciousness and a warning to it. The ravings of the priestess, the inhuman shape of the witches, the voices of trees and birds, dreams and so forth, are not the ways in which truth manifests itself; they are warning signs of deception, of an absence of self-possession, of the singularity and contingency of the knowing. Or, in other words, the opposite power which is violated by consciousness is present as express law and valid right, whether law of the family or of the state; consciousness, on the other hand, followed its own way of knowing and concealed from itself what was openly revealed. The truth, however, of the opposing powers of the content [of the knowledge] and of consciousness is the result that both are equally right, and therefore in their antithesis, which is brought about by action, are equally wrong. The action, in being carried out, demonstrates their unity in the natural downfall of both powers and both self-conscious characters. The reconciliation of the opposition with itself is the Lethe of the underworld in death; or the Lethe of the upper world as absolution, not from guilt (for consciousness cannot deny its guilt, because it committed the act), but from the crime; and also the peace of mind following atonement for the crime. Both are oblivion, the vanished-ness of the reality and the action of the powers of substance, of their individualities, and of the powers of the abstract thought of good and evil; for none of them by itself is the essence, which rather is the repose of the whole within itself, the unmoved unity of Fate, the peaceful existence and con-

sequent inactivity and lack of vitality of family and government, and the equal honour and consequent indifferent unreality of Apollo and the Furies, and the return of their spiritual life and activity into the unitary being of Zeus.

741. This Fate completes the depopulation of Heaven, of that unthinking mingling of individuality and essence—a mingling whereby the action of essence appears as inconsequent, arbitrary, unworthy of itself; for individuality that is only superficially attached to essence is unessential. The expulsion of such shadowy, insubstantial picture-thoughts which was demanded by the philosophers of antiquity thus already begins in [Greek] Tragedy in general through the fact that the division of the substance is controlled by the Notion, and consequently individuality is essential individuality, and the determinations are absolute characters. The self-consciousness that is represented in Tragedy, knows and acknowledges, therefore, only one supreme power, and this Zeus only as the power of the state or of the hearth, and in the antithesis belonging to knowing [of knower and known], only as the father of the *particular* that is taking shape in the knowing; and also as the Zeus of the oath and of the Furies, the Zeus of the *universal*, of the inner being dwelling in concealment. The further moments issuing from the Notion and dispersed throughout the pictorial representation, moments which the Chorus allows to hold sway one after the other, are, on the other hand, not the 'pathos' of the hero; they sink to the level of passions in the hero, to the level of contingent, insubstantial moments which, though praised by the impersonal Chorus, are not capable of constituting the character of the heroes, nor of being expressed and honoured as their essential nature.

742. But also the persons of the divine Being itself, as well as the character of its substance, coalesce into the simplicity of what is without consciousness. This Necessity has, in contrast to self-consciousness, the characteristic of being the negative power of all the shapes that appear, a power in which they do not recognize themselves but, on the contrary, perish. The self appears merely as assigned to the *characters*, not as the mediating factor of the movement. But self-consciousness, the simple *certainty* of self, is in fact the negative power, the unity of Zeus, of *substantial* being and of *abstract* Necessity; it is the spiritual

unity into which everything returns. Because actual self-consciousness is still distinguished from the substance and Fate, it is partly the Chorus, or rather the crowd of spectators, whom this movement of the divine life fills with fear as being something alien, or in whom this movement, as something close to them, produces merely the emotion of passive sympathy. Partly, too, so far as consciousness is involved and belongs to the characters, this union is an external one, is a hypocrisy, because the true union, that of the self, Fate, and substance, is not yet present. The hero who appears before the onlookers splits up into his mask and the actor, into the person in the play and the actual self.

743. The self-consciousness of the hero must step forth from his mask and present itself as knowing itself to be the fate both of the gods of the chorus and of the absolute powers themselves, and as being no longer separated from the chorus, from the universal consciousness.

744. *Comedy* has, therefore, above all, the aspect that actual self-consciousness exhibits itself as the fate of the gods. These elementary Beings are, as *universal* moments, not a self and are not equal. They are, it is true, endowed with the form of individuality, but this is only in imagination and does not really and truly belong to them; the actual self does not have such an abstract moment for its substance and content. It, the Subject, is raised above such a moment, such a single property, and clothed in this mask it proclaims the irony of such a property wanting to be something on its own account. The pretensions of universal essentiality are uncovered in the self; it shows itself to be entangled in an actual existence, and drops the mask just because it wants to be something genuine. The self, appearing here in its significance as something actual, plays with the mask which it once put on in order to act its part; but it as quickly breaks out again from this illusory character and stands forth in its own nakedness and ordinariness, which it shows to be not distinct from the genuine self, the actor, or from the spectator.

745. This general dissolution of the shapes of the essentiality as a whole in their individuality becomes in its content more petulant and bitter in so far as the content has its more serious and necessary meaning. The divine substance unites within itself the meaning of natural and ethical essentiality. As regards

the natural element, actual self-consciousness shows in the very fact of employing things of Nature for its adornment, for its dwelling, and also in feasting on its sacrificial offering, that it is itself the Fate to which the secret is revealed, viz. the truth about the essential independence of Nature. In the mystery of bread and wine, it appropriates this independence along with the meaning of the inner essence; and in Comedy, it is conscious of the irony of this meaning generally. Now, in so far as this meaning contains ethical essentiality, it is partly the nation in its two aspects of the state, or *Demos* proper, and the individuality of the Family; partly, however, it is a self-conscious pure knowing, or the rational thinking of the universal. This *Demos*, the general mass, which knows itself as lord and ruler, and is also aware of being the intelligence and insight which demand respect, is constrained and befooled through the particularity of its actual existence, and exhibits the ludicrous contrast between its own opinion of itself and its immediate existence, between its necessity and contingency, its universality and its commonness. If the principle of its individuality, separated from the universal, makes itself conspicuous in the proper shape of an actual existence and openly usurps and administers the commonwealth to which it is a secret detriment, then there is exposed more immediately the contrast between the universal as a theory and that with which practice is concerned; there is exposed the complete emancipation of the purposes of the immediate individuality from the universal order, and the contempt of such an individuality for that order.

746. Rational *thinking* frees the divine Being from its contingent shape and, in antithesis to the unthinking wisdom of the Chorus which produces all sorts of ethical maxims and gives currency to a host of laws and specific concepts of duty and of right, lifts these into the simple Ideas of the Beautiful and the Good. The movement of this abstraction is the consciousness of the dialectic contained in these maxims and laws themselves, and, consequently, the consciousness of the vanishing of the absolute validity previously attaching to them. With the vanishing of the contingent character and superficial individuality which imagination lent to the divine Beings, all that is left to them as regards their *natural* aspect is the bareness of their immediate existence; they are clouds, an evanescent mist, like

those imaginative representations. The essence of these having been given the form of *thought*, they have become the *simple* thoughts of the Beautiful and the Good, which tolerate being filled with any kind of content. The power of dialectic know-ledge puts specific laws and maxims of conduct at the mercy of the pleasure and frivolity of youth which is led astray by it, and provides weapons for deceiving old age with its fears and apprehensions and which is restricted to life in its individual aspect. The pure thoughts of the Beautiful and the Good thus display a comic spectacle: through their liberation from the opinion which contains both their specific determinateness as content and also their absolute determinateness, liberation, that is, from the firm hold of consciousness on these determina-tenesses, they become empty, and just for that reason the sport of mere opinion and the caprice of any chance individuality.

747. Therefore, the Fate which up to this point has lacked consciousness and consists in an empty repose and oblivion, and is separated from self-consciousness, this Fate is now united with self-consciousness. The *individual self* is the negative power through which and in which the gods, as also their moments, viz. existent Nature and the thoughts of their specific charac-ters, vanish. At the same time, the individual self is not the emptiness of this disappearance but, on the contrary, preserves itself in this very nothingness, abides with itself and is the sole actuality. In it, the religion of Art is consummated and has com-pletely returned into itself. Through the fact that it is the indivi-dual consciousness in the certainty of itself that exhibits itself as this absolute power, this latter has lost the form of something *presented to consciousness*, something altogether *separate* from *con-sciousness* and alien to it, as were the statue, and also the living beautiful corporeality, or the content of the Epic and the powers and persons of Tragedy. This unity, too, is not the *unconscious* unity of the Cult and the mysteries; on the contrary, the actual self of the actor coincides with what he impersonates, just as the spectator is completely at home in the drama performed before him and sees himself playing in it. What this self-con-sciousness beholds is that whatever assumes the form of essenti-ality over against it, is instead dissolved in it—in its thinking, its existence, and its action—and is at its mercy. It is the return of everything universal into the certainty of itself which, in con-

sequence, is this complete loss of fear and of essential being on the part of all that is alien. This self-certainty is a state of spiritual well-being and of repose therein, such as is not to be found anywhere outside of this Comedy.

C. THE REVEALED RELIGION

748. Through the religion of Art, Spirit has advanced from the form of *Substance* to assume that of *Subject*, for *it produces* its [outer] shape, thus making explicit in it the act, or the self-consciousness, that merely vanishes in the awful Substance, and does not apprehend its own self in its trust. This incarnation of the divine Being starts from the statue which wears only the *outer* shape of the Self, the *inwardness*, the Self's activity, falling outside of it. But in the Cult the two sides have become one; and in the outcome of the religion of Art this unity, in its consummation, has even gone right over at the same time to the extreme of the Self. In Spirit that is completely certain of itself in the individuality of consciousness, all essentiality is submerged. The proposition that expresses this levity runs: 'The Self is absolute Being.' The essence, the Substance, for which the Self was [only] an accident, has sunk to the level of a predicate; and in *this self-consciousness* over against which there is nothing in the form of essence, Spirit has lost its *consciousness*.

749. This proposition: 'The Self is absolute Being', belongs quite obviously to the non-religious, actual [or secular] Spirit; and we have to remember which shape of that Spirit it is which expresses it. It will contain the movement, and also the conversion of it, which degrades the Self to the level of a predicate and elevates Substance to Subject; and in this manner, that the converse proposition does not *in itself* or *for us* make Substance into Subject, or, to put the same thing another way, it does not reinstate Substance in such a manner that Spirit's consciousness is led back to its beginning, to natural religion; on the contrary, this conversion is one that is brought about *for* and *by self-consciousness* itself. Since self-consciousness surrenders itself consciously, it is preserved in its alienation and remains the Subject of substance, but since it is likewise *self*-alienated, it still has the consciousness of the substance; or, since self-consciousness through its sacrifice *brings forth* sub-

stance as Subject, the substance remains self-consciousness's own Self. In the first of the two alternative propositions, the substantiality of the Subject merely vanishes, and in the second, Substance is only a predicate, and both sides are thus present in each with contrary inequality of value. Here, however, the result achieved is the union and permeation of the two natures in which both are, with equal value, *essential* and at the same time only *moments*; so that Spirit is simultaneously *consciousness* of itself as its *objective* substance, and simple *self-consciousness* communing with itself.

750. The religion of Art belongs to the ethical Spirit which we earlier saw perish in the *condition of right* or law, i.e. in the proposition: 'The Self as such, the abstract person, is absolute Being.' In the ethical life, the Self is submerged in the Spirit of its people, it is the universality that is *filled*. But *simple individuality* raises itself out of this content, and its levity refines it into a 'person', into the abstract universality of right or law. In this, the *reality* of the ethical Spirit is lost, and having lost all content, the Spirits of national individuals are gathered into a single pantheon, not into a pantheon of picture-thought whose powerless form lets each Spirit go its own way, but into the pantheon of abstract universality, of pure thought, which disembodies them and imparts to the spiritless Self, to the individual person, a being that is in and for itself.

751. But this Self has, through its emptiness, let the content go free, it is only *within itself* that consciousness is essence; its own *existence*, the legal recognition of the person, is the unfilled abstraction. What it possesses, therefore, is rather only the thought of itself; or in other words, in the mode in which it immediately exists and knows itself as object, it is something that is *not actual*. Hence it is only the Stoic independence of thought, which passes through the dialectic of the Sceptical consciousness to find its truth in that shape which we have called the Unhappy Self-consciousness.

752. This self-consciousness knows what the validity of the abstract person amounts to in reality and equally in pure thought. It knows that such validity is rather a complete loss; it is itself this conscious loss of itself and the alienation of its knowledge about itself. We see that this Unhappy Consciousness constitutes the counterpart and the completion of the

comic consciousness that is perfectly happy within itself. Into the latter, all divine being returns, or it is the complete *alienation* of *substance*. The Unhappy Consciousness, on the other hand, is, conversely, the tragic fate of the certainty of self that aims to be absolute. It is the consciousness of the loss of all *essential* being in this *certainty of itself*, and of the loss even of this knowledge about itself—the loss of substance as well as of the Self, it is the grief which expresses itself in the hard saying that 'God is dead'.

753. In the condition of right or law, then, the ethical world and the religion of that world are submerged and lost in the comic consciousness, and the Unhappy Consciousness is the knowledge of this *total* loss. It has lost both the worth it attached to its immediate personality and the worth attached to its personality as mediated, as *thought*. Trust in the eternal laws of the gods has vanished, and the Oracles, which pronounced on particular questions, are dumb. The statues are now only stones from which the living soul has flown, just as the hymns are words from which belief has gone. The tables of the gods provide no spiritual food and drink, and in his games and festivals man no longer recovers the joyful consciousness of his unity with the divine. The works of the Muse now lack the power of the Spirit, for the Spirit has gained its certainty of itself from the crushing of gods and men. They have become what they are for us now—beautiful fruit already picked from the tree, which a friendly Fate has offered us, as a girl might set the fruit before us. It cannot give us the actual life in which they existed, not the tree that bore them, not the earth and the elements which constituted their substance, not the climate which gave them their peculiar character, nor the cycle of the changing seasons that governed the process of their growth. So Fate does not restore their world to us along with the works of antique Art, it gives not the spring and summer of the ethical life in which they blossomed and ripened, but only the veiled recollection of that actual world. Our active enjoyment of them is therefore not an act of divine worship through which our consciousness might come to its perfect truth and fulfilment; it is an external activity—the wiping-off of some drops of rain or specks of dust from these fruits, so to speak—one which erects an intricate scaffolding of the dead elements of their outward existence—

the language, the historical circumstances, etc. in place of the inner elements of the ethical life which environed, created, and inspired them. And all this we do, not in order to enter into their very life but only to possess an idea of them in our imagination. But, just as the girl who offers us the plucked fruits is more than the Nature which directly provides them—the Nature diversified into their conditions and elements, the tree, air, light, and so on—because she sums all this up in a higher mode, in the gleam of her self-conscious eye and in the gesture with which she offers them, so, too, the Spirit of the Fate that presents us with those works of art is more than the ethical life and the actual world of that nation, for it is the *inwardizing* in us of the Spirit which in them was still [only] *outwardly* manifested; it is the Spirit of the tragic Fate which gathers all those individual gods and attributes of the [divine] substance into one pantheon, into the Spirit that is itself conscious of itself as Spirit.

754. All the conditions for its production are to hand, and this totality of its conditions constitutes its coming-to-be, its Notion, or the production of it *in principle*. The circle of the creations of Art embraces the forms in which absolute substance has externalized itself. Absolute substance is in the form of individuality as a Thing, an object of sensuous consciousness that simply *is*—as pure language, or the coming-to-be of a shape whose existence does not go outside of the Self, but is purely a *vanishing* object; as immediate *unity* with the universal *self-consciousness* in its inspiration, and as a mediated unity in the act of the Cult; as a beautiful, self-like corporeality; and lastly, as existence raised into an ideational presentation and the expansion of this existence into a world which finally collects itself together into a universality which is at the same time a pure certainty of itself. These forms, and on the other side, the world of the person and of law, the destructive ferocity of the freed elements of the content, as also the person as *thought* in Stoicism, and the unstable restlessness of the Sceptical consciousness, constitute the [audience or] periphery of shapes which stands impatiently expectant round the birthplace of Spirit as it becomes self-consciousness [i.e. round the manger at Bethlehem]. The grief and longing of the Unhappy Self-consciousness which permeates them all is their centre and the com-

mon birth-pang of its emergence—the simplicity of the pure Notion, which contains those forms as its moments.

755. Spirit has in it the two sides which are presented above as two converse propositions: one is this, that substance alienates itself from itself and becomes self-consciousness; the other is the converse, that self-consciousness alienates itself from itself and gives itself the nature of a Thing, or makes itself a universal Self. Both sides have in this way encountered each other, and through this encounter their true union has come into being. The externalization [or kenosis] of substance, its growth into self-consciousness, expresses the transition into the opposite, the unconscious transition of *necessity*; in other words, that substance is *in itself* self-consciousness. Conversely, the externalization of self-consciousness expresses this, that it is *in itself* the universal essence, or—since the Self is pure being-for-self which in its opposite communes with itself—that it is just because substance is self-consciousness *for the Self*, that it is Spirit. Of this Spirit, which has abandoned the form of Substance and enters existence in the shape of self-consciousness, it may therefore be said—if we wish to employ relationships derived from natural generation—that it has an *actual* mother but an *implicit* father. For *actuality* or self-consciousness, and the *in-itself* as substance, are its two moments through whose reciprocal externalization, each becoming the other, Spirit comes into existence as this their unity.

756. In so far as self-consciousness one-sidedly grasps only *its own* externalization, then, even though its object is for it just as much Being as Self, and it knows all existence to be spiritual in nature, nevertheless true Spirit has still not yet come to be explicitly *for* self-consciousness, inasmuch as being in general, or Substance, has not equally, on its side, *implicitly* externalized itself and become self-consciousness. For in that case, then, all existence is spiritual being only from the standpoint of consciousness, not in its own self. Spirit is in this way only *imagined* into existence; this imagining is the visionary dreaming which insinuates into both Nature and history, into the world and into the mythical ideas of earlier religions, another, esoteric meaning than that which lies on the surface, and in the case of religions, another meaning than the one known in them by the self-consciousness whose religions they were. But this meaning

is one that is borrowed, a garment which does not cover the nakedness of the appearance and merits neither belief nor reverence; it is no more than the dark night and self-delusive rapture of consciousness.

757. If, therefore, this meaning of the objective is not to be mere imagination, it must possess *intrinsic* being, must *originally* appear in consciousness as stemming from the Notion and must come forth in its necessity. It is thus that self-knowing Spirit has arisen for us, viz. through the cognition of the *immediate* consciousness, or of the consciousness of the object in its *immediacy*, through its necessary movement. This Notion which, as immediate, had also the shape of immediacy for its consciousness, has, in the second place, given itself the shape of implicit self-consciousness, i.e. by just the same necessity of the Notion by which *being* or the *immediacy* which is the content-less object of sensuous consciousness, externalizes itself and becomes the 'I' for consciousness. But the *immediate* in-itself or the necessity that simply *is*, is itself different from the *in-itself* that *thinks*, or from the *cognition of necessity*—a difference, however, which at the same time does not lie outside of the Notion, for the *simple unity* of the Notion is *immediate being* itself. The Notion is at once a self-externalization or a coming-to-be of *intuitively perceived necessity*, and also in this necessity is in communion with itself, knows it and comprehends it. The immediate in-itself of Spirit that gives itself the shape of self-consciousness means nothing else than that the actual World-Spirit has attained to this knowledge of itself; it is then, too, that this knowledge also first enters its consciousness. How that came about we have already seen.

758. That absolute Spirit has given itself *implicitly* the shape of self-consciousness, and therefore has also given it for its *consciousness*—this now appears as the *belief of the world* that Spirit is *immediately present* as a self-conscious Being, i.e. as an *actual man*, that the believer is immediately certain of Spirit, *sees*, *feels*, and *hears* this divinity. Thus this self-consciousness is not imagination, but is *actual* in the believer. Consciousness, then, does not start from *its* inner life, from thought, and unite *within itself* the thought of God with existence; on the contrary, it starts from an existence that is immediately present and recognizes God therein. The moment of *immediate being* is present in the content of the Notion in such a way that the religious Spirit,

in the return of all essentiality into consciousness, has become a *simple* positive Self, just as the actual Spirit as such in the Unhappy Consciousness was just this *simple*, self-conscious negativity. The Self of existent Spirit has, as a result, the form of complete immediacy; it is posited neither as something thought or imagined, nor as something produced, as is the case with the immediate Self in natural religion, and also in the religion of Art; on the contrary, this God is sensuously and directly beheld as a Self, as an actual individual man; only so *is* this God self-consciousness.

759. This incarnation of the divine Being, or the fact that it essentially and directly has the shape of self-consciousness, is the simple content of the absolute religion. In this religion the divine Being is known as Spirit, or this religion is the consciousness of the divine Being that it is Spirit. For Spirit is the knowledge of oneself in the externalization of oneself; the being that is the movement of retaining its self-identity in its otherness. This, however, is Substance, in so far as Substance is, in its accidents, at the same time reflected into itself, not indifferent to them as to something unessential or present in them as in an alien element, but in them it is within itself, i.e. in so far as it is Subject or Self. Consequently, in this religion the divine Being is *revealed*. Its being revealed obviously consists in this, that what it is, is known. But it is known precisely in its being known as Spirit, as a Being that is essentially a *self-conscious Being*. For there is something hidden from *consciousness* in its object if the object is for consciousness an '*other*' or something *alien*, and if it does not know it as *its own self*. This concealment ceases when the absolute Being *qua* Spirit is the object of consciousness; for then the object has the form of *Self* in its relation to consciousness, i.e. consciousness knows itself immediately in the object, or is manifest to itself in the object. Consciousness is manifest to itself only in its own certainty of itself; its object now is the Self, but the Self is nothing alien; on the contrary, it is the indissoluble unity with itself, the universal that is immediately such. It is the pure Notion, pure Thought or *being-for-self* which is immediately *being*, and consequently *being-for-an other*, and as this *being-for-an other* is immediately returned into itself and in communion with itself; it is, therefore, that which is truly and alone revealed. The Good, the Righteous,

the Holy, Creator of Heaven and Earth, and so on, are predicates of a Subject—universal moments which have their support on this point and only *are* when consciousness withdraws
into thought. As long as it is *they* that are known, their ground
and essence, the Subject itself is not yet revealed; and similarly,
the *determinations* of the universal are not *this universal* itself. The
Subject itself, and consequently this pure universal too, is, however, revealed as Self, for this is just this inner being which is
reflected into itself and which is immediately present and is the
self-certainty of the Self for which it is present. This—to be in
accordance with its *Notion* that which is revealed—this is, then,
the true shape of Spirit, and this its shape, the Notion, is likewise
alone its essence and its substance. Spirit is known as self-consciousness and to this self-consciousness it is immediately
revealed, for Spirit is this self-consciousness itself. The divine
nature is the same as the human, and it is this unity that is
beheld.

760. Here, therefore, consciousness—or the mode in which
essence is for consciousness itself, i.e. its shape—is, in fact, identical with its self-consciousness. This shape is itself a self-consciousness; it is thus at the same time an object in the mode
of immediate being, and this being, likewise immediately, has
the significance of pure Thought, of absolute Being. The absolute Being which exists as an actual self-consciousness seems
to have come down from its eternal simplicity, but by thus *coming down* it has in fact attained for the first time to its own highest
essence. For it is only when the Notion of essence has reached
its simple purity that it is the absolute *abstraction* which is *pure
Thought* and hence the pure individuality of Self, just as, on
account of its simplicity, it is also the *immediate* or *being*. What
is called sense-consciousness is just this pure *abstraction*, it is this
thinking for which *being* is the *immediate*. Thus the lowest
is at the same time the highest; the revealed which has come
forth wholly on to the *surface* is precisely therein the most *profound*. That the supreme Being is seen, heard, etc. as an immediately present self-consciousness, this therefore is indeed the
consummation of its Notion; and through this consummation
that Being is immediately *present qua* supreme Being.

761. This immediate existence is at the same time not solely
and simply immediate consciousness, but is religious conscious-

ness; the immediacy has inseparably the meaning not only of a self-consciousness that immediately *is*, but also of the supreme Being as an absolute essence in pure thought, or absolute Being. What *we* are conscious of in our Notion, viz. that Being is Essence, is what the religious consciousness is also conscious of. This *unity* of Being and Essence, of Thought which is immediately Existence, is both the *thought* of this religious consciousness, or its *mediated* knowledge, and equally its *immediate* knowledge; for this unity of Being and Thought is *self*-consciousness and is itself immediately *present*, or the *thought* unity has at the same time this [existential] shape of what it is. Here, therefore, God is *revealed as He is*; He is immediately present as He is *in Himself*, i.e. He is immediately *present* as Spirit. God is attainable in pure speculative knowledge alone and *is* only in that knowledge, and is only that knowledge itself, for He is Spirit; and this speculative knowledge is the knowledge of the *revealed* religion. Speculative knowledge knows God as Thought or pure Essence, and knows this Thought as simple Being and as Existence, and Existence as the negativity of itself, hence as Self, as the Self that is at the same time *this* individual, and also the *universal*, Self. It is precisely this that the revealed religion knows. The hopes and expectations of the world up till now had pressed forward solely to this revelation, to behold what absolute Being is, and in it to find itself. The joy of beholding itself in absolute Being enters self-consciousness and seizes the whole world; for it is Spirit, it is the simple movement of those pure moments, which expresses just this: that only when absolute Being is beheld as an *immediate* self-consciousness is it known as Spirit.

762. This Notion of Spirit that knows itself as Spirit is itself the immediate Notion and is not yet developed. Absolute Being is Spirit, i.e it has appeared, it is revealed; this first revelation is itself *immediate*; but the immediacy is equally pure mediation or thought, and it must therefore exhibit this in its own sphere as such. Looking at this more closely, Spirit, in the immediacy of self-consciousness, is *this individual* self-consciousness, and so in an antithesis to the universal self-consciousness. It is an exclusive One or unit which has the still unresolved form of a sensuous 'other' for the consciousness for which it is immediately present. This 'other' does not as yet know Spirit as its own,

i.e. Spirit as an individual Self is not yet equally the universal Self, the Self of everyone. In other words, the shape has not as yet the form of the Notion, i.e. of the universal Self, of the Self that in its immediate actuality is at the same time a superseded Self, viz. Thought, universality, without losing its actuality in this universality. But the proximate form of this universality, the form that is itself immediate, is not yet the form *of thought* itself, *of the Notion as Notion*, but the universality of reality, the 'allness' or totality of the selves, and the raising of existence into an ideational form; as in every case, and to cite a specific example, the superseded *This of sense* is, in the first place, the Thing of *perception*, not yet the *universal* of the Understanding.

763. This individual man, then, which absolute Being has revealed itself to be, accomplishes in himself as an individual the movement of sensuous Being. He is the *immediately* present God; consequently, his '*being*' passes over into '*having been*'. Consciousness, for which God is thus sensuously present, ceases to see and to hear Him; it *has* seen and heard Him; and it is because it only *has* seen and heard Him that it first becomes itself spiritual consciousness. Or, in other words, just as formerly He rose up for consciousness as a *sensuous existence*, now He has arisen *in the Spirit*. For a consciousness that sensuously sees and hears Him is itself a merely immediate consciousness, which has not overcome the disparity of objectivity, has not taken it back into pure thought: it knows this objective individual, but not itself, as Spirit. In the vanishing of the immediate existence known to be absolute Being the immediacy receives its negative moment; Spirit remains the immediate Self of actuality, but as the *universal self-consciousness* of the [religious] community, a self-consciousness which reposes in its own substance, just as in it this Substance is a universal Subject: not the individual by himself, but together with the consciousness of the community and what he is for this community, is the complete whole of the individual as Spirit.

764. *Remoteness in time and space* is, however, only the imperfect form in which the immediate mode [of existence] is given a mediated or universal character; it is merely dipped superficially in the element of Thought, is preserved in it *as* a sensuous mode, and not made one with the nature of Thought itself. It

is merely raised into the realm of picture-thinking, for this is the synthetic combination of sensuous immediacy and its universality or Thought.

765. This *form of picture-thinking* constitutes the specific mode in which Spirit, in this community, becomes aware of itself. This form is not yet Spirit's self-consciousness that has advanced to its Notion *qua* Notion: the mediation is still incomplete. This combination of Being and Thought is, therefore, defective in that spiritual Being is still burdened with an unreconciled split into a Here and a Beyond. The *content* is the true content, but all its moments, when placed in the medium of picture-thinking, have the character of being uncomprehended [in terms of the Notion], of appearing as completely independent sides which are externally connected with each other. Before the true content can also receive its true form for consciousness, a higher formative development of consciousness is necessary; it must raise its intuition of absolute Substance into the Notion, and equate its consciousness with its self-consciousness *for itself*, just as this has happened for us, or *in itself*.

766. This content is to be considered as it exists in its consciousness. Absolute Spirit is the *content*, and is thus in the shape of its *truth*. But its truth is to be not merely the Substance or the *in-itself* of the community, nor merely to step forth out of this inwardness into the objectivity of picture-thinking, but to become an actual Self, to reflect itself into itself and to be Subject. This, therefore, is the movement which it accomplishes in its community, or this is the life of the community. Consequently, what this self-revealing Spirit is *in and for itself*, is not elicited by, as it were, unravelling the rich life of Spirit in the community and tracing it back to its original strands, to the ideas, say, of the primitive imperfect community, or even to the utterances of the actual man himself. This 'tracing-back' is based on the instinct to get to the Notion; but it confuses the *origin* of the Notion as the immediate existence of its first manifestation with the *simplicity* of the Notion. What results from this impoverishment of Spirit, from getting rid of the idea of the community, and its action with regard to its idea, is not the Notion, but rather bare externality and singularity, the historical manner of the manifestation in its immediacy and the non-spiritual recollection of a supposed individual figure and of its past.

767. Spirit is the content of its consciousness at first in the form of *pure substance*, or is the content of its pure consciousness. This element of Thought is the movement of descending into existence or into individuality. The middle term between these two is their synthetic connection, the consciousness of passing into otherness, or picture-thinking as such. The third moment is the return from picture-thinking and otherness, or the element of self-consciousness itself. These three moments constitute Spirit; its dissociation in picture-thinking consists in its existing in a specific or *determinate* mode; but this determinateness is nothing else than one of its moments. Its complete movement is therefore this, to diffuse its nature throughout each of its moments as in its native element; since each of these spheres completes itself within itself, this reflection of one sphere into itself is at the same time the transition into another. Picture-thinking constitutes the middle term between pure thought and self-consciousness as such, and is only *one* of the specific or determinate forms; at the same time, however, as we have seen, its character—that of being a synthetic connection—is diffused throughout all these elements and is their common determinateness.

768. The content itself which we have to consider has partly been met with already as the idea of the 'unhappy' and the 'believing' consciousness; but in the former, it has the character of a content produced from consciousness for which Spirit yearns, and in which Spirit cannot be satiated or find rest, because it is not yet *in itself* its own content, or is not the Substance of it. In the 'believing' consciousness, on the other hand, the content was regarded as the self-less *Being* of the world, or as essentially an *objective* content of picture-thinking, of a picture-thinking that simply flees from reality and consequently is without the certainty of self-consciousness, which is separated from it partly by the conceit of knowing and partly by pure insight. The consciousness of the community, on the other hand, possesses the content for its *substance*, just as the content is the *certainty* of the community's own Spirit.

769. When Spirit is at first conceived of as substance in the element of pure thought, it is immediately simple and self-identical, eternal essence, which does not, however, have this abstract *meaning* of essence, but the meaning of absolute Spirit.

Only Spirit is not a 'meaning', is not what is inner, but what is actual. Therefore simple, eternal essence would be Spirit only as a form of empty words, if we went no further than the idea expressed in the phrase 'simple, eternal essence'. But simple essence, because it is an abstraction, is, in fact, the negative in its own self and, moreover, the negativity of thought, or negativity as it is in itself in essence; i.e. simple essence is absolute *difference* from itself, or its pure othering of itself. As essence it is only *in itself* or for us; but since this purity is just abstraction or negativity, it is *for itself*, or is the Self, the Notion. It is thus objective; and since picture-thinking interprets and expresses as a *happening* what has just been expressed as the *necessity* of the Notion, it is said that the eternal Being *begets* for itself an 'other'. But in this otherness it has at the same time immediately returned into itself; for the difference is the difference *in itself*, i.e. it is immediately distinguished only from itself and is thus the unity that has returned into itself.

770. There are thus three distinct moments: essence, being-for-self which is the otherness of essence and for which essence is, and being-for-self, or the knowledge of itself *in the 'other'*. Essence beholds only its own self in its being-for-self; in this externalization of itself it stays only with itself: the being-for-self that shuts itself out from essence is *essence's knowledge of its own self*. It is the word which, when uttered, leaves behind, externalized and emptied, him who uttered it, but which is as immediately heard, and only this hearing of its own self is the existence of the Word. Thus the distinctions made are immediately resolved as soon as they are made, and are made as soon as they are resolved, and what is true and actual is precisely this immanent circular movement.

771. This immanent movement proclaims the absolute Being as *Spirit*. Absolute Being that is not grasped as Spirit is merely the abstract void, just as Spirit that is not grasped as this movement is only an empty word. When its *moments* are grasped in their purity, they are the restless Notions which only *are*, in being in themselves their own opposite, and in finding their rest in the whole. But the picture-thinking of the religious community is not this speculative thinking; it has the content, but without its necessity, and instead of the form of the Notion it brings into the realm of pure consciousness the natural rela-

tionships of father and son. Since this consciousness, even in its thinking, remains at the level of picture-thinking, absolute Being is indeed revealed to it, but the moments of this Being, on account of this [empirically] synthetic presentation, partly themselves fall asunder so that they are not related to one another through their own Notion, and partly this consciousness retreats from this its pure object, relating itself to it only in an external manner. The object is revealed to it by something alien, and it does not recognize itself in this thought of Spirit, does not recognize the nature of pure self-consciousness. In so far as the form of picture-thinking and of those relationships derived from Nature must be transcended, and especially also the standpoint which takes the moments of the movement which Spirit is, as isolated immovable Substances or Subjects, instead of transient moments—the transcending of this standpoint is to be regarded as a compulsion on the part of the Notion, as we pointed out earlier in connection with another aspect. But since this compulsion is instinctive, self-consciousness misunderstands its own nature, rejects the content as well as the form and, what amounts to the same thing, degrades the content into a historical pictorial idea and to an heirloom handed down by tradition. In this way, it is only the purely external element in belief that is retained and as something therefore that is dead and cannot be known; but the *inner* element in faith has vanished, because this would be the Notion that knows itself as Notion.

772. Absolute Spirit as pictured in pure essence is not indeed *abstract* pure essence; for abstract essence has sunk to the level of being merely an *element*, just because it is only a moment in [the life of] Spirit. But the representation of Spirit in this element is charged with the same defect of form which *essence* as such has. Essence is an abstraction and is therefore the negation of its simple, unitary nature, is an 'other'; similarly, Spirit in the element of essence is the *form* of *simple oneness*, which therefore is equally essentially an othering of itself. Or, what is the same thing, the relation of the eternal Being to its being-for-self is the immediately simple one of pure thought. In this *simple* beholding of itself in the 'other', the otherness is therefore not posited as such; it is the difference which, in pure thought, is immediately *no difference*; a *loving* recognition in which the two

sides, as regards their essence, do not stand in an antithetical relation to each other. Spirit that is expressed in the element of pure thought is itself essentially this, to be not merely in this element, but to be *actual* Spirit, for in its Notion lies *otherness* itself, i.e. the supersession of the pure Notion that is only thought.

773. The element of pure thought, because it is an abstract element, is itself rather the '*other*' of its simple, unitary nature, and therefore passes over into the element proper to picture-thinking—the element in which the moments of the pure Notion obtain a *substantial* existence relatively to one another, and also are Subjects which do not possess for a third the indifference towards each other of [mere] being but, being reflected into themselves, spontaneously part asunder and also place themselves over against each other.

774. Thus the merely eternal or abstract Spirit becomes an 'other' to itself, or enters into existence, and directly into *immediate* existence. Accordingly, it *creates* a world. This 'creating' is picture-thinking's word for the Notion itself in its absolute movement; or to express the fact that the simple which has been asserted as absolute, or pure thought, just because it is abstract, is rather the negative, and hence the self-opposed or 'other' of itself; or because, to put the same thing in another form, that which is posited as *essence* is simple *immediacy* or *being*, but *qua* immediacy or being lacks Self and, therefore, lacking inwardness is *passive*, or a *being-for-another*. This *being-for-another* is at the same time a *world*; Spirit, in the determination of being-for-another, is the inert subsistence of the moments formerly enclosed within pure thought, is therefore the dissolution of their simple universality and the parting asunder of them into their own particularity.

775. But the world is not merely this Spirit cast out and dispersed into the fulness [of natural existence] and its external ordering; for since Spirit is essentially the simple Self, this Self is equally present in the world: it is the *existent* Spirit, which is the individual Self which has consciousness and distinguishes itself as 'other', or as world, from itself. This individual Self as at first thus immediately posited, is not yet Spirit *for itself*; it does not *exist as* Spirit; it can be called 'innocent' but hardly 'good'. Before it can in fact be Self and Spirit it must first

become an 'other' to its own self, just as the eternal Being
exhibits itself as the movement of being self-identical in its otherness. Since this Spirit is determined as at first an *immediate*
existence, or as dispersed into the multifariousness of its consciousness, its othering of itself is the withdrawal *into itself*, or
self-centredness, of knowing as such. Immediate existence suddenly turns into thought, or mere sense-consciousness into
consciousness of thought; and, moreover, because the thought
stems from immediacy or is *conditioned* thought, it is not pure
knowledge, but thought that is charged with otherness and is,
therefore, the self-opposed thought of Good and Evil. Man is
pictorially thought of in this way: that it once *happened*, without
any necessity, that he lost the form of being at one with himself
through plucking the fruit of the tree of the knowledge of Good
and Evil, and was expelled from the state of innocence, from
Nature which yielded its fruits without toil, and from Paradise,
from the garden with its creatures.

776. Since this withdrawal into itself or self-centredness of
the existent consciousness immediately makes it self-discordant,
Evil appears as the primary existence of the inwardly-turned
consciousness; and because the thoughts of Good and Evil are
utterly opposed and this antithesis is not yet resolved, this consciousness is essentially only evil. But at the same time, on
account of just this antithesis, there is also present the *good* consciousness opposing it, and their relation to each other. In so
far as immediate existence suddenly changes into *Thought*, and
the *being-within-self* is on the one hand itself a thinking, while
on the other hand the moment of the *othering* of essence is more
precisely determined by it—[because of this double aspect] the
becoming of Evil can be shifted further back out of the existent
world even into the primary realm of Thought. It can therefore
be said that it is the very first-born Son of Light [Lucifer] himself who fell because he withdrew into himself or became self-
centred, but that in his place another was at once created. Such
a form of expression as 'fallen' which, like the expression 'Son',
belongs, moreover, to picture-thinking and not to the Notion,
degrades the moments of the Notion to the level of picture-
thinking or carries picture-thinking over into the realm of
thought. Likewise it makes no difference if we co-ordinate a
multiplicity of other shapes with the simple thought of *otherness*

in the eternal Being and transfer the *self-centredness* into them.
In fact, this co-ordination must be approved, since by means
of it this moment of *otherness* also expresses diversity, as it should;
and, moreover, not as plurality in general, but also as a specific
diversity, so that one part, the Son, is that which is simple and
knows itself to be essential Being, while the other part is the
alienation, the externalization of being-for-self which lives only
to praise that Being; to this part, then, can be assigned the taking back again of the externalized being-for-self and the withdrawal into self of the evil principle. In so far as the otherness
falls into two parts, Spirit might, as regards its moments—if
these are to be counted—be more exactly expressed as a quaternity in unity or, because the quantity itself again falls into
two parts, viz. one part which has remained good and the other
which has become evil, might even be expressed as a five-in-
one. But to *count* the moments can be reckoned as altogether
useless, since in the first place what is differentiated is itself just
as much only *one* thing—viz. the *thought* of the difference which
is only *one* thought—as it [the differentiated] is *this* differentiated element, the second relatively to the first. And, secondly,
it is useless to count because the thought which grasps the Many
in a One must be dissolved out of its universality and differentiated into more than three or four distinct components; and this
universality appears, in contrast to the absolute determinateness of the abstract unit, the principle of number, as indeterminateness with respect to number as such, so that we could
speak only of numbers in general, i.e. not of a specific number
of differences. Here, therefore, it is quite superfluous to think
of numbers and counting at all, just as in other respects the
mere difference of quantity and amount has no notional significance and makes no difference.

777. Good and Evil were the specific differences yielded by
the thought of Spirit as immediately existent. Since their antithesis has not yet been resolved and they are conceived of as
the essence of thought, each of them having an independent
existence of its own, man is a self lacking any essential being
and is the synthetic ground of their existence and their conflict.
But these universal powers just as much belong to the self, or
the self is their actuality. In accordance with this moment, it
therefore comes to pass that, just as Evil is nothing other than

the self-centredness of the natural existence of Spirit, so, conversely, Good enters into actuality and appears as an existent self-consciousness. That which in the pure thought of Spirit is in general merely hinted at as the *othering* of the divine Being, here comes nearer to its realization for picture-thinking: this realization consists for picture-thinking in the self-abasement of the divine Being who renounces his abstract and non-actual nature. Picture-thinking takes the other aspect, evil, to be a happening alien to the divine Being; to grasp it in the divine Being itself *as the wrath of God*, this demands from picture-thinking, struggling against its limitations, its supreme and most strenuous effort, an effort which, since it lacks the Notion, remains fruitless.

778. The alienation of the divine Being is thus made explicit in its twofold form: the Self of Spirit and its simple thought are the two moments whose absolute unity is Spirit itself. Its alienation consists in the moments going apart from one another and in one of them having an unequal value compared with the other. This disparity is therefore twofold, and two relationships arise whose common moments are those just given. In one of them, the divine Being counts as essence, while natural existence and the Self count as the unessential aspect which is to be superseded. In the other, on the contrary, being-for-self counts as the essential and the simple, divine Being as unessential. Their still empty middle term is *existence* in general, the bare community of their two moments.

779. This antithesis is resolved not so much through the conflict between the two moments which are pictured as separate and independent Beings: their very independence implies that each of them in its own self, through its Notion, must resolve itself. The conflict begins where both cease to be these minglings of thought and of independent existence, and where they confront each other only as thoughts. For then they are, as specific Notions, only in the relation of an antithesis; as independent, on the other hand, they have their essentiality outside of their antithesis. Their movement is, therefore, their own free and spontaneous movement. As, then, the movement of the two sides is an *intrinsic* movement, since it is to be considered in the sides themselves, it is initiated by that side which is determined as possessing being-in-itself as contrasted with the other. This

is depicted as a spontaneous act; but the necessity for its exter-nalization lies in the Notion that being-in-itself, which is so de-termined in the antithesis, has just for that reason no genuine subsistence. It is, therefore, that side which has not being-for-self but simple being as its essence that alienates itself from itself, yields to death, and thereby reconciles absolute essence with itself. For, in this movement, it manifests itself as Spirit; abstract essence is alienated from itself, it has natural existence and self-like actuality; this its otherness, or its sensuous presence, is taken back again by the second othering and posited as superseded, as *universal*. The [absolute] essence has thereby come to be its own Self in its sensuous presence; the immediate existence of actuality has ceased to be something alien and external for the absolute essence, since that existence is superseded, is universal. This death is, therefore, its resurrection as Spirit.

780. The transcended immediate presence of the self-con-scious essence has the form of universal self-consciousness. This Notion of the transcended individual self that is absolute Being immediately expresses, therefore, the establishing of a com-munity which, tarrying hitherto in the sphere of picture-think-ing, now returns into itself as the Self; and in doing this, Spirit passes over from the second element constituting it, i.e. from picture-thinking, into the third element, self-consciousness as such. If we further consider the behaviour of picture-thinking in its progress, we find first of all the declaration that the divine Being takes on human nature. Here it is already *asserted* that *in themselves* the two are not separate; likewise in the declaration that the divine Being *from the beginning* externalizes itself, that its existence withdraws into itself and becomes self-centred and evil, implies, though it does not expressly assert, that this evil existence is not *in itself* something alien to the divine Being. Absolute Being would be but an empty name if in truth there were for it an 'other', if there were a 'fall' from it; on the con-trary, the moment of *being-within-self* constitutes the essential moment of the *Self* of Spirit. That this *being-within-self* and the actuality which follows from it belong to absolute Being itself, this which for us is *Notion*, and in so far as it is Notion, appears to the picture-thinking consciousness as an incomprehensible happening; the in-itself assumes for it the form of *indifferent being*. The thought that those moments of absolute Being and of the

self-centred Self which seem to flee from each other are not separate, *also* appears in this picture-thinking—for it does possess the true content—but this picture-thought comes later, in the externalization of the divine Being who is made flesh. The picture-thought is in this way still *immediate*, and therefore not spiritual, i.e. it knows the human form of the divine Being at first only as a particular, not yet as a universal, form; it becomes spiritual for this consciousness in the movement whereby this divine Being in human shape sacrifices his immediate existence again and returns to the divine Being: only when essence is reflected into itself is it Spirit. In this picture-thought there is depicted the reconciliation of the divine Being with its 'other' in general, and specifically with the *thought* of it—*Evil*. If this reconciliation is *notionally* expressed by saying that it consists in the fact that Evil is *in itself* the same as Goodness, or again that the divine Being is the *same* as Nature in its whole extent, or that Nature separated from the divine Being is simply nothing—we must regard this as an unspiritual way of talking and one that is necessarily bound to give rise to misunderstandings. If Evil is the same as Goodness, then Evil is just not Evil, nor Goodness Good: on the contrary, both are suspended moments—Evil in general is self-centred being-for-self, and Goodness is what is simple and without a self. When thus expressed in terms of their Notion, their unity is at once evident; for self-centred being-for-self is simple knowing, and simple [being] that lacks a Self is equally pure self-centred being-for self. If, therefore, it must be said, that according to this their Notion, Good and Evil, i.e. in so far as they are *not* Good and Evil, are the *same*, it must also no less emphatically be asserted that they are *not* the same, but are utterly *different*; for simple being-for-self, or pure knowing too, is each in its own self equally pure negativity or absolute difference. The whole is only complete when the two propositions are made together, and when the first is asserted and maintained, it must be countered by clinging to the other with invincible stubbornness. Since both are equally right, they are both equally wrong, and the mistake consists in taking such abstract forms as 'the same' and 'not the same', 'identity' and 'non-identity', to be something true, fixed, and actual, and in resting on them. Neither the one nor the other has truth; the truth is just their movement in which simple sameness is an abstraction and hence absolute difference, but this, as difference in itself, is distinguished from itself and is therefore selfsameness. This is precisely the case with the 'selfsameness' of the divine Being and Nature in general, and human nature in particular: the former is Nature in so far as it is *not* essential Being, and the latter is divine according to its essence. But it is Spirit in which the truth of these two abstract sides is made explicit, viz. by reducing them to suspended moments, an explication which cannot be expressed by the judgement and the lifeless 'is' which forms its copula. Similarly, Nature is *nothing apart from* its essence; but this same 'nothing' just as much *is*; it is an absolute abstraction, and thus pure thought or being-within-self, and with the moment of its antithesis to the spiritual unity it is Evil. The difficulty that is found in these Notions stems solely from clinging to the 'is' and forgetting the thinking of the Notions in which the moments just as much *are* as they *are not*—are only the movement which is Spirit. It is this spiritual unity, or the unity in which the differences are present only as moments or as suspended, which has become explicit for the picture-thinking consciousness in that reconciliation spoken of above; and since this unity is the universality of self-consciousness, self-consciousness has ceased to think in pictures: the movement has returned into self-consciousness.

781. Spirit is thus posited in the third element, in *universal self-consciousness*; it is its *community*. The movement of the community as self-consciousness that has distinguished itself from its picture-thought is to make explicit what has been implicitly established. The dead divine Man or human God is *in himself* the universal self-consciousness; this he has to become explicitly *for this self-consciousness*. Or, since this self-consciousness constitutes one side of the antithesis in picture-thought, viz. the side of evil, for which natural existence and individual self-consciousness count as essence—this side which is pictured as independent, not yet as a moment, has on account of its independence to raise itself through its own nature to Spirit, i.e. it has to exhibit in its own self the movement of Spirit.

782. This self-consciousness is *natural Spirit*; the self has to withdraw from this natural existence and retreat into itself, which would mean, to become *evil*. But this side is already *in*

itself evil; its withdrawal into itself consists, therefore, in *convincing itself* that natural existence is evil. For the consciousness that thinks in pictures the world has *actually* become, and is, evil, and the propitiation of the absolute Being was a real event; but in self-consciousness as such, what is thus pictured as happening, as an event, has as regards its form the significance only of a suspended moment, for the *self* is the negative and hence a knowing—a knowing that is a pure act within consciousness itself. This moment of the *negative* must likewise express itself in the content. That is to say, since absolute Being is already reconciled with itself *in itself* and is a spiritual unity in which the parts of the picture-thought are suspended or are moments, what is expressed in the content is that each part of the picture-thought here receives the *opposite* meaning to what it had before; each meaning thereby completes itself in the other, and only through this self-completion is the content a spiritual one; since the determinateness is just as much its opposite, unity in otherness, i.e. the spiritual relationship, is an accomplished fact: just as the opposite meanings were united previously for us, or in themselves, and even the abstract forms of 'the same' and 'not the same', of 'identity' and 'non-identity' were reduced to moments.

783. If, then, in the picture-thinking consciousness the *inwardizing* of natural self-consciousness was the real existence of evil, that inwardizing in the element of self-consciousness is the *knowledge of evil* as something that is *implicit* in existence. This knowledge is, of course, a genesis of evil, but only a genesis of the *thought* of evil, and is therefore recognized as the first moment of reconciliation. For as a withdrawal into itself from the immediacy of Nature which is determined as evil, it is a forsaking of that immediacy and a dying away of sin. It is not natural existence as such that is forsaken by consciousness, but natural existence that is at the same time known as evil. The immediate movement of *withdrawal into self* is just as much a mediated movement; it presupposes itself, or is its own ground: that is to say, the ground of the withdrawal into self is that Nature has already withdrawn into itself; on account of evil, man must withdraw into himself; but evil is itself the withdrawal into self. This first movement is for that very reason only immediate, or the *simple Notion* of that movement, because it

is the same as what its ground is. The movement or othering has therefore still to appear, but in its own more characteristic form.

784. Besides this immediacy, therefore, the *mediation* of the picture-thought is necessary. The *knowledge* of Nature as the untrue existence of Spirit, and this immanently developed universality of the Self is *in itself* the reconciliation of Spirit with itself. For the self-consciousness that does not think in terms of the Notion, this in-itself receives the form of something that possesses immediate being and is imaginatively represented. Comprehension is, therefore, for that self-consciousness not a grasping of this Notion which knows superseded natural existence to be universal and therefore reconciled with itself; but rather a grasping of the imaginative idea, that by bringing to pass its own externalization, in its historical incarnation and death, the divine Being has been reconciled with its [natural] existence. The grasping of this idea now expresses more definitely what was previously called the spiritual resurrection in this same context, i.e. the coming into existence of God's individual self-consciousness as a universal self-consciousness, or as the religious community. The *death* of the divine Man, *as death*, is *abstract* negativity, the immediate result of the movement which ends only in *natural* universality. Death loses this natural meaning in spiritual self-consciousness, i.e. it comes to be its just stated Notion; death becomes transfigured from its immediate meaning, viz. the non-being of this *particular* individual, into the *universality* of the Spirit who dwells in His community, dies in it every day, and is daily resurrected.

785. Thus what belongs to the element of *picture-thinking*, viz. that absolute Spirit *qua* individual, or rather *qua* particular, Spirit, presents the nature of Spirit in its [natural] existence, is here shifted into self-consciousness itself, into knowledge that preserves itself in its otherness. This self-consciousness therefore does not actually *die*, as the particular self-consciousness is pictured as being actually dead, but its particularity dies away in its universality, i.e. in its knowledge, which is essential Being reconciling itself with itself. The immediately preceding element of picture-thinking is, therefore, here explicitly set aside, or it has returned into the Self, into its Notion; what was in the former merely in the element of being has become a Subject.

By this very fact, the first element too, pure thinking and the eternal Spirit therein, is no longer *beyond* the picturing consciousness or beyond the Self; on the contrary, the return into itself of the whole is just this, to contain within itself all the moments. The death of the Mediator as grasped by the Self is the supersession of his objective existence or his particular being-for-self: this *particular* being-for-self has become a universal self-consciousness. On the other side, the *universal* has become self-consciousness, just because of this, and the pure or non-actual Spirit of mere thinking has become *actual*. The death of the Mediator is the death not only of his *natural* aspect or of his particular being-for-self, not only of the already dead husk stripped of its essential Being, but also of the *abstraction* of the divine Being. For the Mediator, in so far as his death has not yet completed the reconciliation, is the one-sidedness which takes as *essential Being* the simple element of thought in contrast to actuality: this one-sided extreme of the Self does not as yet have equal worth with essential Being; this it first has as Spirit. The death of this picture-thought contains, therefore, at the same time the death of the *abstraction of the divine Being* which is not posited as Self. That death is the painful feeling of the Unhappy Consciousness that *God Himself is dead*. This hard saying is the expression of innermost simple self-knowledge, the return of consciousness into the depths of the night in which 'I' = 'I', a night which no longer distinguishes or knows anything outside of it. This feeling is, in fact, the loss of substance and of its appearance over against consciousness; but it is at the same time the pure *subjectivity* of substance, or the pure certainty of itself which it lacked when it was object, or the immediate, or pure essence. This Knowing is the inbreathing of the Spirit, whereby Substance becomes Subject, by which its abstraction and lifelessness have died, and Substance therefore has become *actual* and simple and universal Self-consciousness.

786. In this way, therefore, Spirit is *self-knowing* Spirit; it knows *itself*; that which is object for it, *is*, or its picture-thought is the true, absolute *content*; as we saw, it expressed Spirit itself. It is at the same time not merely the content of self-consciousness, and not merely object *for it*, but it is also *actual Spirit*. This it is because it runs through the three elements of its nature;

the movement through its own phases constitutes its actuality. What moves itself, that is Spirit; it is the Subject of the movement and is equally the *moving* itself, or the substance through which the Subject moves. The Notion of Spirit which had emerged for us as we entered the sphere of religion, viz. as the movement of self-certain Spirit which forgives evil and in so doing abandons its own simple unitary nature and rigid unchangeableness; or as the movement in which what is in an absolute antithesis recognizes itself as the same as its opposite, this recognition bursting forth as the *affirmative* between these extremes—this Notion is *intuitively apprehended* by the religious consciousness to which the absolute Being is revealed, and which overcomes the difference between its Self and what it intuitively apprehends; just as it is Subject, so also it is substance, and hence it *is* itself Spirit just because and in so far as it is this movement.

787. But the community is not yet perfected in this its self-consciousness; in general, its content exists for it in the form of *picture-thinking*, and the duality in this thinking still attaches even to the *actual spirituality* of the community, to its return out of its picture-thinking; just as the element of pure thought itself was burdened with it. The community also does not possess the consciousness of what it is; it is spiritual self-consciousness which is not an object to itself as this self-consciousness, or which does not unfold itself to a consciousness of itself; but rather, in so far as it is consciousness, it has those picture-thoughts which we have considered. We see self-consciousness at its last turning-point become *inward* to itself and attain to a *knowledge* of its *inwardness*; we see it divest itself of its natural existence and acquire pure negativity. But the *positive* meaning, viz. that this negativity or pure *inwardness* of knowledge is just as much the self-identical essence—or in other words, that substance has here succeeded in becoming absolute self-consciousness—this is an 'other' for the devotional consciousness. It grasps this aspect, viz. that the pure inwardization of knowledge is *in itself* absolute simplicity or substance, as the picture-thought of something which is so, not in virtue of its Notion, but as the deed of an *alien* satisfaction. In other words, it does not grasp the fact that this depth of the pure Self is the power by which the *abstract* divine Being is drawn down from its abstraction and

raised to a Self by the power of this pure devotion. The action of the Self retains towards it this negative meaning because the externalization, the kenosis of substance, is taken by the Self to be an action implicit in the nature of substance; the Self does not grasp and truly comprehend it, or does not find it in its *own* action as such. This unity of essence and the Self having been *implicitly* achieved, consciousness, too, still has this *picture-thought* of its reconciliation, but as a picture-thought. It obtains satisfaction by *externally* attaching to its pure negativity the positive meaning of the unity of itself with the essential Being; its satisfaction thus itself remains burdened with the antithesis of a beyond. Its own reconciliation therefore enters its consciousness as something *distant*, as something in the distant *future*, just as the reconciliation which the other *Self* achieved appears as something in the distant *past*. Just as the *individual* divine Man has a father *in principle* and only an *actual* mother, so too the universal divine Man, the community, has for its father its own doing and knowing, but for its mother, eternal love which it only *feels*, but does not behold in its consciousness as an actual, immediate *object*. Its reconciliation, therefore, is in its heart, but its consciousness is still divided against itself and its actual world is still disrupted. What enters its consciousness as the in-itself, or the side of *pure* mediation, is a reconciliation that lies in the beyond: but what enters it as *present*, as the side of *immediacy* and *existence*, is the world which has still to await its transfiguration. The world is indeed *implicitly* reconciled with the divine Being; and regarding the divine Being it is known, of course, that it recognizes the object as no longer alienated from it but as identical with it in its love. But for self-consciousness, this immediate presence still has not the shape of Spirit. The Spirit of the community is thus in its immediate consciousness divided from its religious consciousness, which declares, it is true, that *in themselves* they are not divided, but this merely *implicit* unity is not realized, or has not yet become an equally absolute being-for-self.

(DD.) ABSOLUTE KNOWING

VIII. ABSOLUTE KNOWING

788. The Spirit of the revealed religion has not yet sur-
mounted its consciousness as such, or what is the same, its actual
self-consciousness is not the object of its consciousness; Spirit
itself as a whole, and the self-differentiated moments within it,
fall within the sphere of picture-thinking and in the form of
objectivity. The *content* of this picture-thinking is absolute
Spirit; and all that now remains to be done is to supersede this
mere form, or rather, since this belongs to *consciousness as such*,
its truth must already have yielded itself in the shape of consciousness. This surmounting of the object of consciousness is
not to be taken one-sidedly to mean that the object showed itself
as returning into the Self, but is to be taken more specifically
to mean not only that the object as such presented itself to the
Self as vanishing, but rather that it is the externalization of self-
consciousness that posits the thinghood [of the object] and that
this externalization has not merely a negative but a positive
meaning, a meaning which is not only for us or in itself, but
for self-consciousness itself. The negative of the object, or its
self-supersession, has a positive meaning for self-consciousness,
i.e. self-consciousness *knows* the nothingness of the object, on
the one hand, because it externalizes its own self—for in this
externalization it posits *itself* as object, or the object as itself,
in virtue of the indivisible unity of *being-for-self*. On the other
hand, this positing at the same time contains the other moment,
viz. that self-consciousness has equally superseded this externalization and objectivity too, and taken it back into itself so that
it is in communion with itself in *its* otherness as such. This is
the movement of *consciousness*, and in that movement consciousness is the totality of its moments. Equally, consciousness must
have related itself to the object in accordance with the totality
of the latter's determinations and have thus grasped it from the
standpoint of each of them. This totality of its determinations
establishes the object as an *implicitly* spiritual being, and it does

truly become a spiritual being for consciousness when each of its individual determinations is grasped as a determination of the Self, or through the spiritual relationship to them that was just mentioned.

789. Thus the object is in part *immediate* being or, in general, a Thing—corresponding to immediate consciousness; in part, an othering of itself, its relationship or *being-for-an-other*, and *being-for-itself*, i.e. determinateness—corresponding to perception; and in part *essence*, or in the form of a universal—corresponding to the Understanding. It is, as a totality, a syllogism or the movement of the universal through determination to individuality, as also the reverse movement from individuality through superseded individuality, or through determination, to the universal. It is, therefore, in accordance with these three determinations that consciousness must know the object as itself. However, this Knowing of which we are speaking is not Knowing as pure comprehension of the object [i.e. in terms of the Notion]; here, this Knowing is to be indicated only in its process of coming-to-be, or in the moments of that aspect of it which belongs to consciousness as such, the moments of the Notion proper or of pure Knowing in the form of shapes of consciousness. For this reason the object does not yet appear in consciousness as such as the spiritual essentiality we have just affirmed it to be; and the relationship of consciousness to it is not the consideration of it in this totality as such nor in its pure form as Notion; but it is from one side a shape of consciousness as such, and from the other side a number of such shapes which *we* bring together, in which the totality of the moments of the object and of the relation of consciousness to it can be indicated only as resolved into its moments.

790. For this aspect of the apprehension of the object, i.e. as it exists in the shape of consciousness, we have only to recall the earlier shapes of consciousness already encountered. Thus, in regard to the object so far as it is an immediacy, i.e. is an *indifferent being*, we saw Observing Reason *seeking* and *finding* itself in this indifferent thing, i.e. we saw it equally conscious of its action being external to it, as it was conscious of the object only as an immediate object. And we saw Observing Reason at its peak express its specific character in the infinite judgement that the *being of the 'I' is a Thing*, and, moreover, a sensuous

immediate Thing. When the 'I' is called *soul*, it is true that it
is also represented as a Thing, but as something invisible, intangible, etc., and therefore in fact not as an immediate being
and not as what is meant by a Thing. That judgement, taken
just as it stands, is non-spiritual or rather is the non-spiritual
itself. In its Notion, however, it is in fact the most richly spiritual, and this *inner* significance of what is not yet *apparent* is what
is expressed in the two other moments to be considered.

791. *The Thing is 'I'*; in point of fact, in this infinite judgement the Thing is superseded; in itself it is nothing; it has meaning only in the relation, only *through the 'I'* and its *connection* with
it. This moment manifested itself for consciousness in pure insight and enlightenment. Things are simply *useful* and to be considered only from the standpoint of utility. The *cultivated* self-
consciousness which has traversed the world of self-alienated
Spirit has, through its self-alienation, produced the Thing as
its own self; therefore, it still retains its own self in it and knows
that the Thing lacks self-subsistence, that it is *essentially* only
a *being-for-an-other*; or, to give complete expression to the relationship, i.e., to what alone constitutes the nature of the object
here, the Thing counts for it as something that *exists on its own
account*; it declares sense-certainty to be absolute truth, but this
being-for-self is itself declared to be a moment that merely
vanishes and passes over into its opposite, into a being that is
at the disposal of an 'other'.

792. However, at this stage, knowledge of the Thing is still
not complete; it must be known not only from the standpoint
of the immediacy of being and of determinateness, but also as
essence or *inner being*, as Self. This occurs in *moral self-consciousness*.
This is aware that its knowledge is a knowledge of what is *absolutely essential*, it knows that *being* is simply and solely pure willing and knowing; it *is* nothing else but this willing and knowing; anything else has only unessential being, i.e. not *intrinsic*
being, only its empty husk. In the same measure that moral
self-consciousness lets *determinate being* go free from the Self, so
too, in its conception of the world it takes it back again into
itself. Finally, as conscience, it is no longer this continual
alternation of existence being placed in the Self, and *vice versa*;
it knows that its *existence* as such is this pure certainty of itself.
The objective element into which it puts itself forth, when

it acts, is nothing other than the Self's pure knowledge of itself.

793. These are the moments of which the reconciliation of Spirit with its own consciousness proper is composed; by themselves they are single and separate, and it is solely their spiritual unity that constitutes the power of this reconciliation. The last of these moments is, however, necessarily this unity itself and, as is evident, it binds them all into itself. The Spirit that, in its existence, is certain of itself, has for the element of *existence* nothing else but this knowledge of itself; when it declares that what it does it does out of a conviction of duty, this utterance is the *validating* of its *action*. Action is the first *implicit* sundering of the simple unity of the Notion and the return out of this dividedness. This first movement changes round into the second, since this element of recognition posits itself, as *simple* knowledge of duty, in antithesis to the *distinction* and *dichotomy* that lie in action as such and so constitute a stubborn actuality confronting action. But in forgiveness, we saw how this obstinacy surrenders and renounces itself. Here, therefore, actuality as well as *immediate existence* has for self-consciousness no other significance than that of being a pure knowing; similarly, as *determinate* existence or as relation, what is self-opposed is a knowing, partly of this purely individual Self, partly of knowledge as universal. In this is posited at the same time that the *third* moment, the *universality* or *essence*, counts only as *knowledge* for each of the two sides that stand over against each other; and finally these latter equally resolve the empty antithesis still remaining and are the knowledge of 'I' = 'I'; this *individual* Self which is immediately a pure knowing or a universal.

794. This reconciliation of consciousness with self-consciousness thus shows itself as brought about from two sides; on one side, in the religious Spirit, and on the other side, in consciousness itself as such. The difference between them is that in the former this reconciliation is in the form of being-*in-itself* or *implicit* being, and in the latter in the explicit form of being-*for-self*. In our consideration of them they at first fall apart. In the other in which the shapes of consciousness came before us, consciousness reached the individual moments of those shapes and their unification long before ever religion gave its object

the shape of actual self-consciousness. The unification of the two sides has not yet been exhibited; it is this that closes the series of the shapes of Spirit, for in it Spirit attains to a knowledge of itself not only as it is *in itself* or as possessing an absolute *content*, nor only as it is *for itself* as a form devoid of content, or as the aspect of self-consciousness, but as it is both *in essence and in actuality*, or *in and for itself*.

795. This unification has, however, already occurred *in principle* and that, too, in religion, in the return of picture-thinking into self-consciousness, but not according to the proper form, for the religious aspect is the aspect of the *in-itself* which stands over against the movement of self-consciousness. Consequently, the unification belongs to this other aspect which, in the contrast of the two sides, is the aspect of reflection into self, and therefore the one that contains both its own self and its opposite, and not only *implicitly* or in a universal sense, but *explicitly* or in a developed and differentiated way. The content, as well as the other aspect of self-conscious Spirit so far as it is the *other* aspect, has been exhibited and is before us in its completeness; the unification that is still lacking is the simple unity of the Notion. The Notion, too, is itself already present on the side of self-consciousness. But as it has come before us thus far, it has to be a particular shape of consciousness like all the other moments. It is, therefore, that aspect of the shape of self-assured Spirit that abides within its Notion and was called the 'beautiful soul'. The 'beautiful soul' is its own knowledge of itself in its pure, transparent unity—the self-consciousness that knows this pure knowledge of *pure inwardness* as Spirit. It is not only the intuition of the Divine but the Divine's intuition of itself. Since this Notion holds itself firmly opposed to its realization, it is the one-sided shape which we saw vanish into thin air, but also positively externalize itself and move onward. Through this realization, this objectless self-consciousness ceases to cling to the *determinateness* of the Notion as against its *fulfilment*; its self-consciousness gains the form of universality and what remains to it is its true Notion, or the Notion that has attained its realization; it is the Notion in its truth, viz. in unity with its externalization; it is the knowing of pure knowledge, not as an abstract *essence* such as duty is, but of knowledge as an essential being which is *this* knowledge, *this* pure self-consciousness which is,

therefore, at the same time a genuine *object*, for the Notion is the Self that is for itself.

796. This Notion fulfilled itself on one side in the self-assured Spirit that *acted*, and on the other, in religion: in religion it won for consciousness the absolute content *as content* or, in the form of *picture-thinking*, the form of otherness for consciousness; on the other hand, in the prior shape the form is that of the Self itself, for it contains the self-assured Spirit that *acts*; the Self accomplishes the life of absolute Spirit. This shape is, as we have seen, that simple Notion which, however, surrenders its eternal *essence*, it *is there* [in the real world], or its acts. The *self-sundering* or stepping-forth into existence stems from the purity of the Notion, for this is absolute abstraction or negativity. Similarly, the Notion gets the element of its actuality or the being it contains in pure knowledge itself, for this is simple *immediacy*, which is as much being and existence as it is essence; the former, negative thought, the latter, positive thought itself. Finally, this existence, both as existence and as duty, is just as much the reflectedness into self out of pure knowledge—or the state of evil. This withdrawal into itself constitutes the *antithesis* of the *Notion*, and is thus the emergence of the pure knowledge of the essence, the knowing that *does not act* and is *not actual*. But this emergence in the antithesis is participation in it; the pure knowledge of essence has *in principle* renounced its simple unity, for it is the self-sundering, or the negativity which the Notion is; so far as this self-sundering is the process of becoming *for itself*, it is evil; so far as it is the *in-itself*, it remains good. Now, what at first happens *in principle* is at the same time explicitly for consciousness, and is thus double: it is both *for consciousness* and also is its *being-for-self* or its very own act. The same thing that is already posited *in principle* now therefore repeats itself as consciousness's knowledge of it and conscious act. Each in relation to the other lets go of the independent determinateness with which it comes forth against it. This letting-go is the same renunciation of the one-sidedness of the Notion that in itself constituted the beginning; but it is now its own act of renunciation, just as the Notion which it renounces is its own Notion. That *in-itself* [i.e. the immediacy] of the beginning is in truth, as negativity, no less *mediated*; what it is in truth, it now also makes *explicit*, and the *negative* is, as *determinateness* of each both

for the other and in itself, self-suspending. One of the two parts of the antithesis is the disparity between the Notion's being *within itself* in its *individuality*, and universality; the other, the disparity between its abstract universality and the Self. The former dies to its being-for-self, disowns itself, makes confession; the latter renounces the obstinacy of its abstract universality, and in so doing dies to its lifeless Self and to its unmoved universality; the former has thus completed itself through the moment of universality which is essence, and the latter through the universality which is Self. Through this movement of action, Spirit has come on the scene as a pure universality of knowing, which is self-consciousness, as self-consciousness that is the simple unity of knowing. It is only through action that Spirit *is* in such a way that it is *really there*, that is, when it raises its existence into Thought and thereby into an absolute *antithesis*, and returns out of this antithesis, in and through the antithesis itself.

797. Thus, what in religion was *content* or a form for presenting an *other*, is here the *Self's* own *act*; the Notion requires the *content* to be the *Self's* own *act*. For this Notion is, as we see, the knowledge of the Self's act within itself as all essentiality and all existence, the knowledge of this subject as substance and of the substance as this knowledge of its act. Our *own* act here has been simply to *gather together* the separate moments, each of which in principle exhibits the life of Spirit in its entirety, and also to stick to the Notion in the form of the Notion, the content of which would already have yielded itself in those moments and in the form of a *shape of consciousness*.

798. This last shape of Spirit—the Spirit which at the same time gives its complete and true content the form of the Self and thereby realizes its Notion as remaining in its Notion in this realization—this is absolute knowing; it is Spirit that knows itself in the shape of Spirit, or a *comprehensive knowing* [in terms of the Notion]. Truth is not only *in itself* completely identical with certainty, but it also has the shape of self-certainty, or it is in its existence in the form of self-knowledge. Truth is the *content*, which in religion is still not identical with its certainty. But this identity is now a fact, in that the content has received the shape of the Self. As a result, that which is the very essence, viz. the Notion, has become the element of existence, or has

become the *form of objectivity* for consciousness. Spirit, *manifesting* or *appearing* in consciousness in this element, or what is the same thing, produced in it by consciousness, *is Science.*

799. The nature, moments and movement of this knowing have, then, shown themselves to be such that this knowing is a pure *being-for-self* of self-consciousness; it is 'I', that is *this* and no other 'I', and which is no less immediately a *mediated* or super-seded *universal* 'I'. It has a *content* which it *differentiates* from itself; for it is pure negativity or the dividing of itself, it is *consciousness*. This content is, in its difference, itself the 'I', for it is the move-ment of superseding itself, or the same pure negativity that the 'I' is. In it, as differentiated, the 'I' is reflected into itself; it is only when the 'I' communes with itself in its otherness that the content is *comprehended* [i.e. in terms of the Notion]. Stated more specifically, this content is nothing else than the very movement just spoken of; for the content is Spirit that traverses its own self and does so *for itself* as Spirit by the fact that it has the 'shape' of the Notion in its objectivity.

800. But as regards the *existence* of this Notion, Science does not appear in Time and in the actual world before Spirit has attained to this consciousness about itself. As Spirit that knows what it is, it does not exist before, and nowhere at all, till after the completion of its work of compelling its imperfect 'shape' to procure for its consciousness the 'shape' of its essence, and in this way to equate its *self-consciousness* with its *consciousness*. Spirit that is in and for itself and differentiated into its moments is a knowing that is *for itself*, a *comprehension* in general that, as such, substance has not yet reached, i.e. substance is not in its own self an absolute knowing.

801. Now, in actuality, the substance that knows exists earlier than its form or its Notion-determined 'shape'. For sub-stance is the as yet undeveloped *in-itself*, or the Ground and Notion in its still unmoved simplicity, and therefore the *inward-ness* or the Self of the Spirit that does not yet *exist*. What *is there*, exists as the still undeveloped simple and immediate, or as the object of the *picture-thinking* consciousness in general. Cognition, because it is the spiritual consciousness for which what *is in itself* only *is*, in so far as it is a *being for* the Self and a being of the *Self* or Notion, has for this reason at first only a meagre object, in contrast with which substance and the consciousness of this

substance are richer. The disclosure or revelation which substance has in this consciousness is in fact concealment, for substance is still *self-less being* and what is disclosed to it is only the certainty of itself. At first, therefore, only the *abstract moments* of substance belong to *self*-consciousness; but since these, as pure movements, spontaneously impel themselves onward, self-consciousness enriches itself till it has wrested from consciousness the entire substance and has absorbed into itself the entire structure of the essentialities of substance. And, since this negative attitude to objectivity is just as much positive, it is a positing, it has produced them out of itself, and in so doing has at the same time restored them for consciousness. In the Notion that knows itself as Notion, the *moments* thus appear earlier than the *filled* [or *fulfilled*] whole whose coming-to-be is the movement of those moments. In *consciousness*, on the other hand, the whole, though uncomprehended, is prior to the moments. Time is the Notion itself that *is there* and which presents itself to consciousness as empty intuition; for this reason, Spirit necessarily appears in Time, and it appears in Time just so long as it has not *grasped* its pure Notion, i.e. has not annulled Time. It is the *outer*, intuited pure Self which is *not grasped* by the Self, the merely intuited Notion; when this latter grasps itself it sets aside its Time-form, comprehends this intuiting, and is a comprehended and comprehending intuiting. Time, therefore, appears as the destiny and necessity of Spirit that is not yet complete within itself, the necessity to enrich the share which self-consciousness has in consciousness, to set in motion the *immediacy of the in-itself*, which is the form in which substance is present in consciousness; or conversely, to realize and reveal what is at first only *inward* (the in-itself being taken as what is *inward*), i.e. to vindicate it for Spirit's certainty of itself.

802. For this reason it must be said that nothing is *known* that is not in *experience*, or, as it is also expressed, that is not *felt to be true*, not given as an *inwardly revealed* eternal verity, as something sacred that is *believed*, or whatever other expressions have been used. For experience is just this, that the content— which is Spirit—is *in itself* substance, and therefore an *object* of *consciousness*. But this substance which is Spirit is the process in which Spirit *becomes* what it is *in itself*; and it is only as this process of reflecting itself into itself that it is in itself truly *Spirit*.

It is in itself the movement which is cognition—the transforming of that *in-itself* into that which is *for itself*, of Substance into
Subject, of the object of *consciousness* into an object of *self-consciousness*, i.e. into an object that is just as much superseded,
or into the *Notion*. The movement is the circle that returns into
itself, the circle that presupposes its beginning and reaches it
only at the end. Hence, so far as Spirit is necessarily this
immanent differentiation, its intuited whole appears over
against its simple self-consciousness, and since, then, the former
is what is differentiated, it is differentiated into its intuited pure
Notion, into *Time* and into the content or into the *in-itself*. Substance is charged, as Subject, with the *at first only inward* necessity of setting forth within itself what it is *in itself*, of exhibiting
itself *as Spirit*. Only when the objective presentation is complete
is it at the same time the reflection of substance or the process
in which substance becomes Self. Consequently, until Spirit has
completed itself *in itself*, until it has completed itself as world-
Spirit, it cannot reach its consummation as *self-conscious* Spirit.
Therefore, the content of religion proclaims earlier in time
than does Science, what *Spirit is*, but only Science is its true
knowledge of itself.

803. The movement of carrying forward the form of its self-
knowledge is the labour which it accomplishes as actual History. The religious community, so far as it is at first the substance of absolute Spirit, is the uncultivated consciousness
whose existence is all the harsher and more barbarous the
deeper its inner Spirit is, and the deeper its Spirit is, the harder
the task that its torpid Self has with its essence, with the alien
content of its consciousness. Not until consciousness has given
up hope of overcoming that alienation in an external, i.e. alien,
manner does it turn to itself, because the overcoming of that
alienation is the return into self-consciousness; not until then
does it turn to its own present world and discover it as its property, thus taking the first step towards coming down out of the
intellectual world, or rather towards quickening the abstract element of that world with the actual Self. Through Observation
it finds, on the one hand, existence in the shape of Thought
and comprehends it, and, conversely, in its thinking it comprehends existence. When, to begin with, it has thus expressed the
immediate *unity* of Thought *and Being*, the unity of abstract

essence and the Self, abstractly; and when it has expressed the
primal Light in a *purer* form, viz. as unity of extension and
being—for extension is the simple unity which more nearly
resembles pure thought than light does—and in so doing has
revived in thought the *Substance* of the Orient, Spirit at once
recoils in horror from the abstract unity, from this *self-less* substantiality, and against it affirms individuality. But only after
it has externalized this individuality in the sphere of culture,
thereby giving it an existence, and establishing it throughout
the whole of existence—only after Spirit has arrived at the
thought of utility, and in its absolute freedom has grasped existence as its will, only then does it turn the thought of its inmost
depths outwards and enunciate essence as 'I' = 'I'. But this 'I' =
'I' is the movement which reflects itself into itself; for since this
identity, being absolute negativity, is absolute difference, the
self-identity of the 'I' stands over against this pure difference
which, as pure and at the same time objective to the self-knowing Self, has to be expressed as Time. So that, just as previously
essence was declared to be the unity of Thought and Extension,
it would now have to be grasped as the unity of Thought and
Time. But the difference left to itself, unresting and unhalting
Time, collapses rather within itself; it is the objective repose
of *extension*, while extension is pure identity with itself, the 'I'.
In other words, the 'I' is not merely the Self, but the *identity
of the Self with itself*; but this identity is complete and immediate
oneness with Self, or *this Subject* is just as much *Substance*. Substance, just by itself, would be intuition devoid of content, or
the intuition of a content which, as determinate, would be only
accidental and would lack necessity. Substance would pass for
the Absolute only in so far as it was thought or intuited as *absolute unity*; and all content would, as regards its diversity, have
to fall outside of it into Reflection; and Reflection does not pertain to Substance, because Substance would not be Subject,
would not be grasped as reflecting on itself and reflecting itself
into itself, would not be grasped as Spirit. If a content were
to be spoken of anyway, it would, on the one hand, only be
spoken of in order to cast it into the empty abyss of the Absolute,
and on the other, it would be a content picked up in external
fashion from sense-perception. Knowledge would seem to have
come by things, by what is different from itself, and by the dif-

ference of a variety of things, without comprehending how and whence they came.

804. Spirit, however, has shown itself to us to be neither merely the withdrawal of self-consciousness into its pure inwardness, nor the mere submergence of self-consciousness into substance, and the non-being of its [moment of] difference; but Spirit is *this movement* of the Self which empties itself of itself and sinks itself into its substance, and also, as Subject, has gone out of that substance into itself, making the substance into an object and a content at the same time as it cancels this difference between objectivity and content. That first reflection out of immediacy is the Subject's differentiation of itself from its substance, or the Notion's separation of itself from itself, the withdrawal into itself and the becoming of the pure 'I'. Since this difference is the pure act of 'I' = 'I', the Notion is the necessity and the uprising of *existence*, which has substance for its essence and subsists on its own account. But this subsistence of existence on its own account is the Notion posited in determinateness and is thus also its *immanent* movement, that of going down into the simple substance, which is Subject only as this negativity and movement. The 'I' has neither to cling to itself in the *form* of *self-consciousness* as against the form of substantiality and objectivity, as if it were afraid of the externalization of itself: the power of Spirit lies rather in remaining the selfsame Spirit in its externalization and, as that which is both *in itself* and *for itself*, in making its *being-for-self* no less merely a moment than its in-itself; nor is Spirit a *tertium quid* that casts the differences back into the abyss of the Absolute and declares that therein they are all the same; on the contrary, knowing is this seeming inactivity which merely contemplates how what is differentiated spontaneously moves in its own self and returns into its unity.

805. In this knowing, then, Spirit has concluded the movement in which it has shaped itself, in so far as this shaping was burdened with the difference of consciousness [i.e. of the latter from its object], a difference now overcome. Spirit has won the pure element of its existence, the Notion. The content, in accordance with the *freedom* of its *being*, is the self-alienating Self, or the immediate unity of self-knowledge. The pure movement of this alienation, considered in connection with the content,

constitutes the *necessity* of the content. The distinct content, as *determinate*, is in relation, is not 'in itself'; it is its own restless process of superseding itself, or *negativity*; therefore, negativity or diversity, like free being, is also the Self; and in this self-like *form* in which existence is immediately thought, the content is the *Notion*. Spirit, therefore, having won the Notion, displays its existence and movement in this ether of its life and is *Science*. In this, the moments of its movement no longer exhibit themselves as specific *shapes of consciousness*, but—since consciousness's difference has returned into the Self—as *specific Notions* and as their organic self-grounded movement. Whereas in the phenomenology of Spirit each moment is the difference of knowledge and Truth, and is the movement in which that difference is cancelled, Science on the other hand does not contain this difference and the cancelling of it. On the contrary, since the moment has the form of the Notion, it unites the objective form of Truth and of the knowing Self in an immediate unity. The moment does not appear as this movement of passing back and forth, from consciousness or picture-thinking into self-consciousness, and conversely: on the contrary, its pure shape, freed from its appearance in consciousness, the pure Notion and its onward movement, depends solely on its pure *determinateness*. Conversely, to each abstract moment of Science corresponds a shape of manifest Spirit as such. Just as Spirit in its existence is not richer than Science, so too it is not poorer either in content. To know the pure Notions of Science in this form of shapes of consciousness constitutes the side of their reality, in accordance with which their essence, the Notion, which is posited in them in its *simple* mediation as *thinking*, breaks asunder the moments of this mediation and exhibits itself in accordance with the inner antithesis.

806. Science contains within itself this necessity of externalizing the form of the Notion, and it contains the passage of the Notion into *consciousness*. For the self-knowing Spirit, just because it grasps its Notion, is the immediate identity with itself which, in its difference, is the *certainty of immediacy*, or *sense-consciousness*—the beginning from which we started. This release of itself from the form of its Self is the supreme freedom and assurance of its self-knowledge.

807. Yet this externalization is still incomplete; it expresses

the connection of its self-certainty with the object which, just because it is thus connected, has not yet won its complete freedom. The self-knowing Spirit knows not only itself but also the negative of itself, or its limit: to know one's limit is to know how to sacrifice oneself. This sacrifice is the externalization in which Spirit displays the process of its becoming Spirit in the form of *free contingent happening*, intuiting its pure Self as Time outside of it, and equally its Being as Space. This last becoming of Spirit, *Nature*, is its living immediate Becoming; Nature, the externalized Spirit, is in its existence nothing but this eternal externalization of its *continuing existence* and the movement which reinstates the *Subject*.

808. But the other side of its Becoming, *History*, is a *conscious*, self-*mediating* process—Spirit emptied out into Time; but this externalization, this kenosis, is equally an externalization of itself; the negative is the negative of itself. This Becoming presents a slow-moving succession of Spirits, a gallery of images, each of which, endowed with all the riches of Spirit, moves thus slowly just because the Self has to penetrate and digest this entire wealth of its substance. As its fulfilment consists in perfectly *knowing* what *it is*, in knowing its substance, this knowing is its *withdrawal into itself* in which it abandons its outer existence and gives its existential shape over to recollection. Thus absorbed in itself, it is sunk in the night of its self-consciousness; but in that night its vanished outer existence is preserved, and this transformed existence—the former one, but now reborn of the Spirit's knowledge—is the new existence, a new world and a new shape of Spirit. In the immediacy of this new existence the Spirit has to start afresh to bring itself to maturity as if, for it, all that preceded were lost and it had learned nothing from the experience of the earlier Spirits. But recollection, the *inwardizing*, of that experience, has preserved it and is the inner being, and in fact the higher form of the substance. So although this Spirit starts afresh and apparently from its own resources to bring itself to maturity, it is none the less on a higher level that it starts. The realm of Spirits which is formed in this way in the outer world constitutes a succession in Time in which one Spirit relieved another of its charge and each took over the empire of the world from its predecessor. Their goal is the revelation of the depth of Spirit, and this is *the absolute Notion*.

This revelation is, therefore, the raising-up of its depth, or its *extension*, the negativity of this withdrawn 'I', a negativity which is its externalization or its substance; and this revelation is also the Notion's Time, in that this externalization is in its own self externalized, and just as it is in its extension, so it is equally in its depth, in the Self. The *goal*, Absolute Knowing, or Spirit that knows itself as Spirit, has for its path the recollection of the Spirits as they are in themselves and as they accomplish the organization of their realm. Their preservation, regarded from the side of their free existence appearing in the form of contingency, is History; but regarded from the side of their [philosophically] comprehended organization, it is the Science of Knowing in the sphere of appearance:[1] the two together, comprehended History, form alike the inwardizing and the Calvary of absolute Spirit, the actuality, truth, and certainty of his throne, without which he would be lifeless and alone. Only

> from the chalice of this realm of spirits
> foams forth for Him his own infinitude.[2]

[1] Phenomenology.
[2] Adaptation of Schiller's *Die Freundschaft, ad fin.*

ANALYSIS OF THE TEXT

PREFACE

1. It is impossible to begin a philosophical work with a clear statement of the kind of view it hopes to establish, or of its relation to what others have written. For philosophy aims at a universality which will embrace and sum up particulars, and cannot be expressed till those particulars have been gone through, and have yielded up the universality in question. It cannot be anatomized in advance, without seeing how its parts function in the whole.

2. To state the relation of a philosophical work to others is also misleading, in that it suggests that previous works were false, and have now been cancelled out in truth. But philosophical systems do not replace falsehood by truth: they represent the ever clearer development of truth, which is as much present in earlier forms as in later, and which is only complete in a total development which includes all earlier stages.

3. A statement of philosophical aims and results is only legitimate if it is seen as being initial and superficial, and is not regarded as revealing the essence of the matter in hand. For this essence is not exhausted by aims, but by the way in which they are carried out. It is not concerned with mere results, but with the manner in which they emerge. To state results without saying how one arrives at them is to present the corpse of a system, whereas merely to differentiate a system from others is to remain resolutely on its fringes.

4. General principles and points of view belong only to the beginnings of the life of thought. Once one's mind has become deeply immersed in its subject-matter, they will be relegated to surface-talk.

5. Philosophical truth can only exist in the form of a fully-worked-out scientific system. Philosophy must show up the inner necessity that drives knowledge towards Science, and it must itself embody this drive when the appropriate moment arrives.

6. The true shape of truth is conceptual and notional. This can at present only be asserted as a counter to views like those of Jacobi (*Studies in Spinoza*, 1779), Novalis, Schlegel, etc., which make direct, unreasoning intuition *(Anschauung)* and feeling and central in philosophy, and the very being of the Absolute itself.

7. These latter views arise from the disillusioned desire to return to the peace and security of unquestioning faith which philosophical thinking has rudely shattered. They demand a suppression of thought-

distinctions, not their further clarification. They aim at edification and enthusiasm rather than cool insight.

8. Such views are an attempt to return to the heaven-directed gaze of earlier eras of thought, which has been succeeded by a gaze directed only to empirical detail, which now stultifies and starves the Spirit.

9. True Science cannot, however, be satisfied to see all detail vanish in an insubstantial, edifying mist.

10. The complacency which spurns as finite the exactly defined concepts and necessary connections of Science, is not above but below the level of Science. Its would-be profundities are empty, its sweeping assertions superficial, its prophetic pronouncements arbitrary and superficial.

11. Our own time is obviously ripe for a major intellectual and spiritual advance. This has been 'in the womb' for a long time, and is now about to achieve birth. Its birth-pangs are felt in a widespread sense of disillusion and frivolity, and in the vague foreboding of something unknown at hand.

12. A new scientific spirit is at first only present in general, notional germ. It is the product of an extensive, laborious transformation of previous cultural forms, and their resumption into a new simplicity. It must, to be fully actual, redevelop these forms out of this simple unity.

13. Science, in its new, notional form, as yet ill worked out and ill connected with the rich detail of past thinking, seems to be the obscure possession of an esoteric sect. To be generally intelligible and exoteric, it must connect all this past detail with its new position. To understand is to make familiar material *one's own* by incorporating it in a new scientific structure.

14. When Science first emerges, it has on the one hand a tendency to stress simple intuitive rationality and a relation to what is divine, but also on the other hand to develop this insight into an organized wealth of detail. The second tendency may be held in check by the first, but continues with justification to demand satisfaction.

15. The tendency towards detail may try to satisfy itself by merely running through familiarly organized material, adding to this much that is extraordinary and curious, and then mechanically applying the same 'absolute idea' to all such detail without the least modification to suit special cases. This is a monotonous formalism, applicable only to ready-made differences.

16. The false absolutism just sketched fails to develop difference and detail out of itself, but thinks it has done its task when it has said of anything specific that it is *not* to be found in the Absolute, since there we have only the Absolute's identity with self. Such an Absolute is the night in which every cow is black. As opposed to such a false

absolutism, it will be helpful to give a sketch of a true one. (Aimed at Schelling, but obviously applying to others as well.)

17. In my view, which the full exposition of my system alone can justify, the true Absolute must not merely be thought of as a Substance, i.e. something immediately there, whether this be a knower or something known. It must be thought of as a Subject. We think in terms of Substance if we think in terms of undifferentiated universality, whether this be that of what merely is, or of what merely thinks, or of what (à la Schelling) combines both in a single intellectual intuition.

18. True Substance is a being that truly is Subject, i.e. which only is itself in so far as it alienates itself from itself, and is then able to posit itself in and through what is thus alien. It cannot exist as a simple, positive starting-point, but only as part of a self-departing, self-returning movement, which both negates itself in indifferent, external otherness, and then reasserts itself as the negation of all such otherness.

19. The life and self-knowledge of the Absolute may well be described as that of the divine Love disporting itself with itself, but such an image readily becomes insipid, or sinks into edification, since it fails to emphasize the seriousness, the anguish, and the patient effort involved in thus negating the negation. The essence of the Absolute cannot be separated from its execution, nor its form from the full content of its carrying-out.

20. The true Absolute can only be seen as the *whole* of a self-realizing act or process, and is also the result or outcome of such an act or process. What is present at its beginning can only be emptily universal, and can only achieve specific content through connection with what appears to be other than itself, but what can then be seen to be not really other.

21. There is a horror of mediate connection which stems from a misunderstanding of the role of mediation in absolute knowledge. For mediation is merely the self-negation, and the negation of this negation, involved in the self-identification of the Subject. The Subject only becomes an immediate unity through the denial of its mediate connection with something else. Reflection, or the going from one thing to another, should not be abhorred: it is essential to the return to self which annuls it.

22. What has been said amounts to saying that Reason is purposive activity. External purpose has rightly been banished from natural philosophy, but not so the self-moving purposiveness which is indistinguishable from subjectivity. For in purpose the result or outcome is one with its moving cause, which in departing from self realizes self, and in which even the process of departing from self is a fulfilment of self.

23. Philosophical sentences, e.g. God is the moral order of the world, illustrate the nature of the Absolute. For while they appear to have fixed subjects to which predicates accrue externally, these subjects merely anticipate what is to be predicated of them, and only acquire concrete significance when the predication is completed. Predications analytically anticipated in the meaning of their subjects make predication quite vacuous.

24. Philosophical knowledge is essentially systematic, and a philosophical first principle therefore at once refutes itself by being merely a first principle. Being merely universal, merely initial, its further development is in a sense its own refutation, the clear exhibition of its merely initial character.

25. That philosophical truth is necessarily systematic, that Substance must be Subject, can be expressed by saying that the Absolute is essentially Spirit, both in and for itself. It is at first only in and for itself to philosophical reflection, and is then spiritual Substance, or Spirit in itself. It must become in itself *for* itself, must come to know Spirit, and itself as Spirit, i.e. must become its own object both immediately and reflectively. Spirit thus fully self-conscious is Science, i.e. Spirit fully constituted for itself in its own element.

26. To know itself and be at home with itself in what is absolutely other than itself, is the true 'Aether' of Science. But for the ordinary consciousness, which always opposes itself to its objects, life in such an Aether seems topsy-turvy and unreal. The thinking spirit must gradually accustom itself to such topsy-turvy unreality.

27. The genesis of Science is the theme of the Phenomenology of Spirit. This genesis starts from Spirit immediate or spiritless Spirit, i.e. from the consciousness of sense, and must tread a long road before it can become true Science, can give birth to its true concept or element. Such a genesis will not be a fancied illumination of the road to science, nor yet an actual founding of science, nor yet a pistol-shot of illumination aiming straight at absolute knowledge.

28. The task of proceeding from the uncultured to the knowing mind is really performed by the universal individual, i.e. self-conscious Spirit as such. The particular individual is merely a one-sided, partial expression of this Spirit, an expression in which one trait is emphatic and the rest underscored. The particular individual must, however, run through and repossess itself of all the phases of the universal individual's past development. They will now be seen as part of the environing scene, not requiring the deep research that was previously demanded.

29. It is impossible to state the scientific outcome of all this cultural development without running through it patiently stage by stage. Each stage on the route has been necessary, and has incarnated the

sense of the whole movement in one of its special phases. But such a running-through is eased and abbreviated by the reduction of past stages to explicit thoughts from being merely implicit existences.

30. Past stages have lost the immediacy of existence, but this loss of existence is only a first negation which still retains the immediacy of the mere presentation, the idea that is familiar, and has as such been set aside. This first negation must itself be negated, and the familiar idea brought back into the purview of the thinking self.

31. What is merely familiar is not as such properly known. To build upon familiar concepts of subjectivity, objectivity, God, Nature, etc., without allowing these ideas to develop, is and remains irremediably superficial.

32. The analysis of an idea is the removal of its familiarity, its reduction to elements that are the true possessions of the thinking self. In such reduction the idea itself changes and renders itself unreal. The force which effects analysis is that of the Understanding, the most remarkable and absolute of powers, the power of the thinking self and also of death. It is above all marvellous that this thinking self should be able to isolate, and to look at apart, what can only exist as an aspect or 'moment' in a living whole. Thinking Spirit can, however, only grasp such a whole by first tearing it into parts, each of which it must look at separately for a while, before putting them back in the whole. The thinking self must destroy an immediate, existent unity in order to arrive at a unity which includes mediation, and is in fact mediation itself.

33. Ancient thought differs from ours in that it built directly on the natural consciousness, and reached out to the universal from it, whereas our thought finds the universal lying ready to hand, in hard, fixed form, which it then has to revitalize and restore to fluidity. So vitalized, fixed ideas become self-moving notions, spiritual essentialities.

34. Such a movement of pure essentialities is Science as such, whose content is nothing but their necessary expansion into an organic whole. The notion of Science does not arise out of contingent philosophizing on these or those themes, relations or common ideas, nor from logical manipulations of these or those definite thoughts, but from the rounding-itself-out of the self-moving concept into cosmic completeness.

35. The exposition to be given in the present work is therefore the first part of Science, in that Spirit's first existence is merely the beginning in which it has not yet returned to self. Existential immediacy distinguishes this part of the system. This leads us on to comment on certain fixed ideas which occur in this context.

36. Consciousness, the immediate existence of Spirit, always em-

braces two opposed factors: the element of knowledge and that of objectivity. Together these constitute the experience of Spirit, and there is nothing in the objective Substance given in experience but what falls within such experience. Spirit, however, itself underlies the objectivity which at first confronts it as alien, and which is then repossessed and seen as its own.

37. The disparity between the self and the objective Substance is the void which inspires their movement towards one another. The ancients rightly made the void a principle of motion. The disparity between self and object is at once an inadequacy of the self in understanding the object, and an inadequacy of the object to itself. When the object is fully itself, i.e. fully revealed, the subject–object distinction vanishes and Phenomenology yields place to Logic.

38. There is a temptation to think that, since the standpoint of Phenomenology is superseded as false in the standpoint of Logic, it would have been better to have dispensed with it, and have gone straight to Logic. This argues a false view of truth and of its relation to what is false.

39. Falsehood is not simply the slag or dross which must be rejected to arrive at truth: it is the unshaped metal which must be reshaped and refined into truth, and which is necessarily present in the final shape of such truth.

40. The philosophical dogmatist thinks we can pronounce definitively on a philosophical issue as we can pronounce on the date of Caesar's birth or on the equality of the square on a triangle's hypotenuse to the two squares on its other two sides.

41. The truths of history, to the extent that they are contingent, and concern particular existents, are indeed naked matters of fact, which nothing renders necessary. Even here, however, there are grounds for and against, so that error becomes part of truth.

42. Mathematical truths are not thought to be known unless proved true. Their demonstrations are not, however, kept as parts of what they prove, but are only our subjective means towards knowing the latter. In philosophy, however, consequences always form part of the essence made manifest in them, which returns to itself in such expressions.

43. Mathematical insights, employing constructions and proofs, have to that extent always something false about them. We depart from the triangle in incorporating its parts into other figures, and we only come back to it in the end.

44. Mathematical knowledge is defective in that lines of proof and constructions have to be blindly tried out till we hit on one that leads to the desired conclusion. They are not consequences of the notional content of the theorem to be established.

45. Mathematics may plume itself on its self-evidence, but this self-evidence rests on the poverty of its aim and the defectiveness of its material, in which philosophy should be ashamed to follow it. Mathematics only seeks to establish quantitative relations which belong exclusively to the surface of things. Its materials are space and the unit, an empty, lifeless, repetitive element, set forth in fixed, dead propositions, linked together only by equational identities, and never progressing through opposition to some qualitatively different outcome. The incommensurability of the different dimensions, which for mathematics constitutes a problem, is a luminous necessity to the philosopher.

46. Mathematics is wholly unsuccessful in its treatment of time, which it does not see as standing in a relation of necessary opposition and complementarity to space. Its proofs of the equalization of moments in the lever, and of the relations of time and space in gravitation, are pitifully empirical. Time with its essential, living self-differentiation, is the very Notion present in actual existence. The notionless quantities and equations of mathematics are unable to capture its essence.

47. Philosophy does not move in the inert, abstract, unreal medium of mathematics, but in an actual, living progression of distinct notional phases, some of which negate what went before, and are themselves negated in what follows, but are all necessary steps in the progression, and are recalled in its final conclusion. Philosophical truth is like a Bacchanalian riot where the drunken participants fall down as they try to stand up, but it is also like the enlaced final sleep in which all have collapsed on to the floor.

48. The method of philosophy must be set forth by Logic, and is in fact Logic itself. It is not the method of mathematics, with its definitions, axioms, theorems, proofs, grounds *pro* and *contra* etc., which deals externally with its materials, and does not seek to develop their inner content. Mathematical methods are suited to their abstract materials, and to the fixed identities of concrete sensuous things, which do not change as we consider them.

49. But if philosophy steers clear of the loose methods of ordinary argument and the exact methods of mathematics, it must not therefore let itself sink back into prophetic divinations and enthusiasms which are not scientific at all.

50. Kant has brought back into philosophy the dialectical triplicity which is the essential form of Science. But neither he nor his successors have been able to give it life. They have treated it as an inert schema, and have applied it to the most heterogeneous materials, sometimes grossly empirical, sometimes categorial and notional. Such applications are as void of deep sense as are the category-headings of ordinary chatter.

51. Such unthinking application of the same schema to quite different materials is a pure formalism, though it may call itself a construction. It makes use throughout of a wild series of analogical identifications. The Understanding is linked to electricity, the animal to nitrogen, and so on. There is an appearance of conceptual connection where none is really present. The procedure resembles that of a poor painter who depicts everything in two colours, or, worse still, in one.

52. It is, however, only because dialectical triplicity is felt to be the essential form of Science that it is thus devitalized and abused.

53. True Science is nothing but the self-development of the Notion, which first confronts its own simple universality with a specific, objective other, then takes back the sense of that other into its own simplicity, thereby becoming more determinate. The schematizing Understanding merely catalogues and tables the stages of such self-development, without knowing what they amount to, nor the principle of their growth.

54. Every qualitative nuance of being has its own abstracted self-identity, which is one with the abstract self-identity of a distinct thought. This self-identical, qualitative nuance necessarily brings about its own dissolution, and becomes a mere moment in a wider whole. But this dissolution is not brought about by some alien process of reflection, but is cunningly contrived by the objective content itself, which to preserve itself must move beyond itself. The thought that sees this does not progress by a retreat into subjectivity, but by immersing itself in its object's own development.

55. The abstractive Understanding is not only an aspect of self-conscious subjectivity, but also of existent being. Existence means distinction in quality: this is the Understanding of existence, what Anaxagoras called its Noûs, and what later thinkers raised to the status of an Eidos or Idea or sort. But such a self-identical, distinct sort involves its own dissolution: it may seem to be destroyed by alien violence, but is in fact destroyed by the negation, the reference to another, which it bears within itself. In such becoming the Understanding-aspect of being passes over into its Reason.

56. The being of anything is one with its Notion, and this Notion is at once the necessity of its rhythmic development and the speculative concept which enables us to know it. It is not necessary to *apply* speculative categories to what concretely is, since the latter already embodies such categories in itself.

57. The scientific method of speculative philosophy will show itself to be at once determined by the contents it studies and by its own inherent rhythms. If it is described as we have just described it, resistance will be aroused from the standpoint both of sound common sense and of mystical insight. This is the standard response to what seems an

alien dogma: men prefer to be revolutionary in their own time and manner.

58. To think in pure Notions, e.g. self-identity, being-in-itself, being-for-self, is tiresome and difficult, both to the thought that prefers to think in pictures, in which what is universal is not clearly abstracted, and to merely argumentative thought, which does not immerse itself in its thought-content at all, but satisfies its vanity by pronouncing upon it rather than by allowing it to develop.

59. Argumentative thinking delights in refuting a conceptual content and reducing it to nothing. Such negative reflection is as vain and empty as the content it refutes. It is quite different from the constructive negation which always has a positive outcome.

60. Argumentative thinking connects the content it thinks of with its own self as judging Subject. The determination of subject by predicate seems to it to be its own free doing. But the thought which achieves grasp of its subject only does so when its round of predication is complete. It discovers its subject only in being forced to enlarge its predications, and not in its original reference. But picture-thought, concerned only with points of reference and with what is accidental, resents having to revise its content as it goes along. The revision of the logical subject, however, means the emergence of the thinking Subject, which finds itself in developing the content of the logical subject through various predications, and not in some arbitrary reference-point of which arbitrary predications are made. (Paragraph very difficult owing to identification-in-distinction of the conscious with the logico-grammatical subject.)

61. The conflict we have here is that of the superficial view of the proposition of judgement, which treats it as an external connection of independently significant elements, and of the speculative view which sees it as the self-development, through complementary differences, of a single significant content.

62. It is hard for an argumentative thinker to realize that, until he has decided what has to be said of a given logical subject, e.g. God in his relation to being, he is not truly concerning himself with subject of reference nor with any subject at all.

63. From this springs the objection to philosophical statements that they have to be read over many times before they can be understood. A comfortable enlargement of a familiar subject by the mere addition of predicates has ceased to be possible.

64. To mix argumentative thinking with speculative dialectic can never succeed, since the fixed points of reference necessary for the former are lacking in the latter.

65. Speculative dialectic does not merely dispense with the fixed distinctions of argumentative thought in some high flight of insight.

It shows them breaking down as it reflects on the intrinsic sense of propositions.

66. Speculative dialectic must itself be expounded in propositions, and this might seem to expose it to the same objections as argumentative thought, and to open the way to a critique of speculation. But the propositional form is a mere shell in speculation, since its predications are not meant to be externally added to an already fixed subject of reference. For this reason names like 'God' with a conventionally fixed content are best avoided in philosophy.

67. It is not thought necessary to have a preliminary training before one philosophizes: ordinary information, skills, methods are thought sufficient. But since nothing can be taken for granted until tested by philosophy, philosophy involves its own skills and standards which have to be learnt and practised.

68. Thought incapable of considering abstract propositions or their mutual relations should not be confused with tolerance and freedom of mind, much less with inspired genius. Inexact, undisciplined thinking has all the defects of poetry without its merits.

69. To be a naturalist or a common-sense philosopher is to revert to trivialities that it requires no philosopher to utter. Such trivialities always lead on to antinomies which are neither sophistical nor visionary. To refuse to engage in justifications and analyses is to abdicate human rationality.

70. To rely on common sense supplemented by a little reading of philosophical prefaces and reviews is an easy road to Science. Science, however, requires that truth should be won by the labour of the Notion developing itself in its own medium.

71. Though there have been many who value Plato for his literary myths, there have been times when his *Parmenides* has been seen to be the supreme work of art of the ancient dialectic, and the positive expression of the divine life. There have been times, too, when the philosophy of Aristotle was valued for its speculative depth. We may hope that our system will penetrate public attention, since it has had to wait till its time was ripe and its public in existence. This public does not consist of the *soi-disant* representatives of public opinion.

72. In our age the universal aspect of Spirit has been strengthened, while its individual expressions are less significant. In such an age the individual must forget his individuality and must do what he can, while less should also be demanded of him by society.

INTRODUCTION

73. It is a natural idea that before engaging in philosophical inquiry one should first examine the instrument or medium of such knowledge (Locke, Kant). Perhaps it is a good or a bad instrument, perhaps no good at all for knowledge of what absolutely is, since it modifies or distorts its object. It is quite vain, however, to try to eliminate the refracting and transforming powers of the instrument and so arrive at the intrinsic notion of the thing. For if what absolutely is cannot be reached by our faculty of knowledge, with all its refracting and transforming power, there is no sense in supposing that it can be reached by dispensing with or discounting the work of this faculty and the course it has to take. Remove the way truth affects us and nothing at all remains.

74. But if we doubt the ability of knowledge to reach what absolutely is, why not doubt the doubt and so on? It may be pointed out, further, that the notion of knowledge as a medium or instrument which stands in an external relation to what absolutely is, which is quite separate from it, is a wholly questionable notion which makes knowledge impossible from the start. In our fear of error we are excluding the possibility of knowledge.

75. That we might have knowledge of a sort, e.g. of phenomena, but not of what absolutely is, is a wholly obscure notion to which no one has managed to give any clear meaning. (Even knowledge of *Schein* or *Erscheinung*, Hegel is later to insist, is knowledge of how things really appear to be or manifestly are.)

76. All these confused conceptions which make knowledge inherently impossible must be dismissed: the actual development of knowledge itself sets them aside. But knowledge in its first appearance is itself merely apparent and so defective. Science cannot merely *claim* to be better than such apparent knowledge, for this is to put itself on the level of the latter, and to rely on its mere existence. Nor can it appeal to its own rudimentary presence in apparent knowledge, for this is not, in apparent knowledge, specially distinctive. We must accordingly say what apparent knowledge really is.

77. Apparent knowledge in all its varied forms is the path taken by the natural consciousness till it reaches true knowledge. Along this path Soul becomes purified into Spirit: by a complete experience of itself it comes to know what it in itself is.

78. In philosophy fundamental beliefs are always being shaken and are not restored in the same form as in the case of ordinary doubt. We are not merely trained thinkers who are now trying to think for themselves: we are people who for the first time are really learning

how to think, for whom the results of all training are in question. Philosophical scepticism is radical and not piecemeal.

79. But in philosophy scepticism does not merely doubt: it always arrives at a determinate positive result, a position whose positive truth involves, and is involved by, the negation of the position just considered before. Purely negative scepticism is a delusive form of consciousness which is passed on the way.

80. The goal of knowledge is a situation where there is no longer an apparent element to be discounted and transcended, but where Notion and object are mutually adequate. Consciousness by its very nature presses on to this goal, though it sometimes retreats in terror from this endless self-transcendence, and affects to regard all positions of thought as vain and empty, or as good in their own kind, thereby increasing its own vain self-importance.

81. To progress in self-criticism it seems that there must be a criterion which knowledge can apply to itself. But knowledge does not seem to possess any such criterion wherewith it can test itself.

82. Knowledge is always given as correlated with an independent, self-existent, objective something, *the truth*. This truth may be for consciousness, but it also is what it is in itself.

83. This independent, self-existent truth must, however, itself be a truth for consciousness, and this seems to make consciousness its own criterion, and to point to *another* self-existent truth with which the first truth can be compared, and so on.

84. In reality, however, both the self-existent truth and the knowledge of it fall within consciousness. Or otherwise put, the object as it intrinsically is, its essence, on the one hand, and the object *as* an object for consciousness or a Notion, on the other, both fall within consciousness, and the latter has to be made to conform to the former. Or if we identify Notion and essence, and the object is what this is for us, then we have to see if the object conforms to the Notion. Both these processes are the same and in them consciousness only applies its own criterion to itself. (This paragraph seems pure subjective idealism—consciousness in testing its ideas, its immanent contents, merely confronts them with other ideas, other immanent contents. But it can also be interpreted as saying that what objects 'in themselves' are is always more or less adequately there in and for consciousness, and in knowledge it has merely to replace an inadequate by a more adequate revelation.)

85. Consciousness itself tests itself and compares itself with its own object: we, the philosophical observers, can only observe it at work. Consciousness itself constantly changes its view of the object. What the object was intrinsically [*an sich*] becomes merely what it is for consciousness, and a new *Ansich* develops. We may say that conscious-

ness is adjusting itself to the reality of being, but it is more correct
to say that the reality of being is adjusting itself to consciousness. In
this adjustment the criterion applied by consciousness is *itself* being
tested and transformed.

86. For consciousness to negate what at first seemed absolutely
objective, and for it to regard this absolute truth as a mere truth-
for-consciousness, is for consciousness to have lived through an experience [*Erfahrung*] in the phenomenological sense, which always involves self-transcendence.

87. The progress of consciousness can be progress for consciousness;
it can also be a progress for the phenomenological observer who is
considering and commenting on consciousness. The phenomenological observer sees the links of negation and the resultant positiveness
which springs from negation in the successive phases of consciousness,
whereas for consciousness itself each step involves a surprising transition to a totally new object. The deep dialectic seen by the phenomenological observer goes on behind the back of consciousness itself.

88. Science includes in its content the road to Science, the account
of its own essential experience.

89. The shapes of consciousness are not fully conscious of themselves as shapes of consciousness, nor of their place in a continuous
conscious history, until the end of the road is reached.

I. SENSE-CERTAINTY

90. The knowledge from which our phenomenological investigation starts is absolutely immediate knowledge, which is also knowledge of what immediately is, of what just is there. What just is there
must simply be taken in, registered, we must not try to grasp it notionally, nor add anything to what it lays before us.

91. This sort of knowledge appears to be inexhaustibly rich in content and also in extent. What it lays before us seems to be infinitely
divisible and to stretch away infinitely in time and space. It also
appears to be the truest knowledge we can possess, since it omits no
detail of the object. But this kind of knowledge also shows itself up
(to the phenomenological observer) as the poorest and most abstract
possible: it merely acknowledges the *being* of the object. The consciousness which is aware of what to us merely is there, is likewise
denuded of content: it does no thinking work, it connects nothing
with nothing, it simply registers. It is just I, *this* consciousness, confronting *this* immediate content.

92. When scrutinized, however, sense-consciousness reveals itself
as less purely immediate than it at first seemed. It involves two typical

factors, an indefinite registered content and an indefinite registering self, and these constitute a necessary form or structure. There is a registering self only because there is an immediate content to register, and there is a registered content only because there is a self to register it. We are dealing with a general pattern of experience, not merely with a singular fact of existence. (A tendency to self-correction is inherent in consciousness and this distinguishes its subjectivity from its objectivity.)

93. Not only does sense-certainty embody this subject-object pattern, it also involves a *claim*, something *gesetzt*, posited, that one factor is more true and essential than the other. The object comes before it as the True, the essential, that which is there whether there is knowledge or not. Knowledge, contrariwise, is given as secondary, unessential: it presupposes, depends on, is mediated by the object, which is truly immediate and does not presuppose or depend on it. (Realism is thus not an imposed theory but part and parcel of our most elementary experiences. We are dealing with something whose deeper nature *will* come out as *we* examine it, but is not exhaustively and finally given.)

94. Sense-certainty seems, however, to involve an inherent conflict. Its object as given in it does not match what that object is given out as being. This content is not introduced by a reflective observer, but is part and parcel of sense-certainty itself. (It is because sense-certainty feels itself *not* to be the rich thing it on the surface claims to be, that it tries to *make out*, to *perceive*, what it has before it.)

95. The immediate 'This' of sense-certainty involves the two connected forms of the 'Now' and the 'Here'. If we try to pin the 'Now' down by giving it definite content, that content is quite inconstant. What *now* obtains is night, but (a little later) what *now* obtains is not night, but noon. (Since what is, always changes its appearance, we never get at it: it is the complete thing which *underlies* changing appearances.)

96. The *now* of sense-certainty reveals itself as inherently *universal*, i.e. it cannot be identified with any one definite state of things, though it can also indifferently be any one such state or another. (Universals obey a different logic from their instances. Not only the characters of what is are universals, but its general form is itself universal, i.e. the concrete reality behind changing appearances.)

97. In the use of demonstrative words there is a conflict between what we really say and what we mean to say (our *Meinung, was wir meinen*). We mean to express what is ultimately individual, but this is inexpressible: all we succeed in expressing is what is universal.

98. The demonstrative 'Here' behaves exactly like the demonstrative 'Now', and always changes its application. It is therefore a case

of pure universality. We cannot pin down the individual position *qua* individual, only individuality in *general*.

99. The universality of pure being which has revealed itself as the essence of sense-certainty involves abstraction, but it is not, as it seemed to be, real abstraction from rich contents, but abstraction from the mere meaning or claim to have rich contents. (Individuality on Hegel's view is a mere moment of living, concrete universality.)

100. Since the *object* of sense-certainty is not the definite contentful thing it claimed to be, the phenomenological emphasis shifts to the *Subject*. *My* experience becomes the rich, colourful thing. What I *mean* is important because it stems from *me* [*Meinen* and *mein*]. (Like Descartes, Hegel shifts to the individual Subject as that of which we are certain.)

101. But in the flux of experience the *me* which experiences always has different successive contents to its experience, and cannot therefore be identified with such contents. The *me* of the moment may mean to be definite in content, but it cannot express this definiteness. It is in a sense as much a plurality as a single *me*.

102. The *me* also stands essentially opposed to other *mes* and cannot say how *this me* differs from another. Each man is, as an experient, every man. (The individual as such cannot be understood or deduced.)

103. We now move to a position where not the mere object, nor the mere subject, is the rich, contentful thing, but the whole structured subject–object situation.

104–7. The whole structured subject–object situation is as essentially fluctuating as the mere subject or object considered before. The wholly definite time-situation we try to pin down at once becomes a matter of the past: the only present that can survive is a universal present which remains what it is despite variation of content, and which has subordinate presents within it. From the many 'Nows' which arise and pass away we come to a 'Now' which always is, no matter how long a happening may be. This is of course a universal. (The substantial, the permanent is the Universal not the particular.)

108. The wholly definite 'Here', the point, cannot be seized. Every real 'Here' breaks up into 'Heres', or points to 'Heres' beyond itself. But in all these 'Heres' the universal 'Here' persists. (We cannot get parts, but strictly speaking only the whole of Reality, and the whole of Reality is a universal present in all its so-called parts.)

109. Sense-certainty never grasps definite particulars but always deludes itself into thinking that it does. In the Mysteries bread and wine are consumed to show the nullity of the solid things of sense, and hungry animals reveal the same mystical wisdom.

110. Language, being divine and rational, frustrates the attempt

of sense-certainty to grasp surd particulars: it only expresses universals. The truth of sense-certainty is taking-for-true, i.e. perception. (The dialectic is much influenced by arguments in Plato's *Theaetetus*, where the impossibility of reconciling knowledge with radical subject–object flux is maintained, and the unchanging universal ideas are shown to be necessary. Wittgenstein would regard Hegel's treatment as resting on a misunderstanding of demonstratives, which are unique linguistic instruments, and neither name nor describe.)

II. PERCEPTION

111. Immediate certainty's true object is the universal, but it wants to deal with the immediate 'This'. Perception acknowledges the universal, the general pattern, to be its object, but it does not yet see this to be the essential element in its object: it is *we*, the phenomenological observers, who see this to be the essential element and the necessary outcome of what has gone before. For perception itself, the essential element is again the object, as in the sense-certainty. The object is the essential, constant, independent element, while perception is given as unessential, variable, dependent. Perception does not see that subject and object are equally the unessential forms in which a universal pattern is cast.

112. The object can, however, only be a universal pattern in so far as it unites many distinct elements, i.e. properties, in its pattern. The perceptual object is really given with the interior richness which the object of sense is only taken to have. (Universality is meaningless without specificity.)

113. The thing of perception is sense-given, but its sensuousness is universal, i.e. appears in the form of a property. Sense is *aufgehoben* (destroyed yet preserved) in the perceptual thing. But the universality of perception necessarily diremps itself into a number of mutually exclusive properties which at the same time it brings together. Its structure involves an inherent conflict. From one point of view it is an absolute unity, that of a space–time region, which brings the properties indifferently together, so that where the one is the other is also, while from another point of view it breaks up into the many distinct properties, each of which can be considered in and for itself.

114. The more loose 'Also' of a medium points, however, to some more absolute kind of unity which excludes otherness rigidly from itself. This absolute unity can be attributed to the several properties, or it can be attributed to the thing as such. We have the alternatives, it would seem, of having either a bundle of properties or a metaphysical peg to hang them on or both. (Very uncertain of interpretation.)

115. The perceived Thing represents a difficult compromise of (a) a set of properties loosely together and supplementing each other in the Thing; (b) the Thing as the space–time location or medium in which the properties are brought together; (c) the properties treated as pure universals having a status outside of the particular Thing.

116. The dialectic now takes a new turn. The perceptual object being this curious mixture of internal togetherness and apartness, the subject regards it as essentially constant and selfsame. All departures from *Sichselbstgleichheit* are attributed to the subject, are *its* illusions, and are not to be found in the object.

117. Consciousness now becomes aware of the contradictions in the object which only we, the phenomenological observers, have seen in it. The object first presents itself as a pure unity, but the properties are all universal and could exist outside of it. The unity of the object is therefore *my* confusion or mistake, and the object is really only an association of universals. But in such a loose association the properties are not effectively brought together so as to exclude one another: the object is therefore again a pure unity, and the properties mere sides of it. But the properties are often mutually indifferent, so that the object's unity again vanishes. The properties now become so wholly detached that they no longer contrast with anything, and no longer *are* properties. We are back at the blank being of sense-certainty.

118. Consciousness now repeats the whole circle somewhat differently. It becomes conscious of the essential untruth of all perception, and attributes this untruth to itself, being at the same time made aware of its power to correct perception and arrive at the naked reality behind perception, which corrected picture it again recognizes as its own.

119. The doctrine of primary and secondary qualities is now developed. The object itself is conceived as profoundly simple, but it is perceived with a variety of properties because it affects various bodily organs, eye, ear, etc. The conscious Ego now becomes the common medium in which all the Thing's sense-aspects are brought together.

120. By a new shift in the dialectic it is made plain that, if the Thing is conceived as absolutely One, it will be no longer possible to distinguish it from other things: all will be wholly blank unities and so indistinguishable. A Thing must be what it is only by having its own properties, those proper and peculiar to itself. Since each of these properties has its own separate being, the Thing again becomes a loose association of properties: it is A and also B and also C, etc.

121. Consciousness now, instead of attributing the plurality of the Thing's properties to itself, and making the thing intrinsically One, makes the Thing intrinsically an assemblage of properties, of free

'matters'—the physics of Hegel's day spoke of electrical, calorific, chromatic matters—while the object's unity is a sort of fiction for which consciousness alone is responsible.

122. Consciousness now gets tired of attributing such diverse errors to itself, and simply recognizes that the Thing itself (as reflected into itself) has this diversity of opposing aspects in it. It at one moment shows itself as a profound unity, at another moment as a loose assemblage of properties.

123. Consciousness no longer attributes the object's oscillation between profound unity and dirempted multiplicity to consciousness, but to the object. But a new device occurs to it. The object is put forth as profoundly One, while its diversity of aspects are due to its relations, not with consciousness, but with other objects, which as it were call forth different responses from it.

124. It seems absurd, however, that Things without intrinsic differences should be coaxed into showing difference by their mere relations with other Things without intrinsic difference. We are therefore forced to postulate an internal distinctiveness [*Unterschied*] which is essential to the object, and an external diversity [*Verschiedenheit*] from other objects, which is an unessential consequence of this. It is because Things are intrinsically distinctive that they are also extrinsically diverse.

125. We are, however, unable to distinguish this internal distinctiveness from the external diversity. The Thing's absolute character seems the same as its relatedness to other Things and vice versa.

126. Same point restated. The Thing's absolute self-relation, which negates all otherness, also shows itself up as being no more than thoroughgoing relation to others.

127. Same point. The extrinsic which is none the less quite necessary is really intrinsic.

128. We cannot draw subtle distinctions between 'the object as it intrinsically is' and 'the object as it is in relation to other Things'. The former is the latter and the latter the former: we have a distinction without a difference (i.e. a merely meant, intended, verbal distinction).

129. The Thing is therefore essentially overcome as it was previously overcome on its sensuous side. The latter revealed itself as pure universality, but as a universality infected with several conflicts: that of the universal and the individual, that of the unity of the properties in the Thing and their isolation as 'free matters', that of being intrinsically this or that and that of being something only in relation to other Things. The nature of the Thing is therefore simply the nature of the Understanding which constitutes it, and in which all these tensions are always present.

130. The sophistry of perception tries to save itself by a device of aspects and 'in so fars'. It talks of the perceived object *in so far* as it is one object, *in so far* as it is many properties, *in so far* as it has self-existence, *in so far* as it is related to other things, etc. This sort of device must be abandoned. It is the pure universality of the *Begriff*, of the Notion, which emerges, which involves in inseparable union the universal, the specific and the singular, the separate and the inter-related.

131. Perceptual understanding is dominated by the empty abstractions of individuality and universality, of the essential and the unessential, etc. It despises philosophy for concerning itself with *Gedankendinge*, but in effect deals with nothing else itself, and merely oscillates from one crude abstract thought to another. If it could realize that it is dealing with thoughts, concepts, it would be their master, and shape them as it wills, but it imagines that it is dealing with real matters, substances, etc. In its vain wanderings the perceptual understanding fails to arrive at the truth of things though it plainly reveals its own untruth.

III. FORCE AND THE UNDERSTANDING

132. The Thing of perception has passed away into a universal which is unconditioned since it includes what is specific and individual in itself, and is not merely an essence set over against the unessential. Consciousness has implicitly grasped the notional character of its object, but, not having itself become purely notional, fails to recognize itself in the object before it, which is still treated as an object, alien to itself.

133. The object of consciousness is consciousness's own notional object, but the consciousness *of* this notional character, its *Fürsichsein*, is lacking. Hence it comes before consciousness as freely active in independence of consciousness; consciousness merely watches it in action. It is *we*, the phenomenological observers, who must transform the object for consciousness till consciousness can see and grasp itself in the object.

134. Consciousness has thoroughly identified its object's being-for-self and its being-for-another. This is not merely the object's form but its content as well: it is the sort of object that in being for itself is for another, and vice versa. And this unity of the two aspects is *all* that the object has become.

135. None the less, since the aspects are identified, they are also distinguished, and consciousness therefore has before it the contrast of a number of loosely arrayed elements, on the one hand, and a pro-

found unity on the other. But these aspects are no longer given as rival views which merely oust one another, but each is given as essentially and necessarily passing over into the other.

136. The process of Force is precisely the process in which dispersed, independent elements come out from a unity in which they were lost, and again lose themselves in this unity. The dispersed elements are the expression or manifestation of Force, while Force proper, or Force unexpressed, is the unity out of which these manifestations issue. For thought the distinctions may have no substance, but the thought has to be carried out in the stuff of perception, and for perception Force unmanifest is obviously different from Force manifest. The two forms of Force are always vanishing into each other, for Force exists in so far as they keep up this mutual vanishing.

137. Though it is Force itself which by its nature passes from its unexpressed to its expressed form, these forms appear to be mutually external. Not only is this so, but the passage from one to the other necessarily appears as an external incitation or solicitation. Something external to the unmanifest Force provokes it to manifest itself, and something external to the manifest Force provokes it to retreat into unmanifest latency. This external solicitation is only in appearance external, and is really an inseparable aspect of the Force itself.

138. A Force is thus seen as essentially breaking up, dirempting itself into two Forces, one that is solicited to express itself (or withdraw itself from expression) and the other which solicits it to do just this. On examination, however, the soliciting Force is itself solicited into soliciting by the Force it solicits, and hence both Forces solicit and are solicited by one another.

139. These two Forces solicit and are solicited by one another, each appearing in relation to the other as medium in which properties are distinguished, and as a merely latent power. Each may be said to work upon the other, or to be worked on by it, because that other is not really distinct from its own self.

140. The difference of the two Forces or aspects of Force is both a difference in content (medium of properties and latent power) and form (soliciting and solicited). The distinction of form is given as intrinsic, while that of content exists merely for the observer. But in the actual process of Force both these differences are eliminated. The active solicitor turns into the passive object of solicitation and vice versa. For the phenomenological observer, too, the notional unity of the two extremes is evident: the solicitor *is* also the solicited, and the realized content *is* also the latent form and vice versa.

141. Each aspect of Force is a reality on its own, but its being consists essentially in a movement towards, a vanishing into the other aspect. Its being consists in a *Gesetztsein*, a positedness or being posited

by the other aspect. There is nothing fixed and substantial in either aspect by itself: the Notion of both is found in their essential unity. The true being of Force is not the reality it seems to gain or lose by being expressed or unexpressed, but the universal, the thought, which is present in both these states.

142. Force therefore appears in two guises, as a substantial entity active in the world of phenomena, and as a pure Notion behind or beneath phenomena. The latter is the truer view.

143. Consciousness now sees itself as penetrating beneath the surface show [*Schein*] of things, with its perpetual vanishing of factors and forces, to a true background of which the surface show is the appearance [*Erscheinung*]. In the surface play of Forces everything negates and cancels everything, but the true background is wholly positive. This whole background consists essentially of pure Notions which are part of the Subject's innermost self-consciousness. The Subject does not, however, as yet realize their subjective, notional character, and sees them as an inner essential depth in the objects themselves.

144. The Understanding therefore at this stage conceives of a true, supersensible, permanent world, a *Jenseits* which lies essentially beyond the *Diesseits* of this vanishing world of appearances. This world is a world of notional contents inadequately conceived as alien to the mind.

145. The conscious sphere of appearances is the middle term through which the Understanding penetrates inferentially to the inner, essential nature of things.

146. The inner, essential nature of things is readily conceived as a mere void, a region in which nothing positive can be known. (Kant's thing-in-itself.) Even subjective fancies are better than notions so wholly void of content.

147. But the inner, essential is essentially the *truth* of appearance, the truth in which immediate sense-certainty and perception are overcome, notionally transformed. It stands in a negative, but not merely negative, relation to the world of appearance.

148. Since Force and its expression are through and through dialectical, the soliciting being also the solicited, and the medium of properties also the latent force, the Understanding is driven beyond the play of Forces to the principle present in them all. This is no other than the *law* which governs all the manifestations of one Force.

149. A law is an abiding image of restless appearances, a principle which, in governing change and revealed in change, is itself unchanging. The supersensible world is a tranquil kingdom of laws.

150. The kingdom of laws has an ever varying actual existence in the world under ever varying circumstances. It tends to be thought of in an ever more abstract way and so becomes refined into the mere

empty form of law as such. Hegel thinks that the law of universal gravitation has this empty character: it merely says that everything has a law-determined relation to everything else. This is important only as setting bounds to chance and sensuous independence.

151. Hegel thinks that beyond specific laws is the bare conception of law, which transcends specific laws and even law as such. It reduces all distinctions of content and form which occur in laws into an absolute unity, a pure necessity.

152. The duplicity of Force and expression reappears in the case of laws. Laws have both an explicit specification in which all the differences to which they apply have a distinct expression: they also occur as pure universalities in which all such specification is somehow absorbed and nullified. Simple electricity, e.g., is the absolute unity behind positive and negative electricity and the laws connecting them, simple gravity is the absolute unity behind the factors of mass, distance, velocity, etc., and the laws connecting them. Wherever there are laws there is a deep underlying unity expressed in them, and every deep unity expresses itself in characteristic laws.

153. In the common representation of the deep nature behind laws, a law is readily thought of as a mere by-product of the relation of the factors present in the law, e.g. motion is an accidental relation between the independent variables of distance and time, etc. This is a deeply wrong way of conceiving the matter. Motion is in reality the whole which distance and time alike presuppose, and in which alone they make sense, and so on in other similar cases, e.g. gravitation. There can be no laws except where there is a common deeper nature behind the laws.

154. The Understanding is now tempted to regard the deeper unity behind the law as something that *we* postulate and which is not properly to be attributed to the thing. The nature behind the law is merely the law otherwise expressed. The process of tautologization, of reducing the same to the same, is what we call 'explanation'. Various electrical phenomena arise in a law-governed manner because Electricity is their common ground.

155. We are, however, brought to realize that the distinction between the law and the unitary nature behind the law cannot be regarded as merely a distinction that *we* draw. The thing itself involves the distinction which has therefore a position in the supersensible background of things.

156. The very nature of the intelligible world is thus to draw distinctions which turn out to be no distinctions. It is the selfsame which repels itself from itself, and this element repelled is in consequence attracted to what has repelled it, for it is the same 'at bottom'. (Passage illustrates the essential peculiarities of Hegelian logic.)

157. Hegel now passes to the difficult conception that, in addition to the first intelligible world which is a tranquil kingdom of laws, there must also be a second intelligible world which embodies all the distinctions and exclusions which we find in the phenomenal world. There must not only, to use Platonic language, be single Ideas of essences multiply instantiated, there must also be Ideas of Instances *qua* Instances, and of Instantiation as such. This second intelligible world will be the inverse of the first one.

158. The inversion is now rather fancifully worked out by Hegel in the statement that what is sweet in the first intelligible world is sour in the second, what is a north pole in the first is a south pole in the second, what is revenge here is punishment there, what is honoured here is dishonoured there, what is a disgrace here is a saving grace there, and so on. The inversions of the Sermon on the Mount are used to illuminate the inversions of physical explanation.

159. On examination, however, the inverted world shows itself to be indistinguishable from the sense-world of which it purports (at a second remove) to be the essence. Everything in the sense-world is there only with a nuance of difference that really amounts to nothing. It is quite as one-sided in its way as the sense-world and the first intelligible world are one-sided. All it embodies is in fact present in the tensions and oppositions of the actual sense-world, where there is a real north pole lying side by side with the real south pole, and so on.

160. We progress to a true view of the relation of essential nature to outward manifestation if we see both the profound opposition of the two, which must not be ignored, and the fact that each factor is the opposite of its opposite, and so includes the whole opposition and its opposite in itself. The supersensible world, in particular, in being the inverse of the sensible world, includes the sensible world in itself. (Cf. Plotinus: Everything that is yonder is also here.) Such a distinction within a profound identity is called by Hegel 'infinity', since the thing is not bounded by an opposite alien and external to itself.

161. 'Infinity' means that we have (a) a unitary nature, e.g. motion, electricity, which dirempts itself into (b) a number of distinct, interconnected factors, space, time, positive electricity, negative electricity etc. which none the less (c) show themselves as overcome, cancelled in their common unity. They are inseparable aspects of the common unity in question.

162. There is no problem in the self-diremption of an absolute unity. It can only be an absolute unity if it also dirempts itself and is itself in such diremption. If it merely stood opposed to diremption, it would not be the absolute unity, but be itself dirempted from something else.

163. The truth of all these convolutions lies in the self-conscious Understanding which is in all this merely discovering itself and its varied aspects and internal tensions. (This need not be interpreted in a purely subjective manner. The Understanding has not manufactured the natural world. But both are sides of the Absolute Idea whose function it is to realize itself in self-conscious Spirit.)

164. The Understanding does not, however, realize that all these dissolving distinctions are merely the internal manœuvres of its own self-consciousness; only we, the phenomenological observers, realize this.

165. The two extremes of the Understanding gazing into the inner world of essence, and this inner realm itself, are now merged together. The curtain of appearance is drawn aside, and the Ego, *qua* expression of the Absolute Idea, will come to see only itself beyond. But for it to realize that it is seeing itself, it must itself go behind the curtain, and to do this requires several prior steps and stages.

IV. THE TRUTH OF SELF-CERTAINTY

166. So far certainty has always been outward-turned. It has affirmed the truth of something other than itself. But this reference to sheer otherness has shown itself up as empty and untrue, and a certainty has arisen which measures up to its truth: certainty is certain of certainty, and consciousness has its own truth in consciousness. A residual distinction remains, but it is also a distinction overruled: a distinction between a concept as an act or cognitive motion, and the tranquil content which is itself, or between the concept as the mere self-being of the object and the object as there-for-another. The conscious Ego is both the related subject–object terms and the relation between them: it has an Other which it overreaches and sees as itself.

167. In the new state of self-consciousness the features of the previous other-consciousness are summed up and preserved, but only as insubstantial, vanishing phases. There must be a trace in it of the immediate separate being of the sense-given world, which is, however, given as a mere appearance, and devoid of genuine substance. Self-consciousness feels the unity of this seeming other world with itself in the form of a desire to abolish this seeming otherness and to discover itself in this alien content. (The nature of Desire: to abolish the otherness of the Other.)

168. To desire in the subject, there corresponds in the object life, which, like desire, seeks to achieve infinity and to be itself (without knowing itself) in its other. The living object has implicitly the same

self-transcendent completeness which is explicitly realized in self-consciousness.

169. The essence of life is infinity as the supersession of all distinctions, tranquilly seated at the centre of axial rotation, the moving essence of time congealed into spatial solidity. All distinctions in the living organism pass away in flux, but must have a momentary solidity and separateness in order to pass away in this manner. Fluidity, pure movement, is the essence of the living.

170. The independent members of the living organism have their limited self-existence which, however, is nothing but their relation to the total flux of living, and which itself in its truth is nothing beyond a constant diremption into independent shapes. The unity of life is constantly dirempted, because only as dirempted can it continue to be a unity. Shapes pass away and are superseded by other shapes, because their real Substance is the flux which is constantly being dirempted in them.

171. As fluidity, life always involves a gamut of independent forms, each asserting itself against the others, and against the whole flux itself. Either can be regarded as the *Ansich*, the inner self of life, while the other is merely the other side of this. Life constantly consumes and dissolves its solid structures, and therefore has general dissolution as its constant essence, but again it regenerates such structures out of such consumption and dissolution, and therefore has articulate diremption as its constant essence. This turning and twisting is the essence of life: life indeed *is* absolute turning and twisting. It is an ever developing, ever dissolving whole which, in development and dissolution, simply maintains its being.

172. Life proceeds from immediate unity through articulation and process back to a like unity, which, however, being repeated, is a generic unity. The constant simple genus which is maintained in life points to consciousness, for which alone such a genus exists *qua* genus.

173. Self-consciousness which contemplates genera, and which is itself purely generic, is at first aware of itself as a pure Ego, an extreme abstraction which will however, enrich and differentiate itself.

174. The pure Ego is the simple universal which seeks (at this stage) to assert itself by abolishing the articulate forms which stand or seem to stand opposed to it. It is essentially desire, need.

175. The object which the pure Ego of self-consciousness seeks essentially to abolish is, however, essential to its being as an abolishing activity, and is therefore always regenerated as much as abolished. Self-consciousness can therefore only achieve satisfaction in so far as the object abolishes itself, shows itself *to* self-consciousness as really being self-consciousness. Self-consciousness can only achieve satisfaction in *another* self-consciousness.

176. The manner in which the living organism abolishes articulate otherness and in which ordinary desire does so, are merely undeveloped versions of the abolition of otherness which occurs in the mutual recognition of two self-conscious persons.

177. Only in a self-consciousness for a self-consciousness do we have a true, accomplished case of self-consciousness, where the object of consciousness is also its subject. Animal desire is only universal substance pursuing universal substance: here subject pursues and also finds subject. We have now risen to the level of Spirit, the I which is a We, and the We which is an I. We have moved from the coloured show of this-world sense, and the empty notional night of Understanding, into the spiritual daylight of what is completely present. (Hegel holds that the understanding of other minds, far from being more obscure than the understanding of things, is the model and paradigm in terms of which intercourse with things can assume a limited clarity. In all intercourse with things we are striving towards the complete penetration and lucidity of social intercourse.)

LORDSHIP AND BONDAGE

178. Self-consciousness exists in and for itself inasmuch, and only inasmuch, as it exists in and for itself for another, i.e. inasmuch as it is *acknowledged*. It is therefore essentially one only in duplication, and reveals itself in a number of traits which have to be kept firmly apart, and yet reveal themselves as always melting into one another, and dissolving this apartness.

179. Self-consciousness lives outside of itself in another self-consciousness, in which it at once loses and also finds itself.

180. Self-consciousness is intrinsically set to eliminate this alien selfhood, but, in being so set, it is both set to eliminate the other in order to achieve its own self-certainty, and also to eliminate itself in the process, since it is itself that other.

181. This dual elimination involves, however, a return to self, since what is eliminated is its own other-being, while it at the same time permits the other to be other, since it removes its *own* being from the other.

182. The process just outlined in 178–81 is not, however, carried out solely by one consciousness on the other, but by both consciousnesses on each other. It can only be successfully carried out by either consciousness because it sees the other doing to it just what it does to the other: each in fact demands that the other should treat it just as it treats the other.

183. Each consciousness then acts on itself as much as it acts on the other, and what it does is as much done by the other to it, as by it to the other consciousness.

184. Separate consciousnesses re-enact at a higher level the action of mutually soliciting forces which, in soliciting each other, in effect only put themselves forth. Each uses the other as the means by which it achieves self-consciousness. To mutual solicitation mutual recognition here corresponds, as well as the recognition *of* mutual recognition.

185. The recognition of self in its other at first presents itself in a one-sided form in which only the one side does the recognizing, and the other side is merely recognized.

186. Self-consciousness is at first simple being-for-self which is attached to an immediate individuality which excludes all others from itself. Self at first confronts self, not as an infinite negation of the negation making all its own, but as a simple case of natural being facing another such case, both deeply absorbed in the business of living. Each is conscious only of its own being, and so has no true certainty of itself, since the being of the self is essentially a socially acknowledged being.

187. Self-consciousness must, however, express itself as the negation of all mere objectivity and particularity. This initially takes the form of desiring the death of the other at the risk of its own life. Self-consciousness must be willing to sacrifice everything concrete for its own infinite self-respect and the similar respect of all others. A life-and-death struggle therefore ensues between the two rival self-consciousnesses.

188. For both members to die in the life-and-death struggle would not, however, resolve the tension between them. (Nor would the death of one of them do it.) Death certainly eliminates all opposition, but only for others, or in a 'dead' manner. Death does not preserve the struggle that it eliminates in and for the parties in question. For preservation, it is essential that the parties in question should live.

189. The demotion of another self-consciousness so that it does not really compete with my self-consciousness, now takes the new form of making it thing-like and dependent, the self-consciousness of a bondsman as opposed to that of a lord. That the two self-consciousnesses are at bottom the same becomes deeply veiled.

190. The self-consciousness of the lord is essentially related to the being of the mere things he uses and uses up, and these he enjoys through the bondsman's self-consciousness. The bondsman prepares and arranges things for the enjoyment of the lord. The self-consciousness of the lord is likewise essentially related to the self-consciousness of the bondsman through the various punitive, constraining, and rewarding instruments which keep the bondsman in thrall. The bondsman working on things does not completely overcome their thingness,

since they do not become what he wishes them to be, or not for himself. It is the lord who reaps the enjoyment from the bondsman's labours.

191. We thus achieve an essentially unbalanced relationship in which the bondsman altogether gives up his being-for-self in favour of the lord. The lord uses him as an instrument to master the thing for his own (the lord's) purposes, and not for the bondsman's, and the bondsman acquiesces in the situation, and becomes in fact part and parcel of the total objective situation. This means, however, that the lord cannot get the reciprocal recognition that his self-consciousness demands from a consciousness so degraded and distorted. What the lord sees in the bondsman, or what the bondsman sees in the lord, is not what either sees in himself.

192. The lord therefore paradoxically depends for his lordship on the bondsman's self-consciousness, and entirely fails of the fully realized independence of status which his self-consciousness demands.

193. The truth of independent self-consciousness is therefore to be found rather in the bondsman's self-consciousness than in the lord's. Each is therefore the inverse of what it immediately and superficially is given as being.

194. The bondsman in his boundless quaking respect for the lord becomes shaken out of his narrow self-identifications and self-interest and rises to the absolute negativity, the disinterested all-embracingness of true self-consciousness. He becomes the ideal which he contemplates in his lord.

195. The bondsman has the further advantage that in working on the object he as it were preserves his labour, makes the outward thing his own and puts himself into it, whereas the lord's dealings with the object end in vanishing enjoyments. The bondsman overcomes the otherness and mere existence of material thinghood more thoroughly than the lord, and so achieves a more genuine self-consciousness.

196. The bondsman in overcoming the mere existence of material thinghood also rises above the quaking fear which was his first reaction to absolute otherness as embodied in the lord. Then he achieved self-consciousness in opposition to such otherness, now he achieves a self-consciousness not opposed to otherness, but which discovers itself in otherness. In shaping the thing creatively, he becomes aware of his own boundless originality. Hegel thinks that the discipline of service and obedience is essential to self-consciousness: mere mastery of things alone would not yield it. Only the discipline of service enables the conscious being to master himself, i.e. his finite, contingent, natural self. Without this discipline formative ability would degenerate into a narrow cleverness placed at the service of personal self-will. (Hegel suggests that a period of subjection to others is essential to the highest

magisterial rationality. Not to have undergone such discipline results in a trivialization of self-consciousness which never rises above petty finite interests. It would seem that the permissive bringing-up of children is implicitly condemned, and that 'imperialism' and 'colonialism' at certain stages of development are given a justification.)

FREEDOM OF SELF-CONSCIOUSNESS

197. In the servile self-consciousness we have the moments of pure, universal being-for-self projected on to the lord, and its own implicit self-existence projected on to the particular contentual things it elaborates. These moments are not united in the servile consciousness, but for us, the observers, they are identical, and we are therefore brought to think of an essentially infinite, free, thinking self-consciousness which preserves its selfsameness in the various purely conceptual contents that it envisages. At first, however, its content is not unfolded nor set in motion, and it appears as merely the unfettered universality of thought.

198. The form of self-consciousness now before us can be identified with that historical Stoicism which makes of consciousness a purely thinking essence to which nothing can be of moment except to the extent that it puts its own thinking being into it.

199. In this form of self-consciousness all detailed content of consciousness, natural existences, feelings, desires, aims (whether our own or other people's) becomes unessential; only the pure conscious thought that we put into them counts. The Stoic self-consciousness is indifferent to the master–slave distinction: whether on the throne of the world like Marcus Aurelius, or in the slave's chains of Epictetus, it withdraws into the solitary sovereignty, the pure universality of thought. Such a withdrawal is characteristic of a period in which high culture goes with universal fear and bondage.

200. The pure Ego of Stoicism, though not devoid of content, is inward-turned whatever its content, and has therefore an abstract indifference to natural being which it leaves to take its own course. The freedom of such Stoicism is not, therefore, a living, contentful freedom, but the mere idea of such freedom, drawn away from life and things into itself. This means that unless content is externally given to this consciousness, it cannot by itself determine the True and the Good. It has no criterion other than the wholly empty, abstract one of the reasonable, a notion as tedious as it is superficially elevated.

201. The Stoic consciousness may negate particular content, but it altogether fails to negate this negation, i.e. to appropriate such content to itself. The specificity of its contents still falls outside of its thinking essence.

202. Scepticism carries into realization what Stoicism merely

notionally thinks. It explicitly negates the rich determinate content
of life and action. All tasks and all desires become for it vanishing
quantities.

203. Scepticism carries to the limit the dialectic which has been
sapping Sense-certainty, Perceptual acquaintance, Understanding,
and the master–serf relationship, a dialectic which has steadily eliminated determinateness from our thinking and left us with empty scientific abstractions from the last of which we now withdraw our cre-
dence.

204. Scepticism does not regretfully see the solid world of reality
going up in the flames, nor even its own perception of that world, it
does not even repine at the sacrifice of its professional sophistries
which have framed the bonfire. In seeing all this vanish, it has become
confirmed in the consciousness of its own freedom from conviction,
in the simple negativity of its own thinking.

205. This sceptical freedom from determinate conviction is also,
however, a giddy whirl of disorderly, ever dissolving, ever reinstated,
personal beliefs. The sceptic in fact confesses that, as a finite, contingent, empirical person, he is everlastingly subject to many definite,
unjustifiable convictions. He has to continue with the business of ordinary living, acting and speaking. He oscillates continually between
the high detachment of universal scepticism and a welter of unreason-
able beliefs. Even his pure scepticism is a thesis for which doubtful
arguments are adduced, and he must in practice rely on the deliverances of the senses and the conventions of morality. The sceptical
self-consciousness is in fact deeply self-contradictory, and its reason-
ings and counter-reasonings are like the arguments of children concerned to contradict one another and always to have the last word.

206. Scepticism is self-contradictory but unaware of its inner self-
contradiction. Its 'truth' is a consciousness which makes self-contradiction its explicit principle, which is always conscious of itself
both as selfsame, unchangeable, and free, *and* as confused, variable,
and distorted. In it both the magisterial and the servile elements are
present in uneasy unity. This new emergent consciousness is called
the Unhappy Consciousness.

207. This Unhappy Consciousness essentially moves towards the
accomplished goal of Spirit, which involves the vision of one self-consciousness in another. For the Unhappy Consciousness, however, this
goal is remote and implicit: its two sides are always being forced
together in unity, only to fall painfully apart.

208. The Unhappy Consciousness separates its unchangeableness
from its variability, and regards the former as exclusively essential,
the latter as wholly unessential. Being an unhappy, divided consciousness, it identifies itself with the unessential, changeable element, but

it cannot help having the unchangeable element as its true essence. It is therefore in the paradoxical position of having its true essence outside of itself, and for ever trying to be what, from another point of view, it essentially is.

209. The Unhappy Consciousness cannot unite itself with its unchangeable essence without importing changeableness into that essence and so starting a fresh cycle of struggle and misery.

210. In this movement various identifications and separations of unchangeable essence and variable non-essence occur, which suggest the triune Persons of Christian theology. There is a consciousness, suggestive of the infinitely transcendent Father, which rejects the variable non-essence from the unchangeable essence. There is also a consciousness, suggestive of the Son, which accepts something in the realm of unessential variability as an embodiment, an outer shape of the unchangeable essence. There is also a consciousness of the Spirit as reconciling the eternal essence with the changeable non-essence in a deeply joyful manner.

211. These identifications and separations are for us part and parcel of the unchangeable essence itself, which is not dirempted as the Unhappy Consciousness sees it. But for the Unhappy Consciousness itself they are merely appearances which it attributes to the unchangeable consciousness, and which are all hopelessly beyond itself.

212–13. For the Unhappy Consciousness, having thus turned a necessary relationship into a contingent coincidence, forgets its own relation to the Unchangeable, and only considers its relation to the remote past specification of the eternal essence. It is with this remote past specification (the historic Christ) that it must become united.

214. The unessential consciousness strives to unite itself to its embodied Transcendent in threefold fashion: (a) as a pure consciousness; (b) as an individual with wants and work to perform; (c) as conscious of its being-for-self.

215. As regards (a) the embodied Transcendent seems to the pure consciousness to be posited as it is for itself. But its transcendence means that its present revelation is necessarily imperfect, and refers a perfect revelation to the distant future.

216. The Unhappy Consciousness is itself the bridge between the unchangeable and the changeable consciousness. But it does not as yet see itself as such a bridge.

217. Its relation to the Unchangeable is therefore not one of explicit thought [Denken] but of implicit thought or devotion [Andacht]. It thinks of its Unchangeable musically, or by way of clouds of incense, as a saving union of pure thought with individuality which lies for ever beyond itself, and which it can only yearn towards. Its feeling essence lies for ever outside the notional essence it adores, and

it can only lay hold of its unessential externals. Only the grave of the divinity can be penetrated: the divinity itself eludes it. Only by giving up the search for the ideal in the actual world (*our* non-Hegelian use of 'actual') can it hope to find it.

218. The Unhappy Consciousness's relation to its embodied Transcendent appears further as its own self-feeling connected with its desires and the work it performs. This desire and this work do not, however, give its existence positive meaning, make it confident of itself, enable it to enjoy the Transcendent. All that they bring to light are the Unhappy Consciousness's infinite remoteness and separation from its ideal.

219. What the Unhappy Consciousness works upon is given as having two sides like the Consciousness itself. In one of them it belongs to the Unchangeable, in another to the realm of variability.

220. For the Unhappy Consciousness its abilities are not really its own, nothing whose exercise can give it personal satisfaction: all are gratuitous gifts from the Unchangeable.

221. The activities of the Unhappy Consciousness are given as being as much products of the Unchangeable's free grace as are the passive reactions of the things it works upon.

222. The Unhappy Consciousness only feels one with the Unchangeable when it adopts an attitude of boundless gratitude towards it. But even this attitude separates it from the Unchangeable, and confirms it in its unhappy distance.

223–4. Consciousness must, however, return to itself out of its feeling and its work, and in this return it is conscious of itself as simply nought and null in the sight of its Transcendent.

225. The Unhappy Consciousness affirms its nullity by discovering 'sin', alienation from the Unchangeable, in its most trivial activities, and in brooding continually on its own sinfulness.

226. But in its sinfulness it is always necessarily directed to the Unchangeable, and would not otherwise feel itself as sinful.

227. Its relation to the Unchangeable is therefore necessarily mediated for it by a third (priestly) consciousness which brings it into harmony with its ideal.

228. The Unhappy Consciousness surrenders all the fruits of its personal work and enjoyment, and accepts the direction of this mediating priestly consciousness in all things.

229. Only by the complete sacrifice of all decisions and understanding to this mediating consciousness can the Unhappy Consciousness achieve union with the Unchangeable.

230. It is the absolving act of the intermediary consciousness that must release the Unhappy Consciousness from its sinful schism, establish its oneness with the Unchangeable. This absolution still has a

tinge of unhappy externality but it is in principle a consciousness of the universal, positive, rational mind overcoming and superseding the alienated personal one. Implicitly, though not fully, it has now the consciousness of being, in all its particularity, inherently and essentially absolute, of being all reality.

(Hegel's three exemplary states of Stoicism, Scepticism, and the Unhappy Consciousness need not be given the philosophical or religious content that he gives them. One might, for instance, illustrate them by (a) the empty self-satisfaction of a mechanist who believes that all organic and psychic action can be mechanistically explained, without attempting to show how this is possible; (b) the equally empty self-satisfaction of a theoretical mechanist who also believes that it will never be actually possible to give an adequate explanation of organic and psychic action in mechanistic terms, or who thinks that a non-mechanistic explanation is equally feasible; (c) the tormented state of one who believes that a mechanistic explanation of life and consciousness is possible but despairs of ever finding it, who always dreams *(Andacht)* of an unattainable mechanistic explanation, who always treats non-mechanistic explanations as a *pis aller* for mechanistic ones (Freud), and who drags in the priestly scientist to validate his philosophical and moral opinions.)

V. THE CERTAINTY AND TRUTH OF REASON

231. Consciousness in the experience of absolution has risen to the realization that the individual consciousness is implicitly one with the Absolute Essence which is, however, still placed essentially beyond itself. In this realization self-consciousness has been projected into the world of objects, into the realm of being, and it has also identified itself with the universal. It has become the middle term in a syllogism which reconciles the individual with the unchangeable universal, and which thereby sees itself as all truth.

232. Hitherto (in Stoicism, etc.) consciousness has adopted a purely negative attitude to the world and to its own actuality in it, and has sought to save its pure essence from both. Now, as Reason sure of itself, it tranquilly sees all reality, objective and subjective, as no other than itself. It has achieved the position of idealism. Having done away with graves and abolished abolitions, it sees the world as its own new actual world, as its own truth and presence, which it wishes to see maintained in being and not vanish away.

233. Reason is consciousness's certainty of being all reality: this is the essential Notion of idealism. For Reason, the Ego's object is neither emptily general nor one object among others: it is an Ego which

excludes anything taken as other than itself. It can, however, only be all reality for and in itself, in so far as it shows itself to be such, and this it has done in the dialectical development from sense-certainty to the Unhappy Consciousness. Only in the light of this history, this experience, is the liquidation of other-being and the pure certainty of Reason intelligible. For the reasonable consciousness this certainty is a fact, but it is not an explicitly formulated or comprehended fact.

234. An idealism which merely asserts this certainty (All the world is my idea) without going through the relevant dialectical preparation can neither explain nor understand itself. Its certainty always stands over against other certainties that the dialectical journey abolishes. The certainty of my rational ego always stands over against the certainty of something else existing alongside myself. The dialectical preparation establishes idealism as the only truth, but only in a general, abstract form which will have to be given concreteness in various actual sorts of confrontation.

235. The rational consciousness here considered is merely the *category*, i.e. the wholly general, formal certainty that what is, is for thought, and what is for thought, is; self-consciousness and being are given as being one and the same essence. It is a mere confusion when another being-in-itself (the Kantian noumenon) is postulated as being beyond being-for-thought. The categorial consciousness in question must, however, be such as intrinsically to specify itself in a number of distinct categories, forming a complete system (as in the Logic): to derive these categories from an external source, e.g. the forms of judgement, is a disgrace to philosophy.

236. The categorial certainty in question not only specifies itself in a system of categories but also includes in itself a pure or schematic reference to individuals; though individual things are no part of the categorial framework, individual thinghood *is* part of it.

237. Consciousness essentially moves around among its various moments, seeing the universal from the angle of the species and vice versa. Consciousness *is* this perambulation and what it sees on this course.

238–9. The first simple form of the idealistic consciousness is the consciousness that all I deal with is mine, my own idea. Such an empty appropriation leaves all detailed content to experience and foreign intervention. It passes to and from its empty proclamation of ownership to foreign material, and in fact oscillates like the consciousness of scepticism. It has no power to generate specific content in and by itself, and thereby condemns itself to the perpetual phenomenalism of Kantianism. Such an Idealism is self-contradictory because abstract. It says Reason is all reality but does not show it concretely at work in the world: it requires a further carrying out to be a true idealism.

OBSERVING REASON

240. The consciousness for which what is, is its own, now turns to sense-certainty, perception, etc., not to deal with something merely other, but in the certainty of being that other. Formerly it *happened* to notice and experience much, now it actively determines what it shall observe and experience. It seeks in the world only its rational, conceptual self, its own infinitude.

241. At first it merely divines its presence in the world, but proceeds thereupon to take possession of its inheritance, to plant the ensign of its sovereignty on every height and depth. There must be no differentiation of the real in which it does not discover itself, and its idea of itself must develop as it proceeds in such discovery.

242. The observant consciousness professes to be finding out the essence of things, not of itself: while it *is* Reason, it does not clearly *know* itself to be Reason. To do so it must plumb its own depths, see itself as through and through conceptual, notional. It can then, in transforming the superficial, sensuous being of things into Notions, recognize itself in such Notions.

243. Observation is concerned with Nature, with Spirit, and with the relation between them. These three must be studied in turn.

OBSERVATION OF NATURE

244. The unthinking consciousness treats observation and experience as the source of truth, but forgets that the object of observation is as important as the mere act of seeing, hearing, etc., and that not every perceived content counts as observed, e.g. that this penknife is next to this snuff-box. What is observed must be more than a mere particular: it must instantiate a universal.

245. The universal of observation at first merely stays the same: its movement is a mere recurrence of selfsameness. The Understanding must try to bring difference into this selfsameness through description, a procedure never short of material. But it encounters a check when it begins to wonder whether it is not describing something merely accidental, unworthy of description and lacking in generic meaning.

246. Observation and description are now urged by an obscure 'instinct of reason' to distinguish between the essential and the accidental characters of objects, and to make of the former, not merely marks through which we distinguish them, but marks through which they distinguish themselves. This is successfully done in zoology, where claws, teeth, etc. are the very organs through which specific being

is sustained, less successfully in botany, and still less successfully in the case of inorganic substances, whose description changes in changed circumstances.

247. The difficulties of border-line vagueness and confusion are endemic to the interrelations of species and threaten to reduce observation to unthinking description.

248. An instinct of Reason, however, drives the observing consciousness to look for a law governing the transitions between specific descriptions.

249. The observing consciousness sees such laws as sensuously present in the particulars it observes, which would, however, make them merely contingent and not genuine laws at all. A universal of Reason will, however, retain its notional universality even if it descends into the being of sensuous thinghood. Those thinkers (e.g. Fichte) are wrong, who make laws merely patterns to which things *ought* to conform.

250. The observing consciousness does not take a law to be a universal of Reason, but sees in it something external and foreign. But it denies this foreignness when it refuses, e.g., to identify gravitation with the actual falling behaviour of *all* bodies. It is content to observe bodies falling in a large number of cases, and to infer analogically that this must happen in others. What is inferred remains probable, and never becomes an observed fact. It is only when falling is made part of the *Notion* of a heavy body in its relation to the earth that a law enters the field of the observable.

251. Since a law is a Notion implicit, an instinct of Reason seeks to purify it into a Notion explicit. It sets up experiments which eliminate the irrelevant and highlight the essential. While seeming to sink deeper into sensuous particularity, such experiments really cut off the Notion from the latter. We soon arrive at free-standing 'matters', e.g. positive and negative electricity, which are neither bodies nor properties of bodies.

252. A 'matter', e.g. heat or calorie, is not an existent thing, but an existent universal or instance of notional being. An instinct of Reason rightly draws us to such 'matters', since laws, being general and non-sensuous, necessarily connect universals, things, not sensuous, though given in what is sensuous, and incorporeally present in bodies.

253. The truth of the observable is accordingly something present in sensuous being, but also free to move about in it, and in all change preserving its notional simplicity. What is implicit in such a Notion then renders itself explicit in a new sort of object, whose observation constitutes a new sort of observation.

254. An object explicitly embodying the Notion's shifting sim-

plicity is an organic object. Such an object embodies an absolute fluidity in which all external relations vanish. Inorganic objects depend
on other objects to bring out and to complete what they are, and get
lost in their ramifying relations towards such objects. But organic
objects, despite their openness to external influence, are not essentially
related to what is external and in all relations preserve their unity
and simplicity.

255. An instinct of Reason seeks to discover laws connecting
features in the organism with features in the inorganic environment,
thereby reducing the externality and contingency in which such
features stand to one another. Such laws do not, however, explain
the richness of organic being, and never pass beyond talk of 'great
influences' to exceptionless necessities. Their teleological explanations
remain external, and are therefore the very antithesis of laws.

256. The observing consciousness never goes beyond external
teleology to the true teleology of organic nature, which is Nature's
embodiment of the Notion. In true teleology we do not have one factor
passively produced by another, but a single nature realizing itself and
sustaining its own reality.

257. Teleological processes may seem to be provoked by indifferent, external circumstances, which therefore seem to have
explanatory priority. In reality, however, the circumstances make no
difference to the outcome, of which the true ground is the End itself.
This End feels itself in the final satisfaction.

258. The relation of the teleological organism to external circumstance is analogous to the relation of self-consciousness to external
reality. As the hungry animal assimilates its food, so self-consciousness
understands external objectivity, and makes it its own. But since it
first does so instinctively, its satisfaction seems doubled: it is felt by
itself, but is also referred to a sort of blind understanding in the object.

259. An organism conceals the relation of its manifest actions to
their immanent aim, and so seems to have been constructed by an
outside intelligence. Just so Reason conceals the inner necessity of
its own proceedings, and locates it in the objects that it is studying.
In both cases there is a distinction which is really no distinction: teleology is in the organism, and Reason in the thing studied.

260. The individual performances of an organism in furtherance
of its own maintenance and that of its species are not observed to
have a necessary relation to these purposes, though they in fact
have it.

261. The self-differentiating unity of organic teleology is not obser-
vationally, but notionally, grasped. Observation therefore converts
it into the interplay of distinct factors which suits its thought-style.

262. The organism therefore appears to observation to have an in-

ner, teleological core and an outer, actual crust, the latter being the expression of the former. The Notion here expires in a picture.

263. Neither inner purpose, nor outer expression, nor their unity of essence, are more than formally distinct: we do not have a connection between genuinely distinct terms. Observation recognizes this in talking of a *mere* expression.

264. Observational picture-thought must none the less externalize its formal distinction of outer and inner.

265. Observation finds internal teleology in the unresting fluidity of the soul, while its outer actuality is found in the quiescent, external organism. It conceives of the relations between these two factors in three basic organic properties, at once essences and patterns of interaction. These are the sensibility, irritability, and reproduction only fully found among animals.

266. Sensibility is simply the organism's reference of all to itself, its taking of all into its own fluidity, while irritability is its answering reaction to what invades it, a reaction which affects what is external as much as itself. Reproduction, finally, is the organism's maintenance of its own pattern in the constant renewal of parts by the individual and in the generation of ever new individuals. All three functions stem from the organism's concern with itself as its own sole End.

267. The outwardly actual form of sensibility is the nervous system, that of irritability the muscular system, that of reproduction the viscera.

268. There are peculiar organic laws connecting our three functions, both as regards external structure and fluid, inner character. The latter also has its external side.

269. The laws connecting the outer and inner aspects of the organism elude observation, not because the latter is short-sighted, but because such laws lack all truth.

270. Sensibility is not a function confined to the nervous system nor separable from reactivity or irritability. The latter is inseparable from sensibility, and both enter into organic self-maintenance or reproduction. Hence laws connecting such factors must be spurious.

271. Sensibility, etc. are qualitatively distinct aspects. When made into the terms of an empirical law, they are credited with quantitative differences, and are said to vary inversely or directly. It is as if one made a law of the tautology that a hole increases as its filling diminishes, or as more and more stuff is removed from it.

272. Such laws have nothing to do with sensibility and irritability, but are mere cases of a logical truism.

273. Since reproduction is not opposed to either sensibility or irritability there is even less reason to look for a law connecting it with either.

274. The laws in question are really tautologies, which have been given a false appearance of actual existence. Their outward shapes do not really differ from their inward presence.

275. Organic functions studied as observable existences obey no governing laws, but range over every chance magnitude, e.g. the X's greatly prefer this sort of food to that, they have this or that number of offspring so many times a year, etc.

276. There are no clear relations between vague functions like sensibility, etc. and the structured systems revealed by anatomy, which are much more numerous than the functions in question. Anatomy reveals only dead structures, never their living use.

277. The various functions distinguished in organic being cannot be regarded as distinct existents externally related. They are pervasive aspects of one life-process.

278. There is therefore no place for laws in the treatment of organisms: they cannot be broken into separate determinations united by bonds which determine each differently. Organic being is always dissolving all separate determinations.

279. When the Understanding discovers laws connecting existent aspects of Nature, it is itself the connecting factor among those sides: it does not as yet see them as part of the object. But in the observation of life the interconnection of aspects is itself objective. We no longer have the merely existent aspects between which a law could be found to hold.

280. If we seek to consider organic existence in and for itself, it loses all precise character, and becomes almost indefinitely variable. The necessity of the Notion vanishes altogether.

281. The observational consciousness, while rising above mere Understanding in its treatment of life, always relapses into the manner of the Understanding, treating aspects as fixed determinations, and relating them quantitatively in what it would like to consider as laws.

282. The observational consciousness tries to rise above perceived, sensuous differences by using germanized Latin names for potencies and faculties, to which varying degrees are then attributed. It does not thereby genuinely rise above the senses.

283. We have now to consider the organism's outer aspects.

284. The organism externalizes itself into structures essentially related to the inorganic environment—the object opposed to its being-for-self—but in ways not capable of being brought under strict laws.

285. The actual organism is at once turned towards the being-in-itself of the object and also towards its own being-for-self. In the latter respect it is free, self-determining, and indifferent to the definite shapes it assumes: it is a stream which does not care what mills it drives. This inner side of the actual organism can be expressed only

in the non-sensuous determinateness of number: sensuous qualities, the life-style of the organism, are the outer aspect of such number.

286. The inner side of the actual organism has therefore itself an inner and an outer aspect, the former the restless variability of the essentially abstract, the latter the non-sensuous determinateness of number, in which all movement and relation to the sensuous have been eliminated.

287. Such an abstract treatment of the organism, however, reduces it to the inorganic, which has its essence outside of itself in the self-conscious thinker. We must treat the organism in its own concrete sphere.

288. Specific gravity is, in the concrete, the internal aspect of the inorganic thing, expressible in terms of numerical measures, revealed by comparing observations, and underlying the thing's colour, hardness, and other sensuous properties.

289. Specific gravity is not, however, self-differentiating, and so not involved in process except quantitatively. It is therefore only contingently connected with the multitude of properties that it underlies. In this respect it falls short of cohesion, which involves differences of state and consequent transitions from one state to another. Cohesion, however, only abstractly achieves self-differentiation in the imperfect form of changes in specific gravity: degree of specific gravity is not systematically connected with degree of cohesion.

290. The many other properties of inorganic bodies have no necessary connection with their specific gravity or cohesion, and can only be classified in numerical terms, i.e. unessentially. We cannot discover general quantitative principles underlying the various types of property, whether severally or as a whole.

291. The relation of inner to outer is, however, quite different in the case of organisms. In the inorganic what is internal is a definite numerical measure, quite indifferent to sensuous manifestations, but the organism contains a principle of sensuous differentiation within itself. Its internality takes the form of a natural genus or kind which has the power to determine itself in various alternative ways, whereas the internality of specific gravity has one definite property corresponding to each of its degrees.

292. The universality of the genus is inherently such as to reveal itself in alternative individual ways. But between the universal and the individual the determinate universal or species necessarily has its place. When a process from the universal to the individual via the species takes place we have a case of consciousness: in an inorganic being it does not occur as a process but only as an outcome. In this outcome the universal is represented by a series of numbers over which the individual freely varies. Only if an individual could transcend the

limits of such individuality, could he achieve consciousness. (Being conscious is only logically different from being a case of a species or genus: in a case of consciousness universality *moves* through specificity towards individuality, in unconscious individuality there is no detached universality, and no movement towards individuality, only the sort of fusion which might have been the *outcome* of such a movement.)

293. Generic universality, differentiated specificity, and individual singularity are the three syllogistic terms which, by their inter-relations, explain organic and inorganic being. (Hegel's dynamic Platonism.)

294. The pure genus specifies itself into a set of sorts systematically ordered by quantitative differences. But the individuation of these species is determined in part by the universal individual, the Earth, which contingently determines just where, and to what extent, particular species will be individually instantiated.

295. In the case of self-conscious man the specific forms of consciousness constitute an ordered line of development, a necessary spiritual history. Organic nature has no such history: it falls straight from pure universality into the brute singularity of existence.

296. Organic Nature only actualizes such of its specific forms as the individuality of Earth permits.

297. Observing Reason dealing with organic Nature can therefore never rise above mere opinions, which at best predicate 'great influences', and never achieve the necessity of laws.

OBSERVATION OF SELF-CONSCIOUSNESS IN ITS PURITY AND IN ITS RELATION TO EXTERNAL ACTUALITY: LOGICAL AND PSYCHOLOGICAL LAWS

298. The observation of inorganic Nature finds the Notion split into a plurality of things which are nowhere bent back into simplicity or unity. Organic Nature involves such a simplicity, which does not, however, distinguish its moments clearly. Only in self-consciousness is singularity held apart from universality, yet absolutely held fast in the latter.

299. The 'Laws of Thought' are the first discoveries of observational consciousness turned inward on itself. They are formal expressions of the relations between aspects of the Notion. Being formal, they are not set over against the content which would give them truth and reality, but their form none the less includes an intrinsic reference to such content.

300. The 'Laws of Thought' are given to observational consciousness as a set of existent contents which it merely finds there. As so conceived, they are not so much empty forms as unformed materials,

whose role in thought is not as yet determined. This role will be studied in our speculative system.

301. The observational consciousness does not closely connect the 'Laws of Thought' with the action of consciousness of real materials. It therefore fails to identify the principles immanent in thinking with the same principles used to overcome the otherness of the materials thinking deals with.

302. The varying reactions of consciousness to what it sees as a merely other, found reality are the theme of a new set of laws, those of psychology. These laws concern the effort of consciousness to accommodate its individuality to the ways of objective things, but also to accommodate objective things to its own needs and passions, and thereby to sacrifice its detached universality. The former, 'cognitive' laws merely give reality the universality of consciousness, whereas the latter, 'practical' laws show us reality modified to suit the personal self, and that perhaps in a criminal or revolutionizing manner.

303. Observational psychology never gets past regarding mental faculties, dispositions, etc. as a rag-bag of disconnected items wonderfully churning about in a single container.

304. In treating all these items separately, or as united only in the actual individual, it fails to notice the overarching universality of Spirit. Its pronouncements regarding differences in intelligence, propensities, etc., are for that reason even less valuable than enumerations of the contingent differences of mosses, insects, etc.

305. The laws looked for by observation involve some specific individual, on the one hand, and the environing natural and social circumstances, on the other, both of which are conceived as given particulars.

306. But such an endeavour forgets that the individual, having the universal in him, can freely take up different stances towards circumstances and influences, and that he reflects as if in an inner gallery the same general array of circumstances that play upon him in the world.

307. What the world is for the individual depends on his own active or passive response to it. Hence no clear meaning can be given to the psychological necessity that the world imposes on him.

308. Since environing world and responding individual cannot be neatly separated, there can be no laws connecting one with the other.

OBSERVATION OF THE RELATION OF SELF-CONSCIOUSNESS TO
ITS IMMEDIATE ACTUALITY: PHYSIOGNOMY AND
PHRENOLOGY

309. Since the environing world has been made part of self-conscious individuality, observation must now make the latter its object.

310. In such individuality the existent body is the individuality's being-in-self, just as its activity is its being-for-self. The body cannot, however, be merely external to the individual's activity, but must in some manner express its determining character.

311. The law-governed relation of individuality to environment has now been transferred into the *expressive* relation of a man's bodily shape to his consciousness and movement. We have now to elucidate this 'expressive' relation.

312. An expression at once goes beyond what it expresses by fulfilling and completing it, but it also falls short of it, by lending itself to distortion by circumstances, by an individual's clumsiness, or by his intention to deceive. We must therefore look for some more reliable sign of an individual's inwardness than the use of his bodily organs.

313. Such a sign must be neither an organ nor an action, but some quiescent feature of bodily structure, arbitrarily and contingently related to some inward individual peculiarity.

314. The would-be science of physiognomy wants to make such a contingent relation into a *law* connecting inner with outer, and claims in this to be superior to astrology and palmistry which merely connect one external thing with another.

315. Palmistry can, however, claim to use the hand, in which, after the tongue, a man's individuality is above all manifest, as the in-itself of a man, on which his fate and fortune depend.

316. Though the condition of a man's organs of speech, manipulation, etc. is in a sense external to his inward disposition, yet it is less external than the actions its brings about, and is in fact the middle term from which these follow as conclusions.

317. This middle term covers not only what is done by the organ mainly involved, but by other expressive movements and stances which reveal the individual's inwardness to himself and others.

318. Expressive movements differ from deeds, and can be used to test the seriousness of the latter. But they too are contingently related to the inwardness of which they are the sign, and can, like a mask, be laid aside and replaced.

319. Observation identifies what is inner with a man's intentions rather than his actions: the latter are for it the inessential expressions of the former. It then looks for something observable which will correspond to these inward intentions.

320. Physiognomy does not differ in principle from the unscientific gauging of a man's character from the way he looks and acts. It makes little difference that it speaks in terms of capacities and propensities, and does not merely call someone a murderer or a thief. The individual's inexhaustible nature cannot be set forth in terms of such capacities and propensities.

321. The 'laws' which such a science enunciates are based on personal associations and opinions, like the housewife's 'law' that it always rains when the washing is out to dry.

322. Whenever deeds conflict with physiognomic expressions, they answer the questions raised by such expressions. What we do stamps us as murderers, heroes, etc. Deeds can of course go awry or fail of their purpose, but where they are on target, and persist uncorrected, they are not mere signs but the thing itself.

323. Physiognomy improves psychology by substituting for the provocative environment the individual's own expressive movements. Physiognomy must now be improved by substituting for such movements something fixed, thing-like, and immobile.

324. Since both inward and outward have their own being-in-self, their relation to each other must now take the form of an external causal action.

325. The inward conceived as self-related, yet active in, and not indifferent to, its outgoing manifestations, must have an actual existent organ, not merely instrumental, which is active in such manifestations.

326. The heart, the liver, etc. are frequently conceived as the active centres and sources of certain manifestations. They are not, however, first sources, but rather half-way stations.

327. The brain and spinal cord (minus the nerves) represent the organism's pure self-consciousness, not as such outgoing, but at rest in itself, a fluid pool in which disturbances die away. The diversity of bodily movements having their source in this consciousness must, however, be represented in this fluid pool, which must accordingly be articulated into zones or regions.

328. In the head, the being-for-self of the organism appropriately comes to a head, and that in two extreme forms, the *caput vivens* or brain, and the *caput mortuum* or skull. The skull is the being-for-self of the organism made into a fixed, inert thing. The spinal cord merely conducts action to and from the head, and there are other channels for this as well.

329. Since brain and skull are both expressions of the organism's being-for-self, there is necessarily an accommodation of the shape of the one to that of the other, which we may or may not like to conceive in terms of causal action of either on the other, or both on one another.

330. There is no intelligible connection between the strength or weakness of spiritual faculties and the bulging or contracted size of regions of the skull.

331. For observation the brain only counts as the existent form of self-conscious individuality, while the skull-bones count as its existence-for-another or as a mere thing.

332. The many-sidedness of Spirit necessarily expresses itself in a geography of skull-regions of differing significance.

333. Skull-bones do not express mental states in the way changes of countenance do, nor are they even signs of such mental states. They reduce all reference to self to the purest immediacy.

334. Vaguely localized feelings in the head could possibly show what skull-regions corresponded to what psychic tendencies, e.g. murderous, poetic, thieving, etc. Such diagnoses would, however, be quite ambiguous and indefinite.

335. The propensities and capacities of the mind have to be pared down to a few ossified differences to be arbitrarily correlated with the bumps and hollows of the skull. In such correlations a collection of mental dry bones is correlated with an equally dry physical collection.

336. Anything in a man's disposition can be correlated with a bump or hollow on his skull, even, as in the case of a cuckold, with a bump or hollow on someone else's skull. Such conceptions are pictorial, without genuine notional possibility.

337. If an individual does not behave as his bumps and hollows suggest, one can always attribute such deviations to his exercise of free will. Bumps and hollows are only the foundation for empty possibilities. They never justify definite predictions.

338. Such subterfuges make the skull-bones a sign of everything or nothing.

339. Self-consciousness cannot be made to depend on bone-formations, since such inert existences are everything of which self-consciousness is the negation. A man might prove the absurdity of such a reduction by simply smashing in someone's skull.

340. Observation finds it harder to see through such a gross absurdity as mind–skull identity as to see through much less flagrant absurdities. But the limit of the absurd is here reached, and Reason must do an about-turn in the opposite direction.

341. Retracing our path, we see how we moved from observing inorganic Nature to postulating non-sensible laws behind it: this pure universality, conflated with existent, sensible objectivity, became a new object, the organism. Such existent, sensible objectivity could not, however, be a true expression of such universality, which accordingly became a detached, purposive universality, i.e. self-consciousness as an observed object.

342. Self-consciousness as an observed object at first specified itself in the 'Laws of Thought', treated as existent contingencies. These differentiations, fused into a unit, became the individual self-consciousness, which necessarily contained and related an outward-turned aspect of will and action to an inward-turned self-conscious aspect,

of which it was the sign. These two aspects were externally and contingently related.

343. Recognizing the relation of inner and outer to be contingent, observation ceased to look for an organ, a symbol of Spirit, and pinned down its external immediacy in a dead Thing. The reality of Spirit was thereby made into a thing, and inert being given the significance of Spirit. To treat Spirit as a merely existent, objective thing is certainly to make it into something like a bone.

344. This result had a twofold sense. On the one hand it completed the previous self-extrusion of self-consciousness which we saw in the Unhappy Consciousness, its self-projection into a mere object, which, though embodying a categorial unity stemming from its own conscious selfhood, was seen as having a rationality that self-consciousness could *have* rather than *be*. Such merely *had* rationality was typical of the observer: he saw his Reason out there in the Thing. Such self-projection of Reason could not, however, be sustained. Self-consciousness necessarily felt its gaze reverting from the rationalized object to its own rational activity. (In this difficult paragraph the ordering universality which can lead a detached life as the self-conscious Ego is seen stretching out towards a specificity and individuality which *seems* to lie beyond itself, and in relation to which it *appears* as a set of objective categories. From this self-separation it comes to the realization that this ordering universality, categorially projected into objects, is *the same* as the ordering universality at work in its own conscious efforts.)

345. On the other hand, our outcome is simply the identification of self-consciousness with a sensible, objective thing. Self-consciousness only becomes *real* in a bone. (Self-consciousness, in other words, despite its systematic elusiveness, must have a foothold somewhere in the crust of material thinghood.)

346. What emerges from the observational experience is that the pure universality of the Notion is the ordering principle of the Thing, that thinghood and Notion are the same. This cannot be understood as long as we treat Notion and Thing as independent, self-subsistent realities, and do not see the former as *self*-dirempted in the latter, and so constituting an infinite judgement. ('The Notion is no Thing' is an infinite judgement which, in opposing Notion to Thing, makes their whole being consist in their mutual relevance.) As long as we look on them as sundered, their opposition remains gross and crass: it is like the union of urination and orgasm in a single organ.

THE ACTUALIZATION OF RATIONAL SELF-CONSCIOUSNESS
THROUGH ITS OWN ACTIVITY

347. The true significance of self-consciousness's self-recognition in the external, observed thing, is its self-recognition in another self-con-

sciousness, which, though a duplicate of itself, has the surface separateness from itself characteristic of a thing 'out there'.

348. Observational Reason categorized the observed thing in ways corresponding to its own development from sense-certainty, through perception, to Understanding. It went, that is, from description through classification to lawlike explanation. Reason must now recapitulate its further development from individualistic self-assertion and conflict to the ethical self-consciousness which unites all self-consciousnesses. (This recapitulation is to take place *within* the social medium only implicit in Master and Slave etc., and remote and alien in the Roman and medieval worlds.)

349. The stage of self-consciousness towards which we are now moving is essentially ethical, governed by unwritten laws and social customs, a framework within which the individual lives and moves, and from which he does not think to disassociate himself.

350. The members of an organized social whole not only resemble the differentiated modes of a single substance: they are also more or less conscious of their common membership, of the sacrifice of their individual, to a generic identity.

351. The individual in an organized social whole works for himself in ways practised and sanctioned by all, and performed for others as much as for himself. His most independent efforts are sanctioned and approved for all, and entail a thoroughgoing reciprocity in his relation to others.

352. The customs of an organized society have both the opacity of external thinghood and the transparent self-identity of self-consciousness. One realizes oneself most perfectly by being the perfect embodiment of one's community's social norms.

353. To live as a mere individual in an organized social whole is *not*, however, to be explicitly conscious of one's identity with it. One may either have forgotten it in a mere taking for granted, or may not as yet have fully achieved it.

354. The immediacy of ethical life is not critical of established laws and customs. Much less does it consciously align itself with them, and assert their absolute standing.

355. When self-conscious individuality arises, the bond of trust which links it with the social unity is destroyed. The individual opposes himself to social laws and customs.

356. The self-conscious individual, withdrawing from the social medium, seeks to make his own mark in the world through his practical efforts. He seeks to fulfil himself, to achieve personal happiness.

357. The fulfilment which the individual at this stage pursues is the fulfilment of his own immediate will and natural impulses, not the welfare of society. This individualistic pursuit of satisfaction may

either precede or follow the full development of the ethical consciousness. In the former case, crude impulses are subordinated to the ethical life of custom, in the latter case there is a conscious abandonment of the life of mere impulse, and an advance to the acceptance of an ethic made to fit the individual's own inward sense of morality. Since the individualism most rampant in our own day is of the latter sort, it is this that we shall now consider.

358. Self-consciousness, which has risen to the Notion of Spirit, now seeks to realize itself in an individual's mind or person.

359. Self-consciousness, pledged to individual self-realization, necessarily negates the self-realization of other individuals, and seeks to impose on all the negation of all ends but its own. This universally imposed self-realization assumes three forms: the undisciplined pursuit of pleasure, the undisciplined law of the heart, and the more disciplined cult of virtue. These lead ultimately to the one-pointed self-dedication to the matter or task on hand.

PLEASURE AND NECESSITY

360. Self-consciousness sees the existent, objective thing that confronts it as implicitly itself. It seeks to make what is implicit explicit, and to reshape the objective thing to satisfy its individual self. All the higher intellectual and ethical ends of the community are spurned and set aside.

361. It expresses its individuality in immediate, active living, culling delights where it finds them, rather than creating them for itself. It makes no use of laws and general principles.

362. It does not seek to transform existence practically, but to savour its surface. Its enjoyment centres principally on another self-consciousness, an embodiment of rational categories and laws, which it does not, however, treat as such, but as made for its own gratification, thereby destroying the other's rationality.

363. Pleasure taken in another's person for one's own gratification is essentially self-destroying. The rational categories essential to personality are bypassed, and there is therefore nothing to hold one to an individual object. There is therefore a blind necessity driving one on to seek ever new objects in unending self-frustration. This necessity is nothing but the expression of the sheer emptiness of what is merely individual.

364. The pursuit of one's own satisfaction therefore passes over from sheer individualism to an absolute universalism in which all individuality is shattered.

365. What is now pursued by the individual assumes the form of a necessity, a law, which he cannot understand, but to which he must unconditionally submit.

366. To surrender to a law is, however, to remove its alien character. It will become the individuals' own law.

THE LAW OF THE HEART AND THE FRENZY OF SELF-CONCEIT

367. The individual's satisfaction seen in the form of a law becomes the law of the individual's own heart.

368. The individual must see whether his true essence lies in such a law of the heart.

369. The law of the heart necessarily opposes itself to the law of this world, under which the individual and humanity live oppressed. To the individual the positive, worldly law is something actual and found, whereas we phenomenologists see it as the shadow cast by the law of the heart.

370. The heart-ruled individual necessarily sees his undisciplined personal dictates as pleasing to all, and himself as noble in carrying them out.

371. Oppressed humanity does not seem to the heart-ruled individual to be aware of its oppression by this-world ordinances, or of its nobility in transgressing them. This deference to external authority must be broken down. It is merely accidental if authority and the heart agree.

372. To the extent that the law of the heart becomes an actual ordinance, the heart-ruled individual must cease to find satisfaction in it. It is no longer the law of his heart, but something alien and actual, against which his heart must rebel. To fulfil the heart's law is therefore also to frustrate it.

373. Whatever the individual chooses to do will, through such choice, conform to the law of his heart. But not every individual's heart will concur with the chosen course. Other individuals will condemn what a man's heart dictates, and will therefore become horrible in his sight.

374. The individual who erects the dictates of his heart into a law for all comes to see that the actual law for all is not alien and dead, but a genuine law for all hearts, even though the individual failed to realize this.

375. The heart-ruled individual therefore becomes a living contradiction, and recognizes as a universally valid order one that he, as an individual, does not wish to recognize.

376. To be thus torn between the recognition of a universally instituted, and a personally chosen law, is to be self-alienated or insane.

377. The heart thus torn madly fulminates against the priests and despots who have imposed their alien laws on humanity. But since

it itself wishes to be just such a priest and despot, it comes to see itself as being as perverse and perverting as these are.

378. It comes to see that a universal law is itself perverted if it is merely seen as a law of all *hearts*, as satisfying everyone's selfish individuality.

379. A law for all hearts necessarily becomes a law that all individuals fight over, a way of the world that never achieves a stable, agreed form.

380. But to such a fluctuating way the ideal of a fixed, agreed way of life necessarily opposes itself: the ideal of virtue as opposed to the way of this world.

VIRTUE AND THE WAY OF THE WORLD

381. Both virtue and the way of the world involve a compromise between disinterested universality and individuality. Only, in virtue, individuality sacrifices itself to standards that it has itself set up, whereas, in the way of the world, disinterested universality is realized through the interaction and attrition of individuals.

382. The way of the world is the disinterested order which arises out of the interested actions of countless individuals. Though condemned from the emptily universal standpoint of virtue, it is really what virtue seeks to compass. It is not, however, a blind drift, but one that consciousness can understand and accept, even though it springs from the mad self-assertion of individuals. (Hegel extends the principles of *laissez-faire* economics to all human and social action.)

383. Virtue, however, attempts to reverse the way of the world, and to arrive at a disinterested order through individual effort.

384. Virtue makes its direct aim, what the way of the world achieves by indirection. The aim of virtue is a poor abstraction from what is actually achieved by the way of the world.

385. From the standpoint of virtue there are gifts and powers, of which there is a right and noble use, but which are abused and perverted by the way of the world.

386. But these gifts and powers are precisely the substantive content to which virtue and vice add an insubstantial nuance of difference. One cannot transform the vicious into the virtuous without damaging such content. Hence the whole fight between virtue and vice becomes a mock combat.

387. The way of the world, having no sacred cause to defend, always achieves great richness of content, while virtue, with its special preferences, remains always in jeopardy.

388. Virtue cannot overcome the way of the world by making a

cunning use of the latent good in it. For the way of the world vigilantly fences off such interference. This latent good is either something that virtue dare not interfere with, or is as lacking in reality as are the gifts and powers that can be used in its service. It is no more than an imagined higher consciousness behind the actual natures of men.

389. Virtue is overcome by the way of the world, since virtue aims absurdly at abolishing the individuality which is the very principle of actuality. The ideal of disinterested virtue is either an empty word, or it must achieve actuality by accepting actual men and their interests.

390. Virtue, therefore, as opposed to the way of the world, is an emptily rhetorical, unconstructive form of edification, which may minister to men's vanity, but is ultimately boring. It is not like the virtue of antiquity which accepted ethical existence, and only sought to improve it.

391. When boredom sets in, men drop an ideal of virtue which uproots the individuality and interest essential to practical realization.

392. The way of the world is by the same movement brought to vanish. Self-interest is better than it thinks it is: in realizing itself, it realizes Ends that are universal.

393. The universal End of self-conscious life cannot be separated from the private, personal acts and ends of individuals.

INDIVIDUALITY WHICH TAKES ITSELF TO BE REAL IN AND FOR ITSELF

394. Self-consciousness has now ceased to oppose universal gifts and powers to the individual employment of them. It is subjectively certain of itself in and through its individual acts, which are its objective truth: alternatively, its acts provide the subjective certainty of which its aims are the objective truth. It has become, in active form, the categorial consciousness of Kantianism, in which consciousness of self amounts to consciousness of law-governed objectivity, and vice versa.

395. Self-consciousness no longer observes an apparently independent reality nor takes up practical attitudes towards it. This reality and its responses to it are transparently distinguished in its own practical activity, which is the genus under which its actions fall.

396. All that self-consciousness now aims at is to display itself in the daylight of actual existence, turning an act merely intended into one actually performed.

THE SPIRITUAL ANIMAL KINGDOM AND DECEIT, OR THE 'MATTER IN HAND' ITSELF

397. Real individuality is at first definite and simple, but with no specific content to differentiate its universality. It is the pure thought of a category, rather than its actual application.

398. Such real individuality involves an original given nature with definite qualitative limitations, which do not, however, limit the free action of consciousness.

399. All that the individual does springs from this original given nature, which it would not wish to transgress. But its negativity is not a passive being thus and thus and nothing else, but an active imposition of its whole character on what lies around it.

400. Action involves a subjective object or end, opposed to what is given as actual, then an instrumental transition in which the end achieves the full form of reality, and lastly a realized end which exists apart from the subject and his ends. In such action, the end, the original nature, the original situation, the means, the transition, and the resultant reality, are all only moments in a transparent identity.

401. Original nature, whether considered as special aptitude, talent, or character, is the first aspect of all action. This original nature is as much reflected in the external situation, which seems to evoke and shape a man's aims, as in those aims themselves. It is, moreover, only in action, in given circumstances, that consciousness becomes aware of its aims: its aims, as formed in thought, are merely movements towards action, and only become fully definite in action. The circumstances which evoke action, and the means used in it, are likewise parts of action, and the individual's inner nature is also a sort of means to it. None of the features distinguishable in action is really independent: all count as moments in a single conscious performance.

402. The universal character of a man's active nature can, however, be distinguished from a single, specific performance, and can be compared in respect of such characters as inventiveness, persistence, range, etc.

403–4. A man's actions cannot be judged as good or bad except in a wholly external, comparative manner. Whatever a man does, corresponds to his active nature, and is to that extent neither good nor bad, and neither to be admired nor lamented.

405. The product of a man's action makes explicit what lay in the man's nature, and makes this explicit for the universal consciousness. In this product circumstances, aims, means, procedures are all dissolved, and have become part of an actuality foreign to the agent, and open to all individuals. But it represents what is transitory, rather than what is permanent, in the individual concerned in it.

406. Consciousness in such work experiences the gulf between doing and being. Being precedes doing as the original nature behind action, and being succeeds doing as the work which results from action. It is in its work that consciousness achieves full reality, and gets rid of its emptiness.

407. The elements involved in work—original nature, aim, performance, and result—will, however, at times fall apart, thus contradicting their essential unity. The aim may not express the original nature, nor issue in an appropriate performance, nor yield the desired result.

408. This element of contingent failure in work is itself contingent. The different aspects of action hang together in their Notion, even if they at times fall apart in reality.

409. When a work vanishes, its contingent success or failure also vanishes. What persists in self-consciousness is the attempted performance in which doing and being, intention and execution, are united. It is irrelevant that reality sometimes fails to fulfil a work's intention. When a work is conceived as indifferent to contingent failure it becomes a task as such or 'matter in hand' itself.

410. The 'matter in hand' is the unit, the 'thing', of practical life. It combines aim with execution, circumstances and means with result. In it self-consciousness becomes real in a single performance.

411. The 'matter in hand' unites subjective individuality with objectivity, and puts self-consciousness before itself in the role of a substance. The 'matter in hand' has end, means, procedure and result as its dependent modes or moments: it is the genus which they all specify. But it remains abstractively universal, rather than truly a subject, since it does not generate such dependent moments.

412. Honesty of consciousness demands that the 'matter in hand' should express the agent's best endeavours, no matter what the circumstances or outcome may be. Whatever happens, he will have coped well with the 'matter in hand'.

413. If the agent has not realized his aim, he has at least tried to realize it, and in so doing has dealt effectively with the 'matter in hand'. He has dealt with it, even if others bring his work to nought, or if he can in fact do nothing about things. He has dealt with it even if he has merely approved of something, or taken an interest in it.

414. These emphases on the honest coping with the 'matter in hand' shift their ground from case to case. Sometimes a mere aim suffices, sometimes an act which fails of effect. All attempt to turn an ineffective or bad performance into one that is successful.

415. The honest agent is not as honest as he seems. Being concerned only with *his own* performance, or with *some* 'matter in hand', or with *some* reality, he is not really in earnest about achieving something.

416. The honest performer necessarily moves towards being a deceiver. For what others see him doing never fully embodies what he means to do, and so admits of differing interpretations, from which he may derive advantage.

417. A man appears in his actions to be disinterestedly realizing some 'matter in hand', but may disappoint others by showing that he only cares for this task if done by himself and not by them. Such disappointment, however, shows their own concern to be with their own performance and not with the 'matter in hand'. And if they magnanimously leave each man to do his own tasks, they still interfere with these through comments and criticisms. They care, not for the 'matter in hand', but for their own pronouncements upon it. And those who say that they care nothing for what others do or say, contradict this by submitting their work to the daylight of publicity.

418. A 'task in hand' is essentially such that all feel themselves entitled to share in it, and to make it their own, whether directly or indirectly. Its being a 'matter in hand' does not mean that it is not interesting to individuals: it is disinterestedly pursued only because it is interesting to everyone. The 'matter in hand' therefore becomes the category or categorical imperative, the sort of being demanded by self-consciousness. (Hegel here shows how the practical egoism, in which a man undertakes something to give *himself* something to do, necessarily expands into universal moral egoism, where the task is set by Everyman for Everyman.)

REASON AS LAWGIVER

419. Self-consciousness has now ceased to be the consciousness of a particular individual, and has become a consciousness shared by all individuals, and conceived by all as thus shared. Being thus categorial, it is at once the form and the matter of self-consciousness.

420. Self-consciousness now identifies itself with the absolute 'matter in hand', the task which is of self-consciousness's essence, and which it neither can nor will question. This task is the absolute ethical task or substance, and its consciousness the ethical consciousness. But it differentiates itself into a number of distinct tasks or prescriptions.

421. No justification can be given or sought for these absolute ethical imperatives, the pure deliverances of self-consciousness.

422. The imperatives in question are immediately given as the deliverances of sound reason, and such soundness must be immediately and unquestioningly accepted.

423. But just as the immediate deliverances of sense-certainty become articulate in perception, so the deliverances of moral sense become articulate in various well-known precepts.

424. 'Everyone ought to speak the truth.' This rule has to be quali-

fied in many ways, e.g. if he believes or knows it to be true. An imperative so qualified loses all definite force.

425. 'Love thy neighbour as thyself.' This rule says, if it says anything, that we should try to do what is for the good of others, a Notion at once involved in immense obscurity.

426. It becomes clear that the most we can demand of an ethical precept is not that it should have definite content, but that it should be free from internal contradiction.

427. All that the ethical consciousness can therefore prescribe, as our task itself, is that we should do whatever we usually do.

428. All that it can warn us against is self-contradiction in ethical use and wont. It therefore becomes only the critic of existing or proposed ethical laws.

REASON AS TESTING LAWS

429. Self-consciousness now applies to ethical precepts the sort of criticism which *we* as phenomenologists applied to them. But these precepts are no longer taken to be the authoritative deliverances of self-consciousness, and they are only criticized in regard to self-consistency.

430. Such criticism is, however, nugatory, since any and every content can be made formally self-consistent, e.g. neither the institution nor the non-institution of private property need be formally inconsistent. And both involve conflicts when we descend to the level of specific rulings, e.g. that each should receive as much as he needs.

431. Private property and communism are alike free from contradiction if treated as simple abstractions: in the concrete both involve infinite contradictions. It is ridiculous to think that the mere absence of contradiction, so useless in theory, could provide guidance in practice.

432. Precepts and criticisms of precepts are alike vanishing moments in the ethical consciousness, whose substantial content they never succeed in providing.

433. These moments enter into our consciousness of the ethical task, and are aspects of the honest endeavour to gain clarity and insight into what we should do.

434. But there is in fact no validity in the definite laws they prescribe nor in their arbitrary criticisms of the same.

435. The spiritual essence or substance of a living community gives all the validity that can be given to such one-sided precepts and criticisms.

436. Ethical law is implicit in communal living. It is not grounded on arbitrary individual decrees, which can simply be disregarded. It is what all men in the community accept as *their* standard, and that

without question, and what they do not in any way see as foreign or alien.

437. True ethical law is the unwritten, inerrant, unalterable divine law spoken of in the *Antigone*. It is not anything that an individual can hope either to criticize or to justify, and certainly not in terms of mere self-consistency.

VI. SPIRIT

438. Reason becomes Spirit when it achieves the full consciousness of itself as being all reality. In the previous stage of Observing Reason it merely found itself in an existent object. From this it rose to a stage in which it no longer passively perceived itself in an object, but imposed itself more actively on the world, a stage as one-sided as the previous one. Finally, it rose to an as yet abstract identification of itself with reality in the vocational dedication of itself to the 'task itself', or in the arbitrary institution of moral canons, or in the personal pronouncement upon such canons.

439. The essence of Spirit has already been recognized as the ethical substance, the customs and laws of a society. Spirit, however, is the ethical actuality which, when it confronts itself in objective social form, has lost all sense of strangeness in what it has before it. The ethical substance of custom and law is the foundation and source of everyone's action and the aim towards which it tends: it is the common work which men's co-operative efforts seek to bring about. The ethical substance is as it were the infinite self-dispensing benevolence on which every individual draws. It is of the essence of this substance to come to life in distinct individuals and to act through and in them.

440. Spirit is the absolutely real being of which all previous forms of consciousness have represented falsely isolated abstractions, which the dialectical development has shown them to be. In the previous stages of observational and active Reason, Spirit has rather *had* Reason than *been* Reason: it has imposed itself as a category on material not intrinsically categorized. When Spirit sees itself and its world as being Reason it becomes ethical substance actualized.

441. Spirit in its immediacy is the ethical life of a people, of individuality at one with a social world. But it must advance to the full consciousness of what it immediately is through many complex stages, stages realized in a total social world and not merely in a separate individual consciousness.

442–3. The living ethical world is Spirit in its truth, its abstract self-knowledge being the formal generality of law. But it diremps itself on the one hand into the hard reality of a world of culture, and on the other hand into the inner reality of a world of faith and insight. The conflict between these two modes of experience is resolved in Spirit-sure-of-itself, i.e. in morality. Out of all these attitudes the actual self-consciousness of absolute Spirit will make its appearance.

THE TRUE SPIRIT. THE ETHICAL ORDER

444. Spirit is a consciousness which intrinsically separates its moments, whether in its substance or in its consciousness. In its consciousness the individual moral act and the accomplished work are separated from the general moral substance or essence: the term which serves as middle term between them is the individual conscious agent.

445. The ethical substance, i.e. the system of laws and customs, *itself* reflects the distinction between the individual action or agent, on the one hand, and the moral substance or essence, on the other. It splits up into a human and a divine law. The individual harried by these contradictory laws both knows and does not know the wrongness of his acts, and is tragically destroyed in the conflict. Through such tragic instances, individuals learn to advance beyond blind obedience to law and custom. They achieve the ability to make conscientious decisions to obey or disobey.

THE ETHICAL WORLD

446. Spirit is essentially self-diremptive. But just as bare being dirempts itself into the Thing with its many properties, so the ethical life dirempts itself into a web of ethical relations. And just as the many properties of the Thing concentrate themselves into the contrast between individuality and universality, so too do ethical laws resolve themselves into individual and universal laws.

447. The ethical substance, as individual reality, is the commonalty which realizes itself in a plurality of existent consciousnesses in all of which it is consciously reflected, but which also underlies them as substance and contains them in itself. As actual substance it is a people, as actual consciousness the citizens of that people. Such a people is not anything unreal: it exists and prevails.

448. This Spirit can be called the human law since it is a completely self-conscious actuality. It is present as the known law and as the prevailing custom. It shows itself in the assurance of individuals generally, and of the government in particular. It has a daylight sway, and lets individuals go freely about their business.

449. The ethical substance reveals itself, however, in another law, the Divine Law, which springs from the immediate, simple essence of the ethical, and is opposed to the fully conscious dimension of action, and extends down to the inner essence of individuals.

450. The Divine Law has its own self-consciousness, the immediate consciousness of self-in-other, in a natural ethical community, the Family. The Family is that elementary, unconscious ethical being which is opposed to, and yet is also presupposed by, the conscious ethical being of the people and their devotion to common ends.

451. In the Family natural relations carry universal ethical meanings. The individual in the Family is primarily related to the Family as a whole, and not by ties of love and sentiment to its particular members. The Family, further, is not concerned to promote the well-being of its individual members, nor to offer them protection. It is concerned with individuality raised out of the unrest and change of life into the universality of death, i.e. the Family exists to promote the cult of the dead.

452. The individuality by dying achieves peace and universality through a merely natural process. As regards its timing it is only accidentally connected with the services he performs to the community, even though dying is in a sense the supreme service to the community that a man can perform, in furnishing the Family with its ancestral pantheon, its household Lares. In order, however, that the individual's taking up into universality may be effective, it must be helped out by a conscious act on the part of the Family members. This act may indifferently be regarded as the saving of the deceased individual from destruction, or as the conscious effecting of that destruction, so that the individual becomes a thing of the past, a universal meaning. The Family resists the corruption of worms and of chemical agencies by substituting their own conscious work in its place, by consigning the dead individual solemnly to the imperishable elementary individual, the earth. It thereby also makes the dead person an imperishable presiding part of the Family.

453. All living relations to the individual Family members, while yet in the realm of actuality, are matters of the human law. The Divine Law only concerns individuals no longer actual who have become universal meanings still efficacious in a people's and a Family's life.

454. There are in both laws differences and gradations. In discussing these we shall see them in active operation, enjoying their own self-consciousness and also interacting with one another.

455. The human law has its living seat in the government in which it also assumes individual form. The government is the actual Spirit which reflects on itself, and is the self of the whole ethical substance. It may accord a limited independence to the families under its sway, but is always ready to subordinate them to the whole. It may likewise accord a limited independence to individuals promoting their own gain and enjoyment, but it has to prevent such individual interests from becoming overriding. From time to time it must foster wars to

prevent individual life from becoming a mere case of natural being, and ceasing to serve the freedom and power of the social whole. The daylight, human law, however, always bases its authority on the deeper authority of the subterranean Divine Law.

456. The Divine Law governs three different family-relationships, that of husband to wife, of parents to children, and of siblings to one another. The husband–wife relation is a case of immediate self-recognition in another consciousness which has also a mainly natural character: its reality lies outside of itself, in the children, in which it passes away.

457. A relationship unmixed with transience or inequality of status is that of brother and sister. In them identity of blood has come to tranquillity and equilibrium. As sister, a woman has the highest intimations of ethical essence, not yet brought out into actuality or full consciousness: she manifests internal feeling and the divinity that is raised above the actual. As daughter, a woman must see her parents pass away with resigned tenderness, as mother and wife there is something natural and replaceable about her, and her unequal relation to her husband, in which she has duties where he mainly has pleasures, means that she cannot fully be aware of herself in another. In brother and sister there are none of the inequalities due to desire nor any possibility of replacement: the loss of a brother is irreparable to a sister, and her duty to him is the highest.

458. The brother represents the family-spirit at its most individual and therefore turned outwards towards a wider universality. The brother leaves the immediate, elemental, negative ethical life of the Family to achieve a self-conscious, actual ethical life.

459. The brother passes from the suzerainty of the divine to that of the human law: the sister or wife remains the guardian of the Divine Law. They have each a different natural vocation, a sequel of the vocation considered above in the 'task itself', a vocation which has its outer expression in the distinction of sex.

460. The human and ethical orders require one another. The human law has its roots in the divine order, whereas the Divine Law is only actual in the daylight realm of existence and activity.

461. The ethical system in its two branches fulfils all the imperfect categories that have led up to it. It is rational in that it unites self-consciousness and objectivity. It observes itself in the customs which surround it. It has pleasure in the family life and necessity in the wider social order. It has the law of the heart at its root which is also the law of all hearts. It exhibits virtue and the devotion to the 'task itself'. It provides the criterion by which all detailed projects and acts are tested.

462. The ethical whole is a tranquil equilibrium of parts in which

each finds its satisfaction in this equilibrium with the whole. Justice is the agency which restores this equilibrium whenever it is disturbed by individuals or classes. The communal spirit avenges itself on wrongs done to its members, wrongs which have the mechanical character of the merely natural, by equally natural expedients of revenge.

463. Universal self-conscious Spirit is chiefly manifest in the man, unconscious individualized Spirit in the woman: both serve as middle terms in what amounts to the same syllogism uniting the divine with the human law.

ETHICAL ACTION

464. In the opposition of the two laws we have not yet considered the role of the individual and his deed. It is the individual's deed which brings the two laws into conflict. A dreadful fate (*Schicksal*) here enters the scene and makes action come out on one side or the other.

465. The individual's self-alignment with one law does not, however, involve internal debate and arbitrary choice, only immediate, unhesitant, dutiful self-commitment. There is no quarrel of duty with passion, much less any ridiculous seeming conflict of duty with duty. It is one's sex, Hegel suggests, which decides which law one will obey.

466. In self-consciousness the two laws are explicit, not merely implicit as in ordinary ethical life. The individual's character commits him to one law. The other seems to him only an unrighteous actuality or a case of human obstinacy or perversity.

467. The ethical consciousness cannot (like the consciousness that preceded it) draw any distinction between an objective order and its own subjective order: it cannot doubt that the law it obeys has absolute authority. Nor is there any taint of individuality left over that can deflect it from the path of duty. It cannot conceive that its duty could be other than what it knows it to be.

468. None the less the ethical consciousness cannot divest itself of allegiance to both laws, and so cannot escape guilt when it opts for the one as opposed to the other. Only an inert, unconscious stone can avoid incurring guilt. The guilt is, however, not individual, but collective. It is the guilt of a whole class or sex.

469. The law violated by an individual's act necessarily demands vindication, even though its voice was not at the time heard by the violator. Action brings the unconscious into the daylight, and forces consciousness to bow to its offended majesty.

470. The ethical consciousness is most truly guilty when it wittingly rejects the behests of one law and holds them to be violent and wrong.

Its action denies the demand for real fulfilment which is part of the law, and so involves real guilt.

471. The individual cannot survive the tragic conflict in him of the two laws, neither of which he can repudiate. He cannot merely have a sentiment (*Gesinnung*) for the one. His whole being is consumed in pathos, which is part of his character as an ethical being.

472. In the fateful conflict of two laws in different individuals both individuals undergo destruction. Each is guilty in the face of the law he has violated. It is in the equal subordination of both sides that absolute right is first carried out.

473. A young man leaves the unconscious natural medium of ethical life to become ruler of the community and administer the human law. But the natural character of his origins may show itself in a duplicity of existence, e.g. Eteocles and Polynices. The community is bound to honour the one who actually possesses power, and to dishonour the mere claimant to state power who takes up arms against the community. This dishonour involves deprivation of burial rights.

474. The family-spirit, backed by the Divine Law, and with its roots in the underworld waters of forgetfulness, is affronted by these human arrangements. The dead man finds instruments of vengeance by which the representatives of the human law are in their turn destroyed.

475. The battle of laws, with its inherent pathos, is carried on by human agents, which gives it an air of contingency. The atomistic family has to be liquidated in the continuity of communal life, but the latter continues to have its roots in the former. Womankind, that eternal source of irony, reduces to ridicule the grave deliberations of the state elders, and asserts the claims of youth. The communal spirit then takes its revenge on feminine anarchy by impressing youth into war. In war the ethical substance asserts its negativity, its freedom from all existent arrangements. But since victory depends on fortune and strength, this sort of ethical community breaks down, and is superseded by a soulless, universal ethical community, based on limitless individualism.

476. The destruction of the ethical world of custom lies in its mere naturalness, its immediacy. This immediacy breaks down because it tries to combine the unconscious peace of nature with the self-conscious, unresting peace of Spirit. An ethical system of this natural sort is inevitably restricted, and gets superseded by another similar system. Spiritual communal life necessarily detaches itself from such tribalism, and erects itself into a formally universal 'open society' (term not used by Hegel) dispersed among a vast horde of separate individuals.

LEGAL STATUS

477. The universality into which the ethical substance has now developed is the soulless commonalty which has ceased to be the self-conscious substance of its members. These latter alone, in their atomistic multiplicity, are real and substantial. All are equal and all count as persons. The abstract individuality of the dead person in the tribal state has become the abstract 'I' of self-consciousness, the spirit of the new community.

478. Individual personality is now the acknowledged substantial principle. But it is an abstract principle instantiated in disjoined selves which lack a common substance. (Use of concept of *Sprödigkeit*, brittleness, diremptiveness, non-cohesion.)

479. The world of abstract atomic persons carries out in reality what in Stoicism is a mere abstraction. The abstract right of the individual person depends merely on his being a person, not on any superior inner richness or power.

480. The world of right-endowed persons develops dialectically as does Stoicism. Since it gives no content to personality and personal right, it has to relate it to senseless, external things. Persons become property-owners, and so trivial and contemptible, and their rights are all rights to property. (Stress on property in Roman law.)

481. Since empty individuality is the guiding principle of the right-state, it naturally incarnates itself in an arbitrarily selected individual, an emperor or living god, whose universal ownership can only express itself in monstrous excess.

482. Since legal personality is devoid of content, the abstract individuality that incarnates its principle is such as to destroy it and also itself.

483. In legal personality the person is meant to be absolutely essential, but its abstraction makes it completely unessential, the prey of unlimited caprice. The absolute unessentiality of the individual becomes the heart of a new phase of experience, that of the self-estranged person in a world of 'culture'.

SELF-ALIENATED SPIRIT. CULTURE

484. The ethical substance has, in the state of mere right, put its ethical being outside of itself. As an abstract individual, it confronts the world ordered by law and custom as something alien, from which it feels estranged. The world is its own world, but not seen as its own world, and accordingly becomes objectively different. Ruined is the atomistic assertion of personal rights, it acquiesces in a social order which seems deeply foreign.

485. The ethical substance then opposes to the real ethical order,

which seems deeply alien, a pure, essential order representative of its inward thoughts and ideals. The real order is *this*-world and strange, the essential order is an *other*-world in which it would feel at home.

486. The ethical Spirit thereby comes to inhabit two worlds, an actual world of 'culture' and civilization, and an unreal world, posited by faith, and more truly in harmony with itself. But just as the divine and human laws vanish in the atomistic legal person, so do both worlds vanish in the pure insight of the Enlightenment, with its unknowable god at one pole and its pure utility at the other. This pure insight refines itself into the nullity of revolutionary freedom, from which it must return to repossess itself of its alienated content in the new phase of morality.

THE WORLD OF SELF-ALIENATED SPIRIT

487. Spirit now lives in two worlds, one of self-alienation and the other of faith, where, however, in fleeing from the former world, it is involved in another form of the same self-alienation. The principle of the former world, not being aware of its Notion, has the false limitation of being opposed to faith.

THE REALM OF ENLIGHTENMENT

488. The world we are about to consider is one in which consciousness externalizes itself, which accordingly seems strange to it, and which it has to master. Only by mastering the world can self-consciousness have the universality which is its validity and its reality. This universality involves conformity to general patterns, and is not to be confused with the merely formal universality of the realm of right.

489. In the world we are about to consider the individual counts and is real on account of his *Bildung*, his culture. He is actual, powerful only to the extent that he is cultivated. His natural being and endowment in all its forms is utterly unimportant: only as cultivated are they better or worse.

490. The cultured individual exercises his ability and talents in a cultured world. In 'making his mark in the world' he in effect helps to make the world in which he makes his mark, though he is not conscious of doing so.

491. In the world each man has a place and an opening for his talents, and this place goes with seemingly fixed judgements of good and bad. Since he is part of the world, such judgements always stand over against other seemingly just as definite judgements.

492. As Nature dirempts itself into the elements of Air, Water, Fire,

and Earth so the social milieu dirempts itself into (1) a spirit of over-all uniformity, (2) a spirit of individual diversification, and (3) a spirit which embodies both aspects and unites them in its self-consciousness. There is nothing here analogous to the element of fate which embodies the conflicts of family and state: self-consciousness embodies both.

493. The spirit of uniformity in a society comes before the pure and detached consciousness on the one hand, and the involved actual consciousness on the other, as the *good* element in that society, whereas the spirit of divergent individualism comes before them as the *bad* element.

494. The good element in the society, considered as a reality, is the state power in which all individual endeavours are integrated, while the bad element is represented by the riches aimed at by their personal, self-aggrandizing efforts. But the quest for wealth is in reality as much for the good of the whole as the state power, and both are the same at bottom.

495. Self-consciousness sees its substance, content, and End in two spiritual powers. Its being-in-self is the state power, its being-for-self riches. Self-consciousness necessarily judges these two powers, and sees the former as good, and the latter as bad. But because both involve their opposites, this judgement can always be reversed.

496. What things intrinsically are is what self-consciousness finds them to be, and so the prima facie judgements of self-consciousness will necessarily be reversed on deeper reflection.

497. This reversal makes the state power be an oppressive, interfering, evil thing in which self-consciousness fails to recognize itself, whereas riches becomes a good thing to it, which only harms certain individuals accidentally.

498. This reversed judgement is, however, itself reversible on still deeper reflection. State power is seen as realizing the enduring good of individuals and organizing their activities, whereas riches only ministers to their vanishing enjoyments.

499. Self-consciousness now judges its own judgements, finding goodness in judgements which recognize themselves in state power *or* riches, badness in judgements which regard either as bad.

500. If a man judges state power in a good manner, he takes up a noble-minded attitude towards it, and becomes intent on political and social service. If he judges riches aright, he is grateful towards it and the dispensers of it.

501. To judge badly of either of these powers is to adopt a base-minded attitude, one which secretly rebels against all rulers and uses, while it despises wealth.

502. Both these judgements are immediate and one-sided: they are not brought together in consciousness as they are for us philosophers.

But this immediacy generates a demand for a reasoned, syllogistic demonstration by way of a middle term which will suffice to bring them together.

503. The noble-minded consciousness, positively disposed towards state power and negatively to its own selfish purposes, achieves the heroism of service.

504. The heroism of service endows consciousness with self-respect and exacts respect from others. But it also is the real, ultimate source of state power.

505. At first self-consciousness only gives the state power an impersonal legislative status, not an individual one. The haughty vassal retains his individuality and offers advice, counsel to the state powers.

506. The relation of the haughty vassal to the state power is ostensibly noble and loyal, even unto death, but is none the less always ready secretly to conspire against the state for personal ends.

507. A true self-surrender to the state power gives the latter its own individual will, makes it a monarch.

508. In all cases of self-alienation *language* plays an operative role. Through language the individual makes himself universal and impersonal, and transcends his immediate, changing self. (Cf. the 'divine' universality of language in sense-certainty.)

509. Spirit is essentially such as to be one in and through separated sides, each of which treats the other as an object excluded from itself. As such it will itself express itself as an existent object (i.e. a monarch) distinct from its many sides.

510. The 'universal best' is a poor expression of the profound unity underlying the various 'sides' in a society. An individual, monarchical will is a better, truer expression.

511. The noble-minded consciousness now develops a language of flattery to reconcile itself with the supreme monarchical will. The monarch becomes unlimited and absolute, and is spoken of by his proper name. The monarch identifies himself with the state power (*L'état c'est moi*).

512. The flattery of the subjects really creates the monarchical self-consciousness. But the nobility in practising flattery retains its inner conscious independence, and turns the monarch into a mere dispenser of wealth.

513. The noble-minded consciousness, through its unscrupulous use of flattery, becomes indistinguishable from the base consciousness.

514. For the base self-consciousness the monarch becomes a fount of wealth for which he becomes boundlessly grateful.

515. Wealth represents individual satisfaction but not the satisfac-

tion of a definite individual. It is a form of intrinsic being [*Ansichsein*] in which being-for-self is negated.

516. In the pursuit of wealth the noble-minded individual comes under the sway of an alien power.

517. In the pursuit of wealth an individual's personality becomes enslaved to the chance personality of another. What he personally is becomes utterly impersonal, a commodity like others to be bought and sold. Feeling that everything essential is reduced to unessentiality, the individual becomes profoundly rebellious.

518. The self, seeing itself thus superseded and rejected, supersedes this supersession and rejects this rejection. It is consciously for itself in and through them.

519. In its inner independence the self rises above the distinction of the noble- and base-minded: both become a single attitude. Wealth in being universally dispensed gives self-conscious independence and freedom of choice to all, but these are exercised at the expense of others. An arrogance of wealth arises which generates unbounded resentment.

520. Self-consciousness uses a language of noble flattery in dealing with state power: it employs a language of ignoble flattery in dealing with wealth. But the language which truly expresses its *Zerrissenheit*, its torn state, is one which makes diremption its essence, which in all its judgements unites terms in an utterly irrelevant, external fashion. Its only reason for dealing with things together is that they have nothing to do with each other.

521. The absolute, universal inversion of reality and thought, their mutual estrangement, is the final product of culture. Everything becomes void of substance and confounded with its opposite. All values become transvalued. Spirit in this phase of culture speaks a language of utter disintegration, which takes the novel form of *wit*.

522. Wit runs the whole gamut of the serious and the silly, the trivial and the profound, the lofty and the infamous, with complete lack of taste and shame (see Diderot's *Nephew of Rameau*).

523. Plain sense and sound morality can teach this disintegrated brilliance nothing that it does not know. It can merely utter some of the syllables the latter weaves into its piebald discourse. In conceding that the bad and good are mixed in life, it merely substitutes dull platitude for witty brilliance.

524. The disintegrated consciousness can be noble and edifying but this is for it only one note among others. To ask it to forsake its disintegration is merely, from its own point of view, to preach a new eccentricity, that of Diogenes in his tub.

525. The disintegrated consciousness is, however, on the way to

transcending its disintegration. It sees the vanity of treating all things as vain, and so becomes serious.

526. Wit really emancipates the disintegrated consciousness from finite material aims and gives it true spiritual freedom. In knowing itself as disintegrated it also rises above this, and achieves a truly positive self-consciousness.

FAITH AND PURE INSIGHT

527. Beyond the alienated world of culture seems to stand the unreal world of pure insight or thought. Consciousness does not, however, recognize that it is its own thought that occupies the transcendental medium, but rather fills it with *Vorstellungen*, picture-thoughts. The world beyond is a religious picture-world, unreal but conceived as real.

528. Religious faith, with its simple affirmation of a real beyond, is distinct from the religious phases considered before, i.e. the anguished squirmings of the Unhappy Consciousness, or the family-centred cult of the dead.

529. Since consciousness in religious belief flees the world, it continues to carry something which represents the worldly consciousness in itself. This accompanying voice is that of the never resting critical negativity which has emerged out of the realm of culture, and which destroys all positivity and all objectivity. This negative consciousness is without definite content of its own, but it fastens itself on the pictorial content of religious belief and devours the latter.

530. Both faith and pure insight represent consciousness returning to itself from the dispersed world of culture. Each presents three sides for examination: (a) what it is in and for itself; (b) how it stands to reality; (c) how it stands to its sister mode of transcendence.

531. For faith its absolute object is a pictorial reflection of the real world with the historical character of that real world.

532. In its relation to the real world, the object of faith articulates itself into the Absolute Father, the self-offering Son, and the Holy Spirit in which it returns to its original simplicity.

533. Since the Son and Holy Spirit bring the transcendent religious object into relation with reality, they also bring the believing self-consciousness into relation with the transcendent.

534. The spirit of religious faith lives in the world of culture, but tries to rise above its vanity to the transcendent religious object. It practises acts of devotion which bring it no nearer to its goal which it locates in a remote region of time and space.

535. For pure insight the Notion or concept alone has reality.

536. It seeks to overthrow every type of independence other than that of self-consciousness.

537. In its first appearance the Notion of pure insight is not fully realized. It refers everything to the future, in the form of an aim to be realized. All is to be given a rational reduction which will be valid for everyone. Differences between individuals do not count: they are differences of degree, not of kind. Pure insight is something that all can exercise and possess.

ENLIGHTENMENT

538–40. Pure insight is essentially opposed to religious faith. It is also opposed to the real world and fights against its impure intentions and perverted insights.

THE STRUGGLE OF ENLIGHTENMENT WITH SUPERSTITION

541. Enlightenment unites all the destructive, negative poses of consciousness in one. It is the same as religious faith, but seems utterly opposed to it, since it denies all the pictorial content of religious faith. What content it has, it borrows from religious faith, and causes it all to disappear.

542. To enlightenment religious faith is, in the main mass of the people, unconscious error and superstition. But it also attributes a self-consciousness to this error in the person of deceiving priests and despots.

543. Enlightenment appeals to the insight latent in all to free themselves from the impostures of religion.

544. Enlightenment is essentially ambivalent in its relation to the naïve consciousness, which it sees as a ready prey to imposture, yet capable of achieving insight.

545. Enlightenment thinks that it will win its way to men's minds without a painful struggle, and by a simple infection. One fine day the false idols of religion will simply lie flat on the floor before it. (*The Nephew of Rameau.*)

546. But it also engages in various noisy combats with religious superstition.

547. Pure insight gives a false reality to the superstition that confronts it, and pretends that it is something that it has to defeat.

548. The 'other' of pure insight can only be pure insight: it can only condemn what it is, since beyond itself nothing is admitted to have substance. But it maintains itself by confusedly finding an other in the objects of religion (another form of itself for us, but not for it) which it condemns as irrational lies leading to bad purposes.

549. The object of religion is rightly declared by enlightenment to be a product of the religious man's thought, but it is wrongly supposed that this means that this object is a mere fabrication. The religious man's trust in God is a recognition of the identity of God with

his own rational being. The worship of the religious community is likewise something in which God comes to be as the spirit of that community, and does not remain blandly beyond it.

550. For the religious consciousness talk of priestly deception, etc. is absurd, since its object corresponds to the inmost nature of consciousness. The lie lies rather in enlightenment which makes the object of religion something entirely different from what it essentially is. There can in fact be no delusion regarding the inmost reality in which consciousness finds the direct certainty of itself.

551. Pure insight misinterprets the various aspects of religious belief, i.e. its view of the absolute essence, the grounds of this belief, and the nature of its service to this essence.

552. Pure insight wrongly supposes that religious belief adores a sensuous object, a lump of wood or stone, a wafer made of paste, etc.

553. But religious belief is not really oriented towards a temporal, sensuous thing. It goes beyond this towards a thought-object which alone is self-existent.

554. Pure insight regards religion as basing itself on contingent, historical matters of fact, whose evidence is inferior to that of the newspapers, and which has passed through many distorting media, e.g. inadequate translations. The religious consciousness, however, bases itself solely on internal grounds of certainty. Only when corrupted by enlightenment does it look for historical support.

555. Religious acts really consist in cancelling the individual's particularity, which makes them appear senseless, without definite objective, to pure insight.

556. To pure insight the religious consciousness is foolish when it seeks union with its ideal by foregoing natural enjoyments, etc. For pure insight the religious consciousness is likewise foolish in rising above isolated individualism and renouncing private property. To the charge of foolishness it adds the further charge of moral wrongness, thereby making finite ends the sole ends of action, and being untrue even to its own transcendence of these.

557. The role of enlightenment is to make religious faith aware of what it intrinsically is. What, however, is the positive truth which enlightenment opposes to religious superstition? It removes from absolute being all sensuous properties, and so turns it into a mere vacuum to which no predicate can be attributed.

558. Over against absolute reality stands the individual, whose primary awareness is sense-certainty, which has become the absolute truth through the destruction of all sense-transcending forms of consciousness. Sense-experience is supposed to involve certainty as to the reality of the sensitive person and of other things external to himself, all of which exist absolutely.

559–60. Enlightenment can indifferently place featureless intrinsic being beyond sensible things or in them. It can further combine these two ways of regarding sensible things in which they come to have their whole being in their usefulness for other finite things beyond themselves. Reason is the function which prevents immoderate self-assertion and makes everything continue to be truly useful to everything else.

561. The mutual serviceableness of all things is for pure insight a reflection of their derivation from the absolute essence, which is itself the supremely useful, profitable thing.

562. Faith finds the positive outcome of enlightenment abominable, its empty absolute, its goodness present in everything, its summing-up of religion in utility. It sees in enlightenment nothing but self-confessed banality.

563. Faith has a divine right against enlightenment by which it feels itself utterly wronged. The enlightenment too has a divine right against faith, based on the self-consciousness which it expresses, and which is such as to absorb its opposite.

564. Enlightenment does not attack faith with principles peculiar to itself but with those that faith itself acknowledges. It merely reminds faith of certain sides of itself which in certain situations it tends to forget. What it brings before faith is as much an essential part of it as the aspects that it opposes.

565. In regarding faith as its sheer opposite, enlightenment fails to recognize its own self. It does not see that the thought it condemns in faith is its own. Against faith insight is the power of the Notion, relating distinct moments to one another and bringing out their contradiction. It has right against faith because faith contains both contradictory elements in itself.

566. If faith errs in making its object something alien, quite beyond its own devotional activities, insight reminds it of its error in stressing that its object is its own creation. But insight errs in making the object of faith a contingent fiction. It also itself believes in an unattainable, unsearchable Absolute, and is therefore on a level with faith, which combines the cognate with the unsearchable.

567. Both faith and insight wrongly isolate the sensuous from the notional, the former in looking at both this world and its other-world in incompatible ways which it fails to combine, the latter in seeing this world as abandoned by Spirit and playing no part in the essential process of Reason.

568. As regards the ground of knowledge, faith acknowledges that its knowledge of the Absolute involves an element of the contingent, but forgets this in its face-to-face confrontation with the absolute

essence. Enlightenment, however, remembers only the former and forgets the latter.

569. Enlightenment regards the sacrifice of property and enjoyment by faith as wrong·and inexpedient. Faith, however, recognizes, the merely symbolic character of such sacrifices.

570. Enlightenment sees it as absurd to sacrifice a particular, concrete source of pleasure (e.g. by fasting) if one's aim is to be rid of sensual desire altogether.

571. But enlightenment is here wrongly abstract in seeing the essential element in mere intention or thought, and not in the carrying-out of the latter in the instinctive realm.

572. Enlightenment has irresistible power over faith since it brings into play moments present in faith itself. It seems to destroy the beautiful unity of trust and immediate certainty, to sully spirituality with sensuousness, to disturb calm certainty with the idle play of understanding and self-will. But in reality enlightenment enables faith to overcome its split-mindedness, its dreaming life among notionless thoughts, on the one hand, and its waking life among the realities of sense, on the other.

573. The effect of enlightenment is to empty faith of its imaginative content, and to turn it into a pure yearning for an empty beyond. Its object is the same as the empty Absolute of enlightenment, except that it is not satisfied with this object, whereas enlightenment is satisfied. But enlightenment's satisfaction is, even as such, merely partial, as is shown in its further turning towards this-world utility.

THE TRUTH OF ENLIGHTENMENT

574. Pure insight in its ultimate development frames an object to fit itself, pure thought in the form of a Thing, an Absolute without determinations, in which all distinctions are without a difference. This empty Absolute is the same as the object to which faith sank back when disillusioned of sense-content by enlightenment. The self-alienated Notion does not, however, see the identity of these two Absolutes with each other, and with the self-consciousness which draws these distinctions.

575–8. The fight with faith reproduces itself within enlightenment in the form of a dual Absolute, on the one hand, the pure predicateless supreme being or first cause, and, on the other hand, an Absolute which especially involves the negation of all sensuous quality, and so becomes invisible, intangible, etc., underlying matter. Both are essentially, the same concept, different only in their starting-point. What the one regards as horror, and the other despises as folly, are altogether the same. Thought is being, the copula is here a separation as well as a connection, so that thought becomes opposed to its own shadow, matter. But matter as purely negative is indistinguishable from thought. The Cartesian *Cogito ergo sum* establishes the overriding identity which enlightenment fails to perceive.

579. The universal present in the contracted forms of God and matter is an eternal abstract oscillation within self or the pure thought of self. The oscillation within self is the simple Notion of utility.

580. Utility is a bad word to faith, sentiment, and speculation, but it expresses the ultimate truth of enlightenment—endless restless oscillation from one thing to another. Pure insight is the existent Notion whose being-in-self is not abiding being, but a perpetual being-for-another.

581. Summary. The world of culture ends in the consciousness of its own emptiness and vanity: self-consciousness retreats into self, passing into the two forms of faith and anti-faith (or enlightenment). Faith's imaginative pictures perish in the onslaught of pure insight, which circles between the two empty poles of the supreme being (negative) and matter (positive). Craving the reality which these abstractions exclude, self-consciousness turns to the real world it has forsaken and finds its own reflection in the universal usefulness of everything to everything. The three worlds traversed by Spirit are therefore (a) the dispersed world of culture in all its rich specificity and its hidden basic genus; (b) the genus behind this world seen as faith and insight; (c) the reconciliation of the genus with the specific forms in utility. In utility the rational universal is united with the individual and his satisfaction, and heaven is brought down to earth.

ABSOLUTE FREEDOM AND TERROR

582. Consciousness has seen its very Notion in utility, which is, however, still envisaged as a predicate of the object of consciousness or as End of its pursuit, and not as its veritable being-for-self. There is, however, an implicit withdrawal from objectivity in the Notion of the useful, and when this withdrawal becomes more explicit we have as a new form of consciousness—absolute freedom.

583. In utility all that intrinsically matters in objects is their use for some self, i.e. their use for a subject inherently universal which sees itself in the superficially alien being of the objects it uses. When the seeming distinction of subject, object, and interaction between them is overcome, absolute self-knowledge results.

584. Spirit knowing itself in all its uses is absolute freedom, which sees nothing sensuous or supersensuous beyond itself. The world is its will, and this will is a general will, the will which is a real will and not capable of being mediated by a representative. This general will is the true will, the self-conscious essence of any and every person, so that each does what all do and vice versa (Rousseau).

585. This general will puts itself on the throne of the world without resistance. Since self-consciousness is the principle behind all separately organized social 'masses', all these masses collapse into the unitary will which expresses self-consciousness. What gave the self-thinking Notion existence was its diremption into separated social masses: when the thinking Notion becomes its own explicit object, all such masses go. Each individual consciousness rises above the accidents of its class and place, and desires only to perform the work of the whole. All differences of rank and function are annihilated.

586. Utility as a predicate of a real object vanishes when self-consciousness is its own only object. In this phase of experience there is no room for the distinction between the individual and the general will. The *Être suprême* is reduced to a gaseous phantasm floating above the wrecked world of culture and faith.

587. In the new fusion of individual with social will, the individual can do nothing but enact laws and public resolutions and decrees.

588. Consciousness thus exalted and universal in aim can achieve nothing positive, either legislatively or executively. Its absolute negativity excludes a differentiation into groups having different state functions (legislature, executive, judiciary) or into the variously aligned groups in the world of culture. Being committed only to do the work of the whole, the individual can do nothing at all.

589. But all deeds, however universal their source, are necessarily the deeds of definite individuals, and not of everyone. Only purely negative, destructive work can therefore be the· common work of wholly free consciousnesses.

590. Self-consciousness, being self-consciousness, cannot avoid the differentiation which self-consciousness involves. If it abolishes all groups, it still keeps the distinction between the inflexible universal and the dirempted individual atoms. The only relation between these two extremes can be one of pure negation: the universal will must seek the death of its individual instances, and this in the most brutal and direct and senseless way.

591. The government is necessarily individual, since only so can it will anything definite. But an individual structure necessarily departs from its own ideal of being the universal will, and becomes the will of a faction which may readily be replaced by another faction. It cannot escape the guilt of violating its own principles. Such guilt, being devoid of any objective principle, is indistinguishable from mere suspicion, and its only fit punishment is simple annihilation.

592. In the work of destruction absolute freedom discovers what it is. Implicitly it is the abstract self-consciousness which uproots all distinctions within itself. The terror of death is the intuition of the negative essence, quivering between its empty absolute poles (God

and Matter). The universal will pursuing nothing becomes the elimination of self-thinking self-consciousness.

593. The absolute negativity cannot help generating class- and position-differences within itself which it ruthlessly keeps in their place by sheer terror.

594. From this reign of terror Spirit is unable to return to the concreteness of the realms of culture and faith. It is universal will which in its ultimate abstractness has nothing positive left in it. The unfulfilled negativity of the self, with its senseless pursuit of death, is, however, such as to swing over into absolute positivity in so far as the individual becomes, not something to be destroyed by the universal will, but to be taken up into it as pure knowledge and pure will, the Kantian formal *a priori*.

595. Absolute freedom has as its positive outcome a purely formal moral will, universal as much as individual. The Kantian Categorical Imperative is the other side of revolutionary destruction.

SPIRIT CERTAIN OF ITSELF. MORALITY

596. We have advanced to a position where the individual person, at first alienated from its own 'concept' in the worlds of culture, faith, and enlightenment, and swamped by that universal meaning in the stage of revolutionary freedom, has achieved unity with its own inherent universality.

597. The individual's relation to his own spiritual universality is both immediate and mediate. It is immediate in that the individual simply knows his duty and does it. But it is mediate in that the individual does not do his duty as an unreflecting member of the total ethical substance, nor as an alien prescription of an external authority, but in that he understands and sees why he should do as he should do. This deep rational understanding abolishes all otherness, and becomes the whole being of the ethical world.

598. At the moral level only what is known and present to the conscious agent makes any sense or has any reality. The world as an unknown external set of facts of Nature has been transformed into the world as a known spring-board for action.

THE MORAL VIEW OF THE WORLD

599. Self-consciousness in this phase makes duty the absolute substance and essence, which is also its *own* substance and essence, and which cannot assume the form of anything alien. To this substance an other-being must stand opposed, a Nature morally meaningless, governed by laws that have nothing to do with morality.

600. A moral outlook develops in which the intrinsic being and self-consciousness of morality stands in a relation of stark indifference

to the intrinsic being and self-consciousness of Nature. The moral and natural orders are for it given as mutually independent and irrelevant. From another point of view, however, only duty counts, the natural order being dependent and unessential. The moral life develops the conflict of these two points of view.

601. From the former point of view, the moral consciousness is satisfied by the mere performance of duty: the natural setting merely provides the occasion for this performance, and it may or may not reward the performance with complete success and happiness. From the latter point of view, which is not purely moral, it is a matter of complaint and regret that the natural order so often fails to match the demands of duty and the requirements of justice.

602. The moral consciousness cannot satisfy itself in the fulfilment of an impersonal, universal purpose: it necessarily demands also that the individual person be satisfied. Nature, it is felt, must come into line with morality, and reward the moral individual with personal satisfaction. From the strictly moral point of view, Nature has no true self to oppose to the demands of morality, and its conformity to these demands is accordingly *postulated*. This postulation goes beyond present actualities, but is not a contingent, personal demand. It is a necessary demand of Reason.

603. The moral consciousness not merely demands Nature as something completely external and alien in which it operates, but as something also present in itself in the form of contingent, sensuous urges and tendencies directed to specific and individual ends. These urges and tendencies constitute an internal opposition to the purposes of the pure will. The moral consciousness remains one consciousness, however, and in virtue of this unity is obliged to terminate the conflict between its pure self and its contingent, sensuous urges: its essence lies in ending such a conflict. But the conflict cannot be ended by uprooting the sensuous urges, since they are the *real* element in morality. It must accordingly be ended by making the urges conform to moral requirements. This harmony of urge with morality is a postulated harmony, not as before in the nature of things, but as a harmony consciousness must itself bring about in an endless moral progress. The harmony itself is placed at infinity, since if it came about it would terminate morality. It is not really what we want to achieve, though it must be absolutely carried out: it is a task that must be carried out without ever ceasing to be a task. Infinity is a good place for such contradictory accommodations.

604. Our first postulate was that of an inherent harmony of morality with external Nature, our second that of a self-conscious harmony of morality with internal nature or sensuous impulse. These two harmonies are brought together in the actual movement of action,

and each appears required by the other. We have a harmony both inherent and for consciousness.

605. The moral consciousness has to function in relation to an actuality that presents many distinct 'cases': in relation to these it breaks up into a variety of laws and duties presupposing different objective and subjective situations. These laws of detail have not the sacrosanctness of morality as such, and have to be referred to another consciousness than the one that prescribes the moral ideal as such.

606. There are therefore two moral consciousnesses, one prescribing a law of duty indifferent to special content, and the other particularizing this law into special rules. This second moral consciousness also has the task of harmonizing morality with happiness. What we here necessarily have is the concept of a moral world-ruler who pluralizes duty and connects it with happiness.

607. In actual conduct, however, the agent is always an individual concerned to achieve a result in the real world. He refers the unpluralized law of duty to another consciousness, that of a sacred lawgiver. (This is a strain of the dialectic opposed to 606.)

608. The moral agent, since he places the pure law of duty beyond himself in a perfect lawgiver, necessarily thinks of himself as imperfect in knowledge and will, and a victim to the contingent and the sensuous. He is unworthy to receive happiness and can receive it only through the operation of Grace.

609. The Notion of a full conformity to duty is necessarily postulated by the imperfect moral agent, and he thinks of such a perfection as meting out desert according to merit.

610. The moral consciousness locates its moral ideal in another being, partly as a mere representation in its own mind, partly as something which in its perfection would transcend morality.

611. The moral consciousness does not see its own Notion in the divine lawgiver, nor does it recognize itself as the concept which links all these opposed moments with one another. It operates with picture-thoughts rather than pure Notions. Its object is treated as something merely existent which irrupts upon it in picture-presentation.

612. The moral consciousness also sees its own intrinsic Notion in a quasi-temporal perspective as an original state of perfection to regain which is the aim of the world.

613. The result of these transcendent projections is that the moral consciousness is one of infinite imperfection. There is for it no moral actuality.

614. The accomplished moral actuality is for it merely something 'beyond'.

615. Both the imperfect individual and the perfection it aims at thus become mere presentations, each valid only from the point of

view of the other. The complete moral self-consciousness is and is not, since it exists only in idea. There is and can be no transcendent moral perfection, but an ideal of a moral transcendence is treated as if it were such a perfection.

MORAL DUPLICITY

616. In the moral view of the world consciousness consciously produces its object, i.e. the realm of duty. This it does even if it attributes some aspects of its ideal to a transcendent, divine self-consciousness.

617. The moral view of the world now develops its basic contradiction in several directions. It constantly regards one side of its being as a mere mask for the other, while the latter in its turn merely masks the former. It is, moreover, profoundly conscious of its shifting duplicity and pretence, and its basic lack of seriousness.

618. This masking can be studied in the postulated harmony of morality and Nature. This is not given as actual now, but as to be actualized through moral action. But in so far as it is brought about and the result enjoyed by the agent, there ceases to be the transcendently postulated harmony, and the postulation thereof is therefore shown up as insincere. We only postulate the ultimate harmony to inspire present action.

619. If our postulation of ultimate harmony is insincere, our immersion in action must be sincere. But the End of action is not the individual act but the total betterment of the world, to which the act makes only a negligible contribution. But to place the End in world-betterment is also insincere, since the performance of duty is the essence of action and the only really worthwhile thing in the world. But again the performance of duty essentially relates to the world of Nature: moral laws must become laws of Nature.

620. If, however, the highest good is taken to be a Nature which conforms to morality, morality itself vanishes from this good, since it presupposes a non-conforming Nature. Moral action, being the absolute purpose, seems to look to the elimination of moral action.

621. Morality presumes that morality and reality are in harmony, but not seriously, since it proceeds to bring them into harmony. But it is not serious in doing this, since its action is a mere means to the highest good. But it is not serious with this good, since it involves the destruction of moral action.

622. Morality posits its End as freedom of the pure will from the misleading power of sensuous impulses and tendencies. But in doing so it cuts its connection with reality, since impulses and tendencies alone relate us to reality. It therefore postulates a mere conformity of these impulses to morality. But morality cannot prescribe a direction to the impulses, which alone can give a definite content and direc-

tion to morality. We have therefore to make the harmony of impulses and morality an idea of Reason located in the infinite distance. But this again is not serious, since it would involve the elimination of morality in the struggle with the impulses and contingent desires. The non-seriousness is shown in the introduction of the Notion of infinity.

623. It would seem that a state of moral progress is the true moral goal. But progress towards a condition where morality ceases would be moral decay rather than progress. The Notion of an increase or decrease in morality is, moreover, inadmissible. Either one acts dutifully or one violates duty (Stoicism).

624. Since morality is always incomplete, happiness can never be deserved, only granted by grace. Hence happiness is an independent End having nothing to do with morality.

625. Since morality is always incomplete, it is a mere expression of envy when people complain that the wicked flourish while the good suffer. There are no good and no wicked, and happiness should simply be as widely spread as possible.

626. Pure morality inheres only in a divine legislator, who pluralizes duty. But nothing can pluralize duty if our moral insight does not do so. Not even a holy being can sanctify what is not intrinsically holy. Nor can an arbitrary being be holy.

627. The perfection of moral insight has to be located in a divine legislator untroubled by sensuous impulses.

628. But in such a being the moral struggle would vanish and hence all genuine moral goodness.

629. In God all the contradictions of morality come to a head. The moral consciousness has to abandon God and retreat into itself.

630. The whole valid morality of God is a mere thing of thought and therefore without moral validity. It is opposed to reality and yet ought to be real.

631. Consciousness, aware of its deep insincerity in all these positions, flees to its own inwardness and takes up the position of pure conscience, indifferent to all these transcendent questions.

CONSCIENCE. THE 'BEAUTIFUL SOUL'. EVIL AND ITS FORGIVENESS

632. The antinomy of the moral world-view has given us duty located in the beyond but also demanded down here. It has solved moral contradictions by displacing them into some other, transcendent self-consciousness. Now, however, the moral self-consciousness has reabsorbed this transcendent being into itself, and recognizes itself as absolutely valid in its contingency. Its immediate particular existence is the true reality and harmony.

633. The self of conscience is to be contrasted with its predecessors:

(a) the self of the legal person whose existence consists in being acknowledged by others; (b) the absolutely free self which is the end-product of the realm of culture; (c) the moral self involved in the oscillating displacements of universality and individuality. In conscience we for the first time give content to the empty pattern of duty, right, and the pure will, and lend it authentic existence.

634. Conscience heals the various breaches across which moral displacement has woven its dialectic, the breach between what is intrinsic and what is a matter of myself, between the pure End and the opposed factors of Nature and sensibility. Conscience is morality become complete, which never submits its decisions to the empty arbitrament of some general standard.

635. For conscience [*Gewissen*] the intrinsically right is what it is inwardly sure of [*gewiss*]. It converts the given case before it into something which consciousness itself has produced. It does not dirempt the case before it into a variety of pre-existent duties between which it must decide: it alone can determine its duty in the concrete, making short work of conflicting prima facie claims.

636. Conscience does not consider itself as impure in relation to a transcendent morality, nor does it refer the pluralization of the pure principles of duty to a transcendent consciousness.

637. It abandons all positions which contrast duty with reality. It recognizes duty as concrete action, not as a pure abstraction encapsulated in what is not duty. It is immediately certain of itself, this certainty being its own conviction regarding its own self, and not meant to hold for other persons.

638. The moral consciousness only grasps the underlying essence of the moral, whereas in conscience it is self-conscious. Conscience does not oppose to itself an alien Nature subject to independent laws. As absolute negativity it can identify itself with, and so confer validity on, a finite content.

639. Conscience gives universal validity to the actions of the individual self. This validity is derivatively a validity for others, who recognize its validity for the self in question.

640. Anyone's conscientious action is recognized as absolutely right by the whole community of conscientious persons. Such universal recognition is not found in the moral realm, where the rightness of acts is always in doubt. In the realm of conscience absolute conviction of rightness *is* absolute rightness. At this level there can be no question of good intentions which have gone astray or of misfortunes which attend upon the good. What the individual thinks is admitted as right for that individual by all.

641. At the threshold of the sphere of 'Spirit' we were concerned with the 'honest consciousness' absorbed in the 'cause itself', which

was a predicate of the subject rather than the subject itself. In conscience the 'task' or 'cause itself' *is* the subject. It includes in itself the aspect of social substantiality derived from the ethical sphere, the aspect of external authorization derived from the sphere of culture, and the self-knowing essentiality of morality. In conscience the subject sees all these moments in and as himself, and seeing them as his moments, he has power and sovereignty over them all.

642. Conscience tries in some measure to consider the circumstances and consequences of action in all their detail. But it also knows and is not dismayed by the fact that these circumstances and consequences ramify infinitely in all directions, and that it is wholly futile to attempt to take account of them all in one's action. It is *for others* to pursue the investigation of circumstances ever further: conscience must act on its own incomplete knowledge which, because it is its own, is sufficient and complete.

643. Conscience has to consider all the prima facie duties which come up in concrete cases, but none of them has authority for it. *It* must determine which is overriding. In doing so its own naturalness, its impulses and inclinations, must play a part. Only this can break through the circle of inauthentic prescriptions derived from others. Conscience must exercise its arbitrament, and this must rest ultimately on its own impulsive and emotional make-up.

644. It is the arbitrament of the individual subject which alone determines the content of duty in given cases. Other individuals might regard this determination as a fraud, since they consider other aspects of the matter. An action that seems violently unjust to others may be an act of justified self-assertion to the person concerned, an action that others see as cowardly may be a prudent conservation of oneself and one's usefulness to the man in question. Since morality consists merely in the consciousness of having done one's duty, any content can be moral and must be recognized as such by others.

645. It is no good saying that the content of conscience should have been otherwise. Its essence is arbitrariness. One cannot say that it should have been directed to the general rather than the individual good, for the general good only has definite meaning if one brings in the social laws which override individual conviction, and these conscience will not admit. And any act the individual does for his own good can be plausibly defended as for the good of all. The balancing of goods against goods is moreover something that conscience by its essence cuts short.

646. Conscience is Spirit sure of itself, fully possessed and apprised of its duty. Anything which exists *an sich* is demoted to a mere moment: it is only in so far as it knows of it that it counts. Conscience has no

content: it must decide whether to obey or disobey any law. It has the power to bind or loose.

647. Conscientious acts exist as such for others. They are acknowledged as conscientious by other conscientious persons, and are put on a level with *their* conscientious acts.

648. There is, however, always some doubt whether other consciences will endorse the determinations of the individual conscience. Conscience therefore oscillates hopelessly between self-doubt derived from the reactions of others and its own self-certainty.

649. Conscientious people, trusting the integrity of their own consciences, cannot help impugning the *soi-disant* conscientious deliverances of others, and thinking that they are products of morally bad consciences.

650. Only if an act is *truly* conscientious must it be acknowledged as morally right by all: otherwise it counts as a mere expression of personal preference.

651. Only a man's consciousness of situations, not the real result of his acts, is morally relevant and acknowledged as such by others.

652. Language is the medium in which Spirit or social subjectivity exists. Through language one personal Ego recognizes the Ego-status of another personal Ego, and so transcends its separate individuality.

653. In moral discourse the moral consciousness loses its dumbness and becomes universal. One man utters his conviction of duty which is understood as such by others. Nothing counts except that others are assured that the man himself is assured of doing his duty.

654. The conscientious agent cannot admit questions as to whether or not he is acting from a true sense of duty, since he admits no distinctions of absolute duty from the individual's conscious determination of it. If a man says he is acting conscientiously, he is.

655. Conscience in its sublime majesty can put what content it wills into its knowing and its willing. It is the moral genius which knows the voice of its inner intuition to be divine. It is likewise the creativity that can make any action to be right. To follow conscience is to practise a religion of self-worship.

656. This lonely religion is also communal, and holds for all who speak the language of conscience and are conscientiously pure in purpose.

657. This sort of pure conscientiousness is wholly empty. One is assured of always being right without regard to what one is right about. Consciousness, the relation of mind to something objective, has vanished into empty self-consciousness, and what we have is really the untruth of the moral consciousness rather than its truth.

658. What emerges out of this emptying of morality is the 'beautiful soul', which is too fine to commit itself to anything. It lacks force to

externalize itself and endure existence. It does not want to stain the radiance of its pure conscientiousness by deciding to do anything particular. It keeps its heart pure by fleeing from contact with actuality and preserving its impotence. Its activity consists in yearning, and it is like a shapeless vapour fading into nothingness.

659. Conscience has yet to be considered as acting. It gives empty universal duty a determinate content drawn from its own self, and from that self as a *natural* individuality.

660. Self-certainty is the primary fact for conscience: the universal *Ansich* takes a second place. For the universal consciousness represented by other people the absolute certainty of conscience is essentially evil and hypocritical.

661. The universal moral consciousness represented by 'the others' tries to unmask the hypocrisy of the individual conscience. It tries to show that the universal, impersonal language of morality is both used by the conscientious person, and also serves to disguise his personal contempt for that universality.

662. There is an inherent incompatibility between the impersonal universality of conscious utterances and the claim to obey one's own private standards. To be impersonal about confessedly personal standards is to abuse others.

663. But when the impersonal moralist condemns private conscientiousness as hypocritical, base, etc., he merely sets up one arbitrary personal standard against another. He in fact legitimizes the conscience he attacks by taking issue with it.

664. The judgement of universal morality is unwilling to enter the arena of action, and remains snug within the universality of thought. It thereby itself exhibits hypocrisy, since it wishes its impeccable judgements to do duty for hazardous deeds.

665. The judgement of universal morality is itself a mode of action, and its main concern is to denigrate men's conscientious acts by explaining them by interested motives like ambition, desire for happiness, moral vanity, etc. No act can escape judgement in such denigratory terms: no hero can be a hero to his valet, because the latter *is* a valet.

666. The exalted consciousness which judges the active individual can itself be convicted of hypocrisy. It is afraid to act, and it passes off its cowardice as a wonderful piece of insight. The man of action sees his judge correctly as but another agent, and humbly confesses his imperfections to him.

667. But this confession of moral inadequacy is not met by a similar confession on his judge's part: the judge remains stiff-necked and hard-hearted. Such a retention of uncommunicating being-for-self in the face of the other's renunciation of the same, denies the very nature

of Spirit, which is master and lord over every deed and reality, and can make any of them as if it had never been.

668. The 'beautiful soul' represents no accommodation of the clash here considered. It simply passes away in yearning. It does not insist on its own being-for-self, and merely sinks down to unassertive, soulless being.

669. The true accommodation of the two sides just mentioned occurs when the moralist drops his attitude of stiff-necked judgement and matches the confession of inadequacy of the practical man.

670. The recognition of himself, the moralist, in the erring practical agent involves an act of reconciliation and forgiveness which simply is Absolute Spirit showing itself between the two antagonists.

· 671. The Notion of pure duty and tainted individual practice are two sides of the same Notion in seeming opposition. They are the 'I = I' where the Ego knows itself in its absolute other, another Ego. This is the first full appearance of God, the object of religion, on the phenomenological stage.

VII. RELIGION

672. Hitherto in Consciousness, Self-consciousness, Reason, and Spirit there have been manifold consciousnesses of the Absolute. The Absolute Being has not, however, been aware of *itself* in them.

673. The supersensible inner essence postulated by the scientific understanding was the Absolute, but certainly not a case of Spirit aware of Spirit. The Unhappy Consciousness yearned towards the Absolute, but did not recognize the Absolute as itself. Reason missed the Absolute because it found itself in what was immediately before itself.

674. In the religion of the ethical order fate was an impersonal factor distinct from all selves—they could not recognize themselves in it. The spirits of the dead, on the other hand, may have put off immediate particularity, but had not yet achieved true universality.

675. The religion of the Enlightenment had an empty Absolute quite beyond the wholly satisfactory present. It emphatically failed to see itself in its *Être suprême*.

676. The religion of morality and conscience involved an awareness of the inner universal self, but as having all differentiation and all actuality outside of itself.

677. In religion Spirit is *self*-conscious, as it is not in the phases outlined above. It sees itself objectively as a universal Spirit comprehending all essence and all actuality. It may have an objective natural shape, but this is also wholly transparent.

678. Religion does not, however, completely unify the actual world with the self of which it is conscious, but seems to have only a partial connection with that world, to be clothed by worldly forms as an outer garment. It does not yet see those worldly forms, in all their independent actuality, as simply Spirit itself.

679. Religion presupposes all the previous 'shapes' of Consciousness, Self-consciousness, Reason, and Spirit. But though it contains them all in unity, and not successively, yet, as individually realized in the world, it must realize them in succession.

680. The stages which lead up to religion recur in religion as specifically religious phases, out of which religion in its fullest realization arises.

681. In religion the principles of the pre-religious stages no longer occur in isolation. We do not have a set of linear advances punctuated by nodes, but each node sums up all the advances which occur at other nodes and so is the centre of a radiating system. We have always, i.e., the whole progression, but with one phase emphatic.

682–3. In developed religion consciousness is self-consciousness, but not so at less developed stages. There Spirit first contemplates itself in an immediate natural form, into which it then puts its own creative life, i.e. the Art-Religion of Greece. In Revealed Religion, finally, Spirit is itself given to itself, but only in a form suitable to picture-thought. From this it must rise to a self-consciousness in the pure medium of thought.

NATURAL RELIGION

684. Religion is existence embraced in thought, or thought which is there for itself. Only in the specific way in which this pattern is realized does one religion differ from another. All are phases in the development of religion as such. In this development picture-thinking is steadily reduced. In all stages of religious development there are rudiments or residues of what is present at other stages, e.g. the unity of universality with individuality fully realized in a Christian incarnation is rudimentarily prefigured in the incarnations of other religions. But though all religions contain all sides of religion, we must not confuse rudiments or residues with the full expressions. Only when Spirit is at a certain stage does the religious presentation of that stage have full truth.

THE GOD OF LIGHT (PERSIA)

685. Spirit at first has the consciousness of itself as being all truth and all reality in the form of a mere concept, a dark night of essence opposed to its daylight forms, a creative secret of birth. This secret must be externalized, seen in and through all daylight forms.

686. In its first immediate diremption, absolute Spirit appears to itself in the manner of sense-certainty. It appears as a being pervaded by Spirit, but Spirit in the form of lordship or mastery, the immediate as opposed to the inwardly withdrawn form of self-consciousness. Its shape is in fact shapelessness, the all-embracing light of the morning, which shows itself in the forms of Nature, but continues to play uncommittedly over them.

687. This life of uncommitted surface-play never truly returns to self, nor makes its manifestations truly its own: these latter are merely its attributes, its myriad names, its selfless surface-ornaments.

688. This incoherent life must rise to self-consciousness and give firm subsistence to its vanishing forms. It must come to know itself as itself. Firm subsistence must be dissolved in the gamut of forms it lays before the individual.

PLANT AND ANIMAL (INDIA)

689. Religion goes on from seeing itself in the immediacies of sense-certainty to perceiving itself in a variety of independent forms, first blameless and vegetable, then vicious and animal. These animal spirits become locked in a combat unto death with one another.

690. Out of the self-cancelling attrition of the various animal spirits, Spirit sees itself in a new guise, that of an artificer behind objects. Spirit does not as yet see itself in the material it works upon: this material is already determinate and pre-existent and Spirit merely works upon it.

THE ARTIFICER (EGYPT)

691. Spirit now appears as an artificer, which puts itself into its product, without knowing that it is itself that it is thus producing. It works instinctively like a bee building its cells.

692. The first products of Spirit are products of the Understanding, obelisks, etc. in which the straight predominates and the round is shunned. Spirit imprisoned in these forms is as it were dead, external to itself, not presented as Spirit.

693. Spirit now moves to a better representation of itself in which soul is clothed by body and not merely working on it *ab extra*. At the same time it sees this union externally, and so remains hidden from itself.

694. Spirit takes plant forms and stylizes their freedom into the straight and the round, the severe universals of thought and the elements of free architecture.

695. Spirit mirrors its own individuality in animal forms, which are, however, also hieroglyphs of thought and not given as endowed with language. Even when they rise to the human shape they are still

inarticulate and require the breath of morning to draw from them a tone, not a significant word. ('As morning from the lips of Memnon drew rivers of melodies'.)

696. The artificer himself lingers darkly in the background: when he does represent himself it is in the shapelessness of a black stone.

697. The artificer, conscious of the conflict between his withdrawn self and the outer product, expresses this conflict in a sphinx, half-animal and half-human, articulate but only in wise riddles.

698. Spirit now brings itself explicitly into the product it creates, and becomes an artist instead of an artificer. It creates a product in which its own self-consciousness is manifest.

THE RELIGION OF ART (GREECE)

699. Spirit puts itself into a shape which is that of self-conscious Spirit: it no longer goes in for incongruous mixtures of the natural and the thinking.

700. The religion of Art is closely connected with the ethical Spirit. Not a blind adoration of mastering light, nor an attrition of warring castes, inspires it, but the life of a free people whose customs are also the will of all.

701. In the ethical stage, however, Spirit has not as yet retreated inwardly from its contented acceptance of its position in a society where all have different duties. It must come to detach itself from this happy life of custom, and must come to mourn over the loss of happiness and security, before it can rise to true art.

702. Absolute art is a product of the break-up of merely customary society. Previous art was merely instinctive, not a product of free Spirit.

703. Spirit as artist banishes all that is colourful and substantial from its expression. It wants only to express itself, the fathomless night of self-consciousness in which the ethics of custom is betrayed (Gethsemane). All that it is interested in is form alone. (White marble conception of Greek art due to their loss of colour.)

704. Spirit as artist chooses an individual subject-matter, and there is pathos in such a choice. The universality of Spirit is dominated by the exigencies of the individual, but these in their turn dominate unformed matter. In the end we have Spirit presented in breathing individuality and sensuous presence.

THE ABSTRACT WORK OF ART

705. The first work of art is abstractly individual, because immediate. It must move away from such individualized art towards self-consciousness, which, in the religious cult, overcomes the otherness of its religious object.

706. The artistic product (the statue of the god) stands out as an individual on the universal background that surrounds it and houses it. It has a form which avoids the straight lines of the Understanding and the incongruous imitative mixture of straight and curved derived from vegetable shapes (in Egyptian art). It rejoices in the incommensurability of the straight line and the curve, and uses both.

707. The typical form produced by the art-religion is an idealized human form whose semblance of animal functions stops at the form's surface. Such an idealized human form unites natural existence with self-conscious Spirit. It may contain residues of old untamed forces—the Titans, etc.—but all is dominated by a spirit which is also that of a free, self-conscious people.

708. The restless variety of actual individuals is brought to peace in the idealized individuality of the sculptured god. In this, however, the artist expresses none of his own tortured individuality. But the work of the artist or the onlooker is as essential to the aesthetic situation as the mere art-object.

709. The artist's creative efforts are inadequately shown forth in the art-object. When others admire his creation and even kneel before it, the artist recognizes his superiority to it and to them.

710. Self-conscious Spirit therefore seeks a more adequate artistic expression than the mere art-object. This it finds in language, which is simply self-conscious existence in its immediacy, where production is one with product. The hymn is the essential art-form into which spirit puts its self-consciousness, and it is a self-consciousness shared by all who join in the singing.

711. We may, however, observe that oracular utterance is an even more primitive religious expression of Spirit than the hymn. Spirit has in it, however, not risen to universal self-consciousness, and so takes the oracular sayings to spring from an alien self-consciousness. Oracles tend to match the stage of spiritual evolution achieved, e.g. in the ancient east they utter sublime generalities which seem trivial to developed consciousnesses.

712. In the religion of Art universal truths are not proclaimed in oracular fashion, but are discovered by each man's reflection. Oracles utter the contingencies, whether of fact or practice, that cannot be effectively discovered. (Socrates' daemon only told him trivial matters, leaving him to think out the great generalizations.)

713. After the digression of 711. and 712., the hymn is contrasted with the statue, the latter being extruded from the self and reposefully 'out there', while the hymn forms part of the life of the self and has the vanishing character of that life.

714. In the religious cult the god loses his immobile 'out-thereness',

and the worshippers cease to be humble suppliants before their gods. The god comes down from his pedestal and the worshippers actively commune with him.

715. The abstract cult makes the soul into the temple of the divinity, not merely someone striking attitudes before a divinity which he contemplates from without. The Greeks were not, however, sufficiently conscious of their remoteness from divinity, their sinfulness, and thought a change into white garments and a few penances could purify them.

716. The religious cult involves an actual *rite* and cannot be carried out on the plane of mere thought. In this rite the divine essence comes down into actuality and becomes one with the self.

717. In the cult natural objects, bread and wine, are given a divine meaning and a divine meaning is given concreteness and actuality.

718. The cult begins with the sacrifice of objects which represent a man's own personality and possession. But the god also makes a sacrifice, firstly in creating the sacrificial object, and secondly in entering the sacrificer as he eats the sacrificial elements.

719. A cult is most fully and abidingly realized in the construction of a great temple, which is not only a dwelling for the divinity and its treasures but for the use and enjoyment of the citizens.

THE LIVING WORK OF ART

720. In the art-religion the self-consciousness of the individual is one with that of the national Spirit, not, as in the light-religion, wholly subordinate and lost in the latter.

721. Self-consciousness in the art-religion does not involve the strain of the artist, his dark struggle for expression. His self-consciousness is not the dark, but the peaceful night, the night after sunset, not before dawn. The fruits of Nature have been quietly consumed and appropriated by self-consciousness.

722. In the various religious mysteries of Demeter and Dionysus bread and wine mediate a full communion and revelation of Spirit to Spirit.

723. In these mysteries the absolute Spirit unites with the self-consciousness of his worshippers, or the self-consciousness of the latter is lost in the absolute Spirit.

724. The Absolute in these mysteries is not, however, completely revealed. The mystery of the bread and wine is not the mystery of flesh and blood.

725. At this level the Absolute as artist seeks a more adequate living embodiment, not merely 'out there' and unmoving like the sculptured god. This it finds in the athlete's matchless body displaying his powers at one or other of the great athletic festivals.

726. In the mysteries and the athletic games self-consciousness has been made one with the absolute essence, but not in a balanced manner. In Bacchic revels the self has been rapt out of its body, in athletic beauty spirit has become corporealized. In language alone can there be a perfect balance of interior and exterior. This balanced language is not the charged speech of hymns and oracles, but the luminous language of literature, open to all the members of a contemporary culture.

THE SPIRITUAL WORK OF ART

727. Language unites the various distinct national spirits into a single pantheon, in which, however, there is considerable looseness and independence, not subjected to an overriding unity.

728. The gods preside over all Nature and society: their chief is merely *primus inter pares*. They represent various aspects and powers of self-consciousness. Their essential unity is masked by an external camaraderie.

729. In the epic these various sides of self-consciousness engage in a dialectic which takes the form of a pictorial narrative. The minstrel is the real power which unites the whole picture, bringing all together through the might of his muse. Though not present in the narrative he projects himself into the heroes who occur in it.

730. The various aspects of self-consciousness appear in the epic as separate individuals and forces (including the dead), all spurred into activity by someone's deed. Gods and men repeat each other's work, the divine participants being redundant individuals instead of active universals.

731. The gods thus individualized quarrel with one another in a comic fashion. All that presides over them and over men is the unintelligible power of necessity.

732. Necessity really represents the power of the Notion operating through all these seemingly independent realities. It lurks in the background just like the minstrel. Both must, however, be brought into the picture.

733. This is what happens in tragedy where language ceases to be narrative and where self-conscious human beings are the spokesmen, behind whose mask actual actors are present.

734. The general commentary of the epic reappears in the discourse of the chorus of elders. These never reveal profound reflection or reaction, but practise only general observations, vague wishes, and feeble comfort. Before necessity they are blindly resigned and show only ineffective horror and pity.

735. In tragedy individuals are raised to heroic universality, while

a vaguer commentatorial universality surrounds them in the chorus and spectators.

736. The divine forces in tragedy muster about the two poles of the ethical order, the feminine, family pole, on the one hand, and the masculine, governmental pole on the other.

737. The heroic agents in tragedy live divided between knowledge and ignorance. Even the powers of light which give them knowledge deceive them with ambiguous utterances which they completely trust. (Hamlet and Macbeth are more cautious.)

738. There are in tragedy two standards of right, the daylight standards of Apollo and the underworld standards of the Furies.

739. Zeus is presented as the ultimate reconciler and unity of the two standards.

740. Both forces are equally right and wrong, and their struggle ends in the death of the individual concerned, or his absolution from guilt. Both then vanish in the calm balance of the ethical order.

741. Even in tragedy Zeus tends to predominate over the separate ethical powers, which become demoted to passions in the individual, not impersonal principles which pathetically crush him.

742. Zeus and necessity become more and more the central figures in tragedy, on whom the chorus looks with terrified awe as on something quite alien.

743. The self-consciousness of the heroes is gradually passing beyond their supposed limitations of vision and becoming deeply critical.

744. In comedy the actor doffs his mask, and the individual self-consciousness reduces everything to mockery, even the solemn proceedings of the gods.

745. In comedy the common man asserts himself in his revolutionary disrespect for everything. But he also makes a mock of his own self-assertion.

746. The dialectic of the Sophists and Socrates is a continuation of the dissolving irony of comedy. For conventional opinions and prescriptions it substitutes cloudy notions of goodness and beauty.

747. The truth of comedy is that all the great big essential fixtures that stand over against self-consciousness are really products of, and at the mercy of, self-consciousness. The individual knows himself in his individuality as the Absolute.

REVEALED RELIGION

748. The religion of art has made the great step of making its Absolute a Subject instead of a Substance. It has expressed itself in forms (that of the statue) emblematic of self-consciousness, and in the comic consciousness it has reached a pitch where all, including itself, is at the mercy of the individual self-consciousness.

749. Spirit has inverted the view of the self as a mere apanage of the absolute essence to making the latter, in the comic consciousness, a mere apanage of the former. It now inverts that inversion but without returning to the original priority of mere Substance set over against self-consciousness. Since it *consciously gives* priority to the absolute essence, the absolute essence continues to be itself, i.e. self-consciousness, of which it is in another form conscious. We have therefore two coequal sides of self-consciousness instead of situations in which one of these sides takes precedence over the other.

750. The art-religion and the comic consciousness are the spirit of a time in which the ethical spirit is being eroded, and pure individualism is beginning to run riot. This is a period of abstract right like that of the early Roman Empire, when religion has lost its meaning and a man lives unto himself alone.

751. Abstract right is, however, an empty abstraction, and soon passes over into yearning for a new Absolute. The Roman Empire, the seat of Stoic strength of mind, becomes a prey to the Unhappy Consciousness.

752. What is to the comic consciousness a vast joke is to the Unhappy Consciousness a vast misery. Its own abstract self-consciousness is a miserable refuge, and it cries with Luther (not yet born) that 'God is dead'.

753. The Unhappy Consciousness has lost all reason for respecting itself, whether as legal person or as a rational thinking being. All the religious and artistic expressions of its culture—statues, rites, etc.— have become deeply meaningless, as they are for modern scholars who study them in a merely external, lifeless way, and build up pictorial views of their background. Really, however, *our* reinterpretation of antiquity is more important than antiquity itself, if we will but truly remember and interiorize it [*Erinnern*]. Image of the maiden and the fruits.

754. All the spiritual attitudes engendered in the classical world, from the sculptural to the stoical and the sceptical, can be pictured as in wait about the true birthplace of self-consciousness, half in hope and half in despair.

755. Spirit may be thought of (a) as Substance going out of itself and becoming self-consciousness; (b) as self-consciousness going out of itself and making itself Substance. Spirit, we may say, has a real mother, self-consciousness, and a merely dispositional father, Substance.

756. Spirit is at first one-sidedly conscious of itself as (b). As such it fantastically imposes subjective interpretations on nature, history, and past religions, interpretations that are really not warranted. (The cults of Isis, Mithras, etc.)

757. But Spirit must be aware of (a) as much as of (b), i.e. it must see what immediately is before it taking on the lineaments of Spirit. This will happen at a certain stage in world-history when Spirit sees itself in the objective necessity of external things.

758. At a certain favourable moment in history the belief arises (note stress on belief rather than event) that absolute Spirit has taken on actual, sensuous form. God is taken to exist before the yearning, conscious mind, and not to be merely a projection of it. And God is believed to exist as an individual self-consciousness.

759. God's being made man is the simple content of absolute religion. Spirit is knowledge of self in self-abandonment, and absolute religion knows God as Spirit. Absolute religion is revealed religion because in it God is revealed, and revealed as essentially self-conscious. We do not achieve absolute religion as long as the object of religion is other than the Subject, is thought of merely as the absolutely good, creator of heaven and earth, etc. God must know God in religion: he must know himself in the religious person.

760. To be conscious of himself in a finite, sensuous, human individual does not represent a descent for God but the consummation of his essence. For God is not merely an abstract being, remote from concrete sensuous instantiation: he is only fully and completely himself in an instance.

761. Revealed religion is one with speculative knowledge: both attain to the knowledge of the universal as essentially *in* the individual. This is the message for which all previous ages were thirsting.

762. The individuation of the absolute essence is, however, pictured as achieved only in one case (Jesus), not equally in all, i.e. it is not truly a universal, notional self-consciousness which is everyone's equally. Men are conceived as a lot of perceptible individuals, not as a single concept.

763. But the single exemplification of the absolute essence must die in time in order to become something in which all men can share. If Christ does not go, the Holy Ghost cannot come to the worshipping community.

764. The passing of Christ's life into the remote past merely pictures its translation to the plane of universal meanings.

765. The religious consciousness thinks the truth in pictures which give a false independence to the various sides of what it believes in. These pictures have to be given a notional reinterpretation.

766. The religious consciousness goes astray when it substitutes for its own rich life the brooding upon a historical figure and particular events in the past.

767. Spirit is essentially a process which starts from pure thought (logic), goes on into otherness and pictorial presentation (Nature), and

returns from Nature to complete self-consciousness (Spirit proper). It is also essentially the synthetic connection of these three phases.

768. In the unhappy and believing consciousnesses there was a partial self-consciousness of Spirit. Spirit, however, mistakenly referred itself to a sphere beyond the conscious subject.

769. Spirit conceived in the element of pure thought is meaningless unless it also becomes manifest in something other than its pure self and returns to itself out of such otherness.

770. God is there manifest firstly as the Essence (the Father), secondly as the Being-for-self for whom the Essence is (the Logos or Word which made the realm of Nature), and thirdly as the Being-for-self which knows itself in the other (the Spirit or principle of self-consciousness).

771. Pictorial religion turns the necessary relations of essential moments within the Absolute into external generative relations of paternity and sonship.

772. The relation of the Absolute's moments *in* the pure thought of the Absolute is a relation of pure love in which the sides we distinguish are not really distinct. But it is of the essence of Spirit not to be a mere thing of thought, but to be concrete and actual.

773. Since the element of pure thought is abstract, it necessarily passes over into the realm of intuitive picture-thought, i.e. the realm of Nature. There one has a plurality of substantial things and a plurality of thinking subjects.

774. This passing over into the world of intuitive picture-thought is what is pictorially called 'creation'. The absolute universality requires instantiation to be what it is, and it is this logical requirement which is misleadingly pictured as a temporal requirement.

775. Spirit not only instantiates itself in objects but also in subjects. These are at first not conscious of themselves as spiritual, and hence are innocent rather than good. Their first self-consciousness is as capable of evil as of good. This first self-consciousness is pictorially misrepresented as a historical 'fall'.

776. Evil is the first actual expression of the dirempted self-consciousness, but it is the one that self-consciousness as it deepens must more and more repudiate. Pictorially, therefore, it is referred back to an infinitely remote date, to the fall from heaven of Lucifer, son of the morning. The angelic hosts enter the picture as a valuable pluralization of the being-for-self of the Word. If we add them to the Trinity we get a quaternity, and if we add the fallen angels we get a quinity. Counting in theology is, however, a bad practice. (Note Hegel's incorporation of Evil into the Absolute.)

777-8. Pictorial religious thought tends to extrude evil from God except in so far as, with great difficulty, it credits God with a wrathful side. The activity of God can be nothing but a bringing-together of the dirempted world with his simple essence, each of which is one-sided without the other.

779. Pictorial religion treats the redemption of the alienated world as an act of arbitrary free will. But in reality the absolute essence would be abstract and unreal if it did not exercise itself redemptively, if it did not enter the sphere of alienation and overcome the alienation. This it does by living and then dying, accepting the burden of sensuous instantiation and rising above it to pure universality.

780. That God becomes alienated from himself in angelic and human evil does not mean that such evil really lies outside of God. To be distant from God is to be distantly God: nothing can lie outside of the Absolute Being. The self-centredness, the *Insichgehen*, which is the root of evil, is an essential moment in the life of the Absolute. This religion recognizes in making God redeem the alienated, self-centred beings. Evil is in a deep sense the same being-for-self as absolute good, yet, in a deeper sense, it is not the same, since in fully developed being-for-self evil will be set aside and overcome. The true selfishness will drive out the untrue. It is above all mistaken in this sphere to speak in terms of fixed identity and diversity, and to fail to recognize the dialectical movement which makes everything turn into something else. Nature is and is not God, and God is God only by departing from himself in Nature, and returning to himself in Spirit.

781. Spirit is most essentially itself in the religious community where the Divine Man or Human God is transformed into the members' universal, inward, chastening self-consciousness.

782. Evil lies not so much in an abuse of natural existence as in the very conception of it as other than, remote from, Spirit. It is only for picture-thought that Nature is at first good, then fallen. In the Absolute there is no such history of phases, only moments which entail one another.

783. Evil is nothing but the going-into-self out of the immediacy of nature and is accordingly the first step in the direction of good. To be evil one must be conscious of the norms one rebels against, and will ultimately obey. There is no element of chance in the going-into-self which leads to evil: it is the essential movement of self-consciousness.

784. Instead of seeing the redemption of the alienated world as inherently necessary the religious consciousness sees it as due to a special event, God's incarnation and death. But it also realizes that death to be a resurrection, the universal life of Spirit among the individuals in a religious community.

785. What is really meant by the passion and resurrection is the

elimination of pictorial particularity and its supersession by the life of thought. An existent entity has become a Subject, a universal self-consciousness. The mere idea of self-consciousness has likewise become a concrete reality. God as a picture must die in order that God as a thought may live, one with every man's deepest self-consciousness.

786. Spirit is the mover, the moved, and the motion. It is its nature to forgive and pardon evil, to reconcile it with itself. But the religious community sees this all in pictures.

787. The religious consciousness never fully *identifies* itself with the object of its devotion, but at best pictures itself as coming together with that object at an indefinitely future date. The religious community has an actual father (its own action and knowledge) but a merely felt mother, eternal love which will one day unite it with God.

VIII. ABSOLUTE KNOWING

788. In revealed religion self-consciousness is aware of itself in pictorial objective form, not as yet *as* self-consciousness. It must cancel this form and become aware of itself in all the forms it has hitherto taken up. They must not merely be forms of self-consciousness for *us*, the phenomenological observers, but for self-consciousness itself. It must see how it has externalized itself in various objects, and in seeing this also cancelled the externalization. It must see all its objective forms as itself.

789. The object of religion is at first an immediate existence (given in sensation), a determinate existence (given in perception), and a notion given as behind the immediate (to the scientific Understanding). Consciousness must now grope forward to an understanding of objects in the form of self. But it does so by gradual stages, and dirempts itself into a number of distinct mental postures in which separate sides of the object are gradually brought together.

790. Consciousness assuming the form of observation reaches the point of seeing itself, the Ego, as an external thing given to sense-perception, the bones of the skull.

791. This view of the Ego as sensuous externality is, however, also the view of external things as nothing but the Ego. The full development of this realization arises at the stage of enlightenment or pure insight, when things are considered solely from the point of view of their utility to the subject.

792. A further spiritualization of objective thinghood occurs in the moral self-consciousness, where the Ego's self-certainty extends to the whole of essential being, everything else being a mere husk. As the

oscillation of moral duplicity vanishes, all objective ends are absorbed in a man's own conscientiousness.

793. Spirit certain of itself in its objective existence takes as the element of its existence nothing but the knowledge of self. That what it does is in accord with its ideas of duty makes them its duty. There is still, however, an opposition between pure duty and the external world and what men in it do. But with the act of forgiving another, this last opposition vanishes, and in all human action the Ego only encounters the Ego.

794. In religion this knowledge of Ego by Ego becomes explicit (in the Incarnation). Ego is known both in and for itself (and by itself).

795. In religion, however, the identification of Ego with Ego is still only achieved in the medium of picture-thought. A less pictorial identification was achieved in the case of the beautiful soul, whose pure inwardness really amounts, not merely to an intuition of the Divine, but to the Divine intuiting itself. Only the opposition to realization makes this last form defective. We must progress to a knowledge of self, not as a floating universal, but in its particular externalization.

796. This knowledge must somehow unite the religious consciousness, with its pictorial otherness, and the moral spirit, which is simply the self in action facing the two possibilities of the evil and the good. The religious spirit and the moral spirit must both abandon their rigid distinction from one another. The hard-edged, abstract, out-thereness of religion, its presentative character, must blend with the personal inwardness of the moral spirit. They must in fact both lose themselves in a new spirit.

797. In this new spirit the content of religion must become the action of the self, must be seen by the self as expressing phases of its own interior drama.

798. We now reach comprehending knowledge (*begreifendes Wissen*), or time and knowledge in the form of self. Spirit has reduced all its objective materials to pure concepts which are merely specifications of its own conceptual activity. Purely conceptual knowledge of knowledge in the form of self is *Wissenschaft*, Systematic Science.

799. What we now have, therefore, is a pure knowledge of self, even of *this* individual self, which is also the knowledge of all the moments of content which self distinguishes from self, and in comprehending brings back into self.

800. Systematic Science only appears when Spirit has achieved a purely conceptual self-consciousness and can reduce all objectivity to Notions, and so see itself in them.

801. Consciousness must go through a long process of first enrich-

ing its object, poor and abstract in its first appearance, and then appropriating and conceptually reabsorbing all that it has thus enriched. The pure Notion presupposes all these stages that lead up to it, but consciousness embraces them all in implicit non-notional form. Time is the Notion itself when presented to consciousness as an empty intuition, and Spirit appears to itself in time till it achieves full notional grasp and thereby abolishes time. Time is the destiny and the necessity of the as yet not perfected Spirit, i.e. until it has overcome the externality of objective Substance.

802. Everything we know must come before us in a living phase of experience (*Erfahrung*). The substantial, the solidly out there, must slowly be transmuted into the notional, the subjective. Time simply is the form of this self-realizing process. Until Spirit reaches the end of the requisite temporal process it cannot achieve complete self-consciousness.

803. The final conceptualization and reduction to self of all objectivity began when the religious world-view of the Middle Ages made way for the post-Renaissance philosophers. These ran through an observational phase in Cartesianism, a unified, oriental, religion-of-light phase in Spinozism, an individualistic, monadistic form in Leibniz. Everything became further subjectivized in the utility of the Enlightenment and in the pure rational, noumenal will of Kant. The subjectivization became more absolute in the Ego-positing-the-Ego of Fichte, and the dependent construction of both time and space. This leads on to the imperfectly carried out subjectivization of the substantial natural world in Schelling, the natural being externally and imperfectly integrated with the Ego in one Absolute.

804. The Ego must not, however, be afraid of the substantial world of objective Nature: this is its foil and therefore itself. The power of Spirit lies in remaining one with itself while it externalizes itself in Nature, and that without paring down the elaborate distinction of natural being. It must understand Nature in all its variety as necessary to itself.

805. Spirit is all the phases of content in which it externalizes itself, and the process of leading these phases back to a full consciousness of self. It unfolds its existence and develops its processes in the pure ether of its life and is Systematic Science. In Systematic Science the distinction between subjective knowledge and objective truth is eliminated: each phase always has both aspects.

806–7. Systematic Science cannot, however, remain a pure conceptual development: it must step out of itself and see Spirit developed in space and time and in nature.

808. It must then study Spirit returning to itself in time, i.e. in the long procession of historical cultures and individuals.

INDEX

DATE DUE

Demco, Inc. 38-293